Sociology and Social Life

Sixth Edition

Jean Lloyd
University College
Rutgers University

Raymond W. Mack
Northwestern University

John Pease
University of Maryland

D. VAN NOSTRAND COMPANY
New York Cincinnati Toronto London Melbourne

Cover and text art by William L. Elder, Jr.

D. Van Nostrand Company Regional Offices:
New York Cincinnati

D. Van Nostrand Company International Offices:
London Toronto Melbourne

Library of Congress Catalog Card Number: 79-64607
ISBN: 0-442-23373-6

Manufactured in the United States of America.

Published by D. Van Nostrand Company
135 West 50th Street, New York, N.Y. 10020

10 9 8 7 6 5 4 3 2 1

Preface

The Sixth Edition of *Sociology and Social Life* not only builds on the strengths that made preceding editions successful but also incorporates substantial improvements. In preparing this revision, we have sought suggestions from colleagues who have loyally used the text in the past and from others whose experience in the teaching of introductory sociology was invaluable. The goal has been to make the text increasingly effective and to bring its contents up to date with recent developments in sociology.

Changes in the contents alone reflect the broad scope of this revision. A chapter on research methods called "Doing Sociology" is placed early in the text to introduce students to the tools and procedures involved in research. Included in this chapter is a discussion of ethics in sociology and social sciences.

Two chapters dealing with topics of current sociological research and study were contributed. Chapter 7, "The Sociology of Aging," was written by Professor Jeanne C. Biggar, University of Virginia. Chapter 10, "The Sociology of Health," by Franklyn N. Arnhoff, University of Virginia, presents the issues of health, illness, and treatment in a social context.

Every chapter has been updated and includes the most current research and terminology. In-text features have also been added to increase clarity and enhance student interest. Boxed inserts entitled "Checking It Out" lucidate concepts through the use of excerpts from scholarly journals, newspapers, and popular magazines. A complete and current glossary of sociological terms is included. An Instructor's Manual, prepared by Professor Jon Darling, of the University of Pittsburgh, includes suggestions for audiovisual materials for classroom use, suggestions for further reading, and ten multiple-choice questions for each chapter.

Generally, the guidelines used in preparing this revision have been similar to those used by the prestigious group of authors who have contributed to the text since its original publication by Professor Kimball Young in 1959. To this end, the book continues to offer the student a concise, eclectic overview of the theories, concepts, and research that are basic to the discipline. In this edition, we have attempted to amply illustrate the content with applications from a "real-life" context.

Colleagues who provided suggestions for the preparation of this revision include Professor Kenneth E. Sinclair, Holyoke Community College; Professor David Ermann, University of Delaware; Professor Charles Nanry, Rutgers University; Professor Charles Jaret, Georgia State University. I would also like to acknowledge the support, concern, and helpful criticism of the following colleagues: Lloyd Barenblatt (my mentor at New York University), Charles Nanry, Chaim Waxman, Peter Jackson, and Martin Bierbaum. Among those student associates who helped with the research for the book are Mark Seglin, Samirah Abdul-Alim, and Anthony Haynor. Special thanks must also go to those special people who aid in turning out the manuscript. Among these are Patricia Lang, Naomi Wynn, Eileen Gnecco, and Camille McKay. Finally, special thanks and love to Lula, my grandmother; Gladys, my mother; and Jamie, my daughter, who contributed to this project in many ways.

Jean Lloyd

Contents

Part I The Study of Social Life

Part I

The Study of Social Life

The Study of Sociology
Doing Sociology—Research Methods
Social Structure
Social Interaction and Social Processes
Culture and Society
Personality and Socialization
The Sociology of Aging

1

The Study of Sociology

Sociology is the scientific study of the social aspects of human life. It is a body of knowledge, compiled through the use of the scientific method, about the structure and content of social life, that is, the organization of human interaction. Sociologists study the behavior of people in a group context.

"No man is an island, entire of itself." People everywhere deal with other human beings as members of groups. Only in the most exceptional cases do individuals live in isolation, and such isolation is never absolute. Even being a hermit presupposes some social experience; a person needs to learn many things from other human beings before deciding to be a hermit. The decision to be a hermit is a socially induced decision; a person has to participate in a human group to be able to decide to participate no longer.

Every human being is born into a group and spends a lifetime in patterned social relations. Everything we do—crossing the street, naming a boat, choosing a mate, making a fire, buying new underwear—is closely bound up with what we expect from others and with what others expect and accept from us. How we act under various circumstances is largely a consequence of the expectations created by interaction with others. Each of us expects certain behaviors from our relatives, friends, and even people we see only casually at a traffic intersection, a bookstore, or the coffee shop between classes, and we are aware that others expect certain behavior from us in such situations. Thus group life is patterned. If we are to understand and explain the actions of people, then we must devote considerable study to the ways in which groups are organized and function. Such a study of social life is the subject matter of sociology.

THE SOCIOLOGICAL PERSPECTIVE

The primary focus of the sociological perspective is the fact that human behavior is social. People do not live separate from one another, each seeking a personal and unique solution to life's problems. People live together sharing a common way of life that patterns and organizes their group existence. People live collectively as well as individually.

Any phenomenon can be viewed from more than one perspective and what we see depends, of course, upon the perspective we assume. One need only recall the variety of ways in which sex is viewed to appreciate the difference perspective makes. For example, the sexual behavior of human beings from the perspective of the so-called swinger is "fun and games," a form of play as natural as breathing. From the perspective of those who write marriage manuals, however, it is "hard work," requiring much effort, study, and preparation. From still other perspectives, sex is seen as "sin" or "love" and so on.

The basic premise of the sociological perspective—and a basic premise of all social science—is that the behavior of people is a consequence of the social situations in which they live. "There is no private life," George Eliot (1866) wrote, "that has not been determined by a wider public life." It follows that we come to know ourselves and others by knowing the places we occupy in the social world. The social world of the aristocrat is not the same as that of the agricultural migrant worker; the social organization of the metropolis is different from that of the small town; and the social structure of the prison creates patterns of behavior very different from those created by the social structure of the commune. The point is that

> The facts of contemporary society are also facts about the success and failure of individual men and women. When a society is industrialized, a peasant becomes a worker, a feudal lord becomes a businessman or he is liquidated. When classes rise or fall, a man is employed or unemployed. When wars happen, an insurance salesman becomes a rocket launcher; a store clerk becomes a radar expert; a wife lives alone; a child grows up without a father. (C. W. Mills, 1959, p. 3)

Sociology is a disciplined study of the social world; how it is organized and how it changes; how it varies from time to time and from place to place; how it remains the same; and how it is interrelated and how it is not.

THE METHOD OF SCIENCE

Sociology is a relatively new social science; to understand the material that sociology covers and what sociologists do and how they do it, it is necessary to have some understanding of what is meant by science. When a student speaks of "taking science this semester," he or she usually means that he or she is learning some of the content of a body of knowledge. The body of knowledge may be labeled physics, or chemistry, or biology. A science, then, is a body of knowledge.

But although this definition is correct, it is an inadequate definition because it does not distinguish science from nonscience. English literature, philosophy, and eighteenth-century art are bodies of knowledge, too, but we do not consider them sciences. We need a more precise definition.

People often think of science as a laboratory pursuit, and often it is. Sociologists, for example, conduct some studies of small group behavior in highly controlled laboratory settings. But scientific knowledge need not be compiled through the use of test tubes and Bunsen burners. Volcanoes and protest demonstrations, for instance, cannot be adequately studied in a laboratory, let alone a test tube. Most of the data of political science and anthropology are not gathered in laboratories, but they are sciences nonetheless.

Articles and advertisements in popular periodicals tempt one to equate science with control. The Sunday supplement often has a feature telling the reader how to make other people do what he or she wishes by "using psychology" on them. Other columns assure us that scientists have made it possible to control the environment in myriad ways: we can drive to town on tires that will not endanger life by blowing out; power steering allows us to steer an automobile comfortably with one hand so that, with the other, we can light a cigarette from which scientists have removed the ingredient that used to stain teeth; and finally, having arrived at the drugstore, we can purchase a scientifically compounded toothpaste that will prevent tooth decay. But there are sciences that do not offer us control of either our social or our physical environment. Astronomy, for example, is a body of knowledge that we classify as a science; but the astronomer does not exercise any control over the courses or rates of movement of the heavenly bodies.

What, then, is the common factor that leads us to classify certain bodies of knowledge as science? It is the way in which the knowledge is obtained. The identification of a field of knowledge as a science rests on the method used to acquire that knowledge. Knowledge obtained by what we call the *scientific method* is referred to as *scientific;* those who utilize this method to add to a body of knowledge we call *scientists;* and a body of related knowledge compiled by the method is designated a *science.*

THE CHARACTER OF SCIENCE

Three of the most essential characteristics of science, characteristics which go far toward explaining the scientific method and the activity of scientists, are empiricism, theory, and public verifiability.

Empiricism

Empiricism is the method or practice of obtaining knowledge from observation, experience, or experiment. A valid method of gaining knowledge is through the senses: sight, hearing, taste, smell, and touch. When a man "just has the feeling, deep inside him," that the Chicago Cubs will win the World Series, he is not basing his conclusion on empirical evidence gained through the senses. When Aristotle assumed that a horse had a certain number of teeth because that seemed a reasonable number of teeth for a horse to have, he was not proceeding empirically. Had he looked inside the mouths of a number of horses to find out how many teeth were there, or reached inside to touch and count them, he would have had empirical evidence—straight, indeed, from the horse's mouth!

Sociologists listen to people talking in small groups. They try to hear the difference in the tone of a murmuring crowd during a theater intermission, a cheering crowd at a ball game, and a roaring mob at a lynching. They taste the food which one group selects for picnics and another group defines as ceremonially unclean. They smell the perfume that is said to make a woman attractive, and they observe the smoke from chemical plants that influence people to sell their houses and move. They touch and compare what factory workers describe as a good and a bad welding job, and they watch the facial expressions of teachers supervising disadvantaged students. By no means least importantly, they observe the discrepancies between what people say and what they do. They use their senses to gather data about the behavior of human groups.

1-1 CHECKING IT OUT: The Scientific Method and the Study of Suicide

Emile Durkeim's *Suicide* (1951, originally published 1897) can be called the first real example of sociological research. It is an example of the scientific method. Before Durkheim, some sociologists were writing about social behavior. Also some sociologists had attempted to conduct empirical research, so that some surveys had been attempted. But Durkheim was the first sociological researcher to combine empirical investigation with theoretical assumptions. Let's see how he did this.

In the late nineteenth century when Durkheim was writing and teaching in France, the psychological perspective was very important and much emphasis was focused on the behavior of the individual (remember that Freud and Durkheim were contemporaries). But Durkheim, as a sociologist, had no interest in explanations of individual behavior. For him, the business of sociology was the study of society, its structure and the way in which society changed. Thus Durkheim undertook a study that was breathtaking in its audacity and its originality. He decided to study suicide. One would think that no act is as personal and private as suicide, so that it would be of more interest to the psychologist than the sociologist. Indeed at that time, there was only one explanation for suicide. The person who committed or attempted suicide was accepted as insane (psychopathic). But Durkheim said that the suicide rate is a social fact. Suicides can best be explained in social terms.

Empirical investigation. Durkheim begins the empirical phase of his work by contacting the Chief of the Bureau of Legal Statistics. He needs to get all the data available on suicides throughout Europe. Through the Ministry of Justice he gets information about 26,000 suicides (e.g., social characteristics, such as age, religion, sex, marital status). Durkheim is using existing data or what are called secondary sources. He begins to examine these data carefully and objectively. A startling fact is revealed. If the absolute figures are examined (the actual number of suicides) or if the suicide rates are examined (the number of suicides per 100,000 inhabitants), year after year the numbers are amazingly similar. Durkheim states, "Indeed, providing too long a period is not considered, the statistics for one and the same society are almost invariable. . . . To be sure, more considerable variations occasionally occur; but they are quite exceptional. They are also clearly always contemporaneous with some passing crisis affecting the social state." The hunch or theoretical assumption that Durkheim began with is being confirmed empirically by the statistical facts. There must be social factors to explain why the suicide rates within different countries remain so constant.

Existing theories. Durkheim then begins to look at existing theories to see if they offer explanation. The psychiatrists of the day, or alienists as they were called, have characterized all suicides as insane and have categorized all the varieties of insane suicides (e.g., maniacal suicide is due to hallucinations, delirious conceptions. The patients kill themselves to escape an imaginary disgrace or danger). Durkheim finds this interesting but not helpful because it tells about a certain kind of suicide, while nothing is learned about the phenomenon of suicide as it occurs in groups.

The statistics do not support the pathological theory either. In comparing Catholics, Protestants, and Jews throughout Europe, Jews are found to have the highest rates of insanity. If suicides are committed by people who are insane, then groups with high insanity rates should be expected to have high suicide rates too. But this is not the case. Jews have a high incidence of insanity but a low suicide rate. Durkheim continues to examine his data and discovers that a number of popular notions about suicide are not borne out by the statistics. He rejects the influences of alcoholism on suicide, or geography, or urban–rural differences, of the factor of imitation (e.g., in prisons).

What factors, then, do relate to the rates of suicide? Durkheim's study is a good example of a situation in which the theory emerges from the data. The author begins with only a hunch that the explanation for suicide is social rather than psychological. By eliminating all the popular notions, the actual social factors become apparent. Durkheim develops an important theoretical statement (proposition) to explain one variety of suicide.

Egoistic suicide. Suicide is directly related to the integration of an individual's social groups. If the individual is loosely connected to the family group or the religious or political group, the possibility of suicide is greater. Unmarried males and widowers without children have very high suicide rates.

1. Loneliness is a powerful factor here. Durkheim reasons that the family group formed by parents and children causes integration and a sense of cohesion or union.

2. Among religious groups, Protestant countries have the highest suicide rates, mixed Protestant and Catholic countries are next, and Roman Catholic countries have the lowest rates. Durkheim reasons that, as in the Jewish faith, Catholics are expected to submit strictly to religious requirements. Both of these religions exert much authority over believers. Protestantism leaves much to individual judgment and less to authoritarian hierarchy. The fact that there are so many Protestant sects indicates the degree to which traditional beliefs have been questioned. Protestantism is, then, less integrated and less cohesive.

Altruistic suicide. If egoistic suicide results from loose social ties, altruistic suicide results from ties that are very demanding. In some societies, suicide is a duty and obligation or a means of achieving grace, as in the case of self-immolation by a Vietnamese Buddhist monk or the Kamikaze pilot who crashes his plane into a battleship to destroy it. Hara-kiri in Japan is a suicide intended to restore honor that has been lost. In India, at one time, a widow was required to throw herself on the funeral pyre of her husband and join him in death.

Anomic suicide. Anomic suicide occurs in societies where norms or rules of behavior are unclear. When social morality is changing or when social disorganization is apparent, there is a higher possibility of suicide. Anomie can be defined as normlessness (lack of norms or rules). Durkheim notes that when individuals suddenly become poor or rich the rapid shift in their social fortunes increases the possibility of suicide because in either case familiar norms no longer apply and anomie results.

Public verifiability. Durkheim's study of suicide is a stunning example of the scientific method and remains a classic to all sociologists in the integration of theory and empirical investigation. Public verifiability causes some problems here. In general the notion of checking the findings of research by other researchers working independently is a sound one. But this study was done in 1897. The recording of data at this time was not necessarily complete and accurate. For instance, the recording of births, deaths, and marriages was handled by the church. Since the Catholic church denies burial to the suicide, the accuracy of such recording can be questioned. Public verifiability is therefore not applicable in this instance, because statistical techniques are so much more sophisticated today. However, Durkheim's theoretical conception and research procedures are so excellent they can still serve as a model for any sociologist interested in the phenomenon of suicide.

To be sure, scientists often use instruments in gathering data, but these are devices that serve to extend the senses in much the same way that a magnifying glass extends the eyesight. The most refined gauge must be read by a competent person if it is to contribute to the accumulation of knowledge. The thermometer does not feel temperature; the ruler does not measure distance; the stethoscope does not hear a heartbeat. These are only auxiliary to the human senses; it is the eye and ear of the person using the devices that make of their sensitive indications a scientific observation.

Parenthetically, method should not be confused with technique. Administering a questionnaire is a technique which sociologists use, just as making a microscopic slide is a technique which biologists use. A technique is a tool for gathering or analyzing data. So too, interviewing is a technique; but science is an overall method of gaining knowledge.

Theory

Another characteristic of science is theory. A valid method of organizing knowledge is through the use of reason. We organize knowledge by making statements that relate one fact to other facts—that is, by formulating a theory. A scientific theory is a set of logically related propositions based on empirical data.

There is a widespread belief that scientists are persons who "let the facts speak for themselves." Facts never speak for themselves. Facts have no meaning unless they are seen in relationship to other facts. During our lives we all acquire a considerable amount of information which we may bring to bear upon each new fact we learn. We tend to be unaware that our brains are cataloging the newly presented information by reference to other knowledge which we already possess.

If, for example, a friend tells us that the temperature outside today is 74, we are inclined to think that this fact is meaningful by itself. Actually, it would take pages to list all the facts to which we relate this one. Here are a few. Obviously, each word in our friend's sentence has a meaning for us because we were reared in a society where English is the standard language. Then too, we are familiar with a Fahrenheit scale for measuring temperatures and know that in ordinary conversation we refer to this scale rather than to the centigrade scale. We know that water boils at 212, that it freezes at 32, that normal room temperature in our society is about 70, etc. Our conclusion—that it is unseasonably warm or cool today, or about what one would expect—indicates a knowledge of the time of year, the geographic location, and some information about temperatures in this area at this season in previous years. This simple illustration points up what we mean when we refer to a science as a body of knowledge: it is a body of knowledge because it consists of facts that have been organized with relation to one another by reason.

When we can put in order a set of related propositions—for example, what variations in temperature have to do with variations in air pressure and volume—this set of related statements constitutes a theory.

Public Verifiability

Another characteristic of scientific data is that it is publicly verifiable. A valid method of checking knowledge is through the independent conclusions of a number of competent observers. One of the reasons we sometimes have to wait so long to gain access to a scientific discovery is that a relationship between facts that seems apparent to one competent observer has not been validated by others, and hence is not yet accepted by scientists as part of scientific knowledge. It is not unknown in human experience for one observer to see small winged beings descending from the clouds, to hear them speak to him, and even to touch them.

But because other competent observers cannot see, hear, or touch them, their existence is not accepted as scientific fact. Scientists sometimes agree on the data they observe, but they may disagree on what the data actually mean.

THE VALUES OF SCIENCE

Objectivity

The scientific method is an attempt to be completely objective. Scientists try to separate their own wishes and values from the process of observation. Their own conditioning influences their choices of problems to study, of course, but they try not to let categories of perception that they have acquired in the normal process of living influence observation or interpretation of what they actually find. They have absorbed from society its values, its norms, and its way of thinking. That is exactly why they utilize the scientific method: to attempt to get outside themselves and their milieu in order to see the physical and social environment as they would if they had not acquired a whole set of notions concerning the way it seems to be. There are many jokes that illustrate the scientist's attempt to be completely objective, such as the story of the man on the train who commented to his seatmate, a scientist, "The sheep in that field have just been sheared," and the scientist replied, "They seem to have been, on this side."

This reluctance to overcommit oneself is the caution of a person who does not want to let preconceived ideas bias his or her observations. The stereotype of the absent-minded professor is perhaps not so derogatory as we sometimes assume; it is a portrait of a person who removes himself or herself from the ordinary human world of prejudice and emotion, who strives as a scientist to be an objective, unbiased, rational person.

Relativism

In the world of science knowledge is only true until further notice. There is no theory so sacred, no fact so absolute that is beyond question and further study. Science as a body of knowledge is continually changing, more often because of new discoveries than because of the disproval of previous "facts." When what is learned today is added to what was known yesterday, our total understanding is often altered. Scientific knowledge is cumulative. Einstein's theory of relativity does not show that Newton's scientific facts were wrong; it only explains more about particular phenomena.

Intrinsic Value of Knowledge

Finally, scientists generally assume that knowledge *per se* is worthwhile. The scientist does not assume that only facts about people are important and that facts about animals are not; or that only facts about economics are worth gathering and that information about religion is not; or that only data for which some immediate practical use can be found is worth pursuing and that study in other areas is useless. If the last assumption were held, for example, we would not be able to generate power to heat, light, and operate large factories with atomic energy; for when Einstein worked out the formula which led eventually to the splitting of the atom, his research had no immediate practical use. He was pursuing knowledge for its own sake; as a scientist, he valued the idea of giving humankind more knowledge than it previously possessed.

SOCIOLOGY AND SOCIAL SCIENCE

By *social science* we mean those bodies of knowledge compiled through the scientific method that deal with the forms and contents of human interaction. To be social is to interact, to participate in group life.

Social Environment

All human beings are social. People have to interact with other people in order to survive. Since all human beings live in a society—which is to say that every person is a member of some human group—it is just as reasonable to speak of social environment as to speak, as people more often do, of physical environment. People are profoundly influenced by their social as well as their physical surroundings. The three-year-old son of a steel mill laborer in Pittsburgh who is taken from his home and reared by foster parents in a steel mill laborer's family in Birmingham, England, not only will talk and act otherwise than if he had remained in Pittsburgh, but will think otherwise as well. The change in his physical environment will have been minimal; the alteration in his behavior will be traceable to the difference in the two social environments. As the physicist, the chemist, the astronomer, and the biologist study the universe in which we live and the elements of which it is composed in an attempt to understand our physical environment and to predict what will happen in any given set of circumstances, so the social scientist studies the social environment in which we live in an attempt to understand human society and to predict how people will interact in different sets of circumstances.

Some social scientists concentrate their study on a single aspect of the social environment. Political scientists utilize the scientific method to compile information about the interaction that occurs as people attempt to maintain order in their societies. Economists assemble knowledge about what takes place in the production and distribution of goods and services. Cultural anthropologists seek to ascertain the relationships between the political, economic, religious, and familial behavior of persons within a given society, or to contrast the ways in which people in different societies come to fulfill the same needs.

Other social scientists are concerned primarily with social phenomena that are relatively unique; they observe, record, and attempt to interpret interactions that are not recurrent. Historians may draw parallels between the French Revolution and happenings in other times and places, but their primary concern is the uniqueness of human events; that is why a historian is more likely to be known as an authority on eighteenth-century France than as an expert on revolutions. The field of sociology is different from history in this respect. Its major concern is not with the unique in human events but with the similarities among social structures and the recurring nature of patterns of social interaction.

THE FIELD OF SOCIOLOGY

The difference between the generalizing focus of sociology and the more specialized focus in fields such as economics and political science is well stated by Pitirim A. Sorokin. (Sorokin, 1947) Sorokin suggests that the interactions which the economist studies be represented by letters, *a, b, c, n, m,* and *f.* The human behavior of interest to the political scientist can be called *a, b, c, h, d,* and *j.* Another social science might have as its subject matter those interactions represented by the letters *a, h, c, g, i,* and *q.* The first concern of the sociologist would be those social elements and relationships found among human beings whether they are acting as familial groups, say, or as political groups, or in economic pursuits: *a, b,* and *c.* Sociologists, then, study human interaction as such. They try to learn the likenesses among people in groups, no matter what the particular orientation of the group may be.

Specialties Within Sociology

The general sociologist devotes himself to understanding universal social structures, such as groups and publics, and universal social processes, such as competition and cooperation. Much of what is synthesized into general sociological principles, however, is learned from research carried out in specialized areas of sociology such as the sociology of the family, of law, of the city, of education. Scholars work in these more restricted areas in order to narrow their field of observation. They attempt to gain new insights by exploring one area of interaction intensively instead of making a broad survey of all human groups. This gives them an opportunity to make certain kinds of contributions to general sociology. First, they may uncover previously unnoted social phenomena of the type represented by *a, b,* and *c* in the Sorokin formula. For example, a specialist studying family organization may note that, as the family loses some of its functions to schools, public recreational facilities, and government agencies, it becomes less stable. Second, they may add to the body of knowledge about such interactions. Other sociologists may conclude from the findings of the family specialist that as any group loses functions, it loses stability. Third, specialization permits sociologists to note cases where some variation, say in *h, d,* or *f* is accompanied by variation in *g, i,* or *q*. Thus the sociologist doing research in family organization may find that wherever families are decreasing in size, the literacy level of the population is increasing. This poses the question of whether one of the happenings is causing the other, or whether both are traceable to a third factor or variable.

Just as the delimitation of the scientist's field of observation through specialization has proved a fruitful procedure in the development of many disciplines, such as physics, chemistry, biology, and psychology, a number of the best-established principles in sociology have been derived from research in the fields of population, criminology, industry, the family, and so on.

HANDICAPS TO SOCIOLOGY

Science is the most fruitful way of observing, classifying, and interpreting physical and social environments. We are all aware of the great strides in the physical and biological sciences which have made possible modern industry and agriculture, rapid transportation and communication, and the control of disease. Yet we find people are often loath to take an objective viewpoint and apply the empirical method of science to personal and social problems. We would ridicule a person who, if an automobile did not start, would say that the engine was evil or curse the steel from which it was made. We consider ignorant, at best, the person who attempts to set a broken leg with magic incantations. Many people, however, who consider the scientific method a useful device for establishing the principles on which an automobile is built or a leg is set nevertheless resist with great emotion the suggestion that the same method might reveal knowledge and understanding about how people select mates or why some persons in a society become criminals. There are several reasons why such negative attitudes exist.

Resistance to Social Change

The ways of humans are hedged in by intertia. People stubbornly resist innovations which exert pressure on them to alter their socially shared values and beliefs. We need not go back to Galileo or other medieval examples; it was only some 50 years ago that a schoolteacher in Tennessee was tried in court for teaching his students about the theory of evolution.

Social facts are considerably more emotion-laden, of course, than physical facts. When physicists announce that they have learned something new about the way atoms behave, few people are excited about the discovery. They are not personally acquainted with any atoms; their parents did not teach them that good, moral atoms behave in a certain way; and they feel no obligation to revise their day-to-day thinking or behavior because of the physicists' discovery. But when sociologists announce that they have learned something new about how human groups behave, many people are likely to be agitated. They feel that their own observations of their acquaintances are just as valid as the studies of social scientists. Since their parents have taught them that good, moral people behave in a certain way, scientific knowledge about human behavior may threaten to make them feel obligated to revise their own day-to-day thinking and behavior. It takes a considerable amount of conscious effort to abandon ways of thinking to which one has become accustomed, and most people resist new knowledge, even though rationally arrived at, in favor of old superstitions or prejudices. If we have long believed that people who live in the country are happier than those who live in the city, or that white people are more intelligent than blacks, or that contact between groups of persons who resent and distrust each other will get rid of their hostility, then it is easier to reject the evidence of social scientists who inform us that these beliefs are prejudices and superstitions than it is to abandon our beliefs because the scientific evidence runs counter to them.

That people do resist facts that will force them to alter their thinking can be observed in most college classrooms where knowledge about social life is being presented. The phenomenon has been called the "my Aunt Emma" response: the demonstration of a preference for one's personal experience over observations from scientific research whenever the two are in disagreement. The instructor in a sociology class, for example, reads from a United States Census report, "On the basis of interviews with millions of people, we conclude that the average high-school teacher has a larger annual income than the average factory laborer." A student replies, "Well, I don't think that's true, because my Aunt Emma is a teacher and her husband works in a factory and his income is higher than hers." That his personal observation may be perfectly accurate without disproving the census-based generalization may not occur to Aunt Emma's nephew.

Common Sense

People everywhere develop certain standardized answers to questions about people and society that come to be accepted more or less uncritically. One of the difficulties that many of us experience is learning that some of the facts about which we are most certain are false. Because sociology (and the other social sciences) so often deals with matters about which we all have some knowledge, sociology sometimes confronts people with knowledge that is contrary to their "common sense." But common sense is often vague and contradictory. Suppose, for example, that you were to undertake a research study to determine if the statement "persons who work alone are more efficient than persons who work in groups of two or more" is true or false. If, on the basis of your research you learn that the statement is true, you may be certain that someone will tell you that what you learned is only common sense: "Everyone knows that too many cooks spoil the broth." If you find the statement to be false, you may also be certain that someone will tell you that what you learned is only common sense: "Everyone knows that two heads are better than one." The point is that common sense is usually vague and often contradictory. On the one hand we are told to "look before you leap" while on the other hand we are told that "he who hesitates is lost." Common sense is like calling a spade a spade, all the while confusing cards with shovels.

Not only is common sense sometimes vague and contradictory, it is often false and always socially relative. What is common and sensible to the very poor in the United States, for example, is often surprising and fascinating to the middle classes. What is common sense to the Amish of Pennsylvania may not be common or sensible to social workers in San Francisco. All this is not meant to denigrate common sense. On the contrary, the more common the sense, the better it is. Just remember that "common sense" is often neither common nor sensible.

Confusion of Science and Engineering

Scientists assume that any knowledge, whether or not it is "practical," is worthwhile. There is a crucial difference between the scientist, who discovers knowledge, and the engineer, who applies it. The physicist discovers the laws of mass and volume; the engineer applies these laws in constructing a bridge. Sir Alexander Fleming, a bacteriologist, discovered penicillin; the physician who injects penicillin into a patient is acting, not as a scientist, but as an engineer applying knowledge discovered by a scientist. The social worker does not test hypotheses in order to evaluate a scientific theory; he or she applies the knowledge furnished by sociologists and other social scientists. In other words, the social worker is a social engineer. No invidious comparison between scientists and those who apply scientific knowledge is implied. It is important, however, to understand the differences in what they are attempting to do and how they are attempting to do it. Much of the contemporary criticism of the social sciences stems from the fact that some (amateur?) social engineers try to apply knowledge that social scientists have not yet validated.

The goal of the engineer forces him to be concerned with what will work, with principles that are immediately applicable. The goal of the scientist is to pursue with equal concern projects which have no obvious applicability as well as those that do. If there is a possibility that observations of two sets of physical or social phenomena may lead to the understanding of some significant relationship between them, the scientist is interested in those observations, whether or not they seem to offer a way to control disease, build bridges, or make money. He or she is aware that much of the most valuable information in the storehouse of science, such as that about atomic structures cited earlier in this chapter, had no immediate or obvious applicability at the time research leading to it was initiated. Pressures on scholars to engage only in "useful" research can do much to deter the development of science.

Inefficiency of Terminology

Words are the essential tools of thought, scientific and otherwise. All sciences require a clear and unambiguous terminology. The physical and biological scientists have solved this problem by creating complex technical vocabularies, as any freshman struggling to memorize biological terms well knows. In most of the social sciences, however, the answer has not been so simple. First, many of the terms of the social sciences are words also found in everyday speech, and words in general usage are notoriously vague. Thus the word "instinct" once had a rather technical meaning in psychology and biology but, because of its literary and everyday meaning as any more or less learned but automatic response, it has been abandoned by scientists. Second, the language of sociology and psychology, because it is also the language of everyday speech, tends to be emotionally charged. Thus, if a sociologist asks on a questionnaire, "Are you a political conservative?" he or she may get a stream of disgust or affirmation instead of an answer, and even if the interviewees try to answer honestly, there is no assurance that they and the scientist will be using the term *conservative* in the same way. Thus sociologists must constantly try to prune their speech of even remotely emotionally charged words and to guard against their own human reaction to connotative language.

Science and Religion

In addition to the roadblocks to sociology which we have discussed—resistance to social change, common sense, the confusion of engineering with science, and the terminological inefficiency—there is a traditional block for some persons to the acceptance of the scientific study of society: the notion that science is opposed to religion.

Science and religion have come into conflict in the past over matters of dogma, not ethics. The famous religion-versus-science dramas of history have occurred when scientists turned up evidence which made some theological dogma seem extremely unlikely—for example, the refusal of ecclesiastical authorities in the time of Copernicus and Galileo to consider the evidence that the earth moved around the sun. Science does not challenge the rules of morality of any religion, because such guides for living are outside the province of science.

The dogma that all species of life were created in their present form and have not changed since, scientists can disprove; but they can neither prove nor disprove the moral principle expounded in the Golden Rule, which is a statement of what one *should* do. There is no way for science to determine what one should or should not do; science at its most sophisticated stage can only predict what will happen if one does or does not do a certain thing. A scientific theory is composed of empirically testable statements of relationship: "If *a* occurs, then *b* will result." Scientific theories never contain such propositions as "*A should* occur, because that will be better for most people."

Some people object to social science on the ground that God did not intend us to understand man and that it is therefore evil to attempt to do so. Science does not offer a method for proving that there is or is not a God, much less for fathoming His wishes or intentions. Social scientists simply proceed on the premise stated by Alexander Pope: "The proper study of mankind is man."

THE DEVELOPMENT OF SOCIOLOGY: THE FOUNDING FATHERS

Auguste Comte (1789-1857)

Auguste Comte is generally acknowledged as the "father of sociology." He developed the social science which he called sociology and he analyzed the social world around him to explain why this new discipline was needed. And yet it is incorrect to say that Comte was the first person to grapple with the ideas and problems that constitute the subject matter of sociology. The ancient Greeks had systematically examined social phenomena such as the customs and manners of peoples other than themselves, the effects of physical environment (for example, climate) on the inhabitants of a society, the ways in which ideal societies could be developed, the significance of the stage of infancy for human society. Indeed it was Aristotle who described man as "by nature a social being."

The Greeks investigated social phenomena. It was Comte who examined the theoretical sciences that existed (mathematics, mechanics or astronomy, physics, chemistry, biology) and decided that a new science was needed, sociology, a science of social phenomena or a science of society. Comte ranked these theoretical sciences in a hierarchy based on their complexity. It is significant that he placed sociology at the summit. This is because sociology had a special contribution to make. When Comte was writing, Europe was still recovering from the social dislocations of the French Revolution and was also moving into an industrial age where science and technology were to become powerful influences. Comte, acting as a scientist and a social reformer, wanted sociology to provide the means by which a better and more productive social order could be developed.

Positivism Comte developed **positivism,** a method of observing and analyzing social behavior in order to discover the fundamental laws of historical development. An understanding of these laws would, he felt, accelerate the coming of the new order. Using the method of positivism, the sociologist was expected to employ the techniques of observation (the senses), experiment, logical comparison, and the historical method. Interestingly, Comte's historical method is not the method of the historian, who looks for causal relations. Comte is less interested in causes and more interested in uncovering general laws. His historical method involved arrangement of historical facts to coincide with his views of social evolution. Needless to say, this method has little empirical validity.

Statics and Dynamics Comte, however, made a major contribution to the new science of sociology in delineating the two basic categories to be investigated: social statics and social dynamics. Even today these are still central to sociological research. **Social statics** refers to the analysis of the structure of a society. This analysis is anatomical and it reveals the elements that fuse individuals into a cohesive unit and produce social order. **Social dynamics** relates to the ways in which societies change. Thus, Comte expected the sociologist to chart the development of societies as they progressed toward a new and better order.

Herbert Spencer (1820–1903)

After Auguste Comte, it was Herbert Spencer who next enriched the discipline of sociology with valuable theoretical insights. Although Spencer disavowed any intellectual debt to Comte, he, too, accepted the goal of the sociologist as the attempt to uncover the fundamental laws of social progress. Spencer considered his doctrine of evolution to be such a fundamental law.

The Doctrine of Evolution This theoretical contribution was a further development of the concept of social dynamics stated by Comte; it offered an explanation for the way in which societies change. Spencer was aware of Charles Darwin's biological explanation of man's survival through adaptive physical change. However, he insisted that his own contribution was developed independently of Darwin and was distinctive. Spencer was interested in a theoretical explanation for man's social evolution. He noted the way societies grew, both in size and in complexity. With growth came increased differentiation of functions (i.e., the division of labor). Early, loosely knit groups of wanderers at some point became a tribe in which the individuals subordinated themselves to a leader. Next a group of tribes might accept one paramount chief who controlled the actions of a constellation of subchiefs. In these progressive changes Spencer saw a law of social development operating. The process of social evolution involves the passage from an incoherent homogeneity to a coherent heterogeneity, or to state this in another way, the passage from the uniform to the multiform. A primitive tribe illustrates an unstable and homogeneous entity which has the possibility of developing over time into a complex, heterogeneous, and modern society whose differentiated parts perform many different functions.

Society as an Organism In his theory of evolution Spencer draws an analogy between society and a living organism, systematically developing this comparison with fundamental similarities and differences. One similarity is that in both societies and animal organisms, if the life of the whole is destroyed, the units or parts will continue to live on for a while. While Spencer's argument that society is a living organism is impressively argued, sociologists today do not believe that social phenomena can be explained in the terms of biology. They also reject his deductive explanations rounded out with illustrations. Unlike Comte, he ignored the importance of empirical testing. Contemporary sociologists consider empiricism a cornerstone of scientific investigation.

It would be difficult to overestimate the importance that Spencer had for his contemporaries. His work was an important theoretical force throughout the entire English-speaking world. And yet much of his theory and methodology have been discarded. Whereas Comte expected sociology to aid in developing a better world, Spencer conceived social evolution to be inevitable and not to be interfered with. His personal concern with individualism caused him to resist notions of social reform. He coined the term "the survival of the fittest" and clearly stated that the less fit (the sick, the poor, the less intelligent) should be allowed to die. Spencer greatly influenced certain American sociologists, such as William Graham Sumner, and many of his ideas were used by the industrial barons of the day to justify their positions of power.

Karl Marx (1818-1883)

The theoretical contributions of Karl Marx have been so influential within the social sciences that he has become all things to all scholars. Marx is discussed as a philosopher by modern philosophers, hailed as a seminal economist by economists, profoundly respected as a political scientist by political scientists, and is accepted without question as a sociologist by sociologists. Within the field of sociology, Marx's analyses of social interaction are compelling and useful in understanding group behavior.

Economic Determinism First of all, Marx identified the economic structure as that basic social institution that determined the growth and functioning of all others. Thus, in industrial society the owners of the means of production (i.e., industrial plants and equipment) had the power to control economic output and also political institutions, could significantly influence religious institutions, and could affect education and the quality of life within families. Marx's theory is, then, an example of economic determinism, in which one causal factor explains everything that happens—production, distribution, the balance of power, artistic and intellectual products, and both the evils and problems to be found in contemporary societies.

Social Change A basic concept in sociology is that of social change. Marx's theory of social change is tied to the way economic arrangements change. With immense erudition and a powerful intellect, he reviewed the development of Western capitalistic society using the dialectical process or explanation. It was his belief that social change occurs as opposing elements clash in dramatic ways. One historical order **(thesis)** produces an opposing order **(antithesis).** The industrial society in England, the model best illustrating his theories, developed out of an agricultural society in which ownership of land determined power and influence. The earlier society (thesis) gave way to a new order (industrial capatalism—antithesis).

Class Conflict But Marx was a compelling social reformer committed to the development of a better world. His doctrine of revolution through class conflict offered the mechanism whereby a more positive reorganization of society **(synthesis)** could be achieved. Marx believed that it was in work activity that man most fully realized his potential, both creatively and productively. His powerful analysis of the differences among social classes offers a valuable new analytic concept to social scientists. By losing control of the production process, the class of workers (the proletariat) felt exploited, and alienated by the boring, repetitive, segmented tasks associated with the division of labor on the assembly line. Because the dominant class, the bourgeoisie who were the owners of the means of production, would continue to exploit them relentlessly, the only hope of the workers would be the development of consciousness of themselves as a social class (a political awareness which would prepare them for the coming revolt). Out of the revolutionary conflict, the once exploited proletariat would eventually establish a classless, nonantagonistic, more humane society.

Emile Durkheim (1855–1917)

Emile Durkheim is a towering figure in the development of sociology. He was profoundly affected by Auguste Comte's conviction that positivism offered the most precise method for analyzing social life. Because positivism directs researchers in the social sciences to use the exacting methods of the physical sciences, both Durkheim and, before him, Comte hoped to develop a rigorous new science that would permit the comprehensive examination of social structures.

Social Facts It is possible that Durkheim's own Jewish background and his identification with this cohesive ethnic minority contributed to his ongoing interest in the solidarity of social groups. Contrary to the psychological emphasis of his time, Durkheim rejected the individual as the basic unit of study and focused instead upon the group. He maintained that the character of group life could not be explained using psychological factors. Durkheim used the illustration of a crowd. If an emotional and violent outburst exploded from such a group, it was not merely the common expression of individual sentiments. It was a new thing entirely, a social fact with a reality of its own. Social facts must then be the basic units of analysis in sociology and part of a new methodology devised to deal with this special subject matter. Social facts were external to the individual and consisted of characteristic ways of acting, thinking, and feeling. Social facts were culturally created and had great power over individual conduct. Some examples of social facts were standards of morality, customs, religious requirements, rules of professional behavior (e.g., the Hippocratic Oath). Birth rates, marriage rates, suicide rates were also examples of social facts. All were uniquely social realities and, though we might resist, their coercive power remained for us to react against. Thus, human beings did not in fact create society, but were rather the creations of society.

Social Order A fundamental aspect of Durkheim's sociology is the problem of social order. Like Herbert Spencer, he focused his examination of society on the parts of the whole. However, he rejected the biological analogy. Durkheim was interested in the way the parts functioned in the maintenance of social order. This stress on interrelated social elements and their functions for the whole structure has caused Durkheim to be identified as the father of **functionalism,** still the dominant theoretical perspective in American sociology. Social order was essential in social life or society could not survive. And the division of labor was basic to the foundation of social order. In *The Division of Labor in Society* (1893) which Durkheim wrote in partial fulfillment of the requirements for the degree of Doctor of Philosophy, he identified two processes that contributed to social solidarity. The first of these was **mechanical solidarity.** Mechanical solidarity could be found in early, primitive or traditional societies. Here the pressure for sameness or homogeneity in behavior and attitudes was great. Individuality and differences were muted by a collective conscience, made up of the shared beliefs and sentiments of the group. The repressiveness and coerciveness of such societies could be seen in their penal laws, which were also their religious laws (Bierstedt, 1966). The commission of a crime injured a victim, but it was also an affront against the community. Thus the criminal law dealt with more than punishment; it served social ends by healing "the wounds of the law-abiding, the wounds caused by assault on their common sentiments. Punishment thus serves the community and contributes to the integration of society." (Durkheim, 1912)

Organic solidarity was characteristic of modern industrial society. Because of the division of labor, societies were complex. Labor was divided among numerous occupational groups. But many tasks basic to society's functioning were also assigned on a basis of age and sex. Durkheim agreed with Spencer that societies became increasingly heterogeneous or differentiated as they developed. He called this an "organic" solidarity because the interrelated parts had specialized functions. However, out of this specialization, this difference, cohesion and solidarity grew. Though individuals were less restricted by the group pressure of traditional society and had more freedom, they were also more interdependent. The very division of labor caused us to rely on each other. (And in contemporary society it only takes a social crisis like a garbage strike or a massive power failure to demonstrate this.) Organic solidarity, then, contributes to the integration of society and social order.

Max Weber (1864–1920)

Max Weber is an example of a polyhistor. This is a scholar whose learning is so prodigious in so many areas that his writings cannot be confined to one discipline. Weber is like Marx in this respect. His writings on the sociology of religion, the sociology of law, economics, history, and the methodology of the social sciences are brilliant and still immensely useful to researchers in all of these fields.

Weber's sociological investigations were very original and insightful. He seemed frequently to be responding to Karl Marx, though Marx had died many years before. Weber was definitely not a Marxist. While he acknowledged the relevance of economic conditions on social behavior, Weber found Marx's economic determinism too narrow. He refuted it in a highly creative essay called "The Protestant Ethic and the Spirit of Capitalism."

The Protestant Ethic Marx had developed an economic interpretation of history to account for the rise of capitalism. Weber found the Western form of capitalism to be absolutely unique because it had been shaped by religious influences coming from Protestantism, specifically the precepts of Calvinism. Indeed, Weber noted that the Chinese civilization contained many of the economic elements necessary to the development of capitalism and yet it had not happened. Calvinist doctrine tied the possibility of eternal salvation to the secular activity of work. Religious salvation then became a powerful motivational force which produced:

1. A justification for acquisitiveness. Wealth was a sign of God's blessing.
2. A diligent, internally motivated work force. The rewards were not financial but spiritual.
3. A sober group shunning luxury and consumption so that financial accumulation could continue.

From these conditions, institutionalized within the ascetic branches of the Protestantism religious structure, came the elements necessary to usher in the economic system of capitalism in the West.

Weber had little interest in developing comprehensive scientific systems like Comte and Spencer. He did not believe that it was possible to uncover general laws of human behavior. Weber defined sociology as the science of social action, but he viewed action from two perspectives. This is because he was interested in the individual within society, so on the one hand Weber examines social action in a subjective and individual way; and on the other hand, in a more general and typical fashion. In a blurring of sociology and psychology, Weber is interested in the meaning that the individual gives to social actions. But he also developed a typical or abstract method for examining the elements in a pattern of action. This is Weber's famous ideal type.

The Ideal Type The ideal type is an analytic tool that Weber found useful in historical and sociological examinations. The ideal type can be a historical entity that is unique to an era, like capitalism or feudalism, or it can be an institution frequently found in history, like the bureaucracy. The ideal type offers a model, developed by abstracting elements from an entity so it appears in its purest form. This model can then be compared with reality. For example, the bureaucracy as an ideal type could be compared with the welfare system, thus measuring reality against an abstract reconstruction. Such a method offered the scientist a way of rationally and objectively dealing with phenomena.

THEORETICAL PERSPECTIVES IN SOCIOLOGY

In looking at the world and in doing research, the sociologist is guided by a point of view. What is observed or learned is filtered through a special frame of reference which can be called a theoretical perspective. Each sociologist has such a frame of reference because it offers a way of organizing and understanding what has been amassed through research. In ancient Rome there existed a theoretical point of view called Epicureanism. In this frame of reference, pleasure was the highest good. In day-to-day interactions with others, Epicureans allowed this perspective to influence their behavior so that, during the latter period of the Roman Empire, they gave full rein to every sensual appetite and passion— "Let us eat and drink, for tomorrow we die." Epicureanism, then, provided a frame of reference that influenced the perceptions and behavior of the Romans in unusual ways. Clearly, theoretical perspectives shape what is perceived and the way sense data (the impressions of the senses) will be used.

Functionalism (Structural-Functionalism)

The functionalist views society as a social system, a whole, made up of parts that are interrelated. The parts of the system perform functions (have duties or work) that allow the whole to survive. Sociologists accepting this point of view stress the contributions of the parts to the maintenance of the whole. Earlier sociologists like Herbert Spencer had been guided by a functionalist model derived from biology. But the modern sociologist would avoid the biological analogy, recognizing that Spencer's awareness of parallels between living organisms and society does not prove actual connections between them. However, modern functionalists do accept the view of society as a system of interrelated parts.

The functionalist perspective has been enormously influential in American sociology for nearly a century, because of the influence of Emile Durkheim and later theorists such as Robert Merton and Talcott Parsons. Functionalists have stressed an image of society as a well-integrated whole. The early functionalists conceived of the social system as a closed entity, which could adjust to minor dislocations but which was not able to deal with major social disruptions created by social forces outside the system. Early functionalist theory did not account for sudden crises, such as the gasoline shortage of 1973, within its theoretical framework. This static quality within the theory caused many critics to attack functionalism as a conservative perspective. Contemporary theorists recognized these criticisms and adjusted the theoretical framework. The parts of the **social system** (the family system, the educational system, the economic system) function to maintain a balance or equilibrium. Where there is disruption in one part, the effects are felt in other parts of the system and are perceived as *dysfunctional*, or detrimental, to the whole. Since the system strives for balance, adjustments are made that offer the possibility of a renewed state of equilibrium.

In functionalistic terms the educational system may be thought of as an important subsystem or social institution of society that functions in close relation to other parts of the whole system. For example, in America the educational structures must continue the socialization initially undertaken by the family and provide the cultural knowledge and skills demanded by the economic structure if young people are to successfully fill occupational roles. And yet the campus disruptions of the 1960s can be examined from the functionalist perspective. The eruptions of violence were related to a general disaffection with the power of college administrators to control the lives of students (rigid grading systems and curriculums, and also sex-segregated and rigidly controlled dormitory arrangements). Added to this was student resistance to faculty involvement in war-related government research and the presence of military installations, such as R.O.T.C., on campus. When the Vietnamese war escalated and demonstrating students at Kent State and Jackson State were shot, the educational system became a battleground. Disruptions in the forms of computer blow-ups (with loss of life), student strikes, and confrontations, were dysfunctional because they threatened the equilibrium of the educational system and also the larger society. The functionalist view is that the social system adjusts to disruption through compromise and cooperation. Within the educational structures of the society such adjustive procedures began. Student representatives were added to school governing bodies, curricula were liberalized, "open" dormitories were instituted as higher education officials attempted to restore an equilibrium to the system. On a national scale, the disruptions of students were acknowledged to have influenced American withdrawal from Vietnam and the ending of the draft (reactions within the political subsystem); they also roused opinion within the religious subsystem on the morality of American commitment. There is some question whether or not the lethargy and quiescence of students today is, in fact, an example of a well-integrated educational system. However, the functionalist would stress that disruption in one part of the system affected other parts so that societal adjustments were necessary to restore balance to the whole.

Macro-Theory and Micro-Theory Functionalism and conflict theory are examples of macro-theories. The concept of a macro-theory means that the canvas to be examined and explained is the society as a whole. Using this orientation the theorist looks at the larger elements of social structure (i.e., the political system, patterns of racial discrimination, the effects of prostitution on the institution of marriage, the interactions between unions and corporations). Exchange theory concerns itself with macro- and micro-theory. *Micro-theory* (or small-scale theory) is exemplified in symbolic interaction, in which theoretical explanations of social behavior are limited to small-group interactions in face-to-face situations.

The Concept of Function Previously, the way that the social system functioned has been defined as the way the system operated or worked. Because functionalist theory stresses the interrelationships and interdependence of the parts of the system, the way in which the component parts function determines the stability and equilibrium of the whole. However, the concept of function deserves additional attention. The function of the parts of the system is revealed by the consequences they have for the whole. This examination of consequences rather than purposes is valuable because often the parts have consequences for the whole that have not been anticipated. Robert Merton (1957) has offered an analysis of system functions that clarifies the question in a useful way. Some functions of the social system are **manifest.** This means they are recognizable, obvious, and consciously intended. One function of the political system is the maintenance of public order. The function of the educational system is to prepare the young for adult roles in the society. Merton notes that there are **latent functions** to be considered also. These are functions that are not recognized and are unintended. A latent function of the educational system is to contain millions of physically mature youngsters and keep them out of the job market. The manifest function of a funeral is to bury the dead. A latent function of a funeral is to reintegrate the group, to draw scattered family members together, and reestablish a sense of solidarity—to close the gap in the circle caused by the death.

1-2 CHECKING IT OUT: A Conflict Theorist Views Functionalism

One of the more unfortunate connotations of the word "system" is its closedness. Although some structural-functionalists have tried, there is no getting away from the fact that a system—even if only "for purposes of analysis"—is essentially something self-sufficient, internally consistent, and closed to the outside. A leg cannot be called a system; a body can. Actually, advocates of the system have little reason to be unhappy with this term; abandoning it would rob their analysis of much of its neatness, and above all would leave no function for the "whatever sources"—the villainous outsiders they can now introduce to "account" for unwanted realities. I do not want to carry my polemicizing too far, but I cannot help feeling that it is only a step from thinking about societies in terms of equilibrated systems to asserting that every disturber of the equilibrium, every deviant, is a "spy" or an "imperialist agent." By implication, the system theory of society comes dangerously close to the conspiracy theory of history—which is not only the end of all sociology but also rather silly.* There is nothing logically wrong with the term "system." It begins to give birth to undesirable consequences only when it is applied to total societies and is made the ultimate frame of reference of analysis. It is certainly true that sociology deals with society. But it is equally true that physics deals with nature, and yet physicists would hardly see an advance in calling nature a system and trying to analyze it as such. In fact, any such analysis would probably—and justly—be discarded as metaphysics.

To repeat, the social system as conceived by some recent sociological theorists appears to have the same features that characterize utopian societies. This being so, we are forced to conclude that structural-functional theory also deals with societies from which historical change is absent, and that it is, in this sense, utopian. To be sure, it is utopian not because some of the assumptions of this theory are "unrealistic"—this would be true for the assumptions of almost any scientific theory—but because it is exclusively concerned with spelling out the conditions of the functioning of a utopian social system. Structural-functional theory does not introduce unrealistic assumptions for the purpose of explaining real problems; it introduces many kinds of assumptions, concepts, and models for the sole purpose of describing a social system that has never existed and is not likely ever to come into being.

*It could, for instance, be argued that only totalitarian states display one unified value system, and that only in the case of totalitarian systems do we have to assume some outside influence ("from whatever source") to account for change—an argument that clearly reduces the extreme structural-functional position to absurdity.

SOURCE: Ralf Dahrendorf, *Essays in the Theory of Society* (Stanford: Stanford University Press, 1968), pp. 117–118.

1-3 CHECKING IT OUT: A Functionalist Defends Functionalism

The fact that functional analysis can be seen by some as inherently conservative and by others as inherently radical suggests that it may be *inherently* neither one nor the other. It suggests that functional analysis may involve no *intrinsic* ideological commitment although, like other forms of sociological analysis, it can be infused with any one of a wide range of ideological values. Now, this is not the first time that a theoretic orientation in social science or social philosophy has been assigned diametrically opposed ideological implications.

SOURCE: Robert Merton, *Social Theory and Social Structure* (New York: The Free Press, 1967), p. 39.

Conflict Theory

The sociologist who accepts the conflict perspective might accept the view of society as a whole made up of parts, but because of a personal frame of reference that is very different from that of the functionalist, this sociologist looks at the same social system and events but filters sense impressions differently, asks different kinds of questions, and arrives at different kinds of answers. To the question "How does the whole thing operate?" the conflict theorist focuses, not on the interdependence and cooperation of the parts of the social system, but on the competition and conflict evident as social groups interact. There is little social integration here. Thus the conflict theorist asks

> 1. How do conflicting groups arise from the structure of society? 2. What forms can the struggles among such groups assume? 3. How does the conflict among such groups affect a change in the social structures? (Dahrendorf, 1958)

Conflict theorists, among them Ralf Dahrendorf and Lewis Coser, have been much influenced by Karl Marx. Marx clearly believed that when the workers or proletariat began a revolutionary struggle against the bourgeoisie or capitalists, the outcome would be a beneficial thing, producing a more humane and egalitarian society.

The Value of Conflict Conflict theory recognizes that social conflict is a fundamental mechanism of society. It is not occasional, but omnipresent. It is not unusual; it is constant. The things that people strive for (wealth, power, prestige, fame) are in short supply. Many desire them but few achieve them. Those few who "catch the brass ring" are rarely anxious to share the rewards with others, so that the "haves" will unite to thwart the progress of the "have-nots." The conflict that ensues can take many forms: hostility, disagreement, competition, violence, injury. Marx focused on the conflict resulting from the struggle of social classes within capitalistic society. But conflict theorists today must recognize a variety of conflicting interest groups besides social classes—corporations and unions; consumers and manufacturers; senior citizens and governmental agencies; landlords and tenant groups; competing ethnic, racial, and religious groups. The special contribution of conflict theory to an understanding of social interaction is that conflict is valuable. Though it may sometimes have destructive results, it may often have positive results. It is through social conflict that social change occurs.

The disruptive events on college campuses in the 1960s offer a cogent example of the uses of conflict. The student population had a variety of special interests to expand and protect. They were in disagreement with the administrators who exerted power over them through rigidities of curriculum and grading and who prevented freer sexual expression with peers. They were in disagreement with policy makers in government about U. S. goals in Southeast Asia and particularly angry that middle-aged functionaries in Washington had the power of life and death over them as instruments in a deadly nuclear war machine. Campus conflict accomplished many things:

1. It bound college students more closely together and clarified their common interests.

2. Campus conflict galvanized national opinion about curriculum reform, the special problems and needs of minority college students, the questionable need for college officials to function as guardians of morality (*in loco parentis*) as well as educators, the role of warfare in civilized society. The possibility of constructive change grew as these social problems were debated in a national arena.

3. Social conflict on the campuses and in the urban centers of the society helped to effect important changes within the educational system (e.g., open university programs, life experience credits, affirmative action programs benefiting ethnic minorities and women).

Conflict theorists stress that in the resolution of conflict, social stability is accomplished once again. It can then be suggested that although conflict occurs, society adjusts and returns to stability; therefore social conflict contributes to social stability.

Exchange Theory

Exchange theory examines the process of social exchange in human interaction. Day-to-day living involves a series of exchanges. If A babysits for B it is assumed that at some point B will reciprocate. If one couple has friends in for dinner, the dinner guests may later invite them to the theater. Social relations are based on reciprocity because people act rationally. As they pursue goals and scarce rewards, those around them must be taken into account, because others both influence and often control their access to the goals that are sought. Social interactions are then based on expectations. We give but we also expect to receive eventually. Therefore the concepts of exchange theory are similar to those used in economic transactions (according to this perspective, economic exchanges are thought to be a variety of social exchange). Exchange theorists discuss investments, value costs, rewards, profits, benefits. Thus a marriage may be headed for divorce when there has been a breakdown in the exchange process with the result that there is an unequal distribution of rewards. When an emotional investment has been made in marriage, but one individual feels that he or she is contributing much more to the relationship than the other, a net loss in the investment is perceived.

Social exchange theory is increasing in popularity among sociologists because it offers valuable insights into social interactions. However, it is a theory that is still being developed. Exchange theory owes much to George Homans. (1961) Because he wishes to develop a formal theory, Homans has devoted much attention to developing basic concepts, and also to formulating general propositions or theoretical statements about the exchange process.

Peter Blau (1964) has also added to the body of exchange theory and, with Homans, is considered a leading exchange theorist.

Symbolic Interactionism

Symbolic interaction theory offers a way of understanding social life that is very different from functionalism and conflict theory. Whereas these latter perspectives give attention to large-scale social structures or systems (macro-systems) and to comprehensive events like social equilibrium and social change, symbolic interactionism focuses on a smaller arena of action. Indeed, interactionism may be viewed as a micro-theory. Interaction theorists are interested in the way people behave in face-to-face encounters and carefully analyze the social interactions of everyday living. George Herbert Mead (1863–1931) enriched the content of interaction theory during the years between World War I and World War II at the University of Chicago. In the famous lectures that became *Mind, Self and Society* (1934), he emphasized the importance of human communication through symbols. Words and gestures are symbols. In an earlier stage in human history there may not have been language, but humans could have communicated through grunts, gestures, posturing. However, the uniqueness of the human animal has much to do with the development of communications processes. Humans learned to use symbols to represent objects. The word "rock" represents the object. By attaching symbolic meanings or names to objects, language was developed. The pool of words that people used grew and began to encompass more subtle thoughts. Words for objects—bone, tree, tiger—gave way to descriptive words like angry, flat, dangerous, and to words of action—run, throw, crawl. As words were shared in social situations, the content and complexity of language grew. Mead was sure that the development of the human mind, which he saw as an evolutionary process, was closely linked to the communication of humans through symbols.

The ability to give meaning to objects and experiences in one's environment is accomplished by communicating with others through language, which creates responses. This notion may be illustrated in the following way.

While it is clear that insects live in societies that are complex in organization, their behavior seems to be biologically determined. They are programmed to act. Mead felt that humans are unique in having the ability to interpret actions and give them meaning before acting. Therefore, when one person extends a hand toward another, the intention of this gesture becomes a symbol to be interpreted: "Is it friendly?" "Am I supposed to put my hat on it?" "Is it begging or threatening?" When this gesture is accompanied by the verbal symbol "Hello!" the gesture of the outstretched hand will then be interpreted as friendly. When the second individual then holds out a hand and completes a handshake, he has interpreted the verbal symbol and the gesture, then responded to them. Note that the gesture and the word have been interpreted by both individuals similarly. The consensus that creates human society results from such shared understandings, shared meanings, and similar expectations. We will more fully examine and relate the development of the "self" to society in our discussion of socialization in Chapter 6.

The theorist using the perspective of symbolic interactionism closely examines the interactions and communication processes of those acting and reacting to one another. Thus this sociologist would examine the interactions among family members to discover how decisions are made, how conflict and violence are handled, what factors cause marital dissolution. The interactionist is particularly concerned about the self-evaluation that comes from interaction with others. Thus, if such a researcher got a chance to question a small group of looters after the blackout in New York in 1977, much attention would be devoted to the way the looters viewed themselves as a result of this experience. Do the looters view their actions as deviant? Do they feel ashamed? How do they justify their actions to their peers, to their families, to reporters? Depending on the way the participant has been raised, will he or she now feel deviant or nondeviant?

INTERPRETIVE SUMMARY

Sociology is the scientific study of human group life. Science is distinguished from other fields of learning by its commitment to the scientific method, its insistence upon objectivity, and its interest in knowledge *per se*. Social science applies the scientific method to the study of human interaction. The social scientist wants to form accurate generalizations about how people behave in groups.

The scientific method seeks knowledge on the basis of three assumptions. The scientist assumes that the most valid way of getting, organizing, and testing the reliability of knowledge is through (1) the use of man's sensory-perceptual experience, aided by instruments, to gather data, (2) the use of logic, or human reasoning, to interpret the data theoretically, and (3) agreement among a number of independent observers concerning the reliability of theoretical propositions.

The social sciences are divided into academic disciplines. Some scholars have studied certain important systems which appear, with variations, almost universally; others have concerned themselves with the more specific event or system. Sociology is the social science dealing with human interaction as such. General sociologists attempt to find generalizations about human groups in interaction. Many sociologists specialize, dealing with particular institutions and phenomena existing at particular times and places.

The study of sociology has been handicapped in several ways, not the least of which have been the fact that people tend to fear and resist new ideas and the fact that the terminology of sociology, which should be as precise as that of any other science, is too often vague and emotionally charged.

Early sociologists devoted much attention to the subject matter and methodology of the new science of sociology. *Auguste Comte,* the father of sociology, developed *positivism,* a method of observing social phenomena using the techniques of observation, experiment, logical comparison, and the historical method. Comte also developed the two major categories of investigation in sociology: *social statics* or the analysis of structure, and *social dynamics,* the analysis of social change.

Herbert Spencer further developed the concept of social dynamics in his doctrine of social evolution. As societies grew they changed from homogeneous structures to heterogeneous structures with more differentiation of functions. Spencer accepted this as a law of social development. He also analyzed society using the biological analogy of a living organism. Spencer's theories had great influence among his contemporaries, particularly American sociologists.

Karl Marx brilliantly analyzed the economic structure of society as the dominant structure that determined the functioning of all others. This is *economic determinism.* Marx analyzed the mechanisms of social change using the dialectical process of *thesis, antithesis,* and *synthesis.* As opposing social forces clashed (in Marx's day these were the dominant social classes), he foresaw that a revolutionary struggle would ensue out of which communism, a new and more humane order, would emerge.

Emile Durkheim was primarily interested in those elements of society that promote social order and cohesion. Human beings were coerced by *social facts,* characteristic ways of thinking, feeling, and acting. Durkheim accepted social facts as the basic units of analysis in sociology. He analyzed *mechanical* and *organic solidarity* as processes that contributed to social order, but he felt that organic solidarity was characteristic of industrial society, fostering differentiation of social functions and interdependence.

Max Weber explained the Protestant Ethic as an important contributing factor to the rise of Western capitalism, a religious motivation with economic consequences. Weber also developed the *ideal type* as a methodological tool of analysis for social scientists.

Functionalism and *conflict theory* are macro-theories that explain how societies work. Functionalism views society as an entity made up of interrelated parts, characterized by a striving toward equilibrium through cooperative effort. The conflict theorist sees conflict and competition as basic social mechanisms. Conflict is always present and in the resolution of conflict situations, social stability is accomplished.

Exchange theory views social interaction as an exchange process in which rational beings interact socially on the basis of *reciprocity.* Through trade-offs and exchanges, we pursue social rewards, aware that others influence our access to rewards.

Symbolic interactionism is a micro-theory, which focuses on small-group interactions in face-to-face encounters. Human interaction in society is based on symbolic communication, a communication that involves shared meanings and expectations.

QUESTIONS

1. What are the elements of the scientific method? How are they different from the methods of inquiry used by a learned minister of the church?
2. Would it be wise to discard all ideas and beliefs that cannot be verified scientifically? Is it possible?
3. If a group of college students decided to form a Tibetan monastery on campus they would excite the interest of many scholars. How might they be examined by a team of sociologists? A group of psychologists? A team of journalists? How might the questions asked by each team be different?
4. Compare the contributions of Comte, Spencer, Marx, Durkheim, and Weber. How did each explain the way in which society functions? Are there any similarities among these theorists? What differences do you see?

2

Doing Sociology - Research Methods

PROCEDURES AND TECHNIQUES

Doing sociology can be tremendously exciting. This is because the whole canvas of human activity is there for sociologists to examine: the interaction of members within an unusual new religious sect, the behavior of a group of winos as they pass the bottle, the conflicts of ethnic minorities within a community or a nation, the encounters of strangers in a singles bar, the progress of women in achieving top management jobs, the social characteristics of child abusers. Any of these groups and diverse others offer a special challenge to the sociologist—the possibility of uncovering new regularities in human behavior. Because scientific knowledge is only true until further notice, new and important explanations may be right around the corner. But how to unearth this new knowledge? How can we devise methods to study such dissimilar groups of people?

Doing sociology involves an integration of theory and research. Either of these may come first. In the case of Durkheim's *Suicide*, the theory emerged from the data. However, most of the time the researcher looks for research methods that are compatible with a proposed theory. The methodology of sociology deals with the procedures followed in scientific investigation. A useful set of procedures includes the following steps: (Selltiz *et al.*, 1959; Miller, 1962)

1. A statement of purpose and a selection of an important problem. The researchers hope to add to the store of human knowledge, to offer some new insights to the discipline. A preliminary statement suggests that an area of study has been chosen and the purpose of the research has been thought about. The reasons for that choice may stem from practical concerns, as when a community organization requests a study of the assimilation patterns of an immigrant group new to the region. However, some scientific investigation is prompted by simple curiosity, as when Charles Horton Cooley watched his own children and began to theorize about the process by which children internalize social norms. Part of the sociological endeavor is to examine social interaction or social problems with the hope of understanding them more fully. The researcher does not commit herself or himself to solving social problems.

2. Formulation of hypotheses and description of study design. The researcher generally begins with a **hypothesis**. This is a statement about the relationships between variables. The researcher may have a hunch about some aspect of social life that deserves further exploration. Possible hypotheses might be: (1) College graduates have a higher probability of getting divorced than do noncollege graduates. (2) Warnings on cigarette packages, about the increased risk of cancer from smoking, decrease the consumption of cigarettes by Americans. These statements are constructed using variables—college graduates, divorce, consumption of cigarettes are variables. A **variable** is any social characteristic that can vary. Height (tall, medium, short), social class (upper, middle, lower class), marital status (single, married, divorced, widowed), ethnicity, sex, political party, or other variables. Hypotheses generalize about the influence of one variable on another because the notion of cause and effect underlies hypothesis construction. Hypothesis: If ties to social groups are weak (cause) the possibility of committing suicide is increased (the effect).

3. Selection of methods for data collection. In assembling the **data,** decisions must be made about the kinds of data to be used. There may be data already available that can be used. Documents such as letters, historical writings, official records, or studies that have been conducted by other researchers can be valuable sources of data. Riley (1963) distinguishes between these data and new data that the researcher must gather, based on the objectives of the study. Where new material is needed, the decision may be made to observe group interaction directly, to question group members, or to combine group observation and questioning as in participant observation. Another method of data collection may be survey research, where questionnaires and interviews may be used. A laboratory experiment may best fulfill research objectives.

4. Research results obtained, analyzed, and presented. Once the data have been gathered, the researcher must establish connections between the data. Here there is a constant analysis of the data. Analysis may take the form of reflection and careful examination to establish relationships as in the case of participant observation. Or analysis may result from mechanical procedures as in the use of computers.

5. Conclusions and interpretations specified in terms of implications for theory, further research, and/or solutions to problems. The significance of this step is great. The study must be examined with its larger implications in mind. Study results must be related to the body of sociological research already existing. The conclusions reached in this research may have implications for future research or may suggest new avenues in terms of social policy.

THE EXPERIMENTAL MODEL

The Laboratory Experiment

The ideal model for scientific research is the classical laboratory experimental design (the controlled experiment). (Stouffer, 1955) The value of this model lies in the possibility of constructing an environment and then carefully controlling all variables within that environment. The laboratory experiment can be contrasted with the field experiment (sometimes referred to as the natural experiment). Field experiments are conducted outside the laboratory in settings like factories, schools, prisons. The research design of the laboratory experiment requires the comparison of two groups (**the experimental group** and **the control group**) at two different points in time (before and after). The two groups must be identical at the beginning of the experiment (the "before" stage). A change (the experimental variable) is then induced in the experimental group but no change is effected in the control group. The control group is used to determine what change takes place "normally" with the passage of time and without the introduction of the experimental variable. The effect of the experiment is measured by looking at the change in both groups, and then subtracting the change (if any) in the control group from the change (if any) in the experimental group.

	Before	After	
Experimental Group	X_1	X_2	$X_2 - X_1 = d$ (change in the experimental group)
Control Group	X'_1	X'_2	$X'_2 - X'_1 = d'$ (change in the control group)

$d - d'$ = the difference due to the experimental variable

Scientists are not always able to follow the classical experimental design in their research. Sometimes they research or describe only one part of the situation (X_2 in the figure shown here, for example). Sometimes the research involves a before and after comparison of an experimental group (X_1 and X_2) without comparable data for a control group. Research sometimes constitutes a comparison of two matched groups at one point in time (X_2 and X'_2). And some research is based on observations of one group at one time and a different group at another time (X_1 and X'_2).

The difficulties of doing research that meets the standards of the classical experimental design is one reason that statistical analysis is widely used in sociology. Probability statistics, for example, are used to estimate the "missing data" in situations in which the data are not otherwise available. Although it is not always possible to meet the ideal model of a controlled experiment, one must be aware of the goal and keep it constantly in mind when evaluating research studies.

A Hypothetical Laboratory Experiment Elements of the classical laboratory experiment may be illustrated by a program of prekindergarten education. The researchers hope to confirm a hypothesis about the value of such education.

Hypothesis Early environmental influences that handicap a child educationally are remediable through intensive early childhood experiences. This theoretical statement is then to be tested empirically. A controlled experiment is devised.

Sample An experimental group of children and a control group are selected, then matched on a number of variables. All the children are three and four years old. They are all from lower socioeconomic status homes; this has been established by a SES scale. Only those below a certain income level are eligible. All the children are black and live in the Harlem area. Both boys and girls are chosen. The research assumption here is that the two groups should be as much alike as possible.

Treatment When the experimental treatment is applied to one group, any changes may be assumed to be the effects of the treatment—intensive compensatory education. When the members of the experimental and control groups are chosen, they are both tested. This is to establish what concepts and information they already have. The experimental group enters school and begins learning experiences (exposure to stories, trips, specially constructed learning materials, experiences with tape recorders, and many situations where verbal enrichment is possible). The control group has no such experiences. They remain at home. At the end of one year both groups are tested again.

Results The hypothesis will be confirmed if at the posttest the experimental group demonstrates superior academic performance. But what if the control children perform as well as the experimental group does? This is possible and reveals some of the weaknesses of the experiment as a method. The greatest problem with the experiment is that control of all possible environmental variables is difficult or impossible, so that confounding factors creep in to cloud experimental results. If the control group achieved scores comparable to the experimental group, the researchers would attempt to locate the confounding factors. Suppose the control group children stay home but watch a good deal of educational television. They might perform as well as the experimentals. Such possibilities indicate the difficulties involved in setting up controlled experiments. The best way to validate the result of the experiment is through replication or public verifiability. If another researcher follows the same procedures and gets the same results the experiment has empirical **reliability.**

The Field or Natural Experiment

The field or natural experiment attempts to avoid the artificiality of the laboratory setting. Even though there will be some manipulation of variables in the field, the hope is that those involved will be less likely to change their behavior in more familiar settings. A well-known field experiment is Elton Mayo's research at the Hawthorne plant of Western Electric in Chicago. (Roethlisberger and Dickson, 1939) Here researchers were examining the factors that might affect worker productivity. Productivity was then the **dependent variable** of their study. In cause-and-effect terms, the dependent variable is the effect, the result. The researchers selected an experimental group of female workers to compare with workers who would continue in a normal manner (control group). Certain aspects of the environment of the experimentals were manipulated (coffee breaks, lighting, ways in which payment would be earned, e.g., piece rates, varied lunch arrangements). These were the **independent variables**: Those factors that would cause the resulting effect, productivity. The researchers were amazed to discover that no matter how the setting was manipulated, the experimental women or subjects increased their production levels. Whether changes introduced improved work conditions or worsened them, production levels soared. The researchers realized that there was an unforeseen variable confounding their results. And this was the extra attention that the experimental group was getting. The positive results that are, in fact, the response to special attention have been called the **Hawthorne effect.** Such confounding variables must be anticipated and accounted for in experimental designs.

Advantages and Disadvantages of the Experiment

The experiment is a valuable method because it allows the reseacher to isolate and study the influence of selected variables. This may be difficult to accomplish in everyday situations, where other influences may be distorting social processes. Experiments offer the possibility of uncovering cause-and-effect relationships. However, experiments are not real-life situations. The artificial setting may cause subjects to behave otherwise than usual, so that laboratory or field behavior might not occur in everyday situations.

SURVEY RESEARCH

Surveys are the most common means of gathering data in sociology. Sociological surveys are different from other surveys in that the sociologist expects to relate empiricial findings to a prior hypothesis and an existing body of theory. And indeed surveys are frequently used by researchers in all areas of our society. Daily newspapers regularly carry results from one type of survey, the public opinion poll, that indicate the current feelings of Americans about such social issues as abortion, marijuana, capital punishment. Surveys are continually conducted on college campuses to discover trends and changing values among students. Corporations rely on surveys to give them information about consumer tastes, responses, and needs. Polls have been very influential in charting voter response to candidates in election campaigns.

The great advantage of surveys is that they allow questions to be asked of large numbers of people. The census is an example of survey research. The intention of the census is to question all adults within the society, the total population. Usually the total group that the reseacher is interested in is thought of as the **population.** This could be all college freshmen, all working mothers, all prison inmates. However, it would be incredibly expensive, time-consuming, and perhaps impossible to reach all members of a particular population, so that the sociologist or researcher chooses a **sample,** a part of the population of interest.

The way the sample is chosen is of great importance. The sample must accurately reflect the larger population or the research results are suspect. The results could accurately indicate the opinions of sample members, the respondents, and yet bear no relation to the opinions of the population. A famous example of this is the public opinion poll conducted by the magazine *Literary Digest* in 1936. In that year, a Republican, Alfred E. Landon, was pitted against Franklin D. Roosevelt, the Democratic candidate, for the presidency. The *Literary Digest,* based on responses from 2 million Americans, predicted that Landon would win. A sample size of 2 million is impressive, but size alone is not the key to survey accuracy. Landon lost the election and the *Literary Digest* soon disappeared from the newsstands. How can such a large sample be so inaccurate? The *Literary Digest* sample did not reflect the total population. The magazine had sent 10 million postcard ballots to respondents chosen from telelphone directories and auto registration lists. But during the Depression, who could have telephones and drive automobiles? The *Digest* sample turned out to be composed of mainly affluent Americans and many of these were Republicans. At the same time, George Gallup sampled a smaller group (312,551) and correctly predicted that Roosevelt would win.

Representative Sampling

Gallup had developed a *representative sample;* he had selected the Democrats and Republicans to be questioned, based on their proportions in the entire population. His sample represented not only the feelings of the middle- and upper-class Americans with telephones and cars, but also the poorer folk, without such comforts, who intended to support Roosevelt. (Labovitz and Hagedorn, 1971; Hennessy, 1970) The accuracy of the representative sample lies in the correspondence between the characteristics of those in the sample and in the larger population. This is why pollsters like Gallup and Harris can use samples of 1,500–2,000 people and accurately assess the opinions and feelings of national populations.

Representativeness

How do people get selected so that a sample is representative? One technique is to use a **random sample.** Random sampling from a population is done in a way that insures that every member of the population has the same chance to be selected as a sample member. Suppose the study habits of American college freshmen were of interest to a sociologist. It would be impossible to question every student in this society. But a representative sample could be developed. It would be necessary to assign every student a number and then let a computer randomly select numbers. The sample thus produced would accurately reflect the total population of freshmen, because selection would be the result of chance operating, rather than a possibly biased human selector. The representativeness of Gallup's sample in 1936 resulted from another method, the use of **quota sampling**. This method is most frequently used in public opinion surveys. The population is divided or *stratified* into categories according to criteria that the pollster thinks are important (for example, Democratic or Republican Party affiliation). Sample members are then selected according to quotas (percentages) that reflect the actual divisions of the population. **Stratified sampling**, which often reflects characteristics of the population such as sex, race, socioeconomic status, political preference, and education, yields findings that will also accurately represent the sentiments of the larger population.

Questioning

In doing survey research there are several ways by which data can be obtained. One method is through the use of **questionnaires.** These are paper-and-pencil instruments that can be mailed to sample members, distributed in the field (on the job, in stores). Respondents personally answer these questions, indicating their attitudes and opinions. Some survey data are gathered through **interviews.** Interviews involve conversation between the researcher and the respondent. Interviews may involve questions carefully prepared in advance and asked in a systematic way or they may be designed to allow a free exploration of issues and ideas. Much skill is needed in the development of survey questions and in interviewing respondents, because people may lie, may not remember, or may be trying to please the interviewer. The way questions are framed is crucial. Wilensky (1967) noted that "Do you like your job?" questions were unsophisticated. Because feelings of self-worth were involved, because there might be social class differences in the way workers chose to express discontentment, respondents might choose to hide true feelings. Indirect questions might reveal more (e.g., "Do you think of yourself as intelligent?" "Does your job give you the chance to use your own judgment?" "How do you feel about this?").

In an attempt to discover changes in the values and morality of youth in the U.S., Daniel Yankelovich (1974) and his researchers interviewed 3,522 young people (age 16 to 25). This was a representative sample of college and noncollege youth, including blue-collar workers, minorities, high-school students, Vietnam veterans, the unemployed, and college graduates in the work force. A special

2-1 CHECKING IT OUT: Personal and Social Values Trend Data

	Noncollege		*College*	
	1973	*1969*	*1973*	*1969*
	%	%	%	%
1. Belief in traditional American values				
People should save money regularly	80	89	71	76
Private property is sacred	74	88	67	76
A "strong" person can control own life	70	77	65	62
Competition encourages excellence	66	81	62	72
Hard work will always pay off	56	79	44	57
2. Activities thought to be morally wrong				
Extramarital sexual relations	65	78	60	77
Having an abortion	48	63	32	36
Relations between consenting homosexuals	47	72	25	42
Casual premarital sexual relations	34	58	22	34
3. Restraints willingly and easily accepted				
Prohibition against mind-expanding drugs*	71	79	73	73
Power and authority of the police	60	79	48	48
Power and authority of the "boss" in a work situation	57	71	44	49
Prohibition against marijuana	49	71	38	49
Conformity in matters of dress and personal grooming	42	54	33	33
Outward conformity for the sake of career or job advancement	37	35	20	14
Abiding by laws you do not agree with	24	34	12	15

*Asked about "LSD" in 1969. Asked about "mind-expanding drugs" in 1973.

SOURCE: Daniel Yankelovich, *The New Morality* (New York: McGraw-Hill, 1974), pp. 93–94.

feature of this survey is that a time variable was included. Students were asked the same questions included in earlier samples in other studies so that changes in attitudes could be seen. This is called **trend data.** Yankelovich found startling differences between the responses of the youth of the 1960s and 1970s. New values were being expressed in relation to individual and public morality, in relation to social values (the work ethic, marriage and the family, the importance of money in defining success). New attitudes were emerging relating to self-fulfillment as opposed to sacrificing for family and employer. The re-seachers were amazed at the rapidity with which the values of a "forerunner" college group had filtered down to noncollege and nonmiddle-class youth.

Participant Observation

Participant observation is an often controversial research method. Rather than bringing people together in a laboratory situation for the purposes of an experiment, the participant observer goes into the field and deals with people in social situations directly at system levels. Such a sociologist is not interested in manipulating a situation to discern relationships between variables of interest. Rather, this sociologist wants to become part of the environment, to observe people and question them. Participant observation continues over time so it is a dynamic technique, which allows the researcher to alter the study design in the midst of the research should new understandings warrant the change. This method offers the possibility of surprise and unsuspected experiences and information. It is a technique much used by ethnographers and anthropolgists to gather data.

Observing Deviance Participant observation is a particularly valuable way of shedding light on deviant behavior, of understanding how people behave in situations that are not seen as respectable or usual. Laud Humphrey (1970) was interested in the "instant sex" available to men in public rest rooms. Sex, a usually intimate and personal interaction, appeared to be sought by these men, in this setting, because it was impersonal and avoided involvement or commitment. Obviously, the observation of homosexual behavior by a researcher is not going to be permitted by the participants, so that some strategy was needed that would permit the data collection to go on. However, this strategy had to allow observation without changing interactions because individuals realized that they were being watched.

Control Effect Humphrey avoided the problem of "control effect" or changing events by his presence by taking a role. He acted as a "look-out" and a voyeur, a person who is stimulated by watching, and was thus able to conduct his research. The ethics involved in such research will be discussed presently.

When Herbert Gans (1967) wanted to discover the interactions that changed a group of strangers into a close-knit community he also had to deal

2-2 CHECKING IT OUT: A White Researcher in a Black Community

They knew that I lived outside the area. They knew that I was a college graduate, or at least they associated an advanced education with the work I was doing. Moreover, it was apparent, certainly to me, that I was not fluent in their language. Thus, I was an outsider not only because of race, but also because of occupation, education, residence, and speech. The fact that I was Jewish came up only twice. Once, a man who worked but did not live in the area threw some Yiddish expressions at me because "I thought you looked Jewish." The other time was when I met a soldier in a local bootleg joint. We had been talking for some ten minutes or so when he asked me whether I was "Eyetalian." I told him I was Jewish. "That's just as good," he said. "I'm glad you're not white."

The fact that I was married and a father, and that I was bigger than average size—6′ 1″, 185 pounds—probably didn't matter much, except as they entered incidentally into my personal relationship with one or another individual. Since the people I spent most of my time with ranged in age from twenty to the middle forties, I would guess that my age (thirty-seven) was not significant in itself.

On several different counts I was an outsider* but I also was a participant in a full sense of the word. The people I was observing knew that I was observing them, yet they allowed me to participate in their activities and take part in their lives to a degree that continues to surprise me. Some "exploited" me, not as an outsider but rather as one who, as a result, had more resources than they did. When one of them came up with the resources—money or a car, for example—he too was "exploited" in the same way. I usually tried to limit money or other favors to what I thought each would have gotten from another friend had he the same resources as I. I tried to meet requests as best I could without becoming conspicuous. I was not always on the giving end and learned somewhat too slowly to accept food or let myself be treated to drinks even though I knew this would work a hardship on the giver.

When in the field, I participated as fully and as whole-mindedly as I could, limited only by my own sense of personal and professional propriety and by what I assumed to be the boundaries of acceptable behavior as seen by those I was with.

Occasionally, when I wanted to record a physical description of say, a neighborhood, an apartment, or a social event, I tried to be an observer only. In practice, I found it impossible to keep all traces of participation out of a straight observer role.

*From the outset, I had decided that I would never shoot crap, pool, or play cards for money, or bet money in any way (numbers excepted, since playing numbers is safely impersonal), and would meticulously avoid the slightest suspicion of a personal involvement with any woman. These self-imposed restrictions to some extent did underline my marginality. My explanation that I couldn't afford to chance a fight or bad feelings because of my job was usually accepted and I was generally excused from participating in these activities rather than excluded from them.

SOURCE: From Elliot Liebow, *Tally's Corner* (Boston: Little, Brown and Company, 1967), pp. 252–254. By permission.

with the problem of changing the behavior of residents if they knew he was a sociologist doing research. Gans solved this problem in two ways. He bought a home and moved into the newly developed Levittown community and conducted his participant observation over a two-year period. As a resident attending community affairs, sports events, and celebrations he was constantly in danger of changing events by his presence, so he took on a neutral role. In meetings and social situations, he was careful to avoid dominant roles or controversial opinions. Gans admitted that his lack of candor about his research activities caused him much anxiety and strain.

Some of the unique aspects of participant observation can be seen in the research of Elliot Liebow (1967) as he studied black street-corner men. Liebow had no research design and no stated hypothesis. His study was clearly exploratory. A white male graduate student, he was able to gain acceptance by a group of lower-class black men because he gave aid and advice when one of them was indicted for murder. He then observed their activities on the street corner, in the poolrooms and bars, as well as in family settings in their community. He was thus able to gain an understanding of the street-corner man "as breadwinner, father, husband, lover and friend." (p. 12) Liebow took on the role of a street-corner man, but *control effect* would be difficult to avoid in the case of a white man in a black ghetto. Yet over a period of twelve months, most of the men appeared to accept his presence in a natural way. Liebow discussed his conception of his research role and the restrictions he imposed on himself.

2-3 CHECKING IT OUT: A Comparison of the Three Major Research Techniques

	Experiment	*Survey Research*	*Participant Observation*
Criteria determining selection of subjects	Convenience—often college students	Probability sampling from the larger population	Availability of subjects and nature of study
When is this technique most valuable?	In explanatory research, especially when number of variables is limited or quantitative	In descriptive, explanatory, and exploratory research	Is excellent for exploratory research; sometimes used for descriptive research
Place of research	Usually laboratory, very seldom natural experiment	In the field	In the field

2-3 CHECKING IT OUT: (continued)

	Experiment	*Survey Research*	*Participant Observation*
Environmental setting	Artificially controlled	More or less artificial	Natural
Research design	Very structured	More or less structured	Unstructured
Size of sample	Usually small	Can range from small (about 300) to large	Usually small
Unit of analysis	Individual	Individual	Somewhat ambiguous (groups, and/or individuals, and/or interactions)
Hypothesis	To be tested	To be tested	To be generated; continued revision and testing of emerging hypothesis
A control group needed?	Yes	No	No
Data processing	Data can be converted into numbers	Data can be converted into numbers	Usually filing activity; data are usually not converted into numbers
Interaction	Face-to-face, formal	Mail; indirect interview; face-to-face, formal	Face-to-face, formal and informal
Can independent variable be manipulated?	Yes	No	No
Deviant cases	Avoided	Avoided	Can yield important insights into patterns of behavior usually defined as normal
Observation	At one point in time	At one point in time	Especially appropriate to the study of social processes over time

	Experiment	*Survey Research*	*Participant Observation*
Used for replication purposes (public verifiability)	Frequently	Seldom	No
Can results be generalized to large population	No	Yes	Yes, but only to similar population—weakest of the three methods
Can behavior of researcher influence results?	Laboratory: no; Natural experiment: yes	Mail: no Interview: yes	Yes
Cost (computer cost not included)	Depends on instrumentation used	Depends on sample size Mail: inexpensive Interview: expensive	Inexpensive
Ethical issues a problem?	Possible	Possible	Possibility of deceiving people; subject cannot refuse to be studied; questions of anonymity
Chief advantages	Isolation of experimental variable and its impact over time	Best method available for collecting original data for purposes of describing the characteristics of a population too large to observe directly	Permits creativity, and means of generating theory or hypothesis; taps deviant behavior
Weaknesses	Artificial; situation created does not reflect the real world	Standardization requirements limit possible responses	Possibility of biased informer, control effect

Advantages of the Method The participant observation has the advantage of observing social action at system levels, of being dynamic, and of continuing over time. Because of these features, the possibilities of unanticipated discoveries are always present. This method allows changes in the research design as one proceeds, or tolerates no research design at all. The fact that the reseacher is at the level of the group as it interacts in this dynamic way allows the uncovering of a deviant behavior in a unique way.

Disadvantages of the Method Disadvantages of the method are the following: (1) Participant observation is limited to the present. One cannot get back to the past. (2) it works only with small groups. (3) *Control effect* or changing the action by one's presence is a problem. (4) Biased viewpoint is a possibility, because the placement of the observer in the setting may distort perceptions of the interactions.

ETHICS IN SOCIOLOGY AND SOCIAL SCIENCES

In April, 1965, Hugo Nuttini contacted some prominent social scientists in Chile. Nuttini was a former Chilean citizen who had become an anthropologist on the faculty of the University of Pittsburgh. He sought to engage Chilean social scientists in a multinational research study attempting to understand the causes of revolution. Nuttini represented the study as financed by private American foundations. It was to be called Project Camelot. However, the Chilean scientists were already aware of Project Camelot. They knew that the real sponsor of the program was the United States Army. According to the research proposal, the actual objective of the study was to "devise procedures for assessing the potential for internal war within national societies." The designers of this study were also interested in identifying "those actions which a government might take to relieve conditions which are assessed as giving rise to potential for internal war." In this remarkable document social scientists were being asked to develop procedures that could gauge a country's potential for revolution, and also to suggest actions that governments might take to alleviate conditions that might end in revolutionary struggle. The Army was clearly interested in predicting and defusing revolutions. This appeared to be part of a commitment on the part of the U.S. Army to "assist friendly governments in dealing with active insurgency problems." (Horowitz, 1965, p. 4) Horowitz interviewed many of the social scientists involved, and found that they saw the project as an important research opportunity and even saw it as a chance to educate the Army to the realities of the contemporary world. Critics of the project, among them Myron Glazer, were alarmed that its designers had accepted the fact that the United States military had the right to interfere in the internal affairs of other countries, that U.S. foreign policy could be a factor in determining research sites. These critics were further alarmed at the implication that internal war is always the greatest threat to a nation's well-being. The document offered no alternate views or hypotheses.

Nuttini's misrepresentation of the sponsorship of Project Camelot was unethical. However, many of the social scientists involved defended the value of the research and resisted the accusations by Chileans that the research was merely a cover for espionage. Project Camelot was canceled when Chilean officials protested to the United States government, but it illustrates some crucial ethical issues in doing research.

Since much science research is possible through grants from public and private institutions, social scientists must consider the uses to which research results may be put by those who have funded their studies.

In the case of Laud Humphrey's research for his book *Tearoom Trade* (1970) further ethical questions arise. Nicholas Von Hoffman of the *Washington Post* (1970) is only one of a number of critics of Humphrey's research. In order to study the homosexual interactions in public rest rooms, Humphrey took on the role of "look-out." He also made a note of the license plate numbers of participants and later traced them. He waited one year and then approached the tearoom visitors. He had included them in a larger sample of male subjects for a social health survey and was able to interview 50 of the tearoom participants. Because he was aware of the implications involved if the identities of these men were revealed (many were married), he took care to have only one master list of names in a bank deposit box. He allowed himself to be arrested rather than disclose his identity to the police, and he eventually destroyed his data. However, this research illustrates the use of deception in getting data. Von Hoffman accused Humphrey of invading the privacy of his subjects; he noted that such information could be used for blackmail or extortion if it fell into the wrong hands.

Ethical issues such as these led to the establishment in 1968 of a Code of Ethics by the American Sociological Association. Here it is affirmed that (1) "Every person is entitled to the right of privacy and dignity of treatment. The sociologist must respect these rights." (2) "All research should avoid causing personal harm to subjects used in research." (3) "The sociologist must fully report all sources of financial support in his research publications and any special relations to the sponsor that might affect the interpretation of the findings."

Commenting on Von Hoffman's charges, Horowitz and Rainwater (1970) defend Humphrey's research procedures in the following way:

> Sociologists uphold the right to know in a context of the surest protection for the integrity of the subject matter and the private rights of the people studied. Other groups in society may turn on different pivots: the right of law, the protection of individuals against invasion of privacy and so forth. But whoever is "right" in the abstract, there is a shared obligation for all parties to a controversy to step forth

with fullness and fairness to present their cases before the interested public—and to permit that public to enter discussions which affect them so directly. Without this, a right higher than public disclosure or private self will be denied—the right to full public discourse. (Nanry and Horowitz, 1975, p. 47)

INTERPRETIVE SUMMARY

Doing sociology involves an integration of theory and empirical research. Procedures to be followed include (1) a statement of purpose and the selection of an important problem, (2) the formulation of hypotheses and a description of study design, (3) the selection of methods for data collection, (4) the analysis and presentation of the research results obtained, (5) the conclusions and interpretations, specified in terms of implications for theory, further research, and/or solutions to problems.

The problem or the social phenomena to be studied often determines the research method that is chosen. The *laboratory experiment* will be chosen if the researcher wants to isolate and study variables in a carefully constructed environment. *The field or natural experiment* may be conducted in everyday life situations, thereby avoiding the artificiality of the laboratory experiment; manipulation of variables is attempted here also. *Survey research* is a valuable technique with large samples. However, these must be random samples if they are to be representative of the population of interest. *Participant observation,* involving questioning and observation, is a method useful in generating hypotheses that examine deviant behavior. This method permits much creativity in research design.

QUESTIONS

1. What does a sociologist do? What methods are available for doing sociology?
2. Are classical experiments common in sociology? Why?
3. In what ways does the sociologist studying a political demonstration use the same research techniques as an astronomer studying the stars?
4. If visitors from outer space did land on Earth, how might they be investigated using participant observation, an experiment, survey methods?
5. What are the advantages and disadvantages of experiments, surveys, participant observations as research methods?

3

Social Structure

When architects speak of the "structure" of a building, they are usually referring to three things: (1) the materials of which it is composed (brick siding, asphalt shingle roof); (2) the relationship between the parts (the porch floor that rests on a foundation, the pillars that support the porch roof); and (3) the building as a unit or whole (a split-level house, a Southern colonial dwelling). When sociologists speak of **social structure,** they are talking about the same three sets of features that concern architects in describing a house: (1) the "building materials" (the number of males and females, adults and children, social positions); (2) the interrelationship of the parts (what wives expect from husbands, how employees interact with employers, how parents and children treat one another); and (3) the nature of the society as a whole—that is, the result of the materials of which it is built and the way they are put together.

BASIC UNITS OF SOCIAL STRUCTURE

The building blocks of which a social structure is composed are called *statuses.* A status is a position in a social structure. Whenever we describe a social position without regard to the individual who is occupying it, we are talking about a status. A status (or social position) is analytically distinct from the particular individual who occupies it.

Status

A registered nurse must have achieved an acceptable grade on a licensing examination. Such an individual is responsible for the care of ill patients. A registered nurse is responsible for maintaining a supply of uniforms in order to appear immaculately clean at all times. Doctors and hospital administrators have authority over the nurse. Note that these sentences describe the *status* of nurse; they do not describe a specific person. It does not matter whether the nurse is dull, jolly, or morose; the personality of the individual occupying the status is quite another variable. If Nurse Akins is discharged and Nurse Manganaro is hired as a replacement, the status of nurse remains unchanged. A status is an abstraction, a description of one's place in a social group relative to other positions in the group.

Status-Set The status-set refers to the complex of statuses that describes one individual. Because we interact in so many different social structures all the time (occupational, recreational, familial, political, religious, community-connected, ethnic, cultural), our status-sets are apt to be large. However, people differ in the number and the complexity of statuses that make up their status-sets. Robert Merton, (1957) who developed the concept of a status-set, uses the example of a wealthy scholar who does not need to work, yet who is so committed to research that he has withdrawn from social structures and remains unmarried, unemployed, and unrelated to civic or other associations. Such a person would have a simple and uncomplicated status-set. Complex status-sets often cause the person difficulty when there are many conflicting obligations attached to status positions (e.g., television producer, breast-feeding mother, suburban commuter). Another problem is that one status may function as a master status in relation to other statuses and inhibit or otherwise affect social interaction. In the case of the extraordinary Paul Robeson, his racial

3-1 CHECKING IT OUT: The Status Set of Paul Robeson

1898–1976
American
Black
Male
Husband and father

Rutgers College graduate (1919)
Phi Beta Kappa member
All-American (football)
Law school graduate (Columbia University)
Shakespearean actor
Concert singer
Civil rights and political activist
Movie actor (11 movies)
Recording artist
World traveler

status, "black man," affected the way in which he was perceived by and treated by those bigoted individuals around him, thereby affecting his other statuses. Because varsity members at Rutgers did not want Robeson on their football team, he left the field on his first day of practice with a broken nose, dislocated shoulder, and cuts and bruises; later his fingers were crushed by a teammate. (Gilliam, 1976) Being *black* (status) almost ended his career as a *football player* (status). Yet, he went on to become an *All-American* (status). Later in his career, his activities as an outspoken *political* and *civil rights activist* during the McCarthy era cost him his livelihood as a *concert singer* and *actor*. He acquired a new status—*"nonperson"* (Gilliam, p. 159) and was unable to travel outside the country or make a living within it.

Role A *role* is the function of a status. When an individual occupies a given position, the placement of that position above some others and below still others will have consequences for his interaction in the group. The consequences of occupying that status are called his role. We can speak, then, of the status of foreman, which is a position in a work group above that of laborer and below that of shop superintendent. The role of the foreman is the result of his status in the group: he is expected to give orders to laborers and to take orders from the shop superintendent. Like status, role is an abstraction; it remains the same even if the expectations are being met by different individuals. Retiring one foreman and hiring a replacement does not usually alter either the position (the status) or its consequences (the role).

Role Behavior The component of the social situation that *can* be altered is the *role behavior,* or the way a particular individual fulfills the expectations of the rule. The status of surgeon ranks above that of nurse; the surgeon's role includes the expectation that he or she will tell the nurse what to do. But the role behavior of surgeons varies considerably. Dr. Form gives specific orders in a pleasant voice, whereas Dr. Huber gives very general instructions in a harsh tone. The contrast between them stems from neither status nor role, but from role behavior.

Every person occupies many statuses. A man may be at one and the same time a citizen of the United States, an attorney, a member of the Episcopal Church, a Post Commander in the American Legion, a male, an adult, a husband, a father, an uncle, a son, a nephew, and a member of the local Board of Education. Each of these is one of his statuses. With each is associated a role, a set of expectations he is supposed to fulfill with respect to people in other related statuses, such as minister, wife, Chairperson of the Board of Education, and so on. To each of these roles he brings his personality, which influences some of the patterns of his role behavior. Since, fundamentally, each role and status is derived from social norms, or group-shared expectations of what ought to be, people in the society will evaluate his role behaviors and pass judgment on how he meets the expectations of each of his roles.

Prestige and Esteem Each status in a social structure has attached to it an evaluation. It is considered "good" or "important" or "difficult" or "routine" or "criminal" or "dirty." There is always some judgment in the norms of a society about how desirable a status is. This evaluation of the status is called its *prestige.* The evaluation of an individual's role behavior in a status which he or she occupies is called *esteem.* This is the judgment by one's fellows of how well one fulfills the expectations of a role. Most people in the United States believe that vice-president of a large corporation is a more desirable status than street sweeper. Thus, no matter who is occupying the status or how well that person is doing, it is proper to say that the status of corporation executive has higher prestige than the status of street sweeper. However, people may notice that Jay Hendricks does an excellent job of sweeping the street, while Dick Mathers does not take his work seriously and leaves trash piled up at the curb. Hendricks, then, has high esteem because of his role behavior, while Mathers has low esteem, despite the fact that the two occupy the same status.

Individuals may occupy statuses which have high prestige and earn high esteem by their role behaviors there, but prestige does not ensure esteem. The alcoholic attorney has low esteem even though the status has high prestige; the best charperson in an office building occupies a status with low prestige but earns high esteem. The esteem accruing collectively to individuals in a status can in time alter the prestige of that status. If, over a period of years, only incompetent persons were made deans of colleges, the prestige of deanship would suffer. Each of us is usually proud to point to highly esteemed persons who occupy the same status as we, because we feel (perhaps without being aware of it) that their presence raises the prestige of our position.

The Reciprocity of Roles Since a role is a set of expectations, it is impossible to define one role without referring to another. There cannot be a parent role without a child, or an employer role without an employee. There must be another role doing the expecting. In this sense, roles are a series of rights and duties—that is, they represent certain reciprocal relations among individuals. To understand this interplay, we must define *right* and *duty.* A right is a privilege to act that is reciprocal to another's duty to permit the act. Of course, a duty is not always passive: a duty may sometimes be an obligation to act, reciprocal to another's right to expect the act. The rights of one are always qualified and limited by the obligations of another.

All societies reveal a wide range of such reciprocal relations. The economic structure *is* a structure precisely because the interactions of people in the market express more or less widely accepted rights and duties. A legal contract to work or to deliver a product at a specified time and place is a pattern of reciprocal rights and duties supported by the law of contracts. In family life the interplay of sympathetic identification of parent and child is counterpoised by obligations to provide on the part of the former and by duties of obedience on the part of the latter. Power relations in the operations of government reveal the same pattern.

The king and his subjects, the judge and the accused, the police and the citizen, the elected official and the constituency, all have reciprocal rights and duties.

Of the many patterns of such reciprocities, some operate quite independently of others. Some come into conflict with each other. Many rights and duties associated with family life or religion have little or nothing to do with those outside the home or the church. In contrast, a man's ethical code about killing may cause inner conflict regarding his rights and duties as citizen-soldier when he is called on to engage in war. Or the widely accepted relations of competitive business may, in time, come into conflict with one's humanitarian feelings.

Every person occupies both ascribed statuses and achieved statuses. By **ascribed statuses** we mean those positions assigned to an individual regardless of his or her own abilities or performance. "Princess" is an ascribed status; where there is a hereditary royalty, a girl does not work her way up to being princess. She is *born* a princess, and whether she is pretty or ugly, tall or short, intelligent or stupid, a princess she remains. **Achieved statuses,** on the other hand, are not assigned at birth, but are left open to be filled by the persons who compete most successfully for them. Being male is an ascribed status. It is determined at birth; either you are male or you are not. Being a husband is an achieved status, it does not result automatically from one's being born a male but depends on a male's own behavior. One's racial status is ascribed. One cannot usually change one's race within one's own lifetime.

ASCRIBED STATUSES AND ROLES THROUGH THE LIFE CYCLE

In many societies most statuses are ascribed. This was true of the ancient Incan Empire, where the newborn male infant was classified as "babe in arms," later as "able to stand," and still later as "under six." Then from 6 to 8 years he was termed a "bread receiver," and so on, until at 20 years he became "almost a man," at 25 "able-bodied," at 50 "half an old man," and after 60 years "an old man asleep." (Tozzer, 1925, p. 208) While no modern society draws such sharp distinctions as these, highly authoritarian cultures, both contemporary and ancient, often fix statuses rather rigidly. This was true in feudal Japan, for example, where individual and family status was regulated by minute rules. In contrast one of the distinguishing features of democratic societies is the relative opportunity of individual choice and freedom. While ascription of certain statuses remains, in a wide range of activities status is acquired, not ascribed or fixed in advance.

In highly stable and rigid societies the individual usually does not experience fear and worry over roles and statuses as one does in societies demanding constant struggle for role and status. In the latter, anxiety and a heavy sense of inferiority and guilt often follow if one fails to "make good."

Age

All societies recognize differences in role and status related to age. Adults have more physical strength and more experience than children. In old age, there is some decline of physical capabilities and sometimes mental faculties, and dependence on others tends to limit the range of thought and action. Yet variations in age are defined much more by custom than by physiology. As Ralph Linton puts it, "In the case of age, as in that of sex, biological factors involved appear to be secondary to the cultural ones in determining the content of status." (Linton, 1936, p. 119)

In most societies, however, there are four major categories of age differences as related to role and status: infancy and childhood, youth, maturity or adulthood, and old age.

The Ascribed Status of Child The role and status of infant and child are always related to dependency on and guardianship by adults. Yet how societies regard babies varies among both small nonliterate societies and large industrial ones. In ancient Sparta, where there was heavy stress on the need for a strong body as well as a normal mind, sickly or deformed infants were done away with, usually by being abandoned in the hills. Among some nonliterate tribes, twins were thought to be a bad omen, and they were disposed of lest some evil descend upon the family and the tribe. In other societies, as in the United States, babies are generally idolized and made much of by adults.

Among some peoples the child is regarded as a miniature adult and is expected to act like "a little man" or "a little woman." Among others there is firm demand for silent conformity—children are expected "to be seen but not heard" when in the presence of their "elders and betters." In still other societies a child may be given a very high status. This is the situation among the Marquesans, where the eldest son is considered the head of the family, regardless of his age. Ralph Linton reports seeing a nine-year-old Marquesan boy, son of a chieftain, drive all the adults out of the family house when he became angry over what seemed a trivial matter. (Linton, 1936) Sometimes there is little or no formal direction or discipline of the children until they are ready to pass into adult status.

In Western societies, it is clear that the culturally defined period of dependency and immaturity has been markedly lengthened, largely as a result of these societies' complexity and their emphasis on occupational specialization. Indeed, this prolongation of the occupancy of the ascribed status of child is one measure of the complexity of a culture.

Since each role is defined by reference to another, there are certain reciprocal relations between parent and child. The major rights and duties in this relationship tend to take shape as social norms. Obviously, the duties of the parent to the child cannot usually be enforced by the latter. But failure to provide for the child's care and training according to the group norms may be punished by the group. Failure of parents to live up to the norms of child care laid down by the culture usually results in some other group's taking over this obligation. In small, intimate communities, serious neglect of children by their parents usually leads to gossip as a device to stimulate the parents to do their duty. Sometimes neighbors may help the children. In large urbanized societies there are many formal agencies, both privately and publicly supported, which concern themselves with child welfare. In a society that places a high value on children, failure on the part of the parents to fulfill their duties leads to their punishment by sanctions decreed in the law and to the rise of substitute means replacing parental care.

The Ascribed Status of Youth The break between various "age" periods is largely determined by culture. While some societies recognize changes from childhood to sexual maturity by special ceremonials and overt changes in social status and role, other societies make no such sharp division. In the United States, for instance, a certain age gradation is recognized in the division of schooling into elementary, secondary, and college. Confirmation ceremonies and high-school graduation symbolize a passage of the growing person into a new role and status. The long period of permissive and accepted preparation for adulthood is restricted, for the most part, to the urban, literate societies, largely as a result of their complexity, specialization, and high standards of living.

This transition from childhood to youth is associated with the development of full sexual capacity and the appearance of secondary sex characteristics which further distinguish the male from the female. There are also changes in height and weight, and other physical characteristics which mark the shift toward adulthood. Since there are variations in the age at which the individual passes through puberty, the culture usually provides a certain latitude for fulfillment of the expected roles and statuses related to this phase.

A major expectation of the ascribed role of youth is that one learn the essential skills that prepare one for the adult role and status. In Western societies there is a tendency to prolong this period of preparation, just as there is a tendency to prolong the period of childhood. In the United States, this fact is reflected in the law. Added protection is given to young people by increasing the years of compulsory education, by prohibiting child labor, and by restricting early marriages.

The United States has, however, a curious inconsistency in the treatment of youth. True, the continued emotional and financial dependence of children on parents is evident. Nowhere else in the world is youth given such leisure and opportunity for education. In other societies individuals in this chronological age group have ascribed adult roles. Yet in the United States youth have greater freedom from parental control than formerly. Adolescent boys and girls are more sophisticated and mature in many ways than their parents were in their youth. Opportunities for escaping from family, neighborhood, and community controls afford young people forms of experience that their fathers and mothers often do not understand or approve of. Various factors have created a situation in which the role and status of youth, their rights and duties, and the responsibility of their elders for their future welfare are not always clearly defined. This very confusion reflects changing patterns of differentiation in the society.

The Ascribed Status of Adult In every society the adult assumes rights and duties not expected of children, youth, or old people. The age at which the individual comes to maturity will be determined by elements in the particular culture. Thus, among the American Plains Indians, acceptance as a member of a war party marked arrival at adulthood. In our society political adulthood is assumed when the person acquires voting privileges. The capacity to hold office, too, is assumed to be related to age. In the United States, while most local and state offices are open to any qualified voter 21 years or over, the holding of federal offices is restricted to narrower age limits. A person under 25 years of age cannot hold office as a Representative in the national Congress. One must be 30 years old to be eligible for the United States Senate and 35 years to be eligible for the presidency.

Voting privileges and eligibility to hold office and perform jury service are basic marks of adult political responsibility in a democratic country. With these, of course, go all the obligations of citizenship, which are stipulated, at least on the negative side, by legal codes regarding both private and public conduct. Under a dictatorship the adult may be accorded no voting or discussion privileges but is usually ascribed specific public roles as party member, worker, taxpayer, or soldier—roles assigned only to those considered in this society as adults.

The Ascribed Status of the Aged Old age is determined not solely by the physiological condition of muscles, glands, and brain, but also by the culture. In most nonliterate societies old age carries with it a real distinction in prestige. In many tribes the elders are the most powerful and revered members of the group. In a society like ancient China, where ancestor worship dominated family and community life for centuries, the power of old age over the social order was everywhere apparent. Deference to old age, to the patriarch of the family, and the desire for sons to carry on ancestor worship long retarded the rise of new ideas and new ways of life.

Throughout the history of European culture, old age has retained great power. In the partiarchal family order, as in ancient Rome, the oldest male in the family retained control over all other members. It is so even today in the peasant populations of Europe. Where urbanization has taken place and industry has developed, this reverence for old age has been modified.

A large percentage of our old people become dependent on others for economic support. Until recently, in our individualistic society practically all provision for old age rested on the efforts of the individual and his or her family. Only gradually are we assigning some responsibility to the community and state to provide for the aged through pensions and insurance.

Age statuses are ascribed; they are fixed for the individual at birth, regardless of his efforts in later years. No matter how hard one works at it, an eight-year-old child cannot occupy adult status. And a thirty-year-old man, whether he works at it or not, whether he wants to be or not, is considered an adult. He is an adult because the norms of the society decree that he is; the status is assigned him, not achieved.

Sex

Perhaps because it is a visible, unchangeable physical characteristic, sex also constitutes a basis for ascribed status. All societies have a dual set of rules associated with the two sexes. The first set is related to biological facts: the male and the female have different roles in the reproduction of children. But there are many other statuses ascribed on the basis of sex. Sex is a basic variable, for example in the division of labor. Occupations, religious roles, intellectual pursuits, political responsibilities, and many other activities are often differentiated according to sex. The important social fact about sexually ascribed statuses, however, is the wide range of variation from society to society in the assignment of sex roles.

This variation will be examined more fully in a chapter on sex roles and socialization (Chapter 6), and the interrelationship between sexually ascribed and achieved status will be explored, and the effects of culture and socialization will be examined.

Race

Since an entire chapter is devoted to racial and ethnic inequality, we shall note here only that in the United States and some other societies, race is an ascribed status. Like age and sex, race has a modifying effect on the prestige of an achieved status and often affects the esteem one receives for the performance of achieved roles.

ACHIEVED STATUSES AND ROLES

All societies have some ascribed statuses, though some use ascription more than others. Age and sex are universally used in human societies as a basis for ascription. All societies also have some achieved statuses. Again, the proportion of statuses which are open to achievement varies widely around the world. In the modern world, one significant mark of a free society is the relative number of statuses and roles that are open to achievement.

The more complex a society is—the more specialized its division of labor—the higher the proportion of achieved statuses it is likely to have. An elaborate division of labor offers the individual who is extremely talented a competitive advantage. If every male in a society does his own hunting, his own house-building, and his own toolmaking, a talent for toolmaking in one man or house-building in another is of little importance. But once the society is so structured that one man specializes in house-building and another in toolmaking, allowing these statuses to be achieved offers dividends both for the specialists and for the society. More and better houses can be built, and more and better tools can be made if each man is encouraged to perform the task at which he excels instead of being assigned a status because his father held it before him.

In a society such as ours, most occupational statuses are open to achievement for at least some members of the society. The proliferation of secondary groups means that most organizational memberships also are achieved statuses. Many primary group roles are achieved as well; that is what we are referring to when we say that one is free to choose one's friends. They are not, in other words, assigned to him by something like clan membership. We are even allowed, in our society, to treat church membership as an achieved status, which makes our social structure unusual indeed, from either the historical or cross-cultural point of view. In most societies, one is born into a religious group; it is just as much an ascribed status as a family membership. To leave it is to be excommunicated from the tribe. But in the United States, religion, like occupation, education, marital status, and many other statuses, is left to the discretion of the individual.

In a society in which almost all occupational statuses are achieved, individuals are largely interdependent. The very specialization which leads to a system of achieved statuses produces bonds of essential interaction. The woodworker is dependent on the toolmaker, the weaver is dependent on the shepherd, the grocer on the farmer, and the entrepreneur on the banker. A structure characterized by achieved statuses enhances competition for those statuses, but the specialization of roles also necessitates cooperation.

THE INTERRELATIONSHIP OF ASCRIBED AND ACHIEVED STATUSES

All societies ascribe some statuses and the assignment of each individual to some ascribed statuses provides a certain stability and security; one does not have to face a life in which all one's associates are potential competitors for every bit of prestige and esteem that one may strive for and attain. The existence of some statuses for which one is eligible to compete, on the other hand, accomplishes two things. It permits the individual some latitude in picking what he or she wants to do and is good at doing, and it contributes to the survival of the social structure by motivating people to seek statuses and ultimately fulfill their duties.

The distinction between ascription and achievement is one of the most important and widely used analytical tools in sociology, but the distinction between ascribed and achieved is not always clear and unambiguous. It is difficult at times to differentiate between the two because the opportunity to achieve tends to be ascribed. For example, in the United States, rich parents' children, even if they are not very bright, are much more likely to go to college than the children of the poor even if they are quite intelligent and have received good grades in high school. There is no status in any society that is always equally open to achievement to all members of the society. The presidency of the United States is an achieved status, constitutionally open to any citizen over the age of 35, but the opportunity to achieve the status is not the same for males and females, whites and blacks, the poor and the affluent.

Status Conflict

We have mentioned that every individual in society occupies many statuses with associated roles. An individual may be a mother, friend, accountant, patient. A given status depends upon the person or organization with which one is interacting. Because of the variety of statuses that characterize the social being, it is important to realize that individuals may be subjected to considerable strain in trying to reconcile the demands of different statuses. For example, a mother may experience *status conflict* as she attempts to reconcile the status of motherhood with the status of accountant. The role behavior associated with these statuses may be particularly demanding and the professional may experience feelings of guilt about difficulties in meeting the status-expectations of mother.

GROUPS

Human life is social life. Social life becomes organized when there are established ways of interacting. We indicate these ways of interacting by such relational terms as status and role. When there is persistent interaction among the same people, social collectivities, both large and small, emerge. These social collectivities we call groups. Analytically, a group is not the same as a social structure. Groups exist through the coming together of a number of identifiable people who build and develop their social relations over time into a relatively stable pattern—a social structure—and who identify to some extent with the others with whom they share this particular social structure (i.e., pattern of social interaction). Thus, groups have a social structure.

Each of us is a member of many groups. With parents and brothers and sisters we make up one kind of group, a family. Many of us are tied also to a wider kinship group of aunts, uncles, and cousins. Most young people belong to school groups; many belong to social, athletic, and other special-interest groups. More than half of the people in the United States belong to church groups; many are affiliated with clubs or lodges; others are members of occupational organizations. In addition to such regularized associations, we interact from time to time as members of shopping crowds, concert audiences, or other temporary collectivities. However, it is important to understand that not every classification of people is a social group. All right-handed people do not form a group. In the effort to fully understand the form and content of social groups and to chart their similarities and differences, sociologists have concentrated their study on a multitude of group characteristics. These will be discussed in detail in a specially developed chapter on social groups (Chapter 8).

INSTITUTIONS

Every society in some way is like no other society, like some other society, like all other societies. That the cultures of the world are so numerous and so diverse should not obscure the fact that there are many universal features of social life. Anthropologist George Peter Murdock and his associates have studied more than a thousand cultures, past and present, and have assembled a list of the uniformities of culture, which Murdock calls the "commom denominators of culture." Some of the similarity Murdock has recorded derives in part from the fact that humans everywhere have certain minimum basic needs; the ways in which they organize their patterns of social interaction must satisfy these minimum requirements if the society is to survive. All societies must perform certain basic functions for survival. Every society must have social arrangements to meet these basic needs, but the form and content of the specific social structures may vary from society to society.

Universal Social Functions

Every human society must have some social arrangement to provide five basic functions necessary for survival: (1) replacement of population, (2) socialization of new population, (3) maintenance of a sense of purpose, (4) production and distribution of goods and services, and (5) preservation of order. Some sociologists also consider as basic functions such things as provision of nutriment or maintenance of biologic adequacy, but since these matters are not strictly *social* in the same sense as the functions listed above, we shall not consider them here.

Replacement of Population Sexual reproduction is not, it is true, the only method of bringing new members into a society. Annexation, the acquisition of slaves, and immigration are means of recruiting people. (Each of these three modes of population expansion has occurred in the United States during its history.) Theoretically, it would be possible for society to fill the positions of its dying members by recruiting replacements in one or more of these three ways from people born into other societies. The practical difficulty lies less in the recruitment than in the knowledge and loyalty required to maintain the social order. Teaching new members the basic cultural values and norms of a society is a task most readily accomplished when those new members are born into the society. Being entirely dependent for their survival on the adults in their primary group, small children are much more easily socialized into the accepted behaviors and attitudes than are adult immigrants or captives. American Indians, aware of this fact, in the days of frontier warfare ordinarily took captive for induction into their society only young children, seldom adults. For the bulk of its new members, therefore, generation after generation, a society depends primarily on sexual reproduction.

Many people believe that reproductive behavior is merely a natural biological phenomenon. Actually, the behavior patterns of human beings as they propagate their kind, like their behavior in any other area of social life, are shaped and modified by the culture through which they have been socialized. The basic act of procreation is influenced by the norms of the society concerning size of family, form of marriage, whether the sex act itself is considered exalted or shameful, age at which people marry, and economic obligations parents are expected to fulfill toward their children. There is no society which does not have a set of norms governing reproduction. Every culture contains some set of prohibitions, expectations, and rewards having to do with who should have children and the circumstances under which reproduction should occur. The cultural values patterned around reproduction are enforced by both positive and negative sanctions.

Socialization In any on-going society there must be some structure which has as its function or consequence the teaching of new members. A society would cease to be, and its culture would be lost, if some social organization did not perform the function of socializing its new members. Merely having replacements is not sufficient; the replacements must learn the culture of the society. They must be taught the basic values, or ethos, around which the normative system is organized. They must learn all the thousands of little behavior patterns that are accepted as normal in the society where they are born: what to eat, how to eat it, where to eat it, when to eat it; what to wear, how to wear it, where to wear it, when to wear it; what to say, how to say it; and so on. Each new member must develop, sooner or later, a sense of self.

A Sense of Purpose A major portion of the time and effort expended in socialization, especially of the young, is devoted to teaching the beliefs and goals of society, including the idea that these are good and worthy of practice and defense. But there is a further function which must be universally met. Societies must in some way motivate their members to *maintain* the conviction that life is good and worthwhile. In other words, people must be imbued with a sense of meaning. They must be convinced that fitting into the social structure as they have been taught to do—meeting the expectations of the culture—is worth the effort.

Production and Distribution of Goods and Services A society without a social arrangement for the division of labor does not exist. The fact that new members born into a society are at first unable to provide for their own needs in itself requires such an arrangement if the society is to survive. Actually, of course, the division of labor extends far beyond what is necessitated by differences in age. The cumulative nature of culture results in the assignment of certain socially specific tasks to particular segments of society. In time, this process becomes institutionalized. It is not biologically necessary, for example, that men work as hunters or that women work as construction laborers, although there are times and places in which they do.

The economic structure and the set of values governing it differ radically from society to society, but everywhere people have some set of norms ordering their activities so that the function of producing and distributing goods and services is performed. In even the most favorable environment, some such social arrangements are necessary: even where socially defined needs are minimal and natural resources are abundant, someone has to be assigned the responsibility of picking the coconuts or berries for those unable to pick their own.

Preservation of Order We have seen that if a society is to survive, it must reproduce new members, socialize them, provide them with a continuing sense of purpose, and insure their biological well-being by arranging for the production and distribution of goods and services. Finally, some structure within the society must result in the preservation of order. Two facets of order are essential if the society is to survive: the society must not destroy itself from within, and it must not allow itself to be destroyed from the outside by some other society.

The values and norms that serve to order a society internally are enforced through formal and informal sanctions. Some obedience is essential to the continuity of a society. If a society were to reach the stage where most of its members failed to abide by the basic rules, it would be doomed. If people killed each other wantonly, refused to honor agreements, failed to fulfill social responsibilities, and meted out no punishment to those who ignored the social norms, the society would soon cease to exist. Anarchy may be a fit topic for philosophical speculation but it is not a basis for continued social life for any extended period of time.

The Web of Social Functions Each of these five major and universal social functions is closely interrelated with the others. Each is by no means separate from the others. If any one of these functions is not performed, the society and hence all the other functions come to an end. The functions are an interlocking system which makes the maintenance, stability, and continuity of social life possible. Because of this interrelationship, a change in any one of them is certain to have repercussions in the others.

Social Institutions

The ways in which a society meets the challenges to its social order posed by these universal social functions vary substantially from time to time and from place to place. But in every human society there is some set of social structures and related norms—called social institutions—for fulfilling these basic functions. A social institution, then, is a structure of social interaction and the accompanying folkways and mores that are integrated around a principal function of the society. "We deal with institutions, then, where distinctive value-orientations and interests centering upon large and important social concerns (e.g., education, marriage, property), generate or are accompanied by distinctive modes of social interaction." (Schneider, 1964, p. 339) There are five basic social institutions that can be identified in all societies—the familial, political, educational, economic, and religious institutions. Most modern societies have many more (e.g., scientific, military, etc.).

The Family Throughout human history, the family has been the group primarily responsible for most of these functions. Even today, in small, relatively isolated societies, the family is the basic primary group around which the major tasks of social life are organized.

In all societies, ancient or modern, small or large, the family is the structure which provides for the reproduction of new members for the society. Families may be organized with one husband, one wife, and their children; one husband, multiple wives, and their children; one wife, multiple husbands, and their children. Or they may consist of great-grandparents plus all their male children and spouses for four generations. And so on. Regardless of the concrete form of family organization, all societies have some form of family, and it is that institution that results in the function of reproduction.

Education The family always participates in socialization as well, but the extent varies considerably from society to society. In the United States, for example, many Indian children are taken from their parents at a very early age and sent to boarding schools hundreds of miles from their homes. (Leviton and Hetrick, 1971) In very small, nonindustrial societies, the family may serve the function of the "school," having almost the entire responsibility for inducting the child into the ways of the society.

People are socialized as a result of participation in many social structures. One learns something about one's society by interacting with others in religious groups, whether Sunday School classes or tribal ceremonies. Membership in a peer group of playmates is also a source of socialization; the child here comes in contact with the values of the culture that surround him or her and learns to conform to group expectations. In the twentieth century public schools have been assuming an important part of the socialization process. Some societies do not have "schools," but all societies have an educational institution—some set of social structures and accompanying folkways and mores that performs the function of socialization.

Religion As in the case of socialization, the sense of purpose is taught to people and maintained in them through a variety of social structures. Because of the range of cultural variability, sociologists use the word *religion* in a considerably broader sense than that in which it is ordinarily defined. For one person, a belief that the scientific method offers the possibility for a better life in this world may serve this function; for another person, the belief that service to a supernatural being promises a blissful and eternal afterlife may serve the same function.

Some structures in all societies have as a secondary or even latent function the fostering of a sense of purpose. Groups such as Senior Citizens' Clubs, community centers, and Marine Corps platoons are not religious structures, but are similar to religious structures insofar as they offer the individual something to participate in and believe in, and allow him to convince himself that his behavior is purposive, that his efforts are not in vain.

The Economy In the days of the frontier in the United States, the family was the basic economic unit. Father, mother, and children worked the fields together, producing most of what they consumed. Now father may work for one company, mother for another, and brother and sister for a third and fourth. The corporation has become the major economic organization in our economy, as secondary groups perform the functions of producing goods and services formerly carried out by primary groups.

Whatever the economic organization of a society—corporate and industrial or primary and agricultural—some groups exist which produce and distribute goods and services. They may specialize in economic activity, as does a steel company, or they may meet this need in addition to others, as does a family. But in all societies there are structures that carry out this function.

The Polity Like other social structures, those which preserve the domestic order vary greatly in their complexity, depending in general on the size and complexity of the rest of the society. A tribe may be composed of half a dozen families, with the head of one serving as chief, settling disputes within the group and/or leading warriors in battle. At the other extreme are the large nation-states of the mid-twentieth century, each of which has an enormous formal governmental structure with a military branch, a foreign relations branch, a taxation branch, and police and courts at various levels to maintain order within the society. In every state in the United States, for example, there is (1) a legislature (2) chosen by the residents of that state (3) on a competitive basis (4) with each adult citizen having one vote (5) which he is not required to cast but can use or not as he sees fit. Each legislator (6) serves for a specified period of time, after which he must vacate his status or again compete for it. And (7) the legislature has certain specific powers and is denied certain others. Through this set of related norms, and many others specifying the roles of federal, state, and local executives, judges, policemen, and people in related statuses, the function of maintaining order in the society is carried out.

3-2 CHECKING IT OUT: The Interrelationships of Social Structures and Social Functions

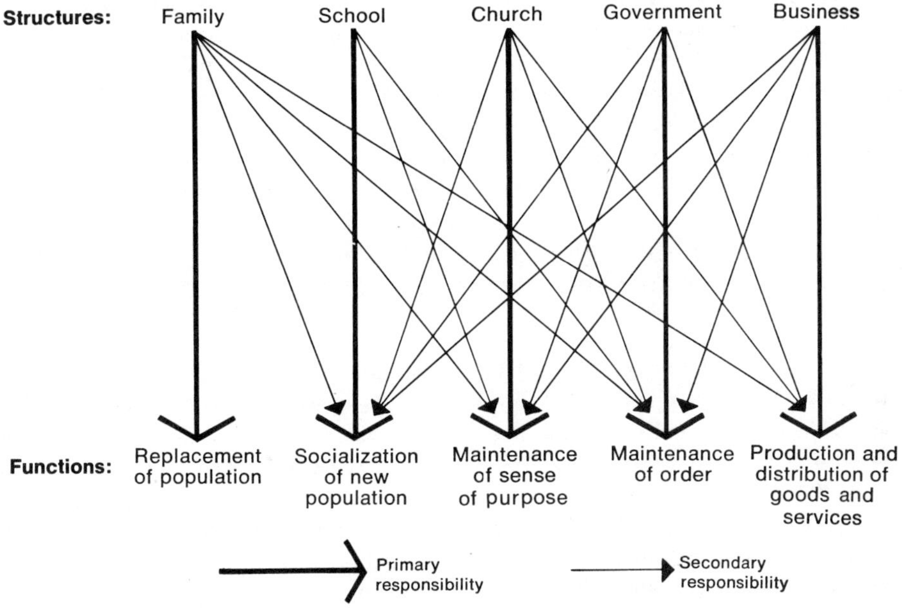

The Web of Social Institutions Each social institution is integrated around a major societal function but each invariably performs supplementary functions. Conversely, a function may derive from more than one structure. "Every institution centers around a fundamental need, permanently unites a group of people in a cooperative task, and has its particular doctrine and its technique or craft. Institutions are not correlated simply and directly to their function; one need does not receive one satisfaction in one institution." (Malinowski, 1931, Vol. 4, p. 262) The crucial nature of these institutions is indicated by the relatively tight balance which obtains among them. A change in the economy, for example, from a homestead agricultural system to a mass-production factory system necessitates a change from an all-relatives-under-one-roof familial group to an immediate family. This, in turn, will alter the early socialization of the child, and so on. Social functions and social structures are so closely interrelated that an alteration in one has repercussions throughout the social system. The integration of social institutions is never perfect, however. It is in a constant state of readjustment as the operation of social processes causes alteration in the social structure. However, there must be some degree of integration of institutions or the society will collapse.

An instance of integration among the institutions of our own society will illustrate this point. The social process of competition is stressed as a positive cultural value in the American economic institution. "Free enterprise" is spoken of favorably; people are urged to strive to "get ahead"; competitive examinations are held for promotion in many jobs; we admire the poor boy who works harder than his fellows and becomes a "success"; we pass legislation to prevent monopoly because "competition is good for the market." The political and educational institutions are integrated with our economic institution: people compete for high political office; children are taught to compete for grades, for athletic honors, for fraternity bids, for scholastic prizes. While there is not a perfect meshing of values (it is sometimes bad taste to compete, as for the last piece of candy in the box), our institutions, in general, like those of any other going society, are so integrated that the norms of one institution support those of another.

Institutional Structures Every institution, in order for its functions to be performed, has a division of labor among its participants. Among the many norms making up the institution are those defining the various roles necessary to the performance of the institutional function. The familial institution, for instance, is responsible for the reproduction of new members for the society; it will therefore specify role behavior appropriate to the statuses of father, mother, son, daughter, suitor, husband, wife, and any other statuses, such as obstetrician or midwife, which are related to the reproductive function in the society.

Of course, not every person who participates in a given institutional structure has exactly the same behavior as every other person in the same role. For one thing, the expectations of one institutional role may interfere with those of another. The expectations of career woman *vs.* those of mother, for example, create role conflict for a person who tries to work and rear children at the same time. Trying to balance the requirements of sometimes conflicting roles, then, can lead individuals to behave differently within the same institutional framework. In addition, each of us brings our own personality to any group in which we participate; we may all conform to its major norms, but our behavior will vary in many small ways. It is obvious that two women who may be described as mothers may behave differently within this role. There are, however, certain major expectations laid down within the familial institutions which lead to a set of similarities in their behavior: the institutionalized role of mother.

Sociologists are especially concerned with the place of each institution in any society; indeed, an emphasis on any one institution or number of institutions is a good indication of the ethics of a culture. A society that demands that its members spend half their time in worship and contemplation leaves them less time for family life, business, and other pursuits than a society with religious requirements that are not so stringent. The dominance of a single institutional structure is less likely for most persons in an urban society, because the urban way of life requires specialization, and each of one's roles tends to be but a segment of his total social life. As Arnold M. Rose says,

> Institutions vary in the degree of specialization expected of persons, and this is often related to the degree of control the institution has over the life of its members. The more specialized and segmentalized the relation of a given member to an institution, the less is its control over him. The teacher is associated with the school only in his occupational life, whereas the nun is associated with the church in most aspects of her life. Even within the same institution this holds true: the religious leader (rabbi, priest, minister) has a less specialized relation to his church than does the average member, and his life is much more controlled by the institution. To the extent that an individual's life is controlled by one institution, he must have fewer relationships to other institutions. A priest, for example, must even withdraw from family life. (Rose, 1956, p. 131)

INTERPRETIVE SUMMARY

Status, prestige, and role are abstractions dealing with society's tendency to differentiate, to evaluate the positions it creates as "high" or "low," and to demand certain behavior from individuals occupying the positions. Each individual occupies many statuses. To a certain extent, a person may "coast" on the prestige of a status he or she occupies, but the role behavior will always be watched by society, and the person will lose esteem if he or she does not conform to expected patterns.

All societies assign some statuses on the basis of such natural categories as sex and age; in fact, all share this age breakdown: childhood, or the period of virtual dependence; youth, the time of increasing sexual maturity and of preparation for adult responsibility; adulthood, the time of broadest rights and full responsibility; and old age, the time of declining powers. The exact age at which an individual is considered an adult, the reverence, or lack of it, that children or old people receive, the tasks youth is required to do vary among societies; but each society ascribes some statuses on the basis of age. Similarly, though physiological differences between the sexes are actually minor, all societies ascribe some statuses, especially those involved with division of labor, on the basis of sex. Some societies tend to ascribe many statuses on the bases of age and sex, while other societies leave many statuses open to achievement. In the United States and in some other societies, race is also used as a basis for ascribed status.

The implications of status and role are important psychologically as well as sociologically. For example, while the reciprocal nature of roles gives the individual a certain security, role conflict may prove overwhelming. The competition for coveted statuses is particularly intense in complex, achievement-oriented societies.

Another structural element within human society is the group. When people come together and develop social relations in patterned ways, they may be identified as social groups.

Several universal social functions may be recognized, since all societies must perform certain basic tasks in order to survive. Each society must replenish its population, must produce and distribute food and other necessities, and must guard against destruction from within or without. Furthermore, each society must teach new members the values, knowledge, and skills of the society, and must convince each individual that life on that society's terms is worthwhile.

Each society must develop some institutionalized means for renewing itself, for distributing goods and services, and so on. Specific structures of social institutions vary with the society. More complex cultures, for instance, have many specific social structures, each having a basic function, each having secondary functions which reinforce the work of other structures. A change in one institution will cause changes in other institutions and functions throughout the society.

QUESTIONS

1. Construct a status-set that illustrates all the social positions that you occupy. Which are master statuses for you, statuses that influence many other statuses?
2. Analyze the role of college student. What role conflicts are related to the status female?
3. Define a social group and describe three social institutions. What characteristics do they share? Which are different?

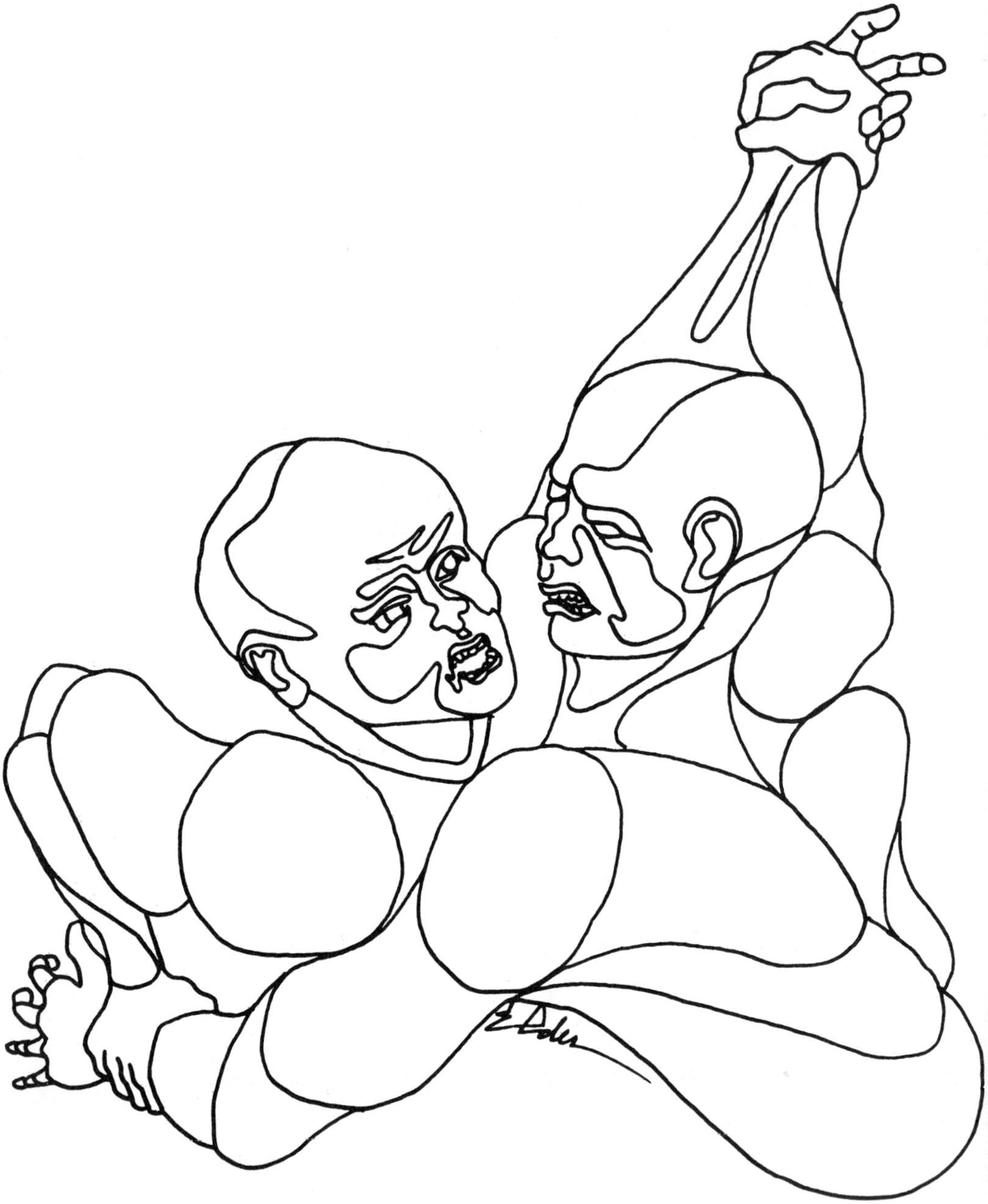

4

Social Interaction and Social Processes

SOCIAL INTERACTION

Social interaction is the key element in all of human life and the concept is crucial to any study of the dynamics of society. Without social interaction there would be no group life. The mere placing of individuals in physical proximity, while usually resulting in a modicum of interaction, does not weld them into a social unit or group. It is when people work or play or talk together with a common end, or when they compete or quarrel with one another that associative life, properly speaking, exists. Social interaction is the basic social process, the broadest term for describing dynamic social relationships.

Basic to human survival is the struggle for material goods and other rewards culturally defined as desirable. The chief forms of such struggle or opposition are competition and conflict. Yet not all life consists of one individual striving against another individual. People also combine to gain goals and rewards. This mutual aid is called cooperation. Then too, the individual learns a variety of distinguishing behaviors that set him or her off from others according to age, sex, occupation, and class. This is the process of differentiation. Opposition, cooperation, and differentiation constitute a base line from which still other more specialized forms of interaction arise, such as accommmodation, stratification, and assimilation. We shall examine first the universal processes of opposition, cooperation, and differentiation, and then we shall turn to the processes derived from them.

OPPOSITIONAL PROCESSES

Opposition, as well as cooperation, occurs in every society, although its form and direction are modified by the culture of the time and place. **Opposition** may be defined as a struggle *against* one or more others for a good, goal, or value; **cooperation** is the joint striving *with* one or more others for a good, goal, or value. A *felt scarcity* or desire for a good or value—money, power, affection, and so on—is basic to both opposition and cooperation. What people fight over, or cooperate together for, is determined in large measure by their culture.

For analytical purposes, opposition may be divided into competition and conflict. **Competition** is a form of opposition in which two or more persons or groups struggle for some need or goal but in the course of which attention is focused chiefly on the reward rather than on the competitor. In **conflict** the person or group thwarts, injures, or destroys the opponent in order to secure a goal or reward. That is, in conflict, interest is often directed initially toward frustrating the opposing individual or group and then toward the ultimate end. It is a two-step process. It is assumed or expected that once the opponent is beaten, the reward will fall to the victor.

Obviously, in real life, competition and conflict sometimes shade into one another. For example, rivals for the hand of a woman may resort to fisticuffs in their efforts to secure the maiden's favor, and for the moment they are more interested in knocking each other about than in courting. Or a business firm unable to compete with another under the usual "rules of the game" may employ gangsters to beat up the competitor's workmen or destroy its goods with a view to forcing the opposing firm to withdraw from the struggle.

The source of competition and conflict is often the frustration which comes into play when quick attainment of a goal or reward is denied. Not only is such activity accompanied by emotions, but the blocking of the movement from desire to consummation sets up intense emotional states that serve to stimulate further the individual's striving toward his goal. Rage, fear, and love are emotions that are particularly linked to ones' efforts to get what one wants.

If an individual is blocked in efforts to secure a desired goal, it may be possible to proceed in various ways to avoid, offset, or overcome the interference. One way is to make a highly emotional direct attack on the object or situation that blocks the way. If this fails, it may be more sensible to set about acquiring the skill and knowledge needed to attain the goal. And in this learning, help from others may be sought. If the individual fails to learn the requisite techniques or does not try to acquire them, it may be easier to find a substitute for the original goal. This is well illustrated in the mechanism called **compensation**, which may be expressed in overt behavior or in daydream or in fantasy. Another way of handling this lack of goal attainment is to give up the effort to reach the original reward or to secure a substitute. Indeed, regression to an earlier stage or avoidance of the situation may be an answer. When confronted by a serious or prolonged crisis, some people make no effort to adapt themselves to the situation. Perhaps the most striking illustrations occur among persons who are mentally ill, especially in severe cases of schizophrenia.

Among human beings, opposition is shaped at most points by cultural learning. For example, a child who from the earliest months of life was deprived of either sustenance or affection or both might well develop certain patterns of reactions to, say, parental authority, or to situations offering the alternative between dominance and submission—might become, for example, a little "tiger" or little "mouse." Later, that child, as an adult, will handle competition and conflict in a way that reflects acceptance of society's rules governing these processes. And yet in a narrower sense, the adult will always be something of the "tiger" or the "mouse" he or she learned to be in the earliest social relationships.

Culture and Competition

While culture or social traditions are rooted in our basic drives and personal interactions, the particular goods—material or nonmaterial—for which we strive vary greatly because of historical factors, accidents, or circumstance of the time and place, as well as local adaptation to resources. In the United States, people take competition and conflict so much for granted that it is difficult for many Americans to understand that a tribe or nation can have little of them.

In fact, however, an examination of the far-ranging variabilities of culture makes it clear that whether whole societies become generally conditioned to competitive or to cooperative forms of economic and community life depends on the value system of the society. An excellent illustration of such variability is found in the survey of the cultures of thirteen widely separated native tribes, prepared under the direction of Margaret Mead. (1937) On the basis of these surveys, Mead concluded that "no society is exclusively competitive or exclusively cooperative. The very existence of highly competitive groups implies cooperation within the groups. Both competitive and cooperative habits must exist within the society." Her analysis is also helpful in indicating the relation of these two basic processes to the tribal structure and to the life organization of the individuals within these societies. Among other significant findings of Mead's survey are the following:

(1) No matter what the nature of the cultural system, strong self-esteem and a sense of power can be found in some members of the society. (2) There is no relationship between the form of the culture and the local problems of sustenance and material resources. For example, there is no reason to assume that lack of food necessarily makes for either competition or cooperation. (3) The concept and valuation of personal success are determined more by the broad and general group emphasis on either competition or cooperation than by the degree of technology or the plentitude of food. (4) "There is a correspondence between: a major emphasis on competition, a social structure which depends upon the initiative of the individual, a valuation of property for individual ends, a single scale of success, and a strong development of the ego" [social self]. (p. 511) This is the sort of pattern that characterizes our own society. (5) "There is a correspondence between: a major emphasis upon cooperation, a social structure

which does not depend upon individual initiative or the exercise of power over persons, a faith in an ordered universe, weak emphasis upon rising in status, and a high degree of security for the individual." (p. 511)

It must be emphasized that in none of these tribes is either competition or cooperation wholly lacking. Such fundamental processes are correlative to each other. As economists long ago pointed out, competition itself rests on certain implicit agreements to follow certain rules in the oppositional relations. Yet when a society tends to stress one process, the other process may be found to be less institutionalized and hence less recognized.

Ralph Linton and Abram Kardiner (1939) cite a striking example of the effects of a basic change in economy on social organization and individual traits. Among the Tanala of Madagascar, the Betsileo tribe found it necessary, because of soil erosion and other changes, to shift from the cultivation of dry rice to that of wet rice. The system of dry-rice farming was marked by communal ownership of land, a high degree of cooperation, and equal distribution of produce under an

4-1 CHECKING IT OUT: The Positive Functions of Social Conflict

What is important for us is the idea that conflict . . . prevents the ossification of the social system by exerting pressure for innovation and creativity. . . . conflict within and between groups in a society can prevent accommodations and habitual relations from progressively impoverishing creativity. The clash of values and interests, the tension between what is and what some groups feel ought to be, the conflict between vested interests and new strata and groups demanding their share of power, wealth, and status, have been productive of vitality; note for example the contrast between the "frozen" world of the Middle Ages and the burst of creativity that accompanied the thaw that set in with Renaissance civilization.

This is, in effect, the application of John Dewey's theory of consciousness and thought as arising in the wake of obstacles to the interaction of groups. . . .

Conflict not only generates new norms, new institutions . . . it may be said to be stimulating directly in the economic and technological realm. Economic historians often have pointed out that much technological improvement has resulted from the conflict activity of trade unions through the raising of wage levels. A rise in wages usually has led to a substitution of capital investment for labour and hence to an increase in the volume of investment. Thus the extreme mechanization of coalmining in the United States has been partly explained by the existence of militant unionism in the American coalfields. . . .

. . . [a] successful reduction of industrial conflict may have unanticipated dysfunctional consequences for it may destroy an important stimulus for technological innovation.

SOURCE: Lewis A. Coser, "Social Conflict and the Theory of Social Change," *The British Journal of Sociology,* VIII (September, 1957), 197–198. Reprinted by permission of Routledge & Kegan Paul Ltd.

extremely authoritarian rule of the fathers. Under this somewhat rigid but paternalistic control, the individual though passive and obedient to authority, was well-adjusted.

The shift to an economy of wet-rice farming brought in its wake some startling changes. Communal ownership gave way to individual ownership. There was a mad rush for fertile acres in nearby valleys. The individual became important and soon began to feel in sharp competition with others over rights, as well as duties. The former family organization broke down, and there was a sharp increase in such deviant conduct as crime, homosexuality, black magic, and neuroticism. In time a whole new social organization emerged, including a rigid class structure of king, nobles, commoners, and slaves. This rapid shift in a basic feature of the culture illustrates clearly how much institutions influence the life organization of individuals.

It is clear, then, that competition may take a wide variety of forms. It may be central to some aspects of a cultural system and not to others. Moreover, under the impact of invention, political revolution, or shifts in the resource base of an economy, striking changes may occur in the interrelations of competition and other social processes.

Conflict

Conflict is characterized by emotionalized and violent opposition, in which the major concern is to overcome the opponent as a means of securing a goal or reward. It is direct and openly antagonistic struggle of persons or groups for the same object or end.

In the struggle to overcome the other person or group, the goal is often temporarily relegated to a level of secondary importance. In contrast to competition, which, at least in its stricter impersonal aspects, is more or less constant and unconscious, conflict is an intermittent but highly conscious process. Of course, in many situations competition and conflict are interrelated, the conflict often arising at critical points in the more prolonged competitive process.

Conflict is affected by the nature of the group and its particular culture. The objects of conflict may be property, power and status, freedom of action and thought, or any other desired value. When economic interests loom large and there are many individuals or groups striving for material gain and power, conflict of economic interests may supplement the competitive process. If sectarianism is rife, we can expect conflict to occur in religion. In other words, the culturally determined values of a society will set the stage for its struggles.

Not only is the form of conflict modified by the particular societal order and its culture, but everywhere there arise regulations to govern it. In feuds, for example, there are certain accepted methods of killing the other fellow. When conflict is infrequent and when no adequate techniques have been worked out, more violent and unpredictable sorts of conflict arise, such as race riots. In war,

4-2 CHECKING IT OUT: Conflict Binds Antagonists

If . . . a fight simply aims at annihilation, it does approach the marginal case of assassination in which the admixture of unifying elements is almost zero. If, however, there is any consideration, any limit to violence, there already exists a socializing factor, even though only as the qualification of violence. Kant said that every war in which the belligerents do not impose some restrictions in the use of possible means upon one another, necessarily . . . becomes a war of extermination. It is almost inevitable that an element of commonness injects itself into . . . enmity once the stage of open violence yields to another relationship, even though this new relation may contain a completely undiminished sum of animosity between the two parties.

One unites in order to fight, and one fights under the mutually recognized control of norms and rules.

SOURCE: Georg Simmel, *Conflict,* trans. Kurt H. Wolff (Glencoe, Illinois: The Free Press, 1955), pp. 26, 35.

of course, there are all sorts of rules more or less agreed upon by the belligerents during the interludes of peace.

At its most rudimentary level, conflict results in the removal or annihilation of the opponent. In human society, however, most conflict ends in some sort of agreement, or accommodation, or in the fusion of the two opposing elements.

4-3 CHECKING IT OUT: Conflict and Social Solidarity

The group in a state of peace can permit antagonistic members within it to live with one another in an undecided situation because each of them can go his own way and can avoid collisions. A state of conflict, however, pulls the members so tightly together and subjects them to such uniform impulse that they either must get completely along with, or completely repel, one another. This is the reason why war with the outside is sometimes the last chance for a state ridden with inner antagonisms to overcome these antagonisms or else to break up definitely.

The fighter must "pull himself together." That is, all his energies must be, as it were, concentrated in one point so that they can be employed at any moment in any required direction.

The well-known reciprocal relation between a despotic orientation and the warlike tendencies of a group rests on this informal basis: war needs a centralistic intensification of the group form, and this is guaranteed best by despotism.

SOURCE: Georg Simmel, *Conflict,* trans. Kurt H. Wolff (Glencoe, Illinois: The Free Press, 1955), pp. 87, 88, 92, 93.

The essential nature of social conflict can be summarized in terms of the following five propositions. (Mack and Syder, 1957)

1. Conflict requires at least two parties (groups, individuals, organizations, etc.) since it is by definition an interaction relationship.

2. Conflict arises from some kind of "scarcity," of desired but limited resources, activities, positions, or goals.

3. Conflict actions are designed to limit, thwart, destroy, control, or otherwise influence another party (person, group, etc.) and a conflict relationship is one in which the conflicting parties can gain only at each other's relative expense.

4. Conflict requires interaction among parties in which their actions and counteractions are mutually opposed.

5. Conflict relations always involve attempts to acquire or exercise social power.

COOPERATION

Cooperation, like opposition, is a basic feature of human interaction. These ambivalent patterns, we have noted, appear to underlie all other more specialized social processes. As Albion W. Small (one of the founders of sociology in America) put it, "Struggle and co-operation are correlates in every situation"—that is, there is either "conjunction" or "conflict" of interests. (Small, 1905) Yet the interplay of these two processes is not always understood. Some writers consider opposition the fundamental form of interaction; others believe that cooperation is the basic social process. For example, some use the term *cooperation* as a synonym for almost all social contact, holding that opponents in fighting must "cooperate" in order to exchange blows, or that traders "cooperate" in their market relations, or that the compromise of disputes between laborers and employers represents a form of cooperation. Such broad and loose use of the term makes it practically identical with the term *social interaction* and thus too vague for effective description and analysis. We shall limit the term *cooperation* to a more specific aspect of human intercourse, one having to do with mutual aid or an alliance of persons or groups seeking some common goal or reward—in short, as some kind of conjoint rather than opposing action.

4-4 CHECKING IT OUT: Cooperation Among the Zuñi

In addition to obligations between kinsmen that are established at birth the Zuñi have institutionalized a ceremonial friendship built around economic cooperation. Such friends are under obligation to lend assistance in all large undertakings. . . .

Strikingly characteristic of all social relations in Zuñi is the relative lack of emphasis upon wealth. Property does not figure in marriage. Individuals do not compete for a fixed supply, and in terms of the prestige an individual may achieve, property in itself is not the determining factor. . . .

Wealth circulates freely, and property rights are neither clearly defined nor strictly enforced. . . .The property that is really valued . . . is the nonmaterial property such as songs, prayers, rituals. . . .

The principles of land tenure reveal further the basic noncompetitive and nonindividualistic property patterns in Zuni. Most of the reservation consists of land unsuitable, at present, for cultivation. These uncultivated areas belong communally to the tribe and any man may stake out new fields wherever he wishes. Such fields, in contrast to those held by the female line of a household, belong to him individually and may be disposed of by him at his pleasure. But so long as he remains associated with a household either by blood or by marriage he cultivates the field for a communal end, the products that he raises becoming the collective property of the women of the household. It is even possible to appropriate land, the title of which is held by another family, providing that it is not in use. For although distinctions are made between ownership and use of a field, these are by no means clear, and it is difficult to dispossess a family that has taken possession.

It is significant, too, that litigations over the ownership of land are rare and in most cases quickly settled. One might expect that disputes would arise frequently among a people whose concepts of ownership are so vaguely defined that boundaries between fields are marked only in one dimension, in width facing the road and not in depth.

The problem of sheep ownership. . . . Here evidently a new individualistic pattern seems to have developed under stimulation of white contact. Yet it is interesting to note that, although the ownership of sheep is individualistic, few Zuñi know how many sheep they own. Nor, in spite of the great value in which sheep are held, do men compete against one another for sheep. Rather, a young man is assisted in developing a flock of his own. A boy who offers to herd for a group of his male kinsmen receives from them at the shearing season a number of sheep as gifts. These belong to him and form the nucleus of his own herd. Next season in addition to the lambs that have been born he is given more sheep by his association until after a few seasons he has accumulated sixty sheep—a sack of wool. At this point he becomes a full-fledged member of the group and he is given no more assistance. Thus instead of attempting to acquire a monopoly, a group of men cooperate to "set up" a young relative, though this is not essential in herding. . . .

Food is shared by all in the household and is based entirely on need, with no account taken of the field it has been grown in or of who has been responsible in producing it. If, for example, *A* should bring in some especially choice melon from his field, his wife does not feel that she has any more claim to it than her sister. A man may, however, take food from his own field to his female relatives, his mother, his sister, or a niece, providing he has not yet brought the food into the house. For then it falls entirely under the jurisdiction of the women in the house.

SOURCE: Irving Goldman, "The Zuñi Indians of New Mexico," *Cooperation and Competition among Primitive Peoples,* ed. Margaret Mead (New York: McGraw-Hill, 1937), pp. 326–329. Reprinted by permission.

Patterns of mutual aid are found among all human groups. Such habits and attitudes begin in infancy and childhood within the family and the congeniality group. Upon the basis acquired in these primary groups, the individual develops cooperative behavior patterns as an adult. In order for rudimentary mutual helpfulness to develop into more deliberate form, people must first be directly motivated to seek a goal that may be shared. Second, they must acquire some knowledge of the benefits of such activity—hence the need for education to foster cooperation. Third, they must acquire a favorable attitude toward sharing both the work and the rewards involved. And finally, they need to equip themselves with the skills necessary to make the cooperative plan work. (May and Doob, 1937)

Cooperation imposes various forms of restraint on the participant. Individuals cannot have their way entirely if they are to work cooperatively with others.

If a self-assertive trend becomes too strong, cooperation will be replaced by struggle. Cooperation always implies inhibition of certain ego-centered tendencies. A child in team play cannot always assume the chief role. The more conscious and complex the form of cooperation, the more evident this fact becomes. From the restraint so imposed there arises a moral control which stands in contrast with the impulsiveness and lack of self-control found in uninhibited conflict. In the struggle of one group against another, this moral order is highly important, as it is also in controlling the relations of persons to one another within the group itself. The function of cooperation is well summarized in the following words of C. H. Cooley (1930):

> Co-operation . . . arises when men see that they have a common interest and have, at the same time, sufficient intelligence and self-control to seek this interest through united action: perceived unity of interest and the faculty of organization are the essential facts in intelligent combination.

Culture and Cooperation

It is not necessary to posit an instinct of sociability or gregariousness in order to explain cooperation. The instances of interaction simply within the family would furnish sufficient ground upon which to construct the cooperative social order which we find everywhere. Beyond the family the neighborhood, the play group, and the whole set of secondary groups call for cooperation. If we say that human cooperation is a form of interaction between two or more persons or groups striving toward some goal or reward that may be shared in material goods, in prestige and power, or in some other accepted satisfaction, we can also say that *culture is what gives cooperation pitch and direction.*

In the United States there appears to be far more teaching of the child, youth, and adult in competitive and conflictive attitudes, habits, and ideas than in those involving cooperation. Yet the society is not given entirely to conflict or to competitive individualism. Within the social class, the team, the trade union, the employers' association, the religious confraternity, interdependence and mutual aid are absolutely essential. Nevertheless, in all these the fundamental and persisting values are frequently those of the competitive-conflictive *ethos*.

An example of a different cultural attitude toward cooperation will illustrate this point. S. D. Porteus (1931), a psychologist, tells of his difficulty in getting certain natives of Australia to work individually and competitively on intelligence tests. The natives turned to him for help to do the task and were clearly upset when he refused. Porteus had earlier been adopted as a tribal brother, and the natives simply could not understand how a person in such a relationship to them could refuse to cooperate in a task put before them.

From an ethnocentric standpoint, forms of cooperation found in other societies may strike us as being absurd and the individuals therein as lacking in ambition and initiative. Some societies, like the one just mentioned, emphasize cooperation as a cultural value much more than we in the United States do, while other societies set less value on cooperation than we. But cooperation, like competition and conflict, is a universal characteristic of human societies; in no society is it completely lacking. Among people, as among animals, there is a good deal of nondeliberate mututal aid, especially in time of grave danger. Even in our highly individualistic, competitive world, people have also learned, especially in primary-group situations, interdependence and mutual aid in times of stress. Certainly such patterns are distinctly culturized through the Judeo-Christian religion. Again, it must be recalled that cooperation and conflict are closely related. For example, members of a group may be highly cooperative with one another and conflictive toward other groups. The ethos of the culture will define the nature and degree of such cooperation and conflict.

DIFFERENTIATION

Some type of specialization or differentiation of role is found in every society. Such differentiation is clearly related to the division of labor. In the industrial economic order, for example, there are the different roles of entrepreneur, manager, and skilled and unskilled laborers. In the political order it is seen in the varying roles of public administrators, and in religion, in the distinctive roles of prophet, seer, and priest. Some form of specialization of role is found in every association of people and, moreover, where such differentiation is linked to basic needs and goals it takes on the permanence and persistence of institutions.

Differences in age and sex are obvious foundations of specialization although how the varied roles are defined depends, of course, on the particular culture. So too, different occupations create conditions for variation in roles and statuses while at the same time fostering interdependence. As the British economist Henry Clay (1918) once put it, "From the point of view of the individual, division of labor means *specialization*; from the point of view of society, it means *co-operation*."

While some specialization is found in tribal societies, highly integrated specialization is associated with extensive agriculture, handicrafts, the marketplace, writing, the political state, and other aspects of a more complex culture. The ancient world, even before the rise of Greece and Rome, witnessed differentiation in economic, political, military, religious, and other areas of human association. Professions and techniques evolved, with their particular knowledge, skills, language, and status. In fact, their development illustrates the emergence of variations in group participation called "specialties."

Economic Division of Labor

The division of labor does not go very far in any society until people begin to produce goods or services in such quantity that the surplus can be exchanged for the goods or services of others. But specialization of economic roles depends not only on the level of technology and the needs of the tribe or society but also on the degree of sophistication in the marketing process. People learned only gradually that division of labor benefits the individual as well as others.

While there was considerable specialization in the ancient world, it was the coming of the factory system that marked the great expansion in division of labor. The modern machine makes it possible to produce small parts that can be combined into a total product. This, of course, involves standardization and further simplification in the making of a particular part. Mechanization also fosters efficient production and the development of a large-scale corporate ownership and control. Finance capitalism and machine-dominated division of labor emerged at the same historical time.

Some of the functions or consequences of a highly differentiated economic structure are the following: (1) Specialization makes it possible to select workers according to their capacity to do a particular job. Both intelligence and temperament may be important. (2) It facilitates the acquisition of high skill in some one craft or phase of an operation. The "Jack-of-all-trades" is displaced by one who can learn the needed skill quickly and accurately. (3) It increases efficiency because it requires concentration of attention and skill on single items of work, and this, in turn, is associated with (4) standardization of product, which makes mass production possible and often—though not always—results in a better product. (5) It saves time and human energy. This is the virtue of automation. (6) It permits classification of skills and products, encouraging in turn effective management. And (7), to repeat, it promotes the factory system and the organization of large-scale units of production. This means the assembly of workers and many machines under one management, making supervision simpler, allowing concentration of raw materials at convenient points, and permitting urbanization with its more advantageous marketing.

Some of the negative consequences of division of labor, especially in the machine age, are the following: (1) Factory work and machine production involve certain dangers and may produce ill-health if not properly regulated. (2) Overspecialization may so concentrate attention and skill on simple muscular responses as to result in monotony and fatigue, destroying incentive and creative interest in one's job. Critics of the modern factory system often contend that such work is unpleasant and disheartening and lowers the morale of the workers. They say that the artisan who made a total product—chair, house, pair of boots, piece of cloth—understood every step in the process, enjoyed putting the material together, and had genuine satisfaction in seeing the finished product. They argue that *the machine dominates the personality.* These critics tend to agree with Karl Marx, who defended the thesis that the machine—an objective, impersonal thing—controlled the spirit, initiative, and freedom of the operator. Instead of being the end or aim of the economic process, the individual, Marx said, becomes merely the means to production, an appendage to a system of machines that reduces him to a nonentity. The impersonality which characterizes much of modern life would thus be traceable not merely to the operations of the market and the wage system, but to the factory system itself. (3) The modern machine tends to destroy the skilled trades and to substitute semiautomatic and automatic machines, leaving the operator only simple movements to perform. (4) In a capitalistic society, such high specialization tends to make the worker increasingly dependent on the owner-manager. Moreover, the business cycle subjects the worker to seasonal and long-term periods of unemployment.

The features which we have just described are, of course, familiar. Efficient and advantageous as the factory system is for our economic welfare, it has not contributed to the larger society and culture without some human costs. Yet human ability to make new adjustments is great; and when there is good health, adequate income with steady employment, and retirement benefits, many of the negative effects of overspecialization tend to disappear. In general, highly industrialized societies make possible a higher level of living than mankind ever experienced in the past.

Social Implications of Specialization

In the study of the division of labor, one is concerned not only with differentiation of activities but also with how the various activities mesh or are interdependent. It is interesting that the individualism associated with a laissez-faire philosophy should produce a social structure so interdependent that the dislocation of any considerable section of it—say a key industry such as steel-making or transportation—threatens the whole society. In other words, specialization promotes not only separateness but also the integration of group life. In this way specialization fosters cooperation. The weaver is dependent on the sheep raiser for wool, and both need a merchant or middleman to market their goods; the entrepreneur is dependent on the banker for capital; and so on. In fact, the economic order consists of a vast network of competition, cooperation, and differentiation.

In societies where all women garden and cook and all men hunt and fish, the total content of the culture is little more than the combined knowledge of any two adults of opposite sex. A second consequence of elaborate occupational specialization, then, is an increase in the content of culture. Bushmen do not have much more to transmit to the next generation than any one Bushman can know; while Western societies, for example, have so much more to transmit than any one individual could possibly know that the concept of the content of culture becomes staggering.

DERIVED SOCIAL PROCESSES

From opposition, cooperation, and differentiation emerge several other social processes. These *derived* processes are also universal in human societies. Out of differentiation grows *social ranking.* Cooperation among varied groups often leads to *assimilation.* Since conflict is not usually continuous between groups, some working arrangement, or *accommodation,* arises. This section describes these processes derived from opposition, cooperation, and differentiation.

Accommodation

The word *accommodation* has been used in two related senses—to indicate a condition of institutional arrangement, and to indicate a process. As a *condition,* accommodation is the fact of equilibrium between individuals and groups and the "rules of the game" which have been developed. Etiquette, or the "proper" way of acting socially, the "agreements" developed between conflicting economic groups, treaties between nations, and the techniques, traditions, and arrangements that define the relations of persons and groups are forms of accommodation. As a *process,* accommodation has to do with the conscious efforts of people to develop working arrangements among themselves that will suspend conflict and so make their relations more tolerable and less wasteful of energy. It concerns the movement toward the accommodated state. It is a means of resolving conflict without the complete destruction or absorption of the opponent—that is, without either party's entirely losing its identity. Accommodation takes place at a conscious—though not necessarily rational—level, and for the most part is in the nature of formal and external regulations or arrangements.

The effects of accommodation may vary somewhat with the circumstances. Accommodation may act to reduce the conflict between persons or groups as an initial step to synthesis of differences into a new pattern—in other words, it may lead to assimilation. It may serve to postpone outright conflict for a specific period of time, as in a treaty between nations or a labor-management agreement. It may permit groups separated by sharp social-psychological distance to get along together. In this function it is closely related to stratification as seen in class or caste systems. It may prevent what the culture considers an undesirable amalgamation or biological inbreeding of two groups and their subsequent assimilation. Sometimes the accommodation is viewed by the parties involved as mutually beneficial. In other instances the arrangements are imposed on one group by another with superior power and prestige.

Forms of Accommodation

Accommodative arrangements between groups or individuals take a variety of forms, from coercion through compromise and conciliation to toleration. **Coercion** is a type of accommodation in which action and thought in social relationships are determined by constraint, compulsion, or force. Coercion implies the existence of the weak and the strong in any conflict. It takes two forms—physical or direct application of pressure; and psychological, or indirect application of pressure. For example, slavery is an arrangement in which the basic social interaction is one of domination by master and subjection of slave. Slavery involves absence of political rights for the slave, compulsory labor, and property rights of the master over the slave as an individual.

Various political dictatorships are coercive accommodations in which a strongly disciplined minority seizes power and inflicts its control on whole populations. We must not assume that such despotism is never welcome as a means of settling conflicts. When older values and practices are lost and a struggle rages among multiple warring interests, the masses come in time to look for a strong person who will bring peace and order.

Compromise, unlike coercive accommodation, implies a fair degree of equality in bargaining power of two contestants or willingness of the stronger party to substitute justice for strength as the basis for agreement. Compromise may be defined as a conscious method of settling a conflict in which all parties agree to renounce or reduce some of their demands in the interest of peace. Readiness to compromise means that groups and individuals are able to view themselves somewhat objectively, and to see themselves as others see them. Intransigent attitudes generated in the heat of conflict give way to more moderate positions. Certain international agreements and management-labor agreements on wages, hours of work, and other conditions of employment are examples of compromise. In a political democracy, too, parties or factions resolve their differences by compromise. This is especially true when they are about evenly matched in social power.

Arbitration is a special device for bringing about compromise when the contending parties themselves are unable to resolve their differences. Disputes are settled by a third party, who may be chosen by the opposing sides or appointed by some large agency of power, as in legalized compulsory arbitration of labor disputes. *Mediation,* which is closely akin to arbitration, is the introduction into a conflict of a neutral agent whose efforts are directed toward bringing about a peaceful settlement. The mediator has no power to settle the conflict; the function of the mediator is advisory only. The use of arbitrators or mediators is common in industrial and religious disputes in the United States.

Closely related to compromise and sometimes involving compromise is **conciliation**, which is an attempt to reconcile disputants as a means of bringing about an agreement. In modern industrial systems certain forms of conciliation have developed as a permanent program for settling disputes between owners and workers. Such organizations, called "works councils" or "shop committees," may or may not exist independently of trade unions. In these organizations representatives of the owners and workers set up institutional devices for handling disputes over wages, hours, and working conditions. Conciliation has also been used in racial and religious struggles. Conciliation always connotes a milder response to an opponent than coercion. In the end conciliation, like toleration, opens the door to assimilation.

Another form of accommodation is **toleration**, or *tolerant participation.* It is an outgrowth of the live-and-let-live policy. It is a form of accommodation without formal agreement. Sometimes it is not entirely deliberate and conscious, but grows up from long-continuing avoidances developed to soften hostilities. There have been many instances of this type of arrangement, such as among various language and nationality groupings in central Europe and among the Navajo and Pueblo Indians.

Social Ranking

Differentiation takes place universally on the basis of age, sex, and other factors. Out of differentiation emerges a division of labor, or assignment of various tasks to categories of people sharing different characteristics. Another process that is derived from differentiation is the ranking of social categories. Social ranking includes both the process of ranking differentiated categories and the resultant hierarchy. As a process, ranking has to do with the forms of interaction involved in the process; for example, ranking wealthy people above poor people, or people who abide by the norms of society above deviants, or people whose tasks are considered important for the welfare of society above those whose work is less highly valued.

Assimilation

If person-to-person, person-to-group, or group-to-group relations remained at the level of accommodation, there would occur no fusion of groups and their cultures. *Assimilation* is the fusion or blending of two previously distinct groups into one. Obviously, assimilation requires more fundamental changes than the "antagonistic cooperation" which we call accommodation. When the process of assimilation takes place, the people in two distinct groups do not just compromise or otherwise agree to get along with each other; they become so much like each other that they are no longer distinguishable as separate groups.

Assimilation occurs only when there is relatively continuous and direct contact. It is a comparatively slow process, though the history of human societies is full of examples of such merging of groups and their cultures. Among the more striking cases was the assimilation of the Anglo-Saxon and Norman societies in Britain in the two centuries after 1066, when the Normans invaded England. The so-called American "melting pot" is a recent and partial instance of assimilation. It is not usually possible today to tell the descendants of Englishmen or Germans who came here in the eighteenth century from the descendants of Scotsmen who emigrated at about the same time. Previously distinct groups have become fused into one, or assimilated. A factor which helps complete the process of assimilation is amalgamation, which is the intermarriage of members of different groups.

Amalgamation

One sometimes hears that a group is partially assimilated, or that Italian Americans, for example, are not as fully assimilated as Irish Americans. The fact that assimilation is not an all-or-nothing condition but rather a matter of degree is simply an indication that it is a process that occurs through time. Complete assimilation always implies amalgamation—that is, accepted intermarriage between the originally divergent groups. Without biological amalgamation, complete assimilation is not possible. If the two groups are still differentiated by the provision that their members shall not intermarry, they then are, *ipso facto*, not fully assimilated.

Mere intermixture of groups to a limited degree does not guarantee assimilation. Amalgamation must be socially accepted; it must become a part of the institutional structure before assimilation exists. For instance, in the United States there has been considerable racial crossing between whites and blacks, but there has been little amalgamation, despite the fact of a common culture. No observer of the contemporary scene in this country would contend that blacks and whites have become fused into one indistinguishable whole. For purposes of most interaction, accommodation and ranking rather than assimilation have been the rule. On the other hand, the rate of intermarriage among European immigrant groups is a definite indication of the fusion of persons from many societies into one new one. The United States is a case study of a society composed, through assimilation and amalgamation, of a variety of social and biological elements.

Acculturation

When two or more cultures come into contact, the subsequent intermixture of shared, learned behavior patterns is called *acculturation.* This process may involve the almost complete absorption of one culture by another, or a relatively equal merging of traits and patterns from both cultures. Acculturation can occur with or without assimilation. The accommodative relations of Christian and Moslem societies through the centuries have resulted in acculturation. Christians have adopted some of the behavior patterns of Moslems, and Moslems have adopted some of the behavior patterns of Christians; but the members of the two societies have not assimilated.

The blending of Oriental and Occidental elements in contemporary Japanese culture is another instance of acculturation without assimilation of two groups. The Japanese way of life has changed considerably in a relatively short time under the impact of Western culture. Not only is there more Western-style clothing in Japan, as well as other evidence of acculturation, such as increased use of telephones, television, and subways, but there are alterations in such basic culture patterns as food consumption and formal education.

Again, the hybrid patterns of Latin-American societies have sprung from the acculturation of Spanish and Indian American cultures, characterized by a degree of both assimilation and amalgamation. Large portions of Greek and Roman culture have become acculturated with Hebraic and Germanic patterns, and have, in turn, contributed to our own culture.

Socialization

Socialization is interaction by means of which the individual learns the social and cultural requirements that make the individual a functioning member of society. This interaction teaches one habits, ideas, attitudes, and values. The person learns to conform to the cultural expectations, traditions, and sanctions, develops a sense of self, and learns to identify with culturally defined in-groups. One acquires the in-group's attitudes toward out-groups—attitudes of opposition, avoidance, or indifference. The initial socialization occurs in the child's contacts with parents, siblings, and playmates, but all through life the individual continues to feel the impact of society (see Chapter 6).

INTERPRETIVE SUMMARY

The word *process,* as used here, describes people interacting: fighting, helping one another, teaching their young, and so on. Like structures and functions, certain processes are universal. One such process is opposition, or struggle over a goal that cannnot be shared or that the antagonists refuse to share. Each faction may calmly concentrate on attaining the goal, it may see destruction of the enemy as absolutely essential to its own success, it may be able to "see the other's side" and be willing to give up part of its demands so that the other faction will not suffer, or it may not even be conscious that a struggle is going on in the first place. The form of the struggle will also be influenced by how the antagonists assess their relative strength; a powerful force may insist on having all its demands met, while equal sides will probably settle for some sort of compromise.

Cooperation, the process of working together for a common goal, is the opposite of competition and conflict. Cooperation leads to acculturation, in which cultures or subcultures adopt behavior patterns from one another, and finally to assimilation, the state in which two groups actually blend into one.

All societies condone both opposition and cooperation under some circumstances. However, a given society may stress one more than the other, depending on the ethos of the society. Furthermore, goals themselves and the rules concerning how one may go about attaining them will differ from society to society.

Two intra-society processes are differentiation and socialization. In assigning specialties, or differentiating, a culture must take into account certain broad biological limitations which members of all societies have in common; beyond this, the culture may follow its own course in dividing necessary labor and deciding how groups should be ranked socially. Socialization is the process in which an individual is taught the ways of his culture, including its ways of carrying out the other processes.

QUESTIONS

1. What social processes might a sociologist observe in a school playground during recreation hour?
2. Is a society without opposition and conflict possible?
3. What is the relationship among accommodation, assimilation, and acculturation?
4. What positive results may derive from opposition, competition, and conflict?

5

Culture and Society

Keep the following characteristics in mind as you read this chapter.
Culture is:

1. *learned* through participation in human groups. It replaces instinct as a means of dealing with the environment.
2. *shared* by humans. The members of a society share a set of common expectations, beliefs, and values.
3. *internalized* and becomes part of us *because of social coercion.* We have no choice (i.e., we must learn to speak the language of our parents). Internalization is aided by sanctions.
4. *immortal* and extends beyond the lives of individuals. The content of culture is passed from generation to generation.
5. *ideational* and is mainly an abstract concept, a thing of the mind. While dealing with abstractions such as belief and values, culture is an integral part of any society and of human reality.
6. *transmitted through* use of *language.*

CULTURE

Definitions and Characteristics of Culture

In every human collectivity, whether a family or a national society, there are certain recurrent, accepted, and expected ways of thinking and acting. Such patterns of behavior when they are common to a society or other large social groups we call culture. The classic definition of culture was written by E. B. Tylor in 1871: "Culture . . . is that complex whole which includes knowledge, belief, art, morals, law, custom, and any other capabilities and habits acquired by man as a member of society" (1924, p.1). Culture is the social heritage of a people. It consists of commonly accepted and expected ideas, attitudes, values, and behavior which people learn in connection with social living. It is, then, that part of the human environment that a group of people itself has created. For the individual, culture provides "a design for living" that is an enormous aid in learning to get on effectively in the world. The members of each new generation do not have to begin "from scratch," but benefit from the earlier generations around them, who also learned how to adjust to the physical and social world largely from their progenitors. Later, this new generation passes on to the next generation what it has learned from the previous generations and what it has added to the cultural whole.

The concept of culture always refers to behavior that is *shared and transmitted through learning*. Behavior in this context refers to thinking and feeling as well as overt actions. Any behavior is part of a culture only when it is shared by most members, or by specifically designated members, of the group. If you are the only person who uses a hairbrush then this behavior is not part of American culture. If most Americans arrange their hair with a hairbrush after they get up in the morning, then this behavior is shared; it is part of American culture. Most Americans share the belief that the United States is the best place in the world to live. This belief is part of the American culture.

It is difficult to exaggerate the importance of culture as a determinant of human behavior. One way to try to grasp the significance of culture is to imagine the human condition without it. Fifty years ago Graham Wallas (1921, p. 16) visualized modern urban people without culture and concluded:

> If the earth were struck by one of Mr. [H. G.] Wells' comets, and if, in consequence, every human being now alive were to lose all the knowledge and habits which he had acquired from preceding generations (though retaining unchanged all his own powers of invention, and memory, and habituation), nine-tenths of the inhabitants of London or New York would be dead in a month, and 99 per cent of the remaining tenth would be dead in six months. They would have no language to express their thoughts, and no thoughts but their revery. They could not read notices, or drive motors or horses. They would wander about, led by the inarticulate cries of a few . . . individuals drowning themselves, as thirst came on, in hundreds at the river-side landing places, looting those shops where the smell of decaying food attracted them, and perhaps at the end stumbling on the expedient of cannibalism. Even in the country districts men could not invent, in time to preserve their lives, methods of growing food, or taming animals, or making fire, or sew clothing themselves as to endure the northern winter. An attack of constipation or measles would be invariably fatal. After a few years mankind would almost certainly disappear from the northern and temperate zones. The white races would probably become extinct everywhere. A few primitive races might live on fruit and small animals in those fertile tropical regions where the human species was originally evolved until they had slowly accumulated a new social heritage.

Cultural Learning *vs.* Instinct

By learned behavior we mean more than attitudes and ways of acting that are formally and consciously taught. Any behavior which is socially acquired (that is, which comes through participation in a human group) is *learned.* Some aspects of individual behavior are determined, of course, by heredity; such behavior is not cultural. If water is thrown in a person's face, the person will blink. This is *shared behavior* (we will all blink), but it is not learned; it is inherited. Another way to describe these built-in or inherited behaviors is to say that they are *instinctive* or *innate.* Most animals exhibit a variety of instinctive behaviors. These are patterns of behavior which are unvarying within the species, and which are generally not subject to alteration or change. Lehrman (1961) describes the rigid behavior patterns of birds in the kinds of nests that they build, the methods used in feeding their young, and the seasonal migration routes they use. Thus, the behavior of birds exhibits a kind of genetic programming. Instinctive behaviors appear in such creatures at appropriate stages of their development or in response to certain stimuli.

Since the period of World War I, it has been generally accepted that the human animal has few such instincts to rely on in adapting to the environment (although Konrad Lorenz [1966] and Nikolaas Tinbergen [1951] have recently led a resurgence of interest in instinct through their studies of animal behavior). Charles Darwin in *The Descent of Man* (1871) makes clear the difference between instinctive and learned behaviors. Darwin notes that a beaver can construct a dam, a spider can spin a web, and a bird can build a nest nearly as well the first time as after long years of experience. These instinctive behaviors do not have to be learned. However, humans cannot rely on inborn behaviors that will be manifest at appropriate times. The human being cannot construct a stone hatchet or a canoe very well at the first attempt. Lacking instinctive behaviors to aid in problem-solving, humans must learn by trial and error, practicing and improving.

Darwin's Theory of Natural Selection

Darwin devoted much time and attention to comparisons of human and other animal behaviors. He saw many similarities between human beings and the higher mammals.

> It has, I think now been shewn that man and the higher animals, especially the Primates, have some few instincts in common. All have the same senses, intuitions, and sensations,—similar passions, affections, and emotions, even the more complex ones, such as jealousy, suspicion, emulation, gratitude, and magnanimity; they practice deceit and are revengeful; they are sometimes susceptible to ridicule, and even have a sense of humour; they feel wonder and curiosity; they possess the same faculties of imitation, attention, deliberation, choice, memory, imagination, the association of ideas, and reason, though in very different degrees. (*The Descent of Man*, p. 456)

Darwin's recognition of similarities between other mammals and humans is integrally related to his theoretical interpretation of evolutionary development. Darwin's theory of evolution accepts human beings as the product of perhaps

5-1 CHECKING IT OUT: Chimpanzees, Closely Scrutinized in Tanzania, Display Resemblances to Humans in Some Gestures, Family Relations and Violent Behavior

We have learned much over the past two years: horrifying new facts concerning infant killing and cannibalism; how the killing of adults from a neighboring community has enabled our main study group to enlarge its range. We have watched Figan, top-ranking male, struggle to maintain his position in the face of vigorous competition. We have learned a whole wealth of information about the role of the female in chimpanzee society.

During recent years we have found that chimpanzees not only resemble humans in some of their gestures (kissing, embracing, holding hands), in their affectionate family relationships (adult sons and daughters may spend much time with their old moms), and, to some extent, in the way they cope with problems, but that there are resemblances in violent behavior also.

In 1974, three vicious attacks were observed between groups of males of our main study group and single males of a small neighboring community. The attacks were about 20 minutes in duration and it is thought that each of the victims died from wounds inflicted. The next attack that was witnessed was certainly the equivalent of human murder.

An old female was attacked by four adult males and although she managed to escape and crawl into thick undergrowth, she died five days later. Her 10-year-old daughter stayed with her until the end, often keeping the flies from her mother's wounds. The field assistants took her some bananas and some water, but she was injured beyond recovery.

Once there were seven males in that community. Now we only know for certain that one is still alive. We do not know what has happened to the other females. By the end of 1976, our main study group seemed to have annexed the country that had been the home range of the victimized community.

Even more horrifying—a high-ranking female and her adolescent daughter were observed three times killing and eating babies of other females of their community. Of the five babies born in 1976 only one survived its first month.

What is the meaning of such behavior? To try to find out more we spent many hours observing females. But though we learned many fascinating things, we came no closer to understanding the killings.

At the end of June 1976, Fifi had her second baby. Fifi was an infant herself when first I arrived at Gombe. I watched her being weaned by her old mother Flo. And I observed Fifi's fascination with her new baby brother Flint.

She played with him, groomed him, and often carried him from the time when he was three months old. I assumed then that she showed normal behavior for an older sister. Through the years that followed, I have learned that in this respect, as in all others, there are great individual differences between one chimpanzee and another.

Other juveniles showed varying degrees of interest in their small siblings, but none of them were preoccupied as Fifi had been. Not until Flint himself became an older brother, when he was almost as fascinated by his sister as Fifi had been by him.

Fifi's first born, Freud, was five years old when Fifi gave birth again. To my delight he soon began to show an unusual interest in brother Frodo. He played with him and, as soon as Fifi allowed it, carried him around. It is clearly a real family tradition.

One day I looked out the window, as the rain was pouring down, and saw Figan arriving with the older Humphrey. Figan, as is his custom, performed a spectacular rain display—swaying the dropping palm fronds, rolling huge rocks, dragging fallen branches. Humphrey watched.

Figan's story is fascinating. From his adolescence he seemed keenly motivated to raise his social status, and by 1973, when he was only about 21 years old, he actually became the top-ranking male. Figan was not so powerful then as Humphrey, the male he overthrew, but he was more intelligent. He only challenged Humphrey when his brother, Faben, was nearby. Then the brothers would display in unison. Eventually Figan dared to attack Humphrey and gained a decisive victory.

SOURCE: Jane Goodall, *New York Times,* September 15, 1977, p. A27.

billions of years of evolutionary change beginning with one-celled organisms. In the harsh struggle for existence, a process of "natural selection" has prevailed, where animals with characteristics that allowed them to adapt to changing conditions were better able to survive. Lehrman, in *The Long Road to Man,* uses the example of the Seymouria, a kind of reptile, to describe natural selection. During one period of the earth's development, swamps covered the earth. Because no two animals are exactly alike, it is possible that there were Seymouria with skin a bit more waterproof, with better lungs than others, with stronger legs. When the swamps began to dry up, those reptiles best able to adapt to the new environment would survive. A natural selection was at work. "The more fit individuals of each generation—more fit for the new conditions—were selected by nature to be the parents of the next. And in the succeeding generations the favorable hereditary features were intensified . . . the average characteristics of the population were pushed toward a new type with thicker skin, better lungs, stronger legs" (p. 71). Such creatures were better able to crawl from water hole to water hole as the earth dried and, with better lungs than their near relations, were able to stay out of water for longer periods of time and finally adapt to dry land.

The evolutionary progression, from amphibians and fishes to reptiles and mammals, seems clearly an adaptive process. At each step a creature evolved that was better suited to life in a particular environment. Within the disciplines of *comparative physiology* and *ethology* (the study of animal behavior), physical scientists have described the ways in which the animals of different species evolved, and have compared them to human beings in physiology and behavior.

Similarities Between Humans and Other Animals

For many generations such studies have been buttressed by theology and ideology. Whereas Darwin catalogued many similarities between higher mammals and humans, modern sociologists have emphasized *homocentrism.* The homocentric approach has been to ignore those things similar between humans and other animals and emphasize our uniqueness, divinity. The human being has been accepted by many philosophers, theologians, and scientists as a supreme creation, a unique phenomenon because other animals "do not have souls or minds, reason or forethought, wisdom or culture, language or opposable thumbs, fire or any one of a host of attributes that set man 'above' nature. . . ." (Tiger and Fox, 1971, p. 8).

By touching thumb and forefinger together, you will have your hand in a position that is valuable for grasping things. This is the opposable thumb that allows the subtle manipulation of objects. Humans have this ability, but so do most other primates, the order of mammals to which men, monkeys, and apes belong. All primates have stereoscopic vision, allowing them to see things in depth because both eyes can see the same object at the same time. All primates are dominated by eye, hand, and brain (Lehrman, p. 101). Their eyes are highly developed so that their sense of smell has diminished. Primates can distinguish colors better than other mammals.

The Unique Human Animal

But humans can be seen to be *unique* primates. Tiger and Fox note that every species is unique in its specializations, so that it is their differences in behavior rather than differences in their anatomy that distinguish them. Other primates are able to walk on two legs but Tiger and Fox emphasize that "Most of the time they do not. Man made this change as he adapted to a hunting life on the hot savannas." So, too, do Tiger and Fox stress the development of the frontal lobe of the brain. As humans evolved, the brain grew; and keener intelligence, speech, the capacity for increased learning, the ability to have foresight, also grew.

> But the other primates have brains with frontal lobes, too. The other primates have spines and a pelvis, too. They are different because they have specialized differently in response to different evolutionary problems. The gibbon has specialized in long arms and the ability to swing gracefully through the trees; the gorilla in great size and the ability to digest stems and roots; the baboon in quadrupedalism [fourfootedness], large canines, and high speed; man in bipedalism [twofootedness], the striding walk, and the enlarged brain. (Tiger and Fox, p. 9)

The anatomical differences between humans and other primates are not as great as was formerly believed. Nevertheless, Theodosius Dobzhansky (1970), the noted geneticist, has described the human species as the most successful product of biological evolution, because, with humans, a new mode of evolution has begun—the evolution of culture. Dobzhansky sees culture as a powerful instrument in the process of adaptation to the environment. While, over the course of time successful adaptation resulted from natural selection that was biological (e.g., a longer neck to reach edible leaves, stronger lungs that could adapt from water to air), with humans adaptation to the environment has occurred through "alteration of culture." Says Dobzhansky, "Many species of animals have become adapted to cold climates by growing warm fur; [the human being] alone has achieved the same end by donning fur coats" (p. 39). But the evolution of culture has not replaced biological evolution. The two processes go on together, reinforcing each other.

Sociobiology, a New Area of Controversy

There is an attempt under way to establish a new scientific discipline, sociobiology, "the systematic study of the biological basis of all social behavior" (Wilson, 1975, p. 4). Some biologists, zoologists, and social scientists believe that the study of culture is meaningless without the study of biology.

Sociobiologists have expanded Darwin's idea of natural selection in startling new ways. Darwin believed that individual organisms with characteristics that facilitated survival did survive and reproduce. These organisms also passed on the characteristics and behaviors that allowed them to survive. Darwin discussed "social instincts," such as sympathy and loyalty, possessed by humans. He noted that as "man is a social animal, it is almost certain that he would inherit a tendency to be faithful to his comrades, and obedient to the leader of the tribe . . ." (*Descent*, p. 481). Homocentric social scientists have argued, however, that, on the contrary, humans have few inherited behaviors or instincts. The sociobiologists now hark back to Darwin and say that human behavior is rooted in biology and that behaviors such as altruism, spite, deceit, are in fact inherited behaviors.

Sociobiologists theorize that if there is a struggle for existence it takes place in the genes, those microscopic units found in the fertilized egg. The genes of male and female transmit information from the parental generation to the developing child. We have long been aware that genes carry information that determines sex, hair, skin and eye color, body build, tendencies to disease, and many abilities. Sociobiologists believe that in addition to messages about characteristics, genetic messages about behavior are also transmitted. They acknowledge that the principal genetic preoccupation is survival, so that organisms do those things that promote competitive advantage. Quite simply this means that the material of the genes (DNA) exist "to protect themselves and their own information" (Pieczenik, 1977). A surprising illustration of this concern with survival relates to altruism, that unselfish devotion sometimes seen in animals and humans. Darwin had difficulty in explaining altruism in organisms if the game of survival was so competitive. Why did some animals risk their lives to save others in enemy attacks? Why do some insects and some birds give their lives to protect their flock or colony? Sociobiologists would argue that what appears to be altruism is in fact genetic selfishness. Both animals and humans are programmed to behave in ways that will promote the safety and well-being of genetically similar relatives.

The claims of sociobiologists are bold indeed. One leading theorist, Robert Trivers, predicts that "sooner or later, political science, law, economics, psychology, psychiatry and anthropology will all be branches of sociobiology" (*Time*, 1977). Unfortunately such confidence on the part of sociobiological theorists about the ultimate influence of their discipline is not supported by a large body of empirical evidence. Much of the theory is speculative. Yet some psychologists, anthropologists, and even theologians are examining this new theory seriously and reviewing their work with the ideas of sociobiology in mind.

Critics of sociobiology point to its weak empirical foundations and predict that in time it will disappear as an area of serious scholarship. However, they are apprehensive about the effects of sociobiology on American culture. If sociobiology is absorbed into the popular culture it may live on with possibly distressing effects. Though sociobiological theorists do not discount the influences of environment, their belief that human behavior is controlled by genetic instructions could be used to advantage by propagandists who favor the status quo. Male supremists could therefore continue to justify their favored status biologically and educators, who have watched compensatory education programs fail to change the academic performance of minorities, could use genetic explanations to explain these failures.

The Importance of Language

The use of language makes the highly developed culture of *Homo sapiens* possible. The fact of human culture is not exclusively the result of intelligence. It is possible to think of many animals that are extremely intelligent (i.e., dolphins) but have only a rudimentary social heritage to share with their young. Other animals also develop intricately organized societies. Indeed, it is erroneous to think of culture as exclusively human. Other animals, like chimpanzees, make an effort to control the environment, use primitive tools, and even attempt to share this learning with their young (Mazur and Robertson, 1972). However, our conception of human culture refers primarily to abstract and intangible entities such as values, beliefs, norms. Culture is primarily a thing of the mind. Culture is intimately tied to symbolic representations. And human language is unique in its **ideational** and **symbolic** nature. Many words that make up human conversation are really symbolic representations for things. The word "shoe" represents a thing that covers the foot. Humans arbitrarily assign meaning to things by attaching labels to them. Symbols may be any words or objects or gestures or sounds that stand for something else. A cross is a symbol that imbues a configuration of metal or wood with specific historic, emotional, and spiritual

5-2 CHECKING IT OUT: The Education of Sarah: Chimps Can Use Language Too!

As the brightest of the big apes, the chimpanzee may be man's nearest intellectual neighbor. How near? Science has long sought to discover in the intelligent chimp the gift of language, the incomparable skill that distinguishes mankind from all other living things. Until now, that search has been fruitless; the chimp lacks the capacity for speech that is innate in every normal human infant. But in *Psychology Today* magazine, Psychologist David Premack of the University of California at Santa Barbara demonstrates that the chimpanzee can converse with man in ways other than by the tongue.

Premack's prime evidence is Sarah, a seven-year-old female chimp with a working "vocabulary" of more than 120 words. Sarah can not only comprehend the

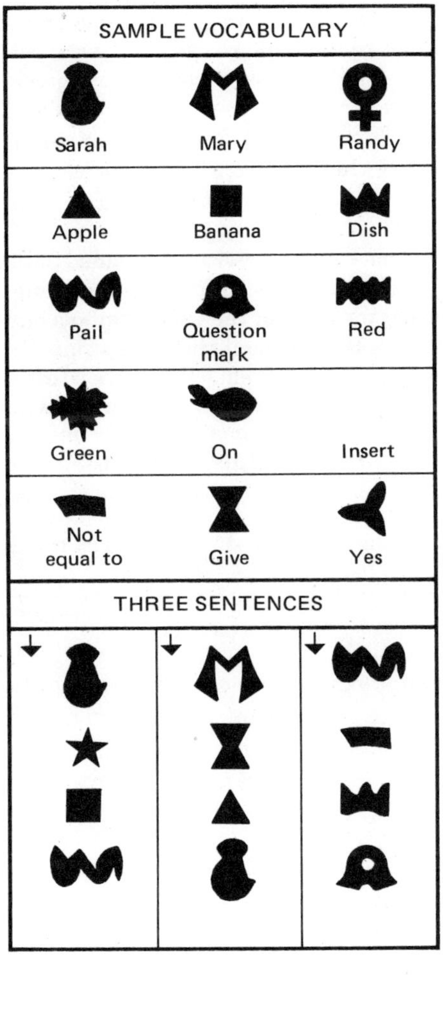

meaning of these words but can dip into her glossary to answer questions and build original sentences of her own.

To teach Sarah, Psychologist Premack devised symbols cut out of plastic and mounted on metal bases so that Sarah could "write" them on a magnetized board. With practice, Sarah learned that a blue triangle meant an apple, a red square a banana. In time she mastered symbols identifying each of her four trainers, plus other symbols identifying colors and familiar objects such as a pail, a cup and a dish. . . . All this was mere rote learning. To develop an understanding of syntax, Premack introduced a new symbol representing the preposition on. Given two familiar color symbols representing green and blue, for instance, and by watching the trainer place the green on the blue and vice versa, Sarah eventually came to understand the preposition's purpose. . . . Before long, Sarah knew how to obey commands in as many as twelve possible color combinations at an impressive accuracy rate of 80% to 90%.

On one memorable occasion, which Premack records with almost parental pride, his pupil invented a sentence-completion game and invited her trainer to play. The trainer had set up some nonsensical physical-relation tests involving objects and colors—red is on (i.e., superimposed upon) green, green is on banana, apple is on orange—to test Sarah's proficiency in word order. Abruptly, Sarah took over. She began a sentence "Apple is on. . . ," and then arranged a number of possible completions, only one of which she considered correct: "Apple is on banana." Then she led her trainer through the multiple choices until her human student caught on to the game.

Over two years, Premack and his assistants trained Sarah in the use of verbs, sentence structure, questions and conceptions, the last being the cognitive ability to grasp not only the root meaning of the word-symbols but their application in totally unfamiliar contexts. Having taught her to associate the color red with apple and the color green with grape, says Premack, "we then tested her comprehension of the conception 'color of.' " He was not surprised when Sarah demonstrated her ability to assign the characteristic "color of" to totally unfamiliar objects: that the redness of an apple, for instance, could also be found—and recognized by her—in a persimmon.

SOURCE: *Time*, September 21, 1970, pp. 51–52. Reprinted by permission from TIME, The Weekly Newsmagazine; Copyright Time Inc. 1970.

associations. We have made of the cross a religious symbol and most people in this culture understand this association. A clenched fist raised over the head has become a symbol of "black power." This symbol also has a shared meaning and most people who see it understand that it represents an expression of rage and a commitment to struggle. The language of humans, then, has this symbolic character, which makes it extremely flexible and rich. Humans may choose "freely and arbitrarily to originate, determine, and bestow meaning upon events in the external world, and [have] the ability to comprehend such meanings" (White, 1973). Several social scientists have attempted to teach human language patterns to animals. A recent attempt centered on Washoe, a chimpanzee. Alan and Beatrice Gardner (Hahn, 1971) have taught Washoe 150 signs from the American Sign Language, most often used by the handicapped. David Premack has successfully taught Sarah, a chimpanzee, to communicate using word symbols so that she was able to answer questions and indeed build sentences of her own.

Culture is based on shared meanings, and symbols are the shared meanings of language. We share a huge vocabulary of words, complex and subtle in their meanings. Our language allows us to transmit ideas about situations from the past to the future. The components of culture are thus *transmitted* through use of language.

THE COMPONENTS OF CULTURE

In his classic definition, E. B. Tylor describes culture as "that complex whole. . . ." This gives a sense of structure to the concept of culture and is helpful in its analysis. Culture must be thought of as a system, an entity or whole made up of interrelated parts. Another word for these parts is components. The following components of culture will be examined: norms, ideas, artifacts or material culture.

Social Norms

Social norms are group-shared expectations or rules about conduct. Such a set of expected behaviors can be associated either with a certain situation or with a given position in the social structure. Examples of the former are "Who ever heard of eating peas with honey?" "A scout is courteous," "A gentleman pays his debts," or, more generally, "You shouldn't have done that." One is supposed to be quiet, respectful, and not to interrupt others in a house of worship. On the other hand, one's trust that one's lawyer need not and thus will not give the court damaging evidence against one is an expectation associated with the lawyer's position in the social structure.

Of course, not everyone in any society abides by all the norms all the time, and no norm is always obeyed. Moreover, not all norms—or even most of them—are written or legalized. Most of the understandings we share with other members of society are informal. There is no law saying that one should not eat peas with a knife, that one should lend money only to friends, or that one shakes hands when introduced. Yet these are shared and learned expectations; they are part of our culture, and most of us conform to them most of the time.

Sociologists differentiate norms, according to the degree of importance attached to the rules by the society, into folkways and mores.

Folkways The most obvious way to determine the importance of a norm for the members of a society is to observe how severely they punish those who violate it. Norms that are not looked on as extremely important—or, to state it another way, norms that can be violated without severe punishment—are called folkways. Adult males should wear a coat and tie to church. People should arrive on time for appointments. Professors should not serve whiskey in their offices. People should not park their automobiles in zones labeled "No Parking." One should not persistently make loud noises late at night in a residential area. People should not smoke in a chapel. We should bathe frequently enough so that others are not conscious of our bodily odors. People should eat three meals a day. We should respect our parents.

Each of the sentences in the preceding paragraph is a statement of a group-shared expectation, or norm, in contemporary middle-class American society. Some norms are covered by formal laws; others are not. Violations of some would be met by fines, imprisonment, or dismissal from one's job; failure to abide by others would be punished only by verbal statements of disapproval or by ostracism. Each of these norms has one thing in common, however: the fact that they are not regarded by most people as moral matters. People who smoke in chapel are regarded as crude, but not as immoral. People who are persistently late for appointments are considered thoughtless; they are not viewed as sinners. People who disturb the peace are nuisances, not lost souls. We may avoid people who do not bathe frequently, but we do not judge them wicked. You may get fined for leaving your car in a no-parking area, but nobody will think the Devil inspired you to park there.

Folkways are rules which most people in the society expect most other people in the society to obey most of the time. They are deemed the "right" way, and "normal" people accept most of them unquestioningly. One can, however, challenge a folkway and suggest that it would not really hurt anything to alter it, without being judged a menace to society. Herein lies the difference between folkways and mores.

Mores The mores are not open to question. The individual so thoroughly internalizes the mores that he or she seldom thinks of them consciously as rules. The professor may be so irked at her warm academic robes that she toys with the idea of going to commencement in a T-shirt, but it will not occur to her to go in the nude. Law enforcement agencies might take seriously a suggestion from a traffic authority for a set of graduated penalties for parking offenses: only a warning the first time, a small fine the second, a larger fine for the third violation, and suspension of the driver's license for the fourth offense. No one would take seriously a similar plan for dealing with wanton murderers: let them off the first time and gradually "crack down" on them. Murder is a violation of the mores, and there is no disposition either to treat it lightly or, for that matter, to discuss whether or not it should be considered a violation of the mores.

Probably the best evidence of how thoroughly we internalize the mores is the difficulty most people would have in thinking of examples. Many generalized maxims that spring to mind are not mores. Taking a human life, for instance, is not necessarily a violation of the mores—it depends on who does it and under what circumstances. On some occasions our society gives medals, rewards, and public acclaim to those who take human life. In wartime, we decorate the man who has shot down more enemy planes than any other flier, and parades are given in honor of the soldier who single-handedly has slain a number of enemy soldiers. A hero's treatment is accorded the policeman who kills a dangerous criminal in a gun battle. A sizable portion of our movies have heroes who, in the course of the story, violate the injunction "Thou shalt not kill." A storekeeper often will not be punished for shooting a burglar in his store. Neither the law nor the mores prohibit killing in self-defense. Unintentional killing is not criminal unless it is the result of negligence on the part of the killer.

While there are laws to deal with wanton murder, some mores are assumed to be so well learned that no law is needed to enforce them. The rare violations are met by community rejection and expressions of loathing of the participants and, if legally catalogued at all, are treated as "acts of indecency." Moral imperatives of this magnitude are so deeply impressed upon the members of society that the average person cannot remember when or how he came to learn that certain behavior is wrong. For example, cannibalism, or the eating of human flesh, is totally unacceptable in American society. Incest is another such prohibition, and is unacceptable in all human societies. Most of us do not know when or from whom we learned that incest is morally wrong, but a father who has sexual relations with his daughter arouses feelings of revulsion and contempt.

Law In most relatively complex societies, some kind of political order serves as an overall seat of authority in which law becomes an important norm of control. Laws are laid down to establish or maintain the rights, duties, and liberties of the members of the state. Rights imply a two-sided relationship, in which one person owes the other a duty and the other person benefits thereby. A person has rights only insofar as others have duties toward him. One's rights set limits on other people's liberties. Freedom and responsibility always go together. In complex societies, the law represents the most certain of all the social norms.

In modern democracies, the law usually falls into three categories: constitutional, statutory, and judge-made. The first sets out the basic features of the political order. The second is the product of legislative bodies and covers a wide range of individual and group activities. The third is the product of the courts—it consists of judicial decisions which are used as the basis of adjudication of subsequent cases.

To adjudicate cases involving legal disputes, courts are established. The judicial system usually has two levels: courts of original jurisdiction and those for appeal. In addition, most courts fall into two legal categories: criminal law and civil law. *Criminal law* deals with such offenses against the public peace, morality, and order as misdemeanors and the more serious offenses, such as murder, treason, rape, housebreaking, and arson. *Civil* cases are suits at law between persons or between duly constituted associations, such as corporations. These relate to such matters as enforcement of contract, titles to property, collections of debts, torts (which have to do with injuries of person to person that may lead to recovery of damages), guardianship of children, marriage and divorce, and many other matters not strictly related to the public peace. The definition of what constitutes a criminal and what a civil case depends on the culture. In many primary-group communities, homicide and feuding, for example, are treated as private, not public, matters. In urban societies these are considered crimes.

Sanctions Sanctions are the rewards or punishments used to establish *social control*—that is, to enforce the norms in a society. Sanctions may be applied in various ways, ranging from the use of physical force to symbolic means, such as flattery. Sanctions are the normative means that are used to force or persuade an individual or group to conform to social expectations.

Informal and Formal Sanctions Sanctions may be either informal or formal. Informal sanctions are illustrated by customs, the mores, and public opinion. The formal sanctions are those worked out by the state through law and administrative devices, those consciously developed within organizations for their own regulation, or those developed between or among organizations to regulate their relations. Sanctions become the standardized codes of conduct, are set down and managed by special groups, and passed on from generation to generation by special agencies. In the rise of the political state, formal lawmaking and the invention of writing, which made possible the keeping of records and the preservation of codes, were especially important. The modern, complex, industrial society is dependent upon formal sanctions, upon impersonal and indirect contacts. In nearly all situations, the formal and informal aspects of control are intertwined, and in many instances of community life, the informal tends to outweight the formal. But in the more highly institutionalized groups, although the informal is not unimportant, the major controls flow through formal channels.

Purpose of Sanctions The basic purpose of sanctions is to bring about conformity, solidarity, and continuity of a particular group, community, or larger society. Sanctions may be used to achieve a balance of power among contending social units, or to deal with the threatened exploitation of one group by another. Sanctions are also used to exact conformity from individuals whose behavior is thought to endanger the solidarity of the group.

To control behavior means to bring about regular and recurrent sanctions. Such regulation makes possible the prediction of behavior. We can usually anticipate what an individual will do or what his punishment will be if he fails to act. For example, a contract usually enables the parties involved to know in advance what to expect and what each party will do. There is no changing of intention from day to day, and the obligation is binding for some specified period of time. Furthermore, control, especially by some overall power, creates an equilibrium between warring factions or groups by obliging them to accommodate themselves to one another and to the needs and values of the larger society. Sanctions thus foster solidarity and integration. So too, sanctions make possible continuity. They form a part of culture that is passed along from generation to generation. Thus each generation gets a pattern of control which keeps the social order running smoothly. If each generation had to develop its own code, there obviously would be waste of effort.

Yet, in a rapidly changing society, this continuity is disturbed, with the result that new codes have to be developed, often coming into conflict with old ones. New conditions demand new definitions, and behavior often far outruns the forms of control. For example, the present growing sense of insecurity, anonymity, impersonality, and dissociation in the individual in mass society is definitely related to the breakdown of the codes and rules of the more traditional social order.

Ideas

Values Values are assumptions, both conscious and unconscious, of what is good, right, and important. Values concern standards of desirability. Some set of values forms the core of every culture. The **ethos**—that is, the fundamental characteristics—of any culture is a reflection of its basic values. During the tremendous industrial and population growth from 1870 to the present, American society, for example, became characterized by a number of culture features, including (1) admiration for individual material success and general national progress; (2) respect for universal literacy and education as a means of solving social and personal problems; (3) delight in the virtue of sheer size, witnessed in ever-larger skyscrapers, schools, industrial plants, and corporations; (4) commitment to rapid movement through space, seen in increased mobility of population and improved means of communication and transportation; (5) love of novelty—constant change to something new and more exciting, as in sensational news, exciting drama, speed racing, crazes, and fads; and (6) the craving for domination—the booster and the "bigger and better" spirit in almost every important aspect of public life.

In contrast to this, in the Orient during the nineteenth century (before Western civilization and its values reached there), human thinking and acting took quite different patterns. There was no insistence on the American value of progress. Mere physical size had no special merit. Certainly no virtue inhered in rapid movement. Instead, the ideal was the calm deliberation of the scholar or sage. In India, among large numbers of the population, instead of desire for personal material success and continued identification of the self with individual striving and "getting ahead," the fundamental desire expressed in religious life was renunciation of self, the abandoning of personal desire, and the elimination of the ambition to be important. Such radical differences in cultural values result, of course, in widely divergent social structures and patterns of expectations in social interaction.

Beliefs If values indicate those aspects of culture that are judged to be good or bad, then beliefs relate to those elements of culture judged to be either true or false. The most obvious illustration of cultural beliefs is the belief systems of religion. Adherents of particular belief systems accept them as truth. Religious beliefs are illustrated by "concepts of deities, afterlife, spirits, and the like, as well as by many ideas about the nature of society and the physical world." (Williams, 1970, p. 27) Robin Williams divides cultural beliefs into (1) those that may not be yet tested but are nevertheless subject to empirical test—these beliefs could conceivably be refuted empirically; (2) Those beliefs that are impossible to verify empirically by known procedures. The existence of heaven is presently unverifiable.

The beliefs of culture reflect the attitudes that social beings have about themselves, about the world they live in, as well as connections with social forces within and outside of the natural world. In addition to theological beliefs, each culture may have beliefs expressed in the form of folklore or legends. Myths and legends are often concerned with the creation of that cultural world, with the gods and heroes of a people. Folklore encompasses the traditional stories and proverbs of the mass of people.

Cultural Knowledge Knowledge applies to that vast body of information that people within a culture know—the principles and truths that are mentally perceived (through, for example, philosophy or literature) and also the empirically certified, generally useful facts, laws, and information that result from understanding combined with experience. Much cultural knowledge is learned in social institutions, such as schools and colleges, created to pass on such knowledge. It is also learned within families, social classes, and occupational groups. The scientific information and skills embodied within a culture must be systematically learned by each new generation so that time will not be wasted rediscovering already known facts (recreating the wheel).

5-3 CHECKING IT OUT: Modernization Leaves Turkey's Culture in Disorder and Its People Seeking an Identity

In 1923, Kemal Ataturk expelled Greek forces from Anatolia and created the Turkish republic from the ruins of the Ottoman Empire. But he then told his people to abandon their Oriental heritage and embrace the culture of the despised Westerners they had just defeated.

Ataturk's main goal was to create a secular state and break the power of Islamic leaders he felt were responsible for the country's stagnation. The Swiss code replaced Koranic law, the Latin alphabet replaced the Arabic, the cap replaced the fez. But most Turks remained poor, backward peasants.

Change came to the village only after World War II, when American aid helped accelerate economic growth and a new government took power. Roads and radios, teachers and politicians began to penetrate even the most remote regions.

"Our 40,000 villages had been cut off from the rest of the world, and all of a sudden they discovered the 20th century," explained Senator Inan. "All the villages had a window opened to the outside world through their workers who went to Germany and France, not to mention Ankara and Istanbul. Then the whole world came into their homes and coffee shops through television."

"We became an impatient nation," added the legislator, who heads the Senate Foreign Relations Committee. "People now want what has been missing from their lives for centuries."

They wanted more jobs and more enjoyment, better houses and health and schools, and the place to look was the cities. Turkey, which was only 25 percent urban 30 years ago, is almost 50 percent urban today.

Migration meant a further change in mentality. "The Turkish peasant discovered that he is not something, he is someone," said Senator Inan. Mayor Vedat Dalokoy of Ankara added, "He sees the value of the work he is selling. He sees it is his right to demand something from the state, and he is using that right."

In response to these demands, the government has embraced the gospel of industrialization, and Turkey's growth rate of 72 percent in 1976 was one of the highest in the world. An organized working class has started to show its strength, and trade unions won wage increases of more than 28 percent last year.

But Turkey's per capita income remains less than 1,000 dollars a year, about one-fourth the figures in the European Economic Community. The population, unchecked by any serious birth control program, is soaring by 1 million every year. Unemployment, 13.3 percent according to official figures, is probably twice that.

Economic growth has been financed partly by rapid expansion of the money supply, and inflation is running at more than 20 percent a year. Heavy foreign borrowing to finance imports has coincided with a sharp slump in Turkish exports and remittances from workers abroad. Foreign exchange reserves have plummeted to $600 million, enough to cover only six weeks of imports, and some foreign banks have stopped honoring checks from the Turkish central bank.

The Turkish crisis goes deeper than economics. "If you go into the house of a newcomer to Ankara," said Mayor Dalokoy, "you see the saz, the traditional instrument of Anatolia, and an electric guitar side by side. One is for the father and one is for the son."

"The culture is in disorder, and it frightens me," he added, as American rock music blared over the restaurant's sound system. "The Turk is like a man who has jumped into the air, and if someone pushes him, he can land almost anywhere."

This disorder is compounded by the weakening of family, community and other traditional restraints. In the permissive confused atmosphere of the cities, young people often look for heroic models and easy answers. The leftists brandish posters of Che Guevara and Mao Tse-tung. The rightists revere Tamerlane and Attila the Hun.

SOURCE: *The New York Times*, May 23, 1977, p. 3.

Artifacts or Material Culture

This component of culture consists of all the objects within a culture that have been made by its inhabitants past and present. The tools, constructed of stone and vines by the Tasaday, that heretofore unknown tribe discovered recently in the Philippines, are examples of artifacts. (Nance, 1975) But so are the computers and skyscrapers of our society. The boomerang of the Australian aborigines, the Eskimo dog sled, science fiction novels, backgammon sets, warm-up suits for jogging. The artifacts of culture must always be related to the nonmaterial components (the values, beliefs, norms). A cast-iron frying pan, a useful but common object, is little valued. A bottle of twelve-year-old scotch is prized. Automobiles, by their price tags and countries of origin, reflect different degrees of prestige and success. As Ely Chinoy (1963) expressed it, "Two crossed pieces of wood may be a religious symbol or fuel to be burned in order to keep warm. To describe cultural objects fully, therefore, it is necessary to know their uses, the attitudes toward them and values assigned to them, and the accompanying body of knowledge and skills" (p. 26). The information, attitudes, ideas, and values of each generation can thus be passed on to the succeeding generation by means of language, and individuals can be prepared for unusual as well as ordinary events.

THE FORMS OF CULTURE

As previously defined, *culture* refers to the total social inheritance of a people. In this sense, the term designates all human behavior which is socially learned rather than biologically inherited and which is shared by most human beings or by specifically designated sets of them. In addition to this general use of the term, we use it more specifically to refer to the shared learned behaviors of a particular group of human beings.

Cultural Traits

Because of the complexity of any culture, it is often useful, for purposes of description and analysis, to examine a culture piece by piece, looking at one part, or a combination of related parts, at a time. Many sociologists follow the lead of anthropologists, who consider culture a master concept. These social scientists analyze culture by breaking it down into small elements or units, called *culture traits.* These represent single combinations of acts and ideas related to a particular need or situation. For instance, fire-making may be thought of as a culture trait involving the use of certain implements and skills. For a nonliterate person this may be the device of rubbing two dry sticks together over a small pile of tinder. For contemporary people it usually means the use of matches or a mechanical lighter. So too, ways of greeting another person—such as a hand shake or "soul slap"—are other illustrations of cultural traits.

5-4 CHECKING IT OUT: Common Characteristics of All Cultures

Age grading
Athletic sports
Bodily adornment
Calendar
Cleanliness training
Community organization
Cooking
Cooperative labor
Cosmology
Courtship
Dancing
Decorative art
Divination
Division of labor
Dream interpretation
Education
Eschatology
Ethics
Ethnobotany
Etiquette
Faith healing
Family
Feasting
Fire making
Folklore
Food taboos
Funeral rites
Games
Gestures
Gift giving
Government
Greetings
Hair styles
Hospitality
Housing
Hygiene
Incest taboos
Inheritance rules
Joking
Kin-groups
Kinship nomenclature
Language
Law
Luck superstitions
Magic
Marriage
Mealtimes
Medicine
Modesty concerning natural functions
Mourning
Music
Mythology
Numerals
Obstetrics
Penal sanctions
Personal names
Population policy
Postnatal care
Pregnancy usages
Property rights
Propitiation of supernatural beings
Puberty customs
Religious ritual
Residence rules
Sexual restrictions
Soul concepts
Status differentiation
Surgery
Tool making
Trade
Visiting
Weaning
Weather control

SOURCE: George P. Murdock, "The Common Denominator in Cultures," *The Science of Man in the World Crisis*, ed. Ralph Linton (New York: Columbia University Press, 1945), pp. 123–125.

Cultural Complexes

Plow agriculture, so important a step in human history is a cultural complex consisting of many culture traits: the way the plow is made, the manner in which the animals or machines that draw it are harnessed or driven, the use of the plant that is domesticated and harvested, how the seeds are put into the ground, and so on through a wide range of activities. The belief in and worship of one god, which we call monotheism, is another cultural complex made up of a wide variety of specific ideas, emotions, and habits. In industrial societies, what the economists call the "market" is a complex and systematic patterning of a wide variety of separate acts and ideas: buying, selling, lending, transporting, and so on.

Universals, Alternatives, and Specialties

An analysis of the place of a culture in the life of an individual or of a group of individuals in a given society reveals wide ranges of participation. Even in small societies, differences in thought and conduct are linked to age, sex, and occupational differences. In a complex industrialized society it is quite impossible for any one person to participate actively in all the many phases of the culture. The way in which the demands of the culture play upon an individual will vary. Three levels of participation in a culture may be distinguished. (Linton, 1936)

Universals are those core features of a culture which are widely accepted and required by the society. They are learned behaviors so widely shared that, without them, one is obviously "different" or an outcast. Examples of universals are the language spoken in the society, the standard patterns of social relationships (such as monogamy in our society), and the deep-seated moral values. In general, ethnocentric beliefs are universals. The term *universal* refers to behaviors associated with a particular culture; a pattern may be universal within one culture and unheard of in another. For example, in some Arab societies, men wear robes, and the wearing of trousers is confined to women and serves as a mark of femininity.

Alternatives are activities in which individuals are allowed a choice. In the recent past, a universal in our culture demanded legalized marriage for couples who wished to live together with the approval of the community; however they were offered certain alternatives: they might be married at home, in a church, or at the city hall, by a minister, priest, rabbi, or justice of the peace. Alternatives are different activities allowed and accepted for achieving the same end.

Specialties are learned behaviors shared by the members of certain social categories but not by most people in the society. The physician, for example, knows things most of us do not know and performs certain activities in which most of us do not participate. In general, specialties are very often a consequence of the division of labor, and are shared according to sex, age, class, or occupation.

CULTURAL DIVERSITY

The uniformities of culture are more easily explained than the variations in time and place. The elements common to cultures everywhere stem, in part, from the fact that all human beings are basically the same biologically, so that their need for survival leads to certain commonalities in behavior. For example, all human beings must eat a certain amount of nourishing food, and a group must reproduce in order to survive as a society. But the patterns of acquiring and consuming food vary greatly from place to place, and the rules regarding who is supposed to have children, how often, and under what circumstances may differ from culture to culture.

Geography and Culture

One explanation for the range of variation among cultures is the diversity of materials provided by the physical environment, by the effect of climate and landscape on the inhabitants. Certain effects of the physical environment on people are readily identifiable. The rigors of winter demand more clothes and warmer houses. To build shelters, people ordinarily have had to use materials near at hand: mud for huts in some places, stone in others, and ice or snow in still others. So too, living in places of rich soil and adequate rainfall produces social arrangements different from those produced by living on a rainless and windy desert or in the hot and humid regions of the tropics.

Reputed Relationships These daily and seasonal effects of the weather, water supply, and soil are obvious enough. Out of such repeated experiences arose popular and often erroneous notions about the impact of geography on human thought and action. For example, one sometimes hears people argue that the Latins, living in warm climates as they do, have "hot blood" and are given to quick anger and impetuous behavior. In contrast, the Finns and Swedes, who live in cold latitudes, are said to be stolid in temperament and slow to action. The fallacy of these and similar views must not mislead us. Geographic factors *do* play an important part in individual and group living. We cannot ignore the influence of climate, topography, and natural resources on human existence. This is especially true of elements of material culture, such as food-getting, housing, manufacturing, and transport. *Yet even in these matters the geographic factors are chiefly limiting rather than directly causative.* The following illustrations bring out the manner in which cultures vary even when the geographic conditions are the same.

Cultural Differences Within Similar Geographic Environments The Eskimo represents a remarkable adaptation to a highly unfavorable environment; and if his were the only arctic culture we knew, we might assume that all arctic inhabitants followed much the same pattern. Consider housing: is anything more natural than that the arctic dweller should build huts from the bountiful supply of snow at hand? Yet if we look across the Bering Sea to the Chuckchee of northeastern Siberia, in a similar climate, we find these people in winter months living not in snow houses but in large, "clumsy" tents of hide stretched over heavy supports. Furthermore, the Chuckchee use the domesticated reindeer for draft purposes, while the Eskimos use dogs to draw their sleds. The Chuckchee apparently borrowed the use of the domesticated reindeer from their neighbors, the Tungus, living to the south of them. The Eskimos domesticated this convenient animal themselves only recently.

The African Bushmen are seed-gatherers and hunters, live in crude windbreaks or caves, and use the bow and arrow. In contrast, their neighbors in the same sections of South Africa, the Hottentots, are a pastoral people, living in mat-covered portable huts and using the spear as their principle weapon, although they have the bow and arrow. While these ethnic groups have many myths and other features of culture in common, the differences in material traits are striking. Once more we must seek the explanation largely in the history of their cultures and not in the physical environment.

The Paiutes, or "Digger Indians," living on the edge of the Great American Desert, considered the Rocky Mountain locust a particular delicacy. The locusts infested these areas periodically in great numbers, and the Indians drove them into brush enclosures to roast and eat them. When the Mormon colonists settled the Great Basin, beginning in 1847, they were greatly troubled during the first decade by plagues of these insects, which devoured every blade of grass, wheat, or corn. The Mormons did what they could to destroy the pests, but were unable to bridge the cultural chasm between themselves and their Indian friends and bring themselves to take up a new dietary habit. Had their own food taboos been less severe they, like the Indians, might have made something of a blessing out of what was to them a curse.

The Effects of Geography These examples show that culture is perhaps the crucial determinant of social behavior. Yet the effects of natural environment, though often indirect and secondary, are nonetheless ever-present and consequential. Even with modern technology, agriculture is limited by soil, climate, and topography. If one wishes to grow bananas, the best chance of success is found in the rainy tropics. And in a humid, continental temperate zone one simply could not raise bananas at all, because killing frosts would destroy the crop. Similarly, coal miners are found in western Pennsylvania, with steel workers nearby, but no such division of labor is found in central Texas. So too, in the developing air age, air currents and degrees of cloudiness and storminess in various regions will affect air transportation and, as a result, the location and function of certain cities.

As human beings have advanced to more complex forms of culture, they have overcome some of the handicaps of the "natural landscape." Not only have they changed the face of the earth and devised new and more rapid means of communication and transportation, but they have partially overcome poor soil by fertilization, provided more adequate water supply for crops by irrigation, insured themselves against some changes in temperature and humidity, and, by the use of refrigeration in transporting and storing foodstuffs, removed earlier restrictions on the use of seasonal foods. In brief, cultural history runs a course from the most rudimentary societies, isolated and tied rather closely to their immediate physical environment, to technologically advanced societies in which there is little left in the physical environment of the ordinary person that has not been altered by culture, including the quantity of clean air and water.

Ethnocentrism

Throughout history, people everywhere have displayed an interest in themselves and other members of their own group. Members of any society tend to believe that their way of thinking and doing things is not only the best way but the only right way. This belief that the ways of one's own group are superior to all others is called *ethnocentrism.* The Navaho of the southwestern United States refer to themselves as "Dineh"–"The People." Germans speak of *das Ausland,* collecting all countries outside Germany into a single noun. The ancient Jews classified themselves as "the Chosen People"; in ancient Greece there were only Greeks and barbarians. When the Greenland Eskimos first had white visitors, the highest compliment they could pay a white man was to say that he was, or soon would be, as good as a Greenlander. We in America have long had a tendency to lump all persons who are not members of our own society into one inferior category: foreigners.

It is easy usually for us to see ethnocentrism among foreigners. But when we read in the newspapers that free enterprise is the best possible economic system, most of us do not recognize this statement as probably an illustration of ethnocentrism. We are usually ethnocentric, too, if we accept the statement as "true." We accept it not because of the evidence–which most of us don't know–but because we *are* ethnocentric. No category of persons, not even scientists, is free from ethnocentrism. That is why it is so difficult for an American scientist to evaluate objectively an experiment contrasting democratic and authoritarian leadership.

Subcultures and Countercultures

Subcultures The place of culture in the life of particular groups and individuals in any given society reveals some range of variation. Even in small societies, some differences in thought and conduct are specific to age and sex. In large and complex industrial societies, it is quite impossible for any one person or group to participate actively in all the many phases of the culture. American society, for example, includes thousands of different occupations and no one person can be a part of all of them. Anyone who has listened to a discussion among a group of medical students knows that they have a special language and a set of values of their own. Such shared, learned behavior that is common to a specific group is called a *subculture.* Railroaders, for further example, share in the general values of the society but they also have a special language, place a special value on time, and know things and have ideas that are not shared among most members of the society. In other words, people who share distinctive occupational specialties can be said to participate in the same occupational subculture. Other subcultures revolve around religion, race, ethnicity, etc., and variously exhibit special modes of dress, food, language, beliefs, and so on that are shared within the group but do not characterize the society as a whole.

Countercultures We have said that subcultures exist within the larger culture but exhibit distinctive norms, values, and beliefs. Subcultures, because they are *ethnocentric* in outlook and believe their way of doing things to be the only right way, generally prefer to stress separateness from the larger culture and frequently choose to ignore it. But countercultures are subcultures in opposition to the larger culture. An illustration of a counterculture may be seen in the youth culture of the 1960s. These young people were in rebellion against the larger culture. In *The Making of a Counter Culture*, Theodore Roszak (1969) described an alternate culture that "continues to be shot through with the spontaneous urge to *counter* the joyless, rapacious, and egomaniacal order of our technological society" (p. 137). The countercultural young are dissenters who have committed themselves to a transformation of the majority culture. They have banded together in diverse groups. Some are communal in orientation

5-5 CHECKING IT OUT: The Central Ideas of Hippie Society (Formerly Called Bohemianism)

The idea of salvation by the child. Each of us at birth has special potentialities which are slowly crushed and destroyed by a standardized society and mechanical modes of teaching.

The idea of self-expression. Each man's, each woman's purpose in life is to express himself, to realize his full individuality through creative work and beautiful living in beautiful surroundings.

The idea of paganism. The body is a temple in which there is nothing unclean, a shrine to be adorned for the ritual of love.

The idea of living for the moment. It is stupid to pile up treasures that we can enjoy only in old age. . . . Better to seize the moment as it comes.

The idea of liberty. Every law . . . that prevents self-expression or the full enjoyment of the moment should be shattered and abolished.

The idea of female equality. Women should be the economic and moral equals of men . . . same pay . . . same working conditions, the same opportunity for drinking, smoking, taking or dismissing lovers.

The idea of psychological adjustment. We are unhappy because . . . we are repressed.

The idea of changing place. "They do things better in. . . ."

SOURCE: Malcolm Cowley, *Exile's Return* as quoted in Bennett M. Berger, "Hippie Morality—More Old and New," *Trans-action,* V (December, 1967), 19–20.

and reject the individualism of the dominant culture; some substitute intriguing religious practices for those of the majority. Some are avowedly political. Some combine several aspects of these. Roszak pits youth against the *technocracy* of modern industrial society, that totalitarian society run by technical experts who respect only scientific forms of knowledge, who ignore ideologies such as capitalism and communism but who subtly control and manipulate us by creating needs and supplying material rewards in return for our docility and compliance.

Although the failure rate of communes and alternate societies has been high, the influence of these groups is yet to be assessed. Some of the norms and values of these groups already appear to have affected the majority culture. The rejection, by the counterculture, of the crushing career demands of bureaucratic organizations appears to be influencing young executives today who choose not to give week-ends *and* weekdays to the corporation but demand time to maintain meaningful family relationships and avocations.

CULTURAL PROCESSES

Cultural Relativism

Cultural relativism describes a principle that guides the sociologist or anthropologist as cultural components are examined.

The researcher must avoid ethnocentrism or the tendency to see the cultural patterns of one's own group as superior to all others. Instead, the customs, values, beliefs of other cultures must be examined and understood as they are understood by members of the group under study. They are never to be evaluated by one absolute standard.

The researcher must seek to understand cultural elements within the framework of a cultural whole, evaluating them in relation to other expectations, values, and norms of the culture.

The Nuer, an East African people, are a society in which the love of cattle and the desire to acquire them totally preoccupy the inhabitants. The Nuer wash their hands and faces in the urine of their cattle. (Evans-Pritchard, 1960) They drink the milk and blood and use dung for fuel. The ashes derived from cow dung are used for dressing the hair, cleaning the teeth, and covering the body. These behaviors and practices have no counterpart among American cattle growers.

However, in observing the Nuer, cultural relativism demands a point of view from which this culture is seen as the result of the group's adjustment to unique circumstances. Therefore, cultural elements can only be evaluated within the context of the culture of which they are a part.

Washing in cattle urine seems less startling if the attitude of the Nuer about cattle is understood. Evans-Pritchard notes that cattle are the Nuers' most prized possession and their chief topic of conversation. The men are often addressed by names that refer to the form and color of their cattle and the women take the names of the cows they milk. Cattle are a basic source of nourishment and also the basic element of wealth. Social relationships and social processes are defined in relation to cattle (for example, contact with ghosts and spirits occurs through cattle). From the time they can crawl, chidren play in proximity to the herd and "the kraal is their playground and they are generally smeared with dung in which they roll and tumble." (p. 38) The relationship between the Nuer and their cattle is "symbiotic." They are intimately dependent on each other. An understanding of this culture is impossible if the Nuer are judged by the standards of our own culture. If such judgments are suspended and the harshness of their environment is understood, the behavior of the Nuer makes much more sense.

Whether we approve or disapprove of social practices, we cannot and will not understand them without reference to the cultural whole. Therefore, an examination of facism demands that this phenomenon be examined within a historical and economic context, and also with attention to beliefs and values of adherents. Once the researcher has objectively embedded facism within a cultural whole, the decision to pass judgment is possible. In other words, having made an objective effort to understand the belief system of facism, the researcher may freely condemn, disapprove, and criticize. Whatever the final judgment, cultural relativism discourages the researcher from making ethnocentric judgments.

Cultural Integration

We have characterized culture as a system, an entity or whole, made of interrelated parts. These parts or components (the norms, values, beliefs, laws) tend to fit together within the whole in an adjustive way. When parts of the system create conflict and tension, there is a strain toward integration of the culture so that the parts will complement each other.

In traditional or preliterate societies the behavior of group members is carefully controlled. The cultural traditions are clearly defined and the stability of such groups results from the good "fit" between the way people believe they should act and the way they in fact do act. These are small, homogeneous societies. Changes occur slowly and cultural traits are well integrated.

However, in modern industrial society different groups may have different values and norms. There may be conflict and tension as changes occur. Because changes in one part of a cultural system affect other parts there may not be a good fit among cultural elements. Modern societies are often characterized by heterogeneity and lack integration of cultural elements. Social disorganization, conflict, resistance to change result from lack of integration.

Cultural Lag

A continuing drama of the present day has centered around the attempts of religious-based groups to prevent or repeal legislation aimed at abortion reforms. Both the issues surrounding abortion and the use of contraception may be analyzed to illustrate *cultural lag.* William F. Ogburn (1966) applied this concept to situations in which some components of a culture are changing more rapidly than other, related parts. Because the different parts change at unequal rates, social strain and conflict often result. Contraceptive devices like "the pill" and the diaphragm prevent pregnancy, and also, for the first time, give women control over the process of conception. In the past, use of contraceptives such as the condom could be controlled by the male partner. Both contraceptives that prevent pregnancy and safe low-cost abortions are the results of modern medical technology. Many women have responded positively to these new aspects of material culture (artifacts), but certain religious interests have seen contraceptive use and abortion as disruptive to religious norms regarding the sanctity of life. Thus, as Ogburn perceived it, material culture (medical technology) has been changing so rapidly that events in the normative culture are lagging behind. The resulting public disagreements and the pressures of appropriate interest groups have illustrated the salience and importance of this issue within the society.

Cultural lag offers a useful way of understanding the effects of social changes, particularly technological change. But Ogburn's discussion shows an implicit "liberal" bias (Martindale, p. 353) that suggests that the lag between material cultural and nonmaterial parts will end as the lagging part adjusts. The underlying assumption is that change is omnipresent and desirable and inevitable. The pressures of interest groups in this controversy are so persistent that the conflicts surrounding contraception and abortion may continue to be contemporary social issues for some time.

Diffusion

Diffusion refers to the process whereby the elements of a culture are diffused or spread to another culture or are spread from one part of a society to another. This is an important process in the cultural development of societies. As soon as two groups come into close contact there will be some diffusion or mutual borrowing of cultural traits. Franz Boas (1948), the noted anthropologist of an earlier day, illustrated the advantages of diffusion by observing that the manufacture of iron did not originate in Europe or America. The use of milk did not originate in Africa. The cultivation of wheat did not begin in Europe. These activities reflect the diffusion of culture. In traditional or early or primitive societies, the means by which diffusion of culture was spread varied. In economic trading with others, group culture is commonly diffused. The kidnapping of brides by one group from

5-6 CHECKING IT OUT: 100 Per Cent American

Our solid American citizen awakens in a bed built on a pattern which originated in the Near East but which was modified in Northern Europe before it was transmitted to America. He throws back the covers made from cotton, domesticated in India, or linen, domesticated in the Near East, or wool from sheep, also domesticated in the Near East, or silk, the use of which was discovered in China. All of these materials have been spun and woven by processes invented in the Near East. He slips into his moccasins, invented by the Indians of the Eastern woodlands, and goes to the bathroom, whose fixtures are a mixture of European and American inventions, both a recent date. He takes off his pajamas, a garment invented in India, and washes with soap invented by the ancient Gauls. He then shaves, a masochistic rite which seems to have been derived from either Sumer or ancient Egypt.

Returning to the bedroom, he removes his clothes from a chair of southern European type and proceeds to dress. He puts on garments whose form originally derived from the skin clothing of the nomads of the Asiatic steppes, puts on shoes made from skins tanned by a process invented in ancient Egypt, and cut to a pattern derived from the classical civilizations of the Mediterranean, and ties around his neck a strip of bright-colored cloth which is a vestigial survival of the shoulder shawls worn by the seventeenth-century Croatians. Before going out for breakfast he glances through the window, made of glass invented in Egypt, and if it is raining, puts on overshoes made of rubber discovered by the Central American Indians and takes an umbrella, invented in southeastern Asia. Upon his head he puts a hat made of felt, a material invented in the Asiatic steppes.

On his way to breakfast he stops to buy a paper, paying for it with coins, an ancient Lydian invention. At the restaurant a whole new series of borrowed elements confronts him. His plate is made of a form of pottery invented in China. His knife is of steel, an alloy first made in southern India, his fork, a medieval Italian invention, and his spoon a derivative of a Roman original. He begins breakfast with an orange, from the eastern Mediterranean, a cantaloupe from Persia, or perhaps a piece of African watermelon. With this he has coffee, an Abyssinian plant, with cream and sugar. Both the domestication of cows and the idea of milking them originated in the Near East, while sugar was first made in India. After his fruit and first coffee he goes on to waffles, cakes made by a Scandinavian technique from wheat domesticated in Asia Minor. Over these he pours maple syrup, invented by the Indians of the Eastern woodlands. As a side dish he may have the eggs of a species of bird domesticated in Indo-China, or thin strips of the flesh of an animal domesticated in Eastern Asia, which have been salted and smoked by a process developed in northern Europe.

When our friend has finished eating, he settles back to smoke, an American Indian habit, consuming a plant domesticated in Brazil in either a pipe, derived from the Indians of Virginia, or a cigarette, derived from Mexico. If he is hardy enough he may even attempt a cigar, transmitted to us from the Antilles by way of Spain. While smoking he reads the news of the day, imprinted in characters invented in Germany. As he absorbs the accounts of foreign troubles he will, if he is a good conservative citizen, thank a Hebrew deity in an Indo-European language that he is 100 per cent American.

SOURCE: Ralph Linton, *The Study of Man: An Introduction*, © 1936, pp. 326–327. Reprinted by permission of Prentice-Hall, Inc., Englewood Cliffs, New Jersey.

another is one means whereby new elements of culture may be introduced into the society of the kidnappers. When Marco Polo returned from traveling in China he brought a noodle dish with him, which he introduced to Italians. Macaroni has subsequently become a favorite in Europe, and also in America as Italians have emigrated.

INTERPRETIVE SUMMARY

Culture is shared, learned behavior created by people and transmitted from generation to generation. A culture is the common way of life among a people. Humanity's basic tool for transmitting culture is language, an ideational and symbolic medium.

Culture is learned. Some human behaviors are not learned but inherited. Such inherited or built-in behaviors are instinctive or innate. Instinctive behaviors, like nest-building in birds, appear in organisms at appropriate stages of their development or in response to stimuli.

Charles Darwin developed a theory of biological evolution to explain the relationships between humans and other animals. From amphibians and fishes to reptiles and mammals, organisms evolved as a result of adaptive responses to the physical environment. Darwin recognized many similarities between humans and higher mammals. Modern social scientists have preferred to emphasize *homocentrism*, which ignores similarities between animals and humans, and stresses the uniqueness of the human species. The uniqueness has been related to an enlarged brain, the capacity for speech, and complex learning.

If the human species is the most successful product of biological evolution it is because humans use cultural learnings to enhance adaptation to the environment. Sociobiology is a recent attempt to relate social behavior and biology. Sociobiologists find behaviors such as altruism to be the result of genetic programming by which behaviors promoting the safety of genetically similar relatives are retained in the species. Critics of sociobiological theory point to a lack of empirical verification on the part of scholars.

Culture must be thought of as a system or whole. Among the components of culture are *norms* (folkways, mores, and laws) or standards of conduct; *ideas* (beliefs, values, and knowledge); and artifacts or *material culture*.

The written and the tacit rules of a society are called norms. A society's most important rules, such as those governing morality, are called mores. Mores may not be challenged, and defiance of them will elicit severe punishment. Folkways are less important, more flexible norms. An institution is a set of mores and folkways having the common goal of facilitating a particular function of a society.

Sanctions are the rewards and punishments employed to enforce a society's norms. Sanctions may be informally invoked or codified by law, may be physical or social, positive or negative. Sanctions themselves become norms when a society decides that a much-used manner of teaching a norm is the "right" way.

The variability of culture is partly related to the physical environment; people develop different cultures as they attempt to survive in their particular environments. However, geography limits rather than determines the course a culture will take. Geographically similar cultures frequently find different ways of adjusting to their environments and hold different values.

QUESTIONS

1. Can you think of beliefs and values that have special significance within your own family?
2. In what ways are folkways different from mores and laws? Give examples.
3. Compare the concepts of counterculture and subculture with the master concept of culture.
4. If you visited the Amish people in Pennsylvania, in what ways might you feel ethnocentric about your lifestyle?

6

Personality and Socialization

There are few questions in all of Western thought that have received as much consideration as the question of the relationship of the individual to society. Much of the discussion has focused around the idea that there is an inevitable conflict between the individual and the groups of which he or she is a member. For many sociologists, however, the question of the person versus society is a false question in the sense that it asserts an autonomy of each which does not exist. As Charles Horton Cooley once wrote, "a separate individual is an abstraction unknown to experience, and so likewise is society when regarded as something apart from individuals." (Cooley, 1902, p. 84) The individual **personality** is shaped and developed within the context of society, not prior to or outside of it. The human being becomes human and social only through participation in the society. The process by which this occurs is known as **socialization.** It is through socialization that the individual is linked to society. The anthopologist Ruth Benedict also argued that there is "no proper antagonism between the role of society and that of the individual." "Most people," she wrote, "are shaped to the form of their culture because of the enormous malleability of their original endowment. They are plastic to the moulding force of the society in which they are born." (Benedict, 1946, pp. 232, 235)

A long-standing discussion concerns the relative importance of heredity and environment in shaping the individual personality. At one extreme are those who attribute almost all variation among human personalities to differential heredity. At the other extreme are those who assume that hereditary differences are so negative that any variations in behavior observed mong people can only be accounted for as resulting from different social environments. Actually, the evidence does not support either one of these extreme positions.

PERSONALITY: HEREDITY AND ENVIRONMENT

Heredity is the transmission of genetic characteristics from parents to their offspring. Hereditary traits, then, are innate; they are present at birth. By

environment people usually mean those forces, situations, and so on that affect the individual from outside. Environment includes the *physical* world external to the individual: the constant threat of starvation facing someone in an arctic setting might contribute to a personality organization different from that likely on a lush tropical island. The *social* environment also molds the personality: a child reared by loving, indulgent, and permissive parents will have a personality different from that of a child with similar inherited characteristics reared by unloving, unconcerned, and restrictive parents.

Heredity

What Do We Inherit? The essential characteristics inherited by all human beings can be classified as follows:

1. physical structure (how tall or short one is, whether one has a long or short nose, large or small feet—briefly, how one is put together)
2. reflexes (direct responses to stimuli, such as withdrawing from a pinprick, blinking when something approaches the eye)
3. innate drives (impulses to act based on physiological tensions; but these must be linked through learning with activities that will reduce the tensions)
4. intelligence (the capacity to learn, to modify responses)
5. temperament (patterned and recurrent responses associated with basic emotional make-up—for example, imperturbability, excitability, or lethargy)

Innate Drives Of the categories above, that of innate drives is probably subject to the greatest misunderstanding. The source of the confusion is the tendency to equate the drive with the activity that reduces the tension. Activity that will reduce tension must be learned. It stems, in other words, from environment. *The innate drive does not need to be learned; one is born with it.* The walls of the stomach will contract in a newborn baby; the hunger drive is present. What to do about hunger must be learned, and hence subject to a certain degree of cultural control. Whether one learns to relish fried chicken or fried crickets depends on the society in which one is reared; either can reduce the hunger drive. Human beings do have socially acquired drives, but these are rooted in social learning, not in heredity. Desires for a college education or for a communal existence are tensions as real and as definite as innate drives, but they are a product of social life, not genes.

Heredity has a limiting influence on personality development. A person can be born severely mentally retarded and therefore so restricted that it is impossible for that person to become as fully a participating member of society as one who is born with the mental capabilities of a "genius" even if they both receive the same social opportunities. The limiting nature of heredity is nowhere more dramatically illustrated than in the observations which were made of an ape and a child reared in an American home as if they were brother and sister.

The Story of Gua and Donald In June, 1931, Professors Kellogg, then at Indiana University, brought into their home a female chimpanzee seven and a half months old, which they named Gua. Their plan was to rear this ape in company with their own ten-month-old son, Donald. (Had the ape and child been reared together from birth, the procedure would have more closely approximated the ideal design for a controlled experiment we discussed in Chapter 2.) The ape and the child lived in the same household and were exposed to more or less the same daily training and kindly care until March, 1932. The regimen included training in postural and body habits, in walking and feeding, play, and all the other habits which a young child in our society acquires. There was little punishment in connection with their training, but a persistent effort was made by word and deed on the part of the adults to facilitate development. In connection with the daily routine, the Kelloggs made systematic tests, observations, and comparison of Gua's and Donald's capacities, traits, and activities. They measured their physical growth and strength, their hearing, seeing, and other senses, and their social-emotional development; and they put them through a number of critical learning tests involving manual skill, memory, recognition, and language. (Kellogg and Kellogg, 1933)

While Gua and Donald had similar reflex organization, the ape was more mature than the child in a number of items, such as strength of the grasping and rejecting responses.

In our society, the fundamental training in habits of elimination ordinarily begins toward the end of the first year, and both ape and child were put on regular schedules shortly after Gua's arrival. From the outset the child was superior to the ape in bladder control (the water intake of the ape was much larger, so that her frequency of urination was about one-third greater than the child's). In bowel control the child was at first superior to the ape, but after four months there was no difference.

At play the ape and child were much alike in handling, biting, and exploring their toys. From the outset, however, Donald showed more interest in examining and manipulating things in the environment. At first their play was of the solitary sort but later simple social games and mutual examination and exploration began. Both were intrigued by the face; they tried kissing and tactile interplay. They became quite protective of each other, holding on to each other, for instance, while riding in a play wagon.

Yet significant differences were early apparent. Gua never got accustomed to older children or to strange adults. In contrast, as Donald grew older he showed increasing interest in both children and grown-ups in the neighborhood. One of the most telling reactions was the growing intensity of the emotional dependence of the ape on the Kellogs. Jealousy also was more evident in Gua than in Donald. Her craving for affection and attention from the Kellogs was much stronger. Donald at 15 months showed distinct bashfulness—evidence of an emerging sense of self. Gua never did reveal such an attitude.

To test their intelligence, a large number of Gesell infant tests were used. In many rudimentary memory tests the ape was superior to the child, but in matters requiring minute manual dexterity, the ape was inferior. Yet taking all the Gesell tests together, the learning of the two was closely parallel.

In vocal communication and the beginning of higher mental powers as seen in the beginnings of language, the child was clearly superior. The ape was at first more correctly responsive to human commands than was the child. She learned to comprehend simple verbal responses by pointing to a picture of a dog on the command "Show me a bow-wow," and she learned to utter certain distinctive bark-like sounds to indicate "Yes" when asked "Do you want an orange?"

However, in spite of nine months of living with human beings and being exposed to kindly and patient teaching, *Gua never acquired a single human word*. That is, she could not use names for objects. Donald, on the contrary, before the first year began using words for objects. He called Gua "Gya" and acquired the usual vocabulary and simple sentences for a child of his age. There is little doubt that, had the ape remained in the Kellogg home, the human companion would soon have outstripped her in acquiring the essential habits of communication and conduct which, in their complex use, so sharply distinguish the *Homo sapiens* from the anthropoid. These involve such characteristics as language and use of concepts, memory expressed in symbolic form, the skilled use of tools and other material objects, and above all else, the self-image which plays such an important part in human personality.

Personality and Society

The comparison of Gua with Donald illustrates how no amount of training can overcome the limitations imposed by heredity on mental capacity. We know too, however, that inherited capacity alone cannot produce a human personality. No matter how impressive the capacities an individual may inherit, he or she becomes a person only through interaction with others. Without society, the individual personality does not and cannot come into being. An individual deprived of all communication with other humans from birth would never become human in any conventional sense of the word. Such an individual would possess no language, and his or her thinking would extend very little beyond momentary recall of sense impressions. Such an individual would have no social status, no loyalties, no beliefs, no love of country, and no worship of God. In this sense, to be human is to be social. Just how essential the social environment is to the development of personality can been seen in the records of children kept in almost total isolation. In the words of one writer, these cases show "what happens when the social environment of a child approaches zero." (Maxfield, 1948, p. 206)

Feral Children There are a number of folks tales and semi-scientific accounts which tell of humans who allegedly were raised by nonhuman animals.

Zeus and Tarzan are probably the two most legendary heroes who were supposedly raised without the benefit of human association. There are also tales that the alleged founders of Rome, Romulus and Remus, were raised by animals. But not all of those who have presumably benefited from such an upbringing have been persons of such high repute; there have also been a large number of lesser mortals who were supposedly raised by animals. In fact, Bergen Evans has learned of accounts of a fish girl of Holland, a swine girl of Bavaria, a bear boy of Lithuania, a chicken boy of Ireland, a badger boy of Winnipeg, a sheep boy of Ireland, baboon boys of South Africa, and a very large number of "wolf-children," the most notable of whom are probably Amala and Kamala (Evans, 1946; Singh and Zingg, 1942)

These tales of feral (meaning wild, existing in a state of nature, or undomesticated) people are sometimes amusing, but none is authenticated. The best *guess* about their authenticity is that some are total fabrications, a couple proven hoaxes, and the rest probably cases of socially unwanted children (possibly mentally retarded or otherwise congenitally deficient) who were mistreated by their families and left in some uninhabited place to die. Bruno Bettleheim is very likely correct when he suggests that the reported behavior of so-called feral children is produced not when wolves behave like human parents, but vice-versa. "The conclusion tentatively forced on us is that while there are no feral children, there are some very rare examples of feral mothers, of human beings who become feral to one of their children." (Bettleheim, 1959, p. 467)

The data regarding the "feral" children are so speculative and insufficient that they are of no value for sociology. There is no creditable case of a person reared from infancy without human influence. There are, however, a few moderately well documented cases of social isolates—persons who had very limited social contact for an extended period of time—which dramatically illustrate much of what is known about the relationship between the individual and society, about the socialization process of preadolescents, and about the extent to which the person is a product of society.

Social Isolation Two examples of social isolation are the cases of Anna and Isabelle, reported by Kingsley Davis. (Davis, 1940; Davis, 1947; Mason, 1942; Bettleheim, 1959; Ogburn, 1959) In the late 1930s and within the span of nine months, in separate states and separate incidents, these two girls were "discovered" by authorities to have been virtually socially isolated for the first six years of their lives.

The Story of Anna On February 6, 1938, the *New York Times* carried a story about a six-year-old child who had been found "tied to an old chair" in an attic room of a farmhouse in Pennsylvania. The child, Anna, had apparently suffered from extreme malnutrition and social isolation and had lived nearly all of her life with only a minimum of human care. When Anna came to the attention of the

6-1 CHECKING IT OUT: Emperor Frederick II and the Effect of Social Isolation

[In the thirteenth century Emperor Frederick conducted an experiment to determine]... what kind of speech and what manner of speech children would have when they grew up, if they spoke to no one before hand. So he bade foster mothers and nurses to suckle the children, to bathe and wash them, but in no way to prattle with them or to speak to them, for he wanted to learn whether they would speak the Hebrew language, which was the oldest, or Greek, or Latin, or Arabic, or perhaps the language of their parents, of whom they had been born. But he laboured in vain, because the children all died. For they could not live without the petting and the joyful faces and loving words of their foster mothers. And so the songs are called "swaddling songs," which a woman sings while she is rocking the cradle, to put a child to sleep, and without them a child sleeps badly and has no rest.

SOURCE: James B. Ross and Mary M. McLaughlin (eds.), *The Portable Medieval Reader* (New York: Viking Press, 1949), pp. 366–367.

authorities, she was removed to a county home and then to a foster home. Later she was placed in a private school for the mentally retarded where she died on August 6, 1942.

Anna was an "illegitimate" child whose grandfather, a widowed farmer in whose house the mother lived, strongly disapproved of the child. Consequently, Anna was shifted from place to place for the first six months of her life. For a short period of time, she was placed in a children's home and various foster homes. But for some reason, Anna was returned to her mother at the age of six months after having lived in ten different places.

Because of the anger and aversion of the maternal grandfather, Anna was hidden in an attic-like room. She received only enough care to keep her alive. Anna was kept in a crib almost constantly until she was "discovered" at six years of age. She appeared to have been moved from one position to another infrequently; she had no toys, no instruction, and no friendly attention. She was almost always alone. Her only contacts were with her mother and occasionally with her step-brother, who reportedly teased and taunted her. She was fed virtually nothing except cow's milk during all of the time she was in her mother's care. She was seldom if ever bathed, caressed, or in any way socialized.

When Anna was discovered, she was extremely undernourished and had skeleton-like legs, a bloated belly, and very little clothing. She could neither walk, talk, nor do anything that remotely showed intelligence. She remained in a supine positon, immobile and indifferent to those around her. She appeared to be totally deaf and her interaction with people was either perfunctory or "openly antagonistic."

As a result of a new diet and massages, her physical condition improved rapidly. Gradually she began to develop some mental and social traits normal for children her age. She acquired visual discrimination of color and improved in posture and motor coordination, including the ability to chew food. Yet after four months she had not learned to speak. By the end of six months, however, she began to walk. In time she learned to control her elimination. She also gradually showed interest in the people around her. Approximately two years after being discovered, Anna could walk, could feed herself, was fairly neat, and could recall people and understand simple commands, but she could not speak. She had, in general, the mental and behavioral characteristics of a child under two years of age.

On April, 1940, at the age of eight, a clinical psychologist reported that she was large for her age, normal in hearing and vision, now able to climb stairs, and had reached the "babbling stage" of speech reactions, with some promise of further linguistic development. At this time it was estimated that Anna had a mental age of 19-23 months.

On July 1, 1941, the school reported that she had grown in height and weight, could bounce and catch a ball, and had made progress in adjustment to group life with other children. Finally, she had begun to talk. The report concluded that there was nothing peculiar about her except that she was mentally retarded. Two months before her death, another report indicated that she could talk, mainly in phrases, and would repeat words and try to carry on a conversation. She was tidy in her personal habits; walked and ran fairly well; and, while somewhat excitable, was good-natured. At the time of her death, Anna's chronological age was ten and one-half years and her estimated mental age was two and one-half years.

It seems evident that Anna's social isolation prevented a considerable amount of the mental and physical development that was part of her capacity. While we cannot know her exact capacity, it is clear that Anna would have never realized the capabilities she actually did develop after her period of confinement if she had remained in isolation.

The Story of Isabelle The second child, Isabelle, was discovered in Ohio under conditions very similar to Anna's. She was born in 1932 and discovered in November, 1938, nine months after the discovery of Anna. Like Anna, Isabelle was an "illegitimate" child and had been secluded at least partly for that reason. Her mother was a deaf-mute, and the best evidence is that she and Isabelle spent most of their time together in a dark room, shut off from the rest of the mother's family. Isabelle had no opportunity to develop speech, although she communicated with her mother by means of gestures. Her diet was inadequate and she saw virtually no sunlight during her period of isolation.

At the time of her discovery, Isabelle was unable to walk; her legs were so bowed that when she was in a standing position, the soles of her shoes came together. At first it was difficult to tell whether or not she could hear, and her estimated mental age was approximately two years.

Unlike Anna, Isabelle was placed in a skilled, systematic program of intensive training immediately following her discovery. At the end of one month she attempted speech, and at the end of one year she had acquired the fundamentals of speech and a moderate vocabulary. At the end of two and one-half years of training she reached the normal level of an eight-year-old child. In other words, she accomplished in two and one-half years what ordinarily requires six years. In 1947, at the age of 14, Isabelle was in the seventh grade of public school and was reportedly doing well both in her school work and in her social-emotional adjustment to her classmates.

The question arises, "Why did Isabelle make a more complete recovery than Anna?" Although no clear answer is available, the differential post-isolation recovery of Anna and Isabelle is probably due to some combination of three factors: (1) The innate ability of the two girls may have been different. Perhaps Anna was mentally retarded at birth while Isabelle was not. (2) It may be that the different social treament received by the two girls following their discovery explains all or part of their differential recovery. Isabelle received prolonged and expert training immediately upon her removal from isolation, while Anna did not. (3) It may be that while both girls were extremely isolated, Anna was more socially isolated than Isabelle. Anna had no human contact except indifferent feedings; Isabelle spent most of her time with her deaf mother and communicated with her, if only through simple nonverbal gestures.

"Moderate" Social Isolation Another study that indicates the importance of society for personal development is one by Rene A. Spitz. (Spitz, 1945) The Spitz study is different from the cases of Anna and Isabelle in that the persons studied had more social contact than either of the girls. The major hypothesis of this study was that prolonged social isolation results in general retardation of such a nature that the subject can never realize his or her full potential. In other words, social isolation results in irreparable mental and physical damage.

Spitz compared four groups of infants in different social situations. One group consisted of infants from urban professional families. All of these children lived at home in a "normal" family situation. A second group of children were from a fishing village of approximately 500 inhabitants which was relatively isolated from other communities and where physical conditions were difficult. These village children also lived with their families. A third group consisted of children born in prison to women who were pregnant at the time of their arrest. The children lived in a nursery annexed to the prison until they were about a year old. The fourth group were children from urban backgrounds who had been placed in a foundling home for orphans when they were just a few days old.

To compare the development of the infants in these four social environments, a series of tests and observations were made for each of the four groups and combined into a "developmental quotient" (roughly analogous to an I.Q.) based upon what might be expected of "average" infants and calculated for three

6-2 CHECKING IT OUT: Developmental Quotients of Infants in Different Social Situations During the Early and Late Periods of their First Year

Type of environment	*Social situation*	*Developmental Quotient* — *Average of first four months*	*Developmental Quotient* — *Average of last four months*	*Difference*
Parental Home	Professional	133	131	−2
	Fishing village	107	108	+1
Institution	Prison nursery	102	105	+3
	Foundling home	124	72	−52

SOURCE: Rene A. Spitz, "Hospitalism," *The Psychoanalytic Study of the Child* (New York: International Universities Press, 1945), I, 53–72.

different periods of the first year of life. In this way, Spitz hoped to obtain a "before-and-after" test of the effects of social environment upon the development of the infants. The average developmental quotient for the first four months and the last four months of each group is shown in the table.

Spitz found that the development of children in the first three social situations was the same at the end of a year as it was during the infants' first four months of life but that the average developmental quotient of the infants in the fourth group had dropped by 50 per cent!

The Foundling Home Why did the developmental quotients for the infants in the foundling home drop so dramatically while it remained relatively constant for the other three groups? Why did three groups continue to develop "normally" when the fourth did not? To learn the answers to these questions, Spitz made a detailed comparison of the conditions in the prison nursery with the conditions in the foundling home. He found that both institutions were the same in many ways. Both provided excellent facilities, medical care, clothing, housing, food, and other items of physical comfort. However, the two facilities were markedly different in four significant ways that offered a clue to the lack of development among the children of the foundling home.

1. Toys. While the infants in the prison nursery regularly played with one or more toys, the infants in the foundling home rarely had any toys to play with.

2. Visual radius. Trees, landscape, and sky were visible to the infants in the nursery. There was also a bustling activity of mothers carrying, tending, feeding, and playing with their infants as well as chatting with each other. The cribs permitted the infants to see everything that was going on around them. They could see into the corridors, look out of the windows, and see infants in other cubicles. In the foundling home, however, the infants' visual field was severely limited except when five to eight nurses came into the room to feed the children. Most of the time there was no activity to attract the infants' attention. Moreover, the foundling home routinely placed bed sheets over the foot and the sides of the railings of each crib. Thus, the child lying in the cot was effectively screened from everything except the interior of the crib and the bare ceiling. The result was that each infant lived in virtual solitary confinement most of the time.

3. Radius of locomotion. The radius of locomotion in the nursery was limited to the space available in the crib; this provides a fairly satisfactory range until a child is about six months old. Theoretically the same situation would have obtained in the foundling home. But because the infants also lacked stimulation, they lay listlessly in their cribs for so many weeks that a hollow was worn into their mattresses. Consequently, this hollow effectively prevented the infants from turning in any direction when they reached an age when they might have turned from back to side. As a result, most foundling home infants were still lying listlessly on their backs at ten and twelve months of age.

4. Personnel. The nursery was run by a head nurse and three assistants whose only duties were to provide medical treatment and to instruct the mothers in child care. The infants were nursed, fed, and cared for by their mothers. Thus, in the nursery each infant had the full-time care and attention of an adult. In the foundling home, the infants were cared for only by nurses, each of whom was responsible for seven to twelve infants. These nurses generally appeared only at feeding and bathing times and did not fondle or play with their charges.

The Follow-Up Study At the time of this study there were 91 children in the foundling home. Two years later only 21 of the original children were still in residence. (Spitz, 1946) Thirty-seven per cent of the original 91 had died, despite the excellent medical care. Of the remaining 21 children, between two and four years of age at the time of the follow-up study, only five could walk unassisted; one could dress himself; and one could speak in sentences.

These data on the consequences of relative social isolation emphasize that individuals who are denied group participation during most of their early years will fail to develop language and other basic features associated with being a person, with having personality. The data also indicate that prolonged and severe isolation from human groups tends to hinder or prevent the development of human potential.

Harry F. Harlow came to much the same conclusions about macaque monkeys raised in isolation after a series of experiments (Harlow and Harlow, 1962; Harlow and Zimmerman, 1959). In one experiment, Harlow removed infant monkeys from their mothers and isolated them. Two surrogate wire mothers were provided, one with the nipple of a nursing bottle protruding from

6-3 CHECKING IT OUT: Level of Development of Twenty-one Children Two to Four Years of Age in Foundling Home

Bodily Development		*Ability to Handle Material Objects*		*Speech Development*	
Number		*Number*		*Number*	
5	Incapable of locomotion	12	Cannot eat alone with spoon	6	Cannot talk at all
3	Sit up alone but not walk	9	Can eat alone with spoon	5	2-word vocabulary
8	Walk with assistance	21	Total	8	3–5-word vocabulary
5	Walk without assistance	20	Cannot dress alone	1	About 12 words
		1	Can dress alone	1	Uses sentences
21	Total	21	Total	21	Total

SOURCE: Rene A. Spitz, "Hospitalism: A Follow-up Report," *The Psychoanalytic Study of the Child* (New York: International Universities Press, 1946), II, 113–117.

its chest and one without a bottle but covered with soft terry cloth. The infant monkeys clung to the cuddly "mothers," preferring them to the "mothers" who provided nourishment. Harlow concluded that without the "contact comfort" derived from the soft mother surrogate, the emotional and affectional development of the young monkeys were stunted. In fear-producing situations those raised with the cloth mothers clung to the surrogate, were calmed, then began to explore the situation. Those raised with the wire mothers never saw them as a source of comfort and either froze or engaged in the convulsive movements and rocking that describe the autistic behavior of institutionalized human children. Harlow concluded that the need for contact and emotional comfort was more important in the development of affection and attachment than nourishment needs. Without this contact the monkeys were unresponsive of their "mothers," fearful, and uninterested in exploration activities.

Human life is group life. People do not live apart, each seeking a private solution to the problems of survival. They live together and share a common way of life that regulates their collective existence and provides methods for adapting to the world around them. The data also suggests that it is the influence of society that really makes individuals different from one another and that contact with other human beings increases the differences between individuals.

If the "true individual" is defined as a person whose behavior is free of the influences of society, past or present, then it must be said that such a person does not exist. The isolated individual is either a philosopher's fiction or a tragic accident.

Which Is More Important—Heredity or Environment?

The cases of Anna, Isabelle, and the infants also make clear that the question of heredity *or* environment is an unproductive question because it presents a false dichotomy, that is, a false choice between one or the other, when in fact both heredity *and* environment have some part in the final process. Heredity is not a factor that acts independently of the social environment. Rather, it helps determine the way an individual reacts in various environments. Inherited capacity is clearly important in the development of the individual, but learning always occurs within a social context. No matter how impressive the capacities an individual may inherit, he or she can become a person only through interaction with others.

6-4 CHECKING IT OUT: Childhood Socialization Among the Manus

In many societies children's walking means more trouble for the adults. Once able to walk, the children are a constant menace to property, breaking dishes, spilling the soup, tearing books, tangling the thread. But in Manus where property is sacred and one wails for lost property as for the dead, respect for property is taught children from their earliest years. Before they can walk they are rebuked and chastised for touching anything which does not belong to them. It was sometimes very tiresome to listen to the monotonous reiteration of some mother to her baby as it toddled about among our new and strange possessions: "That isn't yours. Put it down. That belongs to Piyap. That belongs to Piyap. That belongs to Piyap. Put it down." But we reaped the reward of this endless vigilance: all our possessions, fascinating red and yellow cans of food, photographic material, books, were safe from the two-and three-year-olds who would have been untamed vandals in a forest of loot in most societies. . . .

A good baby is a baby who never touches anything: a good child is one who never touches anything and never asks for anything not its own. These are the only important items of ethical behavior demanded of [these] children. And as their physical trustworthiness makes it safe to leave children alone, so their well-schooled attitudes towards property make it safe to leave a crowd of romping children in a houseful of property. No pots will be disturbed, no smoked fish purloined from the hanging shelves, no string of shell money severed in a tug of war and sent into the sea. The slightest breakage is punished without mercy. . . .

SOURCE: From *Growing Up in New Guinea* by Margaret Mead. Copyright 1930, 1958, 1962 by Margaret Mead. By permission of William Morrow & Company.

SOCIALIZATION

Each newborn human baby is an uncomplicated and delightful little being, full of promise and possibilities. Also, each human baby is totally helpless at birth and dependent on others. Everything he or she eventually will know and be able to do must be learned. The process by which the child does so is called **socialization.** Socialization has two results. First of all, it is through socialization that the individual personality is formed. Second, socialization consists of teaching the person the culture that is to be acquired and shared, thereby producing a participating member in society and its various groups—a person who has been persuaded to accept and abide by social norms. Socialization is a matter of learning, not of biological inheritance. In the socialization process the individual learns the folkways, mores, sanctions, and other patterns of the culture, as well as the skills, ranging from language to manual dexterity, which will make social participation more productive. It is probably true to say that the baby is socialized because loving but coercive parents demand it:

> The infant has only one motive for doing anything: pleasure. What the infant wants (that is, what seems to soothe him when it is present and panic or infuriate him when it is absent) is warmth, dryness, physical support, a full, but-not-too-full stomach, a minimum of pressure on his bowels and bladder, a certain kind of tactile stimulation, and apparently, some exercise and distractions. So far as anyone knows, he would stay infantile all his life if such pleasures were always unconditionally provided for him. "Growing up," which means growing out of this initial Garden of Eden, is other people's idea, not his. (Bredemeier and Stephenson, 1964, p. 62)

All that the growing baby must learn is learned from other members of the society: consciously, from being told what to do by parents, brothers and sisters, friends, or teachers; or unconsciously, by picking up incidental information while observing other people, reading books, watching television, hearing people discuss the behavior of others, and imitating the behavior of others. In all these situations, the learning is social. The whole process of socialization falls within the scope of interaction. It is within the structure of the human group that the individual acquires culture.

The Development of the Social Self

The cases of Anna and Isabelle show that with virtually no socialization, "personality" does not develop. For the infant at birth, there is no distinction between self and not-self. Indeed the newborn baby is probably not aware where the crib sheet ends and his or her body begins. This distinction has to be learned. The individual has no self-concept (no concept of oneself as a unique individual) prior to interaction with others. The self is social, and arises out of interaction with an awareness of others.

It is only when the individual acts with the social expectations of others in mind, that he or she can be said to have developed a social self. When little Kim knocks over a vase and says to herself something like, "Mother will think I should be sorry; I'll apologize," she is developing a social self. This is the major process in the emergence of human personality.

THEORIES OF SOCIALIZATION

Socialization is the price that the baby must pay for parental love and attention. Within the social sciences, this process has fascinated many generations of theorists. They have fashioned a variety of original theories that explain the way in which the unique and individual personality of the child is shaped, that explain the manner in which the social self emerges, that explain the way in which society becomes part of the individual as the elements of culture are internalized. We will examine the theories of Sigmund Freud, Charles Horton Cooley, and George Herbert Mead to learn how each described human socialization.

Sigmund Freud

Whether one agrees with Freud's theoretical conceptions or not, it is generally conceded that this daring and original social scientist made a contribution to psychology that was both profound and revolutionary. An Austrian physician and neurologist, Sigmund Freud (1856–1939) developed a method for treating emotional disorders called psychoanalysis. This technique is based on the assumption that much of human behavior is affected by motives of which the individual is unaware. Indeed one of Freud's major contributions was to identify the existence of the unconscious.

Freud's discussion of the unconscious grows out of attempts to describe and analyze the development of the child's personality. Freud was convinced that events experienced during the period of childhood had a profound effect on the mature adult. Accordingly, Freud divided the personality into three parts or systems. These are the id, the ego, and the superego. The **id** is the realm of the unconscious, that part of the personality that is totally repressed and inaccessible except through the clues given in dreams and slips of the tongue. The id

---

6-5 CHECKING IT OUT

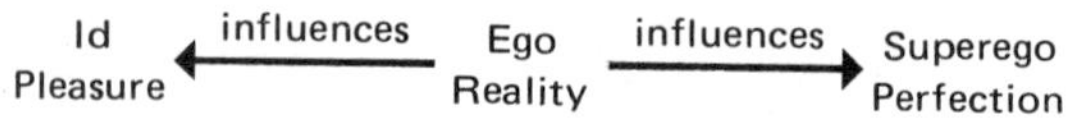

---

is the source of the raw energy that animates us. This energy consists of basic sexual and aggressive drives which Freud called instincts. The id is concerned only with immediate fulfillment of desires and avoidance of pain. The newborn baby is all id in operation as it shrieks and cries, demanding instant gratification. And yet that part of the personality solely concerned with pleasure will be frustrated because there are always obstacles denying us our pleasures. When a toddler sees a toy that looks exciting and proceeds to take it from another child, someone will interfere. In the same way, the pleasure-oriented needs of the id will often be discouraged, refused, and must often be repressed because they are frequently socially unacceptable. Therefore, in the young child the **ego** develops. While the id is pleasure-oriented, the ego is reality-oriented, and is developed specifically to curb the impulses of the id. In describing the ego, Freud likened it to a rider and the id to a horse. The ego guides and influences the id, helping it adapt to the demands of reality.

Freud's third part of the personality is the **superego**. The superego is that part of the personality which concerns itself with behaving properly, with seeking praise. It is similar to the concept of *conscience* and causes the child to feel guilty when the child's behavior has been unacceptable. Like the id, the superego may be compared to a horse and it, too, is a horse for the ego to ride, because the ego must control the demands of the superego as well as the id. The ego is then always in the position of maintaining a balance between the pleasure needs of the id and the demands for conforming behavior coming from the superego.

The Oedipus Complex The way in which the superego develops is a particularly dramatic part of Freud's formulation. This is the period of the Oedipus complex, a controversial and intriguing theory of Freud's. Because the id is tied to sexual drives, this is essentially a psychosexual theory of development, and emphasizes the sexuality of the parent-child relationship. Freud hypothesizes that the young male child between approximately three and six years begins to perceive his mother as a love object. She is the source of all that is pleasurable and he desires her sexually. This same sexual need is experienced in the female child and is characterized as **the Electra complex**. In both cases the child desires the parent of the opposite sex and is jealous of the same-sex parent. Yet this is a no-win situation. The parental rival is bigger, more powerful. It is the ego that seeks a solution to this problem. At this point the superego is developed to end the crisis. The child relinquishes the loved parent and begins to identify with the parent of the same sex. Realizing that "If you can't beat them, join them," the child internalizes the rival parent. By this incorporation of the rival into the personality, the child begins to act in ways appropriate to his or her sex and through imitation absorbs the norms and values of the parent, thereby of the culture. At the same time Freud noted that if this crisis was not resolved properly, the individual would be fixated (or stuck) at this stage and show neurotic reactions.

While many of Freud's ideas have been rejected by modern social scientists, his contribution to the development of psychology is universally acknowledged. His focus on childhood as crucial to adult development has been accepted as valid. While much of his theory regarding instincts has been rejected by modern psychologists, his recognition of the sexuality of children and indeed his awareness of the importance of sexual needs have been of incalculable importance. And certainly his identification of the unconscious portion of the mind and its influence was by itself a monumental contribution.

Erik Erikson

Erik Erikson (1902–) was one of Sigmund Freud's most distinguished students. Nevertheless, Erikson's theory of personality development, while owing much to his teacher, departs in significant ways from Freud's perspective. Erikson accepts Freud's view that there are stages of personality development; also that there is a crisis associated with each stage as the individual grows and matures. But Erikson rejected the psychosexual emphasis that Freud attached to development in describing the Oedipus complex. Also the crises that Freud described, if not successfully resolved, resulted in neurotic problems that plagued the adult. Erikson, on the other hand, was interested in crises that were social rather than sexual; he developed eight stages that demonstrated the emotional growth that extends from birth to maturity (1950). The first stage in the life of the child centers on the need to develop feelings of basic trust, in parents and in oneself. The responses of parents, particularly of the mother if she provides primary care, can lead to either trust in the child and a sense that the world is reliable or mistrust and uncertainty and a sense that the world is a fearful place. If basic trust is firmly established, the maturing ego has the capacity to work through the crises of each stage. Erikson developed the now-common conception of the **identity crisis**, a problem to be met in adolescence, which is complicated by physiological and social changes. It is interesting to note that Erikson sees personality and socialization developing from birth to old age while Freud limits this development from birth to sexual maturity.

Charles Horton Cooley

Charles Horton Cooley (1864–1929) and George Herbert Mead (1863–1931) have been accepted as the cofounders of the social-psychological perspective called **symbolic interactionism**. (See Chapter 1.) Their discussion of the process of socialization and the development of personality is very different from Freud's. Cooley rejected Freud's notion of a continuing conflict between biological drives (id) and social demands (as embodied in the superego). In describing the development of the human personality, Cooley stressed the vital effect of the interaction between the child and those in the surrounding environment. The "self" or "self-concept" emerge from a social context. Cooley was skillful at observing and recording the play activities of children and their relationships with adults important in their lives, and he noted that young children, as they pretended to be mother or father or the supermarket clerk, were carefully imitating sequences of behavior that they had observed others performing. He also realized that such role-playing activities help children to discover much about themselves. In explaining this process, Cooley developed an influential concept which he called "the looking-glass self." The development of the self-concept requires the ability to see one's self reflected in another's eyes. Cooley said:

> Each to each a looking glass
> Reflects the other that doth pass.
>
> (Cooley, 1902, p. 184)

When we, as children, pretend to be teacher or the playground director we are standing in another's position in order to see ourselves as that other person does. We are using the playground director as we use a mirror, to see ourselves. In this way we develop an idea of what we are like to others and at the same time we respond to what we *think* they see. If we believe that people find us bright and alert, we feel proud. If we believe that people find us clumsy and slow in learning, we are ashamed. We interpret their responses to us and use them in developing feelings about ourselves. The looking-glass process, which is begun in infancy, actually continues throughout life. We continue to function as social mirrors for each other. Cooley believed that without this interaction process, no sense of self was possible.

George Herbert Mead

While extending and elaborating on Cooley's theories as he continued the development of the theoretical point of view called **symbolic interactionism**, George Herbert Mead remained in agreement with Cooley's basic notion that the emergence of self and personality is dependent on crucial social interactions. Mead was describing Cooley's looking-glass process when he used the idea of "taking the role of the other" to explain the dynamics of socialization. Mead, however, adds another dimension to Cooley's concept by not only linking the child to important adults in the environment but also linking the child to the larger social community.

In *Mind, Self and Society* (1934), an edition of Mead's lecture notes by his students after his death, Mead stresses that the process of socialization is dependent on interactions that are mainly symbolic; and certainly language is the most important kind of symbolic communication. In the case of the infant, symbolic communications such as gestures, facial expressions, and noises have important meanings to the mother and father. When the infant cries and parents come rushing in, that cry has a symbolic meaning ("I'm hungry," or "I'm wet," or "Where did everybody go?") and the parents respond to it, thus setting the stage for more complex responses.

Mead emphasizes that socialization is accomplished through the use of vocal language. Human beings share a large body of symbolic communications. And while it is true that such a gesture as a slap, such expressions as a frown or a smile, such vocal gestures as a scream or cry have the capacity to arouse in all individuals the same meanings, the use of verbal language is particularly significant. Mead indicates that the development of the human mind or intelligence and the social self depends upon language communication because mind and self develop as ideas are communicated and expressed vocally. For example, every child eventually recognizes the word "cigarette" to be a symbol for an object. And the child quickly takes on the attitude expessed by others about cigarettes (i.e., "They relax you" or "They are dangerous to your health"). As the young child grows, interaction with others helps the child absorb the attitudes and values of the group. And this absorption or internalization is accomplished largely through use of language.

Mead's Stages of Socialization Mead uses three stages to describe the process of socialization. All three stages involve role-playing or "taking the role of the other," so that the child can learn a variety of social roles and the values and norms accompanying these roles. In the first stage, the **preparatory stage,** the child imitates the behavior of adults but does not understand the meaning of what he or she is doing. The little girl perches on the arm of her father's chair and pretends to "read the paper like Daddy." It does not matter that the paper is upside down.

At the second stage, the **play stage**, the child "takes the role of the other" in order to see himself or herself from the perspective of influential adults. When the little boy spanks the teddy bear, saying "Billy is a bad boy for saying bad words," he is learning to understand the meaning of his own actions as well as the actions of others, thereby internalizing social expectations. Mead says that the little boy "addresses himself as a parent or as a teacher; he arrests himself as a policeman." (p. 215) By being another to one's own self, it is possible to understand the meanings attached to behavior and to shape one's own actions and meanings to those of others.

In the **game stage**, the child moves from an awareness of the expectations of specific others, such as parents, to awareness of the expectations of society as a whole. Mead uses the example of a baseball game to illustrate this idea. In order to play the game, the child must "have the attitude" of all the other players. Betty can only be an effective shortstop if she is aware of what the pitcher, the catcher, and the batter are supposed to be doing. What she does is controlled by her assumptions of the actions of the other players. This organization of attitudes (the team) can also be thought of in relation to society or the community. Mead calls it "the generalized other." Says Mead, "The organized community or social group which gives to the individual his unity of self can be called "the generalized other." The attitude of the generalized other is the attitude of the whole community (p. 219). Thus the individual who is socialized has absorbed the general attitudes of the social group or community and uses these attitudes to direct his or her own behavior. In the game stage the self reaches its full development as the attitudes of the community, "the generalized other," become part of the personality, guiding and directing conduct and behavior.

And yet socialization does not create perfect social participants. Mead recognized that the "I" (the spontaneous, idiosyncratic self) is never completely controlled by the "me" (the social self, guided by the internalized norms and expectations of society). The fact that people will violate traffic rules, take office equipment home, or cheat on their income taxes illustrates the capacity of the usually subordinate "I" to prevail.

Jean Piaget

Jean Piaget (1896–), the distinguished Swiss psychologist, has spent half a century theorizing and writing about the moral and intellectual development of children. According to Piaget, cognition, or the capacity to reason, remember, generalize, imagine, or calculate is an important part of the developmental processes of childhood and occurs in specific stages that are universal and unvarying. Piaget differs from Freud, Erikson, and Mead, however, in tying his stages to biological dvelopment. He is convinced that a child moves through four stages of cognitive development, proceeding to each stage only after completing a prior stage successfully. Piaget is also interested in the process during which a child learns to make judgments about what is right and wrong. He considers the development of moral judgments part of the larger process of cognitive development and thus ties the learning of norms to steps that proceed as the intellect grows.

The **sensorimotor stage** extends from birth to two years of age. At this stage children lack symbolic language; thus their intellectual abilities are best discerned from their actions as they establish sensory and physical contact with their environment. For example, because an infant does not understand that objects have a permanent existence, a block hidden under a blanket will no longer exist to the child. At the end of this stage, the older child will find the block under the blanket. At this stage of development the child is egocentric, self-involved, and unable to share the points of view of others. In conforming to rules, the young child sees them as imposed from outside and has no sense of control over them.

The **preoperational stage** occurs between the ages of two and seven. At this stage children are acquiring language. Intellectually they are still unable to understand basic concepts like quantity, weight, number. In the early preoperational stage, when shown two jars, both half full of beans, children will correctly state that both jars contain the same number of beans. When these same beans from the two jars are emptied into two taller, thinner jars, the children believe that the taller jars contain more beans. Only toward the end of this stage do children understand that the number of beans remains constant regardless of the shape of the container. This is still an egocentric stage and the child is unable to take the role of others in play. Piaget notes that in playing marbles at this stage there is no sense of competition. The children do not watch each other or indeed try to win. Playing marbles is a "motor pleasure" rather than a social one (1969).

The **concrete operational stage** lasts from seven to twelve years. Now children are able to apply logic to concrete objects. They can now understand number, quantity, cause, and effect. They easily take the roles of others. In a game of marbles, skill is no longer the only object. Marbles is now a social game with a spirit of competition and cooperation existing. However, the rules of the game exist only for the duration of the game. Generalizing and developing principles, which will apply to all cases in every game, is still not possible.

The **formal operational stage** occurs at the beginning of adolescence. Young people now have the capacity to reason, to handle abstract concepts. They can generalize about whole classes of objects, develop theories and hypotheses. In game situations, rules are no longer seen as exterior and to be respected because of tradition or custom and are therefore subject to change by common consent. At this stage, cooperation results not from what is customary but from a sense of what is right and fair. The fact that the young are now able to think in abstract terms is related to their idealistic goals and utopian interests.

Piaget believes that there are concrete differences in the way children think at different stages of development. Also children move from stage to stage in the same order. The sequence of stages does not vary although the content (i.e., norms, beliefs) varies from culture to culture. Piaget is aware that there are people who never develop beyond the stage of concrete operations and never achieve the ability to reason abstractly. Lawrence Kohlberg (Kohlberg and Gilligan, 1971), who has sought to empirically test Piaget's theories, suggests that 50 per cent of Americans never arrive at Piaget's last stage—the stage of formal operations.

Adult Socialization and Social Control

To the extent that adults imitate the conforming behavior of those around them and incorporate into the personal belief system the beliefs and values accepted as important by the society, they experience the consequences of socialization—social control. Indeed, one cannot fully comprehend the significance of socialization without recognizing the extent to which an ostensibly external process becomes internalized. According to Peter Berger,

> What happens in socialization is that the social world is internalized within the child. The same process, though perhaps weaker in quality, occurs every time the adult is initiated into a new social context or a new social group. Society, then, is not only something "out there," . . . but is also "in here," part of our innermost being. Only an understanding of internalization makes sense of the incredible fact that most external controls work most of the time for most of the people in a society. Society not only controls our movements, but shapes our identity, our thought and our emotions. The structures of society become the structures of our own consciousness. Society does not stop at the surface of our skin. Society penetrates us as much as it envelops us. (Berger, 1963, p. 121)

SEX-ROLE SOCIALIZATION

The Influences of Biology and Culture

The problems surrounding Rose's sports activities highlight some basic issues regarding sex role socialization in Western society. Some of our statuses are conferred at birth. A newborn child is either a female or male, is assigned to one of the three racial groups, and takes on the socioeconomic status of its parents. These are ascribed statuses, and the family is given the responsibilty of seeing that the young child understands the meaning of the statuses that are conferred and adopts the role behavior accompanying each status. Traditionally, boys have been provided with trucks and footballs and guns and have been encouraged toward behavior that is appropriate to the male status. Some norms that boys are taught are these: "boys do not cry"; "boys will be boys and fight"; "boys stand up for their rights." Such norms have been traditionally tied to biological differences in males and females. The basic differences are anatomical: females menstruate, have babies, and produce milk; males produce sperm and can impregnate females. In addition to differences in secondary-sex characteristics (amount of body hair, musculature, differences in voice pitch), there are hormonal differences. Hormones are chemical substances, secreted into the bloodstream from glands, that determine physical development and some behaviors. Although both sexes have male as well as female hormones, the porportion of male hormones (testosterone and androgens) is greater in males and the proportion of female hormones (estrogen and progesterone) is greater in women. While evidence exists that aggression is learned (Bandura, 1973; Patterson et al., 1967), the aggressive behavior of males also seems to be tied to higher levels of testosterone. In animal experiments in which testosterone was administered to infant female rodents, they were more aggressive and showed more fighting behaviors as adults (Edwards, 1969).

6-6 CHECKING IT OUT: When the Football Star's a Girl

Girls participate in sports very much these days. My daughter, Rose, doesn't play tennis or basketball or baseball. She plays football. From the beginning, though, she has been having problems.

Last year, when Rose was 11, she became tall and husky, but that wasn't why I started showing her how to play football. She saw the ball in my closet, where it had been left by Arthur, my son from a previous marriage. He was away at college, and when he came home for the Thanksgiving weekend he was astonished to see Rose throwing and catching his football quite well.

We went to a park and he threw many fast and tricky passes. She caught all of them nicely. Once, when he wasn't looking, she mischievously tackled him and he went down heavily. He was stunned, but he managed to smile as he picked himself up. He complimented her for being so strong and smooth, but a few minutes later he wanted to go home.

That fall, Rose and I started going to football games. She was impressed when a punt was blocked or a pass intercepted. She whooped with joy when a player made a sprint of several yards. She moaned when a ball was fumbled away. The girl was a natural footballphile.

She wanted to be in a game herself, so the next Saturday we went to a park and I rounded up enough boys to form two teams. All were about her size, and we didn't let them know Rose was only 11. They knew she was a girl and they were making wisecracks and acting reluctant. But when I offered $10 to the player who made the most touchdowns, they became eager to play.

Gradually, they saw how she spiraled the ball, how she got it and ran with it, how she kicked it. They were incredulous and now a bit respectful.

"Hey, you're a young Joe Namath," someone shouted to her.

"That's a girl," someone else said. "She's Fran Tarkenton's kid sister."

But a little later in the game she made a flying tackle that actually made the boy's face go flat into the dirt. He spit out dirt when he sat up, and the other boys gaped. Then they turned toward Rose, and I could see their resentment.

When the boy stood, he seemed to be blushing. He dusted himself off, but didn't return to the game. He walked away and we never saw him again. Being rammed into the ground by a girl must have been too embarrassing for him.

Several minutes later Rose tackled someone again, this time gently, and he didn't walk away. But now all the boys quit playing. A pep talk didn't help .They hated Rose.

The following Saturday, Rose and I drove to a park farther away, where we weren't known. I recruited enough boys for a game, offering a $20 prize.

No other girls would join the game. I told Rose not to tackle anyone. She looked puzzled. "You're hurting their male pride," I said. She undersood. "What a disadvantage I'm going to have," she said.

During the game she didn't touch a boy. Twice she threw the ball far and high, and once she intercepted a pass and scored untouched. The boys liked her, and she didn't become a threat to them. We had games in that park week after week.

Now Rose is 12 and 5 feet 6 inches tall and 142 pounds. The boys she plays football with now are 16 and over. They treat her as an equal and do not hestitate to tackle her. However, they never ask why she doesn't ever tackle them. Maybe they think she doesn't have the guts or ability.

Next fall she'll be in high school. Will she be allowed on the team? I doubt it. Yet she might be a star.

Maybe I should talk with the coach. Wearing a helmet and other equipment, Rose would hardly look like a girl. But during practice, who would want to be tackled by her?

SOURCE: Charles Tekeyan, *The New York Times*, March 19, 1978, p. S2.

Biology, however, only supplies part of the answer regarding differences in the behavior of males and females. Money and Ehrhardt (1972, 1970) are convinced that the sex to which a child is *assigned* has much more to do with behavior than hormones. These researchers studied hermaphrodites, individuals born with internal organs of both sexes so that they are not clearly distinguishable as males or females. Money and Ehrhardt emphasize that even though a particular hermaphrodite might have a hormonal and chromosomal makeup that was more female than male, this individual could be raised as either a female or a male. The "sex of assignment" was more important than the genetic makeup. Therefore, Freud's belief that "anatomy determines destiny" is questionable. With sex assignment at birth comes social learning about role behavior. Little girls are expected to be neater, gentler, more passive, nurturant, and less aggressive than boys. They have been traditionally given different toys to play with and discouraged from swearing. Thus they have been socialized to accept behaviors characterized as "feminine," just as boys are encouraged to take on behaviors characterized as "masculine." **Gender identity**, or the assumption of the psychological characteristics associated with masculinity and femininity, becomes clear to young children as adults react to their behavior and praise or punish and as they watch same-sex role models and imitate the ways adults handle crises, express themselves, wear clothes, enjoy leisure activities.

In the case of Rose, the footballphile, we see a vivid example of the effects of sex-role socialization. Rose has a natural ability in a sports activity relegated to males. Rose is as competent as her male teammates, but social practice has made is difficult for them to accept her and their internalization of masculine role behavior makes them downright humiliated when she, a supposedly passive and unaggressive female, successfully tackles them. Their sense of male dominance has been threatened by this "unfeminine" girl.

Females and Males—Cross-Cultural Comparisons

After examining a number of other societies, Barry, Bacon, and Child (1957) concluded that almost all human societies socialize boys differently than girls.

There was a near-universal cultural demand that boys be self-reliant, independent, and achievement-oriented, whereas girls were expected to be obedient, passive, and nurturant. The researchers related the differences in expectations for boys and girls to the division of labor within societies. For example, where there are many tasks that require great physical strength, male children will be socialized differently in preparation for adult roles. Not only do anthropologists point to sex-related socialization patterns, but also to cultural values that give preference to maleness rather than femaleness. Most cultures limit the activities of women to domestic settings. Dorothy Hammond and Alta Jablow (1976) note that the activities of men "dominate the values and ethos of every society." Public life, for example, with its positions of power and prestige, has traditionally been a male domain. Indeed a number of contemporary anthropologists agree that the existence of some degree of male dominance in all human societies could be thought of as a cultural universal (Rosaldo and Lamphere, 1974; Ortner, 1974). Yet this male dominance seems to these researchers to be directly related to the reproductive role of women. In hunting and gathering societies where infant morality is high, if the population of the group is to be stable, women need to be continuously pregnant during the childbearing years. Friedl (1975) notes that in late pregnancy and after the child's birth, the weight of the child affects the mother's balance enough to make even gathering difficult. Lessened mobility stemming from childbearing activities then prevents women from being regular hunters. Friedl did find women fishing and taking part in some communal hunts in some hunting and gathering societies, but the value attached to maleness was clear in such societies where the universal pattern was for males, never females, to hunt large game animals.

There are other anthropologists who are less convinced of universal male dominance. Lamphere finds sex roles more equal where both males and females participate in domestic and political areas. Martin and Voorhies (1975) note that frontier women of the American West won the right to vote earlier than other women because they were regarded as productive economic partners within a system where farming and home industry were viewed as cooperative efforts. Also sexual equality is possible where females control economic production and males are forced to be away (i.e., engaged in warfare). In the case of the Iroquois of North America, women functioned in a matrilineal society where they controlled production and the distribution of crops, participated in the political activities of the tribe, nominated male council representatives, held veto power when war was being proposed, and even had the power to impeach chiefs (Brown, 1975). The economic dominance of women where men are absent is also mirrored in the Igbo of eastern Nigeria (Tanner, 1974). Because the men were frequently away, involved in trading activities, women controlled local production. They grew crops and traded their surpluses in markets which they controlled. Some Igbo women belonged to powerful all-female political associations where they promoted their common economic interests.

The research of Margaret Mead refutes the notion of universal male dominance and describes several societies where the sex-role socialization of children is very different from our own. In *Sex and Temperament in Three Primitive Societies* (originally published in 1935), Mead first observed three tribes of New Guinea. The first was the Arapesh, mountain people who did not expect different role behavior for males and females. Both males and females were expected to be gentle, home-loving, passive, and emotionally warm. The Arapesh rejected competitiveness and aggression in both sexes and derived pleasure in giving and helping activities. Both males and females participated in child care. In general, members of this tribe displayed role behavior that we might call feminine.

The neighboring Mundugumor showed role behavior that we associate with masculinity. Both males and females were aggressive, violent, vengeful. Members of this head-hunting, cannibalistic group were hostile to members of their own sex and only somewhat less mistrustful of the opposite sex. Children were not valued. Women disliked pregnancy and breast-feeding and from the time that they could walk children were expected to fend for themselves.

The third group studied by Mead was the Tchambuli, a tribe where sex-role behaviors of males and females were the opposite of those of the U.S. Tchambuli females controlled economic production and were dominant, practical people who took the initiative in courtship and mating. Tchambuli men were preoccupied with adorning themselves, were artistic, and employed the wiles that we associate with women.

A Functional Analysis

When Talcott Parsons and Robert Bales analyzed the structure of the traditional modern family (1953), they characterized the role behavior necessary as two adults functioned within the family unit. One person, usually the father, could be expected to take on an "instrumental role." In this role, the father interacted with the world outside the family, producing income to support the family. Father's behavior demanded a dominant, aggressive, and competent performance in society and in the workplace. The mother's role was an "expressive" one; she was expected to provide emotional support, warmth, and love and so contribute to the smooth functioning of the family unit. Her role demanded passive, dependent behavior rather than aggression and dominance.

The dichotomy between the "instrumental" or masculine role and the "expressive" or feminine role reflects social expectations about behavior that have been taught to generations of children. There is widespread interest today in the effects of these socialization practices as the women of many nations have begun to resist role expectations that constrict their development and reduce their self-esteem.

Women and Achievement

Contemporary personality research in the United States presents convincing evidence that at all age levels the traditional role behavior demanded of women so lacks the prestige associated with role behavior of males that the self-esteem of many females is low indeed. In a study of young children, Kagan and Lemkin (1960) found that both boys and girls identified the father of the family as the "boss," and as smarter and stronger than the mother. Thus, while female children are expected to use their mothers as role models and learn appropriate sex-role behavior from them, these behaviors are negatively valued. Baruch (1974a) found that the perception of self as having traditionally feminine traits was unrelated to feelings of self-esteem, whereas the perception of oneself as possessing traits traditionally thought of as masculine (i.e., ambition, assertiveness) was related to high self-esteem. This negative self-concept is most poignantly revealed in middle age. Birnbaum (1971) found that middle-aged women, who had not worked since the the birth of their first child, felt less attractive and less competent than did comparable groups of career women. These family-oriented women, while able and productive, ultimately felt unsatisfied with the role that had been assigned them.

This is not to suggest women who are upwardly mobile are free from sex-role anxieties. However, the range of career possibilities has widened as many women have actively resisted motherhood and domestic careers as the "proper" female occupations. Certainly the strength and visibility of the women's movement has contributed much to this change. In this age of female coal miners, jockeys, prime ministers, and corporation presidents, female anatomy is no longer perceived as determining destiny. And yet even women who are academically and occupationally mobile have been socialized in a society that still values the traditional role for females. Matina Horner (1972, 1969, 1968) found that many women still considered success antithetical to feminity and that bright women were particularly afraid of success. Their motivation to avoid success grew out of an anxiety that social rejection, particularly by boy friends, would follow high achievement. Horner reports that in a study conducted by Schwenn (1970) the girls who showed evidence of fear of success and had changed their career plans because of these fears were "straight A averages," (not dating at all) or those dating men who rejected "career women."

Horner asked a sample of female college students to write a four-minute story about Anne, who, after the first term of medical school, was at the top of the class. A sample of male students was presented with the same cue, only the name of "John" was substituted for Anne. The results showed that while 90 percent of males wrote stories exhibiting positive feelings about John's success, 65 percent of females were confused or unhappy about Anne's achievement and found her behavior unfeminine. One respondent described her as being "aggressive, unmarried, wearing Oxford shoes"; some denied that such a person existed.

It might be expected that the women's movement would affect these attitudes of the 1960s. Certainly college women of the 1970s have had a unique chance to observe changes in role expectations as American women have demanded equality of opportunity and social liberation. It is significant that a replication of Horner's study found only a third of the sample of women showed a fear of success. (Katz, 1972).

Whereas Horner examined psychological factors that may inhibit the full development of women, other social scientists have focused on the organizational positioning of women in the social institutions of the society to explain their unequal development with men. Such explanations must relate sexism to the currrent situation of women. **Sexism**, as a cultural ideology, accepts the dominant position of males as the result of their "natural" superiority over women. Economic and social inequalities are closely related to the lack of value attached to femaleness. An interesting example of sexism is to be found in a sample of highly trained chemists, who had received their Ph.D's in U.S. universities between 1955 and 1961 (Reskin, 1978). The sample included 229 females and 221 males. The results of the study showed that there were differences in the productivity of males and female chemists as determined by the number of articles they published and the number of citations they received

6-7 CHECKING IT OUT: Mean Sex Differences in Selected Measures of Scientific Productivity

Productivity Measure	*Men*	*Women*	t-*test*
Predoctoral publications [a]	.85	.76	.55
Early productivity [a]	.57	−.39	.80
First post-Ph.D. year	.51	.41	1.11
Third post-Ph.D. year	.51	.46	.58
Fifth post-Ph.D. year	.74	.48	2.46*
Seventh post-Ph.D. year	.86	.91	−.16
Ninth post-Ph.D. year	.92	.72	1.32
Decade productivity [a]	.087	−.092	1.91*
Early citations [a]	.012	−.012	.26
Total citations	40.14	26.35	1.78*
Recent quality score [b]	.57	−.59	.54
Total quality score [b]	2.27	−2.39	.79
N	229	221	. . .

[a] Standardized by Ph.D.-degree cohort.
[b] Measures described in text.
* $P < .05$, one-tailed test of null hypothesis that male scientists' productivity is greater than that of female scientists.
SOURCE: Barbara Reskin, "Scientific Productivity, Sex, and Location in the Institution of Science," *American Journal of Sociology*, 1978, 83:1235–1243.

in the Science Citation Index. The lower status of women in science is frequently related to differences between males and females in relation to productivity. The table shows that men were somewhat more productive than female chemists but the differences were too small to be statistically significant. The men did outpublish women in the fifth-post-Ph.D. year and after a decade of activity. However, further analysis showed that women were disadvantaged in several important ways. Although acceptance for employment within the university implies ability and promise, women who began their careers in universities more frequently began in nontenure tracks (62 per cent of women, 37 per cent of men). At the end of the decade, women were still in nontenure tracks, whereas almost all the men sampled were moving toward tenure. The productivity of female chemists was more frequently affected by job changes, and for 18 per cent, unemployment. Uneven work histories and unemployment were shown to hamper their productivity even more than marriage and childbearing. It was significant that recognition by colleagues through citations had a greater positive effect on the productivity of women than on men. An analysis of organizational arrangements within science provides clearer explanations for differences in performance than does biology.

INTERPRETIVE SUMMARY

Numerous studies have shown that personality is a product of both heredity and environment. Studies of individuals with widely different heredities who were reared together or in similar environments and studies of individuals with similar hereditary make-up who were reared in different environments both indicate that heredity and environment together have a limiting effect on intelligence, temperament, and physical condition.

The influence of the environment on the development of personality is especially apparent in the cases of children reared in isolation, children living for an extended time in institutions, and monkeys reared in isolation. Prolonged isolation hinders the development of the human potential.

Personality is developed through the process of socialization. Through socialization the individual learns the culture of the group and develops a social self. Freud related the emergence of the self to the development of the id, ego, and superego in the young child. In the resolution of the Oedipus complex in boys and the Electra complex in girls, the child internalizes the norms and values of the culture and begins to identify with the same-sex parent.

Cooley used the image of a "looking glass" to explain the development of the self. Because we see ourselves as others see us, the self reflects the feedback received from those in the child's environment. Mead further developed Cooley's theory but emphasized language as the vehicle through which ideas are communicated (vocally) and through which roles and attitudes can be internalized. Mead's three stages include a preparatory stage, the play stage, and the game stage.

Both Erikson and Piaget explain the process of socialization in stages of development. Erikson's theory, however, is concerned with emotional development and Piaget examines four stages of cognitive development.

Socialization is a continuous process beginning in childhood and continuing in adulthood. We must not assume, however, that socialization is a completely successful process. We have the capacity to make choices and sometimes violate the norms that we have internalized. Traditionally, the socialization patterns for females and males have been tied to biological differences. And while anatomical and harmonal differences do exist, biology alone cannot explain the differing life experiences and sex role behaviors connected with maleness and femaleness. With sex assignment at birth comes social learning about role behavior. *Gender identity*, or the assumption of characteristics associated with masculinity and femininity, is internalized by the young as they imitate same-sex models and are sanctioned positively or negatively.

Cross-cultural studies make it clear that masculinity and femininity are not inherited qualities but acquired through social learning. And while male dominance seems a near cultural universal, this dominance is most apparent where reproduction activity is prolonged because of high infant mortality. Where women control economic production they have social and political power.

In describing modern society Parsons and Bales stress the necessity of sexual differentiation of role functions. Yet current personality research suggests that traditional roles lower the self-esteem of some females. While the women's movement continues to have a significant effect in expanding the role behaviors of modern women, *sexism*, which accepts masculine domination as "natural," continues to limit the occupational and social opportunities of women.

QUESTIONS

1. Compare Mead and Freud in their explanations of socialization. In what ways are Mead's theories very different from Freud's? Are there any similarities?
2. Mead's explanation of the "generalized other" uses the situation of the baseball game. Explain the internalization of norms using the ballgame in your explanation.
3. In what ways do Freud and Erikson differ in their concepts of the stages of socialization?

4. Describe some of the differences between males and females resulting from heredity. Compare them with role requirements in modern and preindustrial societies.
5. How is the "gender identity" of successful career women apt to be affected by sexism?

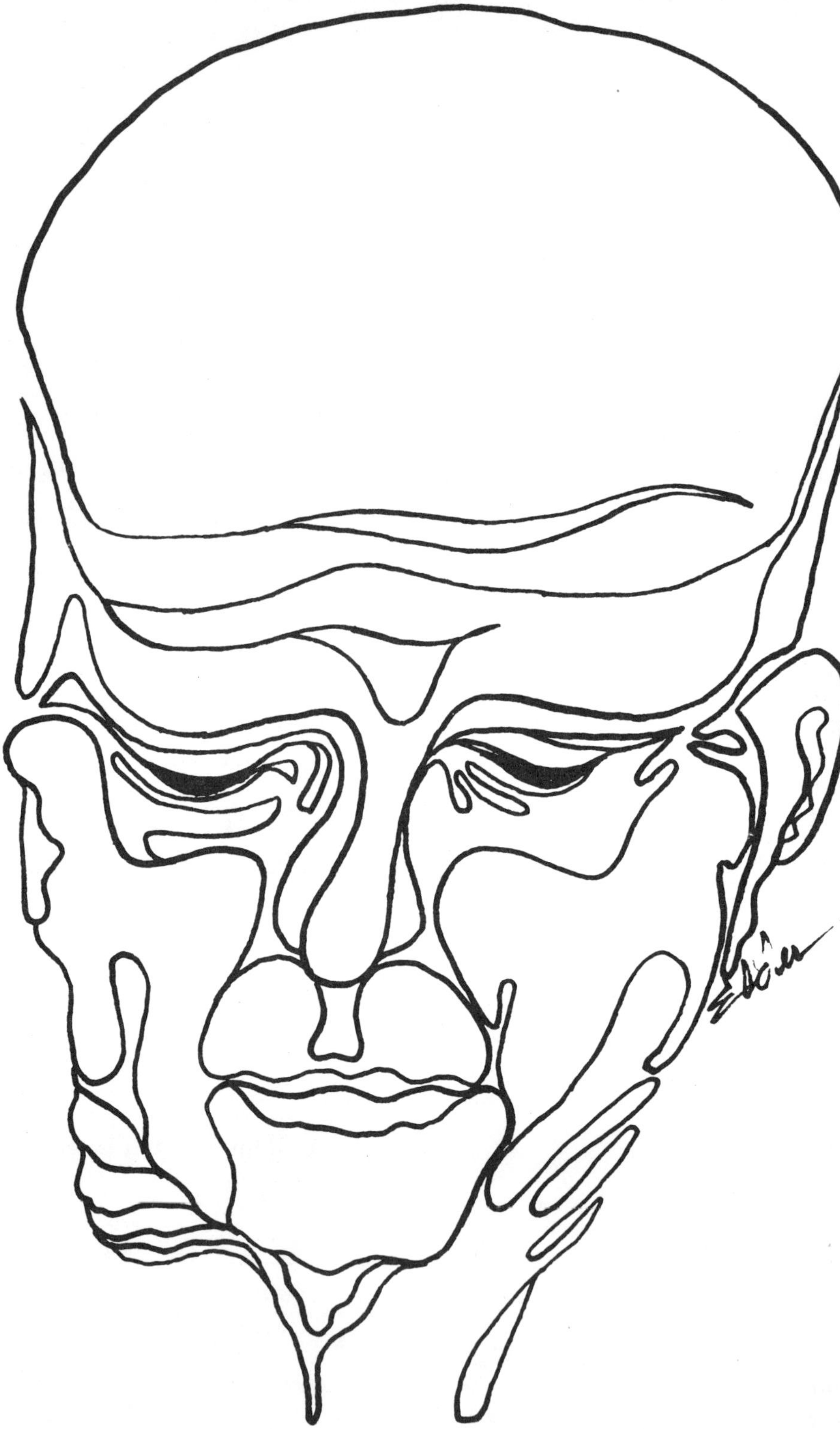

7

The Sociology of Aging

Jeanne C. Biggar
University of Virginia

The conscientious young woman was guiding the senior citizens tour through Monticello. In a high, shrill voice she translated the memorized description of Jefferson's many inventions into grammar school language. As she waited for the tourists to enter the Wedgwood blue dining room, she patronized the gentleman on her right with, "And what were you before retirement?" With no hesitation he retorted, "I still am!"

By the early 1980s it is estimated that there will be more than 24 million people in the United States over the age of 65. These people are referred to in several ways: "the aged," "senior citizens," "the older generation," "the elderly," "those in the golden ages," the "put-down generation," "the put-out generation." Whatever the label used for those over the age of 65, they now represent somewhat more than 10 per cent of the population in this country.

Age is an ascribed status in this society, and given survival to the age of 65, entrance into the aged category is inevitable. Despite our cultural inventions, such as the pacemaker, dentures, hair coloring, wigs and toupees, which either intervene in or disguise the aging process, age 65 brings society's definition of aged status. Increasing concern for the aged stems from two factors: first, the increasing number of the aged; second, a growing awareness of the exclusion of these people from social participation because of age stratification.

DEMOGRAPHIC CHARACTERISTICS OF THE AGED

Since the turn of the century people over the age of 65 have comprised one of the most rapidly growing segments of the population in the United States. Between 1900 and 1970 the total population increased about two and a half times. Over that same period, however, the segment 65 years and older increased more than six and a half times to more than 20 million. Even more dramatic was the increase of the number of people 75 years and older. This segment increased by more than eight and a half times over the 70-year period. Population estimates indicate continued growth for this aged segment until the year 2000, when the number is expected to stabilize. This differential increase of population in the aged category was due not only to the decline in the general mortality rate from over 15 per thousand after World War I to less than 10 per thousand by 1970, but also to the changing base of mortality. Higher standards of living, better public sanitation processes for water and sewer systems, improved maternal and child health practices, central heating, advances in medical technology—particularly the advent of sulfa and penicillin drugs—all contributed to the reduction of mortality from infectious diseases of the respiratory and gastrointestinal tracts which were high risk factors, particularly for children and young adults. The reduction of the mortality rate from infectious diseases is accompanied by an increase in the mortality rate from degenerative

7-1 CHECKING IT OUT: Twentieth-Century Growth of Aged Population

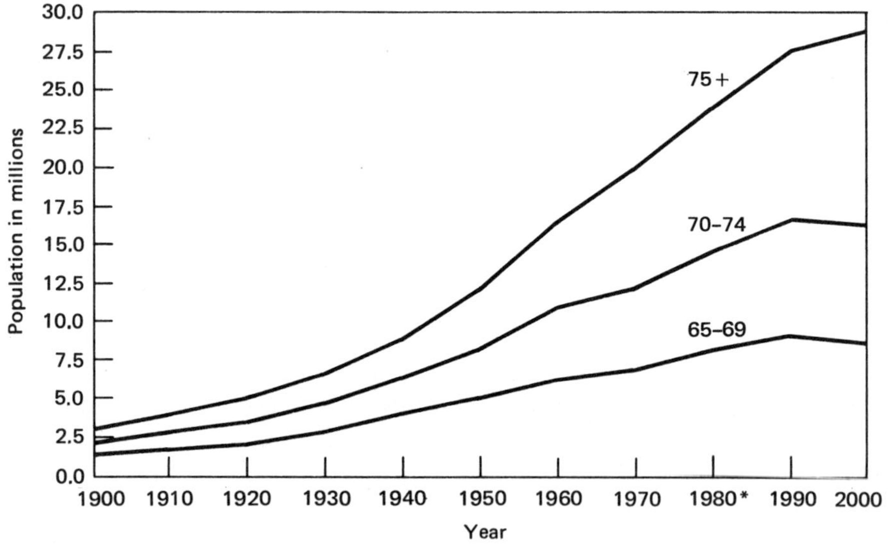

*Based on Series E Projections

SOURCE: Table 53, *General Population Characteristics, U.S. Summary,* 1970, *U.S. Census;* Table 2, *Projections of the Population of the U.S. by Age and Sex,* 1972–2020, Series P-25, No. 493.

diseases such as cardio-vascular problems and cancer, diseases of adulthood. The changes in death rates have increased longevity for Americans. The expectation of life at birth has changed from 54 years after World War II to 73 years by 1977. Furthermore, the expectancy of further life at age 65 is currently an additional 16 years. This means that among those who survive to age 65 there is an even chance of reaching the age of 81.

The increase in longevity for the population in the United States over the last 50 years has shown distinctive differentials by sex and by race. Male mortality rates exceed female mortality rates at every age in both white and nonwhite segments of the population. By the age of 50, male mortality rates are double those of females. The sex differential in mortality does not begin to close until age 72 for whites and age 66 for nonwhites. These mortality differentials

7-2 CHECKING IT OUT: Male and Female Mortality Rates for Whites and Nonwhites, 1975

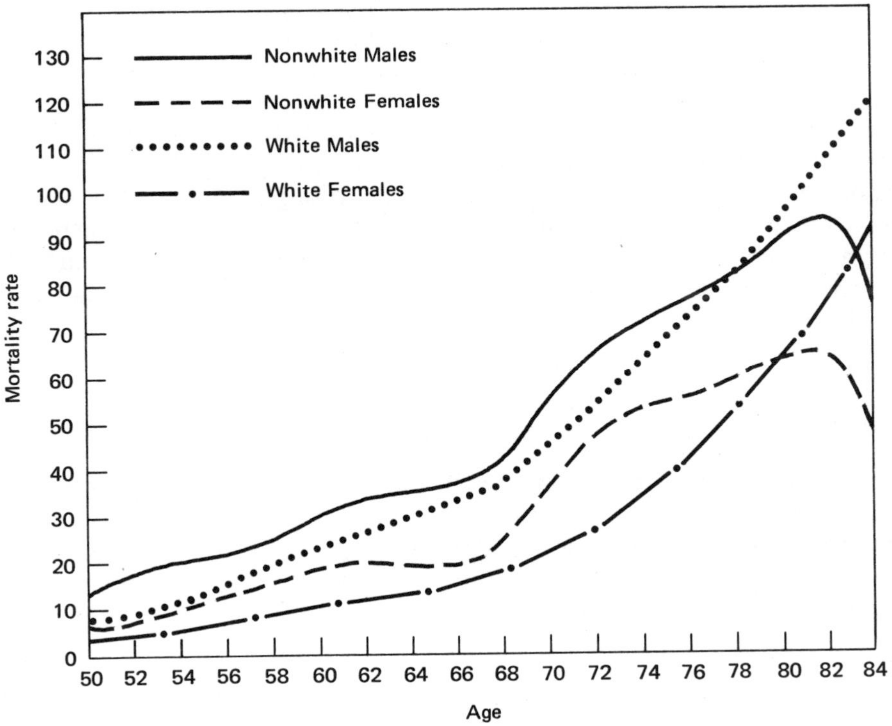

SOURCE: *Statistical Bulletin,* Metropolitan Life Insurance Co., New York, Vol. 58, May 1977, pp. 10–11

have distinct consequences for the age-sex structure of the aged population. For every succeeding age there is larger proportion of females than of males in the population. For example, in the total 1970 population, there were approximately 95 males for every 100 females. That same year there were only 80 males for every 100 females between ages 65 and 69; between ages 70 and 74 there were 74 males for every 100 females; for those 75 years and older there were only 64 males for every 100 females in the population. As we shall see later, the female bias of the aged population has significant socioeconomic consequences for this strata of society.

SOCIOECONOMIC CHARACTERISTICS OF THE AGED

Household Arrangements

Almost half of the population over the age of 65 live with a spouse. The majority of these husband-wife families are in the early period of their retirement years, however. In the first five years of the retirement period more than 80 per cent of the males are married and living with a spouse. The per cent of married males gradually declines until after age 85 when less than half live with their wives. The picture for females is quite different, however. Because of women's greater longevity and because widowed females are less likely to remarry, just over half of the females in the earliest period of retirement are in husband-wife families. The per cent of women living with their husbands drops dramatically in the older ages so that after age 85 three-fourths are widowed and only about one in ten live with a spouse. Of the balance (51 per cent) who do not live in husband-wife households almost half are households headed by women, about one-eighth are men living by themselves, a fourth are older people living with other family members, and a tenth are living in an institution or nursing home.

Work Status

The advent of the Social Security system in 1935 (when approximately 6 per cent of the American population was over the age of 65) had long-range consequences for the older segment of our society. First, the target age, 65, when citizens could qualify for Old Age Survivors Insurance and the age when low-income older citizens could qualify for Old Age Assistance, became the social definition of the aged population. Second, because industry adopted age 65 as the mandatory retirement age, the choice to retire or to continue working at the end of the career was moved from the individual worker to the employer. Third, while it may be that the Social Security model has encouraged pension plans for private industries and retirement plans for governmental agencies, the "rule of thumb age," 65, has become the formal maximum age for work participation. The consequence of mandatory retirement ages, augmented by the "cooling out" process for older workers (informal pressure placed on older workers to leave their jobs), is that about one in five (20.4 per cent) of men, and one in twelve (7.7 per cent) of women continue in the labor force after the age of 65. Those who continue to work after the age of 65 tend to be drawn from the upper-level professional, self-employed, and lower-level unskilled occupations.

Income

Retirement, withdrawal from the labor force, has both economic and non-economic consequences for the aged population. In terms of economic consequences, the amount of income on the average drops to approximately one-half the amount earned in the late working years. In 1969, the median income among working males in the preretirement category (60 to 64 years) was $6,653. Almost three-fourths of these men were still in the labor force. Among women in this age category more than a third were in the labor force, and their median income was $2,373. Median income continues to drop in the older ages in the retirement years so that males 75 years and older, more than 10 per cent of whom work at least part-time, had a median income of $2,140, less than a third of the income of those in the preretirement years. Female median income also continues to drop for each succeeding age category to $1,335 for females over the age of 75. In 1969 the poverty level for the two-person household was $2,215; for the single-person household poverty level was $1,893. At this time one-tenth of elderly white families and one-fourth of elderly nonwhite families had incomes of less than $2,000. Among the elderly living alone three-eighths of whites and three-fourths of the nonwhites had incomes of less than $2,000. Among the single nonwhite elderly a third had less than $1,000 a year to live on.

In an effort to ease the financial problems of low-income households, the Supplementary Security Income (SSI) program was initiated in 1974. At that time all eligible single persons were guaranteed an income of $1,753, eligible couples, $2,672. Eligibility is defined by a maximum of $25,000 real property ownership and a total income less than the guaranteed minimum. In June, 1977, 4.2 million SSI checks were issued by the Social Security Administration. This program has two important consequences for the aged. First, it provides a guaranteed income even though the amount provides little more than a subsistence level living. Second, SSI transformed the former welfare concept associated with such categorical aid programs as Old Age Assistance, which was implemented by the various state governments, into a right of all citizens for minimal income support from the federal government. (Manney, 1975)

SOCIAL PARTICIPATION OF THE AGED

Occupation is the key status for U. S. society. This means that information about the occupation of an individual tells us more than any other type of social information about other social statuses of that individual. Retirement means loss of occupational status. It is in terms of this loss of status that retired people have been labeled the "put-down generation." The consequences of the loss of occupational status for the retired worker are not clearly defined in gerontological literature, however. Some hold that in an industrial society in which work is the basis of social identity, the transition from the productive role to the leisure role is not only difficult but tends to alienate the individual from his or her social milieu. The portent of embarrassment, Miller's concept describing the reluctance of the new retiree to assume the stigma attached to retirement, may result in a reluctance of new retirees to replace work associations that they lost with new acquaintances because of the fear of making mistakes among strangers. (Miller, 1965) Others hold that the majority of older workers are willing to exchange the working role for the leisure role provided there is an assurance of financial security. (Manney, 1975) The transition from the worker to the leisure role is accompanied by changes in reciprocal rights and duties shared in the husband and wife role. A loss of the husband's work associates tends to be replaced by increased activities with the wife's friends. The full-time presence of the husband in the home calls for adjustments in the wife's activities. The authority of the breadwinner in family decision-making is replaced to some degree by the authority of the wife as social engineer in organizing and facilitating relationships with friends outside the family circle. The invasion of the woman's household domain by the newly retired husband often leads to conflict and almost always calls for adjustment by both members of the household to carry on day-to-day activities.

Despite the fact that more than half of the elderly do not have a spouse with whom to share their lives, most do have some type of family interaction. Most of those with children live within an hour's distance of at least one of those children and see them at least once a week. About one in five of the elderly live in the same household with a family member. Such families are more often found in rural, blue-collar, and ethnic households. Another three-fifths of the elderly live in "modified extended family" arrangements. These are people who maintain their own independent dwelling yet interact often with family members. Despite the separate residential arrangements, these families provide mutual support and affection for one another. The remaining fifth who live in the typical nuclear family situation tend to be the elderly who had small families, are well educated, urban in viewpoint, and geographically mobile. (Kerckhoff, 1965) The quality of relationships maintained in the extended families depends to a large degree on the ease with which both parents and children accept the role-reversal which occurs in this life stage. The parents' acceptance of their children's right to make their own decisions and, in fact, to help with decisions for the parents, themselves, is crucial to the maintenance of these family relationships.

The transition from the work role to the leisure role provides freedom and time to foster not only family relations but friendships. Friends are the most valuable resource that older persons find in the community. This is particularly true of those who grow old without the help of the spouse. Friends are a primary means of communication. It is friendship networks that most effectively transmit information about services to the elderly in the local community. Friends prove to be the major source of intimacy and emotional support. Yet it is in this stage of life that friendships are most likely to be lost because of death, involuntary moves, and institutionalization. Health problems, transportation problems, and financial insecurity all erode friendship networks in the later years of life. Many older people find it more difficult than younger people to replace lost friends. In general, older women both have more friends and spend more time with friends than do elderly men. The ability to make friends and keep them is related to the retirement adjustment process. We do not know, however, whether people make a better adjustment to the aging process because they have friends, or whether they have friends because they have made a better adjustment to the changes inherent in this period of life. (Clark and Anderson, 1967)

The growth of voluntary organizations in this century provides many activities for the elderly population. Labor unions, clubs, fraternal groups, religious denominations have no upper age limits to membership. Older citizens depend upon these voluntary associations to maintain connections with the larger community. Organizations specifically formed for older citizens, such as the American Association of Retired Persons, the National Council of Senior Citizens, and Retired Seniors Volunteer Program, focus on the problems of this age group and are involved in developing and implementing solutions to those problems. Participation in voluntary organizations follows much the same pattern as for the larger society. Those who join these groups in the older years tended to participate in groups and associations in their younger years. More middle-class elderly people participate than the working-class elderly; more women participate than men.

Despite the wide variation of voluntary organizations available to old people, by far the most important in terms of both membership and participation, are those that focus on religion affiliations. Cross-sectional studies of church membership and participation indicate increases in membership and participation in late adult years up to the age of 60 and then a gradual decline. However, these findings do not indicate necessarily that older people are more religious than younger people. First, the church was the central institution in the community during the formative period in the lives of those people currently in the retirement years. Second, churches, more than any other single type of voluntary organization, have focused on providing services to elderly people. These services are extended in the form of Friendly Visiting Groups, Golden Age Clubs, and the construction and maintenance of retirement homes. In addition, many local congregations and parishes provide valuable support to local service agencies. Jewish Family Services is a good example of a national organization that specializes in providing services to the elderly at the local level. (Hammond, 1969; Moberg, 1965)

Political participation is another important way for older citizens to become integrated into the community as a whole. Seniors are an important constituency for party politics. Older citizens have more definite political positions than younger people do and they tend to take action on those political positions both in terms of lobbying and in terms of voting. They are important allies, therefore, for they work for the candidates or the issues of their choice and they are less likely to cross party lines in voting. (Glenn, 1969; Glenn and Grimes, 1968) The National Council of Senior Citizens and the American Association for Retired Persons have effective lobbies in Washington and assume a major role in the decisions of Congress on Medicare and Medicaid. The block voting potential of the aged, now about 15 per cent of the voting population, has not, until now, been successfully developed, however. First, there is little consciousness of the aged as a social group. Second, the aged are dispersed both geographically and socially so that it is difficult to develop a voting block. Third, because of their tendency to vote along party lines, it is difficult to persuade them to cross those party lines in support of particular issues, whether or not they are related to problems of aging. Recently, the Gray Panthers have emerged to address these problems of developing consensus on political issues among the aged.

Despite the importance of social participation and voluntary organizations, after the early retirement years, 65 to 69, older men and women become gradually less socially active. Health problems, transportation problems, and financial insecurity keep them from maintaining their activity levels, as well as intervening in the maintenance of friendship networks. Without effective community intervention, the aged become socially isolated. As a consequence of this isolation they are, indeed, the "put-out generation."

THE AGING PROCESSES

Aging is a process, not a life stage. It is the process of passing through life cycle stages; as with cell replacement aging involves the creation of the new and the death of the old. Aging involves physiological, psychological, and sociological development. The essence of the process is the same for those over 65 as it is for those under 65 years of age. The rates of change, however, are different. In general, aging in these later years of life involves a slowing down of biological and sociological functioning.

Physiological Aspects of Aging

Senescence, biological aging, involves a slowing down of body functions so that there is a decline in the viability of the human organism, increased vulnerability to disease, and slower recuperation from illness. The consequences of senescence are familiar, for they are the ways in which old age is defined. The change of hair color, the loss of hair (particularly among men), the wrinkling and roughening of the skin, the appearance of pigment plaques, the slowing of the gait brought about by the stiffening of joints and the loss of muscular strength and coordination, the decrease in height, the appearance of a stooped posture, the loss of hearing and vision—particularly night vision—problems with short-term memory recall—these and other symptoms of the slowing down of the sensory, nervous, circulatory, respiratory, and digestive systems form our stereotype of the aged. These characteristics of senescence can be observed and hence are associated with the aging process after middle life. They have become the expectations of old age and help to define the image that we hold of people in those later years. What often is not understood is that these processes do not occur at uniform rates. For example, gray hair does not indicate the reduced

7-3 CHECKING IT OUT: Kidney Blood Plasma Flow by Age

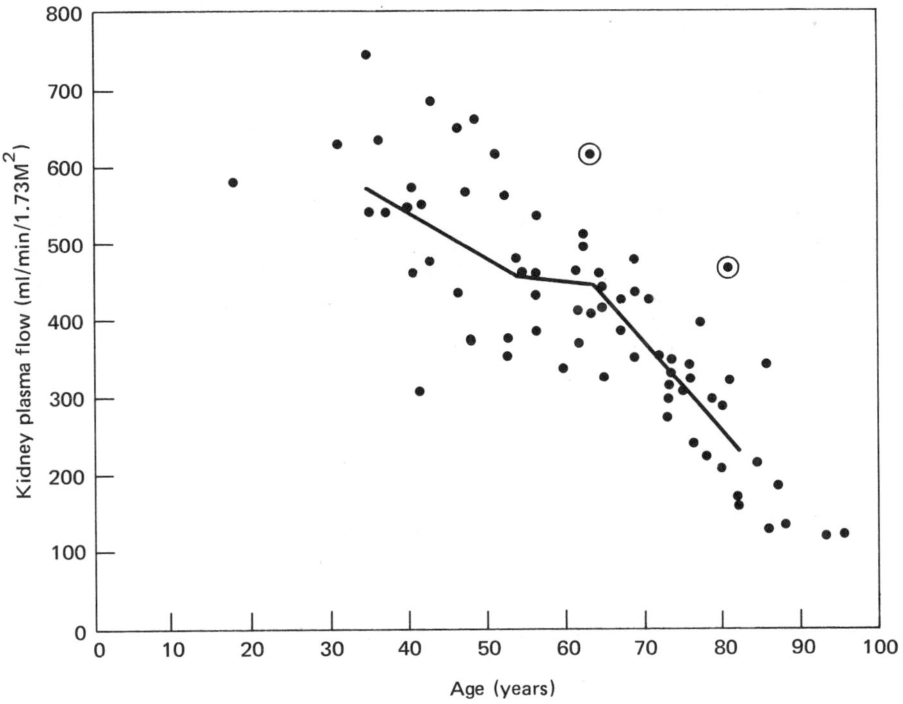

SOURCE: Nathan W. Shock, "The Physiology of Aging," *Lets Learn About Aging*, eds. John R. Barry and C. Ray Wingrove (Cambridge, Mass.: Schenkman Publishing Company, 1977), p. 65.

elasticity, or "hardening," of the arteries; loss of hearing does not indicate the loss of short-term memory. Changes in physiological and psychological functions proceed at quite different rates, so that it is impossible to predict one type of aging by the presence of another. In addition, there is great variation in the rates of change in relation to individual chronological age. Persons with gray hair at age 35 are termed "prematurely" gray. Nevertheless, those 35-year-old individuals exhibit a characteristic which is associated with old age. Box 7-3 shows the individual variability in blood plasma flow through the kidneys of 70 men ranging in age from 19 to 92. The solid line indicates the average kidney plasma flow for men at various ages. Here we can see that as age increases there is, on the average, a slowing down of kidney functioning. At the same time, note the observations which are circled. One man, approximately 63 years of age, had a kidney plasma flow higher than 12 men under the age of 50. Likewise, an 81-year-old man's flow exceeded that of 10 men under the age of 60. (Shock, 1962)

Psychological Aspects of Aging

In general, we know more about physiological aging than we do about psychological aging, and our attitudes toward it are more positive. Negative myths about changes in intelligence and personality are abundant. Because most of the earlier research in gerontology was cross-sectional (that is, comparisons of people of different ages at one point in time) and because so much of this research was carried out in a psychologist's laboratory or in institutions (e.g., nursing homes, where subjects were readily available), there are some misconceptions about these psychological factors and the aging process. Intelligence tests, whatever their strengths or limitations, have shown that learning ability increases to the age of 22 years, stabilizes, and then slowly, but steadily, declines until the years of retirement. More recent research indicates that this is a generational effect rather than an aging effect. This means that our educational systems have changed over the last 50 to 60 years so that the learning patterns themselves are quite different at the present time than the patterns of learning under which our aged population went to school. For example, current educational practices emphasize understanding and conceptualization, while educational systems in the first quarter of the twentieth century emphasized memorization. Recent empirical studies in learning behavior indicate little or no evidence of decline in the ability to learn except in the period just before death. This decline in learning ability, the terminal drop which precedes death, may be more a matter of motivation than actual inability to learn. One panel study examined the cognitive functioning of 301 subjects ranging from 21 to 70 years over a seven-year period. Intelligence encompassing verbal comprehension, numerical skills, and inductive reasoning showed a systematical increase even for people over 70. Cognitive flexibility—the ability to shift among the different types of thinking—and visualization—the ability to organize and process visual materials—were relatively stable over time. Only in the case of physiomotor flexibility—the ability to shift from familiar to unfamiliar tasks which require coordination of visual and motor abilities—was there any clear evidence of decline. (Baltes and Schaie, 1974)

The second misconception about the psychological aging process has to do with personality change. There is little evidence to support the myth that aging brings rigidity and irritability. Recent studies indicate that the individual personality structure persists throughout the individual's lifetime. Despite the fact that the aging process brings with it declining levels of participation in social activities, and despite the fact that some members of the aged category suffer isolation, the basic personality structure tends to persist until death.

Barring the onset of chronic brain disease, even with the changes in biological functioning, the individual in the later years of life is the same individual he was in the earlier years of life. It is, no doubt, in this sense that the old man responded to the guide, "I still am." Alex Comfort describes this persistence of personhood.

> Aging has no effect upon you as a person. When you are "old" you will feel no different and be no different from what you are now or were when you were young, except that more experiences will have happened. In age your appearance will change, however, and you may encounter more physical problems. When you do, these will affect you only as physical problems affect a person of any age. An "aged" person is simply a person who has been there longer than a younger person. (Comfort, 1976, p. 28)

Sociological Aspects of Aging

The third set of changes associated with the aging process is sociological. Both the types and rate of change depend upon the cultural milieu in which the aging occurs. In simple preindustrial society aging meant wisdom, and the people in the later years of life incurred the prestige and deference accorded the most knowledgeable members of the society. In modern industrial societies the pattern of change is quite different. In these societies, as in the United States, for example, occupation is the key to status. Because work and production are so central in the value systems of industrial societies, the occupational or work status is important to the individual's assessment of his own self-worth as well. Despite the emphasis of industrial societies on work and production, or perhaps because of it, a new concept of work cessation emerged in the twentieth century. The retirement concept defined the right of workers to stop work and enter a period of leisure in which some degree of financial security would be provided. The financial security is accommodated by pensions and/or social security.

The loss of the work role is associated with many other sociological changes in the aging process. We know that retirement brings with it a changing level of social participation. Because both formal and informal associations center on

7-4 CHECKING IT OUT: Aging in Simple Agrarian Societies

During a visit to the village of Tamish in the Soviet Republic of Abkhasia, a social scientist raised her glass of wine to toast a new friend who looked no older than 70, "May you live as long as Moses." To her disappointment, the man did not seem happy with her intended good wishes. Later she discovered that he was 119 years old. Moses died at age 120.

And he was not the exception! In the villages of this area approximately 15 per cent of the population were over 80 years of age. Among people over 70, "Most work regularly. They are still blessed with good eyesight, and most have their own teeth. Their posture is unusually erect, even into advanced age; many take walks of more than two miles a day and swim in mountain streams. They look healthy, and are a handsome people." (Benet, 1971, pp. 214–215)

The Abkhasians' agricultural community depended upon tea, tobacco, and vegetables from their collective farms in the valleys of the Caucasus Mountains. This area has been a land bridge traveled by migrants from both the West and the East. Genetic isolation, then, could not account for the extraordinary longevity.

Similar in terms of the agriculturally based economy, but different in terms of geographic isolation are two other pockets of long living peoples—the village of Vilcabamba in Ecuador, and the principality of Hunza in West Pakistan. In Vilcabamba, 16 per cent of the population were over 60 years, and 1 per cent were over 100 years. Here tobacco and sugar cane are the main crops, but primitive farming methods keep the people at a bare subsistence level. (Leaf, 1973)

A system of irrigation canals to bring water from the high surrounding glaciers of the Karakorum Mountains supports the crops of the arid valley of the Hunza. Despite low agricultural production, inhibited by rudimentary farming methods, and the consequent winter deprivation suffered by the people here, a remarkable number of Hunzakuts are known to be over 70.

What are the common dimensions of these communities which could account for the unusual number of the aged? First, vigorous physical activity is a continuing pattern throughout all ages of life. Second, a meaningful work role is maintained so that each individual knows that she or he has a necessary role until death. "Kelkiliana Khesa, a woman of 109 in the village of Otapi, was paid for 49 workdays (a collective's workday is eight hours) during one summer; Bozba Pash, a man of 94 on the same collective, worked 155 days one year. Minosyan Grigorii of Aragich, often held up as an example to the young, worked 230 days in a year at the age of 90."(Benet, 1971, p. 220) Finally, prestige increases as aging procedes. Among the Abkhasians there is no word for old age. Those over 100 years are referred to as "long living people." Aging brings respect and esteem.

the work role of the household head, the frequency of being with friends and associates declines after the worker has retired. Some old people replace lost work-related associates and friends by actively participating in retirement associations such as RSVP (Retired Seniors Volunteer Program) or AARP

(American Association for Retired Persons). Others focus more on neighborhood and family associations. But there are many who find it difficult to replace these work associations and resort to the seclusion of their own homes. The sociological consequences of aging lead to the participation discussed in greater detail in earlier sections of this chapter.

Aging, then, is a process of interrelated changes in physiological, psychological, and sociological realms which develops over the course of the lifetime. These developmental processes vary so much by chronological age that one can predict neither the rate nor the degree of change for any particular individual for any particular age. Likewise, the rates of change for one physiological function vary considerably from the rates of change in another, as we have seen. And similarly there is little relationship between the rates of change across physiological, psychological, and sociological aging. The degree of loss in physical mobility due to degenerative disease does not accurately predict the rate of withdrawal in the sociological realm. Here, we need only witness the political participation of two of our presidents, Franklin Roosevelt, and Dwight Eisenhower, despite the handicaps of cardiovascular disease after the age of 60. Unfortunately then, even though chronological age is society's primary criterion of old age, it tells us little about the stages of development which any particular individual experiences in the aging process. However, because this ascribed characteristic is the primary definition of age, those over 65 are considered to be a societal category. Often the members of this category are treated as if they comprised a social group with distinctive characteristics and social expectations. We call this attitude agism; it imputes social characteristics or expectations to an individual because of his ascribed age status. Agism involves faulty discrimination because it confuses social behavior with a biological characteristic.

THE PROCESS OF RETIREMENT

Considering the long course of the history of man on this planet, retirement is a very recent sociological invention. Cessation of the work role was the privilege of only a small elite who seldom faced the problems of survival to which the masses of human beings addressed most of their waking hours. The emergence of retirement for the worker in the United States in the 1940s was the consequence of several long-term changes. Industrialization brought radical changes in the occupation structure. Large segments of the labor force moved from agricultural and self-employed work to the assembly lines and offices of the great manufacturing centers of urban areas. Higher standards of living and the public health movement of the twentieth century extended the longevity of both men and women so that the probability of surviving to the retirement years was greatly increased. So rapidly have these changes occurred during the lifetime of the current retired generation that few people anticipated either the bonus of leisure years added to their lives or the economic and sociological problems they would meet in making the adjustment to retirement.

Retirement is the exchange of the work role for the leisure role. In the United States we consider retirement both a right and an obligation. The right to retire is assured by the qualifying age accompanying most pension plans and the more comprehensive Social Security Insurance system. The obligation to retire is assured by the mandatory retirement provisions in most jobs. Industry has defended mandatory retirement rules in terms of the rapidly changing technology. The myth that the older worker has difficulty adjusting to changes in work pattern justifies his replacement by the younger, more flexible recruit.

Advocates of compulsory retirement state that such a policy is simple and easy to administer. When there is a clear-cut rule that at a certain age a worker will step down, the employer avoids complicated testing and having to decide whether or not the employee is still qualified for the job. Furthermore, such a policy prevents capricious and disriminatory decisions about individual workers. When retirement rules are clear they provide a predictable structure both for the employee and the employer. They permit the worker to plan ahead for the kinds of activities he will enjoy so that he can enter the retirement years with purpose and anticipation. They also permit the employer to schedule the time when the employee must be replaced and, therefore, facilitate the recruitment of the best replacement. The proponents of this position argue that not only is compulsory retirement good for both the employer and the employee, but that it is necessary in order to open positions so that the young worker can enter the labor market. Because of seniority and tenure provisions (unless the older workers, most of whom the proponents of compulsory retirement believe wish to and can afford to retire, step aside) there is little opportunity for the younger, more flexible worker to compete for jobs. At the same time those who either wish to or need to continue working can find other jobs.

Resistance to compulsory retirement began to crystallize in the mid-1970s. The case for flexible retirement holds that all citizens have the right to work, and that qualifications and performance are the only criteria that should determine both hiring and firing. Any age cut-off for compulsory retirement is discriminatory to those of that age and older. Employers maintain performance standards with which to measure the productivity of workers, whatever their age. To avoid applying these standards to a worker of 65, or even 70, may be to guard against discriminating against that individual, but it discriminates against all older workers. Furthermore, critics of the compulsory rule hold that any adequate time for notice of work termination provides sufficient time for replacement of the worker. The employee should begin to plan for retirement activities during the middle years; a specific retirement age has little relevance to the success of this process. Proponents of flexible retirement maintain that older workers perform as well as younger workers. The myth of declining production has not been supported by studies that compare the performance of older with younger workers under actual working conditions. (Riley and Foner, 1968) To the argument that the older worker must retire to make room for the younger worker, they answer that there are other solutions, such as a shortened work week, longer and more frequent vacations, and the delayed entry of youth into the labor force, which will serve to provide equal or better opportunities to the new worker. While mandatory retirement may have been conceived to save face for the older worker who can no longer perform at required levels of production, it protects a small minority at the expense of the majority. Workers are well aware of their inability to measure up to their employers' expectations. Usually they are "cooled out" by informal pressures before notice of job termination is given. Furthermore, older workers who are unemployed are less able to find a job. The long-term unemployment rate for men over 65 years is more than twice as high as that for men 20–34 years. Age differences in educational level do not account for this unemployment differential. All in all, compulsory retirement discriminates against the many in order to protect the few.

Whether involuntary or voluntary, retirement is withdrawal from the work role; from a societal viewpoint this means withdrawal from productive roles. When work is a central value to the society, withdrawal from productive roles means the loss of the rewards—prestige and income—associated with occupational status. Some critics of the United States hold that our undue emphasis on work and production provides no social status for the retired. While this may be an overstatement of the consequences of the centrality of the work ethic, it does suggest the basis of the problem that some of the aged experience in making the transition from the prestige of the job to the esteem of continuing growth and development in the new leisure world. For those unable to find a continuing basis for high self-esteem, withdrawal from other nonwork roles often accompanies retirement from the work role.

For some people, retirement is a long-awaited emancipation from a hard, and/or boring job. For others, such as the person who retires after 30 years of military service or the retired federal government employee, it is an opportunity for a second career. For many, it provides a long-awaited time to pursue a favorite avocation—hobby, travel. But for others, it is the loss of everything that is meaningful. Alex Comfort states that there are only two types of people who enjoy retirement, those who were too lazy to work anyway, and those who have an unsatiated appetite for avocations which they did not have time to pursue during the working years. (Comfort, 1976)

In fact, most people spend their retired years in the same activities with which they were involved in their younger years. James Manney cites several reasons why retired people seldom use their new leisure freedom to explore new opportunities.

> One may be the lack of well-defined social expectations for retired people. In the absence of social roles, many people probably do not know where to turn when they

> are confronted with a totally free choice of how to spend their lives. Poor health, lack of energy, and limited mobility curtail the options for many retired people, as do insufficient income for food, clothing, bus fares, and membership fees. Finally, a simple desire to disengage from roles, activities, and responsibilities is operative in many old people. (Manney, 1975, p. 59).

The retirement process, then, appears to be highly individual. The only common societal expectation is withdrawal from the work role. The extent of withdrawal from other social roles appears to be related to the lifestyle pattern enacted in earlier years.

THEORIES OF AGING

Up to this point, the discussion of the aged has centered on characteristics of those who have survived to old age and the elements of various aging processes. Explaining why these processes proceed as age increases is more complicated.

Traditional explanations of aging emphasized observed physiological changes. The ancient Greek and Roman believed that aging was caused by the gradual loss of body heat, which was considered the necessary condition of life. In the second century, Galen theorized that the loss of body heat during the aging process was due to the evaporation of humours. (Pythagoras called the body humours blood, phlegm, choler, and black choler.) To offset aging, then, the body must be kept warm and moist. Therefore, hot baths, hot oil, daily wine, and continued activity were prescribed. This theory of aging as a condition between health and illness persisted well into the seventeenth century. At this time the humours theory was translated into the iatrophysicists' notions that the human body was like a machine. Aging was the "wearing out of (body) parts."

Not until the mid-nineteenth century did medicine give specific attention to the older generations. Even then, the main concern was the search for single-cause explanations. Geriatrics as a medical specialization emerged shortly before World War I. Aging continued to be viewed as a medical pathology, however.

About this same time, Frederick Verzà launched gerontology as the science that seeks the explanation of the aging process. Verzà rejected the notion of aging as an illness, a pathology, and conceived it to be continuing life, in which adaptation proceeded at rates slower than those characteristic of younger years. Social gerontology, which focuses on sociological aging, was a well-established specialty by the end of World War II. Three major theories of aging have emerged since that time.

Activity Theory

The first, activity theory, explains sociological aging as a decline in the number and frequency of social activities. Because in their older years people have the same social and psychological needs as in their younger years, they must overcome the obstacles of the aging process to stay "in the swing" of activities in order to stay young. The obstacles to continuing activity for older people stem from the loss of friends and relatives due to death, from the decline in financial resources to pay the costs of such activities, and from decline in physical mobility due to the onset of degenerative disease.

While activity theory has had wide acceptance, it has also had its critics. Two basic assumptions have been questioned. The theory assumes that activity, *per se*, is better than inactivity for everyone at any age of life. In addition, the admonition to maintain earlier activity levels assumes that old age is "bad" and that middle age is "good." The theory explains less about how the aging process occurs and more about how to resist the consequences of the process.

Disengagement Theory

The disengagement theory addressed some of the criticisms of activity theory. In this view, aging is the process of disengaging from social roles and activities incumbent to those roles. This disengagement is functional for the society because it permits the young to replace the old on a gradual basis rather than at the crisis of the death of the old. Likewise, it is functional for the aged person, because it provides that gradual transition to the time of death—the final disengagement from life itself. Successful aging, then, involves gradually disengaging from social roles and the constraints involved with the rights and privileges of other members of the society to enhance the freedom to focus on concern with self and the preparation for death. It involves accepting old age as a life stage beneficial to the individual as well as to the society.

Critics of this position suggest that this explanation of aging may have more validity for the historical past than for the present and the probable future. With the continued vigor and good health of the current generation of the aged, it is doubtful that their disengagement is indeed beneficial to society. There are alternative mechanisms to provide opportunities for the engagement of the young. The wisdom, dependability, and perspective of older people are as important to society as the innovation and creativity of the young. Furthermore, as public support systems are expanded to help older citizens meet the obstacles to continuing interaction in social activities, they continue to engage in the social roles they held in earlier years. Passive acceptance of the aging years as preparation for death has little to offer those who continue in society's mainstream of daily activity.

Development Theory

The third approach to aging synthesizes the best aspects of the two earlier theories but is less encumbered with value judgments. Continuity or development theory views aging as an on-going process of living rather than a declining stage before dying. Studies of older people indicate that neither activity nor disengagement from social roles assures life satisfaction. Conversely, neither low activity nor high social engagement levels were necessarily associated with low life satisfaction. Adjustment to, and satisfaction with, the later years characterized those who continued to live these years as they had lived their younger years. While it is true that older persons were more concerned with the inner self and less sensitive to their social environment, this introspective interest begins with some persons as early as the mid-forties.

Aging, then, is simply a continuing process of development for each individual. The physiological changes—developments—of older persons present new challenges to meeting their basic needs. The slowing down of biological processes and the decreasing flexibility of body tissue call for changes in life-style. Sociological aging involves changes in the ways in which basic needs are met. These changes may mean devoting more time to meeting those persons' basic needs and, hence, less time to social activities. On the other hand, the changes may mean changing the character of social activities by shifting the content of the roles of other persons involved in those activities. Such a shift can be seen in the reversal of the decision-making aspect of the parent-child relationship as the parent ages. When the adult child makes decisions for the aging parent, it is less a matter of the parent's disengaging from the parental role, and more a matter of the child's assuming the decision-making dimension which was formerly part of the parental role. A similar shift in role content occurs when the expressive role of friendship is exchanged for an instrumental role when a friend asks for help from another in meeting a problem.

When aging is viewed as a developmental process in which the patterns of living are a continuation of former patterns of living, the social scientist is free to study the types of changes that occur during aging development without having to decide whether the changes are good or bad, or whether they lead to happiness or unhappiness. These patterns of change that typify the aging years are discussed in the following sections.

DEVELOPMENTAL AGING

If aging is in fact a set of developmental processes, what changes can be expected in the years after retirement?

First, physiological aging calls for changes in the types and scope of physical activities which can be managed well. Vigorous daily exercise is replaced by less vigorous activities—jogging is exchanged for walking. Hard physical work is delegated to others who are younger and stronger. Heavy yard work and seasonal house cleaning, for example, is hired out. When it is no longer financially feasible to hire others to maintain a large dwelling unit, a decision to move to a smaller unit, which minimizes residential maintenance costs, may be called for. As the flexibility of the body declines, a new timetable for daily chores may be necessary. Allowing sufficient time to carry out with ease the activities planned for a day assures more satisfaction in accomplishing the tasks at hand.

Making the changes engendered by physiological aging from a developmental viewpoint makes changes in attitudes important as well. One such change for many is the transition in the evaluation of instrumental as compared to expressive goals. This means relinquishing the emphasis on how much is accomplished during a day (a value highly associated with "success" in U. S. society) and replacing that with an increasing emphasis on enjoyment of the work process itself. Such a change in goal orientation is accomplished only when new criteria for self-evaluation are established. One of the freedoms found in relinquishing the formal work role is the opportunity to appreciate oneself in intrinsic terms of who one is, rather than in extrinsic terms of what one can do.

Finally, because retirement from the labor force usually is associated with a radical cut in income, changes in the standard of living must be effected. This often necessitates moving to a smaller dwelling unit; replacing luxury, prepared menus with simpler, less expensive, do-it-yourself meals; and exchanging costly social club memberships for craft and hobby groups.

In general, then, developmental aging involves continuing life patterns and developing new goals and attitudes which compensate for the changes in what the individual does for himself. As physiological aging progresses, new challenges in terms of subscribing external support systems arise. This usually means a willingness to ask and to receive help from persons and organizations outside the family unit. The degree of success in acquiring such services, however, depends to no small degree on how accessible they are in the community in which the person resides. James Manney describes the changing levels of need for social service in four life cycle stages. (Manney, 1975)

Four Stages In the Aging Process

The later period of adulthood, from 50 to 65, is the time of reorientation. This has been called the "empty-nest" stage for this is the time when children have been launched on their own "flight." Usually the worker has reached the height of his or her occupational career and the work role stabilizes. Often it is the time when health problems emerge. All in all, it is the period of closure for the family and of new opportunities for planning the upcoming changes associated with aging. Education and counseling services are needed in this stage. Both worker and spouse need to know what opportunities and problems lie ahead of them. Retirement education can provide that information. In addition, they need counseling to help them plan wise investments and role transitions in order to assure financial security and continuing social participation appropriate to their particular needs.

The first decade of the aged period, 65 to 75, brings retirement and a radical cut in income. This may also be the time when a spouse is lost through death. Most certainly some friends will be lost through death or migration. Health problems persist and may become chronic. Unfortunately, because of continuing inflation—particularly in the cost of medical services—even the aged who have planned for these years, find they need supplemental income. This is the stage of social intervention when income maintenance programs such as Social Security, health care programs such as Medicare and Medicaid, are needed to augment the resources which the aged have available to them.

The third stage, 75 to 85, brings further challenges to the financial and health status of the aged. Chronic disease limits mobility so that independent living patterns are more difficult to sustain. Now the aged often require support systems at home in order to maintain their daily living. In an effort to keep the aged in their own houses, social agencies have developed friendly visitor, homemaking, and home nursing services.

In fact, however, only a small minority of aged have access to such personal intervention services. Those who move into well-planned retirement communities find these services readily available. But such communities are expensive. Most demand sizable investments to enter, as well as monthly payments which exceed even the highest Social Security retirement benefit. The large majority of old people lack financial resources to qualify for residence in such a community.

Among the aged with low and moderate incomes, access to personal intervention service depends upon the level of social services available in their local community, and their knowledge of such services. The Older Americans Act of 1965 established high priority for the provision of support services in order to maintain the aged in their own homes as long as possible. As a result of this legislation, state and local agencies were established to develop and integrate services to the aged. By 1975, most local communities had an office of this type. However, even in communities with highly developed social service networks, limited staff and budget preclude service to all of the elderly who need it. In addition, service is often impeded by resistance from the aged themselves. Ignorance of how to use the service system and fear of "welfare" dependency negate the efforts of the most skillful social worker.

The final stage of developmental aging calls for personal maintenance services. For those aged who are able to obtain personal intervention services when needed, this stage typically emerges during the mid-eighties. Those who lack social support services in their own homes may be forced to accept institutional care at an earlier age, however. This is the period in which the aged depend upon others to provide the needs of daily living. Some receive personal care from their spouse, family, or friends. The large majority, however, have no alternative to institutional care.

Old age institutions that provide personal care include foster homes, boarding homes, retirement centers, rest homes, nursing homes, and mental hospitals. Personal maintenance varies from minimal custodial care to complex medical care. About 5 per cent of the aged reside in old age institutions. However, in terms of life histories, the probability of entering such an institution is about one in five. Once admitted, few residents leave to return to their own homes and normal living. (Manard and Kart, 1976)

Institutional living is the last-resort choice for most elderly people as well as for their families. It has been said that these institutions are programmed for death. The negative evaluations stem from the poor quality of medical care and from the general absence of nonmedical care. Because licensing regulations focus on safety and the level of medical care provided, the goals of these institutions center on the adequacy of the physical plant and the numbers of medical personnel available. Modern medical practice is dedicated to saving lives. Medicine's greatest contributions have been to treat and to cure acute diseases. Much less progess has been made in treating chronic diseases. Hence, the rehabilitation and adaptation of the patient suffering from chronic disease receive less attention in the medically oriented setting. Because most of these institutions depend on Medicare and Medicaid funds, and, therefore, must conform to their medical standards, they tend to be medically oriented settings. As currently conceived and supported, old age institutions will probably continue to be dedicated to preventing death rather than to fostering meaningful living.

Developmental aging means growing into stages which progressively require supporting services from the larger community. Moving from the role reorientation stage in the preretirement years, through the stages in which social intervention, personal intervention, and, finally, personal maintenance are needed, means changing from relative independence to almost total dependence on the services of others. From this viewpoint, successful aging involves planning, changing attitudes and habits, along with adequate community social services.

INTERPRETIVE SUMMARY

The aged people of our society comprise a significant segment of our population. This segment will continue to increase in number over the coming decades. The aged are a heterogeneous category. In sociological terms they are as varied as the younger members of our society. To treat an aged individual in terms of the aggregate characteristics of that category is "agism."

Retirement changes older people's access to economic and social rewards. Withdrawal from the labor force means a sharp cut in income and lowered social participation levels. For many, this means a loss of self-identity. For many, this means the identification of a "has-been." For many, this means social isolation.

Aging is defined in terms of interrelated physiological, psychological, and sociological processes, which bring change at differing rates. From a developmental viewpoint, aging involves changes in the types of activities undertaken, as well as changes in time orientation, achievement attitudes and goal orientations, and acquisition of social support services. Effecting these changes depends on the ability and willingness of the individual to plan for and go through the aging process. More important, successful aging depends upon society's willingness to provide the social services necessary for the needs of role reorientation, social intervention, and personal intervention and maintenance which characterize later life stages. At the present time, social institutions lack adequate means to facilitate education and planning for retirement. Existing social agencies cannot provide adequate levels of service to meet the needs for social and personal intervention in order to maintain the aged in their own homes and neighborhoods. Finally, as currently constituted, old age institutions lack facilities and funds to provide good living environments for those who need personal care.

QUESTIONS

1. The Gray Panthers maintain that the images of the elderly in mass media perpetuate stereotypes of aging. Discuss the caricatures of the elderly in fiction, magazines, and on TV. How do these images foster agism?
2. Compare activity, disengagement, and developmental theories of aging in terms of their relevance for upper, middle, and lower income elderly.
3. Clearly preretirement education is important in planning the changes to be made in life style after age 65. Who should be responsible for providing that education—industry, governmental agencies, or both?
4. Chronological age is a poor predictor of the various aging processes. With this in mind, discuss the pros and cons of mandatory retirement.

Part II

Social Organization

Social Groups
Bureaucracy and Large-Scale Organization
The Sociology of Health
Social Stratification
Racial and Ethnic Minorities
Population and Society
Ecology and Urbanization
Economy and Society

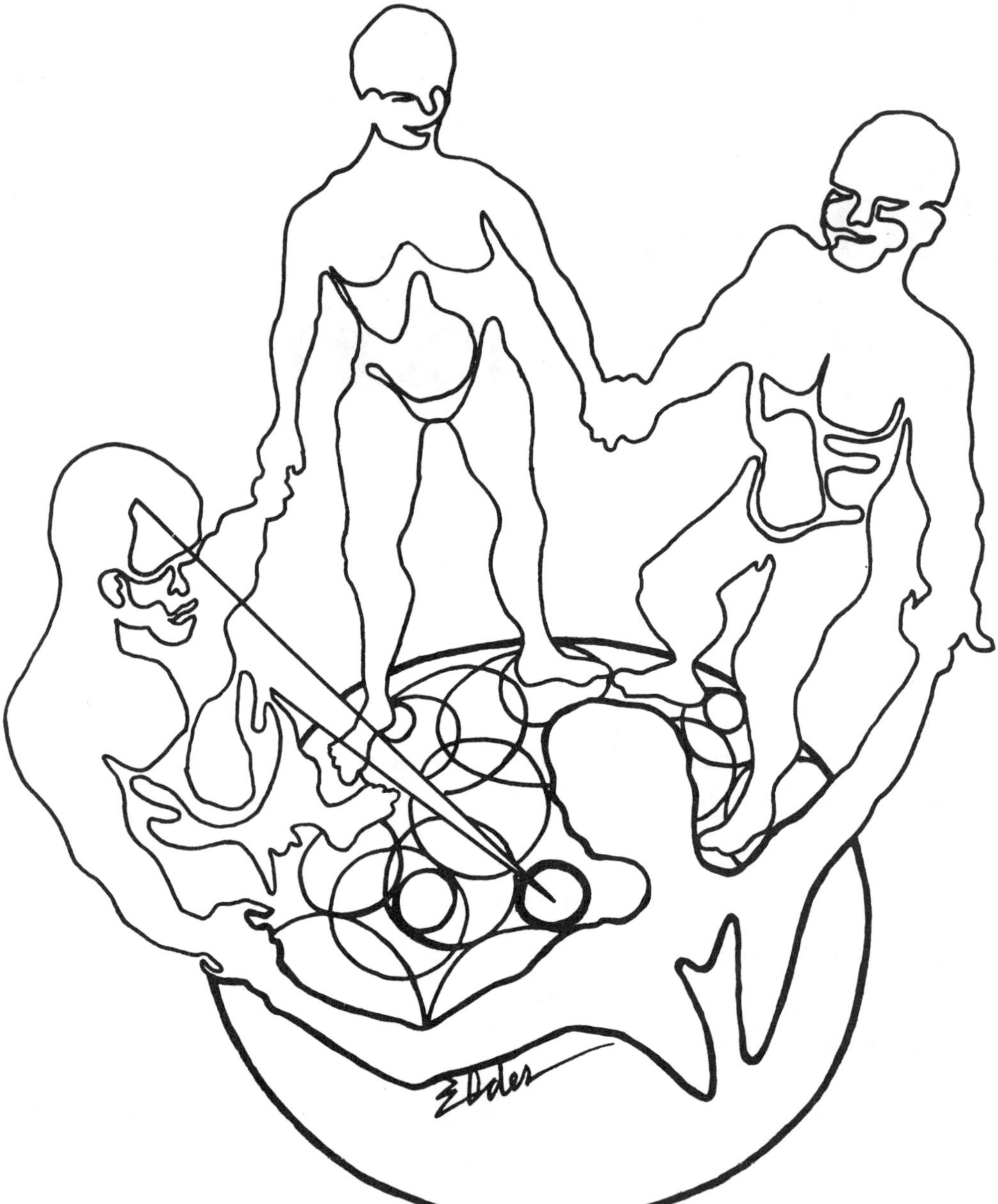

8

Social Groups

Each of us is a member of many groups. With parents and brothers and sisters we make up one kind of a group, a family. Many of us are tied also to a wider kinship group of aunts, uncles, and cousins. Most young people belong to school groups; many belong to social, athletic, and other special-interest groups. More than half the people in the United States belong to church groups; many are affiliated with lodges; others are members of occupational organizations. In addition to such regularized associations, we interact from time to time as members of shopping crowds, concert audiences, or other temporary collectivities. Whenever a collectivity of people interact, whether in the intimacy of a family discussion or in the roar of a bargain sale, they constitute a group. If we attempted to list all of the specific groups in American society the list would be virtually inexhaustible.

In the effort to fully understand the form and content of social groups and to chart their similarities and differences, sociologists have concentrated their study on a multitude of group characteristics. Among the more important characteristics of social groups are (1) the size of the group, (2) the degree of "consciousness of kind," (3) the patterns of interaction among the members, (4) the permanence of membership in the group, (5) the permanence of the group, (6) the nature and specificity of group goals, (7) the basis of membership, (8) the formality of the organization of the group, (9) the degree and intensity of involvement of members, (10) the social similarity of the members, (11) the form of social control within the group, and (12) the extent to which the group is dependent upon or independent of other groups.

CHARACTERISTICS OF SOCIAL GROUPS

Structure and Interaction

Human life is social life. Social life becomes organized when there are established ways of interacting. We indicate these ways of interacting by such relational terms as status and role. When there is persistent interaction among the same people, there emerge social collectivities, both large and small, which we call groups. Analytically, a group is not the same as a social structure. Groups exist through the coming together of a number of identifiable people who build and develop their social relations over time into a relatively stable pattern—a social structure—and who identify to some extent with the others with whom they share this particular social structure (i.e., pattern of social interaction). Thus, groups have a social structure. A **social group** is defined as a plurality of people "involved in a pattern of social interaction, conscious of sharing common membership, of sharing some common understanding, and of accepting some rights and obligations that accrue only to members." (McKee, 1969, p. 124)

This definition makes it clear that not every classification of people is a social group. Sociologists make a sharp distinction between social groups and **social categories**. A social category is a classification of persons who share a common characteristic but who have no social interaction, no common understanding of membership, and no consciousness of kind. Examples of social categories are all seven-year-old girls, all right-handed people, all owners of a new automobile, all bald-headed men, all high-school graduates, all people born on November 10, and all widowed people. Obviously, persons who share a common characteristic have the potential of becoming a social group.

Consciousness of Kind

Membership in a group relates people to one another in a way that is different from how they are related to others not in the group. Common membership subjects them to the expectations governing action in the group—its social norms—and to the culture that emerges from the interactions shared among the members. Members of a group, then, share a common set of cultural understandings about the meaning of membership in the group that emerges from their consensus about the purpose of the group—its functions and objectives.

This sharing of membership in a group, and sharing of its common experiences, develops a sense of group unity that is important for the effectiveness of the group's collective activities. Franklin Henry Giddings, one of the first American sociologists, spoke of "consciousness of kind" to designate this sense of unity that common membership and common experience brings. (Giddings, 1896) The intensity of the consciousness of kind varies from group to group, however. Many large groups suffer an attenuated sense of belonging for their members place only limited value on membership and the heterogeneity of members tends to reduce consciousness of kind. Also, the members of one group have membership in other groups, so that no one group may claim a total loyalty or a full commitment from the individual. Limited though it may be, however, membership in a group does bring some degree of consciousness of kind and some recognition of sharing with others the obligations that participation in a group requires. Without some consensus among its members as to its norms and its expectations of behavior—its definitions of its roles—there cannot be a group. Thus, a group is not merely a system of interaction; it also involves a sharing of membership among those who interact in this way.

People in social groups are not only conscious of belonging together in common memberships, but they also possess some mechanism to determine who belongs and who does not. In formally organized groups, membership qualifications may be spelled out and who belongs may be formally recognized by such means as membership rosters, membership insignia, and access to privileges that go with membership. Even in groups that are not formally organized, the recognition of who belongs and who does not is crucial to the group's sense of its own existence. In small and informal groups, the conferring of recognition upon a person as belonging and another as an outsider may be carried out by forms of address and by obvious ways of inclusion and exclusion in the activities of the group. No human group has any particular difficulty in making an individual feel that he or she is not wanted, that he or she is not "one of the group."

The Effects of Group Size

It has been observed that we are all members of many different groups. Some groups, like families, are small and offer opportunities for intense emotional experiences. Other groups, like unions or lodges, are much larger, and our participation in them is much less demanding emotionally. It is clear that the size of a group, a structural characteristic, may dramatically affect the kind of interaction we experience in it.

The smallest group possible consists of two people and is called a **dyad**. Relating to the other person within a dyad places a special responsibility on each member. After all, the group no longer exists if one person withdraws, so that continuity of the dyad calls forth some effort from both members. And because there are no other members to depend upon, the member of a dyad is less able to abstain from decision-making. This inability to submerge oneself within the group and avoid participation affects the quality of interaction. George Simmel, a German sociologist who examined social forms and the processes occurring within them, concluded that dyadic size causes group members to expose more of their personalities than in large groups. Therefore, the dyad offers the possibility of emotional response, either positive and affectionate, or hostile and full of conflict. This constant need to participate if the group is to survive causes the dyad to provide a group experience that can be unique in its intensity and its intimacy. (Simmel, 1950)

With the introduction of another person, the dyad becomes a **triad**. This new group is less demanding on the emotions of the participants because the group structure is less fragile. If one member of the triad drops out, the group still survives. Also there are interaction possibilities found in triads that are not possible in larger groups, or in dyads. In a group of three, the third person may function as a mediator and help to prevent disruption of the group. Or the third person may actually be instrumental in helping to develop the social group in order to fulfill his or her own purposes. Simmel suggests that in some situations, the third member of a triad may take advantage of the lack of agreement between the other two group members and unite with one or the other to bring about a desired decision or end.

The problem of deadlock is most apparent in the two-person group. This is because there is no source of support in a dyad. Opposition may then create much tension but there must be some control of hostilities if the interaction is to continue. (Hare, 1962)

The most satisfying group size for discussions has been found to be five members. (Bales, 1954: Slater, 1958) Although groups smaller than five would allow more conversation time per person, five-member groups, because of their odd number, have the advantage of making deadlocks impossible. Also if the group of five splits on issues, a majority and a minority is created so that the possibility of isolation on issues is less likely.

Society, the Largest Social Group

The concept of society, like that of the group, has always been a central concept in sociology; sociology is often defined as the study of society. A society is a collectivity of people who share a common culture, live in a definite geographical territory, and consider themselves a social unit. It is the broadest social group to which a people belong and encompasses all the other social groups of which they are members. A society, then, refers to the inclusive networks of social interaction among a culturally defined people that sustain a complex social structure. This social structure provides for the totality of a way of life for that people.

Such a conception of society does not dictate a size requirement. Societies are both large and small. Prior to the emergence and widespread growth of the nation-state, societies were usually smaller entities. In the modern world, however, there is a trend toward large national societies that are politically organized and controlled by a nation-state and that monopolize control over a given territory customarily inhabited by and identified with the people of that society. This transition from small-scale to large-scale forms of social organization is one of the most significant changes in the history of human life.

THE TRANSFORMATION OF SOCIETY

The systematic study of society was spurred by the recognition that human society had been radically altered by the Industrial Revolution. The great Western intellectuals of the nineteenth century realized that the Industrial Revolution involved more than the introduction of a new technology with new and different jobs. It was changing the whole social order: the older forms of social organization were "breaking down;" the social patterns of traditional society were being destroyed; and there was widespread dread of the future of society.

Prior to the Industrial Revolution, people lived in small traditional villages where everyone knew everyone else. The traditional village was more than a geographical site. It was small, personal, familiar, shared, and intergenerational, and allowed for few alternatives in behavior. People knew who they were and they knew their place in the scheme of things. The city, on the other hand, was more impersonal, more rational, nontraditional, new, and not socially intergrated.

The city gradually replaced the traditional and secure village. Although it was not a new social invention, the big city loomed as a new and strange social experience. Being a stranger fast became a common experience as the transition from small-scale to large-scale social organization occurred. The city was regarded as the antithesis of the small, traditional village. People were being "torn from their roots" and the intellectuals of the time described the process as "social disorganization."

The Secular Crisis

During the "secular crisis of the nineteenth century" the world was reshaped. The Industrial Revolution had razed the traditional social fabric and new questions and new assumptions began to occupy the minds of Western intellectuals. Much of their concern was centered on the issues of social solidarity, size (i.e., bigness), and social control. In the transition from the small-scale traditional village to the large-scale diversified city, how can 30,000 strangers move to one restricted place and so coordinate their activities that meaningful social relations will result? How does social solidarity come about? How will people hold themselves together? What unites people? What new social order, if any, will come to exist?

The focal point of concern was the recognition that the Industrial Revolution was a genuine social revolution that totally changed people's lives. There were unanticipated consequences in the alteration of the social world in this transition from an agricultural village society to an industrial society. The urban experience fast became the common denominator with a new and complex division of labor. People became involved in a large pattern of activity for which they had no sense of belonging.

Nowhere was this change more evident than in the change of the character of the family. In the traditional world, work and home life were one and the family was both an economic and social unit. Furthermore, the family was the setting for almost all of the other social functions as well—welfare, recreation, education, religious instruction, and so on. With industrialization the family, as an institution, became separated from most of these functions. Education is now performed almost entirely by schools; recreation is largely handled by commerical enterprises; and welfare is the responsibility of government. The family today is now chiefly charged with fulfilling psychological and emotional needs, and many people say that it is not even performing this function very well.

TYPES OF SOCIAL GROUPS

The challenge to explain and understand the "new kind of society" which was emerging from the apparent dissolution of the older, traditional ways of living has led a number of sociologists to develop a mode of social analysis—a typological analysis—that contrasts the basic characteristics of two radically different social structures. With seemingly endless variety, sociologists have compared and contrasted two ideal-types of societies: (1) that which characterized most of Europe prior to the Industrial Revolution and much of the nonindustrial world today and (2) that typified by the society produced by the Industrial Revolution.

Some of the more prominent of these typologies of society are:

Robert Redfield—folk society and urban society
Howard Becker—sacred society and secular society
Charles Horton Cooley—primary society and secondary society
Robert MacIver—communal society and associational society
Pitirim Sorokin—familistic society and contractual society
Carle Zimmerman—localistic society and cosmopolitan society
Henry Maine—status society and contract society
Ferdinand Töennies—Gemeinschaft society and Gesellschaft society
Emile Durkheim—mechanical society and organic society

Although there are some differences among these typologies, each is primarily concerned with describing and understanding the same social phenomena; each calls attention in different ways and with varying degrees of emphasis to approximately the same social facts. Each is an attempt to analyze the great social transformation wrought largely by the Industrial Revolution. These ideal-types are analytical tools designed to bring into relief the essential features of two polar opposite types of societies.

Primary and Secondary Groups

One of the most commonly used of these typologies is that of primary and secondary groups. The primary group is characterized by intimate face-to-face contacts and direct interaction made possible by common locality. (Cooley, 1909) Social interaction is distinctly personal. Primary groups are the first groups into which the individual is inducted. With few exceptions, the *family* is the first group into which the infant is introduced. In the family the child acquires all his fundamental habits—those of bodily care, speech, morals, obedience, and so forth. He or she learns submission to authority and practices rivalry and cooperation with his or her brothers and sisters. Affections and dislikes are deep within the family. The family is thus *primary* not only in form but also in time, since it is the first group to which the child is exposed and the one in which he or she gets his or her fundamental training.

The *play group* arises out of contact between children of the same family or neighborhood. It is more or less spontaneous in its formation, developing out of new situations not necessarily found in the family. The children in the play group meet other children of like age. Parental authority is often not present. In these associations the child learns to give and take. There may be quarrels and division, but there is also cooperation, teamwork. When the child enters the group, play habits are often influenced by home training. The child's aggressiveness or docility may be habits learned at home. The play group gives the child early training in how to meet his or her peers, how to cooperate and compete, and how to express his or her own self—things not always fully expressed or permitted within the family.

Another primary group is the *neighborhood*, where there is also a direct, face-to-face relationship. Neighborhoods are characterized by such things as borrowing and lending, social control through gossip, and communal recreational activities. Neighborhood gangs, such as the Norton gang in the famous study of *Street Corner Society*, are also primary groups. The gang is based upon friendship that arises out of repeated association and shared interests or experiences. Such groups lack formal organization, rules, charters, or officers; they proceed on informal common agreement. Gang members ordinarily share social activities: attend the movies, play cards, discuss politics, bowl together, and so on. Such a group is characterized by interaction of fairly high intensity, frequent contacts, and a broad general focus resting on sympathetic, affectionate relationships and persisting only so long as the members are in direct contact with one another.

Secondary groups are characterized by much more deliberate and conscious formation than primary groups. Almost always they represent partial and specialized interests. In fact, they are sometimes called "special-interest" groups. They do not necessarily depend on face-to-face contacts. A scientific association may exist for years without the members ever meeting one another. Secondary associations include the nation, the political party, the professional society, the religious body, the employers' association, and the international labor union.

Another feature of secondary groups is that they often outlast any given generation. Because the particular interests or needs they represent may persist through time, more organization is required than is found in primary groups.

8-1 CHECKING IT OUT: The Social Structure of the Norton Gang

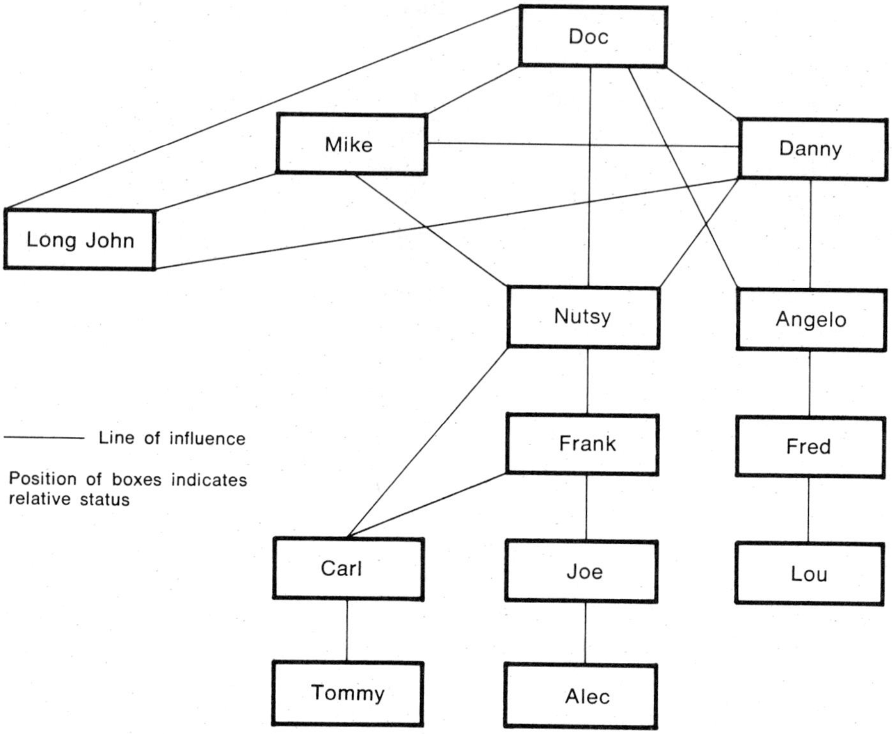

SOURCE: William Foote Whyte, *Street Corner Society: The Social Structure of an Italian Slum*, 2nd ed. (Chicago: The University of Chicago Press, 1955), p. 13. Reprinted by permission.

There develop traditions, codes, special offices, and fixed methods of carrying out the group's activities.

Primary-Secondary Relationships

The Gemeinschaft—Folk Society The family, band, clan, tribe, and small village long antedate urban society. The very first forms of human society, however, can only be inferred. We know, of course, that the primary forms of human grouping are far older than the secondary. Earliest people apparently lived in relatively small groups formed on the basis of family and blood ties. Their economy consisted of seed and root gathering, and hunting and fishing. Their social organization must have been relatively delimited. (Stewart, 1946)

The culture of present-day primary communities stems from the Neolithic Revolution. The domestication of plants and animals and the development of agriculture made possible more permanent settlement. This in turn brought changes in social organization and division of labor, and laid the foundations of rural culture patterns which have come down into our own time.

Even today, from two-thirds to three-fourths of the world's people live in what may be called Gemeinschaft societies with a strong solidarity of family life, importance of religion, and forms of moral control. This social group was first described by the German sociologist Ferdinand Töennies. He contrasted the Gemeinschaft or community with the Gesellschaft or society. These ideal types have many elements in common with primary group-secondary group comparisons.

Among the most interesting forms of the Gemeinschaft in the United States are the "cultural islands" of distinct groups that have persisted in the midst of highly secularized and technologically developed areas. The Amish, Mennonites, Dunkers, and other "plain people" who migrated from Europe have maintained certain cultural traits for generations. Their clothing, agricultural practices, vehicles, and certain social institutions have been carried down with little change from the time of the Protestant Reformation. These groups have regarded the "simple life" as the "good life," and have fought doggedly to keep from becoming "worldly." The more conservative sects, particularly the House Amish, shun all technological innovations except those absolutely necessary to their survival.

The Gemeinschaft, as exemplified by the communities of the Amish, is typically small, with a minimal division of labor and consequently only a limited differentiation of social roles. The role of the male among such primary societies is roughly the same for almost all adult men, with some differences only in terms of age and marital status.

The only important economic differentiation is in terms of sex and age. There are few specialized roles pertaining to religion and leadership. There is no formal structure of political roles. Families and other primary groups make up the important units within the society as a whole. One result of the small population size, the social isolation, and the lack of occupational specialization and social differentiation is the social homogeneity of the population. The different physical types, interests, occupational roles, values, religious groupings, and ideologies so obvious in the urban society are absent from the folk community. While the family and community are the most primary of all associations, even folk societies have some delimited groups which serve the more special interests of their members. Tribal councils, secret societies, and formalized age and sex groups sometimes appear. Nevertheless, in primary communities the number of such organizations is relatively small, and among those which do exist the social contacts tend to be very informal.

Social roles are, therefore, inclusive rather than segmental; they include many aspects of behavior rather than merely some limited segment of an individual's activities. Since members of a folk society perform inclusive rather than segmental roles, they necessarily interact with one another in a wide variety of contexts. Social relationships are, therefore, long-lasting, inclusive, intimate, and personal. Social relationships have intrinsic significance; they are valued (positively or negatively) for themselves rather than as means to other ends. The reciprocal expectations of persons involved in these primary relationships are diffuse and generalized. One must live up to standards of respect, loyalty, or affection, for example, rather than merely fulfilling specifically defined obligations.

Homogeneity of the Gemeinschaft The absence of secondary groups and the homogeneity of values and behavior patterns produces a powerful sense of unity binding the people together. The members of the Gemeinschaft exhibit a strong in-group feeling. Since the whole of their social lives is wrapped up in a society which is essentially a primary group, they are inclined to view the entire outside world as an out-group.

In the Gemeinschaft, behavior is regulated largely by custom; the many aspects of everyday life are governed by a complex array of rules and regulations regarding the activities of eating, sleeping, hunting, fishing, praying, dancing, and love-making. Behavior flows fairly smoothly through conventional grooves. With the informal norms exercising a strong hold upon behavior, there is little need for formal sanctions. Social control is part of tradition; it is not codified or rationalized, not enacted or dictated. Instead, it emerges from the traditional experience of the society. It is incorporated in the folkways and mores known and accepted by its members. There is a strong feeling that what the culture moves one to do is well worth doing.

Primary communities are also notable for the extent to which social control is informal. Sanctions are imposed through gossip, ridicule, or ostracism. Behavior is governed by folkways and mores; there is little formal law. Where everyone knows everyone else intimately, the informal pressures of the community are sufficient to enforce the norms.

In the Gemeinschaft social roles are inclusive rather than segmental; social relationships are personal and intimate; and there are comparatively few subgroups other than family and kinship units. In this typically small, isolated, and homogeneous society, tradition permeates all aspects of life and the range of alternative patterns of behavior open to individuals is inevitably restricted. There is resistance to change and innovation.

The Gesellschaft—the Urban Society The social structure and the culture of the Gesellschaft differ from those of folk societies. The simplest summary of the differences between the two types of social organization is to recall that they are opposites: whereas the Gemeinschaft is homogeneous, the Gesellschaft is heterogeneous, and so on.

Two dominant features are size and population density. There is, of course, no sharp dividing line for classification according to size or density of population. When a community becomes large enough that most of the residents are not able to know most of the others personally, some of the patterns of social relations typical of folk society tend to disappear and are replaced by other forms of social interaction. One function of relatively large population size, then, is impersonality in interaction. An urban society as a whole cannot be primary when there are too many people in it for each to have personal knowledge of most of the others. In most rural communities in the United States, it is considered polite to speak to anyone you meet on the street. But if you tried to greet everyone you met as you walked across Broadway in New York City, you would find that you had set yourself an impossible task, and the people whom you addressed would be divided in their opinion as to whether you intended to fleece them of their money or were mentally unbalanced. Neither can a sharp line be drawn between folk and urban societies simply on the basis of density of population. It is obvious, however, that many of the factors associated with urbanism are closely related to the density of the population.

One characteristic of a city is that it has such a high density of population that it could not support itself by farming the land it occupies. The urban society has a complex division of labor and a proliferation of social roles. Since, unlike mines or farms, cities are usually not places where raw materials are produced, the people living in cities depend entirely on non-city dwellers for these materials. City people thus must support themselves by manufacturing finished products from raw materials, marketing these products, or supplying services, which range from dry cleaning to symphony music. Such economic organization results from specialization for efficient production and service and leads to a more elaborate stratification system than is typical of folk societies.

Heterogeneity of the Gesellschaft Urban differentiation and stratification give rise to a great heterogeneity in the population. The impersonality of urban life allows people with a different skin color or accent or religion to pass relatively unnoticed in a way that could never be possible in the primary organization of a folk community. In addition, the occupational specialties associated with the complex division of labor create differences in the population: variation in training, values, work hours, recreation patterns, and so on.

> In the city the ways of life are legion, and the diversities of its manmade scene admit extreme variations of equipment of opportunity. There is no sense of a common and vital dependence on the aspects of the seasons and the vagaries of the weather. There is no sense of a common fate. There are few common tasks, few incidents all men share.... There are no common hours of work and rest, no common occasions of meeting for personal gossip or public discussion. (MacIver and Page, 1949, pp. 312–313)

Another consequence of the size and heterogeneity of the population is the proliferation of secondary groups. Community-wide organizations to satisfy some of the needs for social contact have long been a part of urban life. Settlement houses, various youth groups, and other organizations aim to provide recreation and education for individuals. Block Association activities and "drives" for the Red Cross and other organizations illustrate how a given crisis may serve to stimulate formal organizations and at least temporarily revive neighborliness in large cities. Sometimes out of these come primary-group relations which did not previously exist.

Mechanical and Organic Solidarity Emile Durkheim was one of the social scientists who watched the dramatic social changes that occurred as nineteenth-century society was transformed by the Industrial Revolution. However, Durkheim was less interested in developing ideal types of the societies that existed than were Töennies and the other social theorists. Rather, he preferred to describe the kinds of relationships that existed in traditional and urban societies. Durkheim's central interest was always social order or social solidarity. He sought to discover ways of relating that produced unity and cohesion in social life. He characterized the kind of unity found in traditional or primary societies as **mechanical solidarity**. Mechanical solidarity was to be found in societies like Töennies' Gemeinschaft. The group exerted much control over behavior and there was order and cohesion in such societies because the pressures toward conformity were great. Individual and unique behavior were discouraged. Being different, being special or unusual, was not valued. Durkheim called the solidarity of such societies mechanical, but he was not referring to machines. He meant rather that in village or traditional society, people are like the molecules of chemistry; they have no actions of their own. Because being alike is valued, the individual personality is absorbed into the collective personality.

Unlike those around him, Durkheim was not alarmed by the changes resulting from urbanization and industrialization. He did not dread the passing of the small homogeneous, intimate Gemeinschaft. He saw folk society as restrictive and discouraging to individuality. Urban or Gesellschaft society, on the other hand, promised much. Urban society was characterized by a division of labor, which encouraged specialization in occupations and activities. Individuality was encouraged. Thus Durkheim rejected the notion that urban society produces disorganization and the destruction of social life. He saw, rather, a new kind of social solidarity resulting from the division of labor. The Gesellschaft produced interdependence. Because urban occupations were so specialized, the smooth functioning of society was the result of differentiation rather than of similarity. In metropolitan areas, social cohesion results from the smooth functioning of such specialized agencies as the postal service, the fire department, the police, the city and state bureaucracies, the hospital services. Durkheim developed an analogy between the physiology of the higher animals and urban society. The individual parts of the society were specialized like the organs of the body (the brain, the heart, the digestive system). The unity of the whole resulted from the specialization of the parts. **Organic solidarity** was then a social unity which grew out of specialization and the division of labor, but which produced interdependence and more freedom for the growth of the individual spirit.

Urbanism as a Way of Life In addition to the social solidarity that grows out of the interdependence described by Durkheim, the Gesellschaft also induces variability, inventiveness, and cultural change. Urban life may and does foster creativeness in basic as well as secondary situations, in personal life organization, and in social movements. Yet, on the whole, the larger the community, the more likely we are to find a sense of personal isolation, loss of intimacy with others, and similar marks of mass society. A central integrating set of values may be difficult to find. "Purchasability of services and things" tends to displace "personal relations as a basis of association." (Wirth, 1938, p. 17) The roles of the individual become so varied and so segmentalized that both competition and cooperation seldom involve the whole personailty. One comes to think of oneself as a combination of bits and pieces, not an integrated participant in society.

One example of the urban type of social relationship is the narrowly contractual relation of buyer and seller in an open market exchange transaction. In this type of social situation everything is formally irrelevant to the relation except considerations of the price, quantity, and quality of the goods being exchanged. The rights and obligations of the parties are specific and definite—neither more nor less than explicitly agreed upon for the specific occasion. The establishment of any particular urban relation does not imply any other social relations between the participants.

Social relations of this kind are essentially **instrumental**; they are not important in themselves but for the goals or ends which they bring closer to realization. As a result there is less of an emotional involvement with other persons than there is in the case of primary relationships. Social relationships in the urban society, therefore, tend to be transitory, superficial, and impersonal. Individuals associate with one another for limited purposes and social interaction tends to be confined to the specific interests involved.

Life in the urban society loses its unitary, cohesive character. Economics and family life are seemingly separated; religion is apt to be confined to particular times and places instead of permeating the whole human existence. Work and leisure are sharply distinguished. As a result, the family does not occupy the same central place in the social structure of the urban society that it possesses in folk society, and people belong to many groups and many bureaucratically organized associations.

In the complex, diversified urban society with its many groups and competing interests, the pervasive hold of tradition has largely been broken. The comparative uniformity of thought has been replaced by an almost endless variety. There are relatively few universally accepted beliefs, values, and

8-2 CHECKING IT OUT: Mass Society—in Spite of Organic Solidarity!

The conception of "Mass Society" can be summarized as follows: The revolutions in transport and communications have brought men into closer contact with each other and bound them in new ways; the division of labor has made them more interdependent; tremors in one part of society affect all others. Despite this greater interdependence, however, individuals have grown more estranged from one another. The old primary group ties of family and local community have been shattered; ancient parochial faiths are questioned; few unifying values have taken their place. Most important, the critical standards of an educated elite no longer shape opinion or taste. As a result, mores and morals are in constant flux, relations between individuals are tangential or compartmentalized rather than organic. At the same time greater mobility, spatial and social, intensifies concern over status. Instead of a fixed or known status symbolized by dress or title, each person assumes a multiplicity of roles and constantly has to prove himself in a succession of new situations. Because of all this, the individual loses a coherent sense of self. His anxieties increase. There ensues a search for new faiths. The stage is thus set for the charismatic leader, the secular messiah, who, by bestowing upon each person the semblance of necessary grace and of fullness of personality, supplies a substitute for the older unifying belief that the mass society has destroyed.

In a world of lonely crowds seeking individual distinction, where values are constantly translated into economic calculabilities, where in extreme situations shame and conscience can no longer restrain the most dreadful excess of terror, the theory of the mass society seems a forceful, realistic description of contemporary society, an accurate reflection of the quality and feeling of modern life.

SOURCE: Daniel Bell, "The Theory of Mass Society," *Commentary, 22* (July, 1956), pp. 75–76. Reprinted from *Commentary* by permission;

standards of behavior. The norms have been weakened and formal law has emerged to regulate behavior and govern both social and sexual intercourse. Therefore, in the urban society, change is rapid. Status is achieved rather than ascribed and there is a constant readiness for change. Indeed, innovation and invention are heavily rewarded in most areas of social life.

Urban society requires more contact among individuals than does rural society, but it is less emotional contact. A superficial observer might imagine that modern cities are by all odds the most favorable places for social interaction. While it is true that city dwellers may talk to many people, it has often been said that persons may feel more lonely in large cities than anywhere else. There is a vast difference between the incidental and temporary contiguity in urban mass society and the shared experience and interstimulation of members of a small community.

The Quest for Community Because of the loneliness experienced in the Gesellschaft, because social relations are fragmented and often impersonal, because within families, the pressures of urban living distort even loving relationships, many individuals hunger for the intimate, caring interactions of the Gemeinschaft. This need to make richer emotional contact with family members and peers led to a revival of interest in social groups such as the commune, and has encouraged the development of new social forms such as the encounter group and the "singles scene."

Communes The coming together of young people in communes during the 1960s was an attempt to capture the intimate stable and inclusive relationships of the primary group and the Gemeinschaft. In the United States if earlier generations of kin (mothers and fathers, and also sometimes aunts, uncles, and grandparents) could live under one roof and share in economic pursuits and recreational and religious activities as members of *extended families*, it might also be possible to develop communities of people, unrelated, but able to share living arrangements that traditionally had been enjoyed by genetically related kin. The substitution of responsive friends for kin might result from the fact that relationships with actual family members and relatives were strained and perceived as unrewarding or were impossible as relatives were living too far away to be seen regularly.

There were often similar goals or intense interests that drew commune members together. Rosabeth Moss Kanter (1974) describes these as the land, the spirit, and the home. Rural communes often grew out of a sense of commitment to nature and a desire to be close to the land. Other communes were organized around religious values and practices. Many urban communes concentrated mainly on developing a smoothly functioning unit. Their main purpose was to share in the communal experience as fully as possible. However, Kanter noted that it was possible for a commune to pursue all of these goals concurrently.

The patterns of relationships within communes are varied but appear to be more stable than is commonly supposed. Bennett Berger and his associates (1972) engaged in participant observations at seven communes in northern California. The purpose of this research was to observe "community-building" or the development of social institutions within communes relevant to the socialization of communal children. Therefore these researchers avoided the transitory urban "crash pad" communes and focused on more stable family-oriented situations. For their purposes, they defined a commune as a structure having five adults and at least two children, all sharing a common household. They only observed situations in which the commune members had lived together for at least six months.

Contrary to more lurid stereotypes, the communes studied were not places where sexual promiscuity was expected behavior. Instead, stability and fidelity were encouraged and these communes were actually broken up into "*nuclear units*" composed of parents and children or couples. Exclusive relationships were encouraged by commune members even though there were instances where each partner might have sexual relations with another person. The general feeling expressed was that "if one spouse wants to, it's better that he (or she) satisfies that want than if he (or she) doesn't"(p. 587) Nevertheless "exclusive sexual access" remained the norm and, where violations of the norm occurred, tensions were created. The researchers had heard of the other communes where sexual intercourse between commune members was viewed as incest. On the other hand, Berger had accounts of one group in which several men of a commune had had sex with a female member when she was considered fertile, so that if a pregnancy occurred the father would be unknown, and presumably the child would be a child of the commune.

8-3 CHECKING IT OUT: Shakerism: A Colonial Vision of Communal Living Fades

The longest and most successful American experiment in celibate Christian communal living is fading away in two remote New England communities where yesterday and today merge in living museums.

Here and in Canterbury, N. H., about 80 miles to the southeast, the last members of the United Society of Believers—commonly called Shakers—are witnessing the end of an experiment that began here in 1774 as an attempt to build "God's kingdom here on earth."

The spiritual leaders of the gentle, aging women who remain in the society closed the doors of their faith to new members in 1964. When the last 14 members die, their experiment, which of necessity was based on constant recruiting, will join a long list of ultimate living experiments that failed to resist the force of the industrial revolution.

At the movement's peak from 1830 to 1860, more than 6,000 Shakers had built 19 communes scattered from Maine to Ohio and Kentucky. From their remote communal farms and workshops flowed a steady stream of products (Shaker furniture, seeds, medicines) and inventions (the flat-sided broom, the clothespin, the circular saw) that made their name synonymous with quality and ingenuity.

"But we feel it is time to close this adventure," said Sister Bertha, one of five elderly Canterbury sisters and an eldress in the society. "Sister Ann Lee, our founder, prophesied that we would one day dwindle until there were not enough of us left to bury our dead. The good we have done will not be lost. Someone will pick up the way."

For many who have studied Shaker history, the decision to conclude the experiment came at a time when some of the principles of Shakerism—long ridiculed and scorned—are becoming fashionable. Equality of the sexes, an effort to avoid personal competition, and generalized love and respect for nature have guided Shakers for more than 200 years. The same characteristics have been catalogued in recent years by writers attempting to describe the alternate life style now being sought by thousands of young people in communes and collectives around the country.

SOURCE: Bill Kovach, *The New York Times*, June 15, 1972, p. 43.

During the 1960s, thousands of communes were begun as social experiments, but failed, often because of internal pressures among members or because of the hostility of neighbors. And yet communes are a recurring phenomenon in U.S. history, and many have lasted for generations. The Shakers are an example of a commune that existed in America for 180 years. Harmony existed for 100 years and the Oneida Community (of silverware fame) lasted for 33 years. Kanter found that successful communes consciously developed commitments to the group in the following ways, thereby insuring their continued existence:

1. Members were expected to give money or property to the community upon joining. This caused the new member to identify with the group and develop a concern about the commune's fate.

2. Communes that lasted over time demanded a renunciation of the outside world on the part of the member. If the commune was to become a true extended family, then the biological family must not be allowed to intrude.

3. Communes that lasted were able to develop new identities for members. The exchange of a former "self" for a new identity that was subject to group control, seems to have been a valuable mechanism in developing group members who conformed to the norms.

IN-GROUPS AND OUT-GROUPS

The primary and secondary associations represent a basic structural and functional classification. Another important and much used typology is that of in-group and out-group. This distinction is found in all societies.

The *in-group* is any association—either primary or secondary—in which there is a sense of solidarity, loyalty, friendliness, and cooperation. It is characterized by a "we" feeling. There is a definite feeling of obligation toward the other members of the group which is especially prominent in critical situations threatening the group. It is in the in-group that we express our deepest sentiments of love and sympathy. We feel at home with those around us. We are familiar with their manner of acting and thinking, and they with ours. We understand their gestures and their words are our words. Often the vocabulary and accent are unique, and are themselves a badge of common membership. Lives center largely around the in-groups to which one belongs.

The *out-group* consists of those persons, whether formally organized or not, toward whom we feel a sense of indifference, avoidance, disgust, competition, or outright conflict. We have no feeling of loyalty, sympathy, or cooperation toward such persons. Rather, we are often prejudiced against the members of the out-group. We may think the family on the next street is inferior to our own, or that our neighborhood is better than the one "across the tracks," or that our race or religion is much superior to another's. One's antagonisms, prejudices, and hatreds usually focus on out-groups. The trade union, for example, opposes the employers' association. Toward other members of the union the individuals feel a sense of solidarity, loyalty, helpfulness, and cooperation. Toward the employer and (especially) toward the strikebreakers, there is intense bitterness.

REFERENCE GROUPS

The attitudes and values of most people are shaped as they grow up within primary groups. It is common to absorb the ideas and norms of those with which we are in close association. Therefore our family functions as a *reference group* when we are children. The reference group is a useful concept in sociology that helps to explain the significance of social groups for the individual. The concept of reference group became well known after elaboration by the influential American social theorist, Robert Merton (1957). He defined a reference group as a social group or social category that the individual uses as a point of reference in the shaping of attitudes, beliefs, values, and behavior. A reference group may be a group of which one is a member or a group of which one is not a member. The important thing is that there is a sense of identity with the particular group. The scout troop may become an important reference group for the young girl or boy who is struggling to understand and absorb socially approved behaviors as childhood is left behind.

A social category such as the Democratic Party may function as a reference group, because voters, aware of the values, ideology, and traditional commitment of this party, identify with it in making voting decisions. However, it is not necessary to be a member of a particular reference group or even to desire to become a member. It is possible to use the glamorous "jet set" of international society as a reference group while knowing that the possibility of ever becoming a member is remote; or to use Chinese Communism as a reference group while functioning as a citizen of the United States. In the 1960s the term "oreo" was bestowed on certain blacks by their peers. This term was used pejoratively to indicate the reference group of individuals. The "oreo" was considered black on the outside; but was presumed to be white on the inside by critical associates. The designation suggested that the individual was racially a black but had accepted the values and norms of middle-class white society, implying that such an individual was rejecting the cultural behaviors, or political style of blacks (e.g., soul music, identification with African backgrounds, militancy). At the same time Native-American youngsters were calling those who identified with white values "apples"; and Oriental Americans were calling group members who identified with mainstream society "bananas."

INTERPRETIVE SUMMARY

Sociologists distinguish between social groups and social categories. They further classify groups according to the frequency, intensity, duration, and focus of the interaction involved. Group size also affect the kinds of interaction possible.

Sociology began in the nineteenth century as an attempt to understand the major social changes brought about by the Industrial Revolution. The Industrial Revolution had a profound effect on the nature of human society. Much of the sociological analysis of these changes has involved a comparison of two polar ideal-types of social organization. The first of these has been called folk society or the Gemeinschaft. Here group interaction is characterized by primary group relationships, intimacy, homogeneity of values and behavior patterns, and a strong in-group feeling. Such societies are small in size and social roles are inclusive rather than segmental. The second ideal-type is called Gesellschaft or urban society. The Gesellschaft is characterized by a large population and a complex division of labor. Social roles are segmented and secondary group relationships predominate. The heterogeneous nature of life in urban society leads to diversity of beliefs, values, and behavior. Social change is rapid and loneliness is common. There is substantial diversity of interests in urban society and social control is formalized in law.

The main purposes of the typological study of societies are to specify the ways in which various aspects of the social structure of a society are interrelated and to provide a basis for the interpretation of social change.

Emile Durkheim was less interested in developing polar ideal-types of social groups and more interested in characterizing the relationships to be found within them. He discussed the mechanical solidarity of the Gemeinschaft with its demand for conformity and homogeneity. Durkheim felt that the organic solidarity of the Gesellschaft or urban society, with its division of labor and specialization, encouraged an interdependence and a unity which produced social solidarity. Durkheim's vision of the Industrial Revolution is positive and hopeful.

However, the urban experience has also been described as producing a sense of isolation and segmented and instrumental relationships. A sense of group cohesion and connectedness is lost. There has been a revival of interest in social groups, such as the commune, which have stressed the intimate, caring relationships of folk society.

The in-group and out-group are additional ideal-types that characterize social interactions, particularly where exclusion of some members of society is practiced by those who are more advantaged. In-groups frequently subject out-groups to antagonism and hostility. In-group members have a "we" feeling and a *consciousness of kind.* Out-groups are composed of those individuals felt to be different from the in-group in significant ways.

A reference group is that group used by an individual as a point of reference in developing values, beliefs, attitudes and in deciding on appropriate behavior in social situations.

QUESTIONS

1. If you joined a rural commune, what kinds of relationships might you expect to have with communal members? What needs cause people to try the communal life?
2. How is the Gemeinschaft different from the Gesellschaft? Give examples of both.
3. What characteristics of groups influence the experiences that we have within them?
4. How does Durkheim respond to the organic solidarity of urban society?
5. Which reference groups most influence your behavior?

9

Bureaucracy and Large-Scale Organization

With the increase in the size and heterogeneity of the population, the proliferation of social roles, and urbanization which resulted from the Industrial Revolution, people came to pursue their collective goals in ever-larger groups and faced new and complex problems of social structure. The Industrial Revolution brought with it a scale of social organization which has steadily increased. Large-scale organizations have become permanent features of industrial societies, commanding an ever-greater share of social resources and exercising pervasive and substantial social power. For example, when the Ford Motor Company began in 1903, it employed slightly more than 100 people and had approximately $150,000 in capital. Though not the largest organization in the country, Ford now has over 300,000 employees and well over $6 billion in assets. (Galbraith, 1967)

The traditional, face-to-face mode of primary group organization that characterizes the small folk society is inadequate to meet the collective goals of huge numbers of people in large urban areas who are engaged in very different activities, at different times, and in different locations. As the population of a society increases, the complexity and the volume of activity necessary for its maintenance also increase.

How do people effectively coordinate their activities to meet common problems without knowing one another and without face-to-face interaction? How is social order possible outside the primary group? The existence of such problems and the need for organizing and coordinating the efforts of large numbers of socially heterogeneous people to meet these problems were noted centuries ago. In his discussion of the Roman Empire of the first century, the historian Dio Cassius wrote:

> The cause of our troubles is the multitude of our population and the magnitude of the business of our government; for the population embraces men of every kind, in respect both of race and endowment, and both their tempers and their desires are manifold; and the business of the state has become so vast that it can be administered only with the greatest difficulty. (Stevenson, 1934)

THE BUREAUCRATIZATION OF SOCIAL LIFE

The Emergence of the Bureaucracy

The major response to the problems of large-scale social organization has been the development and spread of bureaucracy. Bureaucracy is defined as "a formal, rationally organized social structure [involving] clearly defined patterns of activity in which, ideally, every series of actions is functionally related to the purposes of the organization." (Merton, 1957) The term "bureaucracy" originally referred to the administration of government by means of bureaus, that is, special units to care for such matters as taxation, police protection, communications, foreign relations, and military defense. Today, the term is often popularly used to refer to certain negative and "unintended" but nonetheless important features of governmental administration. One such feature is the development of self-perpetuating social patterns in which the means of public service often become ends in themselves and in which administrative personnel are more concerned with their own protection than with the service of the public interest.

Bureaucratic Influence

We are now witnessing the pervasiveness of the bureaucratically structured large-scale organization that Max Weber foresaw when he suggested that this form of the rational coordination of behavior would increasingly dominate people's lives. The pervasiveness of bureaucracy and large-scale organizations is reflected in many ways. The number of white-collar workers, many of whom are engaged in the administration of large organizations and/or the performance of routine bureaucratic tasks, has increased steadily and substantially. Millions of other workers are subject to bureaucratic controls on the job. Consumers who seek redress of their grievances about unsatisfactory consumer products are confronted by a bureaucratic maze.

> Modern man is man in organizations. If the most dramatic fact that sets our stage apart from earlier ones is that we live today under the shadow of nuclear destruction, the most pervasive feature that distinguishes contemporary life is that it

> is dominated by large, complex, and formal organizations. Our ability to organize thousands and even millions of men in order to accomplish large scale tasks—be they economic, political, or military—is one of our greatest strengths. The possibility that free men become mere cogs in the bureaucratic machineries set up for this purpose is one of the greatest threats to our liberty. (Blau and Scott, 1962)

The person in modern society is a person in organizations, so much so that Robert Presthus has dubbed the industrial world the "organizational society." (Presthus, 1965) We live our lives in and through organizations, and we devote large amounts of time, energy, and thought to organizations. Indeed, an increasing lament of our time is that we have become organization men and women. For many persons, the sense of attachment to the organization for which they work is more real than the sense of attachment to their community, their religion, or even their extended family. In the early 1900s more than three-fourths of the population was self-employed—mostly in farming—but today less than five per cent are self-employed. On the other hand, American Telephone and Telegraph employs three-fourths of a million persons; the United States government employs over two million people in civilian jobs and over four million in the armed services.

The state, of course, is a historical product. As populations grew, increasing differentiation of roles led to a change of controls and the need for extension of regulations to new areas of conduct. This meant a shift from a family or kinship basis of social control to one founded on the larger community, with particular individuals, groups, or classes setting down the rules and putting them into effect. More integrated forms of government tended to arise as groups or societies were threatened by, or fell into conflict with, other societies. This tendency was most important in the rise of more complex states: warfare between groups makes for stronger in-group solidarity. Growth of government has meant an increase in the relative importance and role of the administrative structure in comparison with the legislative and judicial branches. This shift has brought with it increased public concern over the nature of the executive structure.

The extension of governmental functions brings people into frequent contact with all sorts of governmental officials: tax collectors, draft boards, plumbing inspectors, unemployment officers, license clerks, policemen, social security representatives, and so on. In many other areas of social life people are continually confronted with large-scale, bureaucratically structured organizations that limit or direct their behavior. People who wish to enroll at a state university, to marry, divorce, vote, travel abroad, buy or repair a house, or obtain a driver's license all confront some form of bureaucracy. Registration at a state university requires the completion of many forms, compliance with a myriad of regulations, and the submission of appropriate papers in the right order and usually in duplicate, triplicate, or quadruplicate. Rules and regulations govern attendance, examinations, grades, the use of university facilities, and many other areas of collegiate life.

In some societies the political organization is such that bureaucratic controls appear to be maximized. The long reach of the state extends into areas once free from or only slightly dominated by political regulations. Bureaucracy is not confined to any one form of political organization or ideology; modern societies—communist, fascist, democratic, and socialist—make extensive use of what Max Weber called "man's greatest social invention." As Weber noted, "the great modern state is absolutely dependent upon a bureaucratic basis. The larger the state, and the more it is or the more it becomes a great power state, the more unconditionally is this the case." (Gerth and Mills, 1946)

Bureaucracy is a form of social structure found not only in federal, state, and local governments, but throughout the institutions of society. Churches, corporations, prisons, armies, welfare agencies, universities, unions, nonprofit research foundations, banks, factories, businesses, political parties, voluntary civic associations, and even some criminal activities are bureaucratically organized.

THE SOCIAL SOURCES OF BUREAUCRACY

Full-scale bureaucracy probably emerged as an answer to the problems of political and military organization in the Roman Empire and in the ancient civilizations of China and Egypt. Bureaucracy was characteristic of the great empires of the past, notably the Roman, Byzantine, Ottoman, and Chinese empires. With the great transformation accompanying the Industrial Revolution, the growth of other large organizations such as the Catholic Church, international labor unions, and business associations, and the increasing size and scope of educational institutions, religious institutions, philanthropic agencies, professional groups, and other associations found in industrial society, bureaucracy came more and more to typify social life.

The Value of the Bureaucracy— Efficiency and Rationality

Although the social conditions which give rise to bureaucracy differ somewhat from time to time and from place to place, the pervasiveness of bureaucracy, according to Weber, is due to its technical superiority.

> The decisive reason for the advance of bureaucratic organization has always been its purely technical superiority over any other form of organization. . . . Precision, speed, unambiguity, knowledge of the files, continuity, discretion, unity, strict subordination, reduction of friction and of material and personal costs—these are raised to the optimum point in the strictly bureaucratic organization. (Ibid., p. 214)

Efficiency alone does not account for the growth of bureaucracy. People must become conscious of the need for a highly rational process of ordering human conduct to recognize the technical advantages of bureaucracy and to be ready to abandon traditional ways of organizing selected aspects of social life.

The increased size, scale, and differentiation of social organization as well as the range and complexity of its activities have made traditional administrative procedures and structures inadequate. The growth of the nation-state and of large-scale economic enterprises strongly encouraged tendencies toward bureaucratic organization. A strong emphasis in Western society upon rationalism in science, philosophy, and Calvinist religion encouraged a rational approach to organization. Calvinism, which Weber demonstrated to be significant in the emergence of capitalism, encouraged hard work as a moral virtue and provided a cultural foundation for the order, the discipline, and the selfless, disinterested conduct required in a bureaucratic structure.

Weber related bureaucracy to the growth of a money economy. He demonstrated the way in which bureaucracy developed more fully when money became the conventional medium of exchange. Money possesses an abstract quality that encourages rational calculation. It permits the payment of regular salaries, a method of remuneration that facilitates the maintenance of control over officeholders. Salaried officials are more likely to depend on their earnings, to count on the security of their position, and to see the possibilities for advancement in terms of constantly increasing income. The emergence of bureaucracy has frequently been accompanied by the transformation of traditional obligations into monetary terms, thus encouraging formal and rational relations between the official and the client.

WEBER'S IDEAL-TYPE OF BUREAUCRACY

The effort to create an organization that provides an efficient coordination of diverse human behavior toward a common goal leads to the formalization of social structure. Bureaucracies differ in the details of their organization and operations, but they are sufficiently similar to construct an "ideal-type" of bureaucratic social structure. This ideal-type, derived from the work of Max Weber, is a conceptual model of a rationally ordered social structure and is useful in analyzing the character and functions of any bureaucracy. (Weber, 1968)

According to Weber, there are six essential characteristics of a bureaucratic social structure, each contributing to the efficient operation of the organization and each functionally related to the others. These characteristics are:

1. The positions become clearly and explicitly defined offices.
2. There is a formal hierarchical order with clear-cut lines of authority and responsibility.
3. Personnel are specialized and are selected on the basis of technical and professional competence.
4. Rules and regulations governing official action are explicit.
5. Social relationships are inherently impersonal.

6. There is security of tenure and the possibility of a career by promotion in the hierarchy.

Offices

Each person in a bureaucratically structured organization occupies an office—hence, is an official. The duties, competence, prerequisites, and tasks expected of the incumbent of each office, as well as the relationship of each office with other offices, are explicitly and clearly prescribed. The set of formally defined offices both dictates and limits the activities of people in a bureaucracy. All offices exist independently of their incumbents and, unlike traditional social roles which can be filled only by particular persons, bureaucratic roles are formally established and can be occupied by anyone with the appropriate qualifications. In the bureaucracy there is no indispensible person; no one has a special claim on any office by virtue of family status or special privilege.

There are important consequences of the sharp separation of the office from the person who occupies it. First, this separation serves to free the organization from the power of or the dependence upon particular persons in particular positions. The separation of the office from the person applies the principle of the interchangeability of parts to human material. No person can monopolize the right to his or her office. Bureaucracy, Weber once noted, compares with any other form of organization "exactly as does the machine with the nonmechanical mode of production." (Weber, 1946, p. 214) If an officeholder were to resign, die, or retire, the functioning of the organization would not be impaired. The organization merely secures another qualified person to assume the duties of the office. So long as the offices are filled by qualified persons, the organization continues to operate effectively.

Hierarchy

The organization of a bureaucracy takes the form of a hierarchy with a "clearly established system of super- and sub-ordination in which there is a supervision of the lower offices by the higher ones." (Weber, 1968, p. 957) The formal organization thus tends to assume a pyramidal form with a few offices at the top, a larger number of lesser offices in the middle ranks, and most offices at the base. The prototype of this kind of social structure is probably the military organization with its ranks of commissioned and noncommissioned officers, its enforced recognition of duties and responsibilities for those with authority, and its insistence upon obedience to superiors. Bureaucracy thus makes explicit the location of authority and its limits for each office. In all large, formal organizations some form of coordination of effort is required.

The major consequence of hierarchy is that it locates responsibility in specific positions and allows for a clear-cut determination of policy. Everyone in

9-1 CHECKING IT OUT: The Peter Principle: "In a Hierarchy, Every Employee Tends to Rise to His Level of Incompetence"

The competence of an employee is determined *not by outsiders but by his superior in the hierarchy.* If the superior is still at a level of competence, he may evaluate his subordinates in terms of the performance of useful work—for example, the supplying of medical services or information, the production of sausages or table legs or the achieving of whatever are the stated aims of the hierarchy. That is to say, he *evaluates output.*

But if the superior has reached his level of incompetence he will probably rate his subordinates in terms of institutional values: he will see competence as the behavior that supports the rules, rituals, and form of the status quo. Promptness, neatness, courtesy to superiors, internal paperwork, will be highly regarded. In short, such an official *evaluates input.*

"Rockman is *dependable.*"

"Lubrik contributes to the *smooth running* of the office."

"Rutter is *methodical.*"

"Miss Trudgen is a *steady, consistent* worker."

"Mrs. Friendly *co-operates* well with colleagues."

In such cases, internal consistency is valued more highly than efficient service. . . .

SOURCE: Laurence J. Peter and Raymond Hull, *The Peter Principle* (New York: William Morrow and Company, Inc., 1969), p. 42.

a bureaucracy is responsible for the behavior of those under his or her authority. Establishing lines of authority facilitates the effective coordination of efforts. Moreover, this arrangement sets up a line of advancement for persons seeking a career within the organization.

Technical Competence

Offices in the bureaucracy are filled by persons who are technically and/or professionally qualified and who demonstrate their technical competence. This makes important the development of tests and other measures of technical achievement by which the qualified can be certified. Examinations were employed in China before the Christian era, and it is reported that in the bureaucracy of feudal China one had to demonstrate excellence in such humanistic skills as writing poetry as part of the "civil service examination." American civil service examinations typically focus upon precise skills that reflect a high degree of specialization of functions. The selection of persons for positions in the bureaucracy on the basis of what they know rather than who they know contrasts sharply with the situation in nonbureaucratic situations in which personal loyalty, kinship, inheritance, tribal connections and such determine the appointment to positions.

The consequence of this characteristic is that trained people are more likely to do their jobs with skill, especially in the highly specialized bureaucracies of today. In addition, it facilitates the independence of the organization beyond the individual.

Rules and Regulations

In the bureaucracy the normative structure is spelled out in a written and codified form that explicitly details the rules and regulations of the organization. "The management of the modern office," wrote Weber, "is based upon written documents (the files), which are preserved in their original or draft form. . . ." (Ibid.) Oral agreements are too easily forgotten and distorted. The formal regulations dictate the appropriate behavior—the official conduct of the officeholders. The rules and regulations in a bureaucracy are specific; they impersonally apply to definite situations and circumstances. Problems are solved by the rules rather than by the personal judgment of an officeholder.

Although there are many complaints about "red tape," there would doubtless be confusion, inconsistency, and inefficiency without rules and regulations. The function of rules and regulations is to minimize the disruptive effects of personal biases and predilections and to provide for continuity and uniformity of treatment both within the organization and for the clients of the bureaucracy. The formality which is imposed by adherence to rules and regulations renders the social relations within the bureaucracy impersonal. Consequently, people can work with one another in spite of any personal frictions that might exist between them. As Merton has noted, "In this way, the subordinate is protected from the arbitrary action of his superior, since the actions of both are constrained by a mutually recognized set of rules." (Merton, p. 195)

Impersonality

Due to the separation of person and office, the hierarchal organization, and the emphasis on technical qualifications and rules and regulations, relationships in the bureaucracy are formally prescribed relationships among offices, not among personalities. The relationships necessary to carry out the tasks of a bureaucracy are impersonal. Personal feelings are subordinated to the demands of the office and are formally contained so as not to impede or disrupt the formally required interaction.

The spirit of impersonality is one of detachment and distance. According to Weber, the ideal-type of bureaucracy is one which "succeeds in eliminating from official business love, hatred, and all purely personal, irrational, and emotional

9-2 CHECKING IT OUT: Closeups of Corporate Bias—Where Impersonality Fails!

Any survey of the corporate world quickly reveals that the dice are still loaded against women executives in a multitude of cases. Herewith are some true stories about companies that, naturally, do not want to be indentified:

A West Coast financial institution rejects a woman computer-marketing expert as head of its new department of computer-marketing services, choosing a less-qualified company man on the ground that it prefers to promote from within. Then it fills his job with an outsider, a male.

Confiding to a senior executive that he doesn't really hit it off with the woman who heads his department, a young manager at a service company gets informal permission to report directly to the senior executive. Comments the department head: "Can you imagine that happening if I were a man? That young twerp couldn't care less that I'm a woman, but he knows it bothers the v-p. So now he has a direct line to top management, and where am I?"

Feeling the effects of economic adversity, a California bank shrinks its corporate lending staff by six. It moves its six women corporate lending officers to less prestigious positions in trust, portfolio management, and other areas. It leaves its 70-odd men corporate lending officers exactly where they were.

The only woman vice-president at a major consumer goods company observes that she is also the only vice-president who has no company car, whose office is off the executive floor, and whose salary (she discovers by discreet detective work) is 20% below that of her counterparts. Taxed with the discrepancies, the boss who appointed her replies indignantly that a woman should be grateful to have the post at all. "Of course I could file suit," says the woman. "And that would be the end of my career."

SOURCE: *Business Week:* November 24, 1975. p. 63.

elements which escape calculation." (Weber, 1968, p. 975) Impersonality promotes equality of treatment, insures cooperation among persons who must interact to meet the obligations of their offices, and enhances the capacity to render rational and objective judgments, uninfluenced by likes and dislikes of particular individuals. Bureaucracy is corrupted when technical competencies are influenced by personal responses to other persons; or, as Weber observed, "Bureaucracy develops the more perfectly, the more it is 'dehumanized'. . . ." (p. 975)

Career and Tenure

Bureaucracy also provides for careers within the organization, typically by fixed steps as in the military or civil service. Officeholders are given security of tenure (usually after a probationary period) in an effort to exact competent and unbiased performance and loyalty to the organization. Security renders bureaucrats less susceptible to outside pressures and the bureaucracy assures itself of continued efficiency by offering the possibility for advancement. Promotion, like initial appointment, is based upon demonstrated ability and/or seniority. An adequate reward system in a bureaucracy ensures continuous and competent performance as well as adequate recruitment of personnel. (Udy, 1959)

BUREAUCRACY'S "OTHER FACE"—THE INFORMAL STRUCTURE

Every large, formal, and complex organization is more than a bureaucratic form of social structure. Bureaucracy is an internal social structure that large-scale organizations use to deal with the problem of achieving effective and efficient operation, but bureaucracy is not synonymous with the substantive organization itself. Any given organization, no matter how highly bureaucratized, is always more than a bureaucracy. Moreover, no bureaucracy conforms exactly to the "pure" type described by Weber. No large-scale organization is exclusively impersonal. Within every large-scale organization there emerges an "informal structure" of social relationships that Charles H. Page has aptly called "bureaucracy's other face." (Page, 1946)

The gap which usually exists between the formal and the informal structure is aptly illustrated in the following report by Peter Blau on a state employment agency in a large Eastern city:

> The trainee learned that requests for workers, when received from employers over the telephone, must be recorded on a form, the job order. The procedure for obtaining all the information needed to fill out the twenty-five categories on this form was fully explained and exemplified. . . . The interviewer was taught the formula "What? How? Why? What is involved?" . . . Two days of training were devoted to the use of the four volume codebook which contained numerical codes for 29,000 occupations. . . .
>
> A series of demonstrations showed how to match the information on the job order with that on the application form in order to select the client best suited for a given vacancy. . . .
>
> . . . Interviewers were taught how to recognize a client's need for counseling and were told about the two types of counseling the agency offers. . . .
>
> . . . All recipients of unemployment insurance benefits . . . [were] required to report periodically to the employment agency. Interviewers . . . [were] responsible for notifying the unemployment insurance agency whenever a benefit client . . . [refused] a suitable job "without good cause."
>
> . . . In Department X, the procedures . . . were quite different from those discussed in the training course. Occupational codes were not used. The "job formula" was never mentioned, Application forms were rarely made out. Selection

> of candidates for jobs was not made from application files but from incoming applicants. Counseling was virtually prohibited....
>
> ... In the case of benefit clients ... refusals [of jobs] could be discouraged by reminders that a refusal might disqualify the client for benefit payments....
>
> ... This interfered with the placement goal of the service agency, which was to help clients find jobs they wanted, not to conscript them. (Blau, 1955)

Anyone who has worked within a large organization knows of the development of cliques and the interplay of personal likes and dislikes. The informal structure can usurp the formal structure of authority and can efficiently block the execution of policy. Middle-level officials sometimes deviate from official policy to aid a friend, to secure a favor from a superior, or to protect their own position within the bureaucracy.

The informal structure does not necessarily obstruct the purposes or weaken the efficiency of the organization. While the informal side of bureaucracy sometimes acts in opposition to officialdom, at other times it parallels and supplements official policy. The efficiency of the bureaucracy may actually be enhanced precicely because the formal requirements are ignored. For instance, intimate personal relationships among employees might deviate from official policy but also promote morale and, in turn, increase the efficiency of the employees.

Informal groups in the large-scale organization are sometimes so important that to secure maximum efficiency the bureaucrat must make use of personal relationships and sentiments. For instance, a superior may overlook minor violations of minor regulations by his or her subordinates to ensure their loyalty and/or friendship, thereby guaranteeing special efforts in their work. Completely ignoring "bureaucracy's other face" may lead to resistance to policy, blocked lines of communication, and even the deliberate sabotage of the goals of the organization.

Leadership and Group Effectiveness

The interrelations of higher and lower echelons will be qualified by the aim of the organization, its particular social structure, the already-existing patterns of control, and a variety of other factors. Numerous research studies have shown how the values, attitudes, and output of a group are affected by the nature of the relationship of the members to the leader and to one another.

The dominance that an individual may exercise will vary according to cultural patterns. The leader of a group anticipates identification, obedience, and deference from the group members. However, it should not be imagined that because dominant individuals in leadership positions are not voluntarily chosen for their positions, their followers are less inclined to do as they say. Whether they are or not depends on their social-cultural training.

Studies of morale and leadership in the United States Army during World

War II show that good morale among the troops was correlated with their having as officers men who were interested in them, understood their needs, recognized their abilities, were just in discipline, job assignment, and promotional policy, and kept them informed—insofar as security permitted—as to the nature of particular missions. The men did not greatly resent dominance and control, but they wanted to know "what the score was," as they put it. (Stouffer, 1949, vols. 1 and 2)

Much the same reactions have been noted in industry and business. A wide range of studies of the interplay of productivity, supervision, and employee morale has shown the importance of a firm but understanding supervisory force. Such a force facilitates the workers' identification with their jobs and with the informal as well as formal organization in the factory or in the store. So too, as Morris S. Viteles remarks,

> It appears that the supervisor who sees the problem of productivity exclusively in the technical terms of work methods and standards is less likely to motivate workers to increased production than one who sees the problem in terms of workers' status, characteristics, needs, and aspirations. The development of "employee-oriented" supervisors, adequately equipped for dealing with interpersonal relations on the job therefore represents one promising approach to the solution of problems of motivation and morale in industry. (Viteles, 1953, pp. 161–162)

To summarize, we may say that among other things important in making a work group or any other group effective are these: the individuals want to feel secure; they want social approval when it is pertinent; they want to know what to do and what is expected of them; they want a sense of participation; they want consistent discipline; and they want to be treated fairly and justly. If appropriate relations are maintained between the workers and their managers and supervisors, even rather authoritarian headship will be effective. But as a survey of the presidents of 171 of the largest corporations in the United States shows, although 50 per cent of the top executives support an autocratic rather than a democratic management, they specify that "the autocrat must listen to the top management group he heads." (Marshall, 1960, pp. 38–40)

Place of Informal Association

In addition to the formal organization of leadership, some kind of informal association and ordering of control often arises. Thus, in a military unit, government bureau, or factory section, voluntary leadership may grow out of the day-to-day interactions of the soldiers, the clerks, or the industrial workers. Sometimes, especially in periods of crisis, these informal leaders wield more power and influence than the formal heads of the operation. Productivity, morale, and sense of participation in the group are all greatly affected by such informal leadership.

The informal groupings that arise within the formal organization perform important functions not only in productive efficiency but in the matter of group morale. Cliques and friendships develop among the workers, and within these leaders emerge. Sometimes these groups have bearing on the work operations of the structure itself, and sometimes they deal only with recreational relationships. With regard to productivity, one important function of these informal groupings of workers is to protect themselves against practices which they consider a menace to their welfare. For example, in one plant, pressure by other employees was put on any worker who tended to exceed a certain minimum standard of output. This pressure consisted of ridicule, name-calling ("rate buster"), and even a certain amount of mild physical punishment. In this particular study, many of the men admitted to the research team that they could have turned out much more work but said they feared that if production were increased too much, the rates of pay would be cut. (Roethlisberger and Dickson, 1939)

On the development of the informal organization, Stogdill had this to say:

> Informal organization comes about as a result of the development of discrepancies (a) between work performances and responsibilities as defined and (b) between informal interactions and formally defined interactions. Thus leadership is ever confronted with the task of reconciling discrepancies—discrepancies between what ought to be done and what is being done, between goals and achievements, between organizational needs and available resources, between the needs of individual members and the requirements of organization, between formal lines of co-operation and informal patterns of co-operation. (Stogdill, 1950)

THE CONSEQUENCES OF BUREAUCRACY

Although Weber regarded bureaucracy as an instrument for achieving maximum efficiency, Blau (among others) has questioned whether impersonality and other characteristics of Weber's ideal-type result in maximal efficiency:

> If reserved detachment characterizes the attitudes of the members of the organization toward one another, it is unlikely that high *esprit de corps* will develop among them. The strict exercise of authority in the interest of discipline induces subordinates, anxious to be highly thought of by their superiors, to conceal defects in operations from superiors, and this obstruction of the flow of information upward in the hierarchy impedes effective management. Insistence on conformity also tends to engender rigidities in official conduct and to inhibit the rational exercise of judgment needed for efficient performance of tasks. (Blau, 1956, p. 33)

Furthermore, Drucker has emphasized that while specialization is not inherently inefficient, the assumption that it is necessarily the most efficient form of the division of labor is questionable.

> [We] have learned that it is neither necessary nor always efficient to organize all mass production in such a manner as to have the majority of workers confine

> themselves to doing one and only one of the elementary manipulations. . . . It was impossible [because of wartime shortages of skilled labor] to "lay out" the job in the usual assembly-line fashion in which one unskilled operation done by one unskilled man is followed by the next unskilled man. The operation was broken down into its unskilled components like any assembly-line job. *But then the unskilled components were put together again with the result that an unskilled worker actually performed the job of a highly skilled mechanic*—and did it as reliably and efficiently as had been done by skilled men. (Drucker, 1946, pp. 183–184)

One bureaucratic dilemma lies in the fact that hierarchy and highly formal relationships and standardized procedures sometimes inhibit the free flow of information and obstruct effective communication throughout the organization. According to Blau and Scott,

> Studies of experimental and work groups have shown that status differences restrict the participation of low-status members, channel a disproportionate amount of communication to high-status members, discourage criticism of the suggestions of the highs, encourage rejecting the correct suggestions of the lows, and reduce the work satisfactions of the lows and their motivation to make contributions. (Blau and Scott, 1962, p. 243)

The point is that formal regulations and procedures will not in themselves automatically yield the desired results. As Blau noted:

> The problem of central concern is the expeditious removal of the obstacles to efficient operations which recurrently arise. This cannot be accomplished by a preconceived system of rigid procedures . . . but only by creating conditions

9-3 CHECKING IT OUT: "You Can't Go Wrong If You Stick To The Book"

According to a ruling of the department of labor, Bernt Balchen [Admiral Bryd's pilot on his historic flight over the South Pole] . . . cannot receive his citizenship papers. Balchen, a native of Norway, declared his intention in 1927. It is held that he has failed to meet the condition of five years' continuous residence in the United States. The Byrd Antarctic voyage took him out of the country, although he was on a ship carrying the American flag, was an invaluable member of the Antarctic expedition, and in a region to which there is an American claim because of the exploration and occupation of it by Americans, this region being Little America.

The bureau of naturalization explains that it cannot proceed on the assumption Little America is American soil. That would be trespassing on international questions where it has no sanction. So far as the bureau is concerned, Balchen was out of the country and technically has not complied with the law of naturalization.

SOURCE: *Chicago Tribune,* June 24, 1931, p. 10.

> favorable to continuous adjustive developments in the organization. To establish such a pattern of self-adjustment in a bureaucracy, conditions must prevail that encourage its members to cope with emergent problems and to find the best method for producing specified results on their own initiative, and that obviate the need for unofficial practices which thwart the objectives of the organization, such as restriction of output. (Blau, 1956, pp. 64–66)

The structure of administrative roles—the "table of organization," as military parlance has it—sometimes becomes so sacred that no deviation from it is permitted. The fixed rules designed to facilitate decision tend to predominate at the expense of variable situations. As bureaucratic members of the military are fond of saying, "You can't go wrong if you stick to the book"—that is, to the rules and procedures laid down by those in the higher echelons of authority. Such emphasis means a tendency to view various activities as fitting neatly into predetermined and rigid categories. Everything has to be labeled, acted on, and reported in formalist fashion, with no deviations. The flow of decisions may become so intricate that the purpose or intent of the action becomes secondary to the proper fulfillment of the procedural rules. This means a high degree of impersonality in handling cases requiring administrative decision. The bureaucrat is symbolic of his organization: he has no power to make personal decisions.

Such stress on "the book" and on cautious following of the rules results in what Veblen aptly called "trained incapacity"—that is, loss of flexibility to meet new situations. Personnel are chosen by examinations to prove their preparation or competence for the job; but once past a usually short probation period, they are protected by various regulations concerning tenure, recurrent promotion, and seniority, whether their competence is maintained or not. The whole structure is a fixed and safe world, marked by rigid rules, methodical and impersonal execution of the rules, and hence a predictable outcome. Once such a scheme gets into operation, it resists modification.

Bureaucratic Personality

The regimen set down in institutions has its counterpart in the human beings who operate the system. There is no neater illustration of the interplay of culture and personality than in the field of bureaucratic administration. The competence needed for a job will vary with what is expected, and the incumbent in a given office must come up to certain standards. But once this person is on the job, there is pressure to be prudent, methodical, and precise in carrying on the work. One needs little or no initiative or imagination, and one avoids responsibility by passing difficult questions on to a higher authority or by hiding behind the rules. In fact, to demonstrate such qualities will usually lead to punishment of some kind, not reward. Innovations are not welcome in a bureaucratic world. Rather, this world encourages and rewards conformity, timidity, and deference to higher authority and regulations.

Yet, living in a safe world, bureaucrats often show arrogance or indifference to their clientele. The officeholders can compensate for their enforced conformity by showing their power over others. This is a feature of bureaucracy which those conditioned to a culture of individualism, personal give-and-take, and flexible decisions find so frustrating in military service and in dealing with corporate and governmental bureaus generally. While bureaucratic features may arise in the economic order, at least under "free enterprise" individuals can "take their business elsewhere." But if you do not like the service at the United States Post Office, you cannot decide to patronize some other firm. There simply is no place else to go for most governmental services.

Some believe there is a drift toward administration by professional bureaucrats in government, just as there is in private enterprise. This drift may be even stronger in societies without representative democracy, because public service there usually is a means of rewarding party members for their political adherence. It is, in effect, a spoils system on a vast scale.

In short, once the administration of government or of business becomes encrusted with bureaucracy, the system tends to perpetuate itself, unless some devices are set up to prevent its doing so. Cautious and "safe" people pick persons like themselves for the jobs. There is a kind of empire-building of the timid to protect themselves. The bureaucrats fear any inroads on their role and status by bold and ingenious people. Officialism, like extreme ecclesiasticism in the church, means that the form of the law remains, but the "spirit," the dynamic function, disappears.

INTERPRETIVE SUMMARY

One of the most significant changes associated with the Industrial Revolution was the increasing pervasiveness of bureaucratically structured, large-scale organization. Bureaucratization has been one of the major responses to the problem of coordinating the social life of large heterogeneous, and physically dispersed collectivities of people.

People in urbanized societies spend a substantial amount of their lives in the influence of bureaucracy, either directly or indirectly. The modern person is increasingly a person in organizations. Churches, political parties, schools, prisons, voluntary associations, corporations, and much more are bureaucratically structured.

A bureaucracy is a rationally organized social structure with clearly defined patterns of activity in which each series of activity is related to the purposes of the organization. Bureaucracy, as an ideal-type, has six essential characteristics set forth by Max Weber: clearly defined offices (positions), a hierarchical chain of command, selection of personnel on the basis of technical qualifications, rules and regulations governing official action, impersonal social relationships, and security of tenure.

Large-scale organizations do not conform exactly to Weber's ideal-type. Formal regulations and procedures do not automatically yield maximum efficiency. The stress on "the book" and the cautious following of rules sometimes results in "trained incapacity" and produces a personality type which is conforming, timid, methodical, and precise. Moreover, every large organization is always more than a social structure and the informal social relationships which emerge within the organization clearly affect its operation.

QUESTIONS

1. How does the university that you attend fit Weber's description of the bureaucracy? What advantages can you see deriving from the use of this organizational model? What aspects of bureaucratic organization seem dysfunctional? Are there ways in which the university departs from Weber's ideal-type?
2. Can you relate Weber's ideal-type of the bureaucracy to a prison? Make some comparisons.

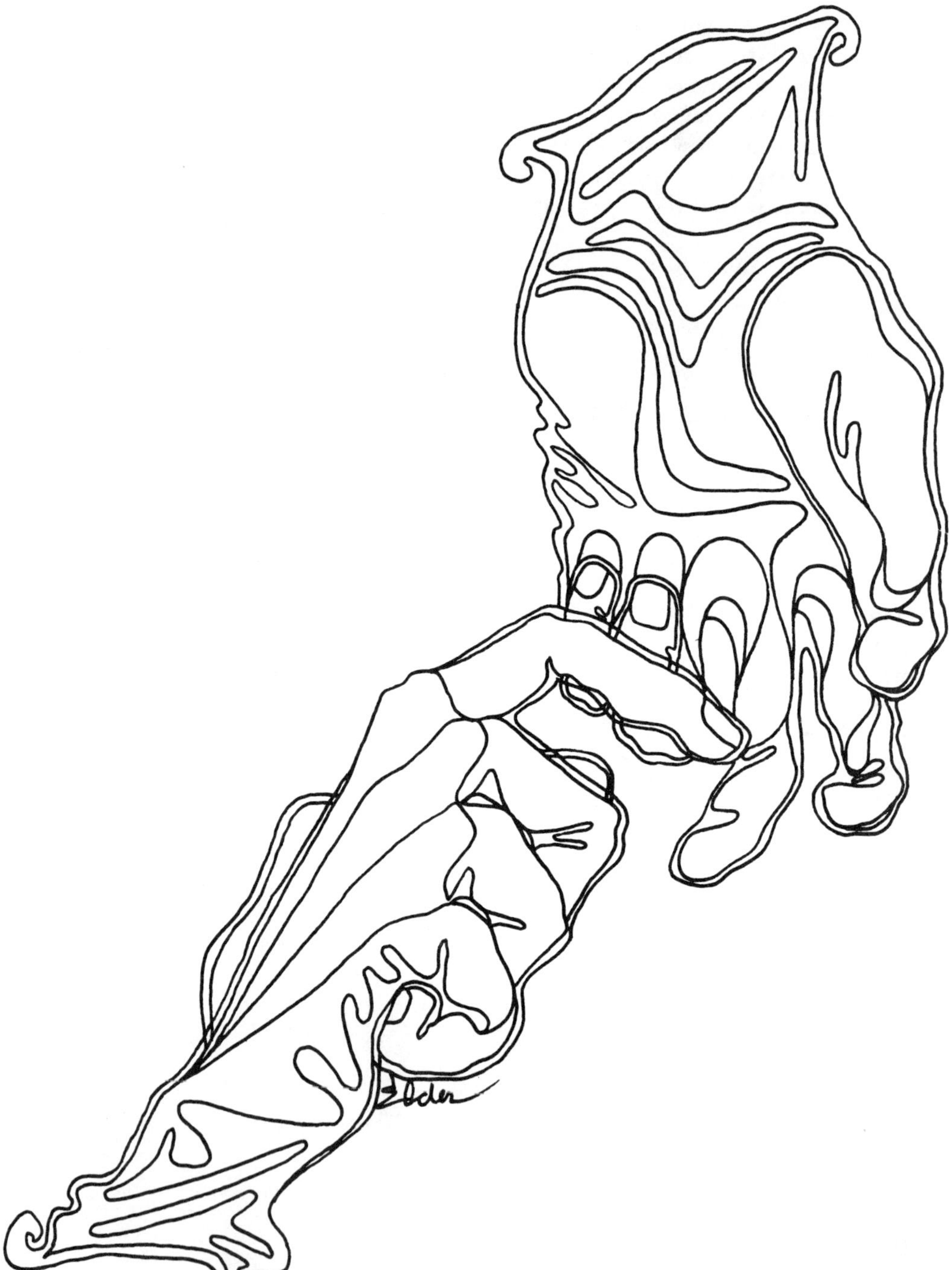
Elder

10

The Sociology of Health

Franklyn N. Arnhoff
University of Virginia

Health, disease, injury, and death are inevitable parts of all our lives, and social arrangements for dealing with these factors are found even among the most primitive tribes. In our own modern, complex society and other similar Western societies, these concerns have evolved into a highly complex, but loosely organized network, which we refer to as the "health system," or the "health-care system." To get some idea of how far this system has evolved from the primitive medicine man or even from the family doctor of television and the movies, consider the following features of the U.S. health system: the health-care system, loosely defined, is now the nation's largest single-industry employer with over 4.5 million employees (including physicians); it is the nation's largest single industry with expenditures of over 130 billion dollars (in 1976) and involves over 422 different kinds of jobs. Clearly, these few facts alone demonstrate our society's concern with health and health-related issues, as well as indicating the tremendous social importance of such a complex of professions, organizations, and economics. Even our everyday language reflects health and disease concerns—one speaks of the health of the family, the health of the community, the health of the nation, the health of the economy; or we refer to a sick society, or sick ideas, or an ailing political system. Obviously, such broad use of these words shows how important our culture finds the concepts of health and illness to be, but it is even more significant to note that none of those examples is really meant to imply biological disease, which is what we usually mean when we say that a person is sick.

We tend to think of being sick in biological (physical) terms—an ache in the back, a pain in the head, an inflamed appendix, or an infection (bacterial and

10-1 CHECKING IT OUT: National Health Expenditures and Percent of Gross National Product, Selected Fiscal Years, 1950-76

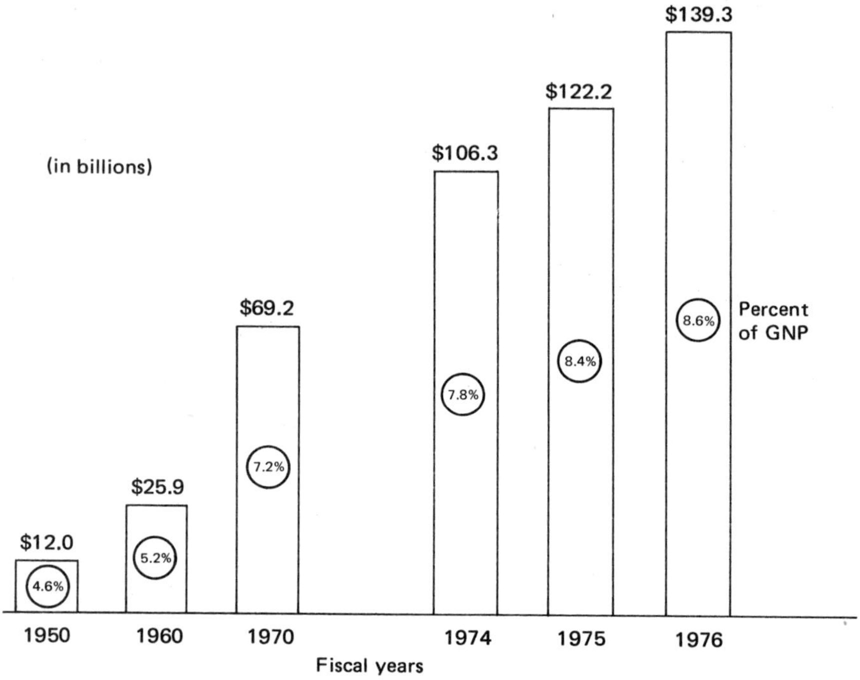

SOURCE: R. H. Gibson and M. S. Mueller, "National Health Expenditures, Fiscal Year 1976," *Social Security Bulletin,* Washington, D.C., USDHEW, 1977, *40,* No. 4 (April), p. 4.

viral). But biological sickness as a social condition is not the aspect usually examined, except in the sense of an analogy, as we mentioned before. Yet the social aspects not only go hand-in-hand with the physical, but even the decision to call something sickness or disease is, in itself, a social convention, and is not necessarily the same for all groups of people in all places.

DEFINITIONS OF HEALTH, DISEASE, AND ILLNESS

Despite the importance of health and disease to our society, it is neither easy to define what is meant by *health* and *disease* nor to establish simple and clear-cut criteria for agreement. The World Health Organization defines health as a "state of complete physical, mental, and social well-being, and not merely the absence of disease or infirmity." While this establishes the importance of the mental and social aspects of life, it is clearly a very idealized definition, for "well-being" is open to many interpretations and judgments. Peter Steinfels has indicated the importance of definitions of health because of what such definitions imply. They denote an attitude toward the particular condition—positive or negative sanction, approval or disapproval. Definitions indicate what particular professions or social institutions are viewed as having primary responsibility for such matters, and they show certain patterns of social action that the society has developed for dealing with issues of health and disease.

Underlying any concepts of disease, health, or illness are assumptions about what is the normal, usual, or ideal state of feeling and function as well as what constitutes deviations from these norms. But what is considered to be normal or usual may differ considerably according to culture, education, ethnicity, religion, age, sex, socioeconomic class, and specific socioenvironmental circumstances at the time; in short, all the various characteristics that make up the diversity of human society shape these definitions and their social consequences. Furthermore, even for a given individual, in a given instance, different definitions may be pertinent, depending upon who is doing the defining. Consider, as an example, a typical individual who does not feel well. Other observers such as family, friends, or co-workers will make judgments about whether or not the person is "really" ill, using their own criteria for accepting or rejecting the complaints. Finally, if the individual seeks the help of a health professional, another judgment is made, one that most certainly will involve additional criteria, which may or may not sanction the patient's complaints and desires. At each step (self, family, health practitioner) the agreement or nonagreement may lead to different social consequences. As we shall discuss later in more detail, the individual's own definition of being sick or healthy, as well as the society's decision to call certain behaviors and conditions disease (for example, alcoholism, delinquency, various behavioral or mental deviations), has profound implications not only for the individual, but for the society as a whole.

The term *disease* is probably best defined in terms of biological processes: that is, as a dysfunction of some part of the body or organ system. *Illness*, on the other hand, is not just the biological dysfunction, but the whole state of the person—the psychological and social experience of being less than what they consider to be their usual or optimal state of being and role functioning. In fact, people can and do feel ill and behave as if they are ill in the absence of any known or discernible physical dysfunction. On the other hand, they may have a biological disease and still consider themselves healthy and show no degree of incapacitation. In many areas of the world where serious diseases such as schistosomiasis (a parasitic disease) are endemic, the majority of the population are afflicted with the disease, and yet the people consider themselves healthy and continue to fulfill their social roles. The studies of Dunnell and Cartwright, for example, found that while 28 per cent of their respondents rated their health as excellent, and 39 per cent as good, only 9 per cent failed to report any symptoms at all from a symptom checklist. People *do* consider themselves healthy and continue to function though at the same time they may have a variety of symptoms and complaints.

While knowledge of what the signs and symptoms one sees and experiences is obviously important in deciding about the biological state of one's body, of equal importance, then, are the individual and social group's belief systems, the meaning and importance they attach to these behaviors, and their perceived implications for life functioning. In recognition of all these factors, modern conceptions of health tend to view it not as a static, ideal state, but rather as a continuing process of adaptation to the changing circumstances, demands, and situations of life and to the meanings that people give to all aspects of living.

SOCIAL FACTORS AND ILLNESS

Centuries before there was a field called sociology, economists, physicians, statesmen, and the social reformers of the times often observed that health and disease problems seemed intimately related to the social and economic conditions of life—that certain groups of people appeared particularly prone to various diseases and pathological conditions. Over the years these observations accumulated, and by the early part of the eighteenth century, the concept of *social medicine* was well established in the minds of many contemporary physicians. George Rosen, the medical historian, has written that these observations were not only of use to physicians, but were part of governmental "policy and organization of which the supreme aim was to place social and economic life in the service of the power politics of the state." (Rosen, p. 31) Thus, the social, economic, and political importance of health and disease was early established. Medical epidemiologists began systematically to refine these observations, building up a large body of knowledge about differential morbidity and mortality as a function of such factors as occupation, social class, imprisonment, sanitary conditions, and alcoholic consumption. Sociologists moved beyond the descriptive relationships between such factors and disease to study the social patterns, interactions, structures, organizations, belief systems, and behaviors of population subgroups. The focus of these studies has been to understand not only where such relationships exist, but *why* they exist: the mechanisms whereby social and cultural factors serve to affect and mediate the underlying biological processes that result in the differential rates of illness, disease, and disability. Here we can see the processes of social adaptation at work and why the modern concepts and definitions of health emphasize these factors. Since man is a social creature, social and cultural structures and organizations are the most important tools at his disposal for survival, adaptation, and pleasure; yet, as we can see, they are also forces that can cause pain, unhappiness, disease, and death. An examination of a simple life expectancy table immediately shows striking

10-2 CHECKING IT OUT: Expected Number of Deaths per 100,000 Population by Age, White *vs.* Nonwhite Males

	15–24		*35–44*		*55–64*	
	White	*Nonwhite*	*White*	*Nonwhite*	*White*	*Nonwhite*
Motor accidents	807	661	351	596	382	628
Other accidents	310	545	321	787	508	945
Suicide	113	82	232	126	348	120
Neoplasms	103	82	507	803	4,697	6,484
Homicide	75	771	98	1,146	62	508
Influenza and pneumonia	29	58	79	422	505	1,210
Heart disease	28	69	999	1,831	9,940	11,679
All causes	1,690	2,777	3,458	9,203	21,902	32,607

SOURCE: Adapted from *Vital Statistics of the U.S.*, U.S. Dept. of Health, Education and Welfare, Washington, D.C., U.S. Government Printing Office (1968).

differences according to age and race. Such tables do not show, however, the underlying reasons for the differences: the economic status of the people and their environmental conditions, whether or not they own automobiles and how they drive them, the alcohol and/or other drugs they may consume, their occupations and the degree of danger in their occupations, whether they settle their disagreements among themselves by discussion or by physical violence, or even whether they go to the doctor when they feel ill, do what they are told to do to get better, and live a life style that is conducive to good health and disease prevention. So our health or illness is not merely a random, chance event depending only upon how fate throws the dice, but is to a very great extent, an intimate part of our very social nature and patterns of living.

Primitive societies and poorer classes of people in all societies have received a great deal of attention for their high rates of infant mortality, generally lower life expectancy, and higher rates of many diseases, especially the infectious diseases. As was discussed in the chapter on Population and Society, societies tend to experience changes in birth and death rates as they become more advanced and industrialized. As Dubos and others have observed, these improvements—in fact the greatest improvements in the health of mankind—generally have come about not because of medical advances but because of improvements in hygiene, sanitation, and the general conditions of life. On the other hand, as we are increasingly learning, civilization and the complex social organization that is characteristic of our current society are accompanied by their own set of disease and illness patterns, patterns that have been called "the diseases of civilization." Our style of life, the food we eat and overeat, the physical and chemical environment we have created, the patterns of education, the nature of employment and working conditions, our political and economic structures, all produce their own characteristic sets of stresses and strains that appear to result in diseases and illnesses that are unknown, or at least far less frequent, among the societies we traditionally have viewed as underprivileged or less modern. Heart disease, cancer, stroke, and various other mental and emotional disorders that tend to be chronic and long-term now pose different new sets of problems for social policy and health policy. Since the nature of these disease and illness patterns is imbedded in our social life, correctives—that is prevention, treatment, and control—are to a marked extent dependent upon detailed social analysis.

PATHS TO TREATMENT—BECOMING A PATIENT

To begin to get a perspective on the ways in which health and illness problems are socially analyzed, we need to examine the broad sociological theory as it has been applied to these issues. Talcott Parsons, as part of his general theory of social systems, approaches illness as a basically social phenomenon; to be ill creates a special social role—the sick role—which represents a particular form of deviance. We recall that in the earlier discussion of the definitions of health and illness, the idea of a normal standard was inherent in any such definition; thus to be ill is to deviate from such standards. This, in turn, places the individual in the particular role of the sick one. This role is characterized by four general role-expectations: (1) The individual is not held responsible for his illness or incapacity; that is, becoming ill was beyond the person's capacity to prevent it. (2) Being defined as ill is viewed as a legitimate basis for being exempted from one's usual or normal role and task obligations. (3) It is assumed that being ill and occupying the sick role is undesirable to the person and that there is a desire to get well. The sick role is, therefore, a conditional one. (4) The sick individual is expected, in fact, has an obligation to seek competent medical advice and to comply with whatever treatment recommendations are made to assure a return to good health. These basic role-expectations provide a useful framework for examining the manner in which particular types of illness or social circumstances may alter the sick role. For example, to be acutely ill and confined to bed with a high temperature has a crisis quality to it—the patient is dependent, incapacitated, and given much attention and special privilege, but the assumption is that this is short-lived and that soon she/he will be well again. But a long-term, chronic illness that leaves partial disability and partial incapacity presents a different set of role circumstances; the crisis is not there, life for others must go on, and the patient is expected to perform as many role obligations and responsibilities as possible to lessen the burden upon others. The expectation outlined by Parsons that the person will seek competent medical advice, etc.

may be mitigated by a lack of knowledge that the condition is treatable, by geographic lack of treatment facilities, or by a simple lack of financial resources, but in such instances we would expect that some other behaviors are expected in its place such as prayers, folk remedies, etc., to indicate the commitment to return to health.

The two most important aspects of Parsons' approach to illness are the emphasis upon the social role that ensues as a concomitant of being ill and the characterization of this role as deviance. Since being ill does alter role obligations and functions, it often produces many stresses and strains within the family, the occupational structure, and other aspects of social life. To define something as deviance also immediately implies the corresponding actions of society to control the deviance and/or to return the deviant to normal functioning. The data on the growth and number of resources devoted to the health-care system presented at the beginning of the chapter is an indication of the importance our society attaches to the prevention and control of this form of deviance.

While Parsons focused on the sick role and illness behavior, the questions remain as to how, why, and when an individual defines himself or herself as ill and adopts (or does not adopt) the sick role. Illness behavior, defined as the manner in which "symptoms are differentially perceived, evaluated, and acted upon (or not acted upon) by different kinds of people and in different social institutions" (Mechanic, p. 116), has been extensively examined. Some of the important factors identified by Mechanic are: the perceived seriousness of the symptoms (the greater the assumption of seriousness, the more likely it is that some action will be taken); the extent to which symptoms disrupt family, work, or other social activities (more disruption brings greater likelihood of pressure by others, and/or personal responsibility to minimize disruption by seeking help); the frequency and intensity of the symptoms (very infrequent symptoms may tend to be ignored, but a very intense one, even if infrequent, is more likely to get attention); the economic costs of seeking help (in addition to the cost of medical care, for many people taking time off from work means they don't get paid); the tolerance of others toward these deviant symptoms (the more others accept, minimize, or ignore symptoms, the less social pressure there is to take action, and the less likelihood that action will be taken). We often forget when thinking or talking about illness and treatment that before, and if, a decision is made to see a health professional, the initial diagnosis that something is wrong is made by a layman (meaning each of us). Having knowledge about illness (in the technical medical sense) is only one factor that may enter into adopting the sick role or in being considered ill by others. Mechanic's focus on the various factors that differentially enter into this decision-making process is quite important for the variety of dimensions they indicate.

Once an individual has decided that something is not quite right, a variety of resources may be utilized. These resources form what has been referred to as the "lay referral structure," which usually never even reaches the point of finally seeking a legitimate health professional. This lay referral structure may include seeking advice or merely discussions with family, friends, etc., including the proverbial talking to the bartender or barber, taking folk remedies suggested in the local or ethnic structure, purchasing over-the-counter medications advertised on radio or television, or even resorting to quacks. It is important to remember that all of our statistics are obviously based upon people whom the authorities become aware of primarily because the patients seek help from a legitimate practitioner or facility, or because their deaths are officially recorded. But physicians have long known that for every case of any disease or illness that comes to their attention, an unknown number of similar cases exists in the community and never comes to light. In various household research surveys it has been shown that only one in three persons who *report* illness will actually see a physician, and estimates from similar surveys conclude that for a given month, even for illness reported as being serious by the respondents, only about nine of 750 ill persons will actually be hospitalized. This information is backed by a vast research literature demonstrating the importance of economic, class, racial, and educational variables in determining both utilization and availability of formal health resources. From this same literature, it is also clear that most health and illness concerns of the society are *not* encompassed by the formal health-care system, despite its current staggering size, but are rather contained and maintained through lay networks and other structures and institutions in the society at large.

Since most people who are ill or who suffer from various diseases do not enter into the formal health-care system, understanding health requires study of their behavior as well as of those who do seek treatment. Over the years, a number of social scientists have used the previously discussed factors in conjunction with additional demographic and medical factors and incorporated them into a theoretical framework called the "health belief model." This model has been especially useful in helping to answer the broad question of how people handle their health problems within specific social institutional frameworks. Two types of health behavior are particularly important: preventive health behavior (what people do to keep well) and compliance behavior (following professional advice to get well when sick, and/or to prevent further illness). As one comedian used to say, "people are funnier than anybody," and their behavior, even when they are suffering serious disease or illness, frequently defies simple explanation. Consider, for example, people who travel many miles to a medical clinic for treatment or other patients who suffer from major respiratory disease. Many studies of the compliance behavior of patients such as these report essentially the same findings. Only about 50 per cent of the patients were found to have actually filled their prescriptions (even if the medicine was free). Even more astounding was the finding that of those who filled the prescriptions, only about 20 per cent actually took the medicine. Subsequent research has found that explanation for such behavior can be found by examination of the various factors in the health belief model, particularly those we mentioned earlier. When these types of data are also used in household surveys about health and illness, a more complete and even predictive picture emerges of when, why, and under what circumstances various groups and classes of people will seek formal treatment, and how well they will comply with prescribed advice.

Preventive health is, of course, a matter of concern for all, since, at least in theory, we all wish to stay well and do what we can to prevent serious illness in the future. Yet here again, despite the constant barrage of mass media information about disease prevention (balanced diets, low fat intake, avoidance of junk food, the dangers of obesity and smoking, etc.), we find that what people know they should do does not necessarily correlate very well with what they actually do. (College students, for example, often maintain diets that are as deficient as those among the poor and underprivileged.) While such findings are, naturally, important, particularly since explanations are usually found imbedded in the social and cultural structure, the implications of our knowledge about preventive health behavior have even more profound significance. Despite national studies demonstrating generally poor preventive health behavior, peoples' expectations about, and demands upon, the health-care delivery system continue to grow, while at the same time increasing evidence shows that individual responsibility for many facets of health is the only answer. No system can provide what people will not do for themselves. This, of course, is only one small (but important) part of a very large, complicated issue in the health-care delivery system; but it does serve to show the linkage between our own beliefs, values, and behavior and social institutions.

MENTAL ILLNESS AND DISEASE

The terms *mental illness* and *mental disease* are used rather interchangeably to refer to a wide range of conditions involving peoples' thoughts (expressed or inferred), behavior, and role functioning. Such a wide range of human functions do not have much in common, resulting in a lack of precision in these concepts to date. The terms are used with impunity by laymen as well as by experts as a social label to describe putative deviations from social, ethical, moral, and legal norms. There are, of course, many known medical conditions in which disturbances and imbalances in hormonal, brain, or other bodily functions underlie such behavioral deviance, but in the majority of people to whom these labels are applied, no bodily dysfunctions of any kind are known to or can be demonstrated to exist. Consequently, considerable debate and controversy continue in the professional literature on the use, misuse, definitions, and applicability of these terms. Much of the debate focuses on the very applicability of the disease concept, which by its very nature invokes assumptions of physical disease and places the issue within the realm of medicine. Furthermore, since the terms are used to describe and explain such phenomena as delinquency, crime, alcoholism, drug abuse, deviant sexual behavior, and even divorce, all of which clearly involve other social institutions (law and criminal justice, education, marriage and the family, and the church), and the behaviors involved are so heavily laden with moral, ethical, and legal judgments, the resolution of the definitional confusion has considerable societal importance. It makes a great deal of difference whether one defines oneself as sick and sees a physician or as immoral and seeks the clergy; or whether one is defined by others as sick and sent to a hospital or as criminal and sent to prison. Depending upon how the deviance is considered, different social forces are set into motion, different social institutions become involved, and different social consequences result.

As is true of the history of disease in general, the social nature and the social context of mental illness have also been noted since antiquity. Two very broad approaches (other than the biomedical) to this subject can be outlined although they have come to overlap considerably. The first and much older approach is that of epidemiology, while the second, more clearly sociologic approach, focuses upon social institutions (medicine and psychiatry), social organization and disorganization, and mental illness as one aspect of the sociology of deviance and social control. One particular variant of deviance theory (labeling theory or the societal-reaction perspective), has received much attention and will be briefly discussed, particularly as it relates to some consistent epidemiologic findings.

In the late eighteenth century, an American physician, Edward Jarvis, made the observation that the "pauper class" contributed disproportionately to the mental hospital populations. These same observations continued to be made over the years, and with more systematic and sophisticated refinements in research, not only the poor but other disadvantaged groups and ethnic, racial, and other minority groups were found to show higher rates of hospitalization in public mental institutions, to have poorer access to treatment, to receive less desirable forms of treatment when they did come to official attention, and to be treated by less experienced physicians. It has been shown consistently that the elderly also receive disproportionately fewer psychiatric services despite their higher illness rates. Some of the other social factors associated with higher rates of some forms of mental illness are: divorce, single status and living alone, lower education, death of spouse, downward social mobility, and inner city and/or ghetto residence. Communities with a low state of social organization (few and poorly supported schools, church groups, civic organizations, etc.) tend to show higher rates of psychiatric symptoms when studied by household or community surveys.

Here again, the previously discussed factors outlined by Mechanic and others are extremely pertinent in determining why these differences occur, why different paths to treatment are sometimes utilized, and why differences in access to help exist. There are, however, additional considerations that are of extreme importance in explaining and understanding these behavioral conditions. The conditions labeled as mental illness, particularly some of its more extreme behavioral forms, frequently involve breaches or violations of culturally sanctioned rules and norms about behavior which are in sharp conflict with established middle-class values. The consequences for the individual often involve severe social stigma and involuntary treatment and/or incarceration. In view of these considerations, analysis of the mechanisms for the social control of deviancy, the social power structure, and the distribution of resources in society have proven essential. For example, it was mentioned above that the rates for psychosis (a severe form of mental illness) tend to rise sharply as social-class level decreases. Research has also revealed that there is a much greater tendency for this diagnostic label to be applied to lower-class and racial and cultural minorities than to middle-class whites showing essentially the same behavior: is there more illness in these groups, or is the medical diagnosis due to cultural ignorance, a discriminatory bias, or a mechanism for the social control of deviance?

The societal-reaction perspective (labeling theory) is concerned with the social forces that structure, organize, and continue patterns of deviance, and gives less attention to the initial origins of the deviant behavior. Deviant behavior is seen as reinforced by the manner in which it is labeled, by the social reactions to it, and by the ensuing patterns of discrimination, exclusion, and isolation that result. Mental illness, in particular, is viewed as a residual form of deviance—no other appropriate labels exist, and when the label is used and applied to a person, it helps organize the behavior into a specific social role with predictable consequences (Scheff). Since the past two decades have seen a continuous broadening of the use of psychiatric labels for deviant behavior as part of a general medicalization of social problems, this perspective has proven very useful in emphasizing the social forces at work in this process.

Historically, the treatment of the severely mentally ill has generally been marked by public neglect and the isolation of patients in mental institutions away from the rest of the community. It was not until 1946 that the U.S. Government began an active role in attempting to correct this pattern by making funds available for research on human behavior, for increasing the supply of treatment personnel, and for the expansion of treatment facilities. The traditional, isolated mental hospital came to be seen as detrimental to the patient, and hospitalization to be avoided if at all possible. Treating patients in the community as out-patients led to the expanded development of community treatment centers, which were only part of a larger therapeutic program of Community Mental Health. The ideas that provided the basis for the Community Mental Health movement were part of a social philosophy that focused on those problems and inequities of the society at large which were thought conducive to poor mental health and to be instrumental in causing mental illness.

Since social conditions were viewed as playing a major role in causing deviant behavior, the idea of prevention through community action and community organization became a major goal of the mental health professions; treatment of those already ill was now only one of their roles. Total elimination of the mental hospital and discharge of the existing patients became the immediate task. In 1956 there were 550,000 patients in the country's state mental hospitals, and by 1972 these had been reduced to 300,000. While the average length of stay in the hospital in 1956 was 8 years, by 1972 this had been reduced to 17 months. By 1972 California had closed 5 of its 10 mental hospitals. However, for this same period it was found that admissions to the hospitals *continued to rise* although the average length of stay was now shorter, and the *readmission* rate for patients who had been discharged rose from 54.4 per cent in 1956 to 65.1 per cent in 1972. Patients were, therefore, not necessarily being cured but were being quickly returned to the community to be treated there. The high readmission rates and the decreased length of stay led Greenblatt and Glazier to conclude that the base of mental illness care had broadened to include less severe forms of personal and social disabilities. They felt that the tolerance of deviant behavior in the community had actually *decreased* as the kinds of behavior seen as requiring care and treatment had been *increasing* over the past twenty years.

Repeated studies of discharged mental patients, especially the aged, those without families, the poor, and those suffering from the severe psychoses, find that these people tend to live in isolation and neglect in substandard housing in deteriorated sections of the city or in unsupervised nursing homes, rejected and resented by the larger community. The community mental health centers have been found to devote most of their efforts to more interesting social problems and less severely ill patients. Minimal attention is given to those most in need.

It is for these reasons, in conjunction with the ever-widening use of the label "mental illness," that the subject of mental health remains extremely controversial. The more forms of behavior that are viewed as deviant and in need of treatment, the farther we move from traditional concepts of disease and the more pertinent become the issues of ideology and values relating to the social control of deviancy and the maintenance of the social order. At this time there are no simple or satisfactory solutions to these problems, but we can expect that they will continue to change and evolve as part of the larger pattern of social change.

HEALTH-CARE ISSUES

The special role of the healer, represented by the physician, has reached its most developed and specialized form in our society, a role characterized by the highest occupational and social prestige, maximum autonomy in structuring role performance, and very high financial remuneration. Despite the growth of ancillary health-care occupations, the physician remains the central figure of authority and power within the health-care delivery system. Within the broader theory of the sociology of professions, medicine has been the most extensively studied profession. Particular attention has been given to examining medical education as part of the professional socialization process, the doctor-patient relationship, and the profession's role and functions in the delivery of health care.

Traditionally, the medical profession has been characterized as altruistic and idealistic, noteworthy for its capacity for self-regulation, its devotion to the common good, and its rigid code of ethics. American medical care, primarily because of these factors plus the amazing advances in biomedical technology of the past few decades, was generally felt to be the best in the world. Over the past decade or so, however, many of these assumptions and values have come to be questioned as part of a broader process of social change. While all costs have been rising, medical care (especially hospital costs) has risen precipitously. The United States, alone among comparable Western societies, has no form of National Health Insurance and, although an increasing percentage of the population is covered by private or occupational health insurance plans, many people are still without coverage. Longevity and infant mortality data in the United States do not compare favorably with many other comparable countries. This raises the question of why this should be so when our national per capita health spending is greater than that in other countries. The civil rights programs and women's liberation movements have added to the growing national awareness of the continuing social inequities and injustices reflected in the differential health and disease rates discussed earlier. Many of the defects of the broader society are also present in the health-care system, particularly in the medical profession, with its disproportionately few racial and ethnic minority members and the small number of female physicians—a pattern caused by long-standing exclusionary practices. The code of ethics of the medical profession itself has been shown to apply far more to intraprofessional rules of conduct than it does to doctor-patient relationships and obligations. Many studies have shown that there is a tendency for the medical education process to diminish the feelings of altruism in medical students and to increase their attitudes of impersonality toward patients, while at the same time to overvalue research at the expense of patient care. The frequent complaints of the public reflect just these findings: overspecialization of practice, high costs, impersonal treatment, unavailability of physicians, etc.

During this same period, the attitude of the government has been undergoing a change also, to the position that health is a right, rather than a privilege, and that equal access to quality health care at a reasonable cost must now become a national priority. There is growing recognition that the development of health services is an important part of the effort to improve social and economic conditions. Through government sponsored initiatives and broad gauged legislation, most of the problems just discussed are receiving corrective attention, ranging from revisions in medical school education programs to an examination of the entire health-care system, but much remains to be done.

Some health problems, however, particularly those that relate to individual perceptions and behavior, may be even more difficult to deal with. Earlier we mentioned that chronic diseases (heart diseases, cancer, stroke, mental illness, etc.) pose new problems for health policy. No cures as yet exist for these conditions, but much evidence points to many things that may be done on the individual level to reduce the probability that in later years we will suffer from these conditions. But individual attempts at healthy living require special effort, plus a belief in their efficacy, plus care: care to exercise, to eat properly and moderately, not to smoke, not to drink to excess, etc. There are, however, many social pressures which work against these efforts: the temptations offered by an economy geared to high production and high consumption, peer group values and pressures to conform, "macho" role models, the uncertainty of the future, and the long-range view of benefits for good behavior. Lurking in the minds of many is the continued belief in the biomedical miracles to come—the cures for these illnesses and "diseases of civilization" which will make such preventive health behavior an unnecessary waste and absolve us of individual responsibility. For now and for the foreseeable future, however, the health-care system is charged with treating and preventing through its social organization those diseases we create through our social processes. This is what the sociology of health is all about.

INTERPRETIVE SUMMARY

No matter how primitive the society, social arrangements are made for dealing with disease, injury, birth, and death. In modern, industrialized society these provisions have evolved into complex and costly health-care delivery systems which involve many professions and occupations in addition to the physician. In the United States, the health-care system is now the nation's largest single industry employer as well as being the largest single industry—an indication of the importance we attach to matters of health and disease. Yet defining health and disease is not a simple matter, since we find that people's beliefs, attitudes, values, and knowledge enter into their definitions of health, disease, and illness. Illness has come to be seen as not just the physical dysfunctions of the body, but the total psychological and social experience that accompanies bodily dysfunction. To be ill, whether it is one's own concept of self or the way others consider one, is to occupy a special social role, the sick role, which carries with it special role alterations and obligations. Since the definition of illness is based upon departures from normative standards of usual functioning and behavior, illness constitutes a form of deviance and the sick role is a deviant social role. As is true for all forms of deviance, various types of social action may be brought into play to control the deviance and/or to return the individual to normal functioning.

How people come to adopt or reject the sick role is a matter of considerable importance and one that has received intensive study. Social, demographic, economic, and medical factors have been incorporated into the "health belief model," a theoretical framework that sociologists use to study health behavior: not only when and why people occupy the sick role, but the circumstances under which treatment is sought, how well patients comply with treatment recommendations, and the steps people will take to prevent illness and disease. Since the rates of illness and disease have been found to vary according to factors such as occupation, social class, age, sex, race, ethnicity, and so forth, analysis of the social interactions, structures, organizations, belief systems, and values of these population subgroups is essential in order to understand why these differences in disease rates occur. Research has consistently shown that the poor, the aged, and underprivileged ethnic and minority groups tend to have higher rates of illness and disease. On the other hand, a variety of disease and illness patterns, "the diseases of civilization," are linked to modern, complex social patterns and structures, and many of these conditions tend to increase with affluence.

The terms "mental illness" and "mental disease" are used to label a vast range of conditions which involve throughts, behavior, and role functions. In contrast to most diseases, these conditions rarely show bodily dysfunctions but are deviations from established social, ethical, moral, and legal norms. Consequently, there is considerable controversy and debate over the term "mental illness," focusing on the appropriateness of calling such conditions "disease," with its implied medical connotations. Furthermore, it has been shown that an increasing array of behavior has come to be included under the label of mental illness, a trend that is viewed as implying a decreased tolerance for deviancy in the community. Changing conceptions of mental illness have been accompanied by changed ideas about how and where the illness is to be treated. The traditional mental hospital is no longer seen as desirable for treatment. Out-patient treatment in the community in a local treatment center has become the desirable approach as part of a larger program of community mental health. Social forces and processes that result in inequities, injustices, discrimination, and poor distribution of economic resources are among the factors that community mental health theory relates to poor mental health and the causes of mental illness.

As part of a broader movement of social analysis, criticism, and social change, the American health-care system has come to be the subject of national focus and controversy. While popular belief has long viewed this system as the best in the world, many deficiencies have been noted including the continuing increase in the costs of health care, the unavailability of care for a large percentage of the population, and the poor comparability in rates of various diseases between the United States and other Western nations. The medical profession itself, as the dominant health-care profession, has been the object of a vast amount of research as well as a vast amount of criticism. The government has now come to view good health and economical access to health care as a right and is attempting to foster changes and improvements in all aspects of the health-care delivery system.

Although public demand for health care continues to grow, increasing research relates many disease and illness patterns to the conditions of modern Western society, and particularly to our styles of living, food preferences, overeating, drinking, smoking, etc. Consequently, any decrease in the rates of disease will depend upon alterations in individual behavior. However, such personal responsibility takes special effort in the face of many social pressures that work against such attempts. Since the patterns of illness and disease, the delivery of services to attempt to deal with them, and the life styles of all of us are an intimate part of the very structure of contemporary society, continued social analysis along with continuing social change will, it is hoped, provide better understanding and better means for correction.

QUESTIONS

1. It is quite clear that our concerns for health and disease have tremendous implications for our society's economic system. Suppose all diseases were suddenly curable: What might be the social implications for the economy, jobs and careers, etc.?
2. Concepts of disease, illness, and health are based upon assumptions of what is normal or usual, and these assumptions in turn differ widely according to many factors. What are the implications of this for medical diagnoses? for data comparisons between countries? for attaining the World Health Organization's concept of health?
3. As we have seen, social factors and conditions are intimately linked to both the types of disease and the rates of disease in populations. Why are attempts by the U.S. Government to change disease patterns in other countries a largely *non*medical problem? Why do third-world countries often view our medical efforts in their countries as interference and/or imperialism?
4. The "lay referral structure" handles far more health problems than does the formal health-care system. What virtues and what dangers do you see in this?
5. What social implications do you see in the trend to include an increasingly broad array of forms of deviance under the label of disease or illness? Do you see this as creating problems for our various social institutions—medical as well as nonmedical?
6. What aspects of mental health and mental illness cause this subject to be controversial? What political implications do you see as pertinent to the society's "tolerance of deviancy"?

11

Social Stratification

WHO GETS WHAT AND WHY?

In any human society people rarely, if ever, accept all others as social equals. In every society some people are identified as superior and others as inferior: there are aristocrats and commoners, masters and slaves, elites and masses, the privileged and the disadvantaged, the rich and the poor, the esteemed and the demeaned, and the rulers and the ruled. Social inequality is probably a universal feature of human society. In all or nearly all societies the good things in life, the things that people desire, are unequally distributed; some have more and others have less. Social stratification refers to the persistence over time of the inequality of valued rewards—as when parents pass on their wealth to their children or when children "inherit" (socially speaking) the same position as their family. When the opportunity for education and good health and social respectability is dependent upon whether or not one's parents are impoverished or affluent, social stratification exists. Underlying and permeating the study of social stratification, therefore, is the question "who gets what and why?"

The rigidity of social stratification varies considerably from society to society. In some societies, males and females cannot change from the class into which they are born, and must marry a person born into the same class. Class position is the prime determinant of the amount of education such people receive, and the occupation that they pursue. In other societies, one's position in the stratification structure is relatively changeable. In such a situation, it is possible for the son of an accountant to quit high school, never go to college, become a garage mechanic, and yet marry the daughter of his employer. Furthermore, there may be some disagreement among members of the society as to whether the accountant is upper class or middle class, and whether the garage mechanic is middle class or lower class.

The more complex the division of labor becomes the more opportunity there

11-1 CHECKING IT OUT: Economic Surplus and Societal Inequality

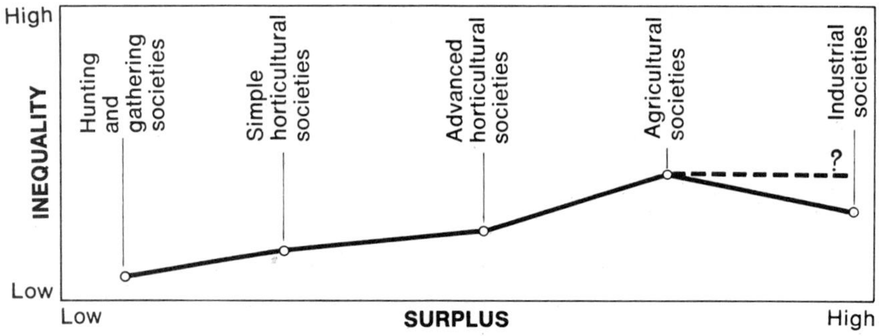

SOURCE: Gerhard E. Lenski; *Power and Privilege* (New York: McGraw-Hill, 1966).

is for class structure to develop; therefore, settled communities are likely to have more complex stratification systems than nomadic tribes, and all urban industrial societies invariably have some form of class stratification. The degree of social inequality in any society is also dependent upon the level of technology and the amount of economic surplus (the goods and services over and above the minimum required to keep producers alive and productive) of the society. According to Lenski, (1966) the amount of societal inequality increases as the surplus of a society increases. Since social stratification is related to the distribution of scarce and valued resources in society, those societies with a very small amount of economic surplus have little inequality. As technology improves and agricultural techniques are developed, the economic surplus rises and inequality reaches a peak. This process is exemplified in such great agrarian societies as the ancient empires of Rome and China. According to Lenski, inequality begins to decline with industrialization because of the nature of the industrial economy: (1) workers at various levels of expertise have skill monopolies and therefore more power in industrial societies than in agrarian societies; (2) managers and other experts have considerable authority in the industrial system and thus command great economic rewards; (3) workers organized into large factories have the power to strike and slow down production; (4) industrialism requires mass distribution and consumption of its products. The industrial system, in short, simply demands more equality than the agrarian system.

The stratification system of a society is partially dependent on the normative order of the culture, since this will determine the criteria upon which statuses are ranked: the power they have, the wealth associated with them, and so on. When we speak of a stratification structure it is easy to sound as if it were a static, permanent thing. Actually, of course, stratification, like any other feature of social organization, is constantly changing. To achieve some perspective on the wide variation in social stratification and the dynamics of the stratification process, we shall look briefly at stratification in various times and places.

A CROSS–CULTURAL VIEW OF STRATIFICATION

Stratification in Preindustrial Societies

In North America the Kwakiutl had a rather rigid scheme, as did the warring Plain Indians. The Pueblo groups, on the other hand, had a somewhat flexible stratification structure. There were caste systems in both Peru and Mexico. In a large part of Africa, Asia, and Oceania, stratification is common. For example, in many parts of western Africa the king and his nobles make up a rigid, inheritable class rationalized as of divine sanction. Below them are various political ranks, specialized craftsmen, commoners, and slaves. There are other forms of stratification structures, as among the cattle-raising Wahuma or Tutsi of eastern Africa, who are the top class ruling the horticultural Bantu, whom they had originally conquered.

In Polynesia there are many castes. The Maori nobility of New Zealand trace their descent through primogeniture back to the highest gods. Every man of distinction has to memorize his lineage so that on occasion he can recite his pedigree. There are five groups of freemen: chiefs, priests, landed gentry, large landholders, and commoners. Moreover, the gradations of rank within these castes are numerous. Complex forms of address and carefully detailed rituals are worked out to control the relations of the various castes and ranks to one another. Somewhat similar caste systems exist elsewhere in the South Pacific.

Caste in India

The Hindu caste system has long been of great interest to Western peoples, and around it has grown up a host of myths and legends. In actuality it is more flexible, more dynamic, and more complex than is generally recognized. The Hindu word for caste is *varna*, meaning *color*, and there is little doubt that in India color and racial differences have had some part in setting up caste lines.

Hindu tradition relates that the major divisions were established about 600 B.C. The ancient Laws of Manu gave the four chief castes as follows: (1) the *Brahmans*, or priests, who were "assigned the duties of reading the Vedas [the sacred books], of teaching, of sacrificing, of assisting others to sacrifice, of giving alms if they be rich, and if indigent of receiving gifts"; (2) the military chieftains, or overlords, called the *Kshatriya*; (3) the agriculturists, herdsmen, and traders, called the *Vaisya*; and (4) the servile class of menials and industrial workers, or *Sudra*.

The Laws of Manu mention 50 castes besides these major *varnas*. Outside these four orders, and outside the bounds of Hinduism, is a varied mass of outcastes, the lowest of whom, the *Chandalas*, are regarded about on a par with such "unclean" animals as dogs and donkeys. (O'Malley, 1932, p. 13) The four divisions, indeed, are but the skeleton of a highly complex system of castes and subcastes. When the local differences in subcastes are taken into account, the number in fact reaches nearly 5,000. Castes and subcastes are constantly forming and reforming by division and unification. When we come to study the system closely, we find, not the static, stereotyped picture of fiction or popular legend, but a living, changing social organization. Castes are formed on the basis of occupations, sectarian groups, races, tribes, or other associations of people with distinctive cultural traits or social roles.

To people of Western culture, some of the regulations seem extreme indeed. For example, one may not sit down to eat with another who is not of the same caste. All meals must be prepared by one of his own caste or by a Brahman. No man of inferior caste may touch the cooked rations of one of higher caste or, for that matter, enter into the latter's culinary quarters.

The severity of social pressure on the man who has been put out of his caste is striking. When a Hindu is expelled from his caste, his friends, relatives, and fellow townspeople refuse to accept his hospitality; he is not invited to their houses; he cannot secure brides or bridegrooms for his children; his own married daughters scarcely dare visit him lest they also lose caste. His priest, barber, and washerman will not serve him. Fellow members of his caste even decline to assist at the funeral of one of his household. With group codes felt so strongly by the individual, it is no wonder that such a system persists even in the face of many forces that tend to disintegrate it.

Although the caste system remains dominant in most of rural India, many changes have weakened its hold on the urban population. The urbanization of population affords the person who has lost caste a chance to change his identity in a great city, to take up another occupation, and perhaps to marry outside his caste. Travel and mobility throw the castes together in situations that were not likely to arise before the coming of the railroad and the crowded conditions of large cities. Schooling has helped alter the attitude toward caste, especially among persons with a higher education. Christianity and other foreign religions have gradually had some effect on attitudes toward caste. The spread of nationalistic and democratic ideas has had a powerful influence on the attitudes toward some features of the caste structure. In fact, in the very first years of Indian independence, measures were introduced in the national legislature to abolish many features of the caste system, including a 1955 law which made discrimination against untouchables (the lowest caste) a crime and a 1956 law which permitted intercaste marriage. Yet the inertia of custom and tradition is powerful. (Green, 1957; Berreman, 1960) The village, the heart of the Hindu social organization, is the seat of caste at its strongest. Family life, religion, and occupation still provide powerful support for the system.

Estates of Feudal Europe

With the breakup of the Roman Empire following the "barbarian" invasion, society in western Europe was refashioned along somewhat different lines. The feudal order which emerged was a more or less legally fixed system of class, sometimes called *estates.* There were various gradations: overlords, lesser lords, knights, burghers, guild members, freemen, and serfs. A shift from one level to another was difficult. Gradually economic and political changes came about, and the seeds were sown for the disintegration of the old order and the rise of a more flexible class system. (Mayer, 1955)

Classes in Modern Europe

The Emergence of Classes The commercial and industrial revolutions disrupted the feudal order and set in motion cultural and social changes that not only produced a shift from primary to secondary organization of society but influenced Western class structure. While the landed aristocracy, the military class, and the ecclesiastical hierarchy remained in the upper brackets, new classes emerged; first, from the large industrial entrepreneurs, bankers, and merchants; second, from the petty business groups; and third, from the rapidly growing urban industrial masses. The last became increasingly numerous and socially more powerful than the peasant and gradually declining serf classes. The shift in the strength of the lowest class was slow. Serfdom did not disappear in France until shortly before the French Revolution, until Napoleon's time in Germany, and in Russia not until after the middle of the nineteeth century.

The most important elements in the modern world which tended to alter the class system were (1) the capitalistic business enterprise and its close associate, the factory system; (2) the political order, which stressed nationalism and, later, democracy; (3) the coming of religious tolerance and freedom following the Protestant Reformation; and (4) the expanding spirit and practice of free inquiry, which led to modern science and technology and had a marked effect on political democracy, business, and even religion.

Revolutions and Elitism The liquidation of former social classes following a great political-economic revolution is well documented in history. For example, in contrast to Czarist days, the present pyramid of power in Soviet Russia follows the pattern of a dominant-party elite: a vast range of administrative officials at the top and below this the masses, within which there are

11-2 CHECKING IT OUT: Social Stratification in Russia

Food shortages are among the most nagging problems of the Soviet economy. In many rural towns, meat is unavailable in the winter and it is often scarce even in the cities. The shortages of food—and many other goods—have fostered a complex stratification of society in which membership in the elite is based less on monetary wealth than on access to consumer items and services in short supply. Money can be a factor, but often as not connections, in Russian called "blat," are more important in acquiring such coveted items as permission to reside in the big cities where shopping is comparatively abundant—and access to special stores with imported and other hard-to-get commodities. The result is a barter system in which people whose positions enable them to hold out rarities from public sale distribute them under the counter to friends who reciprocate with other scarcities. The goods and services bartered range from skilled surgery to ballet tickets to auto repairs.

Elitism is reinforced by policy as well as by inefficiency. Directors of research institutes, for example, receive 500 to 700 rubles a month ($690 to $966) while their junior researchers get 105 to 125 rubles ($145 to $172). The right of inheritance, abolished by a 1918 decree based on Marxist tenets, has been gradually reinstated over the years until now it is basically as uncontrolled as in the West.

Aside from cash, other benefits define class differences. Key officials are paid part of their salaries in so-called certificate rubles, which can be used in special stores carrying imported goods unavailable in regular shops and scarce Soviet-made items at as little as one-fifth the normal price. Travel abroad, highly prized and reserved for the select few, brings with it the privilege of special stores, because payment received in dollars or other hard currency may be converted to certificate rubles upon return home. Other stores exist only for those hand-picked officials and their families who hold special passes. Access to the better hospitals and clinics, restaurants, country dachas, apartment houses and vacation centers are similarly based on one's position in the party, the university or the factory.

Whatever this is, it is not Marxism. Yet it agrees with the traditions of Russian society, and therefore it seems to provoke no real domestic dissent from the left, no Chinese-style criticism of the system. "Mao said we should reject material incentives and motivate our people with revolutionary ideas," Khrushchev declared in his memoirs. "But you can't make soup out of an idea." The remark says something about Soviet ideology today. . .

SOURCE: David K. Shipler, *The New York Times,* November 6, 1977 p. 5.

recognized gradations. (Dallin, 1944; Inkeles, 1950) Wars, like revolutions, often bring about considerable shifts in the class organization; World War I induced many such alterations in Europe, and World War II resulted in even more drastic changes.

CLASS STRUCTURE IN THE UNITED STATES

The United States is one example of a relatively open-class system in which birth or lineage is only one element in the determination of class position. Despite variations in the degree to which achieved status is overshadowed by ascribed status, the open-class system has been increasingly identified with the common man and the democratic process. Yet, social stratification persists in the United States. A major aspect of our stratification structure is the fact that, along with this open-class system, there existed human slavery, which later, under military-political pressure, gave way to a caste-like system based on color. The persistence of the white-black caste relationship not only is an intriguing cultural paradox, but continues to present the United States with one of its most serious and pressing local and national dilemmas. Similarly, opportunities for women in this society continue to be restricted in many ways, and sexism, like racism, pervades the society.

Social stratification is so complex and mutifaceted that the criteria of class position in modern urban-industrial societies are sometimes vague and usually changing. Consequently, classes are not clearly delineated in the minds of many Americans and tend to overlap. There is, for example, general consensus in the United States that it is better to make much money than little, that is better to be educated than ignorant, that professional occupations have higher prestige than unskilled occupations. But consensus declines when more criteria than one are involved. Who ranks higher in the class structure, the person with a moderate income and a great deal of education, or the one with a moderate amount of education and a high income?

The Distribution of Wealth

Social stratification refers to the unequal distribution of the valued items of the society. In modern industrial societies few things are more valued, more consequential, and more unequally distributed than wealth. Valid and reliable data on wealth are not plentiful partly because most people, especially wealthy people, are reluctant to discuss the subject with researchers. One of the most careful and reliable studies of wealth in the United States is by Robert J. Lampman. (Lampman, 1959, 1965) According to Lampman's estimates, persons with assets in excess of \$50,000—only 2 per cent of the population—held nearly 30 per cent of all the wealth in 1953 while 50 per cent of the population held only 8 per cent of the wealth. In 1929 the richest 2 per cent of the population held 33 per cent of all privately held wealth. More current reports indicate that the distribution of wealth has not changed significantly in recent years. In 1972, for instance, 12,815 persons who reported gross assets of \$60,000 or more had a total net worth of \$1,852 billion while 28 per cent of the population had a net worth of less than \$1,000 apiece.

The Distribution of Income

Because most Americans do not have substantial wealth, they must depend upon earned income. Income is more equally distributed than wealth, but as late as 1976 when the median income for all families was $14,958, nearly one-fourth of the population earned less than half that amount (*Statistical Abstract*, 1977). Moreover, the distribution of income has changed very little in the last quarter century. In 1976 the 20 per cent of the population that had the highest incomes received 41 per cent of all income while the poorest 20 per cent of the population

11-3 CHECKING IT OUT: Total Money Income of Families and Unrelated Individuals in the United States, 1976

Income Category		*Per Cent*
Less than $1,000		4.4
$ 1,000–$ 1,999		0.4
2,000– 3,999		10.9
4,000– 5,999		9.5
6,000– 7,999		8.8
8,000– 9,999		4.3
10,000– 14,999		18.7
15,000– 24,999		25.4
25,000 and more		13.5
Median Income	$11,923	

SOURCE: U.S. Bureau of the Census, *Current Population Reports,* Series P-60, No. 114 (Washington, D.C.: U.S. Government Printing Office, 1978), p.43.

11-4 CHECKING IT OUT: Percentage of Income Received by Each Fifth of Families and Individuals in the United States, 1944 and 1976

Families and Individuals Ranked from Highest Income to Lowest	*1944*	*1976*
Highest Fifth	46	41
Second Fifth	22	24
Third Fifth	16	17
Fourth Fifth	11	11
Lowest Fifth	5	5

SOURCE: U.S. Bureau of the Census, *Historical Statistics of the United States* (Washington, D.C.: U.S. Government Printing Office, 1960); and U.S. Bureau of the Census, *Statistical Abstract of the United States,* 1977 (Washington, D.C.: U.S. Government Printing Office, 1977), p. 443.

received only 5 per cent. Taxes, it should be noted, do not have a significant effect on the equalization of income. Persons with less than $2,000 are the most heavily taxed; they pay about 44 per cent of their income in federal, state, and local taxes. (Pechman, 1968) Persons with incomes between $2,000 and $15,000 pay about 27 per cent of their income in taxes, and persons with incomes over $15,000 pay 38 per cent in taxes.

Income and Occupation

The most frequently used measures of class are occupation, wealth, income, and education. Many other items associated with or dependent on these variables have also been used: type of home, "quality" of neighborhood, monthly rent, and the like. The two that are most often used are income and occupation. (Warner, 1949) Income and occupation are, of course, closely interrelated. Table 11-5

11-5 CHECKING IT OUT: Occupation and Median Wage or Salary Income of Year-Round, Full-Time Male Workers in the United States, 1976

Occupation	*Median Wage-Salary*
White Collar Occupations:	
Managers, officials, and proprietors	$17,246
Professional, technical and kindred workers	16,401
Sales workers	14,299
Clerical workers	12,778
Blue Collar Occupations:	
Craftsmen, foremen and kindred workers	13,708
Operatives and kindred workers	11,784
Service workers (except private household)	10,131
Laborers (except farm and mine)	10,080
Farm Occupations:	
Farmers and farm managers	2,010
Farm laborers and foremen	6,270

SOURCE: *Current Population Reports,* Series P-60, No. 114 (July, 1978), p. 244.

shows the relationship between wages and salary income and occupation for full-time, year-round male workers. Table 11-6 shows the association between education and the total money income for all year-round, full-time male workers aged 25 and older.

Furthermore, there is a considerable agreement among Americans about the relative prestige of various occupations. The National Opinion Research Center conducted a public-opinion poll of people in the United States which

11-6 CHECKING IT OUT: Education and Median (Total Money) Income of Year-Round, Full-Time Male Workers* in the United States, 1976

Education	*Median Income*
Elementary	
Less than 8 years	$8,991
8 years	11,312
High School	
1–3 years	12,301
4 years	14,295
College	
1–3 years	15,514
4 years	18,236
5 years or more	20,597

* Males aged 25 and older.

SOURCE: *Current Population Reports,* Series P-60, No. 114 (July, 1978), p. 193.

ranked 90 different occupations on a five-point scale: excellent, good, average, below average, and poor. From two-thirds to three-fourths of all people gainfully employed in the United States were in one of the 90 occupations rated. The ratings were scored so that an occupation receiving exclusively "excellent" ratings would score 100, while one unanimously rated "poor" would score 20. Table 11-7 shows the results of this research.

11-7 CHECKING IT OUT: Occupational Prestige Rankings in the United States, 1963 and 1947

Occupation	*1963 Rank*	*1947 Rank*
U.S. Supreme Court justice	1	1
Physician	2	2.5
Nuclear physicist	3.5	18
Scientist	3.5	8
Government scientist	5.5	10.5
State governor	5.5	2.5
Cabinet member in the federal government	8	4.5
College professor	8	8

11-7 CHECKING IT OUT: (continued)

Occupation	*1963 Rank*	*1947 Rank*
U.S. representative in Congress	8	8
Chemist	11	18
Lawyer	11	18
Diplomat in the U.S. foreign service	11	4.5
Dentist	14	18
Architect	14	18
County judge	14	13
Psychologist	17.5	22
Minister	17.5	13
Member of the board of directors of a large corporation	17.5	18
Mayor of a large city	17.5	6
Priest	21.5	18
Head of a department in a state government	21.5	13
Civil engineer	21.5	23
Airline pilot	21.5	24.5
Banker	24.5	10.5
Biologist	24.5	29
Sociologist	26	26.5
Instructor in public schools	27.5	34
Captain in the regular army	27.5	31.5
Accountant for a large business	29.5	29
Public-school teacher	29.5	36
Owner of a factory that employs about 100 people	31.5	26.5
Building contractor	31.5	34
Artist who paints pictures that are exhibited in galleries	34.5	24.5
Musician in a symphony orchestra	34.5	29
Author of novels	34.5	31.5
Economist	34.5	34
Official of an international labor union	37	40.5
Railroad engineer	39	37.5
Electrician	39	45
County agricultural agent	39	37.5
Owner-operator of a printing shop	41.5	42.5
Trained machinist	41.5	45
Farm owner & operator	44	39
Undertaker	44	47
Welfare worker for a city government	44	45
Newspaper columnist	46	42.5

11-7 CHECKING IT OUT: Occupational Prestige Rankings in the United States, 1963 and 1947 (continued)

Occupation	*1963 Rank*	*1947 Rank*
Policeman	47	55
Reporter on a daily newspaper	48	48
Radio announcer	49.5	40.5
Bookkeeper	49.5	51.5
Tenant farmer	51.5	51.5
Insurance agent	51.5	51.5
Carpenter	53	58
Manager of a small store in a city	54.5	49
A local official of a labor union	54.5	62
Mail carrier	57	57
Railroad conductor	57	55
Traveling salesman for a wholesale concern	57	51.5
Plumber	59	59.5
Automobile repairman	60	59.5
Playground director	62.5	55
Barber	62.5	66
Machine operator in a factory	62.5	64.5
Owner-operator of a lunch stand	62.5	62
Corporal in the regular army	65.5	64.5
Garage mechanic	65.5	62
Truck driver	67	71
Fisherman who owns his own boat	68	68
Clerk in a store	70	68
Milk route man	70	71
Streetcar motorman	70	68
Lumberjack	72.5	73
Restaurant cook	72.5	71
Singer in a nightclub	74	74.5
Filling station attendant	75	74.5
Dockworker	77.5	81.5
Railroad section hand	77.5	79.5
Night watchman	77.5	81.5
Coal miner	77.5	77.5
Restaurant waiter	80.5	79.5
Taxi driver	80.5	77.5
Farm hand	83	76
Janitor	83	85.5
Bartender	83	85.5
Clothes presser in a laundry	85	83
Soda fountain clerk	86	84

11-7 CHECKING IT OUT: (continued)

Occupation	*1963 Rank*	*1947 Rank*
Sharecropper	87	87
Garbage collector	88	88
Street sweeper	89	89
Shoe shiner	90	90
Average	71	70

SOURCE: Robert W. Hodge, Paul M. Siegel, and Peter H. Rossi, "Occupational Prestige in the United States: 1925–1963," *The American Journal of Sociology*, 70 (November, 1964), 286–302. © 1964 by The University of Chicago.

THEORIES OF STRATIFICATION

A Functional Analysis

Kingsley Davis and Wilbert Moore In 1945, Davis and Moore developed a theoretical explanation for the stratification of all existing societies that is now regarded as classic. They began by accepting social inequality as universal. No society was "classless"; no society was unstratified. Davis and Moore concluded that all societies differentiate between people and accord some more status and prestige than others. From a functionalist perspective this inequality was in every society, from the most simply organized to the most complex. The social positions that were available (i.e., chief, witch doctor, lawyer, garbage collector) had differing amounts of social honor or prestige attached to them. Davis and Moore sought to discover why this was so. They identified two functional problems of societies: (1) getting people to fill essential positions, and (2) getting them to perform well in these positions. Regarding the first of these, the positions that were most important for the functioning of the society were generally most richly rewarded with high income, unusual deference, and other benefits, thereby insuring that such jobs would be filled. Together with this, rich rewards were attached to positions that were hard to fill. Where extraordinary talent was needed and where prolonged training was required to develop the talent, few persons would be available. But this was why the difficult and extended training demanded of a doctor might be expected to provide unusual inducements encouraging potential doctors to persevere. Preparation for this occupation was difficult, but the rewards attached became an important source of motivation. Whether the rewards were those things that contributed to sustenance and comfort, or that offered diversion, or that added to self-respect, they were differentially accessible in order to attract personnel to the essential positions of society, where, because of innate ability and training, they might be expected to perform conscientiously and well.

Criticisms of the Functionalist View Melvin Tumin (1953) is one of the sociologists who raises several important objections to Davis and Moore's analysis of the reason for social inequality. Where Davis and Moore accord social rewards to positions difficult to fill by virtue of scarce talent and rigorous training requirements, Tumin points out that the supply of talent is difficult to know. The stratification system with its structured inequality hampers the discovery of talented individuals. For example, where the development and training of the talented depends on the financial resources of parents who must provide for the educations of their offspring, the differential distribution of wealth causes many disadvantaged youngsters to lose the chance to discover or develop their talents. Tumin is particularly aware of the tendency of occupational elites to restrict equality of opportunity by providing a demand for occupational services (i.e., doctors) while at the same time restricting the numbers of individuals who will be available to fill the positions. Tumin remains unconvinced that the differential allocation of rewards is the most functional way of recruiting talent for important positions. Tumin wonders if the motivating force of "social duty" or "social service" or "intrinsic work satisfaction" could be institutionalized so that individual needs for rewards might provide a better fit with the needs of society. However, in a later critical evaluation of Davis and Moore, Dennis Wrong (1970) notes that Davis and Moore have not called sufficient attention to the power element in stratification. Wrong argues that individuals in the most important and skilled positions have the power to influence the reward structure (i.e., to demand greater rewards) and to protect and increase their privileges.

A Conflict View of Stratification

In the writings of Karl Marx, a different explanation for the stratification patterns of modern history is to be found. Marx's conflict approach recognizes the value of struggle and conflict as competing social groups seek either to preserve their advantages or to create a new order. Nevertheless, conflict is omnipresent and basic to social interaction. In *The Communist Manifesto* (1848), Marx and Friedrich Engels identified the two great social classes of capitalistic society as the bourgeoisie and the proletariat. The former consisted of the modern capitalists, the owners of the means of production (factories, railroads, technology). The latter consisted of the working class or laborers, a disadvantaged and propertyless group who sold their labor-power for wages. Just as history has been the chronicle of conflict between those that exploit and the exploited, modern industrial society has been created out of the exploitation of the proletariat by the bourgeoisie. Marx also included several other groups within his system of social hierarchies. Capitalist society also contained "the lower strata of the middle class—the small tradespeople, shopkeepers, and retired tradesmen . . . the handicraftsmen and peasants. . . ." Marx predicted that the members of this class would eventually "sink" into the proletariat, unable to compete with the richer capitalists. And so the proletariat, drawn from all parts of the society, was expected to grow, to organize itself politically, and, after a revolution, establish itself as the ruling class. In the new society forged by revolution, Marx expected the competition and antagonism of social classes to end as all individuals freely developed, first in a socialist society where the means of production would be publicly owned and finally in a communist society where structured social inequality or stratification no longer existed.

It is ironic that Marx, the brilliant analyst of history, should so misjudge the direction of change within industrial society. One example of this is evident in Marx's notion of the "pauperization of the proletariat." The revolutionary struggle was expected to grow out of an oppressive situation in which the proletariat would be continually impoverished so that the overthrow of the exploitive bourgeoisie was the only possible result. Tom Bottomore is one of the influential contemporary sociologists who has indicated the degree to which Marx's predictions were inaccurate. Bottomore notes that even when Marx was alive, movements had already begun whereby political and social rights (i.e., suffrage, old age benefits) would be extended to the masses. Also, with the growth of unions the relations between the two classes has changed dramatically. Marx also underestimated the effect of nationalism on the working classes. Certainly it was easy to understand the development of nationalism and patriotism in the bourgeoisie of industrial Western societies as they began imperialistic empire-building. It is more difficult to understand how the exploited members of the working class in industrial European societies could also support the imperialistic efforts of their country's elites. Also contemporary events have strengthened nationalistic allegiances. Bottomore notes that during the World Wars, socialist and communist parties diverted their attention from revolutionary struggles and "unanimously" supported their national governments. In this case, nationality created a unity that seriously weakened the Marxist notion of a "class antagonism" that would lead inevitably to revolution.

Marx had predicted the abolition of structural lines as the lower part of the middle class (i.e., the small businessmen) sank into the proletariat, having lost ground as the richer capitalist concentrated and expanded their enterprises. Theodor Geiger (1970) suggests that rather than an increased identification with the working class as they have been "pauperized," the lower middle class has shown a determined prestige-need to be separate from the working classes. The new middle class of white-collar workers also seeks to disassociate itself from the working class, further illustrating the failure of the development of Marx's model of social class structure.

CONSEQUENCES AND CORRELATES OF CLASS

Research such as the nationwide public-opinion poll on the prestige of occupations offers useful information about the existence of a status structure and the consensus among members of society about the criteria of status. Other research shows that various occupations, incomes, and amounts of education lead people to share different norms and behave differently. In other words, the existence of a class structure leads to the development of class subcultures. And in time, the patterns fostered in the subculture themselves become criteria of placement in the class structure. Not just one's income, but the way one spends it; not just one's occupational status; but one's attitude toward it—these become factors partially determining social status.

Style of Life in Community Studies

W. Lloyd Warner and "Yankee City" Some of the most detailed descriptions of the styles of life of people in different social classes are found in the work of W. Lloyd Warner and his associates. (1941, 1942, 1945, 1947, 1949; Davis, 1941; Hollingshead, 1949) The best known of these exhaustive investigations was of "Yankee City," a New England community of about 17,000. On the basis of the research, Warner identified social classes in Yankee City.

1. **Upper-Upper:** the elite, based on inherited high family status and wealth, socialized in aristocratic etiquette, and comprising 1.4 per cent of the population.
2. **Lower-Upper:** families with patterns of income, occupation, and participation similar to the upper-uppers, but with more recently acquired wealth and hence lacking old-family prestige; professionals and businessmen; making up 1.6 per cent of the total.
3. **Upper-Middle:** moderately successful business and professional people without distinguished lineage; respected civic leaders but not "society people"; constituting 10.2 per cent.
4. **Lower-Middle:** small businessmen, white-collar workers, craftsmen and foremen, living in neat houses; conservative, self-conscious about respectability; comprising 28.1 per cent.
5. **Upper-Lower:** lower white-collar employees, semiskilled factory workers, and service workers; "poor but hardworking"; comprising 32.6 per cent.
6. **Lower-Lower:** not "respectable" people; unskilled workers, families on relief, transients; making up 25.2 per cent.

Plainville and Burlington Warner found numerous variations in style of life among the six classes. For example, some social clubs were exclusively upper-upper; upper-middle-class men belonged to luncheon clubs; fraternal lodges were primarily lower-middle; and labor unions were upper-lower.

Similarly, members of the different classes attended different churches, read different magazines, and in general showed evidence of participating in a number of different aspects of community life.

There are striking similarities between the conceptions of the class structure held by residents of Yankee City, with their assumptions of differences in morals and "respectability" among classes, and the description of the stratification structure of Plainville, a rural community in Missouri studied by James West. (1945, p. 117)

An investigation of class structure in Burlington, Vermont, showed that nationality and religion in the subculture played important parts in the class system. In this community the families of old Yankee stock, although a definite numerical minority of the total population, were at the top of the stratification order. The other broad category is made up of "foreigners" and "newcomers." The "foreigners" are not necessarily individuals or families born outside the country but rather those not of the Yankee tradition. The "newcomers" are families of perhaps acceptable New England background who have not yet been thoroughly assimilated into the local community. But within this wide division there is a "maze of classes and cliques" resting, for the most part, on three kinds of distinction: (1) economic, divided between professionals and proprietary versus laboring groups; (2) religious, with Protestants considering themselves better than Catholics; and (3) "ethnic" (or nationality) differences, "which serve to enhance the divisions based on religion or economic status and also to create division within the religious worlds or the economic levels." (Anderson, 1937, p. 125)

These investigations and many others show (1) a considerable flexibility in standards, which may include income, occupation, nativity, education, religion, and length of residence; (2) a patterning, at least in regions of older settlement, that gives the residents of long standing—provided they have some wealth and education—the highest ranking; (3) only a gradual acceptance into the top class of people of recently acquired wealth; and (4) moral values and style of life as frequently important standards of judgment, though these are often linked with religious and economic distinctions.

11-8 CHECKING IT OUT: The Children of Affluence

A New Orleans black woman said to me in 1961: "I don't know how to figure out these rich white kids. They're something! I used to think, before I took a job with this family, that the only difference between a rich kid and a poor kid is that the rich kid knows he has a lot of money and he grows up and becomes spoiled rotten. That's what my mother told me; she took care of a white girl, and the girl was an only child, and her father owned a department store in McComb, Mississippi, and that girl thought she was God's special creature. My mother used to come home and tell us about the 'little princess'; but she turned out to be no good. She was so pampered, she couldn't do a thing for herself. All she knew how to do was order people around.

"It's different with these two children. I've never seen such a boy and such a girl. They think they're the best ones who ever lived—like her. They're never asking me to do much of anything. They even ask if they can help me! They tell me that they want to know how to do everything. The girl says she wants to learn how to run the washing machine and the dishwasher. She says she wants to learn all my secret recipes. She says she'd like to give the best parties in the Garden District when she grows up, and she'd like to be able to give them without anyone's help. She says I could serve the food, but she would like to make it. The boy says he's going to be a lawyer and a banker, so he wants to know how much everything costs. He doesn't want to waste anything. He'll see me throw something away, and he wants to know why. I wish my own kids were like him!

"But these children here are special, and don't they know it! That's what being rich is: you know you're different from most people. These two kids act as if they're going to be tops in everything, and they're pleased as can be with themselves, because there is nothing they can't do, and there's nothing they can't get, and there's nothing they can't win, and they're always showing off what they can do, and then before you can tell them how good they are, they're telling the same thing to themselves. It's confusing! They're not spoiled one bit, but oh, they have a high opinion of themselves!"

SOURCE: Robert Coles, "The Children of Affluence," *The Atlantic Monthly* (September, 1977), *240:* 52–66.

The evidence of differences in style of life includes variations by class in sexual behavior (Kinsey, 1948; 1953), in family interactions and child-rearing styles, religious participation (Pope, 1948), and many other culture patterns. "The Children of Affluence" represents a personal evaluation of upper-class socialization.

Life Chances

One's social class, with its concomitant income, education, and style of life, affects greatly the likelihood that certain things will happen to one. As we have noted, the odds for or against one's having any given experience, as they are influenced by class, are called *life chances.* Life chances include a vast array of variables. An individual's position in the class structure alters "everything from the chance to stay alive during the first year after birth to the chance to view fine arts, the chance to remain healthy and grow tall, and if sick to get well again quickly, the chance to avoid becoming a juvenile delinquent—and very crucially, the chance to complete an intermediary or higher educational grade." (Gerth, 1954, p. 313)

The crucial effect of income on life chances is dramatically illustrated by the fact that the life expectancy of infants born into the high-income strata is nearly ten years greater than that of children born to parents in the lowest-income class. (Mayer, 1953) Upper-class children are larger and grow faster than lower-class children, a fact apparently related to differences in diet, which depend on both income and style of life. (Mack, 1951)

People in the lowest-income strata spend nearly three-fourths of their total income for food, while those in the higher strata spend less than one-fourth for food. Obviously, this leaves lower-class families with not only less money but a lower *proportion* of their total incomes available for education and other expenditures that might improve their class position. The smaller amount of money available for purposes other than groceries is reflected in the fact that a sample of lower-class people exceeded those in wealthier classes both in symptoms of illness and in the proportion of those symptoms which are not being treated by a physician. The class structure tends to perpetuate itself. People having high incomes and college educations are more likely to be in favor of having their children get college educations. (Hyman, 1953) And those who received a college education are considerably more likely than those who did not to be able to afford to send their children to college.

Poverty in America

Amidst all the present wealth of the United States, poverty persists, a stubborn backwash that resists the leavening influence of industrial development. Unlike the poverty of yesterday, the poverty of today seems needless. We do not believe with Arthur Young that "the lower classes must be kept poor or they will never be industrious." The growth of income has made poverty expendable and its persistence, therefore, all the more aggravating.

The quantitative scope of poverty in the United States today depends on how one defines it. The Social Security Administration has established a poverty-income standard that takes into account family size, composition, age of family head, and place of residence. The 1976 poverty-income line for non-farm, four-person families was $5,815. If we apply criteria like these to the structure of income in the United State in 1976, we find there were 25 million poor persons, representing 11 per cent of the population. The poverty-income standard is hardly munificent, as anyone must realize who contemplates the urban family of four trying to survive on an annual income of $5,815.

Moreover, the aggregated data on poverty conceal the extent to which it is concentrated in particular subsets of the population. It is the aged, the non-white, and women and children that bear the burden of poverty—"The Other America" in Michael Harrington's phrase or "The Invisible Poor" in Dwight MacDonald's—whose separation, indeed alienation, from the mainstream of life in the United States seems to perpetuate the condition. Two-thirds of all the poor are either under 22 years of age or over 64 years old.

SOCIAL MOBILITY

By social mobility we mean movement within the social structure. When a person leaves a job paying $5,000 a year to accept one paying $80,000 that person alters his or her class position. That person has become socially mobile. Since one's class is determined originally by the class of one's parents, when one acquires a fundamentally different amount of education from that of one's parents and moves into a different occupation,with a different life style and different life chances, one has been socially mobile.

Individual Mobility

An alteration in status can be either upward or downward in the stratification structure. A truck driver's son who wins a college scholarship, joins a law firm as an accountant upon graduation and is later elected chairperson of the board of a large corporation, has achieved upward mobility from the status into which he was born. If his children become waiters in a restaurant, they are downwardly mobile. Individual mobility, however, is always relative; one can be upwardly mobile only if someone else is downwardly mobile.

Structural Mobility

Most mobility is structural mobility, not individual mobility. Many persons have occupations different from those of their parents because of technological changes and shifts in the division of labor. As farming occupations have decreased, many farm children have been "forced" into other occupations and thus do not "inherit" the occupations of their parents. As machines do more and more tasks in the factory, the number of "unskilled" workers decreases and the children of former "unskilled" workers are "forced" into service occupations and white-collar clerical jobs. These kinds of changes in the social structure tend to benefit the entire society. Since the social structure, rather than individual persons, is directly responsible for improvements in the situation of individuals in relation to others, we refer to these changes as structural mobility.

Sometimes a person experiences mobility simply by being a member of some social category if a change takes place in the prestige accorded that category. In time of war, for example, career military men without any alteration in their education, income, or occupation, are suddenly more sought after as party guests, luncheon club speakers, and subjects of feature articles. The occupational status of soldier understandably holds more prestige for many people during a time of war than in peacetime; hence incumbents of the status are automatically upwardly mobile. Similarly, after the stock market crash of 1929 and during the depression of the 1930s, the prestige of bankers and brokers suffered. It was not necessary for individual bankers to alter their occupation or income or style of life to experience vertical mobility; the occupational status itself was downwardly mobile.

Immigration Another source of structural social mobility in the United States has been immigration. The millions of immigrants who entered the United States in the late nineteenth and early twentieth centuries made a certain amount of upward mobility virtually automatic for the people already here. Mass immigration increased the size of the population dramatically, and thus contributed to a growth of the economy. Such growth meant that there was an increase in the number of occupational statuses to be filled at all levels in the stratification structure. The filling of the statuses at the bottom of the structure by immigrants working as low-paid unskilled laborers allowed "native" citizens and their children to move up and fill some of the higher statuses in the social structure.

As a factor in the rate of vertical mobility in the United States, immigration is less important now than it once was. Yet, even with legislation which has slowed greatly the rate of immigration, there is still a steady stream of people entering the United States from other countries. Furthermore, the internal migration from rural areas to urban centers, particularly the movement of blacks from the South to the North, has had much the same effect on the total stratification structure that immigration used to have.

Mechanization Some of this internal migration is symptomatic of another factor that has contributed to a high rate of upward mobility in U.S. society: technological change. The constant trend toward replacing human energy with machinery, culminating in automation, has reduced the proportion of occupational statuses that call for unskilled labor and increased the number of semiskilled jobs. With this have come the growth of bureaucratic industrial organizations and the expansion of government services, both of which require more white-collar personnel. Mechanization of larger and larger proportions of the labor force has allowed the expansion of service industries.

The creation of new occupational statuses in the middle part of the stratification structure and the reduction in the number of occupations at the lower end of the structure necessitate some upward mobility. There is a historical tendency for the division of labor to change as the economy becomes more mechanized and more bureaucratic. That is, there is a contraction at the bottom of the occupational structure as fewer and fewer people are engaged in unskilled work and an expansion in the middle as more and more people enter semiskilled and lower white-collar statuses. This means that if every family had just enough children to assume the jobs the parents had occupied in the stratification structure, there would still be some upward mobility, since there would not be enough lower occupations for the children of the poor, and there would be more middle occupations than middle-class children to fill them.

Differential Fertility Actually, people in each class do not have exactly the same number of children. There are marked differences in the birth rates in the various income classses, with the reproduction rate of the lower income classes being higher than that of the top strata. Professionals and other managerial people typically do not have enough children to replace themselves in the labor force. Farmers and farm laborers, on the other hand, have as much as 50 per cent more than enough children to take their places. This would be true even if there were no changes in the number of people needed to fill each occupational category from generation to generation. Actually, we know that clerical and professional personnel have been an increasing proportion of the labor force, while unskilled laborers and farm laborers have become a small portion of the total number of workers. The openings created in the stratification structure by the relatively low birth rates of the professionals are filled by the children of farmers and manual workers. This differential fertility, like mechanization and immigration, induces a certain amount of vertical mobility.

By far the most frequently used indicator of mobility in sociological research is change in occupation; the next most common indicator is change in income. (Mack, 1957) As we have seen, occupational status is closely correlated with educational status, income, style of life, and other aspects of social class. Occupational mobility may be measured in either of two ways: (1) career mobility may be studied by charting a person's work history in order to see whether he or she has been upwardly mobile, stable, or downwardly mobile since he or she entered the labor force; or (2) one's occupation may be compared with that of one's parents to determine the direction and degree of intergenerational mobility.

Social Mobility and Social Structure

Sociologists study social mobility in order to ascertain the relative "openness" of a social structure. In other words, they are interested in the relative difficulty which different persons, groups, or categories experience in acquiring the goods and services that are valued in the culture and are objects of unequal distribution.

In slave and caste societies, the stratification system is closed to individual mobility. There is relatively no mobility because status is ascribed at birth. The occupational status one will enter, the amount of education one will receive, one's income, and one's whole style of life is known at birth. In an open-class society, status is initially ascribed, but opportunities are available for some individuals to change their initial position. The life chances of a streetsweeper's son born in the slums differs considerably from those of a broker's son born in the suburbs, but the culture does not exclude the former from achievements equal to or greater than those of his contemporaries. On the contrary, the ethos of an open-class society will encourage him to try to achieve statuses carrying higher prestige than those into which he is born.

Just as there is some mobility, even though very little, in India, so that it cannot be referred to as a perfect example of immobility, so there is some ascription in open-class societies. Our own structure is only relatively open; race, for example, is an ascribed status, and members of racial and gender minorities are often blocked in their attempts to achieve certain statuses. In general, however, United States society emphasizes the open-class ideal, and people are socialized into a belief system that encourages them to try to be upwardly mobile.

THE MOBILITY ETHIC

The emphasis on vertical social mobility in the social structure in the United States is one of the most striking features of our class system. Kurt B. Mayer (1955, p. 69) points out that

> . . . the United States has placed greater emphasis on social mobility than any other large nation in modern times. Americans have firmly proclaimed the idea of equality and freedom of achievement and have acclaimed the large numbers of individuals who have risen from humble origins to positions of prominence and affluence. Indeed, the belief in opportunity is so strongly entrenched in the culture that most Americans feel not only that each individual has the "right to succeed" but that it is his duty to do so. Thus we are apt to look with disapproval upon those who fail or make no attempt to "better themselves."

This mobility ethic, or cultural value attached to improving one's position, has roots both in a normative structure growing out of political revolution and frontier economics and in a religious heritage from the Protestant Reformation in Europe. The relative importance of achieved status so characteristic of the open-class system has permeated the ethos of the United States for several reasons. First of all, this country afforded economic opportunties for the ordinary person—free land for settlement, other natural resources for easy exploitation, and a rapidly expanding economy. Second, political freedom was an essential tenet almost from the beginning of our country, and it became increasing significant as the population expanded under favorable material conditions. Third, religious tolerance and freedom not only furnished an outlet for individual choice but gave democracy a strong supporting noneconomic, nonpolitical ideology and practice. And fourth, freedom of research and invention, of personal migration, and other associated features of individualism and liberalism became deeply and firmly embedded in the value system of American culture.

SOCIAL MOBILITY IN THE UNITED STATES

The mobility ethic, the belief that upward mobility is both possible and desirable in our society, has probably led to an exaggerated general notion of the number of cases in which the poor laborer's son becomes president of a corporation. A study comparing more than 8,000 top executives in the largest firms in the United States in 1952 with the top business leaders in 1928 shows that, in both periods, more than 50 per cent of the business leaders were sons of owners or executives. (Warner, 1955, p. 45; Taussing, 1932)

Intergenerational Mobility

Most of the research on occupational mobility indicates that while many sons experience *some* mobility, very few experience *much*. (Hunter, 1953; Davidson, 1937; Centers, 1948; Lipset, 1952; Rugoff, 1953; North, 1947) They move, but not far. If a young man is not in the same occupational category as his father, the next most likely place for him is in the occupational category either immediately above or immediately below that of his father. If a semiskilled worker in a mass-production factory has a son who is mobile, that son is most likely to move one step down to unskilled work or one step up to skilled labor; it is unlikely that he will become an executive or a professional man. In summary, we can say that more sons are mobile than are not, but that most sons work at either the same occupational level or one immediately adjacent to that of their fathers.

11-9 CHECKING IT OUT: The Son Also Rises

Mr. Parks has one son, Mark, Jr., who is now the more active member of the team he and his father represent. He is an alert and capable man, as active in a variety of civic affairs as his father is said to have been some years ago. His rise in the company was from the bottom up. Several of the leaders in Regional City who have inherited businesses have followed the pattern of beginning at the bottom of the ladder in the company. The rise of these men has been meteoric, in many instances, but the newspapers in biographical accounts of the lives of such persons solemnly report that they have "worked their way to the top." The occupational ascent of Mark Parks, Jr., illustrates the rapidity of such a rise up the ladder of success. The pattern is in the American tradition, but most men find the ascent a longer process than did Mark, Jr.

Young Mark, upon graduation from college, came into his father's business as a shipping clerk. He became successively a stockroom clerk, a stock foreman, and an office manager for one of the branch warehouses. Two years after he started as a shipping clerk, he was elected a director of the corporation and placed in charge of one of the major subsidiaries of the company. Three years later he was named treasurer of the company, and in three years more he became operations vice-president. After two years in this position he was made president. His father then became chairman of the board and has since gradually relinquished active control of the business in favor of his son. He still retains a firm control in matters of general policy, however. Mark, Jr., is the authority on administrative matters. So we see that within ten years this young man rose from stock clerk to company president.

It is claimed, and rightly so, perhaps, that by dint of hard work he made good. Certainly it cannot be denied that so young a person as he was in the earlier years of his service in the business shouldered considerable responsibility and has continued to do so increasingly. It may be surmised, nevertheless, that his father's position in the company was extremely helpful in his business success.

SOURCE: Floyd Hunter, *Community Power Structure: A Study of Decision Makers* (Chapel Hill: University of North Carolina Press, 1953), pp. 27–28. By permission.

In the light of the effects of immigration, mechanization, and differential fertility on the openness of the class structure, it is not surprising that there is more upward than downward mobility. One study of the mobility of a representative sample of white urban males showed that nearly 30 per cent of the sons of manual laborers moved up to nonmanual occupational statuses, while fewer than 20 per cent of the sons of fathers in nonmanual work were downwardly mobile into manual occupations. (Centers, 1949, p. 180) Nevertheless, a recent study reported that over two-fifths of the sons of self-employed professionals enter one of the professions and one-third enter some other white-collar job. On the other hand, only 5 per cent of the sons of laborers enter a profession and one-sixth enter other white-collar jobs. The opportunity to attain the economic security of an upper white-collar professional or business occupation is inversely related to one's initial class position. It has been shown that the chances of a professional or managerial career are nearly five times better if one's father was a professional than if one's father was an unskilled laborer. (Blau, 1965) The point that most mobility is into adjacent strata still holds: sons of manual laborers who move up into white-collar work are more likely to become salesmen or clerical workers than professional men or business executives.

Despite the mobility between white-collar and so-called blue-collar occupational statuses, the line between them remains a major hurdle in the class structure. There is more mobility within the manual strata and within white-collar categories than there is between the two.

Career Mobility

Studies of the mobility experienced by individuals during the time they are in the labor force point in general to the same conclusions as do intergenerational studies. They reveal more mobility than stability, but most mobility is horizontal rather than vertical, occurring within occupational categories, not between them. (Lipset, 1952; Davidson, 1937) While it is not unusual for a person to change occupation four or five times during his or her career, about half these moves are from one semiskilled job to another, or from one managerial post to another, and so on. Those shifts which do involve vertical mobility are usually limited in extent, the most common pattern being a move to an immediately adjacent occupational category in the class structure. Career moves from the bottom to the top of the occupational hierarchy are as exceptional as intergenerational mobility of this type. Research on career mobility further confirms the studies of intergenerational movement indicating that there is slightly more upward than downward mobility.

Trends in Social Mobility

Many social scientists have speculated that the mobility ethic might become a norm inconsistent with the facts of American class structure. They have said that the rate of upward mobility has been declining, that the strata are becoming more rigid; the holes in the sieve are becoming smaller. Certainly one can cite arguments that suggest that the chances to work one's way up in U.S. society are diminishing: the passing of the frontiers days of free homesteading, the decline in immigration, the fact that the fertility rates of the different classes are not as disparate as they used to be. As early as 1948, however, Edward Shils (1948) pointed out that "In spite of the oft-asserted claim that opportunites for ascent into the upper strata are diminishing in the United States, no conclusive evidence has been presented on either side of the issue by social research."

Since that time, a considerable amount of research has been published on trends in rates of social mobility in the United States. These studies certainly offer no evidence that the class structure is becoming rigid. Rogoff (1953) has concluded that the rate of upward mobility was about the same in 1940 as in 1910. If the mobility rate was about the same in 1940 as in 1910, even if one does *not* count the mobility which is an automatic result of changes in the occupational structure, then the actual mobility rate would seem to be higher now than it used to be. The conclusions reached in the research comparing the social origins of U.S. business leaders in 1928 and 1952 confirm this fact.

The study of social mobility by Jackson and Crockett showed that "... no striking changes have occurred in mobility patterns and [in the decade following] World War II.... what movement has occurred ... is in the direction of increasing rates of movement." (Duncan, 1965, p. 498) In a recent and definitive study of the trend of occupational mobility in the United States, the author concluded that there is "... little immediate cause for anxiety about whether the American occupational structure is providing more restricted opportunities." (Duncan, 1965, p. 498) However, the author goes on to caution that the data used in his study refer to a ". . . historical experience in which the transition to complete industrialization was rapidly nearing its end. If the movement off farms has been a major factor in inducing upward mobility from nonfarm origins in the past, it is not clear what its counterpart may be in an era when few persons originate on farms." (Jackson, 1964, p. 25) Undoubtedly a significant proportion of this mobility is traceable to the changes in the distribution of occupations growing out of mechanization.

Class Consciousness

How do most people perceive the class structure? How conscious are ordinary citizens of the differential prestige accorded to various statuses?

The fact that there is a high degree of consensus on such things as occupational rankings indicates that people have been socialized into the stratification structure. Research showing that children between the ages of four and six years have already learned to respond to racial differences as a criterion for evaluating people demonstrates that socialization concerning this part of the stratification structure is powerful and effective. (Goodman, 1952) Yet, despite the evidence that Americans are aware of the stratification system, many polls indicate that the overwhelming majority consider themselves to be "middle class." Part of the explanation for the fact that people polled in these studies identify themselves as middle class probably rests in the mobility ethic itself, the norm that says that everyone is supposed to want to move up and that makes it self-derogatory to identify oneself as lower class. On the other hand, the American distaste for aristocracy makes it snobbish for one to claim that he or she is upper class. In a nationwide poll Centers found that Americans saw themselves as follows: upper class—3 per cent; middle class—43 per cent; working class—51 per cent; and lower class—1 per cent. (Centers, 1949, p. 180)

The significance of class consciousness for social mobility lies in the fact that attitudes and values have consequences in behavior patterns. If one believes he or she can be mobile, one will try to be. One's level of aspiration depends on what one has been socialized to believe about one's present status and the chances and desirability of altering it. Research has shown that manual workers are aware that most of them are not going to rise to managerial positions and that, reconciled to the status in which they find themselves, they do not plan upward mobility for themselves but project their ambitions onto their children. (Chinoy, 1952) Of course, the ones most likely to be upwardly mobile are those who actively seek to achieve upward mobility. (Scudder, 1954) One reason for the high degree of occupational inheritance in business leadership statuses is that businessmen's sons are taught to expect to fill these occupational statuses and manual workers' sons are socialized to believe that there is little chance of their attaining such positions. The higher the prestige of the father in the hierarchy of occupational statuses, the more likely the son is to aspire to high occupational status himself.

Thus, just as race can become an ascribed status through the social definition imposed by the culture, so can class subcultures make education and occupation, and hence income, tend to be ascribed. Coates and Pellegri (1956, p. 125), after comparing top-level executives with lower-level supervisors, conclude as follows:

> The social origins and socio-cultural backgrounds of executives and supervisors are significantly different. These variations are basic factors in differential occupa-

tional opportunities and placement. Occupational placement and early career experiences lead individuals to adopt attitudes, values and behavior patterns which function as important positive or negative influences in subsequent career progress and occupational mobility.

. . . Subjective factors, such as attitudes and values which affect occupational behavior patterns, are extremely important influences in determining comparative levels of occupational aspiration.

Levels of aspiration, as they result from attitudes and values, not only affect occupational behavior but also determine occupational plans and goals and condition mobility drives.

INTERPRETIVE SUMMARY

Some tribal societies, particularly nomadic ones, have no complicated class structure; but most societies have either a rigid system called a *caste* system, or a more flexible system called a *class* structure. Broad changes occurring toward the end of the Middle Ages brought an increase in social mobility in European societies. These changes—the rise of capitalism in the economic realm and, in the realm of thought, the emergence of scientific method, religious tolerance, nationalism—had in common the assumption that individuals and their achievements are supremely important.

The United States has a flexible class system, with the exception of its treatment of minorities. Important indicators of class position in our society are income, wealth, and occupation. It is frequently difficult, however, to determine the social class of a particular individual, since in a given situation one factor may outweigh other usually important ones. Then, too, regional differences in class structure exist, some communities placing emphasis on statuses that other communities minimize or do not even recognize.

Though a given individual's position in the hierarchy may be difficult to pinpoint, that position is not likely to change much in his or his children's lifetime. This is true because, first, his position will determine his style of life; and the behavior patterns he learns from others who share his style of life will in turn indicate his position and pinion him to it. Second, he will teach his children his own way of life, since it will be the only way he knows. Third, if he is poor, he will find it difficult to help his children find a better way of life even if he wants to.

In U.S. society, people have had highly favorable, even unique conditions for upward social movement. Political freedom and democracy were held sacred from the beginning of the nation. The country afforded unprecedented opportunities for agricultural and industrial pioneering. The Protestant Ethic, embraced by most Americans, taught that achievement in this world is not only justifiable but morally obligatory. As the country developed, immigration and mechanization led to increasingly skilled and "important" jobs for people already here, while the tendency of the upper classes to have fewer children than others also provided for some mobility. Even though many of these factors have become less important in our century, factors such as increasing mechanization continue to provide some opportunity for mobility.

Vertical mobility is generally not dramatic, however. Many sons succeed in reaching the occupational category immediately above that of their fathers; few go higher, and some go lower. The most difficult gap to bridge in one generation is that between blue-collar and white-collar jobs. One reason for the lack of great intergenerational mobility is class consciousness. While class consciousness, combined with a good dose of the Protestant Ethic, may lead to a longing for a better life, it may also lead to a sound recognition of what is possible, based on what has generally been possible for members of one's class. Then too, class consciousness may lead to pride in one's class, and thus a father may socialize his child to want to put on a white or a blue collar.

QUESTIONS

1. America has been frequently described as a "middle-class" country. Is this an accurate description? Why? Which critics disagree with this statement?
2. An aim of the Russian Revolution was the elimination of social and economic inequalities. What evidence do we have that inequalities still exist in Russia?
3. What factors determine the kind of stratification systems that exist in other parts of the world?
4. Of which social class are you a member? Which of your qualities or achievements are similar to those of others in your social class? Which social class is your reference group?
5. Which realities to be found within our society are not explained by Davis and Moore's functional explanation of the stratification patterns?

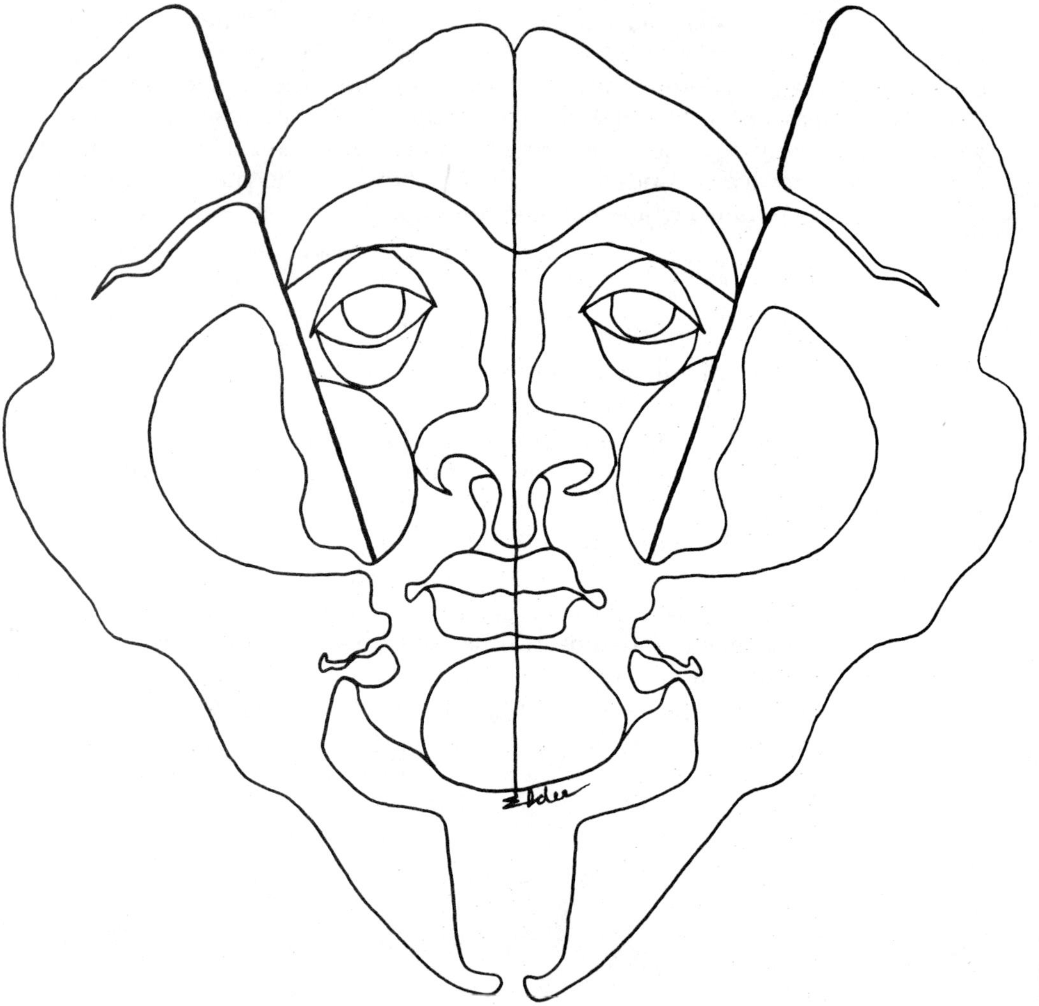

12

Racial and Ethnic Minorities

MINORITY STATUS

There are few issues that have occupied the minds of people more than the issue of equality. The two great revolutions of the eighteenth century, one in France and the other in the United States, were directed toward extending equality. The two major revolutions of the twentieth century, one in Russia and the other in China, were aimed at establishing "complete equality." For more than a decade, the central political question in the United States has been the question of equality for persons of minority status. In recent years the discrimination and prejudice directed against women, blacks, Chicanos, Indians, Puerto Ricans, and others have become increasingly prominent in the national consciousness. Concern about racism and sexism are commonplace. Indeed, one of the defining characteristics of our time is that masses of people no longer concede their "exclusion" from society. This situation is being dramatically expressed by black Americans and increasingly echoed by women, Chicanos, Native Americans, gays, and others.

A black may be a college graduate and an experienced pilot in the United States Air Force and yet be rejected as a job applicant by a commercial airline needing pilots. A woman may have graduated from college with high honors and a degree in chemistry only to be offered a typing job when she applies for work.

A private club with a membership composed exclusively of wealthy businessmen who are graduates of New England universities may refuse to admit a wealthy businessman with whom some of its members attended college because he is Jewish. A political party caucus may refuse to run an intelligent, willing young attorney for the legislature because his name is Colucci. Obviously, other factors may override income, occupation, and education in determining one's position in the class structure. It is not true that two people occupy equal statuses merely because they have the same income and education and occupy similar occupational statuses—not true, that is, if one is Protestant and the other Jewish, or if one is white and the other black. Two persons with the same qualifications and the same educational backgrounds who are of the same religion, race, and age have very different chances for a high-paying executive position if one is a man and the other a woman. Opportunities in society are not the same for all people. The discrimination against people of minority status varies from time to time and from group to group, but it is always reflected in their life chances and life styles.

The term *minority status* is used to designate those members of society who are prevented from participating fully and equally in all phases of social life, who are subordinate to the majority, who can be distinguished on the basis of physical or cultural characteristics, and who therefore have poorer life chances and fewer rights and privileges than the majority. Persons who are discriminated against, who are accorded unequal treatment on the basis of their religion, sex, race, or national origins, occupy a minority status. (Schermerhorn, 1949) The sociological meaning of the concept "minority" is sometimes misunderstood because the term minority also has a quantitative meaning. Many people are likely to speak of white Americans as a majority because they constitute more than one half of the population. The sociological meaning of minority status, however, is a matter of social status and social power, not of numbers. The Bantu people of the Republic of South Africa have minority status even though they are more numerous than the whites in that country. The whites are in power; they control the institutions of society; and they subordinate the black Africans to a minority status. The aristocracy, the rich and powerful, the royalty, and the ruling elite always constitute a numerical minority of a society, but they never occupy minority status.

MINORITIES AS SOCIAL CATEGORIES

Who Are the Minorities?

If the members of a society are to exclude some people from full participation in the culture and define them as a minority, the members of the majority and minority groups must be readily identifiable to one another. The black Africans of the Ituri Forest can treat the pygmies as a minority because they can tell by a man's stature that he is a pygmy. (Coon and Putnam, 1948) New England Yankees can treat local French Canadians as a minority because the latter's speech and family names set them off from the majority group. A minority identification may result from speaking a different language, having a different skin color, possessing different eye color, or attending a different religious institution from the people in the majority group. In other words, minorities can either be physically or culturally different, but one or the other is necessary to be discriminated against as a minority. The Nazis forced German Jews to wear arm bands so that they could be more easily identified.

If it is cultural behavior that makes people identifiable, they can become socialized into the dominant culture and be assimilated. But physical differences are more permanent; if it is skin color or sex that identifies the minority status, no amount of socialization into the culture of the dominant category removes minority status. If physical differences such as skin color or hair type make a person identifiable, the only thing that will remove one from minority status is a change in the beliefs and practices of the dominant group.

ETHNIC GROUPS AS MINORITIES

Ethnic Status

Whereas some minority group members are treated differentially because of their racial status, others may experience differential treatment because of their ethnic status. Individuals are classified within races on the basis of physical characteristics. Ethnic status results from cultural characteristics such as national origin, language, or religion. Members of ethnic groups have a sense of a common ancestral past, whether real or imagined, so that they think of themselves as a cultural unity. Ethnic identification may be imposed by the majority or may be generated within the minority group. Ethnic groups frequently have unique family styles, languages, recreations, customs that cause them to be thought of as distinct entities. Sometimes by choice and sometimes because of majority group hostility they are segregated into separate neighborhoods or ghettos. Ethnic groups have a "consciousness of kind," have a "we" feeling that causes them to group together, realizing that they share a common fate.

In the United States, some ethnic groups are composed of members whose ancestors came here from the same country. The Irish Americans, the Polish Americans, the Mexican Americans are examples of people who share a common national past. However, some ethnic groups transcend nationalities. Jews may be found in many nations, where they have existed for generations. However, their ethnic status is not derived from identification with a country or nation, but rather from a religion (Judaism) and/or a shared cultural heritage and origin. The use of the term La Raza (The Race) by Chicano Americans is an attempt to identify as one ethnic group all those of Spanish origins and language regardless of national background.

Some minority groups, such as Afro-Americans and Japanese Americans are both racially and ethnically different from the majority group. Others, such as Scandinavian Americans are physically indistinguishable from the original American settlers, but may form separate subsocieties based on a distinctive cultural heritage.

RACES AS MINORITIES

Race as a Biological Concept

A race, as the concept is used by geneticists and physical anthropologists, is a number of people who share a set of innate physical characteristics. Non-scientists often assume that members of a race share an unchangeable set of physical characteristics that set them apart permanently from other races. This is not so; races are subject to the processes of genetic change common to all other living organisms.

All human beings belong to a single species. The races of people that today inhabit the earth probably developed through a combination of mutations (some of which permitted survival more easily in one environment than in another), long periods of relative isolation which facilitated inbreeding, and a selection resulting from various cultural standards of what were and were not desirable physical traits. (UNESCO, 1952) The major groups of races formed through mutation, isolation, adaptation, and selection have not remained unchanged, because the peoples have not remained absolutely isolated. Since the earliest period of human history, individuals, armies, traders, and whole tribes have migrated and have intermarried with other physical types, thus breaking up the distinctive hereditary patterns.

As a result, there are no pure races within the human species. It is therefore impossible to devise a system of classification on the basis of inherited physical traits. Physical anthropologists have been trying for years to develop such a classification. In the past, it was acceptable for anthropologists to separate human beings into three distinct groups: the Caucasoid, Mongoloid, and Negroid. However, the magnitude of difficulties in this system of classification can be seen by noting the vagueness of the categories in Box 12-1. Loose as this three-way classification is, it does not cover all the races of people. African Bushmen-Hottentots, for example, have "Mongoloid" eyes. Australian aborigines have "Negroid" skin and "Caucasoid" hair. Some Polynesians have white skin and some dark brown skin; most of them have wavy hair; but there are many with straight or kinky hair. Some have broad and short faces; others, long and narrow. Since there is no such thing as pure race among human beings, one obviously cannot set up a classification scheme for pure races and expect the data to correspond to the theory.

The most important thing to realize about racial classifications is that they

12-1 CHECKING IT OUT: Physical Characteristics of the Three Main Races of Mankind

Trait	*Caucasoid*	*Mongoloid*	*Negroid*
Skin color	Pale reddish white to olive brown; some dark brown.	Pale yellow to yellow-brown; some reddish brown.	Brown to brown-black; some yellow-brown.
Stature	Medium to tall.	Medium tall to medium short.	Tall to very short.
Head form	Long to broad and short; medium high to very high.	Predominantly broad; height medium.	Predominantly long; height low to medium.
Face	Narrow to medium broad; no projecting jaw.	Medium broad to very broad; cheek-bones high and flat.	Medium broad to narrow; frequent projecting jaws.
Hair	Head hair: color light blond to dark brown; texture fine to medium, form straight to wavy. Body hair; moderate to profuse.	Head hair: color brown to brown-black; texture coarse; form straight. Body hair: sparse.	Head hair; color brown-black; texture, coarse; form light curl to woolly or frizzy. Body hair: slight.
Eye	Color: light blue to dark brown; occasional side eye-fold.	Color: brown to dark brown; fold of flesh in inner corner very common.	Color: brown to brown-black; vertical eye-fold common.
Nose	Bridge usually high; form narrow to medium broad.	Bridge usually low to medium; form medium broad.	Bridge usually low; form medium broad to very broad.
Body build	Slim to broad; slender to rugged.	Tends to be broad; occasional slimness.	Tends to be broad and muscular, but occasional slimness.

SOURCE: Adapted from Wilton M. Krogman, "The Concept of Race," *The Science of Man in the World Crisis*, ed. Ralph Linton (New York: Columbia University Press, 1945), p. 50. By permission.

do not correlate with either social structures or culture patterns. High cheekbones show some relationship to reddish-brown skin, and brown-black hair is associated with brown-black skin, but none of these characteristics is associated with intelligence, or a caste structure, or musical ability, or inventiveness, or a belief in one God, or the practice of polygamy, or anything else except other physical characteristics. Such an expression as "It's Arnold's Negro blood that makes him dance so well" is simply a holdover from the era before scientists discovered genes, when people believed that traits were transmitted through the blood.

Berry summarizes nicely the biological concept of race:

> The term "race," as used by most biological scientists, refers to a set of categories rather than to discrete, invariable entities. Races are not so much real things which man has discovered as they are pigeon-holes which man has constructed. These categories, to be sure, are based upon clusters of hereditary, physical characteristics. . . . The criteria upon which racial classification is based are non-adaptive, physical, secondary, and have little survival value. Certain societies, however, have come to attach great social significance to these biological trivia. (Berry, 1958, p. 49)

12-2 CHECKING IT OUT: Race and Culture

School children brought up in a Western heritage do not know about the Zulu conqueror, Chaka, or about his heroic opponent, Moshesh, or about Shamba Bolongogo, king of the Bakuba, who after three centuries is still remembered for his great reforms and inventions and for his love of peace. Few people have heard of the Liberian prophet Harris or of Kamehameha, King of Hawaii, or of the Mandingo Emperor, Gongo Musa, who is said to have embellished his cities with buildings of a style still used in the mosques of the Western Sudan. These, and a score of others, may well have been prevented merely by their isolated environment from achieving recognition as "great" men in the Western sense of the term. . . .

Cultures have flourished and waned in the past, undoubtedly they will continue to have their ups and downs in the future. . . . All that science can say is that no connection has been found between the biological constitution of the peoples and the level of their past or present culture; nor is there any hereditary or other biological reason for supporting that, just because White civilization is leading in the development of the present highly technical age, some races have less aptitude for learning technological skills. There is no reason, for example, why an African, because he is a Negro, cannot learn to drive a tractor or be a soil chemist, or any other of the tasks necessary for underdeveloped countries to help themselves. Such abilities cannot be considered racial ones.

Of course, children of a highly technical civilization have an enormous advantage over those who live in . . . isolated cultures. At an early age they learn the logic that two and two make four, they unconsciously learn the principle of cause and effect, they tinker with machines to see how they work. A . . . child born in the . . . Congo is brought up in a world with a different image of nature and its forces. If he is to adopt Western culture he has to learn, not only how a machine works, but also to interpret natural phenomena according to rigid laws which no longer permit the intervention of spirits or magic. But these are cultural, not racial, differences.

SOURCE: Department of Mass Communication, UNESCO, *What Is Race?* pp. 62–63.

THE SOCIAL DEFINITION OF RACE AND ETHNICITY

What we call "race" in the United States depends on social belief, not on biology. Whether or not one is classified as a white, Indian, or black depends upon which of these groups other people think one belongs to, and not on any specific hair color, hair type, head form, or skin color. It is obvious that the criteria used are not biological, since the biological characteristics overlap among the races—for instance, some people considered white have darker skins than some people considered black. Racial assignment is clearly a matter of social definition. Marvin Harris (1964), Gloria Marshall (1968), and others have shown racial designations to have political overtones. Harris notes that the rule of "hypodescent" assigns individuals of mixed parentage to the race that is politically least powerful. Thus the child of oriental and white parents is oriental. The social meanings attached to racial status are, then, very real and have enormous effects on social experiences. Therefore the sociologist studies race as a social fact, exerting great influence over social conduct. In sociological terms it is, then, valuable to define a race as a number of ethnic groups who, for geographical or social reasons, have isolated themselves long enough to develop distinctive physical characteristics or long enough to regard themselves and be regarded by others as biologically different. Social definition also decides whether or not one is a member of an ethnic minority. Suppose a woman is the daughter of a family known in their community as Jews. Even if their name is Smith and they do not attend a synagogue, their parents were Jewish and they are considered Jews. But what happens if the woman moves to a new community and does not tell anyone that she is a Jew? She is no longer Jewish: she is the same person, but the social definition of her status has been altered. When we say that the descendants of nineteenth-century German Americans are almost completely assimilated, we mean that most of them are identified by the members of American society not as Germans or as German Americans but as Americans.

Minority status, then, is as changeable as the characteristic that is used to define and identify the minority. If the only thing that confers minority status on a person is her or his surname, one can change the name and no longer be identifiable as a member of the category. If, however, it is one's sex or skin color that is the basis for discrimination, one is more permanently consigned to minority status because one is visibly different.

THE CAUSES OF PREJUDICE AND DISCRIMINATION

Prejudice and Discrimination

Prejudice is an emotional, rigid attitude toward a group of people. Prejudice is a misjudgment that one defends. Discrimination, on the other hand, relates to behavior. Discrimination may be defined as the differential treatment of minorities. Discrimination involves behavior based on a prejudiced attitude. The crux of minority status is the capacity of one category of people to impose discrimination upon another. Many people think of prejudice and discrimination as one and the same process; many more believe that whenever prejudice exists, there must be discrimination and vice versa or that an absence of discrimination necessarily means an absence of prejudice. However, there are times when people who are not prejudiced persons are unable to act upon their beliefs and attitudes. For many of us, law, custom, and organizational policy intervene between our individual attitudes and our capacity to act accordingly. Indeed, persons usually do not behave on the basis of their own personal prejudices and individual whims but are constrained in their behavior by law, custom, and the social situation. Most individuals do not act according to their attitudes in any sphere of life; and behavior—whether it is discriminatory or not—is more likely an organizational or social decision than a personal one. Most people function in situations in which prevailing situational requirements control and constrain their behavior; and the structure of the situation is more important than an isolated attitude. People in the armed forces, on the job, in school, in a traffic jam, and at a social function generally find that they cannot do what they want but must acquiesce to the social requirements of the situation they are in. Social scientists have found that once the social structure is changed, attitudes and beliefs reform themselves in the crucible of the new conditions. Thus, Ruth Benedict argues that racial beliefs and prejudices came *after* the onset of slavery to justify existing behavior. (1940)

The Self-fulfilling Prophecy: a Sociological Explanation

In either case, the definition of the status is social, and the members of the minority are a social category—that is, the characteristics associated with the minority are present because people *believe* they are present. Statuses are, among other things, simply sets of rights and duties assigned to people by other people. A role is a set of expected behaviors, and this is as true of a minority role as of any other. By expecting certain social behaviors from members of a minority, therefore, the people in the dominant category tend to make their own beliefs come true. (Merton, 1968) "The majority group asserts that the minority group is inferior and incapable of achievement, then acts in a discriminatory fashion to ensure that such inferior performance will be the outcome." (McKee, 1969) As Merton has pointed out, "the self-fulfilling prophecy is, in the beginning, a *false* definition of the situation evoking a new behavior which makes the originally false conception come true." (p. 423)

For example, white Americans for years accepted the stereotype that black Americans were less capable of learning than whites, that they were innately less intelligent. What, given this belief, was the course of action for the dominant whites? Provide inferior schools and inferior teachers for blacks. Then compare the scores of whites and blacks on intelligence tests and blacks will average lower than whites. By the very fact of believing that blacks cannot perform as well as whites, whites have made this true. Similarily, part of the stereotype of the Jew is that he is aggressive or "pushy." Because the members of the dominant category believe this, they set up extra hurdles for the Jew, such as quotas for admission to medical schools. Thus, if a Jewish person wants to become a doctor, he has to be not only as good as his non-Jewish competitors, but better. He has to work hard enough and perform well enough to overcome discrimination. In other words, he *has* to be aggressive and "pushy."

The same tendency holds for women who apply for a "man's" job, for blacks who seek occupations traditionally held by whites, and so on. As Robert Merton has noted, "the systematic condemnation of the [minority status person] continues largely irrespective of what he [or she] does." (p. 428)

> [O]bserve how the very same behavior undergoes a complete change of evaluation in its transition from the in-group Abe Lincoln to the out-group Abe Cohen or Abe Kurokawa. We proceed systematically. Did Lincoln work far into the night? This testifies that he was industrious, resolute, perseverant, and eager to realize his capacities to the full. Do the out-group Jews or Japanese keep these same hours? This only bears witness to their sweatshop mentality, their ruthless undercutting of American standards, their unfair competitive practices. Is the in-group hero frugal, thrifty, and sparing? Then the out-group villain is stingy, miserly, and penny-pinching. All honor is due the in-group Abe for his having been smart, shrewd, and intelligent and, by the same token, all contempt is owing the out-group Abes for their being sharp, cunning, crafty, and too clever by far. (Merton, 1968, pp. 428-429)

The sociological principle involved is described by Merton: "the moral virtues remain virtues only so long as they are jealously confined to the proper in-group. The right activity by the wrong people becomes a thing of contempt, not of honor. For clearly, only in this way, by holding these virtues exclusively to themselves, can the men of power retain their distinction, their prestige, and their power. No wiser procedure could be devised to hold intact a system of social stratification and social power." (Ibid., p. 429)

It should be clear that self-fulfilling prophecies and majority status require the exercise of social power.

> The pattern of majority-minority relations in any society is not to be explained primarily in terms of some set of prevailing prejudices; rather, minority status can be understood only as one kind of social inequality, and this is a structural arrangement that is sustained by more than just attitudes. Indeed, the domination of a minority group by a majority group cannot occur except through the exercise of *social power*. To be a majority group and to confine a minority group to a subordinate position within the social structure requires the majority group to have the instruments and mechanisms of power necessary to sustain its dominant

position. To discriminate in employment requires that the majority group have control over the distribution of jobs. To discriminate in education requires that the majority group control the educational process. (McKee, p. 294)

The Authoritarian Personality, a Psychological Explanation

In the aftermath of the horrors of Nazi Germany, a group of American scholars began a monumental study to attempt to understand the kind of collective hatred that would cause members of the German majority to destroy 6 million minority group members. For two and one half years researchers attempted to answer this question. What is there in the psychology of the individual that causes the person to be prejudiced? What would make a person respond favorably to the racist ideology of the Ku Klux Klan or the American Nazi Party? The result of this research is a series of studies that reveal the *The Authoritarian Personality* (Adorno *et al.,* 1950). Adorno and his associates found that intense prejudice is more than an accidental development in the lives of some people. It is not the result of a negative experience or parental teaching. For some, prejudice is "lock-stitched" into the fabric of the personality. The opinions, attitudes, and values of such people show a consistent pattern that ties the hatred of other groups to the psychological needs of the individual.

One of the important results of the project was the construction of several questionnaires that were designed to reveal the hidden beliefs of respondents. They were called the E-scale (to tap the rigid feeling toward out-groups as well as positive feelings toward in-groups), the AS-scale (the anti-Semitism scale), the PEC (the Politico-Economic Conservatism scale), and the F-scale (to uncover the potentially fascistic person who would be highly susceptible to antidemocratic propaganda). The test results showed that those who tested high on one of the scales tested high on all the others. However, the authoritarian personality is most closely related to the F-scale. In devising this measure, researchers developed a series of variables that indicated trends to be found deep in the authoritarian personality. These include:

1. A rigid adherence to conventional values. Here the acceptance of conventional values shows itself in unquestioning obedience given to those in power, regardless of ideology.

2. Uncritical submission to authority figures (parents, national leaders, supernatural powers).

3. Readiness to condemn and punish those who violate norms. Individuals who show such a pattern can be aggressive and sadistic.

4. A fear of inner examination or introspection, avoidance of the subjective.

5. A readiness to shift responsibility for events from inside to outside forces which cannot be controlled.

6. Admiration of power and toughness.

7. Strong underlying hostility and aggressiveness, looking for a target.

8. A tendency to project suppressed impulses onto other people. Unconscious urges of sexuality and destructiveness projected onto others.

9. Strong unconscious sex drives; therefore an exaggerated concern with punishing violators of sex norms (homosexuals, sex offenders).

In general, those who score high on tests of prejudice reveal anti-intellectual traits, have a tendency to think in absolute terms (good or bad, right or wrong), and reveal a deep-seated insecurity. Prejudiced subjects reported childhood experiences in homes characterized by harsh discipline, bigotry, "fearful subservience to the demands of parents and by an early suppression of impulses not acceptable to them." (Adorno *et al.*, p. 385)

Simpson and Yinger (1972) raise some questions about the research findings of the Adorno group. Because representative sampling was not used, the possibility of generalizing findings to a larger population becomes questionable. Also some of the measures used were based on verbal responses. The reliability of this method presents problems because in follow-up studies, over time, different responses to the same questions were given. In addition, the failure to control for variables such as education causes serious limitations. It is possible that the responses of a person who scores high on the scale of prejudice may reflect limited experiences and lack of education, rather than a biased attitude. More recent research suggests that the F-scale is not **unidimensional.** This means that it is not based on a pattern of traits that "hang together" to represent the *single* dimension, authoritarianism, or tendency to fascism. Rather it measures several things at one time. It is possible, therefore, that it does not measure any of them very well. However, regardless of their deficiencies, the Adorno studies are accepted as an impressive achievement. The different kinds of measures used strengthen the significance of the results. And while some of the methodology is questionable, there is little doubt of the importance of such personality research.

Racism

Frequently we hear the term *racism* used to mean hatred of one racial group for another. However, this definition is imprecise and not the way the term racism is defined by sociologists. Sociologists know that the world is full of societies in which certain minorities are exploited by dominant groups who treat them as inferiors. Such unequal treatment results from the belief held by the more powerful group that it is superior to the minority. This is the case in South Africa where apartheid is the prevailing system. White racism in South Africa is the belief, built into the culture, that whites are superior and blacks and "coloreds" are inferior. These beliefs become the basis for political and economic differentiations. Joel Kovel, in his psychohistory *White Racism* (1970) describes the pattern of South Africa as "dominative racism." In America he finds the dominative type with its intense effort to control racial minorities but he also finds patterns of "aversive racism." Aversive racists practice avoidance of minorities. "The dominative racist, when threatened by the black, resorts to direct violence; the aversive racist, in the same situation, turns away and walls himself off" (p. 121).

Racism in the History of the West Although it is safe to suppose that ethnocentric attitudes have existed since time immemorial, racism has many characteristics that make it a relatively modern invention. Ethnocentrism or the belief in the uniqueness and superiority of one's group has existed since

12-3 CHECKING IT OUT: Racist Laws—South African Style

It is unlawful for a White person and a non-White person to drink a cup of tea together in a tea room anywhere in South Africa, unless they have obtained a special permit to do so. . . .

Any policeman is entitled, without warrant, to enter and search, "at any reasonable time of the day or night," premises in a town in which he has reason to suspect that an African boy eighteen years of age is committing the criminal offence of residing with his father without having the necessary permission to do so. . . .

A White person living in a town who employs an African to do any carpentry, bricklaying, electrical fitting or other skilled work in his home, commits a criminal offence unless special exemption has been granted by the Minister of Labour; so also does any African who performs such skilled work in a town elsewhere than in an area set aside for occupation by Africans. Each is liable to a fine not exceeding one hundred pounds, or to imprisonment for a period not exceeding one year, or to both such fine and such imprisonment. . . .

Any policeman may at any time call upon an African who has attained the age of sixteen years to produce his reference book. If a reference book has been issued to him but he fails to produce it because it is not in his possession at the time, he commits a criminal offence and is liable to a fine not exceeding ten pounds or imprisonment for a period not exceeding one month. . . .

If an Indian (or a Coloured or an African) sits on a bench in a public park, the bench being set apart for the exclusive use of White persons, by way of protest against the apartheid laws, he commits a criminal offence and is liable to a fine not exceeding three hundred pounds, or to imprisonment for a period not exceeding three years, or to a whipping not exceeding ten strokes, or to both such fine and such imprisonment, or to both such fine and such whipping, or to both such imprisonment and such whipping. . . .

If there is only one waiting-room in a railway station, it is lawful for the station master to reserve that waiting-room for the exclusive use of White persons, and any non-White person wilfully entering it commits a criminal offence and is liable to a fine not exceeding fifty pounds or to imprisonment for a period not exceeding three months or to both such fine and such imprisonment. . . .

Any policeman may, without warrant, enter premises in which a meeting is taking place, if he believes, on reasonable grounds, that the internal security of the

Union is likely to be endangered as a result of the meeting, and that obtaining a warrant would cause serious delay. . . .

No African, lawfully residing in a town by virtue of a permit issued to him, is entitled, as of right, to have his wife and children residing with him. . . .

Any unmarried man who "in appearance obviously is or who by general acceptance and repute is a white person" and who attempts to have carnal intercourse with a woman who is not "obviously in appearance or by general acceptance and repute a white person," is guilty of an offence and liable on conviction to imprisonment with compulsory labour for a period not exceeding seven years, unless he can prove to the satisfaction of the court that he had reasonable cause to believe, at the time when the alleged offence was committed, that she was "obviously in appearance or by general acceptance and repute a white person". . . .

SOURCE: Leslie Rubin, *This is Apartheid* (London: Camelot Press, 1959), pp. 8–16.

human beings first identified physical and behavioral differences in groups other than their own. And yet in the ancient world, racial differences were not considered reasons for racist attitudes. The domination of one group by another was most frequently justified on religious grounds. As Simpson and Yinger (1974) express it, "If, at first the white European did not condemn the Negro because he was a Negro, he could condemn him because he was a pagan." (p. 108) In earlier times before religious tolerance had developed as a cultural belief, religious differences were thought to be the crucial differences between social groups. Racism as an ideology must be connected to the emerging African slave trade in which the immense profits possible caused a new system of beliefs to be developed. In eighteenth-century South Africa (MacCrone, 1937) slaves who had been baptized might be freed, since they were then no longer despised pagans. However, the Church Council of Capetown reflected the interests of slaveowners when it ruled that "neither the law of the land nor the law of the church" (p. 135) required that baptized slaves be manumitted or freed. Stanley Elkins (1954) demonstrates that by the year 1700 in the United States a series of laws had eliminated the possibility that converted slaves might be freed. And yet, involvement in the slave trade caused moral problems for Christian Europeans. Buying and selling human beings was sinful according to religious scripture. Such moral conflicts were increasingly resolved as racial theories appeared which declared the enslaved people to be subhuman. If they were biologically inferior, exploitation by the majority group was deemed more justifiable. Simpson and Yinger note that once racial differences were established designating one group as superior and the other as inferior, the differences were used as weapons in economic situations. Thus, ". . . it is apparent that to understand race conflict in the modern world one must understand conflict, not race." (p. 109)

In the nineteenth century, conflicts based on racial ideology were numerous. Darwin's theory of evolution and Herbert Spencer's expression of "the survival of the fittest" gave justification to imperialist European powers as they continued their exploitation of less powerful nations. Colonialism and the annexation of territory was encouraged wherever the racist belief in the "white man's burden" was accepted. This belief emphasized the responsibility of the white Western nations to bring the benefits of their more advanced civilization to nonwhite nations—to land and resource-rich nonwhites, that is. The conquest of the Native Americans as well as the annexation of territory was justified by the federal government, in the same period, as the result of "manifest destiny." It was judged our destiny to expand our borders as well as our control of ancestral Native American lands. The rights of the minorities were not considered.

Institutional Racism Racism is generally associated with the prejudiced attitudes and discriminatory actions of individuals in society. And yet another kind of racism exists that is more subtle and extremely damaging to minority group members. This is institutional racism. Institutional racism results from the day-to-day operations of social institutions in such a way that discrimination is the result, although this may not be the policy of the institutions involved. Carmichael and Hamilton (1967) described as individually racist the actions of white "terrorists" who bombed a black church in Birmingham and killed five black children who were worshipping there. However, when, in the same southern city, "five hundred black babies die each year because of the lack of proper food, shelter, and medical facilities, and thousands more are destroyed and maimed physically, emotionally, and intellectually because of the conditions of poverty and discrimination in the black community, that is a function of institutional racism."

A significant thing about institutional racism is that it results from indirect processes. For example, as Blauner (1972) has observed, jurors are drawn from voting lists. Black people are underrepresented on such lists; therefore blacks are less apt to be found on juries. The practice of selecting jurors from voting lists is probably not intentionally used to exclude blacks, but, in an indirect way, the consequences of this practice may in fact be racist. In the same way culturally biased IQ tests, which are frequently used to develop tracking systems in educational institutions, demonstrate institutional racism by discriminating against lower-class black children, although this may not be the policy of the schools.

MINORITIES IN THE SOCIAL STRUCTURE

Minorities, then, are social categories of people who have poorer life chances than members of the majority group. In this sense, minorities are similar to classes in the stratification structure. A businessman has higher prestige than a laborer, but a Protestant businessman has higher prestige than a Jewish businessman. Any citizen who meets the age and certain other Constitutional

12-4 CHECKING IT OUT: Size and Proportion of the Black Population in the United States, 1850-1975

Year	*Population (millions)*	*Percentage*
1850	3.6	15.5
1870	4.9	12.3
1890	7.5	11.9
1910	9.8	10.7
1930	11.9	11.4
1950	15.0	10.0
1960	18.9	10.5
1970	22.7	11.2
1975	23.8	11.5

SOURCE: *Statistical Abstract of the United States*, 1971, 1977, U.S. Bureau of the Census, Tables 2, 101, 102, 32; *Historical Statistics of the United States, 1789–1945*, 1949, p. 25; *Seventeenth Census of Population* (1950), *Characteristics of the Population*, Table 35 (Washington, D.C.: U.S. Government Printing Office). 1960 data from preliminary census reports.

Size and Proportion of the Foreign-born Population in the United States, 1850-1960

Year	*Foreign-born (White) (millions)*	*U.S. Population (Census) (millions)*	*Percentage of Foreign-born*
1850	2.2	23.2	9.5
1870	5.5	39.8	13.8
1890	9.1	62.9	14.5
1910	13.3	92.0	14.5
1930	14.0	122.8	11.4
1950	10.2	150.7	6.8
1960	9.3	179.3	5.4

SOURCE: *Statistical Abstract of the United States*, 1953, U.S. Bureau of the Census, Tables 2, 101, 102; *Historical Statistics of the United States, 1789–1945*, 1949, p. 25; *Seventeenth Census of Population* (1950), Vol. II, *Characteristics of the Population*, Table 35 (Washington, D.C.: U.S. Government Printing Office); 1960 *Census of Population*, Volume 1, Characteristics of the Population, Part 1, United States Summary.

requirements may be President of the United States of America, but the chances of realizing that goal are significantly lower for persons of minority status. Indeed, there is considerable evidence that the chances to achieve the positions that offer the most prestige and power and the highest rewards are relatively low for women, blacks, Mexican Americans, Native Americans, Jews, Puerto Ricans, and other minority-status persons.

In 1970, there were more than 22 million black Americans; more than 9 million foreign-born white Americans; more than 5 million Jewish Americans; more than 5 million Mexican Americans; more than 1 million Puerto Rican Americans; more than a million Japanese Americans, Chinese Americans, Filipino Americans, and Korean Americans; and at least 85 million women not included in other minority groups. Clearly, more than three-fifths of the American population occupy minority status and experience some amount of social discrimination.

To be sure, not all life chances are exactly the same for all persons of minority status, for there are important variations both between and within the many minority statuses. For example, black Americans have been disproportionately burdened with very low incomes, but some blacks are quite wealthy. Similarly, the opportunity for a white-collar job is higher for Jews than for Native Americans and the chance for good medical care is higher for Japanese Americans than it is for Puerto Rican Americans. The amount of occupational segregation is higher for women than it is for blacks, and so on. Nonetheless, *all* persons of minority status are denied full and equal participation in all phases of the society.

As recently as 1910, racial and ethnic minorities accounted for more than one-fourth of the population of the United States, as can be seen from Box 12-4. In this century the black population has remained a fairly constant 10–11 per cent of the total while the foreign-born population has diminished markedly. How do people become minorities? What places some people in a society in racial or ethnic social categories? Ordinarily, a racial or ethnic population becomes defined as different and placed in a social category as the result of majority group policy.

Policies of the Majority toward Minorities

Simpson and Yinger (1972) have discussed the types of policies that dominant groups have developed toward minority groups. The six types listed below demonstrate the wide range of responses possible and also illustrate that in some cases the majority policy adopted parallels the goals of minorities and in some cases opposes their goals.

Assimilation Assimilation can either be forced or permitted by the majority. Where assimilation is forced on minorities it reflects an extreme ethnocentrism on the part of the dominant group. Majorities have frequently forced minorities to abandon their own languages, customs, and religions and to take on the cultural traits of those in power. Simpson and Yinger have borrowed the term, coined by Milton Gordon (1964) to describe the most common form of assimilation in the United States, *Anglo-conformity*, a demand that immigrant groups quickly absorb the "Anglo-Saxon" cultural patterns of the majority. Underlying this pressure from the majority is a determination to maintain English institutions, the English language, and English cultural patterns (respecting those modifications resulting from the American Revolution) as dominant and most acceptable.

Where assimilation has occurred peacefully and without force, the majority has recognized the right of the minority to absorb new elements of culture at its own speed. Also in such cases the majority accepts the notion that assimilation may be racial as well as cultural, a two-way process which may lead to a mixed population. Simpson and Yinger note that "Brazil has an ideology that looks with favor on the eventual blending of diverse racial types into a Brazilian stock." (p. 17) In the United States, racial minorities have been discouraged from assimilating (See Box 12-5). Indeed, the majority of white Americans still oppose racial intermarriage. In the past, many states had laws against intermarriage between whites and blacks or orientals. All the culture patterns that keep racial

12-5 CHECKING IT OUT: National Opinion on Marriage Between Whites and Nonwhites

Nation	*Approve*	*Disapprove*	*No opinion*
Sweden	67	21	12
France	62	25	13
Finland	58	34	8
Netherlands	51	23	26
Greece	50	36	14
Switzerland	50	35	15
Austria	39	53	8
Canada	36	53	11
West Germany	35	47	18
Norway	35	44	21
Uruguay	30	44	26
Great Britain	29	57	14
United States	20	72	8
United States:			
non-South	25	70	5

SOURCE: *The San Francisco Chronicle*, November 11, 1968.

minorities separate from the dominant category—segregated housing, schools, churches, and so on—are a deterrent to total assimilation.

Pluralism Where minorities do not want to be assimilated, do not want to lose their unique culture, they press for pluralism. If pluralism is accepted as public policy by the majority, then the minority-majority relationship may be expected to disappear. The truly pluralistic society is, then, composed of culturally different groups, all accorded equal rights and privileges. For several hundred years, the ethnic groups of Switzerland (the French, Italian, and German Swiss) have retained their individual languages and cultural patterns. No group has been treated as a minority as we have defined the concept. Cultural differences have been balanced by considerable political and economic cohesiveness. Tanzania is another example of a society in which pluralism is encouraged. The cultural differences among its African, Asian, European, and Middle Eastern groups are recognized and respected.

Simpson and Yinger have described the policy of the United States to be contradictory regarding pluralism. The demand for "Anglo-conformity" has caused the majority to expect conformity to its cultural patterns. And yet, pluralism is also valued. Minorities such as the Chicanos, Native Americans, blacks, and Asian Americans have been encouraged to emphasize their cultural distinctions. It appears that although America has not been as equitable in her treatment of minorities as her ideology suggests she should be, neither has she been as indifferent to the cultural diversity of her people as her harshest critics have suggested.

Legal Protection of Minorities The legal protection of minorities would not be necessary in a truly pluralistic society, because minorities as we have defined them would not exist. Where such protection must be accorded by legal and constitutional means, it is clear that groups must exist in the society that resist equality of treatment for the minority. Simpson and Yinger note that after World War I, the constitutions of Bulgaria and Turkey accorded autonomy and equality to minorities. Also, in the United States, the Thirteenth, Fourteenth, and Fifteenth Amendments to the Constitution, "although not pluralistic in aim, sought to protect the equal rights of minorities, primarily Negroes, in a situation that had been unfavorable to that aim. Recent fair-employment practices legislation has similar objectives" (p. 21).

Population Transfer Population transfer has been used throughout history as a majority group strategy. In some cases, the removal of minorities has been considered an answer to intergroup tensions. Indeed there have been times when the minority has viewed the transfer positively, desiring secession and self-determination. Intergroup tensions between Hindus and Muslims in India led to the creation of a new state and the movement of Muslims out of India. Frequently population transfer has been an expression of hostility on the part of the majority and has been forced on the minority. For instance, the transfer of Japanese-Americans to relocation camps during World War II was a clear expression of majority group hostility.

Continued Subjugation In some cases, majority group members avoid any opportunity to treat minorities justly yet have no desire to drive them out because they are an exploitable asset. In South Africa, the white majority has made it clear that it will use every means possible to maintain its domination over the black minority. In the United States, there are many Americans who depend on the labor of illegal Mexican immigrants or "wetbacks." Such people do not want to pay standard wages to farm workers and they continue to profit from the powerless position of the "wetbacks."

Extermination The total destruction of a minority group or **genocide** has in some cases been chosen as a solution when intergroup conflicts have been continuous. The extermination of the Native American population was agreed upon by the United States government at several points in our history. The murder of 6 million Jews by the Nazis in Germany is a more recent blight on modern history. In 1972, an example of genocide was reported in Burundi, East Africa, where the Tutsi, the dominant group, were accused of taking the lives of 50,000 to 100,000 Hutus, a Bantu people who had traditionally been accorded minority status.

Minority Status and Life Chances

By definition, minorities occupy a distinctive position in the stratification system and they experience the life chances that accompany that position. (See Table 12-6.) At the turn of the century, for example, the maternal mortality rate

12-6 CHECKING IT OUT: Maternal Mortality Rate, by Race (Per 10,000 Live Births), 1900–1970

Year	*White*	*Nonwhite*
1900	60.1	105.6
1936	51.2	97.2
1950	6.1	22.2
1960	2.6	9.7
1968	1.7	6.4
1970	1.4	5.6

SOURCE: *Maternal Mortality Statistics, United States, 1950*, National Office of Vital Statistics, U.S. Public Health Service, December 3, 1953 (Washington, D.C.: U.S. Government Printing Office), p. 368, and *Historical Statistics of the United States, Colonial Times to 1970* (Washington, D.C.: U.S. Government Printing Office, 1975), p. 57.

among nonwhites was nearly twice as high as it was among whites. The maternal mortality rate has been reduced in this century and the relative advantage of whites has increased to the point that the maternal mortality rate is nearly four times as high for nonwhites as it is for whites. (Black Americans constitute 94 per cent of the nonwhite population of the United States).

Such variations in life chances extend throughout the stratification system: "only 13 per cent of the black men are professional or managerial workers compared to 30 per cent among whites; 17 per cent of blacks, in contrast to 6 per cent of whites, work as laborers." (Farley and Hermalin, 1972, p. 353)

The conflict between the cultural values of political equality and opportunity for economic advancement as opposed to the ascribed status of blacks constitutes what Myrdal has called the "American dilemma." (1944) Attempts to solve it have changed the class status of the black in the United States radically in the past few decades. Many Americans, mostly blacks, have made major attempts in recent years to solve the dilemma, and although racial equality is not yet a reality in America, the efforts of the last few years have helped to close the gap between the races.

THE MINORITIES OF AMERICA

Black Americans

The Period of Slavery The first black Africans arrived in America in 1619. They had been brought from Africa as slaves and sold in Virginia by one of the Dutch trading companies that monopolized the slave trade at that time. (Du Bois, 1896) Because slavery did not exist in the American colonies, these blacks became indentured servants. Like the many white indentured servants, they would remain in servitude for a specified time and then become free. Other blacks who were brought here as slaves gained their freedom by converting to Christianity. However, the demand for a cheap labor force in an agricultural economy led to the introduction of chattel slavery for blacks in America. In the system of chattel slavery, the slave is regarded as portable property, as subhuman and inferior. This is very different from the ancient Roman, Grecian, and African concept of slavery, in which enslavement is a matter of chance, and even slaves have certain rights and privileges because they are human beings. Stanley Elkins (1963), in his analysis of the development of chattel slavery in the American colonies, suggests that the American variety of slavery was developed in a society without prior traditional institutions. The colonists were coming from England where a revolutionary struggle in the mid-seventeenth century had diminished the power of the king (Charles I had been beheaded) and the church (the Puritans had defeated the Anglicans). These institutions did not have the power to exert strong moral leadership as the English wrested the slave trade from the Dutch. In the colonies competing religious denominations again lacked the power or the will to exert any influence as a racist ideology was developed which declared blacks to be biologically inferior to whites, irresponsible, promiscuous, and lazy, and therefore deserving continued subjugation. A very different experience was accorded black slaves in Latin America where the church and the crown were powerful institutions. Though very much a part of the slave system, the Catholic church demanded control over the religious education of slaves and guarded their personal and family rights (slaves could hold property, could work for themselves, could rest on Sundays). A tradition of freeing slaves (manumission) also existed, on special holidays and during festivals. (Freyre, 1963; Tannenbaum, 1947)

In the American colonies, the "peculiar institution" of slavery narrowly restricted the activities and opportunities of slaves. Slaves could not own property, could not be educated, could not be witnesses against whites in court, could not get married legally. Slaves could not be abusive to any white person. Any meeting of more than five blacks, away from home, was illegal unless a white person was present. Sexual relations between white females and black males were forbidden; if such relations were discovered death was often the punishment for the black male. (Stampp, 1956)

There is a current debate among scholars about the slave experience and its consequences. Traditional interpretations have emphasized the separation of families in a system in which human beings were sold on the auction block. Also in order to cope with the harsh system under which they lived, blacks developed behavioral strategies. They feigned illness, they clowned, they sabotaged. Rose (1974) notes that they tried to shield their children from the horrors of the slave experience (sometimes actually taking the child's life). Slave revolts were known to be common occurrences. The insurrections led by Denmark Vesey, Gabriel Prosser, and Nat Turner are well known. When slaves did not revolt, Elkins suggests that their docility can be compared with the adjustment patterns of concentration victims under Hitler. The quiescent, subservient plantation black had, then, accepted the "master" as a "significant other" in order to survive. A recent study of the institution of slavery by Fogel and Engerman questions many of the traditional interpretations about slavery (1974). As economic historians, these researchers produce data to show that under slavery black families were not habitually split up, that the stable nuclear unit was the norm. Nor did the slave system undermine black self-conceptions and destroy the independence and sense of accomplishment of individuals. Functioning in a variety of economic roles, from managers and professionals to fieldhands, their slave experience exemplifies the ability of blacks to survive. Thus the Fogel-Engerman view has been accepted by some black Americans who see a strength and endurance in blacks today that has historical roots.

By the second quarter of the nineteenth century, a vigorous campaign had begun to end American slavery. This campaign was led by northern white abolitionists and ex-slaves who had escaped, among them Frederick Douglass, the most influential black of the period; Sojourner Truth, a black woman who spoke dramatically against slavery; and Harriet Tubman, who helped over 300 blacks to escape to freedom. Eventually the question of slavery was decided by the defeat of the South in the Civil War and the adoption of the Thirteenth Amendment to the Constitution, outlawing slavery.

The Period of Reconstruction The period following the Civil War was a fruitful one for blacks. This era is known as the Reconstruction and was a period of singular achievements for blacks. Under the watchful eyes of federal troops stationed in the South, free public schools were established for newly freed blacks and, for the first time, for poor white children. During this period, black males gained the right to vote and in addition to the election of black sheriffs, state senators, judges, and state representatives, twenty-two black men were elected to the United States Congress. Two blacks served in the Senate. The period of Reconstruction ended in the late 1870s with the election of Rutherford B. Hayes as President. In return for Southern support in his bid for election, Hayes removed the federal troops from the South and returned local autonomy to the state governments. The southern states quickly instituted a system of legal segregation in an attempt to strip blacks of their newly won freedoms. While the Fifteenth Amendment guaranteed them the vote, "grandfather clauses" were introduced, denying the vote to those whose grandfathers had not voted. Fear was also used as a mechanism of control. Terrorist organizations such as the Ku Klux Klan used threats and violence to prevent blacks from voting and holding office. In 1896, in the Plessy *v.* Ferguson case, the "Jim Crow" laws and system of segregation of the races was legitimized by the Supreme Court when it ruled that separate-but-equal facilities were constitutional. Ignoring the fact that separate facilities are never equal, this decision justified the separate schools, hospitals, drinking fountains, and cemeteries of the United States for many decades.

Blacks in the Twentieth Century In 1900, 90 per cent of black Americans lived in the South, predominately in rural areas. Today almost half of black Americans live in the Northern cities; and of those remaining in the South, the vast majority now inhabit Southern cities. In the twentieth century, blacks became an urban people. Between 1910 and 1920 a half million blacks migrated to the North where they were then "locked" into patterns of residential segregation and economic and social discrimination. Whereas economic gains were made during World War I as job opportunities increased, conflict erupted after the War when competition for jobs became keen. Blacks refused to be pushed back into low-paying menial jobs. One of the forms of this conflict was the race riot. Peter Rose (1974) cites thirty-three "interracial disturbances" between 1915 and 1949. Eventually it took the threat of a march on Washington, which was organized by A. Philip Randolph, president of the most powerful black union, to achieve more equitable occupational opportunities for blacks. In 1941,

President Roosevelt issued Executive Order 8802, which promised blacks more participation in defense industries and which established a federal Fair Employment Practices Committee.

An event of unparalleled significance for black Americans was the action of the Supreme Court in 1954 to reverse the Plessy *v.* Ferguson decision. In Brown *v.* the Topeka Board of Education, separate and segregated school systems for blacks and whites were ruled unconstitutional. This decision set the stage for widespread desegregation. It also set in motion an intensified struggle for equality of treatment. This protest movement produced the remarkable Dr. Martin Luther King, Jr., the leader of a nonviolent mass movement in the South that used economic boycotts and demonstrations to effect change. It produced the Student Non-Violent Coordinating Committee (SNCC), an organization of college students who actively attempted to desegregate libraries, swimming pools, and churches. Originally interracial, SNCC became an all-black organization stressing a separatist ideology and a demand for "black power." The Congress of Racial Equality (CORE) founded by James Farmer developed "freedom riders" to challenge segregation on interstate buses. Black and white "freedom riders" met with violence in Alabama in 1961. Another protest group was the Nation of Islam, which under the leadership of Elijah Muhammad and his chief spokesman, Malcolm X, accepted the beliefs of Islam. These Black Muslims developed their own system of parochial schools, businesses, and mosques. Originally, this group expressed contempt for integration efforts, Christianity, and the white race. When Malcolm X broke with the organization in 1964, his antiwhite expressions had moderated. He was assassinated in 1965. Some years after his death, the Muslims agreed to accept Caucasian members.

As the largest and most visible minority in America, as the only immigrant group which came involuntarily, as slaves, black Americans have experienced progress in the twentieth century that has been revolutionary and dramatic. The movement from auction block to Congressional legislature, from assimilationalistic aims to pluralistic demands, has described an odyssey both historic and of significance to all Americans.

Native Americans

The years from 1849 to 1900 mark a crucial change in the history of the Native American. At the beginning of this period, Native Americans still had the power to resist the American government as they were being systematically stripped of their land. By the end of this period, they were a conquered people, impoverished, demoralized, and without hope.

The Native Americans of the northern hemisphere have traditionally been organized into ethnic groups and cultural groups. Individual tribes have had their own belief systems, family structures, and other cultural traditions. While the earliest contacts between the northeast tribes and the European settlers had been friendly, the relentless encroachment of the land-hungry whites alarmed and then angered the Native Americans. In understanding the "Indian wars" of the nineteenth century, it is necessary to remember that the Sioux, the Cheyenne, the Apache, and the Comanche were actively resisting an invasion of Europeans bent on expanding their settlements across the continent. In 1876, at the Battle of Little Big Horn, the Sioux massed and in an intertribal effort, destroyed the military force of General Custer. Their leader, Crazy Horse, the strategist of this campaign, is now acknowledged as a military genius. However, in most cases the written histories of these years are notable for their biased viewpoint. Native Americans have been painted as "savages" and the settlers have been described as "pioneers." The Battle of Little Big Horn has been generally called a "massacre," while expeditions against Native Americans have been hailed as "military victories." While southwest tribes such as the Apache and the Comanche have never been defeated militarily, they were eventually subjugated and forced onto reservations far from their ancestral lands. Governmental policy regarding these groups has frequently indicated that genocide or a systematic extermination of the group was intended. (Marshall, 1972) Removed from ancestral territories, subjected to broken promises and treaties, swindled of remaining lands, Native Americans have been reduced to desperate circumstances.

At the present time, Native Americans are probably the most disadvantaged minority in the United States. For this group, the average family income is just over $1,500 a year. Their unemployment rate is 45 per cent. Suicide among Native American teenagers is three times the national average. The average life expectancy is more than twenty-five years below the national average, and their infant mortality rate is the highest of any minority group. Living conditions on reservations are dismal; people are forced to exist in tents, shacks covered with tarpaper, log houses without heat, caves, and even abandoned automobile bodies. (Burnette, 1971; P. Rose, 1974)

Of the 600,000 Native Americans in this country, the majority now live in urban areas. With almost 60 per cent of the group having less than an eighth-grade education, occupational mobility has been difficult. While many have flocked to cities, such as Chicago, Minneapolis, Los Angeles, and San Francisco, hoping for a better life, what has happened is that, lacking education and skills, they have frequently become welfare recipients. The urban experience has had one positive effect. Exclusive associations with tribal members have broken down as Native Americans have begun to realize that they share common problems. Their awareness of the struggles of blacks and Hispanics has caused the development of a "red power" movement and a militant new spirit. Indigenous movements such as the American Indian Movement (AIM) have begun to confront the society and demand justice, respect, and the right of self-determination.

Asian Americans

Chinese Americans The Chinese began coming to the United States in significant numbers at the midpoint of the nineteenth century. Immigration for this group increased after the discovery of gold in California. Although some Chinese developed their own gold mines, many others were used by whites as a cheap labor source in the mining industry and during the widespread construction of railroads. Because women were in short supply in the frontier areas, Chinese men were hired to do much of the work usually done by women, such as cooking, washing, and gardening. (Vander Zanden, 1972) However, such work was considered unmasculine. Also, the Chinese, who retained their Eastern habits and dress, were treated with contempt. With their hair braided in long cues, and wearing their felt slippers and cotton blouses, they were not thought of as Americans. Anti-Chinese feeling grew as white miners banded together to remove the Chinese immigrants as economic competition. The immigrants became frequent victims of harassment and mob violence. Chinese laborers responded to this hostility by withdrawing from the occupations in dispute. D. Y. Yuan indicates that in 1870, 27,045 Chinese were working as miners and laborers. By 1920 there were only 151. In 1870 there were 9,349 Chinese functioning as domestic servants. By 1920, this number had increased to 26,440. (Yuan, 1970) Majority group hostility against this group reached its height when, in 1882, legislation was passed to prevent the immigration of Chinese laborers for ten years and declaring those Chinese born in China as unacceptable for American citizenship. In 1904, Congress voted to prohibit Chinese immigration indefinitely and this was not repealed until 1943. Because the Chinese were subjected to everything from beating, murder, and lynching, as well as to legislative discrimination, they were rendered powerless. They withdrew into segregated communities where, until recent times, they have remained isolated from the American mainstream. It is interesting to note that although the Chinese were already in America many years before the waves of European immigration around the turn of the century, their isolation in urban "Chinatowns" and the public perception of the Chinese as exotic and "inscrutable" have hindered their opportunities for social contact with majority group members. The Chinese notion of the "sojourner" also contributed to the isolation of this group. In the nineteenth century, Chinese immigrants were mainly males who saw their experience in this country as a temporary one. They expected to make money here and then return to China. They had no desire to internalize majority group norms and values. The inability to return to China at the time of the revolution and the arrival of large numbers of females in the 1950s, led to a change in the "sojourner" orientation. As immigration of orientals began again, the increased commitment of Chinese-Americans to some degree of cultural assimilation has caused this ethnic minority to prosper and achieve social mobility. In recent years, Chinese Americans have frequently left their urban Chinatowns for the more affluent suburbs, making room for a new group of immigrants (i.e., Chinese from Hong Kong). This new group is experiencing problems as some of them collide with the demands of "Anglo-conformity."

Japanese Americans When Japanese immigrants arrived on the American mainland in the 1880s, they had an experience that was somewhat different from that of the Chinese. Whereas the Chinese had been poor and unskilled, the Japanese came with skills that made them economically mobile as a group. Whereas the Chinese retreated in the face of economic and political discrimination, the Japanese displayed ingenuity and boldness in their attempts to overcome differential treatment. Marden and Meyer (1978) note that legislation prevented aliens who were ineligible for citizenship from owning land. Japanese farmers who were leasing land began to buy land in the name of their American-born children. Such adaptations caused the majority population to form a stereotype of the Japanese that was different from the Chinese. The Chinese were believed to be "inferior, humble, and ignorant [people] who could be condescendingly tolerated." The Japanese came to be regarded as ". . . aggressive, cunning, and conspiratorial, requiring more active and outright dominance to keep them 'in their place.' " (p. 197) The Japanese prospered in America. They exhibited cultural values that were similar to the majority. They encouraged their children to excel in school. Many adopted the Christian religion. Indeed, a generation gap developed as the Nisei, the first American-born Japanese, sought to evade the rigid discipline of the Issei, their foreign-born parents, and became even more fully integrated into American life.

However, the experience of Japanese Americans changed drastically when the United States entered a war against Japan in 1941. By August, 1942, over 110,000 West Coast Japanese had been transferred to detention or relocation camps. Because those Japanese Americans who might have posed a military risk had already been taken into custody, the relocation of a whole population which included 70,000 American citizens could only be interpreted "as an act of unprecedented official racism." (Simpson and Yinger, 1972, p. 119) The effects of relocation were catastrophic as businesses and farms had to be abandoned or sold hurriedly at a loss or relinquished to non-Japanese "managers" who could not be supervised. (Bloom–Riemer, 1949; Nishimoto, 1946; Grodzins, 1949)

The experiences of Japanese Americans since World War II have been peaceful and progressive. Like the Chinese Americans, they have shown commitments to many of the same middle-class values as white Americans. Japanese Americans have the highest per capita income of all the racial minorities.

The Chicanos

In past years the term Chicano was a derogatory term used by white Americans (Anglos) to mean "Mexicano" or Mexican-American. This practice illustrates the anti-Mexican prejudice that has been particularly virulent in California and the Southwest United States. However, Mexican Americans now identify themselves as Chicanos, using the term with a sense of ethnic pride, aware of themselves as *La Raza* (the race), a Spanish-speaking people, increasingly demanding respect for their culture and traditions. Of the more than five million Mexican Americans in the United States, some are the descendants of Hispanic families who have lived in the Southwest for over four hundred years. This Spanish-speaking, Catholic group became Americans when formerly Mexican territories were ceded to the United States after the Mexican-American War of 1848. In the twentieth century other Chicanos have been both legal and illegal immigrants, who have come to work as migrant farm laborers. The "wetbacks" were those workers who had entered illegally to find work; the "braceros" were those with legal work permits as farm labor recruited from Mexico. Bracero labor was intended only for the agricultural sector, and use of these imported workers at very low wages drove native-born Chicanos out of farming and to the cities. Peter Rose notes that distinctions between braceros and wetbacks are no longer valid as all Mexicans must now enter legally under the provisions of the revised Immigration and Nationality Act (1974).

However, the exploitation of migrant agricultural workers who would work for lower wages than local workers and a growing sense of cohesiveness have caused Mexican Americans to unite to improve their condition. Charismatic leaders like Chicano César Chavez have unionized agricultural workers and captured the imagination of a national audience as they have lead successful boycotts of fruits and vegetables in order to secure economic gains for farm workers. Through community organization and increased activity in Mexican American political parties like La Raza Unida, Chicanos are determined to resist the stereotyping and discrimination of the majority group and have begun to reject the demands of Anglo-conformity as they intensify their interest in Mexican history and culture and Chicano art, music, and life styles.

White Ethnics

We have said that the immigrant peoples who came to America were expected to relinquish their own cultural behaviors and languages and become Americans. Anglo-conformity demanded that the cultural patterns of the majority group be absorbed as quickly as possible. And for generations this acculturation has proceeded, perhaps painfully, but unquestioningly. However, the stormy events of the sixties produced an unexpected reaction in a hitherto quiescent segment of the population. White ethnic group members began to speak out as a new minority, expressing dissatisfaction with their current experiences in contemporary society. This minority was, at its core, made up of Catholics who were non-Anglo-Saxon whites and largely of the working class (Burkey, 1978). Andrew Greeley, a sociologist and director of the Center for The Study of

12-7 CHECKING IT OUT: Characteristics of White Ethnics

Here is an attempt at catching a profile of these groups.

1. White ethnics are not far removed from their immigrant experience. They are caught between a powerful loyalty to the United States and deep insecurities about whether they are even now accepted by the Republic.

2. In addition to the social insecurity that comes from being still relatively close to the immigration experience, ethnics tend to be economically insecure.

3. They are profoundly committed to family, home, and neighborhood in a fashion that those of us who are part of the cosmopolitan elite find very difficult to understand.

4. Much of the rhetoric of social reform currently being used in the United States not only is lost on white ethnics but actually creates a greater sense of alienation and confusion among them.

5. White ethnics are afraid of violence. There was much of it in their own past, both in this country and in Europe. They have worked hard to achieve a modicum of security.

6. The white ethnics are deeply committed to American society; they are close enough in memory to the poverty and tyranny in their own pasts to be extremely grateful to a nation which has provided them with both affluence and political freedom.

7. While there are few things more valued by ethnics than a college education, there are also few things which they suspect more than intellectualism.

8. The ethnic is also deeply concerned about primary and secondary education, since all of his children will attend at least these schools.

9. The ethnic groups tend to be conservative both morally and religiously; permissiveness, the death of God, and the sexual revolution are all associated in the minds of ethnics with the liberal, cosmopolitan elites.

10. Finally, the ethnics find themselves increasingly isolated from their own political leadership. The problem is most acute in cities where so-called "good government" has cut the liberal elites who run the city off from the ethnic hinterlands.

SOURCE: Andrew Greeley, "The Alienation of White Ethnic Groups," *Sign,* May, 1971, p. 20. By permission of E. P. Dutton & Co.

American Pluralism, identified white ethnics as those Americans of Polish, Italian, Irish, Greek, and Slavonic ancestry (1974). Although Greeley points out the substantial numbers of white ethnics who are college graduates and professionals, others like Stephen Adubato, an Italian American politician of Newark, stress the working-class base of this minority. "We are the working-class people who haven't made it in America, like the blacks, and we are still in the inner city competing with them" (Butterfield, 1971). Such people feel that majority group members have little sympathy for their problems. They see themselves treated stereotypically in the media (Italians are typically "gangsters," and Polish jokes abound) at the same time that the heritage of blacks, Puerto Ricans, and Native Americans is being made much of. Michael Novack (1971), a writer of Slavonic origins, expresses the belief that the traditional policy of Anglo-conformity has robbed white ethnics of their history. Such people, having relinquished many of their ethnic traditions, are increasingly afraid of the homogenizing effects of America's technocratic culture. Certainly in their perception of themselves as a minority that is treated differentially, and in their vocal dissatisfaction, white ethnics owe something to the organized protests of blacks in the nineteen sixties. As blacks have asserted themselves politically and culturally and captured federal funds and national attention, white ethnics have developed similar strategies and they have begun to demand their piece of the pie.

12-8 CHECKING IT OUT: The Direction of Change—The New Ethnicity

Back in 1909, Jewish Immigrant Israel Zangwill had an idea whose time had come. Zangwill wrote a play about American immigrants and called it *The Melting Pot.* It ran for months on Broadway, and the phrase entered the language as an expression of faith in American homogeneity. That faith lasted until the 1960s, when blacks first challanged its homey apple-pie vision and prepared the way for a similar awakening among other ethnic groups.

The latest challenges to the old melting-pot theory come from the "new ethnicity," a movement that began in the early '70s and is continuing to spread among the descendants of Southern and Eastern European immigrant groups, including Italian-, Polish-, Portuguese- and just about every other variety of American but old-line Anglo-Saxon Protestants and the well-publicized blacks, American Indians and Hispanics. "White ethnics have been ignored in favor of blacks and Hispanics," claims Mary Sansone, executive director of New York's Congress of Italian-American Organizations. Now, taking a cue from the blacks, the white ethnics argue that what is good for blacks is good for other minorities. They too are demanding public recognition, federal funds, their own school and college studies—like "The Armenian Immigrant Experience" to be taught in Belmont, Mass., public schools—proportional representation in local government and television time. Among their gains to date: bilingual elementary-school courses for Portuguese Americans in the San Francisco area, and 42 "ethnic heritage" grants to the Belmont Armenians and similar groups from the Department of Health, Education and Welfare.

Prophet of the white-ethnic movement and founder-editor of EMPAC (Ethnic Millions Political Action Committee) is Michael Novak, 42, a Bayville, N.Y., Catholic intellectual and former seminarian, who hopes to shape the new white consciousness into a "creative and progressive force." Novak, author of *The Rise of the Unmeltable Ethnics* (1972), attributes traditional animosity between

Catholic blue-collar whites and blacks to "elite Protestant politics" that pitted the two groups against each other in a war for economic survival.

Novak wants a coalition of minority whites and blacks based on equal ethnicity for all. Others disagree. Harvard Sociologist Orlando Patterson, himself black, thinks ethnicity was "possibly the only way blacks could mobilize" but sees white ethnicity, its successor, as an alarming "sympton of fragmentation" in society, and he believes it is tacitly or potentially anti-black. Some white minority groups would actually rather be all-American than be seen as a separate ethnic group. Carlos Almeida, whose Portuguese Union of the State of California pushed through the Bay Area bilingual program, says that all Americans should learn English, "but if you're going to have a Spanish program and use federal funds for one ethnic group, we should have it for all."

Then there is Englewood, N.J., where to strengthen support for an imperiled minority-employment program in a population that is almost 50% black and Spanish-speaking, the city council has also designated Jews, American Indians, Asian-Americans and women as minorities. According to Rabbi Isaac Swift of an Orthodox Englewood synagogue, the "absurd conclusion" is that "no one will be a minority because we'll all be a minority. And then we can start from ground zero again."

INTERPRETIVE SUMMARY

Minority status persons are those who are discriminated against because they have physical features and/or behavioral patterns which differ from those of the dominant culture. Minority assignment has less to do with the numerical size of a group and more to do with the social status and power of its members. In the case of ethnic groups, differential treatment is accorded because of cultural characteristics (e.g., national origin, language, religion). Where discrimination occurs because of race, differential treatment is accorded because of identifiable physical characteristics, distinguishing members from other races. Any classification scheme developed to categorize races is imprecise because of overlapping categories and because many groups do not fit into existing categories. However, many people accept races as distinct, genetic entities and treat group members accordingly.

Prejudice refers to negative attitudes toward a social group, while discrimination refers to behavior resulting from a prejudiced attitude. These two related phenomena lead to "self-fulfilling prophecies" and stereotyping, as majority group members seek to control the opportunities of minorities. The existence of "authoritarian" personalities as identified by Adorno suggests that some strongly prejudiced individuals possess personality traits that reveal a consistent pattern. Hostility toward other groups may be tied to the psychological needs of such people.

The ideology of racism reflects the attempts of majority groups to defend their prejudiced attitudes and discriminatory behavior. Such groups identify their race as superior and other races as inferior. These distinctions are then used to keep less powerful groups economically and politically disadvantaged. A more subtle kind of racism is institutional racism. In this case, racist practices are not the result of policy, but are rather the consequences of indirect processes, of the way institutions function. (For example, because blacks are underrepresented on voting lists, the practice of choosing jury members from such lists is racist in its result.)

Because majority groups generally have political as well as economic power, their treatment of minorities may range from attempts to exterminate the group to some form of accommodation. Some types of policies developed by majorities toward minorities include *assimilation*, which may be forced or permitted; *pluralism*, in which groups retain their distinct cultural patterns and minorities, as we define them, disappear; *legal protection of minorities*, in which they continue to exist; *population transfer* to ease intergroup tensions (in some cases welcomed by the minority, in some cases resisted); *continued subjugation*, in which majorities are determined to continue their exploitation of minorities; *extermination*, which involves the total destruction of the minority.

Minority status has serious consequences for group members. The life chances of minorities, from surviving childbirth to achieving high socioeconomic status, are more limited than are the chances of members of majority groups.

Among the minorities who have experienced unequal treatment and have engaged the attentions of social scientists are black Americans, Native Americans, Chinese and Japanese Americans, Hispanic Americans, and European Americans or white ethnics.

QUESTIONS

1. How is discrimination different from prejudice? Which is easier to change? Why?
2. In what way would a majority group policy of assimilation be different from a policy of pluralism?
3. Can you think of a situation in which you witnessed an act of discrimination against a minority group member? How did you react?
4. In what way does the self-fulfilling prophecy apply to patterns of relationships between racial groups?

13

Population and Society

The culture patterns of a society are always influenced by the size, composition, and distribution of its population. **Demography**, the scientific study of population, deals directly with analyses of such topics as birth and death rates, migration, marriage, health conditions, and the interrelationship of population and social structure. The study of population also entails a consideration of the actual and potential pressures of population on such resources as food, water, timber, and minerals, the relation of population size to industrial and military manpower, and the quality of the population and the optimum population for a country in the light of problems of resources.

The study of population, therefore, deals directly with (1) trends in population size; (2) birth and death rates; (3) distribution—spatial and cultural; (4) composition and characteristics, such as age, sex, marital status, race, religion, and occupation; (5) movement—that is, in- and out-migrations; and (6) the dynamic aspects of culture and social structure which require analysis. Of central concern in the study of population are such questions as how the character of a population is influenced by fertility, mortality, and migration; how the culture of the time and place affects population trends; and how the values and institutional arrangements of a people influence the size and composition of the population.

WORLD POPULATION GROWTH

In the eighteenth century, after centuries of only relatively slight increase, the world experienced an enormous increase in numbers. In the nineteenth and twentieth centuries, the increase has been even greater. In 1650 the estimated population of the world was approximately 500 million. Within the next 100

13-1 CHECKING IT OUT: World Population Growth*

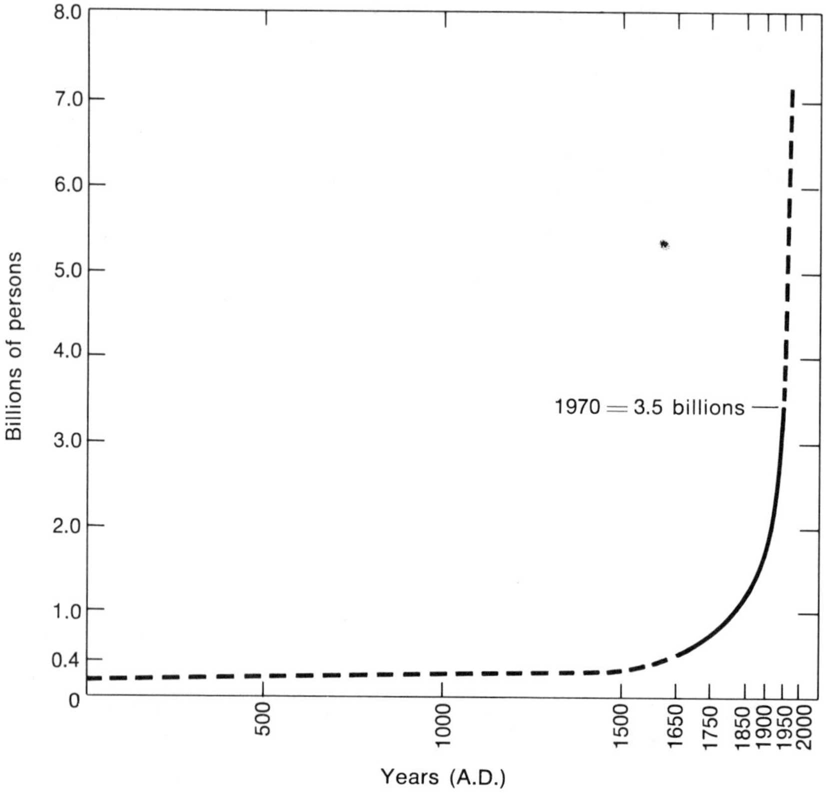

*Estimated population of the world from 1 A.D. to 1960, and the projected population to 2000 A.D.

SOURCE: Harold F. Dorn, "World Population Growth," *The Population Dilemma,* ed. Philip M. Hauser. © 1963 by the American Assembly, Columbia University, New York, N.Y. Reprinted by permission of Prentice-Hall, Inc., Englewood Cliffs, N.J.

years it had risen to about 700 million. By about 1830 it had reached 1 billion. Estimates for 1971 had put the global population at about 3.6 billion—almost three times that of a century ago. It is worth noting, moreover, that nearly two-thirds of this last increase has taken place since 1900. By 1970 the world had added 2 billion people since the turn of the century.

This growth has not occurred uniformly over the earth. Between 1850 and 1950 the population of Europe more than doubled while that of the American continents and Oceania quadrupled. At the time of the writing of the Declaration of Independence, the United States population was just under 4 million. In 1900 it was 76 million, nearly 19-fold increase in a little more than a century.

The total population of the United States was about 217,739,000 as of January, 1978. This figure represents an increase of 13,405,000 in the population since the last census. (U.S. Government Printing Office, 1978)

Similar upsurges have taken place elsewhere in the world, although not at such a marked rate. In fact, as the population in many industrialized countries of the Euro-American culture tends to become more or less stationary, the growth in other regions and countries has accelerated. At the present rate of increase, India, which now has a population of over 500 million, will more than double by the turn of this century (unless limitations are imposed.) Accurate figures for China are hard to obtain, but a census taken in June, 1953, showed a total population of 602 million and the estimate for 1970 was 740 million. Japan has a population of over 100 million, considerably more than twice its population in 1900. During much of the first half of this century, Japan added more than a million people a year. The Soviet Union already has a population of 241 million.

For the world as a whole, not only have the total numbers increased, but the annual rates of increase have risen steadily. It is estimated that the rate of growth in 1650 was 0.25 per cent per year. By 1800 the rate of increase had risen to 0.4 per cent per year and in 1970 it was estimated that the rate of world population growth was about 2.0 per cent per year.

Reasons for Population Growth

Almost all this tremendous increase in the world population is the result of a *reduction in the death rate*, not a rise in the birth rate. This reduction of the death rate derives from numerous causes, among the most important of which are the following: (1) Advances in modern medicine led to the reduction of infectious and contagious diseases, improvement in maternal and infant care, and the introduction of public sanitation. These advances all acted to cut the death rate. Only indirectly did they influence the birth rate. (2) The Commerical and then the Industrial Revolution increased the production of manufactured goods and their transportation and distribiution. Moreover, these changes in the economic patterns of culture provided jobs for an increasing number of people. All this, in turn, created a higher standard of living. (3) New lands in the Americas and elsewhere not only provided an outlet for the expanding populations of Europe and Asia but also, in time, furnished foodstuffs and raw materials to feed the industrial system and to provide a market for goods manufactured in Europe. (4) Because of scientific advances, plant and animal stocks have been greatly improved, while commerical fertilizers and power machinery have greatly increased the production of the world's foodstuffs and commodities, such as fibers and lumber, useful in providing clothing and shelter.

Variations in Population Increase

There is considerable variation in the rates of increase by countries and world regions. The most notable differences are those between highly industralized regions and those that have not experienced an industrial revolution, the "third world" countries. Most of the countries of northwestern Europe seem to be approaching a relatively stable population. In these countries the rates of population growth are clearly associated with rapid industrialization, which began about 1760. It is the nonindustrial areas that now show the most striking increases in rates of growth.

Unlike the historical situation in northwestern Europe in the nineteenth century, when industrialization and improvement in medicine went hand in hand, many present-day "third world" countries have been influenced dramatically by modern medical care without at the same time going through industrialization. In other words, the diffusion of one set of cultural patterns—scientific medical care—has occurred without the spread of a second set of patterns that historically had been associated with the first. In fact, the application of medicine in reducing the death rate—without, however, reducing the birth rate—has produced a decline in mortality rates "much sharper than any ever experienced in the history of the presently industrialized nations." (K. Davis, 1956, p. 55) Kingsley Davis (p. 57) describes what has happened:

> The amazingly accelerated reduction of mortality has . . . been accomplished by international disease control, not by economic development in these areas themselves. It required no essential change in the customs and institutions of the people, no advance in general education, nor growth in per capita income. . . .
>
> Since disease control has not involved basic changes in social institutions, education, and real income, fertility has remained high in nonindustrial regions. . . . The industrial countries began lowering their birth rates *before* their sharpest declines in mortality, but the backward areas will do so long *after* their mortality has reached a low modern level. As a result the densely settled and impoverished countries of the world are experiencing an unprecedented population growth which does not reflect economic development but in fact creates strong impediments to it.

Davis doubts that "social modernization," as he calls it, can really "match the three percent population growth per year found in these areas, much less exceed it." (p. 59)

Industrialization and modern medical technology offer cogent explanations for the decline in population growth in many societies. However, cultural patterns also strongly influence population rates. Among these are societal beliefs and values. For example, where men measure their virility by the number of children they produce, fertility will be high. "The Mysterious Drop in Japan's Birth Rate" tells of a situation in which societal beliefs brought about a decline in birth rate.

13-2 CHECKING IT OUT: The Mysterious Drop in Japan's Birth Rate

In 1966, the birth rate in Japan suddenly plunged to a record low of 13.7 per thousand—down almost half a million births from the preceding year. This decline in births—26 percent in one year—was extraordinary. Such a birth-rate plunge would have exceeded the wildest hopes of the countries that are frantically trying to limit their populations. But in Japan, a prosperous and heavily industrialized country that is not trying to limit its population, the drop seemed to make no sense.

None of the usual explanations for a rapid birth decline seemed to work. A quick survey of the country showed that Japan in 1966 was no different from Japan in 1965 or 1967—and the number of births in 1967 increased by 50 percent over 1966. The year 1966 was marked by no war, no sudden shifts in prosperity, and no change in the legal codes that might have influenced reproductive behavior.

Furthermore, the decline could not be ascribed to any lack of sexual activity. In fact, during the last half of 1965 the number of induced abortions rose sharply. This suggests that people were still engaging in their sexual activities but that, for some reason, they were determined not to have children.

This determination first became evident in the birth statistics for January 1966. In December 1965 the birth rate stood at a steady 17.3; by the end of January it had falled to 14.6. In a single month, the Japanese made their birth rate fall by a spectacular 16 percent. True, with modern contraceptive methods (and, as last resort, modern abortion methods), people have greater control over their reproductive lives. But under no normal circumstances do they choose to exercise this control to the extent that the Japanese did in the last nine months of 1965 and the first three months of 1966. . . .

Why then, against all logical expectations to the contrary, did the Japanese apparently declare a moratorium on child-bearing in 1966? The answer lies in an ancient superstition.

The superstition is rooted in the ancient lunar-solar calendar of Chinese origin. This old calendar, although abandoned by the Japanese in 1872 in favor of the Gregorian calendar used in the West, is still very much a part of Japanese thinking. It is composed of two circular systems—one a decimal system of 10 "trunks" and the other a duodecimal system of 12 "twigs." The trunks carry the names of natural objects or elements, and the twigs carry the names of animals. Every 60 years, when the "fire" period of the first system coincides with the "horse" period of the second, a new cycle of history begins. The first year of each new cycle is called a year of Hinouema.

What explains Japan's sudden birth-rate decline in 1966 is the fact that 1966 was a year of Hinoeuma. For according to the superstition, any girl born in such a year will be of harsh temperament and invite misfortune—in other words, she will have great difficulty finding a husband. The Japanese just weren't taking that chance. Rather than conceiving children on the chance that they would be boys and thus immune to the misfortunes of Hinoeuma, many Japanese decided to wait till next year. During 1965 and early 1966, they practiced rigorous birth control. And failing that, they were quite prepared to resort to abortion to make certain that they brought no unlucky daughters into the world.

SOURCE: Koya Azumi, "The Mysterious Drop in Japan's Birth Rate," *Transaction,* 1968, *5:* 46–48. Published by permission of Transaction, Inc., from *Transaction,* Vol. 5, No. 6,

Malthus' Theory

Such men as the idealistic Marquis de Condorcet in France and William Godwin in England expressed the growing faith of the period in the steady march of mankind toward perfection. Once poverty, misery, vice, crime, and war were removed by proper social reforms, all would be well. According to Godwin, "Make men wise, and by that very operation you make them free . . . There will be no war, no crime, no administration of justice as it is called, and no government. Besides this, there will be neither disease, anguish, melancholy, nor resentment. Every man will seek with effable ardor the good of all." (Hertlzer, 1928)

Others, seeing poverty and the sordid conditions of the peasants and urban masses, were not so optimistic about man's perfectibility. In 1798 a controversy broke out with the publication of one of the most famous books of all time, *An Essay on the Principle of Population as it Affects the Future Improvement of Society, with Remarks on the Speculation of Mr. Godwin, M. Condorcet, and Other Writers,* written by Thomas Robert Malthus, an English clergyman. Malthus contended that Godwin and others were wrong in blaming circumstances for our social ills. It was man's original nature that was at fault. The sexual urges leading to reproduction tended to people the world more rapidly than people could increase their sustenance.

In a time when romantic reformers were preaching doctrines of unlimited human progress, Malthus had begun making calculations concerning the relation of food supply to population increase. He argued that there is a "constant tendency in all animated life to increase beyond the nourishment prepared for it"—that is, animal life is endowed with the capacity for constant rapid reproduction, but the food supply has definite limits.

Applying this principle to human beings, Malthus worked out the following formula: "Population, when unchecked, goes on doubling itself every twenty-five years, or increases in geometric ratio." Food supply, which he called the "means of subsistence," under circumstances the most favorable to human industry, could not possibly be made to increase faster than in arithmetical ratio. (Spengler, 1945 p. 245) In other words, a population would increase every twenty-five years in the ratio of 1, 2, 4, 8, 16, 32, 64, 128, 256, and so on, while the food supply would increase, at best, in the ratio of 1, 2, 3, 4, 5, 6, 7, 8, 9, etc. According to this computation, in 300 years the ratio of the population to the means of subsistence would be 13 to 4,096.

Population does not increase at the highest theoretically possible level, however; and Malthus recognized that there were two kinds of checks on population increase—positive checks and preventive checks. The *positive* checks are those that increase the death rate and arise from poverty, disease, starvation, war, and want of adequate subsistence. The *preventive* checks include celibacy, deferment of marriage, and moral (that is, sexual) restraint, leading to reduction in the number of births. Malthus argued that no devices of political or economic organization or of emigration would stop the positive checks from operating, but only moral restraint of the biological passions. This did not imply, so rationalized the pious Malthus, that God has not our welfare at heart, but rather that "natural and moral evil seems to be the instrument employed by the Deity in admonishing us to avoid any mode of conduct which is not suited to our being and will consequently injure our happiness."

The doctrine of progress and man's perfectibility was not easily dismissed. Nineteenth-century enthusiasts arose on every hand to denounce Malthus. Significant expressions of optimism were found in the works of those who denied that population necessarily outruns the food supply. Karl Marx argued that the problem of feeding the population results from the exploitation of the masses by the ruling class. Once the injustices of faulty distribution of wealth were remedied, there would be food enough for all. Henry George, best known for his theory of the single tax on land values, argued that "nowhere can want be properly attributed to the pressure of population against the power to procure subsistence in the then existing degree of human knowledge; that everywhere the vice and misery attributed to overpopulation can be traced to warfare, tyranny, and oppression, which prevent knowledge from being utilized and deny the security essential to production." He thought it was only a faulty economic and political order that "in the midst of wealth condemns men to want." (Ross, 1931, p. 8)

Throughout the nineteenth century, while the theorists argued, population continued to increase at a rapid rate. And in spite of "free" land and increased industrial production, poverty, misery, crime, and vice persisted. With a view to improving the condition of the masses, there arose in England about 1880 a movement known as *Neo-Malthusianism.* It aimed to educate the masses consciously to reduce the number of births. The leaders, Annie Besant and Charles Bradlaugh, argued that the spread of contraceptive practices in order to reduce the birth rate would lead to an improvement in health, in family life, in the standards of living, and in morality.

But the critics of birth control were not far behind. As birth rates did decline, especially in the Western world, the cry of "race suicide" was heard. One of the most vocal exponents of large families and rapid increase of population was Theodore Roosevelt, who expressed the beliefs and attitudes of millions who saw in the declining birth rate a threat to man's very existence. Then too, many feared that the price of a Neo-Malthusian program might be loss of the white man's supremacy in the world.

The debate still goes on. Thirty years ago, the world heard such dictators as Hilter and Mussolini in Europe and the militarists of Japan calling for larger populations in their countries. Since their downfall and in the face of postwar problems, most students of the issue have stressed the dangerous implications of the continuing growth of population as it relates to food and other resources and to standard of living. In the face of some divergencies of interpretation about the seriousness of the present-day population problem, and especially in view of some of the sharp differences in rates of growth in various areas of the world, let us examine some of the facts about the relation of population to resources. (K. Davis, 1963)

Food Supply and Population

Population and food supply are related, but these are not the only factors to be taken into consideration in discussing the increase in world population. The densely crowded countries of northwestern Europe could not possibly have supported themselves on the food raised on their own land; they furnished goods and services to other regions which, in turn, provided them with foodstuffs and raw materials. Technological advances provided work for millions in the production, manufacture, and distribution of goods and services. So long as commerce between nations of the world went on freely, large massing of population in industrial centers did not appear to be a serious problem.

Yet in spite of the tremendous improvement in agricultural production (most of which has come from mechanical devices and not from improvement in natural fertility of land), in spite of the rising consciousness of the need to conserve water and forest and mineral resources, in spite of the possibility of synthetic foods produced by applied chemistry, and in spite of increased industrialization, the population in many parts of the world is still pressing on the means of subsistence: foods, timber, coal, iron, and oil. Clearly, land and climate distinctly limit the range of man's habitation. Of the total land surface of the earth, little more than one-third is available for raising food and other necessary articles of consumption. Yet the number of people that the world will support is, of course, definitely related to the standard of living. The earth would support at a bare subsistence level a great many more people than there are now. Improved use of present arable lands and their extension—for example, the use of rich tropical lands in South America and of the semiarid regions of Asia—could add measurably to the available food supply. But whatever else happens, nearly all authorities agree that there must be a reduction in the birth rate and an increase in the practice of birth control. Those supporting the latter measure are up against formidable opposition, however.

THE DEMOGRAPHIC TRANSITION

On the basis of what is known about the changes in population which accompanied the industrialization and urbanization of Western societies, students of population have developed a generalization called the demographic transition. It is a generalization that holds that societies experience similar demographic changes in birth, death, and growth rates as they become industrialized. Generally speaking, there are three major stages in the demographic transition.

13-3 CHECKING IT OUT: The Demographic Transition

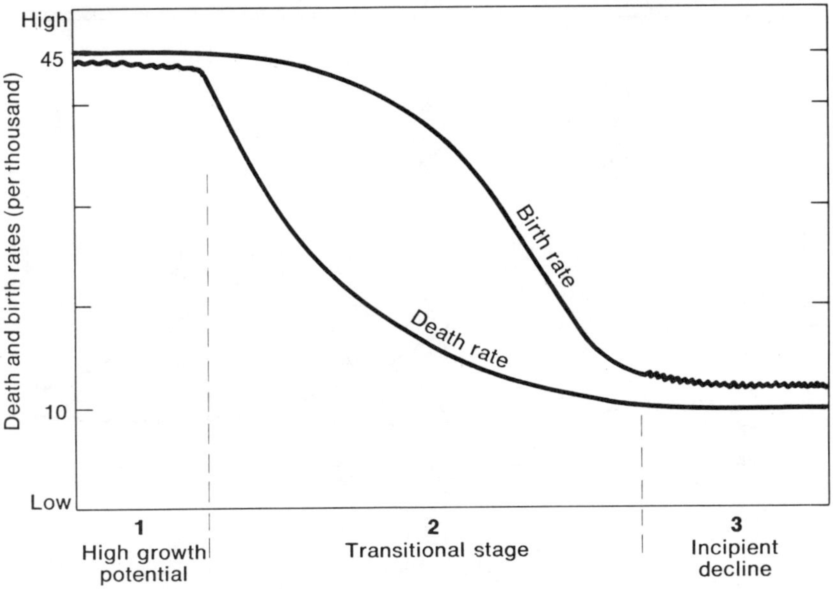

Stage I Societies in stage I are in a situation of "high growth potential." This stage characterizes the demographic balance of preindustrial societies in which there is a high birth rate and a high death rate. Consequently, the rate of population growth is quite low. Since in these societies the birth rate remains high, the rate of population growth depends upon the death rate which varies with the positive checks of droughts, natural disasters, and so on. Life expectancy in these societies is relatively low, typically less than 35 years, and the median age of the population is relatively low—approximately 15 years.

Stage II Stage II is the stage of the "demographic transition." This stage characterizes the demographic situation of societies undergoing industrialization. In the early phases of industrialization the death rate begins to fall but the birth rate remains high. As industrialization continues, the death rate plummets and the birth rate begins to fall. Since the death rate decreases first and much more rapidly than the birth rate, the rate of population growth is very high—indeed, there is a "population explosion." Life expectancy is about 45—50 years and the median age is about 21—23 years.

Stage III The third and final stage characterizes "mature" industrial societies and is called the stage of "incipient decline." Societies in this stage have relatively low birth and death rates and therefore the growth rate is low and

13-4 CHECKING IT OUT: The Demographic Transition in the West

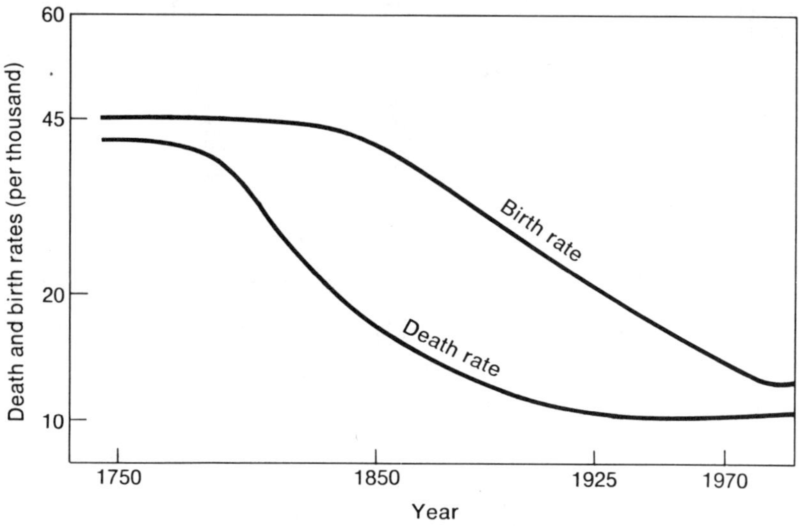

relatively stabilized. The life expectancy in these societies is about 70 years and the median age is about 30 years.

A Population Crisis in the Third World

Obviously, a major question for people concerned with the population crisis is whether or not one can predict the future of population in the "third world" on the basis of the Western experience. Two-thirds of the world has not completed the demographic transition. In considering this question, a number of factors must be taken into account. First of all, as noted above, there has been a rapid increase in population in a number of countries that as yet have not become industrialized. This is the result of the diffusion of modern medical care independently of any basic change in the economy and education of these areas. Moreover, conditions in these regions are not precisely like those that existed in the nineteenth century when the cycle began in western Europe (and the United States). While far more efficient technologies for rapid industrialization are available today than in 1800, there is a dearth of resources and little new land for expanding agriculture.

As to voluntary restriction of births, the whole force of culture in some regions is contrary to such practices. It is questionable whether measures of birth control will be adopted before the industrialized culture patterns and demands for higher standards of life have become widespread in all classes and ancient and

13-5 CHECKING IT OUT: The Demographic Transition in the Third World

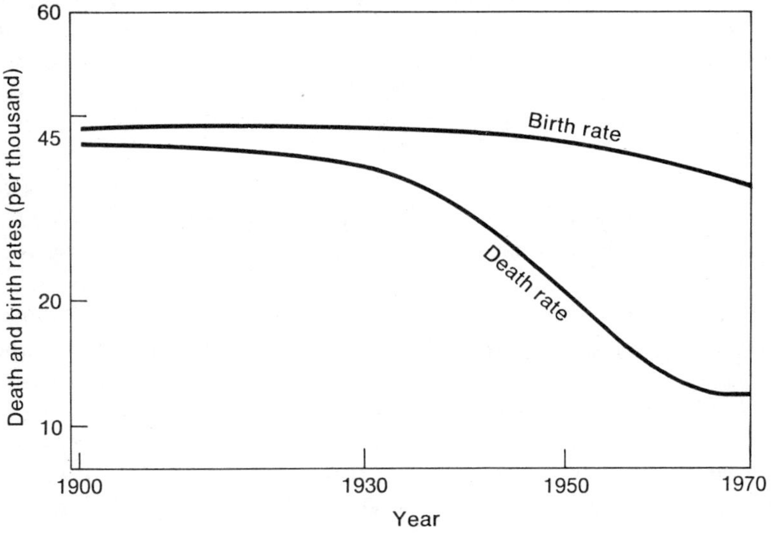

sacred folkways have largely disappeared. Moreover, the third world will have to make the transition in a much shorter time than Western societies did. In the West, the demographic transition took place over a period of about 125 years and many authorities argue that the world cannot now wait that long for the current population explosion to end.

Density of Population

Population is by no means evenly distributed over the earth. Nor are all areas equally blessed with good climate, soils, and other resources that make them acceptable places to live. For example, the wide steppes, the deserts, and the extensive mountainous sections of Asia make up at least half of its land mass. These regions support very few people. In contrast, the rich valleys of India and China support millions. In other regions—the United States, Canada, and the Soviet Union in Europe—there are ample soil and other resources but relatively fewer people.

A measure frequently used in studies of population is density of persons per square mile of land area. Population density, however, must be interpreted in relation to the degree of industrialization, extent and kind of soil resources, and rates of growth. For example, Java and India are chiefly agricultural, and yet the pressure of numbers on the food supply is mounting year by year and the pressure on the arable lands is also increasing. Sumatra, an island neighbor of Java, has rich untapped soil resources, but the Javanese for the most part do not look with favor on migration to Sumatra. So too, there are some excellent unused areas in parts of southern India, but the millions in the congested sections of the country are not interested in moving to these distant areas. Australia, long a target of expanding oriental populations, has recently been stimulating immigration from Great Britain, but so far is unwilling to accept Far Eastern people.

Highly industrialized countries, such as Britain and Belgium, are able to support relatively high concentrations of population. Both countries raise only a part of their own food, and export manufactured goods in exchange for a heavy amount of foods and raw materials. If they had to depend on their own farming, both these countries would probably soon feel the pinch of famine. The population density per square mile of arable land in Britain is about 2,500 persons, in Belgium about 2,200. A similar situation exists in Japan, whose growth in numbers has been possible only because it has been the only highly industrial nation of the Far East. Japan's attempt to get more and more of the trade of that region was one reason for its entry into World War II. With a density of about 3,200 persons per square mile of arable land, Japan probably could not provide its own food.

It seems clear that the matter of population density can be understood only in relation to the amount and nature of basic resources—agricultural and otherwise—and the extent of industrialization as these, in turn, are related to absolute numbers of people and rates of growth. Yet the future of many industrialized nations, especially in Europe, is not altogether certain, despite their relatively stable populations. Without external markets they may face a lowering of standards of living as other nations become industrialized and no longer import manufactured goods from Europe.

FERTILITY AND MORTALITY

The two basic determinants of population size are birth and death rates. These, together with the rates of in-and out-migration, are the only immediate determinants of population change in a society. All other factors such as wars and famines make their influence felt through one of three factors—fertility, mortality, and migration.

The size of a population at any given time can therefore be stated algebraically as:

$$\text{Population}_{t_2} = \text{Population}_{t_1} + \text{Births}_{t_1\text{-}t_2} - \text{Deaths}_{t_1\text{-}t_2} + \text{or} -\text{Net Migration}_{t_1\text{-}t_2}$$

where t_1 and t_2 refer to an earlier and later point in time respectively, and where t_1-t_2 refers to the interval between the two times.

Birth Rates

In discussing rates of growth, it is necessary to distinguish between fecundity and fertility. *Fecundity* is the potential power of reproduction in a population—the birth rate if every woman of childbearing age bore all the children she possibly could. Fertility is the actual rate of reproduction. It is measured by the birth rate, but we must distinguish between the crude birth rate and the specific birth rate. The *crude birth rate* is simply the number of births per 1,000 people at a given period. The *specific birth rate* is the births per 1,000 women of childbearing age, usually considered to be from 15 to 44 years. The crude birth rate gives an estimate of the fertility of any population, but it does not take into account the age and sex distribution of the population.

For long-range comparisons of population growth or decline, the *net reproduction rate* is a better index than either crude or specific birth rates. Such a rate is based on the average number of daughters that will be born per 100 females starting life together if birth and death rates at different age levels remain constant. Thus a net reproduction rate of 1.00 means that, on the average, the survivors of a group of 100 females of the same age will give birth to 100 daughters. An index of 1.00 means that a given population is replacing itself; anything less means that it is not.

As we noted earlier, until the fourth decade of this century, there was a steady decline in the birth rate in countries of western Europe, in the British Dominions, and in the United States. In fact, in some countries the new reproduction rate fell to less than 1.00. But during World War II and subsequently, both the marriage rate and the birth rate increased for a time. As a result, the net reproduction rate in most countries of the same world areas has gone up. Reliable data from the Soviet Union and its satellites is not easy to secure, but there are indications that birth rates in these countries also rose after World War II.

Death Rates

Mortality may be measured by the *crude death rate,* which is the ratio between the number of individuals who die in a given time and the median number of individuals alive during that interval, usually stated in thousands. Thus a death rate of 12 means 12 deaths per 1,000 of the population. Specific death rates may be computed for age, sex, and other factors.

Throughout history the births in many societies have just about balanced the deaths, so that the population size remained practically stationary for generations. This was true for long periods in the Orient and, until three centuries ago, in Europe. In fact, until recently, in all countries outside western Europe, the United States, Canada, New Zealand, Australia, and the scattered European colonies, high death rates have accompanied high birth rates. Among nonliterate peoples the birth rates and the mortality rates are both unusually high by our standards.

Recent decades have witnessed a rapid decline in the death rate. This trend has been going on in Europe for well over a century. There has been a similar decline in the death rate in the United States, where the annual average in 1906–1910 was 15 per 1,000. The death rate has fallen off considerably since then, except in 1918, when it was 18 per thousand because of an influenza epidemic. By 1920 it had dropped to 13 per thousand. Since 1950 the death rate has varied between 9.3 and 9.7 per thousand. In 1976 the death rate was 9.0 per thousand.

While the principal decline in the death rate has occurred among Western nations, the phenomenon is worldwide. Although birth rates are also falling, mortality rates in many regions are falling somewhat faster.

Medical science has dramatically influenced the death rate for the early years of life. A noteworthy decline in infant and child mortality is evident in every large country and in most small ones. The decrease in child mortality is due in large part to: (1) improvement in child care at home, especially in feeding and sanitation; (2) decrease in the number of children born to the average mother, permitting more adequate care of those who are born—studies in France, England, and the United States bear out the fact that infant mortality is much lower in small families than in large; (3) improvement in economic status of large sections of the population; and (4) control of diseases of childhood and early adult life. Additional progress in the conquest of disease the world over makes for the reduction of death in all age groups.

INTERNATIONAL RELATIONS AND POPULATION PROBLEMS

The survival of humankind has always rested on a somewhat precarious balance between the size of population and the means of subsistence. This balance is maintained largely by fluctations in the death rate, as Malthus pointed out. It is quite clear that at least half of the world's population is living at or below a mere subsistence level. World affairs and the future of peace and welfare of the world are closely bound up with differences in rates of growth as they are related to food and other resources, health, and extent of industrialization.

Income, Food, and Death Rates

While it is difficult to secure completely accurate information on the relations of death rates to standards of food consumption and income, estimates have been made. These give a rather grim picture. The countries of high mortality are also those of low income and inadequate diet. The "developed" countries of the world have about one-third of the world's population and four-fifths of the world income. The world is really separated into two great population pools: one is relatively contracting; the other is extending itself rapidly. In the one, the ratio of population to resources has been brought under control. In the other, the Malthusian factors continue to operate. The problem is how to reconcile this disparity. To meet the present difficulty a number of changes appear to be necessary.

Increase in Food

One crucial and immediate task is to increase the world production of foodstuffs to take care of the increasing and undernourished populations. Considerable advances have been made, but in India and Indonesia—to note two of the most needy regions—the race between people and production goes on apace. Only 7 per cent of the land area of the world is under cultivation and there are wide varations in the per capita density of land used for food production. In eastern and southern Asia there are, respectively, less than 0.5 and 0.8 of an acre of cultivated land per person. Yet these are the very regions where the pressure of population on food resources is becoming most severe. By way of contrast, in North America there are nearly 4 acres of cultivated land per capita. Moreover, the yield in calories per acre is much higher so that the output of food per person is vastly greater.

Industrialization

The development of industry is also thought to be an important step in relieving the pressure of population. The argument is that the cycle of growth which resulted in stabilization of population in the Western world, represents a pattern of change essential for the rest of the world. However, the inadequacy of

13-6 CHECKING IT OUT: Population Change In Japan

Japan constitutes one case study in the demographic correlates of modernization of a predominantly industrial type, albeit a peculiarly significant one. Japan's historic culture is Eastern. Her industrial and urban transformation was thus divorced from a base in the nonmaterial culture of the West except in so far as specific elements were deliberately selected for imitation or diffused through more informal mechanisms. . . .

The population growth that accompanies indigenous and comprehensive industrial development and the slowing of that growth through a progressive limitation of childbearing are alike products of the changes in ways of living and thinking that are precondition and product of industrialization. The relations of culture and demography proceed through the intermediation of the economic process itself. Political stability, a disciplined labor force, and rapid capital accumulation are necessary aspects of substantial industrialization. Cultural factors exert a major influence on the extent and speed of the economic transformation, for there are cultural preconditions to indigenous economic transformations and cultural limitations to imposed transformations. As industrialization extends over time and expands over wider segments of a nation, the demographic transition of declining mortality and declining fertility becomes a necessary consequence of the accompanying economic pressures and cultural stimuli. But industrialization regarded as economic, political, or social process is in turn modified by the changing dynamics of population. The relationships are complex; the particular constellation of factors that produced the population growth of Imperial Japan will not be duplicated in detail elsewhere. The fundamental fact, though, is that experience within the East corroborates the hypothesis deducible from Western experience: substantial increases in the size of the total population is a correlate of industrialization, but the social and psychological transformations implicit in industrialization result eventually in a lessened rate of reproduction and a slowing growth. Given the technologies and the basic values of the twentieth century, both population growth and the ultimate slowing of the growth are predictable consequences of the industrial and urban transformation of agrarian cultures.

If the experience of the one nation in Monsoon Asia that has achieved a substantial degree of industrialization can be transferred to project the future of the other cultures, industrialization and urbanization will lead eventually to declines in fertility that will first lessen and then eliminate the growth that accompanies modernization.

SOURCE: Irene B. Taeuber, "Population and Labor Force in the Industrialization of Japan, 1850–1950." *Economic Growth: Brazil, India, Japan,* eds. S. Kuznets, W. E. Moore, and J. J. Spengler (Durham, N. C.: Duke University Press, 1955), pp. 358–359. By permission.

resources for furthur industrialization and the constant need for new capital are two of several problems that obstruct industrialization in many countries. Moreover, the shift of large numbers of persons from peasant agriculture to skilled and semiskilled industrial occupations would not be easy. As has been demonstrated by the experience of the Soviet Union, it takes time to train the workers of a peasant economy to become factory hands and time is crucial. J. J. Spengler (1948, p. 265), studying the relation of economy to population and resources, was not optimistic about the future.

> The evidence presented . . . lends no support to the easy optimism of those who see in industrialization a simple and ready solution for the overpopulation that already affects more than half the world. Countries marked by intense overpopulation must virtually raise themselves by their own bootstraps. They lack land, capital, and the opportunity to make up this lack. They can get only limited relief through trade and capital imports.

Migration

One of the oldest proposals to alleviate, if not solve, the world's population difficulties is to get people to go somewhere else. Some contend that, instead of transferring capital goods and setting up new industries, people should emigrate to other, less crowded areas. One should view with some suspicion schemes to stimulate the migration of large numbers of people from crowded to less crowded areas. It has been shown that, unless the country of origin is cutting its own birth and death rates at the time of out-migration, emigration will only temporarily relieve the pressure. The places of those who go somewhere else will be taken by the newborn of those who remain at home. As Notestein (1944, p. 150) puts it, "... emigration will not check growth in the most important areas of population pressure at the present stage of their demographic evolution. It would be unfortunate to waste the open spaces of the world in a fashion that could only intensify future problems of adjustment." Radhakamal Mukerjee believes that "a complementary program of birth control and 'open door' " should be undertaken. The expanding and preindustrial countries would practice birth control, but in the meantime the industrialized countries would permit immigration to relieve the present pressures of the Orient especially. (Mukerjee, 1941)

Population Pressures, War, and Peace

Although imbalances of peoples and means of livelihood have been known in history, the present problem of disproportion between population and means of survival is particularly acute. The "have-nots" are pushing on the "haves" for a redistribution of resources, a "push" which the latter resent and resist. As Thompson (1953, pp. 359–360) says,

> In order for population pressures to become dangerous to peace, the people of a given country must feel this pressure and believe (rightly or wrongly) that something can be done about acquiring larger resources by force.... When ... a people comes to feel that it is being kept from lands and resources it really needs by peoples who are not using them or are using them in only a limited way, we have a dangerous situation.

The problem is sociological, rather than strictly biological. When disease, vice, poverty, and early death are taken for granted, people are not likely to bestir themselves to raise their level of living. It is when hope, not despair, is generated that pressures arise. Individuals and nations come to feel discriminated against because they do not have free access to the world's resources. They view with envious eye the great expanses of sparsely settled lands in Australia or the Americas and they object to the laws in those countries which discriminate against the immigration of Orientals.

Population imbalances and pressures are bound up with economic and political trends. Strong nationalist states, many with imperialist ambitions, have dominated the world's resources and industrial development for more than

300 years. It is very doubtful that the world, split into warring sovereign states which precariously fluctuate between peace and war, will realize a full and permanent peace so long as gross inequities in resources continue to increase.

POPULATION PATTERNS

Certain aspects of community life reflect or are affected by variations in the sex and age composition of the population. If, for example, there are a great many more males than females, as was true in most pioneer communities, marriage rates will be affected, and there will be a high percentage of unmarried men but few unmarried women. If the proportion of children is high, as in residential

13-7 CHECKING IT OUT: Selected Population Characteristics of the United States, 1620–1970

Year	*Population (in millions)*	*Rate of Population Increase in the Preceding Decade*	*Population Density**	*Median Age*
1620	.002			
1650	.05			
1700	.3			
1750	1			
1790	4		4.5	
1800	5	3.0	6.1	16
1820	10		5.6	17
1840	17	2.8	9.8	18
1860	31		10.6	19
1880	50	2.6	16.9	21
1900	76	1.9	25.6	23
1910	92		31.0	24
1920	106	1.4	35.6	25
1930	123	1.5	41.2	27
1940	132	0.7	44.2	29
1950	151	1.4	42.6	30
1960	179	1.7	50.5	30
1970	203	1.3	57.4	28

* Population per square mile of land area.
SOURCE: U.S. Bureau of the Census, *Statistical Abstract of the United States, 1971* (Washington, D.C.: U.S. Government Printing Office, 1971); and U.S. Bureau of the Census, *Historical Statistics of the United States, Colonial Times to 1957* (Washington, D.C.: U.S. Government Printing Office, 1960).

suburbs, the problem of education will certainly be different than if there are very few children, as is true of certain sections of our major cities inhabited largely by adult males. Again, when the population has a disproportionate number of people in the older age groups, a host of conditions involving the labor force and medical care will exist that are not found when the population is younger.

13-8 CHECKING IT OUT: Population Characteristics of the World's 25 Largest Countries, 1969

Country	*World Rank*	*Estimated Population (in millions)*	*Estimated Annual Per Cent Increase (1963–1969)*	*Estimated Population Density*
China	1	740	1.5	200
India	2	537	2.8	425
U.S.S.R.	3	241	1.2	28
United States	4	203	1.2	57
Indonesia	5	116	2.7	201
Pakistan	6	112	2.2	306
Japan	7	102	1.1	716
Brazil	8	91	3.2	28
Nigeria	9	64	2.6	179
Germany, Fed. Rep. of	10	59	1.0	612
United Kingdom	11	56	0.6	591
Italy	12	53	0.8	458
France	13	50	0.9	237
Mexico	14	49	3.8	64
Philippines	15	37	3.8	321
Thailand	16	35	3.4	175
Turkey	17	34	2.7	114
Spain	18	33	1.0	169
Poland	19	33	1.0	259
United Arab Republic	20	33	2.7	84
Korea, Republic of	21	31	2.6	819
Iran	22	28	3.2	44
Burma	23	27	2.3	103
Ethiopia	24	25	2.2	52
Argentina	25	24	1.6	22
World total		3,552	2.0	68

SOURCE: U.S. Bureau of the Census, *Pocket Data Book, USA, 1971* (Washington, D.C.: U.S. Government Printing Office, 1971), p. 38.

The importation of foreign-born adults into a community produces problems of accommodation, acculturation, and assimilation that will not be found when the population is recruited from births within the community. From about 1820 to World War I, the United States experienced an increasing influx of foreigners. Because the chief call was for a vigorous labor force, the age and sex distribution of the foreign-born tended to be skewed in the direction of the males and concentrated in the middle range of age classes. After World War I, severe restrictive laws were passed to reduce the number of immigrants to be admitted in any one year. As a result, foreign-born people have become an ever-smaller part of the population of the United States.

Internal Migration

Throughout the history of the United States, the basic pattern of migration has been from east to west. This was true when the early colonists landed on the east coast and moved inland; it was true when the pioneers pushed west to homestead land and it is still true.

Young adults account for most of the migration in the United States.

> People in early adult life constitute the most mobile segment of our civilian population. They generally migrate to take advantage of job opportunities and to provide better living conditions for their families. In recent years there has also been an increasing tendency for people at the older ages to settle in areas with mild climates, particularly southern California and Florida. (*Statistical Bulletin,* 1955, 36:8)

The other basic pattern of internal migration has been from farm to city: the nation has become more and more urbanized. The extent of movement from farm to cities varies greatly from region to region, but in general it involves from one-fourth to one-half of all farm youth. For the country as a whole it has been estimated that about two-fifths of all individuals between the ages of 10 and 19 years who lived on farms in 1920 had migrated from there by 1930. The cityward drift of population continues as commercialization and industrialization of agriculture expand and as contacts between cities and farms continue to grow. A particularly interesting phase of this migration had been the shift of blacks from the rural South to Northern industrial centers and to employment areas in the West. However, in recent years, a reversal of this trend is becoming apparent. With increased industrialization in the South, blacks are beginning a new migration southward.

Median Age

The populations of western Europe, the United States, and the British Dominions are growing older—that is, there is an increasingly higher ratio of individuals in the older age groups. A common measure of this shift is the increase in median age. (This is the age that 50 per cent of the population falls above and 50 per cent below.) For the United States, to cite only one example, the median age in 1800 was 16 years; in 1860 it was 19 years; in 1900 it was 23 years; and in 1960 it was 30 years. During the last two decades the median age in the United States has declined. In 1970 the median age of the U.S. population was 28.3 years.

Growth Rates—Zero Population Growth

The events of the 1960s and 1970s have revealed an amazing change in American population patterns. The nation had experienced a rising birth rate after World War II (the baby boom); this, added to the low death rate of the period, produced a population in 1966 in which young people made up 66 per cent of the total population. If this group contented itself with whatever numbers of children its sexual activities produced, a perilous situation would result in the size of the future population. However, a far different trend has developed. The United States is experiencing a rapid decline in fertility. This may be illustrated by the following: Demographers accept 2.11 as the number of children each family should produce to maintain the native-born population. The statistic 2.11 (birth rate) indicates the *replacement level* or **zero population growth** (when the population through births and immigration is equal to the population that is lost from deaths and emigration). With ZPG a population merely reproduces its numbers in succeeding generations. Amazingly, in spite of the size of the child-bearing population, in 1972 the number of U.S. children declined to 2.03 per family, less than the replacement level. In 1976, the birth rate was 1.8 per family.

As we have noted, the decline in fertility together with low death rates is a phenomenon currently found in highly industrialized societies. Certainly factors like industrialization, urbanization, inflation, contraceptive technology, and the availability of abortion are social factors contributing to this decline. However, if the population problem seems resolved as birth rates drop, let us remember that the U.S. population continues to grow at an astonishing rate. Even with ZPG, there are so many women from the "baby boom" group that even a population below replacement level increases our numbers dramatically. It will take several generations (probably 50 years) at this lowered birth rate to reach the point where the population stops growing.

Residence and Fertility

On the average, city families have fewer children than farm families. Such variations in fertility rates are not a recent phenomenon. They seem to have appeared as early as the eighteenth century in Europe, and they became increasingly evident as the Industrial Revolution spread, first throughout Great Britain and then on the Continent. They have been characteristic of the United States for a long time.

Stratification and Fertility

Differential fertility is also associated with social status. A study by Berent indicates that both social class and social mobility affect fertility. Both upper-class position and upward mobility have a marked effect on lowering the birth rate. It is highly probable that a similar pattern is found throughout the industrialized Western world. An analysis of census data shows the persistence of differentials in fertility as related to occupation, income, and education. Persons in the upper economic categories tend to postpone somewhat longer the birth of their first child and to have their last child after fewer years of marriage than persons in the lower economic categories. Beginning in the last quarter of the nineteenth century and continuing to the present, there has been a steady decline in family size in all classes in Western industrialized countries. The rate of this decrease has not been uniform by class, however, as a number of studies of differential fertility have indicated.

> The classes that first gained control over fertility lived predominantly in the cities and were of better than average socioeconomic status. However, the knowledge of conception control spread gradually—first, to other urban groups of lower socioeconomic status, and later, to rural groups. As this took place fertility declined in all classes, but for some time it continued to decline more rapidly in the upper socioeconomic classes. . . . Since it seems likely . . . that economic considerations are going to play a more and more important role in determining the size of the family as voluntary control increases, it seems not improbable that the less favored economic groups will soon have as small families as the more favored groups, or perhaps, even smaller. (Thompson, p. 195)

Mortality

During the past century, there has been not only a general decline in birth rates in Western countries but also a marked decrease in the mortality rates. For example, the crude death rate in Sweden during 1808—1812 was 33 per 1,000 and 26 in France for the same period. In 1950 the corresponding rates were 13 and 10. In 1848–1852 the crude death rate in England and Wales was 23; in 1970 it was 12. These rates vary widely from country to country, but in some countries they are dropping quite sharply. Comparable demographic data for some sections of the world are still inadequate. This is true for most of Africa, Southeast Asia, China, and certain areas in the Near East. Nevertheless, what evidence we have seems to support the idea that in these regions, too, the death rate has been going down in recent decades. For the United States as a whole, adequate mortality statistics were not available before 1900. In that year the crude death rate was 17 per thousand. Since the end of the Second World War, the U.S. crude death rate has stabilized between 9 and 10 per thousand. In 1973 the death rate was 9.4.

Other trends in the reduction of the death rate in the United States since 1870 show these facts: (1) The mortality rate for infants (persons under one year of age) did not decline materially until after 1900, when the infant death rate was 162 per thousand. By 1975 the infant death rate had dropped to 16.1. The infant death rate for blacks and other nonwhites in 1975, however, was 24 per thousand, thus reflecting one major consequence of racial discrimination. (Bogue, p. 177) (2) The death rate for individuals over four years old but under middle age has moved slowly downward. And (3) the mortality rate for persons in the upper-age brackets has remained about the same.

One factor that has long influenced the death rate has been high maternal mortality. This has been drastically reduced by advances in medical science. In 1920 the maternal mortality rate was 80 per 10,000 live births and even as late as 1940 the maternal mortality rate was 32 for whites and 77 for nonwhites. In 1975 maternal mortality for whites was down to 9.1 and to 29.0 for nonwhites.

Age, Sex, and Mortality

The influence of disease on the death rate is qualified in most instances by age. Some diseases, such as diarrhea, whooping cough, measles, diphtheria, and scarlet fever, occur chiefly in infancy and childhood. In addition, earliest infant mortality is affected by congenital defects. Other diseases, such as typhoid and pulmonary tuberculosis, attack middle life most frequently. Adults in the later years are most susceptible to pneumonia, cancer, diabetes, and to such organic breakdowns as heart and circulatory disorders, nephritis, and Bright's disease.

With the decrease in infant and childhood mortality and the aging of the population, there has been a change in the relative seriousness of acute and chronic diseases. Modern medicine and sanitation have largely eliminated the incidence of the acute diseases of childhood and have restricted the incidence and spread of typhoid, diphtheria, smallpox, and other acute disorders that formerly attacked young and old alike. In contrast, chronic diseases—that is, those that persist or recur with such virulence as to need continued medical and nursing care—have become more prevalent in the last half century.

For the younger ages, the disasters of disease and death tend to be related to poor living conditions, inadequate health care, and infectious diseases due to lack of adequate public health measures. Death in the later years seems most often related to organic breakdowns, which may have various causes—earlier infections, congenital defects, occupational hazards, poor medical care, and so on.

Changes in the causes of death are related not only to the advances of medical knowledge and skill, but also to shifts in the age distribution of the population and to improvement in levels of living. In the United States, there were more than four times as many people 65 years old or over in 1960 as there were in 1900, which means that disorders related to aging have become increasingly significant. At the beginning of the century, the leading causes of death were influenza and pneumonia, tuberculosis, and diarrhea and enteritis.

In 1969 nearly 40 per cent of all deaths were due to diseases of the heart and about 17 per cent to cancer and related maligancies. The fourth major cause is death by accidents. (*Statistical Abstract of the United States,* 1971, p. 58)

Sex, Marital Status, and Mortality

Demographic data show that women have a higher survival rate than men. Apparently a lethal selection begins almost from the start of life. More males are conceived than females, in a ratio of about 125 to 100. However, even prenatally, the death toll is higher for males than for females. At the time of birth the sex ratio is about 106 males to 100 females. But even this slight advantage does not last. Among infants under one year, death takes a higher toll of boys than girls. And right on through the age brackets, the death rate is lower among females. Up to age 65, the female rate is about half that of the male rate; at 65 years and over, the female rate is about one-third lower.

Another differential is evident when we compare the mortality of single, married, and widowed persons. Studies both in Europe and in this country reveal the general fact that married persons live longer than single persons. In general, however, single people have a lower death rate than widowed and divorced people.

Occupation and Mortality

The kind of work a person does will determine in part his exposure to various kinds of illness or accidents, and thus play a part in affecting type and time of death. Obviously, construction workers, truck drivers, and miners are more exposed to hazardous working conditions than are bookkeepers or schoolteachers. In discussing various studies of occupational mortality made in Great Britain, Thompson (p. 254) points out a vicious circle:

> ... poor pay makes decent living impossible. The inevitable result of... circumstance is an extremely high death rate in certain occupational groups. It is, perhaps, the living conditions enforced by poorly paid work, even more than the nature of the work itself, that cause the high death rates in many occupations.

Residence and Mortality

For many decades, rural communities have had lower death rates than urban communities. In the United States the rural areas still have lower rates, but with the extension of public health facilities, sanitation, and improved medical care in the cities, the differences are lessening. An important element in the dropping of the death rate has been the sharp decline in infant mortality. One Census Bureau report notes that "Between 1915, the first year for which a comparable figure is available, and 1953, the infant mortality rate dropped 72 per cent." (*Vital Statistics–Special Reports,* 1956, p. 327) The rural-urban differentials, however, continue. "The contrast in infant mortality rates between the metropolitan counties and the nonmetropolitan is greater than that between urban and rural areas. . . . The small cities show slightly lower rates than the large cities and the rural areas." (*Vital Statistics–Special Reports,* p. 329)

INTERPRETIVE SUMMARY

Since the eighteenth century, and particularly in our century, the world has experienced a rapid growth in population. In industrial societies, the decline in the death rate as a result of medical progress and improved standards of living has been somewhat offset by the concomitant decline in the birth rate. Other societies have reaped the benefits of medical knowledge, which are relatively easy to administer as far as lowering the death rates is concerned, without managing to keep births down.

One problem stemming from the population explosion in such countries is, of course, lack of food. Sharing knowledge about improved methods of agriculture, conservation, and birth control, and migration of people in underdeveloped countries to places with extra resources have been suggested to help solve the problem. Those who see industrialization as essential to improved standards of living would lend money and technicians to help countries to industrialize. All these suggestions have been tried and all have worked to some extent, though factors such as poor resources, cultural inertia, and widespread lack of education in the countries needing help have impeded improvement.

Western industrial societies are experiencing a long-range decline in fertility. However, rates of fertility vary among different groups and social categories. In the United States, though several interrelated factors affect birth rates, differences among groups are declining. For example, though city families on the average still have fewer children than do farm families, the differential is decreasing. Though birth rates still vary considerably among religious groups, the number of individuals of all faiths who are apparently planning family size is increasing. Again, though upper economic groups still tend to have fewer children, starting their families later and finishing earlier, this differential also has decreased markedly as contraceptive education has been made available to poor people and secularization has become widespread.

The death rate in Western countries, as well as in many non-Western countries, is also declining. The most striking decrease has come in the lower age groups, as medical science has conquered or restricted the diseases of childhood. Medical advances have also increased life expectancy. The fact that people are living longer has had consequences throughout the society.

QUESTIONS

1. Do members of some religious groups habitually have larger families in this country? What do statistics say about this?
2. What was Malthus' theory about the way population expands? Is this theory out of date now? Explain.
3. What social factors contribute to the growth of the population? What social factors account for any decrease in population?
4. Using the demographic transition as a model, can you describe the population problems of third-world countries such as Africa and South America?

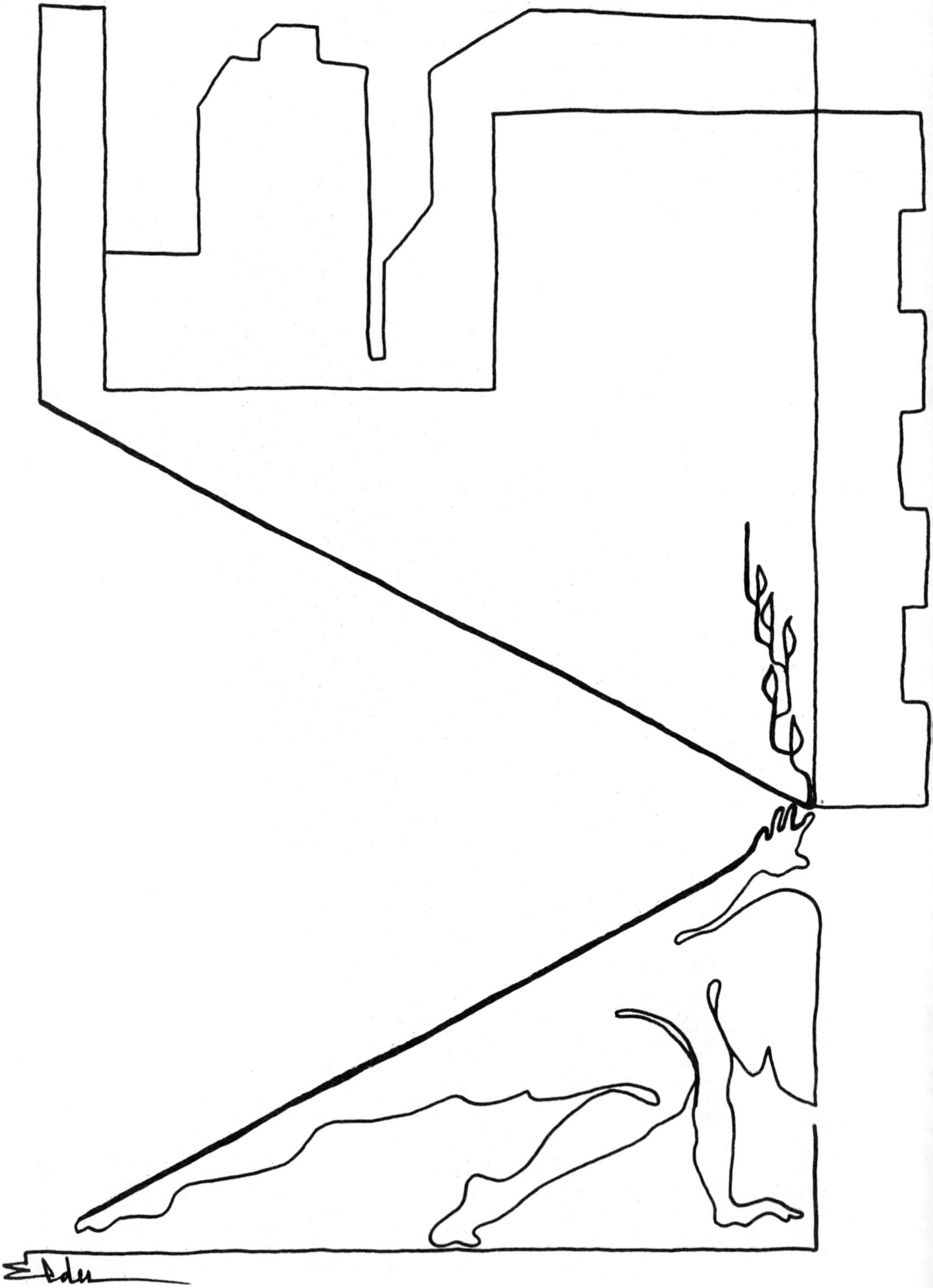

14

Ecology and Urbanization

When a traveler arrives by bus in the center of a large U.S. city, he or she often finds himself or herself in an area containing pawnshops, all-night theaters, and "cheap" bars, hotels, and restaurants. Bus stations are usually located in the section of the city with relatively inexpensive services for transients. If the traveler wants to find the largest theater or department store in the city, he or she can assume with confidence that it will be only a few blocks away, near the center of the city. If he or she is on the way to visit a schoolteacher who lives in a single-family house, he or she can assume that his or her destination will be a considerable distance from the bus station: middle-class single-family dwellings are ordinarily built farther away from the central business district, near the periphery of the city. The person can make all these predictions because human activities are patterned spatially as well as in other ways.

Human ecology is that part of sociology that studies the spatial distribution of human groups and social institutions. Geography is not the only factor determining spatial distribution of a population. The north side of town may not be topographically different from the south side, but if early settlers on the north side are or become wealthy and influential, certain other people will want to live near them and be associated with them, and property on the north side will become culturally desirable. Poor laborers, ethnic minorities, and other lower-status people are often not able to afford homes on this side of town. Nor will they have enough influence to keep polluting factories from being built in their neighborhood. The cultural character of the area of residence will determine social space: residence within these geographic boundaries will be taken as a status symbol and will be a factor in defining social relations.

Ecologists are interested in the spatial distribution of any social phenomenon: what part of the community has the most suicides, where the areas of high and low economic status are located, where minorities live, whether people go to church in the neighborhood where they live, and so on. The ecologist regards spatial relations as an index of social relations and thus is interested in the spatial structuring of human activities in order to learn about the social structure and social groups.

Ecologists, like other sociologists, are concerned with both structure and process. Ecological structure is represented by a map showing the distribution of some social activity, such as gambling or fertility or wholesale trade. Ecological processes include changes in the ecological structure, such as the expansion of the area devoted to retail trade or the change of a Polish-American neighborhood to a Puerto Rican neighborhood.

THE ECOLOGY OF SMALL COMMUNITIES

Because small communities and rural areas emphasize primary rather than secondary group relations and because they have fewer people and are more homogeneous, the ecology of the small or rural community is less complex than the large urban metropolis. (See Chapter 8 for a discussion of the small community or Gemeinschaft.) Nevertheless, communities are not identical. The institutions and organizations found in small communities vary in their ecological setting and culture.

Ecology and Land Settlement

The family has traditionally been the basic social unit in all agricultural societies, but the spatial distribution of farm families has varied greatly. In some regions farm families are dispersed throughout the entire area. In others the population is relatively concentrated in a hamlet or village and work the adjoining land. Probably most of the world's farmers follow the latter pattern. While the concentrated village is the principal dwelling place of farmers in Europe and the Orient, exceptions are found in Great Britain, France, Germany, the Low Countries, the northern part of Scandinavia, and sporadically in southern Europe. The village is the chief pattern in India and China, but there are variations. In Latin America and Africa, rural settlements are usually of the village type.

The ecology of an area is usually influenced by historical developments and the United States is a case in point. The clustered-village type of community was brought to the colonies from England and the Continent. But local differences began to evolve as settlers moved into the interior. Individuals and single families crossed the Alleghenies and squatted on "new" lands, and their claims were later validated by legal action. In the Southern colonies the plantation system emerged out of commercial agriculture supported by slave labor. Later, federal laws influenced the form of land settlement. In 1785 the rectangular survey was established, and public lands were divided first into townships of 36 square miles each. These were then subdivided into sections of 640 acres and quarter sections of 160 acres. In 1841 the requirement was made that, to obtain title to such land, the individual had to live on it. Still later the Homestead Act (1862) provided for settlement and payment for public lands at a low cost per acre.

The rectangular division of land made for a gridiron form of farms and fostered the separation of farmsteads from each other by considerable distances. As a matter of fact, much of the best agricultural land of the United States was settled under this pattern. It is a neat illustration of how a culture trait, in this case law, may influence the ecology of a community. However, there are some variations in the types of farm settlement.

The Rural Community Since the small, spatially isolated community is based upon face-to-face relationships, the neighborhood is probably more primary than any other group except the family. The characteristic feature is that families live near one another and that they are bound together by intimate and personal relationships. The greater the number of bonds, the more distinctive the community. Frequently neighborhoods in highly urbanized areas are built around a single interest or institution, such as a country school or a mill. In contrast, the community is formed around common interests and the means of satisfying most human needs or interests.

Historically, the community has been a very significant organization. In preindustrial times the whole social life of open-country groups centered there. Most manufacturing was done at home, and the economic system was largely one of the direct exchange of goods and services. Today the community has declined for many people as wider ranges of interaction have developed. The traditional rural community is changing its function as the bonds of mere locality are being replaced by urban forms of social organization, such as special-interest groups. Wherever good highways and proximity to trading centers permit, urban services, such as commercial baking, laundering, dry cleaning, and the like, are affecting the patterns of both family and community life.

In the United States, rural communities, as they have related to agriculture, may be divided into four types: the open-country, the village or town-centered community, the agricultural village, and the plantation community.

The Open-Country Community Ordinarily one thinks of a community as composed of more or less definite social structure and population located within some relatively defined space. Yet there are some communities where the stores, garages, schools, and churches are dispersed rather widely. The people who live in such an area and trade in these stores or send their children to the schools or attend the churches do, however, regard themselves as members of a distinct community. Though widely diffused, these communities have names and they are thought of by the inhabitants as distinct communities, within which are to be found relatively traditional patterns of social interaction. Such communities are common in the South and in some parts of the Great Plains, and are found sporadically elsewhere.

Landaff, New Hampshire, for example, is largely of this type. Landaff has a church, a garage, a school, and some scattered service agencies, but it has no nucleus, no fixed center. Yet there is no doubt that, in the thinking of its residents, Landaff is a community. (MacLeish, 1942) Like Landaff, most communities of this kind consist of farmsteads dispersed throughout the area, with various service agencies located at more or less convenient points.

However, unless they are bound together by some emotional tie, such as a common religion or a common ethnicity, many open-country communities are likely to have a limited sense of unity and less sense of belonging together than communities with more concentrated populations—especially in this time of mass community and increasing urbanization. Furthermore, most open-country communities are far from self-sufficient. As good roads have been built, people in these places go to larger localities to satisfy most of their economic and recreational needs.

There are scattered examples of open-country communities which are closely integrated by religious, kinship, linguistic, and ethnic subcultures. Such are the Amish in Lancaster County, Pennsylvania, and the Amana of Iowa. Somewhat similar are certain other pietistic denominations, such as the Mennonites. But for the most part, such integrating factors are not present in the open-country communities of the United States.

Town-Centered Communities Most rural inhabitants in the United States tend to be oriented toward a village or town. But the degree of centralization and the ratio of open-country to actual town members are highly variable. Where the gridiron land survey encouraged dispersal of farmsteads on rather widely scattered farms, the town may have grown up at an important railroad stop or at the junction of two important lines of traffic, rail or highway. The townspeople may be both farmers and persons concerned with providing services connected with the rural economy.

Everywhere the earlier relations of farm families to town centers have undergone many changes. The automobile and hard-surfaced roads made it possible to buy goods and services at longer distances from the farm than formerly. So, too, the development of mail-order buying enabled farm families to get goods which might not be easily available nearby.

Yet the school, the church, the grocery store, and the garage continue to provide important services within easy reach. Some believe that in time the shift to larger centers will eliminate the need for these smaller places near the farmstead. While the relative importance of the hamlet and small town is declining, these centers will probably long continue to provide many goods and services for the farm family and other rural families.

Agricultural Villages The settlement of farmers into more or less compact villages is not as usual in most of the United States as it is in so much of the world elsewhere. Yet the main features of the agricultural village deserve brief comment. The best-known instances of agricultural villages in the United States are those established by the Mormons when they settled in the Great Basin—western Utah, southern Idaho, and parts of Nevada.

The basic pattern was developed by Joseph Smith and first used in Nauvoo, Illinois. A community was arranged on the gridiron pattern, with streets 8 rods wide at right angles and square blocks of 10 acres each, divided into half-acre lots for single dwellings. The plan was later applied when Salt Lake City was laid out by Smith's successor, Brigham Young. And as other communities were established up and down the central valleys of Utah, the same general pattern was followed, though the street widths and size of blocks were often modified.

The necessity for protection against hostile Indians and the cooperative effort to obtain water for the farms by irrigation were not the determining factors, for the farmers lived in the village or town and the farm properties which they worked were adjacent to it. Rather, this was an interesting example of deliberate community planning. Between 1847 and 1877 more than 360 such communities were established, reaching from southern Idaho through Utah into Arizona.

In keeping with the overall program for these communities, the Mormon Church set up a colonization plan to make sure that in each new community sufficient carpenters, blacksmiths, and other specialized workers would be available, as well as enough farmers. Since the entire orientation of these activities was to make the Mormons economically self-sufficient and independent of the "gentile" (non-Mormon) world outside, many communities were *instructed* to develop various industries in addition to their agriculture. Iron works were built in some places, woolen mills in others, salt plants in still others—usually where the necessary raw materials were at hand. These local industries were to supplement the home manufacturing which—at least ideally—was as much a part of family life as farming itself. Actually, the Mormon communities were planned to be more than strictly agricultural villages. They were to be not only the centers of farming and local industry but the seats of all major religious, civic, and other noneconomic community affairs.

Another nucleated community widely distributed throughout the world is the "line village." This type of community is common in southern Louisiana, where French influence was great. Among the rivers where frontage is particularly valuable, houses occupy small areas near the river, with the accompanying farmlands extending back in narrow strips.

It is worth noting that there have been many attempts to establish agricultural villages in the course of American history. Most of them were born of the utopian socialistic or cooperative movements of the nineteenth century. Few remain.

Certainly as far as the Mormon villages are concerned, they are marked by a high degree of community solidarity and integration. Here it is not farming but religious and other cultural elements which furnish the basis for a strong sense of belonging. Of the socialistic or cooperative settlements in this country, it is worth noting that most of them failed because those who took part in them lacked or lost the moral and religious zeal that inspired the founders and leaders. (Bestor, 1950)

The Plantation As a system of agricultural production, the plantation is widespread. It is found in parts of Latin America—as in coffee-growing parts of Brazil—and in the production of rubber in Malaya and Africa. Allen D. Edwards defines a plantation as a "form of social organization in which labor, under unified direction and control, is engaged in the production of an agricultural staple which is usually sold on a world market." Plantations predate the capitalistic economic system and may be described as a quasi-feudal form of organization. (Edwards, 1947, p. 158)

The plantation pattern was introduced into the United States from the West Indies. Before the Civil War, cotton and tobacco cultivation in the South was largely organized under this system. The center of the large holdings consisted of the master's house, houses for his supervisors, outbuildings, and huts for slaves. And the whole economy more or less revolved around this nucleus. Even at this late date, many of the earlier managerial features remain. Sometimes the plantation is organized under the sharecropper system. In other cases the work is done by hired laborers.

In the South, smaller plantations often operated as parts of a larger plantation community. But whether large or small, the plantation was the focus and center of life for many people in the South. Moreover, the influence often reached beyond the plantation itself. Writing in the middle 1930s, Woofter (1936) reported that "Plantation customs and ideology set the pattern for relationships in small farm units. . . . Large planters persistently emerge as the political and economic leaders of the cotton areas . . . and the plantation stands out as the basis for a hereditary oligarchy in southern community life."

Modifications of the plantation system are found in some of the large-scale corporation farms of California and elsewhere. These are what Carey McWilliams has called "factories in the fields." The vast vegetable acreage of the Imperial Valley is owned largely by corporations. The farms are operated by managers and supervisors, who hire laborers at low wages to do the work. The aim is high profit, and farming is made into as efficient a business system as possible. Certainly the communal aspects of social organization tend to disappear under such circumstances, except insofar as it continues in the noneconomic aspects of the lives of workers. So too, the collective farms of the Soviet Union are adaptations of the plantation system.

WORLD URBANIZATION

The widespread and rapid urbanization of the world is one of the most significant trends of our time. Worldwide urban expansion is bringing about great changes in the major patterns of social organization. In many ways it is as revolutionary in its effects on society and institutions as the domestication of plants and animals and the emergence of village life.

The striking growth of cities in the nineteenth and twentieth centuries is a novel event in human history. Although cities existed five or six thousand years ago, the cities of the ancient world were generally small towns by modern standards. The largest of them contained only 1 or 2 per cent of the total population of their society, and it has been estimated that it took from 50 to 90 farmers to produce the surplus needed to enable one person to live in an urban center. (Davis, 1955) In fact, it is here, in the ratio of farmers to urban dwellers, that the explanation can be found for the recency and suddenness of urbanization. Not until the Industrial Revolution, with its factory system, improvement of farming, and tremendous speed-up in the transportation of goods, was it possible for whole societies to become urbanized. Only when one farmer can raise enough food for many people besides himself can a society exist in which the majority of the people live and work in cities.

Only in the past century and a half has the world known truly urban *societies*, in which a high proportion of the total population lives in cities. Box 14-1 shows that as recently as 1800 only 2.4 per cent of the world's population lived in cities of 20,000 or more; today more than one-fifth of the people live in such cities. Furthermore the proportion of people living in large cities has risen even more dramatically. By 1950 the proportion of people in the world living in cities was higher than that in even the most urbanized country before modern times. (Davis, p. 433) Davis describes the increase in urbanization as follows:

> In 1800 there were apparently less than 50 cities with 100,000 or more inhabitants. This was less than the number in the million [category].... By 1950 there were close to 900 cities of 100,000 or more people....
>
> As yet there is no indication of a slackening of the rate of urbanization in the world as a whole. If the present rate should continue, more than a fourth of the earth's people will be living in cities of 100,000 or more in the year 2000, and more than half in the year 2050. For places of 20,000 or more, the proportions at the two dates would be something like 45 per cent and 90 per cent. Whether such figures prove too low or too high, they nevertheless suggest that the human species is moving rapidly in the direction of an almost exclusively urban existence.... When ... more than a third of the population of a country lives in cities of the 100,000 class (38.4 per cent of England and Wales in 1951), the country can be described as almost completely urbanized (81 per cent being designated as "urban" in the English case in 1951). We thus have today what can be called "urbanized societies," nations in which the great majority of inhabitants live in cities. The prospect is that, as time goes on, a greater and greater proportion of humanity will be members of such societies. (K. Davis, 1955, p. 434)

14-1 CHECKING IT OUT: Percentage of World's Population Living in Cities 1800–1950

	Cities of 20,000 or More	*Cities of 100,000 or More*
1800	2.4	1.7
1850	4.3	2.3
1900	9.2	5.5
1950	20.9	13.1

SOURCE: Davis, "The Origin and Growth of Urbanization in the World," *American Journal of Sociology*, 1955, 60: 434.

These figures are even more impressive when one realizes that urbanization is very low in Asia, Africa, and Latin America. This fact underscores the close relationship between urbanization and industrialization. The bulk of the urbanization, as the table shows, has occurred in Oceania, Europe, and North America and the greatest amount of urbanization is still to be found in northern Europe.

14-2 CHECKING IT OUT: Percentage of World's Population Living in Cities

	In Cities of 20,000 Plus	*In Cities of 100,000 Plus*
World	21	13
Oceania	47	41
North America (Canada and U.S.A.)	42	29
Europe (except U.S.S.R.)	35	21
U.S.S.R.	31	18
South America	26	18
Middle America and Caribbean	21	12
Asia (except U.S.S.R.)	13	8
Africa	9	5

SOURCE: Davis, p. 433.

Urban Ecological Structure

Cities tend to locate on trade routes, and trade tends to follow the topography of least resistance. People float their goods down streams to remote markets.

Land routes along valleys, over low passes in mountains, by way of a chain of oases in a desert—all represent the effort to overcome nature's obstacles with the least expenditure of energy, time, and social resources. Wherever there is a break in this flow, cities are likely to arise: where the sea trade must be transferred to river travel, or where there is a break in land travel because of topography, political barriers, or other factors. Paris, France, grew up where trade routes north and south met the Seine River. As Charles Horton Cooley phrased it, "Population and wealth tend to gather wherever there is a break in transportation." Usually the larger the tributary or supporting area, the larger the central city. But factors of topography, population density, and political and economic organization also influence the pattern of location and growth.

An examination of a large map of any city shows how its structure and growth are first of all dependent on the nature of the site itself. Richard M. Hurd (1924, p. 33) remarks:

> The first step in studying the ground plan of cities is to note the topographical faults which normally control the shape of cities, by interfering with their free growth in all directions from their points of origin. These are of two kinds: water surfaces, such as harbors, lakes, rivers, creeks, and swamps, or sharp variations from the normal city level, such as steep hills, deep hollows, and ravines.

Where the land is flat, with no marshes or interfering contours, a city will tend to grow outward from the original center unless man-made factors, such as highways, defense walls, and railroad trackage, interfere. Topography gives the most obvious structure to a city. The towns and cities located on waterways must follow the lines of growth laid down by the water barriers. In hill-and-valley topography, the valley tends to be the seat of easiest communication and of industrial and commercial locations, while residential sections are found on higher ground. If the hills are too steep, travel between homes and work is difficult, so that even residential growth tends at the outset to follow the line of least resistance. Hurd summarizes the major influences of topography: "Level land attracts business, moderate elevations attract residences, land below the normal level attracts transportation lines, and filled-in land is generally used for warehousing, manufacturing, and cheap tenements." (Hurd, p. 36) Of course, the longer people have been settled in a locality, the less important the influence of the natural topography becomes and the more important the man-made "cultural landscape." People level or cut through hills, drain and fill swamps, build dikes, dredge river mouths and harbors, construct canals, and otherwise alter the natural landscape.

The site of a city soon develops a structure or form, with the layout of streets playing a determining part. Unless there is a definite plan, when a city is founded the streets are laid out in conformity with natural topography, and the best available land tends to be taken for retail stores and residences. The ground plan is thus settled, more or less, once and for all. Thenceforth streets tend to become obstructions to further development. Cities with narrow or winding streets, like

Boston, Massachusetts, or cities with many diagonal streets, like Washington, D.C., or Madison, Wisconsin, produce unusually serious automobile traffic problems.

Unless modified by a plan or unusual topography, cities tend to develop in either an axial or radial fashion. Where the streets are laid out with regularity, in squares or rectangles, the city's growth is usually restricted to the direction determined by two main intersecting streets or thoroughfares. There are some advantages and some disadvantages in the rectangular form. It allows the plotting of about equal-size blocks, makes easy the division of the city into administrative districts, and facilitates adequate police and military control. Also, with rectangular blocks there are no main thoroughfares to facilitate circulation between the center and the periphery, although within the center itself movement may not be difficult.

The radial pattern arises when there is a natural center at the end of a number of converging thoroughfares. As the city grows, it tends to follow these major traffic lanes, producing star-shaped cities like Tokyo, Nuremberg, and the older sections of London. This is perhaps the most efficient form of development.

Sometimes one finds a combination of rectangular and radial patterns. Often there were originally a number of highways leading to the village or town, and as the city grew it was laid out in regular rectangular form superimposed on this system of highways. Washington, D.C., was deliberately planned to combine the radial with the rectangular scheme.

In Europe, some streets were developed around certain sections of cities as walls were torn down, moats filled in, or parks cut up. In Paris there are at least four sets of circular streets which arose as old walls were torn down and new ones were built farther away, only to be razed and themselves turned into streets. The Ringstrasse in Vienna was cut out of a series of public parks which had replaced older fortifications.

While the streets provide the basic ground structure of a city, railroad lines also contribute to it. In Chicago, for example, rail lines have tended to break up and isolate certain districts from others, though for the most part the lines have followed either the lake shore or the Chicago River and its branches. Wholesale trade areas and, more particularly, industrial sites call for much trackage, and in these areas slums are likely to develop. Often railroad tracks located on the outskirts of a city later become a barrier to further growth. The geographical distribution of cities over the world reflects various developments in commerce, industry, transportation, government, religion, and agriculture. Those cities most fortunately located have flourished and today stand as large metropolitan centers more or less dominating a surrounding hinterland area. For the most part, such growth has been a concomitant of industrialization. The percentages of population which fall into the urban category vary widely, from Great Britain, with 80 per cent, West Germany, 72 per cent, and the United States, 74 per cent (in 1970), to countries showing little urbanization, such as Pakistan, with 11, and Thailand, with 10 per cent.

Although most of us have an intuitive notion of what is rural and what is urban, the distinction of rural communities and urban communities is not always an easy one to make. The United States census classifies essentially all places with more than 2,500 residents as urban and all other places as rural. In 1970, 74 per cent of the American population was in urban areas (compared with 51 per cent in 1920). Moreover, in 1970 the population density of the United States was 57 persons per square mile. The population density in the Middle

14-3 CHECKING IT OUT: Urban Population and Population Density in the United States, 1790 to 1970

Year	*Per Cent Urban*	*Population Density**
1790	5	4
1800	6	6
1810	7	4
1820	7	6
1830	9	7
1840	11	10
1850	15	8
1860	20	11
1870	26	13
1880	28	17
1890	35	21
1900	40	26
1910	46	31
1920	51	36
1930	56	41
1940	59	44
1950	64	43 †
1960	70	50 †
1970	74	57 †

* Resident population per square mile of land area.
† Includes Alaska and Hawaii.
SOURCE: U.S. Bureau of the Census, *Statistical Abstract of the United States, 1971* (Washington, D.C.: U.S. Government Printing Office, 1971), pp. 5, 17.

Atlantic states of New Jersey, New York, and Pennsylvania was 371; in New York City, it was 26, 343; and in the Manhattan Borough alone, it was 67,808. If the entire land area of the United States had the population density of the Manhattan Borough, the population would be 240 billion!

There were 150 urbanized areas of more than 200,000 population in the United States in 1970 and 50 per cent of all Americans lived in counties that are located at least partly within 50 miles of the coasts. More than one-third of the four dozen large industrial-commercial cities are located on the coasts of the Great Lakes, a fact indicative of the importance of accessibility of water transportation to the development of cities.

A very high population density does not necessarily lead to intimate social relations. Urban life represents not only a certain massing of people but a different kind of interaction. As Louis Wirth (1940, p. 57) put it, "The city is not merely the point at which great numbers are concentrated into limited space, but it is also a complex of human beings exhibiting the most extraordinary heterogeneity in almost every characteristic in which human beings can differ from one another."

Centralization of Services The concentration of services in strategic places is an important ecological aspect of urban life. These services satisfy such common interests as work, education, government, religion, and recreation. Centralization is directly related to transportation and communication: service centers tend to be located where these intersect. The focal point of most cities, or of any community for that matter, is the retail shopping center. Many additional services are provided in this central area. Large cities in particular may provide centralized services for a wide hinterland. Organizational headquarters for a region, governmental offices for a state or nation, or other specialized functions may be located in a particular city.

Centralization may occur first by the sheer addition of activities in a common location, as when a rural trade center at a crossroads becomes, gradually, the locus of schools, churches, post office, garage, and bowling alley. Centralization may also take place through an increase in the number of individuals who find gratification of some interest at the same location. The foci of centralization are in constant competition for patronage, and changes in either the services or transportation facilities may upset any working balance that may have been attained.

Urban people tend to think of distance not in miles but in the amount of time required for movement. As concentrations persist along with population mobility, a kind of territorial specialization of activities follows. An urban community becomes studded with centers of varying sizes and degrees of specialization. These in turn act as magnets to attract the appropriate age, sex, economic, and class groupings. Specialization occurs in time as well as in space, as when an iceskating rink is converted to a swimming pool or meeting hall during the summer. More frequently a specialized business might find it worth its while to remain open only during certain months.

Decentralization There is, of course, a point beyond which concentration and centralization cannot go. Competition for space in the central section of a city leads to such high land values that further expansion of business or other services becomes impractical. And while the construction of more and more skyscrapers keeps adding space for offices, there are physical limits to such

14-4 CHECKING IT OUT: An Ecological Pattern of Community Growth

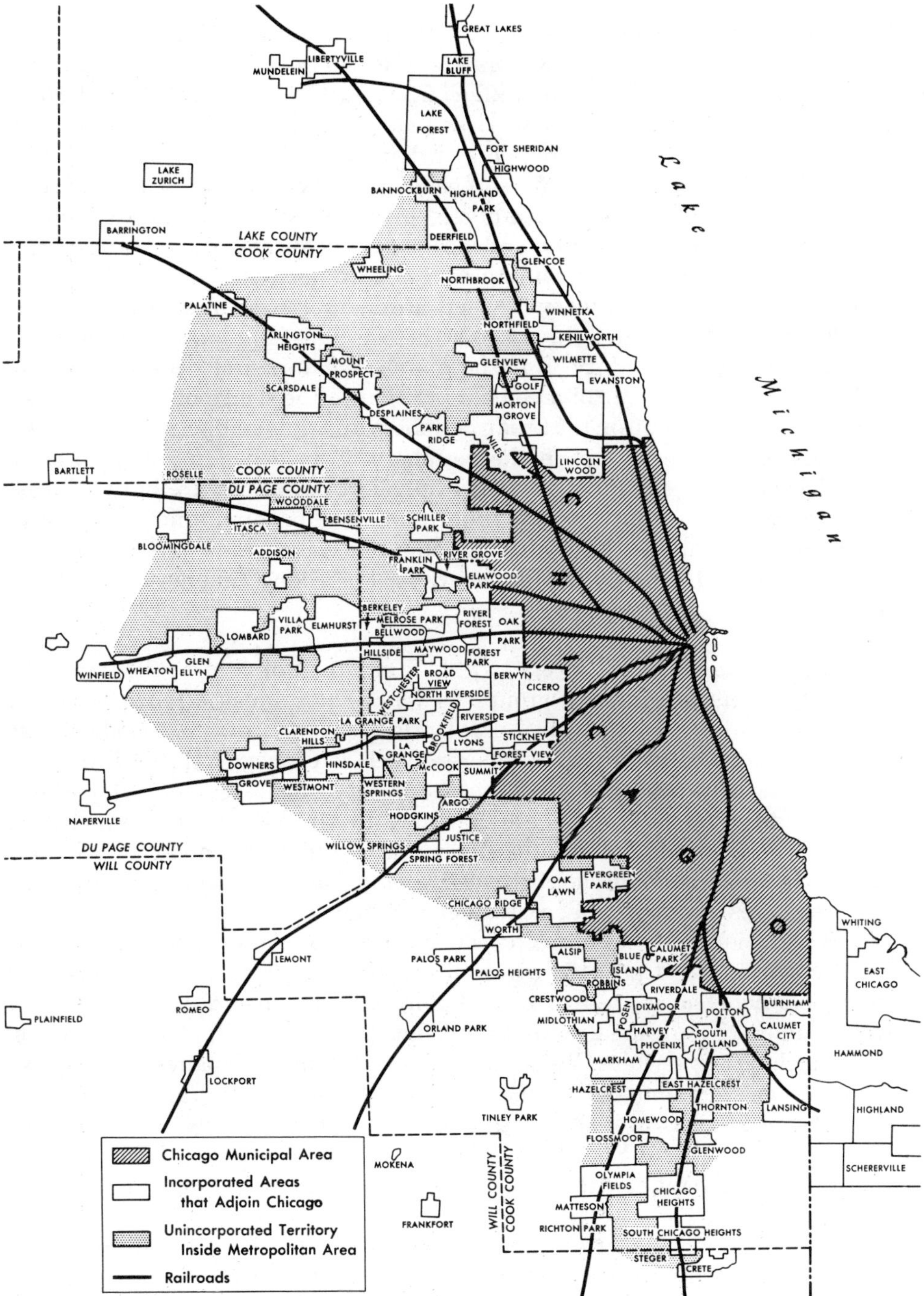

SOURCE: The *Chicago Daily Tribune,* May, 17, 1948. By permission.

facilities. The most obvious fact is that the higher the building, the more the space that must be used for elevators and other service fixtures and the less for commercial purposes. Then too, traffic congestion reduces the gains which come from concentration of goods and services. Loss in time and patience is, in the end, not offset by advantages of shopping or doing business in such centers. As a result, the process of centralization of goods and services appears in new areas. These changes, however, do not signify less urban domination, but the extension of urban culture. One of the first and most common forms of decentralization is the development of large retail stores, gas stations, and garages in or near residential areas. Large cities everywhere are characterized by such subcenters, which duplicate in many ways the structure and function of the original centralized area of the city. But there are other forms of decentralization. Industries may move out of a central position to the fringe of a city, or new industries may be set up on the urban periphery and thus foster a new subcenter.

Suburbs may grow up on the periphery of an expanding city as more desirable locations for families. Or as transportation lines are built nearby, smaller communities may become suburbs or satellite communities of a larger community. Sometimes these outlying communities become a part of the larger municipality and sometimes they continue for a long time as independent political units.

Segregation Almost every large U.S. city has not only wealthy suburbs but settlements of minority groups as well. These areas often carry such descriptive names as Little Italy, Little Harlem, or Chinatown. Areas given over to vice or occupied by transient laborers, such as Chicago's Hobohemia, also have unique features. Such segments of the urban ecological structure have been called "natural areas," to indicate that they are the outcome of competition, conflict, cooperation, and group differentiation and accommodation. Similar variations are to be found in all great cities but may represent quite different culture groups: occupational, caste or class, religious bodies, or others.

Segregation is never complete as to culture group or occupation. There is usually a mixture of peoples, especially around the fringes of the area. For example, where blacks are an overwhelming majority, one finds a few scattered white families. There are also what Paul Hatt (1945) called "polyethnic" areas, which include Jews, white Christians, Chinese, Filipinos, Japanese, and blacks living in close proximity. In some cities where many immigrants of like nationality reside, however, the areas tend to be more nearly homogeneous. Sometimes, as in New York City's Harlem, there is something akin to a self-contained community, with its own ecological structure along class and occupational lines.

Low-income areas often encircle the center of the city. Interspersed throughout the zone are often light manufacturing and business concerns, which "invade" the area because of cheap rents and the hope of an expanding central zone. There are high ratios of poverty, delinquency, and other indices of social disadvantage, as well as many recent foreign immigrants, high birth and death rates, and a high population density.

Assimilation and Segregation The processes of assimilation are both helped and hindered by residential concentration of subcultures. A subcultural area often serves as a cultural island for the newcomers. It gives them a certain sense of security and so helps introduce them to the new culture. The effects of spatial segregation and retention of immigrant heritages may be characterized as follows: (1) Continuity with the old culture is maintained. (2) Immigrants see the new country and its culture through the eyes of their own culture, especially as reflected in the ideas and attitudes of relatives and friends already settled there. The newcomers accept the definition of the situation offered them by their fellow countrymen already here. (3) This continuity of the old and interpretation of the new through their fellow countrymen softens the severity of the change and profoundly influences the process of assimilation itself. (4) However, it is only as immigrants are introduced into more and more of the features of the new culture, and especially as their children come into contact with the school, with agencies of recreation, with family life in this country, and with other patterns, that the effects of the earlier culture wear off and assimilation really gets underway.

The reactions of the established population to an immigrant are often those of avoidance and prejudice. Fear of economic competition and misunderstanding of different culture patterns were common during the period when large numbers of immigrants were coming to the United States. But in time came various accommodations which were steps to cultural assimilation and structural pluralism.

The rates of assimilation have differed. Oriental immigrants for the most part have retained considerable residential concentration, and their relations with the whites continue to be of an accommodative character. Most European immigrants, and especially their children and grandchildren, have largely broken through the barriers of discrimination and segregation and have become assimilated. Public education, improvement in economic status, intermarriage, and moving out of the immigrant area itself have been important factors in this process of change.

Invasion and Succession Population distributions seldom remain fixed: in a highly dynamic society, invasion and succession come into play. The invasion by one group of an area occupied by another leads to segregation and finally to displacement or succession by the intruding group. In some cases lower economic classes invade an area being abandoned by the well-to-do. Sometimes the reverse is true, as when apartment houses spring up in neighborhoods which have long been occupied by families of low incomes but which afford easy access to work or have other attractive features. Good illustrations of the latter are found along the East River in mid-Manhattan or in the "near-north side" in Chicago.

Succession tends to be marked by rather sharp changes in the composition of the resident population. Not infrequently in American cities there has been a long series of intrusions and displacements. The process is acccompanied by continuous competition between groups.

Migration Residential movement follows the spatial expansion of the city toward its periphery. As one would expect, the rate of residential change is higher in hotel and rooming-house areas than in tenement sections and higher in the latter than in districts farther out, where people own their own homes. There is a definite inverse relationship between home ownership and residential mobility. Among the many implications of high residential movement are lack of participation in community organizations, impersonal nature of human contacts, and high degree of occupational specialization, characteristics of the secondary-group organization of urban society.

The erection of skyscrapers increases congestion in movement by adding greatly to the number of persons and goods that must be moved into or out of an area and within the area itself. Some of the most striking facts about urban traffic congestion are these: (1) Between 1922 and 1944 there was an actual decline in the total passenger-carrying capacity of public utility equipment in the United States. It rose somewhat sharply in 1945 but decreased steadily through 1955. When one considers the kinds of transit equipment, there are notable changes and variations. Thus from 1935 to 1940, surface railway cars declined from 40,050 to 5,300 units, while subway and elevated cars decreased from 10,416 to 9,232. In contrast, trolley coaches increased from 578 to 6,157 and motor buses from 23,800 to 52,400. (2) With these changes has come a decrease in the use of public urban transit facilities. From 1924 through 1955, this was about one-fifth. For suburban and related areas the drop has been greater, about one-half for the same period. (3) However, the larger the city, the higher the proportion of the total population that use various means of public transportation.

In addition to public transportation, privately owned automobiles carry thousands of people over our city streets. Every major city of the United States has been harassed by the problems of mounting congestion and pollution from such traffic. There have been many schemes for building multiple-deck expressways into and through the heart of our cities, some of which work, some of which are impractical. But even if all urban workers possessed and were to use their own cars on fast highways, they would have to find places to park them before they could "function at the point of which they . . . transported themselves." Modern elevator or ramp garages have limited possibilities. "Crediting each vehicle with the average loading in city traffic of 1.75 persons" and assuming that a modern office building allows an average of 150 square feet of floor space per worker, estimates show that it would take practically as much floor space to park a person's car as he has in which to do his work. To provide parking space for workers, not shoppers, under the assumptions stated, would meaning doubling *"the cubage requirements of present central area buildings."* (American Transit Association, pp. 24, 25)

Social Area Analysis Several sociologists have employed a method for the analysis of urban social structure by spatial units. Social area analysis, as the method is called, is a technique for the study of social and economic data in the local sub-areas of a city through the use of data collected by the United States Census Bureau on census tracts within the city.

Census tracts are combined into neighborhoods on the basis of their similarity in three factors: social rank, urbanization, and segregation (or, as Bell prefers to call them, economic status, family status, and ethnic status). The social rank of a neighborhood is computed on the basis of two measures: the proportion of people in white-collar jobs and the proportion of the population over 25 years of age with more than eight years of schooling. Social rank therefore is based on two major stratification variables: occupation and education. Three measures are used in calculating the index of urbanization: fertility, the proportion of adult females in the labor force, and the proportion of dwelling units which are single-family houses. Segregation is measured by the percentage of the population which is nonwhite or foreign-born from countries of eastern and southern Europe.

Social area analysis has enabled the sociologist readily to relate divorce rates, suicides, voting behavior, church attendance, or any other factor for an area to the basic structural variables of economic, family, and ethnic statuses in that area.

ECOLOGICAL STRUCTURE OF CITIES

There have been a number of attempts to discover the ecological structure of cities, but each has been only partially successful. Three of the most important theories which have been set forth are the concentric zones theory, the sector theory, and the multiple nuclei pattern.

Concentric Zones

The first and best known of these efforts, known as the pattern of concentric zones, was presented by Ernest W. Burgess in 1925. According to his construct, the center of modern U.S. cities is the point of chief concentration of specialized services. The center, Zone I, is characterized by skyscrapers, department stores, big hotels, motion-picture houses, transit lines, and daily mobility of population as it goes about its business or pleasure. In Zone II are found rooming houses, some light industry, and certain other services. In general, the second zone is

14-5 CHECKING IT OUT: The Concentric Zones of Chicago Circa 1925

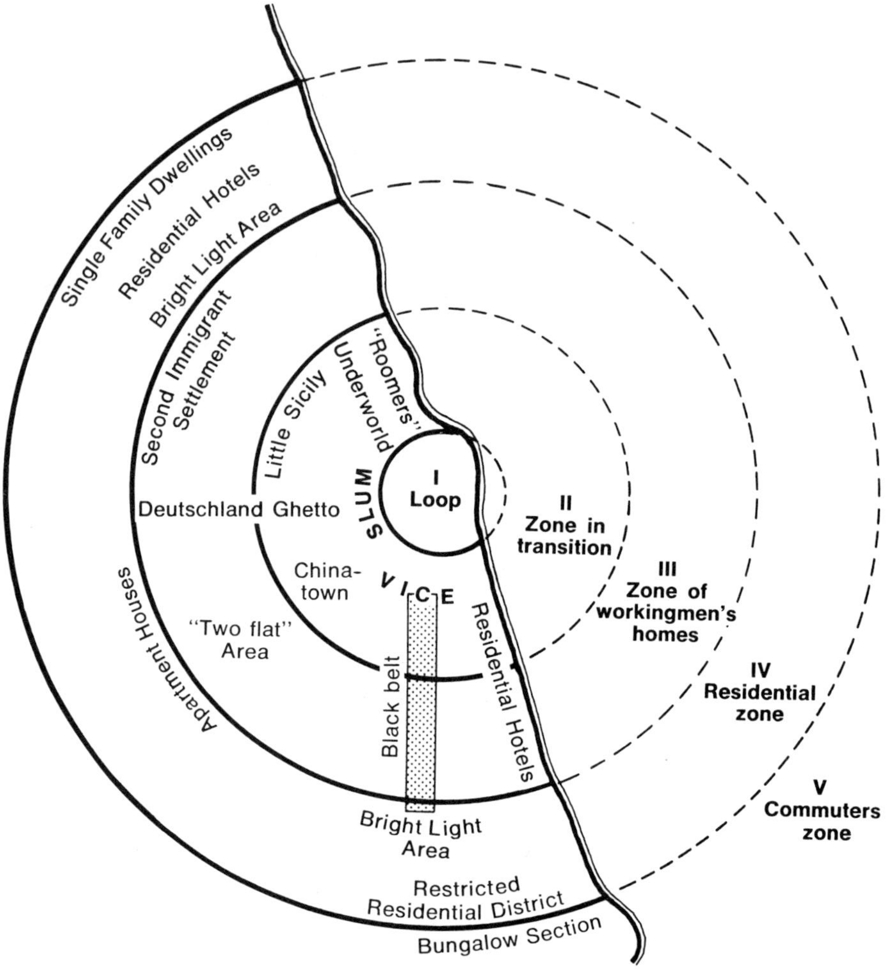

SOURCE: Robert E. Park, Ernest W. Burgess, and Roderick D. McKenzie, *The City* (Chicago: The University of Chicago Press, 1925), p.55. Reprinted by permission.

characterized by rather rapid change or "transition." In Zone III are working people's homes, and shopping centers, schools, and occasional parks. In the fourth zone are better residences, and beyond this is Zone V, the suburban and commuter area. Typically, there is an upward gradation in such features as income and status from the center to the periphery.

Burgess developed his theoretical construct from studies of urban communities, chiefly Chicago. The actual ecological structure of cities seldom conforms precisely to the pattern Burgess described. Topography, waterways, lakes, harbors, and so on all influence the direction and extent of a city's development. Certainly for Chicago, Lake Michigan cuts sharply through the middle of Burgess' circles, so that there we have a series of only half-concentric rings. Morover, the Chicago River, the railroad lines, the highways, and the desirability of lake-front residences also affect the spatial distribution.

14-6 CHECKING IT OUT: Three Generalizations of the Internal Structure of Cities

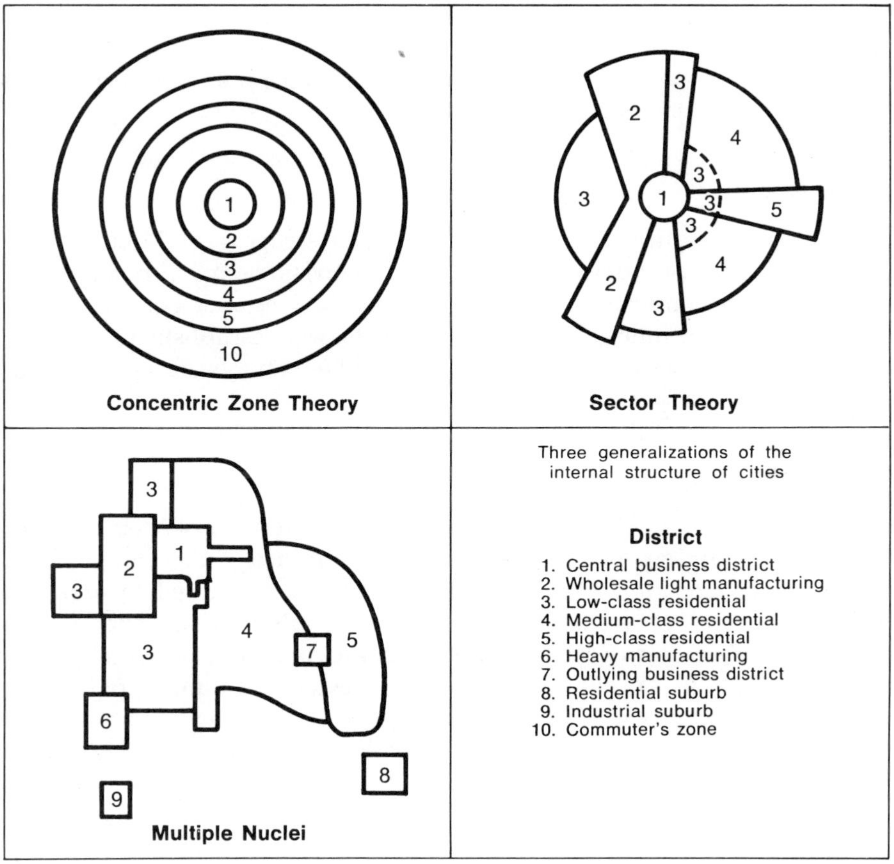

SOURCE: Chauncey D. Harris and Edward L. Ullman, "The Nature of Cities," *The Annals of the American Academy of Political and Social Science,* CCXLII (November, 1945), 13. Reprinted by permission.

Sectors

A second formulation, proposed in 1939 by Homer Hoyt (1939), is the so-called sector theory. This is a modification of the concentric zones pattern suggested by Burgess. Hoyt's proposed sector pattern gives more consideration to the influence of topographic factors and major travel arteries, sometimes producing sectors in wedge-shapes extending outward from the city center. According to Hoyt, high rent and high income sections of a city tend to be on the outer fringes of one or more quadrants or sectors of the community. These areas also tend to be furthest removed from factory districts. The low-rent areas sometimes extend from the very center of the city to its periphery. The growth of population is marked by an outward movement of the high-rent areas along any given sector, which may be initially determined by topographic factors and travel routes. Whether a city shows a sector or concentric zone ecological structure depends in large part on the natural landscape and the initial changes made by people. Where there are no serious natural or man-made barriers as in flat terrain, cities tend to conform to the concentric zone pattern.

Multiple Nuclei

A third major generalization regarding the internal structure of the city is Harris and Ullman's multiple nuclei pattern. According to Harris and Ullman, land use within the city is organized around a number of distinct nuclei or centers, each with its own special function. Most of the nuclei were established early in the city's history. As a city increases in size, the number of nuclei also increases and each becomes more specialized in its activities.

Critique of Ecology

Some criticism of these theories has been made by a number of people. Milla A. Alihan (1938) raised significant questions about the lack of clear-cut criteria in relating the concentric zones to various gradients, measured by indices of population, crime rates, and the like. Her doubts about the assumed homogeneity of population and culture within the zones may be applied equally to sectors and nuclei. On the basis of a careful review of a number of studies of American cities, Maurice R. Davie (1937) also has questioned the applicability of the concentric-zone theory. He says it "clearly does not apply to New Haven," nor to Greater Cleveland, nor to sixteen "self-contained cities." For Davie, the Burgess thesis is too simple for the complex factors of urban development. He points out that it neglects the importance of man-made topography, which follows the building of railroads and industries. Both the sector and multiple nuclei were attempts to improve upon the idea of concentric zones by taking such factors into account.

Another far-reaching critique of all three generalizations has been made by

Walter Firey (1947), who stresses the need to recognize the place of sentiment as it affects urban growth and functions and argues that economic competition for land is not the key variable in determining changes in business and residential locations. In his study of land use in Boston, Firey attempts to document his thesis. Actually, as John James has pointed out, his findings do not entirely refute Hoyt's thesis. And despite the topographical character of Boston, some features of the population movement are not entirely incompatible with the concentric-zone theory. Certainly there are a nucleated center and certain gradients in social-cultural features as one moves from this center to the suburban areas. (James, 1948)

On the whole, the concepts and tools of ecological research have been an aid to understanding how cities arise, grow, and change their features. The importance of cultural factors must not be so overstressed as to lead us to ignore the place of either the natural or man-made landscape of a given locality. The ecological and the cultural are intertwined at many points. As Richard M. Hurd, one of the initiators of modern human ecology, put it, "Underneath all economic laws . . . the last stage of analysis of the problems of the structure of cities, the distribution of utilities, the earnings of the buildings which house them, and the land values resulting therefrom, turns on individual and collective taste and preference, as shown in social habits and customs." (Hurd, p. 18)

METROPOLITAN AREAS

There have been two significant changes in urban comunities in the United States: first, the clustering of central cities and their suburbs, and second, their steady expansion to form what are known as metropolitan areas.

By 1910 the growth of cities beyond their legal-political boundaries led the United States Bureau of the Census to establish the category "metropolitan districts." By 1950 such a large proportion of people were part of the social structure of cities while residing outside them in suburbs that the concept of Standard Metropolitan Area (SMA) was introduced. A Standard Metropolitan Area consists of a core or central city and all of the contiguous area meeting certain Census Bureau standards of density of population, specialization of labor force, and social and economic integration with the central city. In the 1960 census these areas were officially designated as Standard Metropolitan Statistical Areas (SMSA).

In 1950 there were 162 Standard Metropolitan Areas in the United States, totaling a population of 85 million. A decade later there were 212 SMSA's with a total of 112 million people. In 1970 there were 243 such areas with a total populaton of 139 million. Although most of the population increase in the past twenty years has occurred in the metropolitan areas, the bulk of the increase has been in the suburbs, not in the central cities. The United States population increased 28 million from 1950 to 1960 and 89 per cent of that increase took place in metropolitan areas. Only 22 per cent of the increase was in the central cities. From 1960 to 1970 the population increased by 24 million and 83 per cent of that increase was in the metropolitan areas and only 16 per cent in the central cities (and the white population in central cities declined by 600,000 from 1960 to 1970).

In certain sections of this country, especially along the upper Atlantic seaboard, a great many metropolitan areas overlap or adjoin each other. This is particularly evident in the 600-mile stretch from Boston, Massachusetts, to the far tip of Fairfax County, Virginia. This complex, which will contain 80 million people by the year 2000, is typical of a new phenomenon in ecological growth. This is the **megalopolis**, which results from the joining of metropolitan areas into an uninterrupted belt. Another example of the megalopolis is the Great Lakes chain, which stretches from Buffalo to Milwaukee and even further west.

Suburbs

Even casual observation reveals that not all suburban communties are alike. Various attempts have been made to work out a classification. One such attempt classifies suburbs of 10,000 population or more as either residential or industrial. Industrial suburbs have the following characteristics: (1) they are "employing centers" which attract workers from other sections of the metropolitan area; (2) they are concentrated in the northeastern and north-central regions of the country; (3) they tend to be older than residential suburbs; (4) while they are found throughout the entire metropolitan area, they are often located beyond the limits of the densely populated urban core; indeed, (5) they are found in greater frequency as the distance from the central city increases; and (6) they are typically known as low-rent localities.

Residential suburbs of comparable populations are found in all metropolitan areas. They differ from industrial suburbs in that (1) their chief economic activity is retail trade, usually local in scope; (2) they tend to develop with increasing frequency as the size of the central city increases; (3) they predominate among the more recently incorporated communities; (4) very few of them are found outside the densely populated urbanized area or farther than 30 miles from the central city; and (5) they have higher rents than average among suburbs. (Schnore, 1956)

The expansion of economic and other functions depends on changes in the central city as well as the suburbs. The residential populations of industrial suburbs grow less rapidly than those of residential suburbs, and this is directly traceable to the specialization of function in the industrial suburbs.

> Residential suburbs are growing rapidly because they are becoming even more residential in character, by means of large increments of housing construction. At the same time, employing suburbs are growing less rapidly because they are becoming more exclusively devoted to industry and other employment-providing

> activities. In these employing places, the net effects of this increased specialization in production and employment is (a) to drive out pre-existent residential uses of land, and (b) to discourage new construction of housing. (Schnore, 1957, p. 171)

Such differentiation and specialization of land use in suburbs is but a part of the larger changes going on throughout metropolitan areas. In time some kind of working balance will probably arise between shifts in population in the central city and the suburban fringe and changes in the socioeconomic functions.

Moving to Suburbia

There are a number of social and sociological elements involved in the shifts in residence. First, a high proportion of the urban workers who live in the suburbs came originally from rural areas. (Gist, 1952) Suburban residents engage in more "neighboring" than their urban counterparts, and there is considerable retention of the values and attitudes of small primary communities. (Fara, 1956) Suburbs differ in several ways, however, from small communities of similar size which are not part of a metropolitan area. Residential suburbs tend to show higher than average incomes per family and a higher proportion of persons in white-collar occupational statuses; they spend proportionally more on schools, and in general have a higher level of living than do nonmetropolitan communities of like size. (Ogburn, 1937)

Several studies indicate that migration to the suburbs is motivated by the desire for primary group interaction and higher level of living, while still being able to work at urban occupation and procure urban services. A sample of informants who had moved from the central city of Milwaukee to unincorporated areas outside gave as the most important reasons the following, listed in order of their importance: "better for children," "less congested," "cleaner," "larger lot," "lower taxes," "forced to move," and "cheaper land." (Dewey, 1948) From interviews with suburban dwellers in the metropolitan area of Chicago, Wendell Bell (1956, p. 283) concludes

> If anonymity, impersonality, defilement of air and land by industry, apartment living, crowding, and constant nervous stimulation are inherent in "urbanism as a way of life," as some writers say, then the findings of this study necessitate the conclusion that the suburbanite *is* seeking an escape from many traditional aspects of city life. The suburbanite seems to be seeking a way of life in which family, community, and immediate enjoyment through living the "good life" are dominant and interdependent ends.

CONSEQUENCES OF METROPOLITAN EXPANSION

A number of serious problems result from the expansion of metropolitan areas. Some, such as those concerned with highways, streets, and parking space, are physical; some, such as those involved in industrial decentralization, are economic; others are governmental—taxation and schools; and some are exclusively sociological—housing and recreation problems, for example.

Transportion Problems

The automobile played a key part in the extension of suburbia and the development of metropolitan areas. Yet the automobile has created problems of congestion and pollution. These problems are becoming steadily more serious, for both the population and the number of cars per capita are increasing. Since 1930 the number of motor vehicles has multiplied three times as fast as the number of people. The number of registered motor vehicles in the U.S. in 1950 was 49 million; in 1960, 74 million; and in 1970, 109 million.

Superhighways facilitate the flow of traffic in the open country and usually bypass the core of the larger cities. Belt routes which circle downtown business districts also help reduce congestion in some areas, but the street congestion, parking problems, and pollution inside the central city are growing more serious. "The deficiency of parking space is more easily correctable than the acute highway congestion in and around urban centers. At the edge of the city limits the so-called modern highway degenerates, and the once broad expanse of adequate roadbeds narrows to nothing more than antiquated city streets." (Ingraham, 1957)

Economic Changes

Accompanying the growth of the suburbs has been the decentralization of retail business and industry. Shopping centers have spread to the fringes of larger urban communities or into the suburbs themselves. Factories, too, are rising in the suburbs of many metropolitan areas, though some localities make strenuous efforts, chiefly through zoning, to keep industrial plants out. The metropolitan fringe is particularly desirable for manufacturers who use long assembly lines since these require a great deal of space, and large tracts of low-cost land are not available in the central city.

The future advantages for industry and business in the suburbs are likely to be somewhat limited. The core cities tend to keep highly specialized service. Moreover, taxes in suburbia have continued to rise as a result of inflation and increased demands for police and fire protection, utilities, schools, roads, hospitals, and recreational facilities. Nevertheless, a marked movement back to the central cities does not appear likely in the future.

Educational Problems

One of the strong appeals of suburbia has been the fact that, for the most part, these communities had better teachers, newer and more modern school buildings, and, as a rule, higher educational standards than the central cities. But these very advantages have led to rapid growth in the suburbs, and this expansion has partially nullified the advantages. As suburban communities have mushroomed in size, school costs have risen; it has been more and more necessary to set up double sessions of classes; and there has been a mounting shortage of good teachers. In some sections of the country these difficulties have been met, in part, by consolidation of two or more school districts and by centralizing school facilities at key points. The threat of increases in taxes needed, however, has encouraged taxpayer "revolts" and community rejection of necessary programs for the extension of school facilities.

Housing Problems

As metropolitan areas have continued to increase in population and expand in space, there have been widespread efforts to clear slums, stop neighborhood deterioration, and initiate programs for orderly urban development. Within the central cities this has meant replacing slums with housing projects, both public and private, of "vertical design"—that is, multiple-storied apartments which permit a considerable density of population per unit of ground space. Such a development is the Corlears Hook section of New York City. At the time this project was undertaken, the existing tenements housed 878 families. The taller apartments which replaced them provide space for almost double that number of families. The vertical design in cities, however, is not without its limitations. Such construction invariably tends to aggravate traffic congestion and without provisions for security (i.e. doormen, security guards) may be related to escalating urban crime. Newman (1972) warns that such "high rise" buildings may prevent residents from securing control of their environments.

14-7 CHECKING IT OUT: A Plan to Recapture Urban Residential Areas from the Criminal

. . . The time has come to go back to first principles, to reexamine human habitat as it has evolved, to become attuned again to all the subtle devices invented over time and forgotten in our need and haste to house the many. For even within the widespread chaos of our cities, it is still possible to find isolated examples of viable living environments that are crime free, even when located in the highest crime precincts of cities. Architectural design—by the physical layout—can emphasize that an area is the shared extension of the private realm of a group of individuals. . .The form of buildings and their arrangement can either discourage or encourage people to take an active part in policing while they go about their daily business. "Policing" is not intended to evoke a paranoid vision but refers to the oldest concept in the Western political tradition: the responsibility of each citizen to ensure the functioning of the polis.

"Defensible space" is a surrogate term for the range of mechanisms—real and symbolic barriers, strongly defined areas of influence and improved opportunities for surveillance—that combine to bring an environment under the control of its residents. A defensible space is a living residential environment that can enhance the inhabitants' lives while providing security for their families, neighbors and friends. The public areas of a multifamily residential environment devoid of defensible space can make the act of going from street to apartment equivalent to running the gauntlet. The fear and uncertainty generated by living in such an environment can slowly eat away and eventually destroy the security and sanctity of the apartment unit itself. On the other hand, by grouping dwelling units to reinforce assocations of mutual benefit, by delineating paths of movement, by defining areas of activity for particular users by juxtaposing them with internal living areas, and by providing for natural opportunities for visual surveillance, architects can create a clear understanding of the function of a space, and who its users are and ought to be. This, in turn, can lead residents of all income levels to adopt extremely potent territorial attitudes and policing measures, which act as strong deterrents to potential criminals. . . .

. . . The 150 New York families trapped in apartments that open onto the double-loaded corridors of a 17-story high-rise building—whose elevators, fire stairs, hallways and roofs are freely roamed and ruled by criminals—find it hard to believe that the project across the street, composed of three-to-six-story buildings in which two or three families share a hallway and six to twelve an entrance, actually accommodates people at the same densities and could be built at the same cost. The families in the 17-story building are continually aware of the fact that they are the constant prey of criminals and are equally aware that things are a lot better across the street. They find it incomprehensible that the design differences between the two projects are predominantly the result of the whims of each particular designer. . . .

. . .It is possible to design a multi-family housing complex in which as low a number of units as possible share a common entry off the street. Designers can position units, windows, and entries, and prescribe paths of movement and areas of activity so as to provide inhabitants with continuous natural surveillance of the street and project grounds. The street comes under surveillance from the building, the building entries and lobbys under the surveillance of the street. As with the fortress, this design also provides security. But instead of relegating the responsibility to others, it is assumed by the residents in the natural flow of their everyday activities. Moreover, the building complex and the residents are integrated into the community. The complex protects the street as well as itself. The street life helps, in turn, to protect the complex. Instead of being an act of withdrawal, this design reinforces residents in their expression of concern for their own domain and for the streets and activity areas to which it is tied. In this way, residents do not achieve internal security at the expense of the surrounding area, but by insuring that the surrounding area is equally secure. Their concerns are in harmony with those of the community. This is defensible space design.

SOURCE: Oscar Newman, *Defensible Space* (New York: Macmillian, 1972). Reprinted by permission.

One of the most serious aspects of rapid suburban growth is the fact that cheap construction and crowding of single-family dwellings create neighborhoods which in a few years may take on the features of village slums. As one observer puts it,

> Assembly-line construction of thousands of one-family houses in a single development, smaller plots, increasing commutation rates, swamping of suburban facilities by newcomers, and poorly regulated commingling of residential and industrial use of former farmland has taken the promise out of the suburbs for many. . . .
>
> When blight starts spawning in a suburb it may spread faster than in a central city. This is particularly true in suburbs lacking either the plan or governmental structures to support parks, transit, sanitation, and other services. (Grutzner, 1957, p. 16)

Political Lag

Our governmental units are largely the products of historical factors sometimes no longer applicable to the modern metropolis, and recent cultural changes have made their inflexibility more apparent than ever. The emergence of politically independent suburbs and satellite cities has resulted in overlapping and often competing governmental units. More than three decades ago, a government report stated

> Overlapping . . . cities and suburbs of the metropolitan districts are several layers of different-sized, bewilderingly bounded governmental areas with separate legal and fiscal identities—counties, townships, school districts, and special districts of all kinds including sanitary, sewer, library, health, park, forest preserve, street lighting, utility, water and even mosquito abatement districts.
>
> While metropolitan life overflows the artificial network of urban boundary lines, each little bailiwick of government preserves its independent island of authority, with odd results. . . . Criminals hop over jurisdictional lines which local police dare not cross without elaborate devices for administrative coordination which are only now beginning to develop.
>
> Similarly, urban planning, highway construction, transport facilities, parks and recreational preserves too frequently must await the pleasure of minor suburbs. . . . Equally serious is the political indifference and neglect arising from the retirement into the suburbs of large blocs of urban citizenry who . . . lose all civic concern in the city governing the core of their urban community. . . . (National Resources Committee, 1939)

Various means have been used to eliminate at least some of the most flagrant overlapping. The interplay of state and federal rights has led to the setting up of joint boards for certain administrative functions. Such an agency is the Port of New York Authority, which has charge of the bridges and tunnels that connect New York and New Jersey. It also manages various airports, bus and truck terminals, and certain shipping and storage facilities. In some instances—in Denver, Colorado, for example—city and county governments have been merged. Separate cities have been federated: the present City of New York came about from the unification of the five boroughs in 1898. No doubt the coming decades will see increased coordination among government agencies in our metropolitan areas.

In many instances the metropolitan area reaches out to include a very extensive hinterland, so that the problems of the metropolitan areas—in the narrow sense—merge into those of still larger and more extensive regions.

REGIONS

Large regional areas often possess considerable geographic and cultural unity where there is a correlation between geographic homogeneity and patterns or subculture. A region may be described in terms of the following three criteria: (1) There is a physiographic foundation in climate, topography, natural resources, and plants and animals. (2) There are always basic economic patterns linked to these "natural" environmental elements: for example, the ship-building, importing, exporting, and fishing of the New England coast, or the cotton and rice economy of the Mississippi Delta. (3) The people in the region tend in time to take on certain distinctive patterns of thinking and behaving. Because of their shared experiences and activities, they develop a set of shared, learned behaviors peculiar to their area—a regional subculture.

There may or may not be some governmental counterpart to the region. In the United States, region is recognized only informally in politics, as when the "Southern bloc" of Senators holds a policy meeting, or when the governors of the Appalachian region discuss their common problems with the President. France, in contrast, is a country where, in spite of a strong central government, regions have been linked rather closely with provincial and local administrations. (Hintze, 1934) On the international scene, large "natural" regions have often been cut up by political states which have periodically struggled for full control of these areas. The Ruhr and Saar valleys in Europe are good examples.

Regionalism

The word *regionalism* refers sometimes to a theory of, and sometimes to an action program regarding, the place of the region in national and international affairs. Some persons concerned with national planning have characterized regionalism as "a clustering of environmental, economic, social, and governmental factors to such an extent that a distinct consciousness of separate identity within the whole, a need for autonomous planning, a manifestation of cultural peculiarities, and a desire for administrative freedom are theoretically recognized and actually put into effect." (National Resources Committee, 1935)

Regionalism arose in France and elsewhere as a reaction to centralization of economic and political power. In the United States, on the contrary, it seems to have emerged in part from felt social differences, in part as a counteraction to the serious interstate barriers to economic and other unification of larger "natural" areas.

American Regions

Regional differences in the United States were apparent almost from the beginning of the country's history. The conflict between the South and the rest of the nation is often ascribed to political differences, notably to the degree of emphasis on states' rights, but this ignores other factors—geographic, economic, and cultural—which were correlated with political conflict. The climate which allowed a plantation economy to flourish in the South, the stratification system of slaves and an ascribed aristocracy which accompanied that plantation economy—these regional differences divided the country, and the political views of the industrial North and the plantation South were more symptom than cause of regional conflict. Important as political forces are, they do not operate independently of economic and other societal conditions.

The United States has three large physiographic regions: the rough mountains and desert of the West, the Mississippi-Missouri-Ohio drainage basin, the lesser eastern mountains with their coastal plain. These three great regions subdivide into small agricultural regions determined by the length of the growing season and the amount of rainfall. The principal industrial regions are in the Northeast, in the Great Lakes states, in scattered sections of the South, and increasingly in the Pacific states. Naturally, the economic attractiveness of a region for industry depends on a number of factors: availability of raw materials and labor, sufficient power, convenience of transportation, and accessibility to markets. The extension of commercialized and mechanized farming, the decrease in proportion of the population engaged in agriculture and the concomitant increase in those employed in manufacturing and services, and the shifts of industries to new locations as new resources are found, all contribute to residential migration of the population.

INTERPRETIVE SUMMARY

The distinction between rural and urban societies made earlier is an important and useful distinction for ecologists and other students of the spatial distribution of human groups and institutions. Primary agricultural societies are classified according to the degree of centralization of residential and service areas. The plantation and its variations are distinguished from other agricultural communities by their "big business" aspects which lead to unique patterns of community contact and stratification systems.

Historically, cities have tended to locate at important trade crossroads and to develop in axial or radial fashion, following the natural topography except as people modified the pattern. Well-located, industrialized cities grow especially quickly; for example, in the United States, a relatively small number of states have a high proportion of large cities. Business and service areas in the city tend to become centralized until land in the main area becomes so expensive and access to the areas so difficult that decentralization sets in. Industries, shopping areas, and whole suburbs may move to the periphery of the city bringing the city's ways with them. Cities tend to be structured in terms of concentric zones, multiple nuclei, or sectors.

The United States is characterized by an increasing number of metropolitan areas and an increasing number of people in such areas. Most of the increase has been in suburban areas. Such areas may have an industrial, commerical, or residential orientation, but in any case the consequence is that the values and behavior patterns of city dwellers are extended to ever-widening areas.

Metropolitan expansion has been accompanied by a number of problems including traffic congestion, pollution, inadequate mass transit systems, and conflicts between the various political divisions of the city that lead to overlap and lack of effective coordination in the provision of public services.

Metropolitan areas, and indeed all areas in the United States, belong to larger areas called regions. The three major regions of the United States have distinct physical environments, economic patterns, and subcultural characteristics. In many societies, region is recognized as a basic political and administrative unit. In the United States, there have been some attempts at regional administration, but economic and other problems still tend to be treated at the local, state, or federal level.

QUESTIONS

1. What factors lead to the development of slums within cities? Within suburbs?
2. Which ecological pattern best describes the city in which or near which you live (i.e., concentric, sector zone)? Trace the growth pattern of this city.
3. Describe some ecological patterns found in rural communities (i.e., the agricultural village).
4. Why is urban planning so difficult? How can urban planners achieve more success as they confront the future?

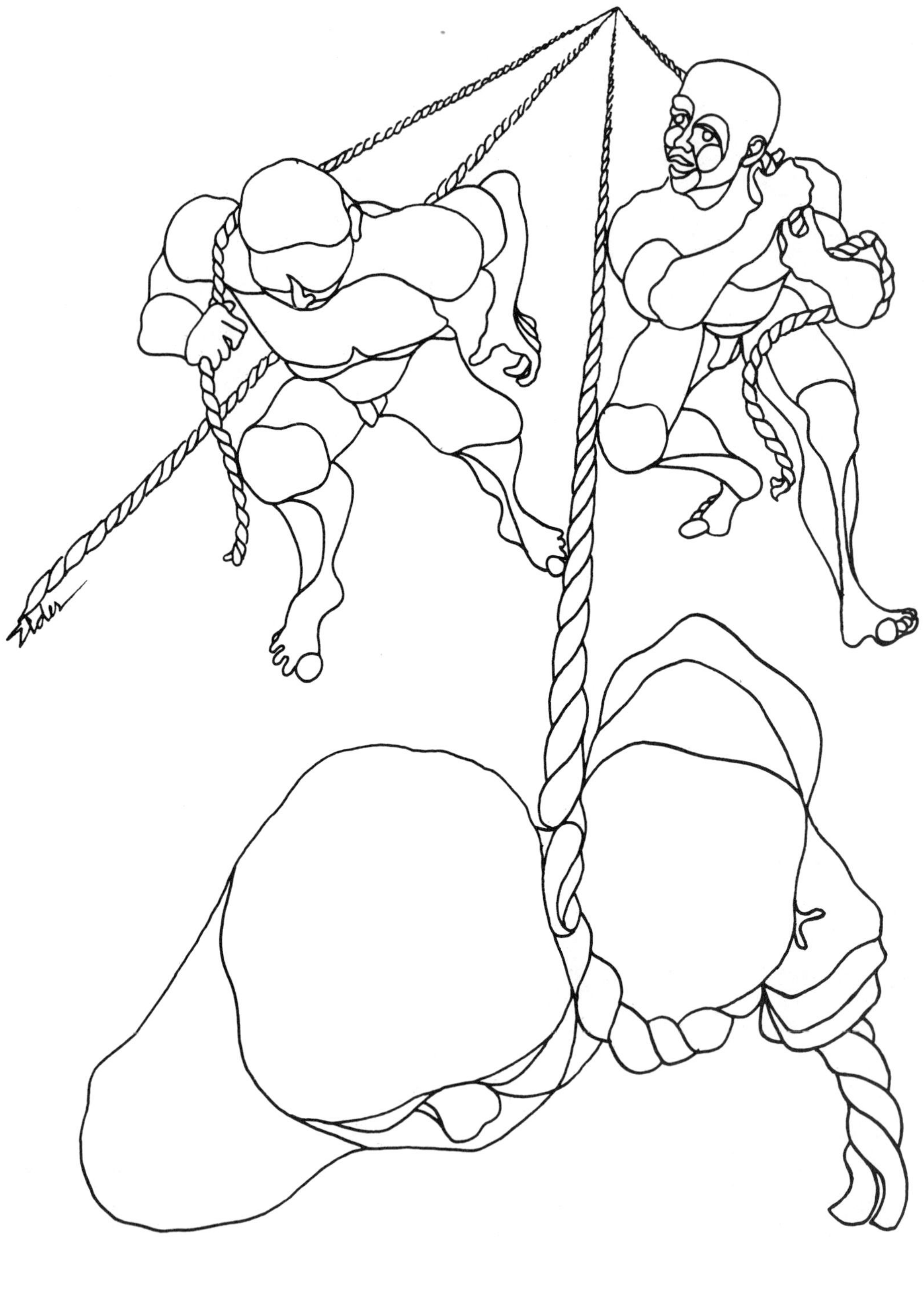

15

Economy and Society

In folk societies (the Gemeinschaft) there typically is no formal organization of economic endeavor. That is, there are no secondary groups, such as labor unions or manufacturing corporations, whose chief reason for being is related to the production and distribution of goods and services. In a folk society, it is more likely that the economic function will be performed by a group already in existence than by one created especially for that purpose. Ordinarily, the economic institution is just one of the many sets of norms which define the familial roles. A father fishes because one of a father's duties is to provide food for his family, not because he is an employee of the Apex Seafood Corporation.

The form of property ownership varies from society to society. In some societies it may be divided among members according to some ranking system by age, sex, and social position. In other societies, individuals considered responsible for creating an item may be recognized as entitled to own it. The development of Western capitalism has gone through certain phases which reflect the shift from a primary-group organization of society to an industrialized, impersonal mass society and culture. Capital is wealth devoted to the production of commodities or services. The accumulation of capital depends on some form of abstinence, some restraint of the impulse to consume goods at once. Long ago people learned to forego immediate consumption so that they might secure more goods at a later time. Even in nonindustrial economies, people save meat they might otherwise eat in order to use it for bait to trap more meat.

Whether or not an item is capital is determined by the use to which it is put. Coal burned in a grate to heat a living room is a consumer's good; used in a blast furnace in making steel, it is a capital good. Capital or producer's goods are easily distinguishable in machines, plants, railroad equipment, and the like. A box of breakfast cereal and a dress are obviously consumer's goods when they are in the hands of those who actually will make use of them.

ECONOMIC STRUCTURES

One of the most important changes in the transition from folk to urban society is the change from status to contract. In medieval times the serfs were bound to the land because of their status, because of who they were. A baron was a baron

15-1 CHECKING IT OUT: From Status to Contact—From Craft Manufacture to Factory

[In] the so-called "putting out" system [which preceded the "Industrial Revolution"] a merchant or group of merchants undertook to organize and finance certain production. The actual techniques of production were unchanged; craftsmen worked at their traditional tasks in a familiar shop environment, or farm families plied their household crafts, without any direct or regular supervision from the merchant-employer who hired their services and supplied materials. In craft manufacture, relations between masters and servants were personal and close. Though the master was senior, he too must conform to the custom and opinion of his peers: he worked with his journeymen and apprentices in an avuncular if not paternal fashion. The latter were protected in their ascribed status by craft tradition and local usage. Unmarried dependents lived in domestic quarters, taking their meals at the place of work. The journeyman could aspire to his own premises and elevation to a master's rank. He might cherish designs on his master's daughter and thereby inherit the shop and its good will. The pace of work and the job routine accorded with this intimate round of everyday life. But as the master withdraws from the shop, as the numbers of journeymen increase and their labor is casualized, so the establishment is more of a factory. Work discipline is less habitual and more contrived: rules and regulations become impersonal and objective. The master departs from the center of the scene, one eye is fixed on the employees, the other on competitors. The position of the journeyman is correspondingly reduced, his status lowered. . . .

It is easy to romanticize a golden age of the crafts before the hectic pace of the machine or the factory's insistent whistle. There is a familiar image of the benign master guiding his trusty servants through their daily tasks with youthful novices romping at their feet. It was never like this. But, leaving aside the tyrannical masters, sullen journeymen, and cringing apprentices, craft and merchant-employer organizations functioned within the accepted custom and domesticity of their less hurried age. The factory brought a furious pace and shaped a relentless discipline, broken only when the crude machines fell apart or the waters ceased to flow. As more processes were integrated under one roof and when, during the industrial revolution, the factory moved into town, men found themselves living in a stark and unfamiliar world. The essential but elusive quality of the factory seems to reside in the relations of employer and employed and in the style of job routine. . . .

SOURCE: Eric E. Lampard, *Industrial Revolution: Interpretations and Perspectives* (Washington, D.C.: American Historical Association, 1957), pp. 24–25.

for the same reason: his grandfather had been a baron, and it was his right. The serfs owed him certain obligations and he owed them certain obligations, not because of some peculiar training they had had, not because of achievement, but because each man was born into his status. The whole society was structured on ascribed statuses.

From Status to Contract

By the time the cottagers were moved into town to work in factories, this structure was crumbling. No longer did people owe these kinds of obligations simply because of the positions they occupied. The nearest thing to the old system in an industrial situation is the small one-company town that survives for generations. Here the owner is the grandson of the original owner; the odds are that the foreman is the grandson of the original foreman and that many of the laborers are grandchildren of the original laborers. Everybody knows everybody else; people speak to one another on the street; and everybody knows what church everybody goes to and whose daughter is being courted by whose son. Suppose a worker in this kind of situation falls ill. There is no unemployment compensation. But none is needed, because a system of mutual obligation exists. When a man is ill, the owner's wife comes by with a basket of groceries and asks if there is anything she can do to help, and a couple of people who work with him will have their wives or daughters over helping nurse him. When he has recovered, he returns to his job. This is a system of mutual obligations. In a larger economy, in which most people work for big organizations, contracts are substituted for this kind of status system. Wherever there is a social need which the baron would have met for the serfs or the serfs would have filled for one another, the trend is toward contracting an obligation.

We are no longer a society of rural villages and independent entrepreneurs. The economic and political institutions of an urban-industrial society are inextricably interwoven because, in the shift from status to contract as a principle of social organization, a wage contract alone replaces only a small part of the total system of mutual obligations. The history of our learning to live with urbanization and industrialization is a history of the process of negotiating supplementary contracts. We start with a wage contract, but we supplement it with a Social Security contract, an unemployment insurance contract, and so on. This is the method which industrial societies—democratic or totalitarian, capitalist or socialist—have devised as a substitute for the mutual-obligation system found where institutions tend to be coterminous—where familial, economic, and political functions derive from the same group.

The economic institutions of modern states are generally labeled "capitalist" or "socialist" according to whether or not the state controls the capital goods. A society in which most of the capital goods are owned and controlled by individuals is called capitalist; when the state takes over ownership and control of capital goods, the economic structure is said to be socialist. The two may be (and usually are) some combination.

The Marxist Analysis of Capitalist Society

Karl Marx wanted to revolutionize human society. He exhibited all the zeal of the reformer in his desire to make the world a better place. So in his monumental work *Das Kapital,* he began by analyzing the history of human society; then he examined contemporary Western society and the way it functioned. Ultimately, using the past as a guide, he sought to predict the direction that industrial societies would take. Because Marx saw himself as a theorist of the philosophy of history and an economic theorist, he was interested in discovering the general laws governing the economic development of societies. This attempt to generalize, to uncover underlying principles or laws, is a legitimate pursuit for the social as well as the physical scientist. Marx's analysis of the historical process underlying the economic development of societies reveals a dialectical process—thesis, antithesis, synthesis (see Chapter 1)—which he accepted as a law. Marx had borrowed the dialectical scheme from the German philosopher

15-2 CHECKING IT OUT: A Contribution to the Critique of Political Economy

. . . The mode of production in material life determines the general character of the social, political and spiritual processes of life. It is not the consciousness of men that determines their existence, but, on the contrary, their social existence determines their consciousness. At a certain stage in their development, the material forces of production in society come in conflict with the existing relations of production or—what is but a legal expression for the same thing—with the property relations within which they had been at work before. From forms of development of the forces of production these relations turn into their fetters. Then comes the period of social revolution. . . .

. . . No social order ever disappears before all the productive forces, for which there is room in it, have been developed; and new higher relations of production never appear before the material conditions of their existence have matured in the womb of the old society. Therefore, mankind always takes up only such problems as it can solve; since, looking at the matter more closely, we will always find that the problem itself arises only when the material conditions necessary for its solution already exist or are at least in the process of formation.

SOURCE: Karl Marx, *A Contribution to the Critique of Political Economy* (Chicago: Charles Kerr & Co., 1918), pp. 11–12.

Hegel. However, he rejected Hegel's assumptions about the forces that cause the process to begin. Marx substituted *economic forces* for Hegel's use of *ideas* as the generating forces of the dialectical process. He proposed, instead, that the dialectical process is generated within the economic structures of society. It is possible to tie together the sociological, the historical, and the economic elements of his theory in the following way:

Economic Determinism Marx was convinced that economic factors determine social behavior in Western society, because the economic institution was the dominant social institution, which influenced the character of all others (e.g. the family, education, the polity, religion). In his lifetime, the dominant economic institution was capitalism and Marx's harsh criticism of capitalism stems largely from his view of human beings as rational individuals with the capacity for creativity and productivity. Capitalism was distorting important social relationships; and drastic remedies were needed to make life in society move productive and meaningful for all.

The Production of Commodities Before Capitalism The basic problem in capitalistic society lay in the capital-labor relationship. In earlier societies, for example, during feudalism, those who labored and produced commodities (cloth, jewelry) might produce in order to meet personal needs, or might produce more than enough in order to exchange the surplus for other desirable items. We may then say that commodities can be produced for use or produced for exchange. The *exchange value* of a product is generally related to the labor involved in producing it for a market. Thus the exchange value of coal, which must be dug out of the earth, is different from granite, which may be taken from the earth's surface. In earlier societies, the tradesman acted as intermediary and facilitated the exchange of commodities with the expectation of making money. Marx gives the example of the tradesman who in the seventeenth century, sold the wool to the weavers, and then bought their products. Here the weavers remained independent, each in his little workshop. (Marx, 1959) Yet the economic order began to change as the tradesman took control of the production process. The tradesman was now the capitalist who owned the looms that the weaver worked on. The worker had then lost control of the means of production (tools, machines). If exchange value was associated with the production of commodities for markets, *surplus value* was now dominant, as a new social arrangement appeared in which capitalists controlled the labor power of workers.

Labor and the Marxist Model of Economic Organization The work situation had a special meaning for Marx. Thus the changing conditions, under which workers had lost their independence, had dramatic implications. This was because Marx saw labor as a central activity of human life. It was through labor that the individual realized his or her human potential. Social relationships grew out of labor activities. Therefore, there should be joy in work experiences. However, the new relationship of the worker to the capitalist was changing the character of labor. There were now two social classes whose members functioned as the major forces in production. They were the capitalist class or bourgeoisie, who owned and controlled the means of production (factories, technology) and thereby dominated capitalistic society. There was also the worker class or proletariat, the disadvantaged group, dominated primarily by an exploitive bourgeoisie that bought and sold their workers' labor-power in return for inadequate wages. The enormous profits available to the owners of the means of production resulted from the fact that the labor-power of the workers produced more than was necessary for the maintenance of the workers. This situation has led to the alienation of the workers.

Alienation Alienation occurs when what the worker has created, through his actions, comes to dominate him. In the past, our need for food, clothing, and shelter provided the reason for labor. With industrialization, our need for such commodities has created a need for wages, not labor. We need wages to get commodities. Also the wage-laborer has lost control of a once formidable labor-power. The industrial worker, unlike the craftsman of the feudal society, had been increasingly separated from the means of production (tools, technology) which were no longer owned or controlled by the worker. Because of the reliance on machinery, because of the division of labor (e.g., the assembly-line process), the work process had lost its special satisfactions. The worker had become "an appendage of the machine." Marx described the situation in the following way:

> Modern industry has converted the little workshop of the patriarchal master into the great factory of the industrial capitalist. Masses of laborers, crowded into factories, are organized like soldiers.... Not only are they the slaves of the bourgeois class and of the bourgeois state, they are daily and hourly enslaved by the machine, by the overlooker, and, above all by the bourgeois manufacturer himself. The more openly this despotism proclaims gain to be its end and aim, the more petty, the more hateful and the more embittering it is. (*Manifesto,* p. 328)

The Reorganization of the Economic Structure Marx, the social reformer, sought to point out the direction of change that industrial societies must take if the quality of life is to change for the proletariat. If meaningful human progress is to take place, "the dictatorship of the bourgeoisie" must be replaced by "the dictatorship of the proletariat." (Lichtheim, 1969, p. 87) By this Marx meant that only through the rise to power of the proletariat could a total reorganization of the economic structure take place. This social change could only occur after a revolutionary struggle. Marx hypothesized that revolutionary struggles were inevitable in industrial societies in which the dominant class thrived as a result of the exploitation of the working class. In the communist society that would eventually develop after the revolutionary struggle, there would be no social classes, hence no class conflicts. Only where there were no classes could social evolution take place without revolution.

Formal Structures in Capitalistic Society

Varieties of Property Ownership One highly important form of ownership and control is *individual (or sole) proprietorship.* As capitalist enterprises expanded, one person joined with another and systems of partnership arose. This enabled two or more individuals to pool their resources, capital, and labor with a view toward making a profit. Sociologically, a *partnership* represents a particular form of cooperation.

In time, a third kind of ownership, the economic **corporation**, emerged. As a kind of secondary group, the corporation enables individuals to act under a common name in order to own, hold, and manage property or an enterprise. The benefits of such an operation are distributed among the associated stockholders. The corporation operates under a charter from the state, which defines its rights, duties, and obligations. The individual stockholder ordinarily is not liable for the debts of the corporation, and the life of the corporation is usually independent of the lives of those who own the stock.

There is perhaps no other phenomenon of our time that typifies mass society more adequately than the corporation. Although recognized in law as a legal unit with many of the rights and duties of an individual, it operates in complete anonymity and impersonality. While it may enter into a contract, the controls which may be exercised over it are not exactly those that society may exercise over an individual. A corporation may be fined or enjoined by the courts, but it cannot be put in jail; nor can it suffer from a sense of guilt and conscience. Yet corporations are the property of multiple individuals, and particular persons run them. (As seen in 1961, though a corporation cannot be put in jail, the individuals who run it can be, and several officials of General Electric were so punished for price-fixing.) They make decisions on policy and practice and hence affect the lives of workers, consumers, and many others. In fact, present-day corporate organization influences productive capacity, the financial system, the employment of labor, and the buying habits of consumers.

The corporation is not confined to capitalistic economies; it is found also under socialism. For example, the nationalization of banking and coal mining in Britain modified only slightly the essential corporate forms of organization and control of these enterprises. The Soviet Union has developed most of its state-controlled and state-managed economy along corporate lines.

The Dominance of the Corporation

In the United States, 95 per cent of the business firms have fewer than 20 employees. A glance at this statistic might lead one to the conclusion that small businesses dominate the economy, but this is not true. The firms with fewer than

20 employees account for less than one-fourth of the wage and salaried workers in the economy. The other three-fourths are employed by the corporate giants which comprise only 5 per cent of the total number of firms. The size and wealth of these mammoth organizations has much to do with the influence that they wield in domestic and foreign economies and in national and international politics. For example, the top 100 industrial corporations together employed 8,679,000 people in 1975. In addition, they revealed assets totaling more than 400 billion dollars and net incomes of 27 billion dollars (*Statistical Abstracts,* 1977). Such incredible profits cause these 100 corporations (out of almost 2 million in the U.S.) to own more than half of the manufacturing assets in this country.

One classic study of corporations reported that as of January 1, 1930, the 200 largest corporations (each with assets of 90 million dollars or more), other than banks, controlled nearly one-half the total corporate wealth, two-fifths of total business wealth (other than banking), and somewhat more that one-fifth of all the national wealth. (A. A. Berle and G. C. Means, 1933) Even today if we define as "small" those companies with assets of less than a million dollars, the small companies have less than 13 per cent of the market. Small companies operate on a smaller profit margin than large companies. Furthermore, companies with fewer than 500 employees (and that includes over 99 per cent of the firms) receive less than 20 per cent of the military contracts from the federal government. Finally, one should note that, in all three of these areas—per cent of market, margin of profit, and share of military contracts from the Department of Defense—the trend seems to be running against the small firm. Economic concentration in manufacturing has increased substantially during the past twenty years.

15-3 CHECKING IT OUT: Ralph Nader on Corporate Power

The management of power in a complex society is built around institutions. In our country, the most enduring, coordinated and generic manager of power is the corporate institution. Controlling great wealth and metabolized by the most fungible of factors—the dollar—the modern corporation possesses a formidable unity of motivation and action with great stamina. Much of what passes as governmental power is derivative of corporate power whose advocacy or sufference defines much of the direction and deployment of government activity. The federal government is replete with supportive programs—subsidies, research, promotional, contracts, tax privileges, protections from competition—which flow regularly into the corporate mission of profit and sales maximization. So much of government resources is allocated and so much government authority is utilized to transfer public wealth into corporate coffers that Washington can be fairly described as a bustling bazaar of accounts receivable for industry-commerce.

It is important to recognize the multiple approaches to power which characterize the modern corporation, particularly the top two hundred companies that lead the ecomony. With limited liability for its owners and diffused responsibility of officers and directors, the corporation derives its strength at the outset from what it gets, not from what it receives. Its inherently acquisitive nature permits easy justification for wide discretion as to when and how to use or not to use the many permutations of its power. Critical impacts on other people and institutions proceed both from the use and non-use of corporate power. How clear have been the consequences, for example, of the historic non-use of insurance industry leverage vis-a-vis the auto industry's hazardous vehicle designs.

The non-use of legitimate power has rarely been popularly evaluated for accountability. So many direct or indirect corporate impacts are of this order. Introducing the internal combustion engine early in the century for mass production in automobiles did not cause much of an air pollution problem. Year after year of rising automotive production with 100 million motor vehicles on the road, the same engine becomes a health menace to Americans. Inaction in 1910 and inaction in 1970 toward the same engine type are completely different displays of corporate behavior. Different magnitudes of hazards to health and property and greatly enhanced industrial capability produce vastly different ethical conclusions. As Alfred North Whitehead wrote: "Duty arises from our potential control over the course of events. Where attainable knowledge could have changed the issue, ignorance has the guilt of vice."

SOURCE: Morton Mintz and Jerry S. Cohen, *America, Inc.* (New York: Dial Press, 1971), Introduction.

Corporate Control Corporate concentration has been accompanied by a separation of ownership from control in U.S. industry. Most of the functions which used to be performed by an entrepreneur—an owner-proprietor—are now performed by a salaried manager. The large individual business is owned, not by one man who can run it but, as some of the institutional advertising tells us, by millions of people. The stockholders among whom this diversified ownership is spread do control their companies.But they delegate control of the corporation to salaried management. The *owners* of the corporation do not dominate it as individuals. As a matter of fact, we have here a sort of collectivization of ownership. It is voluntary and so is extremely different from state collectivization; but it is collectivization nonetheless. In some respects, the differences in the occupational role of the manager of a Soviet factory and of a U.S. factory are not as extreme as they seem at first glance. Modern industrial systems, no matter what their economic norms and political goals, are staffed and run by salaried managers.

The modern type of managerial control has produced distinctive variations within the corporate world. One of these is the phenomenon of "interlocking directorates," where the same top-level executives serve on the boards of directors of many powerful corporations. Their presence in key policy-making positions throughout many industries gives them unique leverage and power.

A second economic form which has developed in recent years is the *conglomerate,* a super corporation made up of a variety of interlocking corporations of different kinds, producing different products and services. The fact of diversity offers the conglomerate the prospect of continued profits though individual companies might falter. A disturbing extension of the conglomerate is the *multinational corporation,* which spans whole societies in its drive for economic dominance. Just as conglomerates may be composed of many corporations, such entities may reach around the world, buying foreign companies, acquiring raw materials in one nation to process in another. ITT (International Telephone and Telegraph) has 400,000 employees operating in 93 countries. Because multinational corporations like ITT have become so powerful internationally, they can operate outside the legal control of any one country and may attempt to direct the political affairs of nations.

Economic Interdependence

The economic interdependence of modern nations has been greatly increased by the rise and spread of industry, which requires raw materials from widely scattered sources. In the century preceding World War I a sort of economic world order arose despite the persistence in some nations of tariffs and other limitations on free trade. The restrictive nature of much of the world's trade is related to shifts in the balance of political power which have been under way for some time. Nonetheless, economic interdependence is clear. People purchase and use articles of food, clothes, implements, tools, machines, and recreational objects that are made of raw materials from all over the world. One's breakfast coffee, tea, or cocoa is imported, as are the tin and bauxite which go into kitchen utensils used in preparing the meal. People ride to work in motor vehicles that could not be made without imported tin, bauxite, chromium, and rubber.

The United States, for example, exports great quantities of coal, copper, gypsum, lead, petroleum, phosphate, rock, silver, and zinc. So too, meats, dairy products, apples, tobacco, wheat, and lumber are shipped abroad in large quantities. Of manufactured articles the most important exports are automobiles, electrical machinery, engines, hardware, farm equipment, sewing machines, firearms, cotton goods, motion pictures, and rubber products.

One instance of the extent of economic interdependence is the extensive United States investment in Latin America. In one sense, it is a fiction to speak of "the" economy of "a" society when the economies of many societies are intertwined. What happens to production or to the market in one society is bound to have repercussions in other societies.

In order to move the needed goods and services from region to region and from country to country, the world is covered with a network of land, sea, and air transport and communication lines. The story of air transport is striking. In the two decades separating the two world wars, airplane lines reached into every part of the globe. Almost overnight remote regions came within relatively easy flying distance. In 1947 an aviation treaty established the International Civil Aviation Organization, with 26 nations participating. The institution set up basic standards for global air traffic.

The international postal service, known as the Universal Postal Union, was established in 1874 and, except during wartime, embraces practically the entire habitable globe in a single worldwide postal area. The development of radio communication followed a somewhat similar course. After early monopolistic trends, international agreements were made regarding commercial radio and the use of radio in shipping. Since World War II, television has become not only commerically but politically one of the most important means of communication to the masses.

The telephone and, later, the radio-telephone have made possible worldwide conversation. The Americas have taken the lead in the international use of the telephone. As early as 1938, through a combination of radio, cables, and land transmission lines, the United States could reach every continent and the major islands of the sea by means of 74 different telephone circuits.

It is evident from all this that, in transportation of raw materials and manufactured goods and in communications, the world has moved toward an international order. In fact, we find a rather paradoxical situation in which we have international traffic and communication rules but national ownership and national control determining the final decisions. The isolationism which has become linked to nationalism stands in sharp contrast with the interdependence of economic structures and functions.

THE INDUSTRIAL GROUP AS A COMMUNITY

Large organizations, whether they are voluntary associations, business firms, or whole societies, eventually reach a critical point of complexity where they assume formally organized hierarchical structures. Such structures, of course, create more rigidly specified roles. Adolph Berle, Jr. (1959) called attention to a problem that occurs when a conflict in values leads to friction between the economic institution and the maintenance of a sense of purpose. Ownership and proprietorship, which have traditionally been parallel, are becoming separate occupational specialties. This trend is probably the source of much of the complaining about "the organization man"—when a complex organization has socialized replacements to perform its specialized roles, it is not likely to be tolerant of deviance. While such a man has the prestige that goes along with wearing a white collar, there are plenty of white collars above him.

Situs

However, individuals have a way of "building in" compensations. Such a bureaucratic division of labor through a whole society leads to what some sociologists have called *situses*—sets of related occupational specialties arranged hierarchically and separated from other sets of related roles, which also are arranged in hierarchies. Each situs or family of related occupations builds up a set of norms peculiar to it. These occupational subcultures insulate their participants from the members of another situs. Doctors and nurses hold values not shared by railroaders and truck drivers; the occupational norms of longshoremen are not those of laboratory workers.

Societies with elaborate occupational differentiation, therefore, while bound together by a common culture, are at the same time fragmented by occupational subcultures. People who share an occupational history develop norms, enforce an in-group ideology, and come to serve as a reference group for one another. We see this at its extreme when physicists from the Soviet Union and from the United States have more to talk about with one another than either group has with the farmers from its own country.

But role segmentalization is not synonymous with a fragmented social structure. The stuff of occupational subcultures can serve as the specialized urban-industrial worker's social substitute for community. Occupational codes can contribute to what Durkheim called organic solidarity; they can help replace the mechanical solidarity of the rural village. Occupational groups, with their shared values, can contribute to the sense of purpose which formerly was a function of the small community, or Gemeinschaft. Certainly the Industrial Revolution has brought drastic changes in economic institutions.

In economic organization as in other areas of social life, it is not always easy to separate formal from informal structures. In industrial groups, as elsewhere, the people who come to fill roles in the formal organization soon develop informal social relationships and groups that emerge within the industrial plant. A factory, department or other retail store, business office, or any other aggregate of individuals concerned with economic production or distribution develops many features of a community, though not all of them. Since the aim of the plant is narrower and more specialized than that of the community, and since its population consists only of members of the labor force, it necessarily lacks the breadth and scope of the community as usually defined. Yet in many of its features the resemblance is close. The factory, like the community, or Gemeinschaft, is characterized by a given locus, and certain functions are carried on by individuals in particular roles and statuses. In both cases—factory and community—some of the relations of individuals and groups are formal and institutionalized; others, of an informal sort, develop naturally from the very circumstance of people living or working together in close proximity.

The personnel have certain contractual relations to one another. The most obvious division is that between management and labor. The former may be the owner but under corporate organization is usually an agent of the owners. The relations of management to workers are those of graded authority and responsibility. Within this large framework there is a ranked status system. In management it ranges from the chief executive downward through subordinate management personnel to the foreman. Among the workers there are gradations in skill, seniority, and other accepted criteria of differentiation of role. These gradations are measurable not only in wages, working conditions, and various work privileges but in patterns of social interaction and socially shared definitions of the situation. For example, among railroaders, engineers and conductors are at the top of the prestige pyramid, section hands and repair workers are at the bottom.

Spatial arrangements are made in accordance with management's decisions as to what makes for highest industrial efficiency. Thus a plant has a certain ecology related to the roles of the various workers. To keep the plant operating successfully, all sorts of rules are laid down as to where to do one's job, skills expected, use of materials, avoidance of wastage and spoilage, compliance with safety measures, provision of light, ventilation, rest periods, devices for handling grievances and suggestions for improvement of product or working conditions, and so on.

Primary Relationships

On the informal side, workers tend to develop cliques or groupings among themselves depending largely on spatial proximity, similarity of work, and level of skill, especially as related to the status factor, commonality of outside interests, and other situations which serve to bring about associations not recognized in the formal organization of the plant as an economic unit. Such groupings may and often do result in certain informal status systems that may influence the morale of the workers.

For example, in spite of the rapid development of mechanization and even automation in industry, there are certain sections in which hard physical work is performed today under almost the same conditions as a century ago. One of these sections is dock work. H. J. Helle worked among longshoremen in five major European seaports in order to study hiring practices and the formation of groups in relation to the danger of accidents on the job. He used multiple-choice questionnaires to collect comparable data on "organization," "attitudes," and "accident rates" in the five ports. Where hiring procedures disregarded both friendship and antipathy among longshoremen by assigning workers to gangs according to their registration number, attitudes toward the work environment were comparatively negative and accident frequencies were high. Conversely, where longshoremen themselves had the opportunity to choose gang members and foremen and where association with able and popular foremen was related to good work performance, work attitudes were comparatively positive and accident rates were lower. (Helle, 1960)

Thus failure of management to take informal associations into account by using them or breaking them up in the interest of efficiency may result in loss of efficiency. These informal groupings are often powerful factors in influencing the level and amount of production. There are norms of plant performance involving

15-4 CHECKING IT OUT: Democratization of the Workplace

Changing attitudes that influence the function of managers result from changes in the economic, social, political, and technological environment.

The view that the manager has the right to set norms, standards, or objectives unilaterally has softened. Presently, managers are permitting nonmanagerial employees to establish group norms. Labor unions have inputs in the manager's decision process, for example. So do scientists, accountants, engineers, and other professionals.

The old attitude of managerial elitism is being eroded by an attitude of egalitarianism. Employees seek an equality of results in place of an equality of opportunity pertaining to employment, promotion, pay, health, and retirement. Employees seek rights based on being members of the community rather than rights based on individual productivity and property.

A prevailing attitude considers business both an economic and a social institution that should contribute to the quality of life in addition to providing goods, services, and employment. Consequently, employees must receive values and satisfactions from their work in addition to compensation.

SOURCE: John A. Mee, "Understanding the Attitudes of Today's Employees: An Interview With Dr. John Mee," *Nation's Business,* 64, 1976, p. 24.

how much work to do for a day's pay, avoidance of speed-up which may affect other workers' wages, protection of one another from foremen in matters involving wastage and spoilage of machines or materials, and many other features of work activity. Failure to conform to these norms usually leads to various forms of punishment: ridicule, ostracism, and at times even bodily injury. However, managers today have actively begun to involve employees in decision-making about norms. (Argyle, 1970)

While such patterns, formal and informal, arise and continue in most plants, they are further influenced when labor unions are organized and collective bargaining comes into operation. Union contracts frequently not only act to modify the formal features of the plant in such matters as wage rates, hours, conditions of work, insurance benefits, amount of product to be turned out per worker per day, and so on, but also may influence the informal features of life in the plant by affecting status relations. And in plants not completely unionized, divisions of workers along lines of membership or nonmembership may make for conflict.

ECONOMIC FUNCTIONS

The essential function of the economic system is, of course, the production and distribution of goods and services. In even a very simple economy, such as one that requires only picking coconuts or catching fish, there is usually some organization in which roles are assigned. There is some normative order governing who gathers coconuts, who is responsible for dividing the catch of fish, at what age one is obligated or expected to enter the labor force and support oneself, what is to become of persons who are too old to gather their own food, and so on. This is simply another way of saying that one function of the economic system is division of labor.

The Division of Labor

The restriction or expansion of role differentiation depends on the complexity of the economic structure. A society which depends solely on hunting for its sustenance will have a relatively small number of economic roles. Not much economic differentiation can take place in a community where every able-bodied person must devote most of his waking hours to throwing spears at rabbits in order to keep from starving. A sedentary agrarian culture frees more people from full-time food production, allows some members the leisure to become priests or craftsmen, and generally implements differentiation of roles. In an urban, industrial society, the economy requires so many specialists and provides so many different roles that it becomes a major criterion for social stratification. One consequence of the economic structure is social stratification. While a small agricultural community is likely to rank its members on the basis of family lineage in industrialized societies position in the division of labor is a major basis of social rank.

The Distribution of Power

Like other social structures, the economic order has many consequences in addition to its manifest function of producing and distributing goods and services. Important among these is the effect which economic organization has on the distribution of political power. (Mills, 1956) One example of the potential of economic position as a political factor may be seen in the fact that more than 20 million Americans belong to labor unions. There is a high correlation between a state's having a low percentage of union members in its electorate and the likelihood that the state has a tradition both of conservative state administration and of sending conservative legislators to Congress. There is also a correlation between the personal wealth of legislators and their voting interests. Another example of association between economic position and politics is shown in the expenditures in national election campaigns. People with corporate interests, as well as those with labor interests, seem to have definite ideas as to which party best represents those interests. The Republican Party receives donations largely from persons with big business investments, while financial aid from organized labor goes usually in large part to the Democrats.

15-5 CHECKING IT OUT: Disinterested Representation?

Everyone "knows" that ours is the age of the limousine liberal. Conservatism, we've heard on all sides, is now the voice of the common people while social justice is a plaything of the privileged.

Vulgar Marxism, though, may better explain the conduct of the United States Senate than sophisticated "new majority" thought. For a recent study released by Ralph Nader's Citizen Action Group (CAG) confirms that the Senate remains a millionaire's club, a conservative club at that. CAG asked each Senator to estimate his personal wealth in one of five broad categories. Fifty-nine Senators replied; reasonable estimates of the worth of 19 Senators were calculated, "leaving 22 Senators for whom no realiable information was available." At least 21 Senators are millionaires; only five share the material condition of most Americans, i.e. of holding assets worth less than $50,000.

The following graph offers a breakdown of the political views of Senators at various levels of wealth, based on the 1975 ADA ratings for each group:

Wealth group	*# in Group*	*Average ADA rating, 1975*
under $50,000	5	92
$50,000-$250,000	30	59
$250,000-$500,000	18	53
$500,000-$1 million	4	53
$1 million or more	21	29

For every liberal millionaire like Ted Kennedy or Phil Hart, there are a half dozen James Eastlands, Barry Goldwaters and Russell Longs. And thanks to the Supreme Court ruling on the Campaign Reform Acts which restricts all donors in the amount they can give, except the candidates themselves, who may spend an unlimited amount in an attempt to be elected, we can expect the Senate to become an even more exclusive preserve of the wealthy.

Can we reasonably expect an assembly whose average member is worth half a million dollars to shift the economic burdens of our society? On the other hand, imagine the attitude of the Senate on tax reform if all Senators, not just five out of one hundred, owned as little as most of us do?

SOURCE: Jim Chapin, "The Rich Are Different," *Newsletter of the Democratic Left,* (November, 1976), IV, p. 3.

The fact that radio and television costs have constituted the largest single item of expenditure for both parties in recent Presidential election campaigns means that greater wealth gives greater opportunity to plead one's case before the electorate. In 1972, over 59.6 million dollars was spent for radio and television broadcasts in the primary and general elections. (*Congressional Quarterly,*

1973) To the extent that the mass media were molders of public opinion, wealth is power.

ECONOMIC PATTERNS IN THE UNITED STATES

The labor supply of any society consists of all its potential workers, male and female. At what age an individual is counted as a potential worker is a matter of cultural definition. For example, adolescents under 14 years of age are not considered to be in the labor force of the United States. Earlier, and still in some societies, younger children were considered part of the labor force. The actual *labor force* may be defined as that fraction of a population which is engaged in producing or distributing goods or services. Those persons temporarily unemployed are also included.

Composition of the Labor Force

In the United States the labor force in 1900 consisted of 29 million persons. In 1950 it was 63 million, and by 1977 it was 97 million. Not all people who are in the labor force are employed, however. In 1976, 7.7 per cent of the total labor force was out of work and among female, black, and young workers, unemployment ranged from 6 to 35 per cent.

15-6 CHECKING IT OUT: Labor Force Participation of Women, 1890–1977

	Per Cent of Women in Labor Force					
	Year					
Marital Status	*1890*	*1940*	*1950*	*1960*	*1970**	*1977*
Single	37	48	51	44	53	59
Married	5	17	25	32	41	47
No children under 18					41	45
Children aged 6–17					49	55
Children under age 6					29	39
Widowed or divorced	29	32	36	37	36	39
All women	18	27	31	35	43	48

* Women age 16 years and older. Per cents for 1890–1960 are based on data for persons 14 years and older.

SOURCE: U.S. Bureau of the Census, *Statistical Abstract of the United States,* 1978 (Washington, D.C.: U.S. Government Printing Office, 1978); and U.S. Bureau of the Census, *Historical Statistics of the United States, Colonial Times to 1957* (Washington, D.C.: U.S. Government Printing Office, 1960).

15-7 CHECKING IT OUT: The Most Outstanding Phenomenon of This Century

Eli Ginzberg, the Columbia University economist who is chairman of the National Commission for Manpower Policy, describes what is happening as "a revolution in the roles of women" that "will have an even greater impact than the rise of Communism and the development of nuclear energy."

"It is the single most outstanding phenomenon of this century," he said, "It is a worldwide phenomenon, an integral part of a changing economy and a changing society. Its secondary and tertiary consequences are really unchartable."

SOURCE: *The New York Times,* November 29, 1977, p. 7.

Females in the Labor Force One important feature of the U. S. labor force is the increasing number and proportion of workers who are women. In 1870 slightly less than 15 per cent of the work force was female; in 1970 there were 31 million women workers, 43 per cent of all women over the age of 15 and 37 per cent of the total work force. In 1890 just 18 per cent of women (over the age of 13) were part of the paid labor force. Most of the increase in the number of working women has been the increase in the proportion of married women who work for pay (in addition to housework). Five per cent of all married women were in the labor force in 1890, while one-fourth of all married women worked in 1950. In 1976, 45 per cent of all married women were employed in paid jobs.

The increase in the number of gainfully employed women—married, divorced, widowed, and single—is, of course, a major aspect of the changing status of women in our society. It should be noted, however, that women are generally discriminated against in employment and promotions, and women who are equally qualified generally receive less pay for their work than do men. Moreover, women contribute an enormous amount to the society in the form of unpaid (house) work, child care, and volunteer work for the community.

Age and the Labor Force

In many societies, particularly the agricultural, productive work begins fairly early in life: the child and the youth arc part of the labor force. In urban industrialized areas of the U. S., the work period tends to be confined to a rather limited part of the life cycle. With the extension of life expectancy, of course, the working period is much longer for the average person than it was in the past. But the age at which one enters the labor force is also later than heretofore. In fact, viewed historically, the most striking changes in the age composition of the labor force have been in the youngest and the oldest age groups. Both male and female child labor increased steadily from 1870 to 1900, when the number of children gainfully employed reached 1,250,000. In 1900 in the United States, 26 per cent

15-8 CHECKING IT OUT: Presence of Women in Selected Occupations as a Percentage of Totals (Figures are numbers of such workers, in thousands)

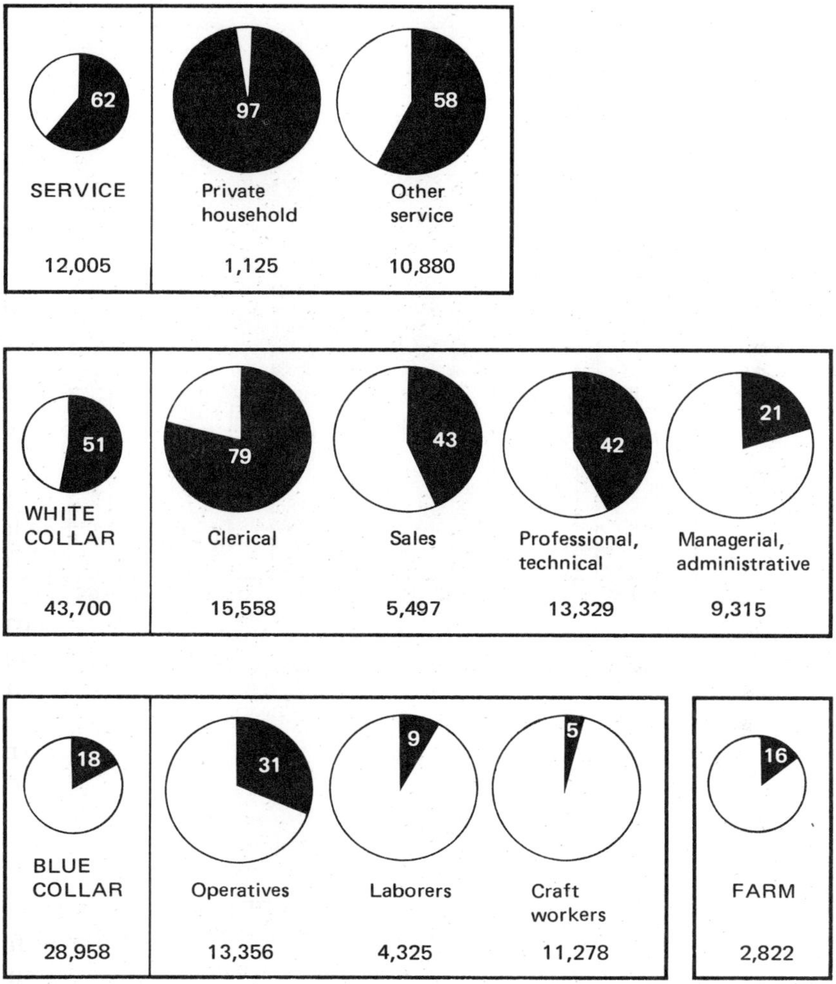

SOURCE: *The New York Times,* November 29, 1977, p. 7.

of all boys 10 to 15 years old and 10 per cent of all girls in this age bracket were in the working force. By 1940 the gainful employment of young children had practically ceased, and it remains rare today.

At the other end of the age scale, there has been a marked decrease—though less than in the case of children—in the percentage of men aged 65 and over in the

15-9 CHECKING IT OUT: Composition of the Labor Force by Age and Sex

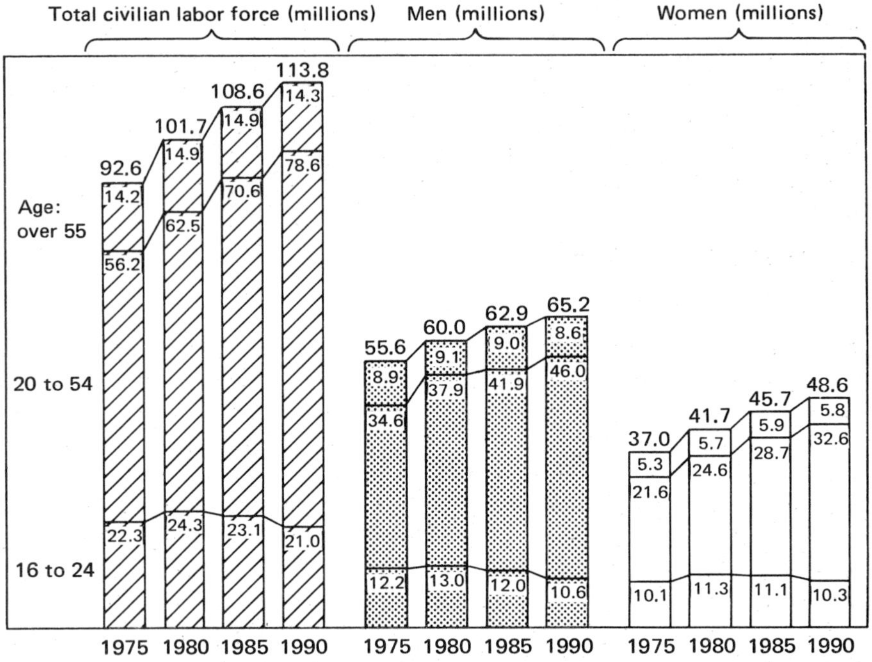

SOURCE: Eli Ginzberg, "The Job Problem," *Scientific American* (November, 1977), 237, p. 51.

labor force. The proportion of men 65 and older who are in the labor force has declined from more than two-thirds in 1890 to about 20 per cent in 1975. This long-term trend is correlated with the changing nature and declining importance of farming, an occupation adapted to the capabilities of both young and old; with the decrease in self-employment; and with the substitution of semiskilled for skilled labor. Moreover, the private pension programs and old-age security programs have made earlier retirement possible and many employers have made it compulsory.

One of the most significant features of the labor force in this country is the high number of persons in the 16-24 age group who are kept out of the working cohort because they remain in school. At no time in the history of mankind and in no other country has there been such a high proportion of individuals in this age bracket still engaged in getting an education. The situation reflects both our high prosperity and our great faith in the value of an education. Associated with the progressive aging of the population is the fact that our labor force has come to consist largely of individuals from 35 to 64 years old. This may change if current efforts to end forced retirement are successful.

The total amount of time expended in work in the United States society has also decreased for most workers. Not only are many workers limited to part-time work, but the length of the work week itself has been reduced over the years. The most reliable estimates are that the standard work week was 70 hours in 1850, 55 hours in 1900, and slightly less than 40 hours per week in 1970. A person steadily employed in a manufacturing plant in 1900 worked 3,000 hours a year. Today such a worker averages about 2,000 work hours a year.

Distribution of the Labor Force

In the last century there has been a major industrial shift from the production of goods to the production of services. In 1870 about three-fourths of the people in the labor force were engaged in producing tangible goods; by 1950 the proportion was less than half. The figures include employers and the self-employed, as well as wage and salary workers. This shift in the distribution of the labor force has been brought about largely by technological improvements. Heavy manual labor has given way to machine production, which has freed a larger portion of the labor force to run laundromats, rent out evening clothes, provide package delivery services, give pedicures to French poodles, be tree surgeons or public stenographers—in short, to enter service industries.

Of course, agriculture too has become more mechanized. At the time the United States was founded, farming was the most important income-producing activity, and as recently as 1870 more than half the labor force was engaged in agriculture. Today farmers comprise only 3.3 per cent of the labor force. The trend in agriculture is toward fewer farmers and larger farms. Individuals who under other conditions might have been farmers are entering the urban labor force, particularly the service industries.

Since 1900 clerical workers in the labor force have increased nearly sixfold, professional and technical workers threefold, proprietors and managers twofold, and sales workers by almost one-half. Household workers declined 60 per cent, but other service workers, such as barbers, beauticians, cooks, firemen, janitors, policemen, and waitresses, have nearly tripled.

The nation's economy is less and less dependent on muscle power and more and more dependent on professional, technical, and clerical skills. The shift from brawn and manpower to education and brain power reflects a basic trend in American economic life.

Automation

Another economic trend with implications for the labor force is automation, which may be defined as mechanization to the point where machines run other machines. Most of our engineering technology in the last century and a half has been put to inventing and perfecting machines that produce a product—that is, production machines. It is only recently that machines have been developed that will do such formerly expensive and time-consuming tasks as quality testing and readjustment of the production line machine. With a whole factory automated, fixed capital will take on new meaning.

By the standards of an automated economy, the present fixed capital of the United States is inadequate. The Industrial Revolution is just beginning. The concept of fixed capital brings to mind huge factories, with big steel machines that cannot be picked up and moved. Think of the meaning of fixed capital when one machine is running another machine, so that the greatest expense is not turning out the product but stopping the machine. Here fixed capital reaches the point where the costliest thing one can do is cease production. A stable market, a steady demand, become essential.

ECONOMIC INSTITUTIONS

Competition is a basic value in American culture; there are norms structured around the value of competition in each basic institution. In courtship, young people compete for dates with the members of the opposite sex considered to be the most desirable. Through missionaries and revivals, churches compete for members. Major political offices are filled by the process of competition: office-seekers compete for popularity with the voters. In the area of socialization, we motivate children to learn by having them compete for grades.

Economic Competition

Economic competition is rivalry and struggle to get possession of those things that a given culture considers wealth. It is one phase of the larger universal struggle for goods, tangible and intangible. There exists, on the one hand, a limited resource, and, on the other, a population with a seemingly ever-increasing number of wants, both basic and culturally defined. The traditional view of economic competition assumes complete self-interest on the part of buyers and sellers. It takes for granted a rational judgment of wants and of the means of satisfying them. It postulates the principle that each person acts to get the most he or she can from others while giving as little of oneself as possible.

This view of competition clearly reflects the whole social-cultural period in which modern capitalism developed. Capitalism assumed a self-regulating interrelation of price, demand, and supply. This, in turn, rested on the simple notion of rational motivation directed "*to economizing* or *utility-maximizing* behavior" believed to flow directly "from the fact that human wants are comparatively unlimited in relation to the resources available for the satisfaction of such wants. (Spengler, 1940)

It was the contention of laissez-faire economists of the eighteenth and nineteenth centuries that the free flow of goods and services through rational and unhampered competition would result in the most efficient production and distribution of goods, capital, and labor supply—all to the ultimate benefit of the consumers. They fully believed in the competitive practice of their time—that the institutions of private property, contract, profit-making, and laissez-faire freedom of action were a true and objective operation of universal forces in nature and society.

Modern social psychology does not support this view of human behavior. People have impulses and interests that do not completely correspond to their rational needs. Political and religious views, class, and lifestyle also influence economic behavior. Love, sympathy, hatred, anxiety, and indifference, tied to irrational attitudes and values, enter into the economic choices people make.

Consumer Activity

The Effects of Advertising Modern technology and complex business enterprise have profoundly altered the market situation in which the ordinary consumer finds oneself. Such changes are due to mass production, to the disappearance of the earlier competitive pattern with the rise of many near-monopolies, to the shift from an agricultural to an industrial economy, to the high degree of division of labor, and to urban life. The consumer has become more and more dependent on the institutions of the market place. At any earlier date, say 1900, the ordinary person in a small town or rural trading center purchased goods that were usually of a quality not very difficult to determine. On the basis of what he could see, touch, or taste, he could decide whether or not to buy. Today in modern retailing the quality, durability, and utility of goods are not well standardized in relation to price. The research of consumers' testing agencies indicates that the less expensive of two competing products frequently is the one of higher quality. The more expensive product may capture a sizable share of the market, however, by skillful advertising and packaging. Advertising profoundly influences consumer preferences and habits of buying. Some advertising is useful in informing prospective buyers about available materials or services, but much of it is emotional and status-appealing. "Keeping up with the Joneses" is an old motive, and all sorts of advertisements stimulate people to buy so that they may have a product popular with the "best people."

Popular Retail Outlets The nature of retailing has changed greatly over the years. The department store, the mail-order house, and the chain store all give witness to the growing complexity of the market, to alterations in the earlier competitive patterns, and to changes in the role of the ultimate consumer. The chain store is a good reflection of business enterprise in mass society. It is efficient—it eliminates the middleman and handles standardized goods—but its merchandising tends to be impersonal.

Installment Buying Finally, alterations have been made in the use of credit. Many consumers no longer pay cash or use an open charge account. Rather, they pay on some sort of fixed installment plan. Credit card shopping has become, indeed, a culture pattern for large sections of the population, and the charges for this service are passed on, in one form or another, to the consumer.

The difficulties for the consumer can be traced to the transition from an old to a new method of distributing consumption goods. While many critics decry advertising, chain-store, and other aspects of contemporary selling, all these activities are intimately interwoven with the whole fabric of modern business enterprise.

Consumer Protection The government of the United States, acting as an agency for the consuming public, has taken some interest in consumer protection. There are laws providing for pure food and drugs, for standard methods of packaging and labeling, and for licensing and inspection. Most of these laws attempt to control the conditions surrounding the production of a good or a service rather than the nature of the product itself. Such regulations are found in public transportation systems, in restaurants, packing houses, and so on. So too, governments attempt to set up standards regarding such matters as weight, freshness, chemical composition, and quality. In addition, various private consumer organizations have been set up to inform prospective buyers about quality and price. Such organizations often publish buyers' guides.

THE SOCIAL MEANING OF WORK

People are socialized to participate in economic activity. People are motivated to work for other reasons in addition to supporting themselves. If not, why would the person who earns 50 thousand dollars a year put in extra hours striving for a promotion and a raise, or why would the person who inherited enough wealth to live comfortably do the work necessary to get through professional school and then show up at an office every day? Why do sociologists who study industrial organization find it not unusual for a member of a small work group in a factory to turn down a chance for a job as foreman, accompanied by a pay raise?

15-10 CHECKING IT OUT: Some Major Value-Orientations in America

Achievement and Success: American culture has long been marked by an emphasis upon personal achievement—"making good"—especially secular occupational achievement.

Activity and Work: "Active" people are held in high esteem and people encourage each other to "get busy." It has been said that few Americans "find it easy to be happy unless they are doing something." To a large degree, work is regarded as an end in itself.

Moral Orientation: Americans tend to see the world in moral terms, to think in terms of right or wrong, good or bad, etc.

Efficiency and Practicality: "Efficient" is a word of high praise in a society that has long emphasized economic expansion, mass production, up-to-dateness, practicality, expediency, and "getting things done." Similarly, "impractical" has long been one of the strongest pejorative words in America.

Progress: The rich vocabulary of epithets ("backward," "outmoded," "old-fashioned," "stagnant," etc.) in America can be understood as epithets only against the unquestioning assumption that the new is better—that "forward" is better than "backward" and that progress is "just around the corner."

Material Comfort: "Americans," a French observer once remarked, "consider it only natural that their slightest whim should be gratified."

SOURCE: Robin M. Williams, Jr., *American Society,* 2nd ed. (New York: Alfred A. Knopf, 1961), pp. 414–468. The descriptive comments borrow generously from Williams' text.

Both the wealthy person who continues to work and the worker who rejects a promotion illustrate the fact that there are incentives governing work which are not exclusively economic. People pursue economic activity not only to make money but to gain power and prestige, to cultivate and maintain primary group relations, to contribute to a sense of purpose, and to fulfill the expectations of other social roles, such as parent and citizen. The worker who would rather stay with the production gang than be promoted is willing, perhaps, to forego economic gain for the feeling of "belonging" which he or she enjoys as a member of the primary group. Many people who have enough wealth to permit them to enjoy full-time leisure continue to work because they have been socialized in American society, where the norms of the culture have convinced them that healthy adults ought to be engaged in some productive activity. It is common for people who have retired to complain of feeling useless; they have lost a sense of purpose which their work gave them.

INTERPRETIVE SUMMARY

The Industrial Revolution has had a profound effect on the economic structure. It influenced the production and distribution of services as domestic industry gave way to the entrepreneur and finally to the large-scale organizations of modern industrial society. Karl Marx analyzed the historical process underlying the rise of capitalistic enterprises as they developed after feudalism (his dialectical process of thesis, antithesis, synthesis). Marx described the problems inherent in the capital-labor relationship.

The corporate system of modern industrial society is characterized by separation of ownership and management, productivity per person, increased employee income, generally improved working conditions, and a gradually decreasing hourly work week. Automation, the industrial system in which machines run machines, is already demanding increased amounts of fixed capital and bringing further changes in the way this basic function is carried out.

Although workers are free to leave a job and employers free to make dismissals, for the term of employment the two interests are required to make contracts for every obligation which in earlier times would have been fulfilled by each as a matter of status.

In an industrial-urban economy, where the person works away from home, individual sense of purpose or lack of it is greatly dependent on how one views oneself as worker. The hierarchical structure of large corporations, especially the management structures, would seem at first glance to stifle creativity, freedom, and thus dignity. However, stratification has also led to the development of situses, occupational "in-groups."

In mass societies, the production and distribution of goods and services tend to be handled by a few large corporate structures, state or private. These structures resemble community structure in several ways: individuals have roles and statuses, in this case related to the division of labor; informal groups supplement the formal structure; and both tacit and stated norms govern behavior.

Besides being a sort of community unto itself, the corporation has profoundly affected the larger community. For one thing, an individual's job status is likely to be the determining factor in his ultimate status in the community. Moreover, one will identify oneself so strongly with members of similar occupational strata that one may vote for and help finance political figures and parties who seem sympathetic to that stratum; thus the economic institution influences the political institutions of a culture. Under systems of free enterprise, the existence of highly mechanized corporate giants has led to many minor culture patterns affecting consumers: the emergence of big retailing combines, the extension of advertising and credit, and even the extension of protective government control, an action that was not contemplated in the days of widespread trust in laissez-faire economics.

In the United States, both the composition and the distribution of the labor force have changed over the years, largely as a result of technological advances which were in turn made possible by the existence of large amounts of corporate capital. The labor force presently has more women than ever before, fewer very old people, many more people performing white-collar jobs, and more occupied in performing services. On the world scale there is increased economic interdependence. Though concern for the political balance of power has dictated caution, the general trend is toward increased cooperation, a cooperation which has been implemented by vast international communication and transportation networks.

QUESTIONS

1. In what way is Marx's concept of alienation related to the hostile reactions of modern automible workers on the assembly lines of Detroit?
2. What is meant by the statement that secondary-group relationships characterize the relationships to be found within modern industrial corporations? Are primary relationships possible? Explain.
3. In which ways are the industrial corporations of capitalistic, socialistic, and communistic countries similar? What common problems do they share?
4. What are some of the theoretical insights that cause Marxist analyses of social interaction to continue to capture the attention and respect of social scientists?

Part III

Social Institutions

Polity and Society
Family and Society
Education and Society
Religion and Society

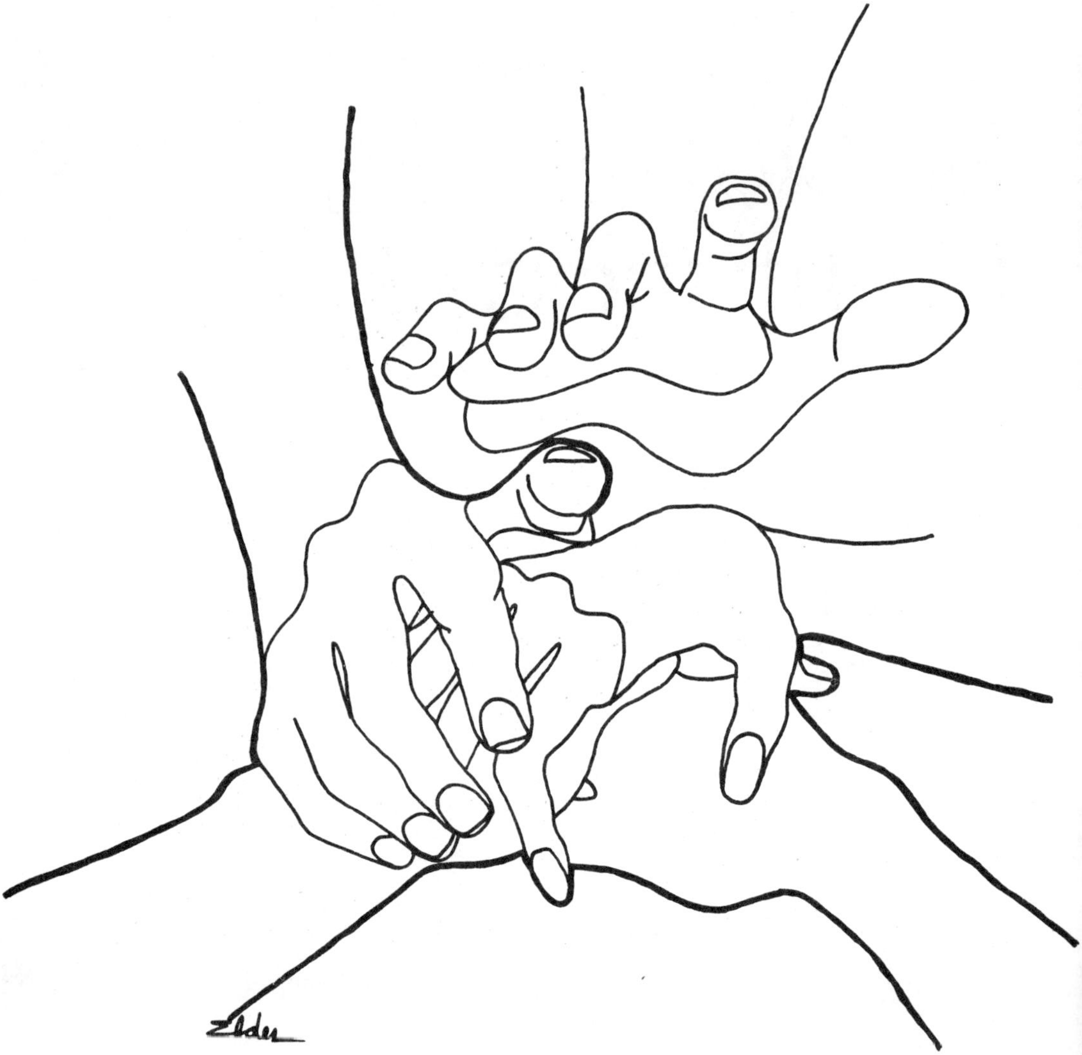

16

Polity and Society

All societies have some sort of larger, overall regulations dealing with the general welfare of the tribe or the community. Usually there are designated groups or persons who set up the rules and act to see that they are enforced. In its broadest sense, this wider regulatory force may be called the government. In more rudimentary societies such controls are largely informal. In more complex societies they are both informal and formal. Generally, the more complex the community, the more formalized the controls. More definite organization is reflected in special personnel—legislative, administrative, and judicial—whose roles are to operate the various control agencies. In the strict sense, the concept of political order or government refers to these special regulations and the operating personnel.

Political scientists specialize in the study of the structure and processes of government. Yet some political aspects of society have considerable interest for sociologists. These include the nature of power itself; the relationship of the society to the nation-state; the way in which mores and public opinion influence political interaction; the place of political revolution in social change; and the functions of political structures for other institutions.

Before discussing specific political patterns and structures, it is necessary to examine the nature of political power and the concept of government. One man who has developed a theory of power and devoted much study to the question of power and its relationship to political structures is Max Weber.

WEBER, POWER, AND THE STATE

Max Weber recognized that there are various kinds of power which affect the lives of human beings. There are, of course, many individuals who pursue goals expecting economic or financial power as a reward. But Weber saw that others strive for power even when the possibility of economic gain is absent. There are those who might relinquish economic power where social power (prestige or social honor) is possible. As he noted, "Naked" money power is by no means a recognized basis of social honor." (Weber, 1958, p. 180) And yet he found that regardless of the sphere in which power might be courted the behavior involved is always the same. Power could be defined as the ability of "a man or a number of men to realize their own will in a communal action even against the resistance of others who are participating in the action." Power, then, is the ability to control and dominate others, even if they resist.

According to Weber's theory the polity or the modern state is based on two unique assumptions about power, First, Weber discerned that the state is the social institution which monopolizes the use of violence. This means that the state is the single institution in society with a right to use violence. Second, the use of violence by the state is *legitimate*. Here Weber is talking about the coercive nature of political power. All political institutions have this potential for coercion and force. But, if the institution is to exist successfully, the power of coercion must be seen as legitimate or lawful by those who are governed. Most Americans grumble and grouse but accept the fact that part of their wages will be withheld by the state as taxed income. The right of taxation by the state is generally seen as legitimate and will continue to be so as long as the majority of citizens believe that the existing political structure is the most effective one for this society.

The state, then, has **authority**. Authority is power that is seen as legitimate. It differs markedly from the power of coercion possessed by organized crime. The power of the mob or syndicate is considered illegitimate by most Americans, for the mob attempts to operate outside the range of governmental scrutiny and refuses to be accountable to the citizens of the society. And indeed from time to time the power of elected officials comes to be regarded as illegitimate because of questionable behavior. Such was the case of Richard Nixon, who resigned in 1974. In resigning, he recognized that the power he exercised in controlling the affairs of state was no longer regarded as legitimate by the populace because of activities that were defined by the populace as criminal. The legitimacy of his authority had declined.

Weber's Ideal-Type of Authority

Weber's ideal-type of authority provides an analytic tool—that is, a model or an abstraction that we can compare to actual power structures and relationships in order to understand and analyze them. According to Weber's theory, ideal authority, or legitimate power, rests on the consent of the governed and the willing submission of the majority. He distinguished three types of this ideal: traditional, legal-rational, and charismatic.

Traditional Authority From earliest times traditional authority has existed. Throughout history the power of a prince or chieftain or lord has been bestowed through ancient custom. Traditional authority is seen as legitimate in societies whose systems of norms are believed to be sacred. Because in such societies things are done in the same way that they have always been done, the norms cannot be violated without the expectation of danger to the society. In traditional societies, then, the authority of the ruler rests upon a belief in the sacredness of what has always been and a deeply ingrained habit of conformity among those who are governed.

Charismatic Authority This type of authority is based on special qualities possessed by an individual. Those that are governed submit because they believe in the unusual abilities of the leader. Weber used the concept *charisma,* "the gift of grace," to describe the extraordinary personal qualities of certain individuals, regardless of whether these qualities are real or presumed. These qualities cause the individual to be treated as if he or she possesses supernatural, superhuman, or exceptional powers. And yet, charisma is a value-neutral term in that it may apply to someone who is later judged saviour because of remarkably fine character or a monster because of cruel and inhuman behavior. Individuals possessing charisma have appeared throughout history. Jesus, Joan of Arc, Gandhi, Hitler, Mao, Martin Luther King, Jr., and César Chavez are examples of charismatic leaders. Such individuals have been thought by their followers to possess qualities that go beyond the normal, to in some cases, the supernatural. The authority of such rulers is, then, related to the beliefs of their followers in "magical powers, revelations and hero worship." Charismatic rulers are expected by their followers to change things, to conquer adversities, make miracles, improve the condition of their followers.

And yet charismatic authority is inherently unstable. This is because the

16-1 CHECKING IT OUT: Anwar el-Sadat, A Charismatic Leader

Before Sadat flew to Israel, the Middle East appeared to be on another of its terrible swings toward war, another violent spasm in the tragic politics of the region. But by one act, the Egyptian President has broken through the seemingly predestined cycle of hatred and killing. Not since the founding of Isreal in 1948 has the will for peace in the Middle East been stronger. If his specific initiative proves unfruitful, there remains a danger that both sides might once again gear up for war. And yet it seems unlikely that the past's bitter patterns of stagnation and violence could return. The very memory of Anwar Sadat at Ben Gurion Airport, at Al Aqsa mosque, at the Knesset, will serve as an enduring reminder that a better way for the Middle East is possible.

SOURCE: *Time,* January 2, 1978, p. 17. Reprinted by permission from TIME, The Weekly Newsmagazine; Copyright Time Inc. 1978.

leader must constantly prove his or her personal strength. In his essay on "The Sociology of Charismatic Authority" (1958) Weber finds this kind of authority to be revolutionary and important in bringing about dramatic and immediate change. The charismatic leader breaks through existing structures, has no allegiance to the legal and traditional norms that have existed. Weber quotes Jesus who said, "It is written, but I say unto you . . ." This statement suggests awareness of the laws or norms but imposes a personal interpretation of what exists, possibly because of a different vision.

The Routinization of Charisma Charismatic authority is also unstable because power resides in an individual, who is mortal. With the death of the leader the crisis of selecting a new leader begins. Because the charismatic leader is unique, the possibility of finding a successor with such unusual qualities is slim indeed. Weber found that problems of succession had been settled in many of the world's societies by the establishment of a belief in hereditary charisma. Here the new ruler comes to power, not through personal qualities, but because of inherited qualities or because of "an act of charismatic election. The process of routinization . . . has set in." (p. 297) The western European notion of "the divine rights of Kings" is an example of this bestowal of charisma through inheritance. There are two important points that Weber is stressing here. The first is that with the advent of hereditary charisma, the new leader may not be the extraordinary individual with "the gift of grace," but this gift now resides in the position the individual inherits. The new leader is elevated because of ascribed characteristics (i.e., kinship) or group designation. This has nothing to do with unusual personal qualities of the leader. Rules or norms have begun to govern in questions of succession. Second, the authority of the charismatic individual, based on a legitimacy rooted in personal power, must ultimately give way to routinization as followers move into the structure that exists and become priests or officials.

Legal-rational Authority In the case of legal-rational authority, the power that the leader exercises is derived from a system of rules and procedures defining rights and obligations. Another way of saying this is that the power of the leader to command is defined in specific laws or norms. Therefore legal-rational authority is power accepted as legitimate because it is bound up in the office or position, not in the leader's charismatic qualities. The President of the United States is one of the most powerful men on earth, yet his power results from the status that he holds and the norms, regulations, and privileges connected with it. Like the United States, many modern societies have political structures developed around systems of norms (constitutions); and the extent of the power wielded by political leaders and officials within these structures has been defined legally. Because the rules guiding behavior within particular positions are explicit, those who abuse their power can be legally removed from office.

Max Weber found legal-rational authority to be the most efficient and the most rational. Traditional and charismatic authority seemed more appropriate to earlier ages when there seemed to be much magic and mystery surrounding human affairs. However, the coming of science, with its emphasis on empirically tested results had swept away many of the mysteries. The **rationalization** of the modern world really resulted from increasing systemization (doing things in a systematic way) with a particular concern for efficiency. Systems of norms. clarify accepted behavior and aid in the efficient conduct of business. Therefore, in political systems where legal-rational authority is established, those who are governed delegate authority to their elected officials, fully expecting them to observe the rules and regulations as they exercise power.

Watergate as Abuse of Power The tragedy of Watergate is very much bound up in the uses and abuses of power. The authority of U.S. Presidents and their bureaucratic staffs is legally-rationally based. A special report requested by the Senate Select Committee on Presidential Campaign Activities (Mosher, 1974) describes the manner in which legitimate authority can become illegimate. Certain actions taken by the Nixon staff were criminal. Among these were the burglary of offices, forgery of a letter, and the so-called laundering of money in Mexico. The Committee to Reelect the President and the White House Staff seemed so obsessed with reelecting Nixon that a tendency developed "to override many other considerations including the public interest and normal ethical and legal constraints." (p. 8) How could these abuses have occurred? The answer seems grounded in the desire for power. We have defined authority as power that is seen, by the people, as legitimate. In the Watergate scandal the assumptions underlying the conferring of power were disregarded.

> The prime motivating drive behind both political and administrative activities seems to have been Presidential *power*, its enlargement, its exploitation, and its continuation ... The zest for power in the Presidential office is perfectly expectable, normal and proper behavior of Presidencies, particularly in the current century—but within limits and constraints, many of which are embedded in the Constitution, and always subject to accountability. (Mosher, p. 7)

The report concludes with the observation that those involved in Watergate had distorted perceptions of their roles and responsibilities, perceptions which "were at best simplistic, and at worst venal and dangerous." (p. 124) This is because a democratic government operates under the assumption that the people are sovereign and that elected officials must regard themselves as servants, not masters, of the people. Officials must have and must exercise power, but only as public servants, fully accountable for their actions.

Overlapping Types of Authority It is possible for the types of authority to overlap. In the case of Queen Elizabeth I charismatic authority and traditional authority were combined. Elizabeth (1533–1603) had a charismatic effect on the London crowds that hailed her as "Good Queen Bess" or "Gloriana." Her rule was accepted as stemming from "divine right" and seen as part of the sacred tradition that gave powerful authority to her reign. Franklin Delano Roosevelt (1882–1945), the only U.S. President elected to a fourth consecutive term, had great personal magnetism and charm and was certainly charismatic. He also had an authority based on the traditional respect and loyalty connected with the Presidency, and the authority stemming from the legal-rational norms guiding his conduct.

POLITICAL STRUCTURES

The Emergence of the State

In ancient Greece a citizen was a full member of the city-state, with a certain role and status in public life. These stood in contrast with his culturally deep-rooted relations with his family, kin, and occupational or other associations. The distinction between public and private matters is historically important because it indicates the shift from a kinship to a territorial basis of control, from private vengeance to public punishment, from small, primary-group obligations to larger obligations based on secondary contacts.

In modern times the political order is centered in the sovereign state. As a social myth and as a set of practices, the state is the core of contemporary nationalism. The sovereign state has become the principal instrument of public order and reflects, in fact, the continuing need for some overall agency of control in an industralized mass society.

One may look at the *state* as an organized power structure the functions of which are the management and control of the society. This involves such things as external and internal security, justice, and welfare, and varying provisions for individual freedom, depending on the nature of the state and the national society. The state also has sole power to levy taxes to pay for these services.

Formal Structures

The state is, of course, a historical product. As populations grew, increasing differentiation of roles led to a breakdown of controls and the need for extension of regulations into new areas of conduct. This meant a shift from a family or kinship basis of social control to one founded on the larger community, with particular individuals, groups, or classes setting down the rules and putting them into effect. More integrated forms of government tended to arise as groups or societies were threatened by, or fell into conflict with, other societies. This tendency was most important in the rise of more complex states: warfare between groups creates strong in-group solidarity.

It seems a far cry from the simple tribal or village council of the elders to the elaborate operations of modern government, and yet these institutions have much in common. Both revolve around a power structure and its functions. Someone or some group makes the rules and laws (or at least standardizes those at hand) without which there could be no social order. This is the legislative structure. Second, somebody or some group enforces the regulations. This is the executive or administrative structure. Third, some group is responsible for settling controversies when the meaning and application of the laws or codes are in question. This is the judicial structure.

16-2 CHECKING IT OUT: Units of Government in the United States, 1930–1933 and 1967

Type of Government	*1930–1933*	*1967*
The Nation	1	1
States	48	50
Counties	3,053	3,049
Municipalities	16,366	18,048
Townships	20,262	17,105
School Districts	127,108	21,782
Special Districts	8,580	21,264
Total	175,418	81,299

SOURCE: U.S. Bureau of the Census, *Statistical Abstract of the United States, 1971* (Washington, D.C.: U.S. Government Printing Office, 1971), p. 397; and U.S. Bureau of the Census, *Historical Statistics of the United States, Colonial Times to 1957* (Washington, D.C.: U.S. Government Printing Office, 1960), p. 694.

In the United States there are over 80,000 governments, each with the power to tax and otherwise influence the lives of people. (See 16-2.) And although the number of governments has been reduced substantially in the past four decades, due mostly to the reduction of the number of school districts, there is an increasing number of social analysts who are convinced that the number and character of formal government structures in the United States will have to be drastically changed before the society will be able to effectively deal with such major social problems as pollution, transportation, and education. Problems such as these are increasingly regional rather than state and local problems. The complexity of the problem can be seen from the fact that the Chicago metropolitan area includes some 250 local governments, small villages, and school districts each with its own administrative powers. In the New York metropolitan area, there are over 1,500 such local governments. Thus, it is argued, local and state government boundaries are inadequate to present-day social needs and some form of regional government is increasingly required.

Regional Planning

Yet even a regional form of government is a questionable solution. The meaning of "region" varies with different functions: a water region, a transportation region, and even an economic region have very different overlays. It is no surprise, then, that there has been frequent and at times bitter debate about the criteria to be used in setting up "regions." Some experts have advocated that such regions be delimited around the major metropolitan areas. Others suggest that regions be delineated according to administrative convenience, such as transportation facilities or proximity to state institutions and federal administrative offices. This does not always create realistic regions.

Still another plan calls for combining groups of states. Actually, the earliest recognition of regional differences grew out of the traditional division of the country into such geographic divisions as the Northeast, Southeast, and North Central. While recent proposals would not follow the traditional combination of states, such a scheme would still be open to the criticism that states and combinations of states cut across too many regional differences in climate, soil, industry, and ways of life. As one commentator puts it, "States or groups of states are not particularly suited to function as planning regions." (National Resources Committee, 1935)

Another proposal is to base regions on single functions and then combine single-function areas when it is administratively feasible to do so. The division of the United States into drainage basins is one illustration of this approach. But here again, overlapping obviously would be increased. One practical plan, though not the easiest to draw up, was suggested in the 1930s. The suggestion was to develop regions around a composite of physiographic and cultural data. Physiographic data include such things as climate, soil, topography, flora and fauna, and mineral resources. Cultural data include population density, metropolitan influence, major types of productive operations, commerce, farm income, and the like. It is evident that the boundaries of such composite regions are not sharp, and certainly would not follow states lines.

Setting up a specific regional area is clearly bound up not only with physiographic, economic, and political factors, but with the whole subculture of the area. If the region is to become a vital unit in social organization, it must be supported by the consciousness of shared subcultural patterns among its inhabitants. Unless regions develop the supporting attitudes and values of group solidarity and common action, the economic or political aspects will be largely superficial. A viable social structure requires the participation that stems from commitment.

16-3 CHECKING IT OUT: Regions and Geographic Divisions of the United States

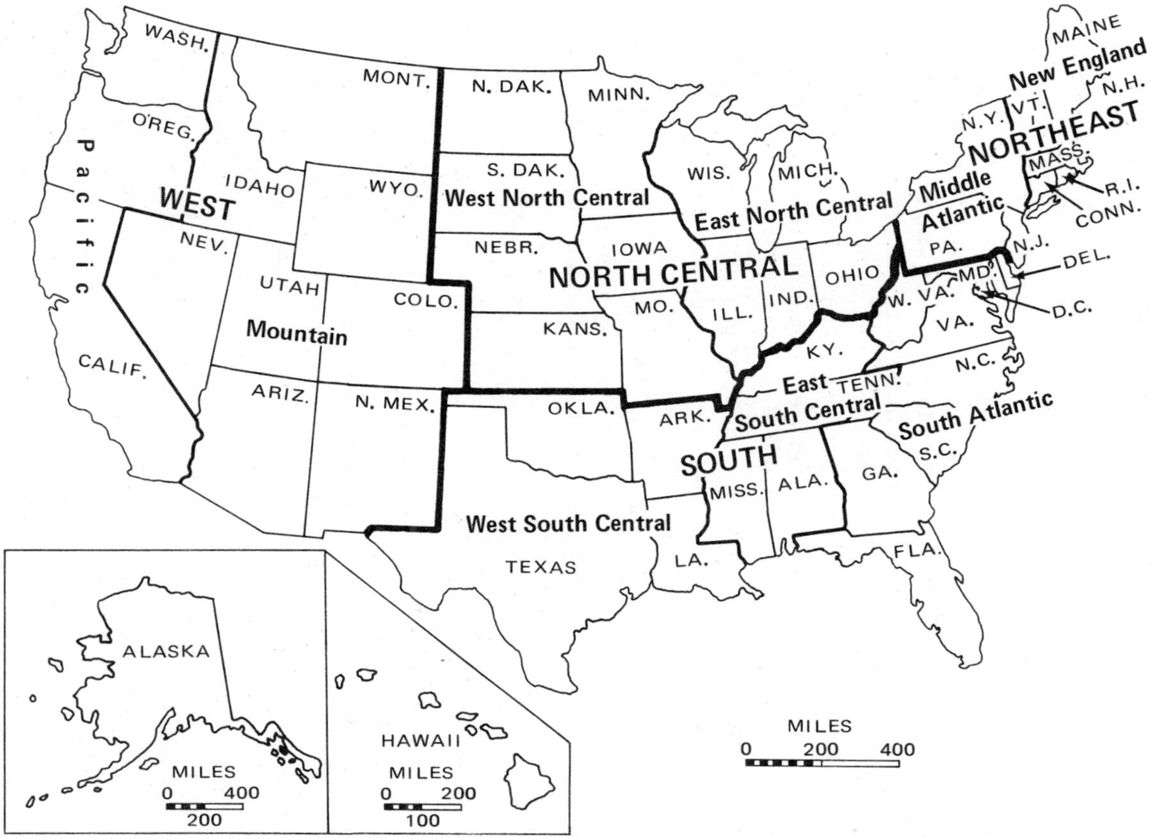

SOURCE: U.S. Bureau of the Census, 1970 *Census of the Population* (Washington, D.C.: U.S. Government Printing Office, May, 1972), p. 7.

POLITICAL FUNCTIONS

We have mentioned three major types of formal political structures: legislative, executive, and judicial. These need not, of course, be operated by separate or distinct groups. In a totalitarian society, one man and a handful of subordinates can make the laws, enforce them, and arbitrate disputes about them. In U.S. society, there is usually a regulation separating the three structures. One cannot at the same time fill the status of a Senator who makes laws and that of a Supreme Court Justice who adjudicates disputes about those laws; nor can one assume the role of a Representative who makes laws and simultaneously act as Attorney General charged with enforcing them. What is called a system of *checks and balances* in the government of the United States is an arrangement whereby the three major functions of government are the responsibility of three separate groups, each of which exercises some limitation on the powers of the others.

The three principal internal functions of government (as opposed to its external function, the protection of the society against other societies) are (1) the institutionalization of norms, or decreeing the rules under which the society shall operate; (2) the adjudication of conflicts, or settling disputes between groups within the society about the application of institutionalized norms and their sanction; and (3) the planning of the state's operation and the enforcement of its institutionalized norms.

Institutionalization of Norms

The central role of legislative bodies is to make laws that become the governmental controls of the society. Other chief functions are taxation and investigation of administrative personnel to see that they carry out the mandates of the legislature. In some systems legislators may act, on occasion, as a judicial body, as in the impeachment of public officials. The legislative group—parliament, assembly, congress—set up to make laws usually does so in accordance with some written or unwritten constitution. Law-making, however, need not be confined to the legislative structure. In the United States, law is also made by judges in rendering court decisions, by administrative action, and by the machinery of initiative and referendum which permits direct legislation by the voters.

In democratic countries, legislators are elected by various systems of voting, sometimes directly and sometimes, as when one legislative body chooses the members of another, indirectly. Representation is usually on the basis of territory, such as the precinct, county, or other geographic district. And in this country at least, prospective legislators must live in the local residential area where they stand for office, for it is traditionally held that persons who live in a neighborhood, city, or region will serve its interests best. The British hold a different view and nominate and elect persons to the House of Commons regardless of their home address. Despite practice in the United States, there is little doubt that the older theory of geographic locus breaks down under modern conditions. It reflects the primary-group culture from which it sprang. Today individuals and groups believe they should also be represented in accordance with the secondary-group interests of their professions, businesses, labor unions, and the like. The lobby and the pressure group show the extent to which modern legislatures must deal with problems other than those which are confined to primary groups living in limited localities.

The Soviet system of representation on the basis of one's occupation—a worker in a plant, or in a railroad system, or a member of a labor union, or a farmer—illustrates a shift from a strictly territorial to a more functional basis of representation. And indeed, the American pressure group or lobby is a kind of unofficial functional representation.

The Adjudication of Conflicts

While the law—constitutional, statute, or judge-made—fixes the rules of human conduct, conflicts of interest constantly require some adjudication. Hence courts are set up, usually at two levels: those of original jurisdiction and those for appeal, the latter culminating in our society in the United States Supreme Court.

The selection and qualifications of individuals to operate the courts vary with the culture. In Anglo-American practice, judicial functions have been divided between those of jury and those of judge. The jury system goes back to the primary-group theory of democracy, that an individual accused of crime has the right to be tried by his equals—his "peers," as the legal language puts it. Though the jury system of the United States has been much criticized and though there has been a trend to abandon trial by jury except in more serious criminal cases, it still represents an important link between citizenry and government.

The Enforcement of Norms

A third basic function of government is to put into effect the "will" or laws of the state. Where government is at all complex there are usually several levels of administrative power and function. First, there is the *head of state.* He or she may be elected by popular vote, or may derive role and status from being a member of a ruling family or from heading a dictatorial clique or party. He or she is charged with the responsibility of enforcing the power of the state. The dictator-head may be both law-maker and law-enforcer, though this situation exists less often than popular notion imagines.

Heads of the state usually have some kind of council or cabinet to advise them. Sometimes the council itself is the head of the state in the sense that its decisions are binding, as in Britain. Sometimes it is only advisory, as in the United States. In Soviet Russia the real head of the country is the Politburo of the Communist Party, although it is not even mentioned in the published constitution. This is a case of single-party dominance of the executive and legislative functions. The various congresses and presidia are largely window-dressing for the real control exercised by the Communist Party.

The second-level administrators are the heads of major governmental departments or bureaus. They are charged with carrying out the executive policies determined by the head of the state and his or her advisors. Below this second level are several other layers of administrators: division and bureau chiefs, and a mass of specialists of various qualifications, duties, and responsibilities.

In democracies it was once common to draw practically all administrative personnel from the membership of the political party in office. (The "spoils" system, as it is called, has also existed under authoritarian and dictatorial forms of government.) But as the duties of administrators became more complex and required special skills and experience, and as the abuses of patronage mushroomed, devices such as the civil service were set up to limit the spoils system. The function of the civil service is to take much public administration out of the hands of politicians and set up professional standards for the selection, continuity, and promotion of most governmental personnel.

Protection from External Forces

The first three functions of government are necessary to the preservation of order within the society. But it is also essential that the society defend itself against outside attack. The two principal means for accomplishing this end are war and diplomacy. The accommodation of conflicts with other societies can be implemented by bargaining, compromise, or threats, or the societies can attempt to subjugate or destroy each other through warfare.

Facile solutions of the problems of war and peace too frequently neglect the fact of peoples' intolerance of those who are different.

People are not only intolerant but inconsistent. Many may desire a world order based on law or rule of reason; but countering this, as always, is the play of nationalist myths and legends which may serve to block movements to establish a global legal system with one central structure for enforcing norms. It is very doubtful that the masses of people in the countries with a high standard of living will voluntarily submit to plans that would take from them what they now hold. Given what we know about the distribution of population and resources in the world, we can expect competition and conflict among states to continue. Each society, therefore, will have some structure with the function of protecting it from external threats.

POLITICAL PATTERNS IN THE UNITED STATES

In highly dynamic periods such as the present, political patterns do not remain static. They are influenced by technological inventions, the relative decrease of primary-group forms of living, and the related extension of secondary and mass-society patterns of action. These changes have been associated particularly with an extension of governmental controls, especially in the area of the planning function of the executive structure.

The Growth of Government

One of the most striking changes in modern life is the expansion of government into areas long considered outside the direct scope of the state. This is particularly true with reference to economic situations, but it is evident in almost all other important phases of our society. The manner in which a state tends to become the all-embracing, controlling agent depends on the cultural values and practices of the time and place. In most democratic countries the trend has been chiefly in the direction of administrative regulation of capitalist enterprises and of furnishing certain public services. On the whole, such trends have influenced the familial, religious, and economic institutions. In some societies the state has taken over property and economic enterprise almost entirely, with more and more regimentation and planning of nearly every aspect of both public and private life.

There are various ways of measuring the expansion of functions in the political order. The most obvious are increases in the cost of government and in

16-4 CHECKING IT OUT: Government Employment in the United States, 1816–1970

Year	*Federal Government Employment*	*State and Local Government Employment*
1816	4,800	NA
1851	26,300	NA
1901	239,500	2,532,000
1929	579,600	NA
1950	1,960,700	4,285,000
1970	2,881,000	10,147,000

NA = data not available.

SOURCE: U.S. Bureau of the Census, *Statistical Abstract of the United States, 1971* (Washington, D.C.: U.S. Government Printing Office, 1971), pp. 388–389; and U.S. Bureau of the Census, *Historical Statistics of the United States* (Washington, D.C.: U.S. Government Printing Office, 1960), pp. 710–711.

the number of public personnel. Others are the growth in services and regulation. The extension of the political structure in the U.S. is easily seen in the increasing proportion of the labor force employed by the government. In 1970 there were nearly 13 million persons employed by various branches of government. Contrary to popular opinion, however, there are three times as many state and local employees as there are federal employees. (See 16-4.) Moreover, the rate of employment among the state and local governments is increasing more rapidly than it is in the federal government.

Another indication of the trend toward government's increasing responsibility for many aspects of social life is revealed in the fact that United States citizens pay an average of 31 per cent of their income in local, state, and federal taxes.

It is true that American society is much larger in population and in geographic areas than it used to be, but the major share of governmental expansion in personnel and budget is attributable to increases in services provided by the government. The state now takes at least some of the responsibility for caring for the aged, the mentally ill, and the unemployed, as well as providing all of the citizenry with postal service, highways, schools, parks, and many other services. It also regulates the currency, the mass media of communication, interstate transportation, the quality of foods and drugs, and numerous other enterprises regarded as needing supervision in the public interest.

The single largest expenditure of government in the United States is for the preservation of external order through the diplomatic and military structures. In addition to financing our own military forces, we spend billions of dollars annually helping support the military forces and economies of other societies. The economic aid that we furnish to other countries accounts for considerably less than half our foreign expenditures, the bulk of which goes to military aid.

The Party System

Those who want direct political power have two simple but basic aims. The first is to get into office—legislative, administrative, or judicial. The other is to stay in office. In democratic societies these purposes are institutionalized in the multiple-party system. In some societies either a ruling class or a single party, which soon takes on the features of a stabilized ruling class, retains this power by various devices, such as tradition, physical force, and propaganda.

Under the democratic system, parties seek election by a plurality of the citizens under certain rules laid down in the law and the mores. As a means of securing the general support of popular "will," political parties become organized in a hierarchical fashion and develop codes, leadership, tactics, and strategy for capturing elections, including membership drives, propaganda, and "getting out the vote."

While parties struggle in the larger public arena in an effort to best their opponents through elections, there is also frequent competition and factional conflict within the party organization itself, aiming at domination of policy. Inner cliques develop, which furnish continuity between one campaign and the next. These political factions are usually more thoroughly organized than the party itself. It is generally believed that the most successful parliamentary governments have operated through the two-party system. In countries of many political parties, the conflicts for power are often hard to resolve by compromise and other accommodations. This is particularly true in periods of grave crisis, such as prolonged economic depressions or war.

Under ordinary conditions of stable society, election of a party to manage the governnent does not mean that the party defeated at the polls has no influence. Rather, it represents an important minority for the period—"His Majesty's loyal opposition," as the British phrase it. It influences public opinion in favor of its countersuggestions to proposed legislation. It acts as a balance to and an alert critic of the party in power. Both parties operate under mutually accepted rules of the political code. In time the parties have to face the national community again to seek election for a new term of office. In U.S. society, the citizenry typically awards control of the government first to one party, then to the other. Never has one party kept control of the national government for more than twenty consecutive years.

The political institutions of the United States are unlike those of the French and British, as well as most other representative systems, in that they do not guarantee a legislature with a majority from the same party that elects the executive. A president from one party may stay in office even when the other party wins control of the legislative branch or branches.

Politics and Stratification

One might expect that, under the system in the United States, parties would tend to represent the interests of certain secondary groups and, indeed, the voters apparently feel that they do. There is a direct relationship between the status one occupies in the stratification structure and the party that one feels best serves one's interest. In general, the lower one's position in the stratification system, the more likely one is to believe one's interests are best represented by the Democratic Party. This set of beliefs is carried into the polling booth. Professionals, white-collar workers, and businessmen, including farmers, are more likely to vote Republican; while manual laborers more often vote Democratic.

In the United States as well as in other industrialized societies political affiliation, political participation, and political choice are all very much related to one's position in the stratifiation order. Although there are notable exceptions, the poor and the minority groups tend to identify themselves with, and

16-5 CHECKING IT OUT: Political Party Affiliation

Question: "In politics, as of today, do you consider yourself a Republican, Democrat, or independent?"

	November, 1974 — March, 1975		
	Republican	*Democrat*	*Independent*
National	*22%*	*46%*	*32%*
SEX			
Male	21	44	35
Female	24	47	29
RACE			
Whites	25	41	34
No. Whites	26	40	34
So. Whites	20	46	34
Non-Whites	8	72	20
No. Blacks	4	72	24
So. Blacks	12	74	14
EDUCATION			
College	27	35	38
High School	21	46	33
Grade School	20	59	21
REGION			
East	25	43	32
Midwest	23	41	36
South	18	51	31
Deep South	15	52	33
West	24	47	29
AGE			
Under 30 years	15	40	45
18–24 years	15	39	46
25–29 years	14	42	44
30–49 years	21	45	34
50 & older	29	50	21
INCOME			
$20,000 & over	30	35	35
$15,000–$19,999	24	42	34
$10,000–$14,999	21	45	34
$ 7,000–$ 9,999	21	44	35
$ 5,000–$ 6,999	21	49	30
$ 3,000–$ 4,999	20	55	25
Under $3,000	22	56	22
RELIGION			
Protestant	27	43	30
Catholic	15	53	32
Jewish	11	59	30

	Republican	Democrat	Independent
National	*22%*	*46%*	*32%*
OCCUPATION			
Professional & Business	27	35	38
Clerical & Sales	24	40	36
Manual Workers	16	50	34
Skilled	17	49	34
Unskilled	16	50	34
Farmers	33	36	31
Non-Labor Force	29	49	22
CITY SIZE			
1,000,000 & over	22	47	31
500,000–999,999	16	50	34
50,000–499,999	18	49	33
2,500– 49,999	25	42	33
Under 2,500 Rural	27	42	31
Labor Union Families	16	51	33
Non-Labor Union	24	44	32

SOURCE: The Gallup Opinion Index, "Campaign '76," Nov.–March, 1975.

vote for, "liberal" politics, and they tend to vote less often than other members of the society. Generally speaking, men vote more often than women in U.S. society; people who live outside of the South vote more often than Southerners; the middle-aged vote more often than the young; the rich and affluent vote more often than the unemployed; the college educated more than those without a grammar school education; the whites more often than blacks and Indians; and the urban more than the rural. The rate of voting is always higher in presidential elections than it is in "off-year" elections, indicating perhaps that people see the executive branch of government as more important than the legislative branch of government. In the presidental election of 1968, nearly 68 per cent of the eligible voters went to the polls whereas only 55 per cent voted in the "off-year" election of 1970.

POLITICAL INSTITUTIONS

The relation of the national community or public to the party system and government—at least under a democracy as we know it—is characterized by a number of important theories and practices. The core of these is stated in the "Bill of Rights," including such items as the rights of free speech, free assembly, petition, trial by jury, the writ of habeas corpus, and a number of others.

Mores and Law

The mere fact that the Bill of Rights is the law of the United States does not mean, of course, that its provisions are known and accepted by all citizens. As a matter of fact, research indicates that even most college students are unfamiliar with its provisions. Furthermore, when students were given an opinion questionnaire about the provisions of the first ten amendments to the Constitution without being told the source of the questionnaire items, most of them indicated disagreement with some of the provisions, and a majority disagreed with several of the amendments. Despite this demonstrated lack of information about the Constitution, when these people were asked whether or not they agreed with all of the provisions in the Bill of Rights, an overwhelming majority said yes.

What is the sociological significance of widespread ignorance of a statute basic to the government of United States society? The traditional position of sociologists has been that the mores and community opinion precede law; and

16-6 CHECKING IT OUT: Extent of Agreement with Bill of Rights Among 560 University Students

		Per Cent Indicating		
Amendment	*Provision*	*Agree*	*Disagree*	*No opinion*
I	Freedom of speech, press	82.5	14.3	3.2
I	Freedom of religion	77.1	13.6	9.3
I	Peaceable assembly	56.8	35.7	7.5
II, III	Bear arms, quartering of troops	63.6	20.3	16.1
IV	Search and seizure	81.8	14.6	3.6
V	Self-incrimination	56.1	33.2	10.7
V	Due process	70.0	25.7	4.3
V	Double jeopardy	23.6	71.8	4.6
VI	Public trial	54.3	34.3	11.4
VI	Confront accuser	23.9	67.5	8.6
VI	Informed of accusation	94.8	2.3	2.9
VI, VII	Trial by jury	89.6	9.3	1.1
VIII	Excessive bail and punishment	61.4	32.2	6.4
IX, X	Reserved rights of people	44.3	51.1	4.6

SOURCE: Raymond W. Mack, "Do We Really Believe in the Bill of Rights?" *Social Problems*, 1956, 3:267. By permission. This research, originally done at Northwestern University, has since been replicated by J. Harold Ennis at Cornell College, Linton C. Freeman and Sherwin J. Feinhandler at Syracuse University, Robert McGinnis at the University of Wisconsin, and Paul Lasakow at the University of Alabama. See also Hanan C. Selvin and Warren O. Hagstrom, "Determinants of Support for Civil Liberties," *British Journal of Sociology*, 1960, 11:51–73.

the classic illustration has been the Eighteenth Amendment—"You can't legislate morality." Many sociologists have moved to the position that, while morality cannot be legislated in a democracy through the enforcement of law to which the majority stand opposed, legislation *can* guide the development of community opinion on matters regarding which the bulk of citizenry have not taken a strong stand one way or the other. An act outlawing reading cannot be enforced and will not be obeyed, because most people believe that they have a right to read. Most Americans indicate that they are unwilling to vote for members of the Communist Party (93 per cent), the Ku Klux Klan (84 per cent), or the John Birch Society (61 per cent) and would probably not react negatively to government action designed to curtail the activities of these groups. (Harris, 1966) On the other hand, a law forbidding the manufacture, sale, or use of sulphur matches could probably be enforced simply because of the indifference of public feeling in the matter of sulphur matches. In other words, most people tend to obey the law if it does not run counter to some strongly held value. Table 16-7 shows, for example, the dramatic increase in black voter registration in the South under the impetus of federal civil rights legislation, especially the comprehensive law adopted in 1965. In 1960 only 29 per cent of the voting age blacks in the South were registered to vote. In Mississippi only 5 per cent were

16-7 CHECKING IT OUT: Black and White Voter Registration in Eleven Southern States, 1960 and 1970

	Per Cent of Eligible Persons Registered to Vote			
	1960		*1970*	
States	*Blacks*	*Whites*	*Blacks*	*Whites*
Alabama	14	64	66	85
Arkansas	38	61	82	74
Florida	39	69	55	66
Georgia	29	57	57	72
Louisiana	31	77	57	77
Mississippi	5	64	71	82
North Carolina	39	92	51	68
South Carolina	14	57	56	62
Tennessee	59	73	72	79
Texas	36	43	73	62
Virginia	23	46	57	65
All Eleven States	29	61	62	69

SOURCE: U.S. Bureau of the Census, *Statistical Abstract of the United States, 1971* (Washington, D.C.: U.S. Government Printing Office, 1971), p. 365.

registered; only in Tennessee were more than half of those eligible registered. By 1970 black voter registration in these same 11 states had increased to 62 per cent and in no state was it less than 50 per cent. In two states, Arkansas and Texas, the proportion of eligible blacks who are registered exceeds the registration among whites. The majesty of the law can be employed to create and strengthen community mores and is, for that reason, of sociological significance.

The End of Colonialism

The diffusion of western European patterns of culture around the world has had political consequences. The colonial patterns of the eighteenth and nineteenth centuries brought more than technology to Africa, Asia, and Latin America; they also brought colonialism. Intentionally or unintentionally, the colonial administrators, the missionaries, the traders, and the settlers taught the natives of these continents many of the values of European cultures. We know enough about the integration of institutions not to expect Asians or Africans to learn our economic institutions, adopt Western notions of education, and so on, without changing some of their political norms.

Africa especially has been a continent of extreme changes. Since 1950, when there were only four independent states in Africa, it has developed into a complex of independent countries and countries moving rapidly toward self-rule. Change has been effected through referendums, war, U.N. intervention, and realignment.

Society and Government

The norms of representative democracy prescribe that the state shall not be identical or coterminous with the society in which it is embedded. Under this theory, in the words of the usual Fourth of July oration, "The state is the servant, not the master, of the people." The theory means, in brief, that ultimate power in a democratic society rests with the citizens, not with the state. (Young, 1946) When we call a democracy "representative," we mean just that. Individuals "represent" the members of the national society and, in the last analysis, are responsible to them. The party system is only a convenient device to implement this basic relationship.

The theory of representative government is not, of course, uniformly and universally accepted. But that is not to say that even dictatorships neglect the matter of support from the wider national society. Certain modern dictators attempt to win popular support and conformity by education and propaganda, as well as by coercion. Stable society and governmental order rest on human acceptance and expectations; and skillful leaders realize that to get this in revolutionary times, changes in values and patterns of social interaction must occur. Although concentration camps, machine guns, and the secret police are effective as controls, nothing but minimum participation in government can be expected unless people share the political norms and are a viable part of the institutional structure of the society. As Mosca once wrote:

> ... ruling classes do not justify their power exclusively by *de facto* possession of it, but try to find a moral and legal basis for it, representing it as the logical and necessary consequence of doctrines and beliefs that are generally recognized and accepted. . . . (*Ruling Class*, 1939, p. 70)

INTERPRETIVE SUMMARY

Most societies have some structure responsible for maintaining internal order. Historically, the same structure or groups of structures have been responsible for protecting the society from outside attack; and this function will undoubtedly be necessary as long as people remain nationalistic and mistrustful of cultural differences, and as long as the needs of certain societies outstrip their resources.

Max Weber, in his examination of the modern state, focused on the phenomenon of power. The state monopolizes the use of violence and this use of violence is seen as legitimate. The state then has authority. Weber described three kinds of authority of power accepted as legitimate. These were traditional, legal-rational, and charismatic authority.

In modern times, the political order is typically centered in the sovereign state. There are two main types of states: the dictatorship, in which a dominant minority imposes its will on the people; and the democratic state, in which elected officials serve the people. Both types of government have gradually become more complex and bureaucratic in administration.

While dictatorships tend to centralize all functions in the hands of a small group, modern democracies have generally divided the three main internal functions of government—the creation of law, administration of law, and judging of disputes involving law—among three structures, though functions of the three structures may overlap somewhat. The legislative branch codifies existing mores into law and, less frequently, may initiate legislation for the purpose of changing mores. It usually acts under some sort of constitution. The executive branch consists of an elected chief executive, various advisers, the extent of whose influence varies among countries, and various administrative sub-heads. It is this branch of democratic governments that is generally criticized for being bureaucratic. Judicial systems show variations in numbers of authority levels, as well as in provisions concerning who shall be judges.

Democratic officials are elected by plurality, after first being nominated by parties. The two-party system, in which the minority retains considerable influence, has generally been the most stable form of parliamentary government.

The United States has a three-branch government with some overlap of functions among the branches. The system contains some checks against bureaucracy and "spoils" appointments. One unique feature of the system is that the election of a chief executive from one of the two major parties does not guarantee a majority of that party in the legislature. Another pattern involves the extension of government control to new areas, especially the areas of economics and welfare. A final feature is the American emphasis on defense spending. Defense is the United States' biggest single expenditure, enormous sums going for economic and military aid to allies as well.

A world trend toward self-government is now in progress; note especially the patterns in former colonies of the huge European empires. Even in authoritarian countries, dictators who would remain in power generally cannot rely on coercion, but must give some attention to indoctrinating people into at least *thinking* they are getting what they want.

QUESTIONS

1. Give current examples of Weber's three types of authority that can be found in the United States. Can you think of examples from another part of the world?
2. In what ways can Watergate be considered an abuse of power? What assumptions underlie the exercise of power by the President?
3. Describe the polity as a social system. Of which interrelated parts is it composed? How does the governmental system of "checks and balances" work?

17

Family and Society

The family is the basic primary group and the natural matrix of personality. "The family is a social group characterized by common residence, economic cooperation, and reproduction. It includes adults of both sexes, at least two of whom maintain a socially approved sexual relationship, and one or more children, own or adopted, of the sexually cohabiting adults." (Murdock, 1965) The precise facts about how the human family originated are unknown. Certain theorists contend that the original human grouping consisted of "group marriage," or a number of males and females living indiscriminately together, with the children of these unions considered the offspring of the whole group. Others have held that the original family was made up of only mother and children, the father, aside from his sexual function, playing a very insignificant role. Actually, no such condition as these theorists assume has ever been found, though in some societies male relatives in the mother's line have played a more important role than the biological father.

FAMILIAL STRUCTURES

In every society there is some form of regulation of family relations, not only fixing—within certain limits—the roles and statuses of the father and the mother but also making the child a legitimate member of the group. The father or his surrogate normally has a family function, and the children have an approved role and status. This status carries over into the child's relations with the wider community.

Systems of Descent

While biologically each individual is the product of two streams of genes—one from each parent—in many societies, social lineage is counted in only one family line. When descent is traced in the father's line, or is **patrilineal**, the child takes the father's family name, becomes associated formally with the paternal family and clan, and has little or no relation with the mother's relatives. When descent is **matrilineal**, the child takes the mother's family name and is customarily more closely associated with her blood relatives than with the father's.

The **bilateral** family system, which we practice, seldom permits the solidarity and continuity possible in a unilateral scheme. Here the adults come together without the restrictions and binding influences found in the unilateral cultures. Although in our own bilateral system the children take their father's family name, both the mother's and father's relatives are considered kin of the child.

Structures of Authority

When the father or his family exercises control of the family, the organization is called **patriarchal. Matriarchal** families are those where control is exercised by the mother or her relatives. Matrilineal families tend to be matriarchal in control, patrilineal to be patriarchal. Although in matriarchal families the mother has considerable power over the children, it is more often her family, rather than she alone, who regulates family contacts, as in the case of the Zuñi.

Types of Families

Particularly in folk societies, we find extended families, in which the household unit consists of grandparents, married children, and grandchildren. (In patriarchal societies, such families are usually **patrilocal**—that is, a woman lives with the family of her husband. In matriarchal societies, households tend to be **matrilocal**; the husband moves into the wife's home.) Such extended families are called **consanguine**; their boundaries are determined by blood relationship rather than by generations. In U.S. society the families are conjugal or **nuclear**. An ordinary household consists of parents and their dependent children. When the children marry, they establish separate households.

Types of Marriage

Marriage is the institution or set of norms which determines the particular relation of parents to each other and to their children. The chief forms of marriage are monogamy, polygyny, and polyandry. (In popular usage *polygyny* is known as "polygamy.") Under any of these forms of marriage, the children's descent may be matrilineal, patrilineal, or bilateral, depending on the particular culture.

Monogamy, the marriage of one man to one woman, is the most widespread form of marriage. Since males and females are everywhere about equal in number—barring some special culture pattern such as infanticide—perhaps it is not surprising that monogamy is so universal. In an analysis of some 250 human societies, however, Murdock found that monogamy was the sole choice in only 43. Two societies practiced **polyandry**, in which two or more men are married to one woman, and the remaining societies recognized **polygyny**, a form of marriage in which two or more women are legitimately married to one man. (Murdock, 1965) In most societies that recognize polygyny as a legitimate form of marriage, most men have one wife, largely because of the economics of supporting two or more.

The only extensive instance of polygyny in recent times in Western society was among the Utah Mormons, from about 1850 until 1890, when it was officially given up by the Mormon Church as a result of legal and moral pressures from the outside. It is estimated that about 5 per cent of the marriages in this group were polygynous. (Anderson, 1942; Young, 1954; O'Dea, 1957)

It is a mistake to assume that polygyny arises from any marked sexual urges of the male. In most societies there is ample opportunity for sexual gratification outside conventional mating. Polygyny is really a form of multiple, if interrupted, monogamy. In most instances, each household is separate, and the husband rotates his attention among his wives. In some societies, however, there are joint households, where two or more wives and their children live together.

The most important motivations for polygyny are economic need and prestige. In certain parts of Africa, for instance, wives are added to the household as the husband demands more help in order to increase his wealth. In the Trobriand Islands of Melanesia, a chief's income consists of the annual endowments from the families of his various wives. Among the Tupis of South America, prominent men keep several wives for their prestige value, as well as for domestic service and labor in the fields. The same is true in Madagascar, in large sections of Africa, and among the Kai of New Guinea. Often the first wife urges the husband to take additional wives, each new one lightening the burden of the others, adding to the economic benefits, and improving the social status of the husband. The first wife frequently retains a certain position of favor and dominance over the other wives.

In polyandry several men are legally bound to one woman. This is the least common form of marriage, there being apparently but four or five localities in which it is found: in the Arctic among certain Eskimo tribes; in Central Asia, especially Tibet; in the Marquesas; occasionally among the Bahima of Africa; among the Nayars of southwest and the Todas of southern India.

FUNCTIONS OF THE FAMILY

Of all the many attempts to explain the importance and universality of the family, few have been as persuasive as the thesis that the family is functionally necessary.

> In the . . . family . . . we see assembled . . . functions fundamental to human social life—the sexual, the economic, the reproductive, and the educational. Without provision for the first and the third, society would become extinct; for the second, life itself would cease; for the fourth, culture would come to an end. The immense social utility of the . . . family and the basic reason for its universality thus begin to emerge in strong relief. (Bell and Vogel, 1968, p. 43)

In modern industrial societies the family shares some functions with other social structures. For example, socialization is a consequence of the familial structure, but it is a function which is also fulfilled by religious structures through Sunday School classes, by formal educational organizations, by economic structures through on-the-job training programs, by informal neighborhood play groups, and so on. Conversely, the family participates in the maintenance of a sense of purpose, in the production and distribution of goods

17-1 CHECKING IT OUT: Changing Functions of the Family

What is a man? A man is nothing. Without his family he is of less importance than that bug crossing the trail, of less importance than the sputum or exuviae. At least they can be used to help poison [sorcery—black magic] a man. A man must be with his family to amount to anything with us. If he had nobody else to help him, the first trouble he got into he would be killed by his enemies because there would be no relatives to help him fight the poison of the other group. No woman would marry him because her family would not let her marry a man with no family. He would be poorer than a new-born child; he would be poorer than a worm, and the family would not consider him worth anything. He would not bring renown or glory with him. He would not bring support of other relatives either. The family is important. If a man has a large family and a profession and upbringing by a family that is known to produce good children, then he is somebody and every family is willing to have him marry a woman of their group. It is the family that is important. In the white ways of doing things the family is not so important. The police and soldiers take care of protecting you, the courts give you justice, the post office carries messages for you, the school teaches you. Everything is taken care of, even your children, if you die; but with us the family must do all that. *A Pomo Indian*

SOURCE: B. W. Aginsky, "An Indian's Soliloquy," *The American Journal of Sociology,* XLVI (July, 1940), 43–44. © 1940 by The University of Chicago.

and services, and in other functions, even though it may not be the structure to which primary responsibility for these activities is assigned. We shall look first at reproduction, the one social function unique to the family in all societies, and then examine some of the other functions in which the family plays an important part.

Reproduction and Norms Regulating Premarital Sex

The sexual life of people is not confined to the marriage situation, but all societies have norms attempting to guarantee that reproduction shall take place within a family framework. Everywhere there are variations in regard to premarital relations, and various extramarital patterns may be permitted along with more formalized family life.

In some tribes prenuptial intercourse is not only permitted but expected, though there is no evidence of complete promiscuity in any society. Everywhere incest taboos, kinship, age, and class rules limit the relations of the sexes both before and after marriage. While many peoples encourage, or at least tolerate, premarital relations, such relations are considered preparatory to marriage.

17-2 CHECKING IT OUT: Control of Premarital Mating in 250 Societies

Control	*Number*	*Per Cent*
Fully permitted (except incest)	65	26
Permitted under specified conditions	43	17
Mildly disapproved	6	2
Forbidden	44	18
Inadequate data	92	37
Total	250	100

SOURCE: Compiled from data reported in George Peter Murdock, *Social Structure* (New York: The Macmillan Company, 1949), p. 265.

There is no uniformity of attitudes toward premarital relations. In contiguous tribes, for instance, one group may put a high value on chastity, while their neighbors consider it of no consequence at all. Some pre-industrial societies, such as the Veddahs of Ceylon, have as strong taboos against prenuptial sexual relations as our own Christian society, where chastity is a high virtue. In the Christian culture the sense of sin and guilt associated with sex affects not only premarital conduct but profoundly influences subsequent marital relations as well.

Among Christian peoples, however, rather striking differences often occur between ideal and practice. Kinsey's research indicates that a considerably greater amount of sexual activity takes place outside the marriage relationship than the ideal norms of our society would lead one to expect. (Kinsey *et al.*, 1948; Kinsey *et al.*, 1953) Since the patriarchal system, with all it implies about male dominance and female submission, was carried over into Christianity, it was very easy for the "double standard of morality" to arise. In many Christian communities the unmarried male is permitted prenuptial sexual freedom, but only with women whom he would not marry. The marriageable women of the community, in contrast, are held to strict taboos on premarital sexual relations. In such a society virginity is rated high, but male continence is neither expected nor often valued, in spite of theological taboos.

17-3 CHECKING IT OUT: Cultural Variation in Punishment of Sexual Behavior

Number of Societies Measured	*Percentage Punishing Given Behavior*	*Type of Behavior and Person Punished*
54	100	Incest
82	100	Abduction of a married woman
84	99	Rape of a married woman
55	95	Rape of an unmarried woman
43	95	Sexual relations during the postpartum period
15	93	Bestiality by an adult
73	92	Sexual relations during menstruation
88	89	Adultery (the paramour punished)
93	87	Adultery (the wife punished)
22	86	Sexual relations during the lactation period
57	86	Infidelity of the fiancée
52	85	Seduction of another man's fiancée
74	85	Illegitimate impregnation (the woman punished)
62	84	Illegitimate impregnation (the man punished)
30	77	Seduction of a prenubile girl (the man punished)
44	68	Male homosexuality
49	67	Sexual relations during pregnancy
16	44	Masturbation
97	44	Premarital relations (the woman punished)
93	41	Premarital relations (the man punished)
12	33	Female homosexuality
67	10	Sexual relations with own betrothed

SOURCE: Julia S. Brown, "A Comparative Study of Deviations from Sexual Mores," *American Sociological Review* (1952), 17:138.

A study of 110 nonliterate societies around the world revealed that among the least frequently and most lightly punished of deviations from the sexual mores is that of having premarital sexual relations. This is especially true when the partners are betrothed. The sexual offenses most frequently and severely punished are "incest, abduction, and rape." Moreover, the punishment increases with the likelihood of the offender's causing a child to be born outside the familial structure. Since a pregnancy arising from premarital sexual relations is likely to be followed by marriage, such relations are less severely punished than rape. In some Western societies, the mother of an "illegitimate" child is scorned, and the child is often denied the right of inheritance. In all societies, some set of sanctions encourages the confining of reproduction to the family.

Socialization

Normally, the basic socialization of the child takes place in the family. All the fundamental ideas, muscular skills, and norms are acquired in the home. Some of the things thus learned are deliberately and consciously taught the child by the parents, older siblings, and other close relatives. The child also learns a great deal nondeliberately—that is, unconsciously. This is especially true of basic attitudes and values.

The religious and moral training of children has always been bound up with the home; and though in much of Western society formal religious education has reached into the earliest years, the family still furnishes basic notions of God, of salvation, and of morality.

The home also provides the first recreational patterns for the child, though play groups furnish important connections with the wider world. In earlier times the family as a unit frequently participated in recreation together: games, picnics, family reunions. Today the commercialized and individualized nature of recreation has increasingly removed this function almost entirely from the home, though radio, television, and the automobile provide some basis for the family in recreation.

As to education, the family provides the bases of all the child's later formal learning. In earlier societies the home furnished much of what is now in the hands of formal education; in spite of great changes, the family still gives the children their basic training in the social attitudes and social behavior important to adult participation in social life.

Habits of bodily care, of social relations, and of seeing the material world are learned in interaction with one's parents. Mother and father symbolize to the child forms of personal power. The child's own wishes must give way in the face of demands for obedience and conformity to these powers external to him or her. The manner in which the child learns how to get along with his or her family will be carried over to interactions with school authorities, religious leaders, the police, and other agents of social control. So too, the way children learn to look at the material forces around them will influence their future interests and attitudes toward science, religion, and art.

Normally, as the child grows up, it is necessary to learn to manage situations outside the home and family. As interests extend beyond the home, the intelligence, emotions, and social habits develop until the child is weaned from the original dependence on the mother, father, and other family members, who have served as principal sources of socialization.

Another important function of the family is to provide a sense of self for the child. Since the child is born helpless and incapable of managing his or her own behavior, it is highly important that a sense of security develops out of the earliest social contacts in the family. The foundations of the sense of safety are laid as the child is shown love, care, and protection, and trained in regular habits of eating, sleeping, bodily care, and play. Consistency of training accompanied by love is of first importance; it provides the stability needed for further learning. It is basic to making the child's world friendly, understandable, and predictable. Every child must learn that contacts with mother, with father, with brothers and sisters, and with others fall into more or less comprehensible and regular patterns—patterns marked by both affection and authority.

The sense of security is related to the child's definition of her or his own role. A clear assessment of the child's own position in the family is fundamental to all future relations in groups outside the home. Very often feelings of rejection, of difference, and of inferiority arise in the family and may carry over to later life. The self- or ego-ideal of the child will be affected at every point by the quality of contacts with parents. Parents may talk about honesty, truthfulness, perseverance, and other virtues of our culture, but it is their overt conduct more than their words that provide the model.

The Economic Function

Present-day family life in the United States reveals changes in the relations of parents and children that grow out of current economic conditions. In urban communities particularly, the absence of the father from the home for long hours has often left to the mother nearly all duties of child training and discipline, a condition not true of the earlier family in the society nor even now so true in rural areas, where the father and children—at least those old enough to work—are often together for long hours daily.

The contrasts in the early and recent economy of the household are striking. In pioneer and early rural America, the husband and wife shared most economic activities. The household was the center of many work activities in which the wife played a definite role. Spinning, weaving, and making clothes continued for a long time to be her duty, and even when machine industry replaced a great deal of home manufacture, she made the clothes for the family. Then too, she took charge of curing meat, of preserving vegetables and fruit for winter use, and usually of the milk, eggs, and garden produce. The household members were concerned with making a living rather than with *earning* wages. The money economy had but slight place in the scheme of things.

Today the family is less and less an economic unit, especially in urban localities. In rural-farm families some of the older patterns remain. But the commercialization and mechanization of agriculture are dissolving the older rural home-centered economy.

Historically, the child has often been considered an economic asset. Among peasant peoples everywhere children are put to work at early ages in the fields and in the household. Even in some pre-agricultural societies boys are initiated early into fishing and hunting activities and girls into household duties. Today in the more industrialized societies child labor is nearly nonexistent and children are noted for consuming rather than producing.

Status Ascription

One's position in the stratification structure is determined by the statuses filled by one's parents. The achievements of one's parents, therefore, can profoundly affect a person's life chances.

> At birth one acquires a variety of initial statuses, and most of these are determined by the family and kinship organization into which he is born. As the individual passes through childhood into adulthood, he continues to possess some statuses which flow from his membership in a family group. Both child and adult, then, receive certain statuses because of their membership in a family. . . . Statuses conferred by the family consist of: (1) those which orient one in his relations with other members of the family (as designated by such kinship terms as brother, father, niece, etc.) and (2) those shared with the other members of the family which orient one with members of the society outside the family (urban, Protestant, middle-class, etc.). (Winch, 1952)

Psychological Relationships Among Family Members

It is easy to overemphasize the reproductive and socializing functions and to overlook the fact that the familial structure has functions as well for the many married couples who are childless. Some couples never have children; others live together for years before having children. In a society that has conjugal families, many couples live together for years after their children have left to form households of their own. What, then, is the function of the institutionalized set of social relations between husband and wife?

A strong need for dependency and security seems to be present in every human being. This is built up in the child within the structure of the family.

Adults carry over into later life this same need for confidence, reassurance, and emotional support from others. Today, with fewer children per family and with the increasing disappearance of economic and educational activities from the home, husbands and wives are more and more dependent on companionship and sexual attraction to keep them together.

There is an especially important interaction centering in the sexual life. At the purely biological level this relationship among human beings is not far removed from that of the anthropoids. Actually, however, human sexual activity is profoundly influenced by culture. While in some societies relatively little emphasis is put on the emotional aspects of sex, among many groups the act is bound up with mutual admiration, respect, and the desire of each mate to please the other in every way. As society removes from the family other functions, including much of the former heavy burdens in connection with child training, these more intimate relations are becoming more important.

FAMILIAL PATTERNS IN THE UNITED STATES

Historical Influences on the American Family

Our basic familial organization has its roots in the Gemeinschaft culture of western Europe, where family control was patriarchal in form. In addition to the major functions of childbearing and child rearing, the family was the important economic unit of the community. It also performed other important functions in education, religion, recreation, and the development of proper values about the community and other aspects of culture.

The Christian church arose within the older primary-group organization of Europe. The church's position regarding family life was expressed in the doctrine of other-worldly asceticism, the doctrine of sexual sin, and ascription of low status to women. Christian taboos against sex were supported by all sorts of notions about its being sinful, lewd, nasty, and debasing. Women were thought chiefly responsible for man's downfall with the first instance of sexual knowledge. Marriage, while by no means man's highest state, was encouraged for the average person; and the church made marriage one of the sacraments in order to keep family life under its rule. This view continued for centuries, until disrupted by romanticism, individualism, and economic changes.

Romanticism fostered the idea of free choice of mates on the basis of love. The Renaissance, with its general enlightenments and criticism of tradition, influenced both theory and practice in regard to sex. Though the Protestant Reformation, especially its Calvinistic branch, laid heavy taboos on sexual freedom, its emphasis on individualism in other areas had the long-term effect of loosening the taboos. The Commercial Revolution furthered the trend, which expressed itself in business enterprise, in freedom of thought and expression, in the growth of the idea of the right of the individual to take part in the affairs of government, and in a general loosening of the older rigid class system. As individualism developed, as eighteenth-century rationalism began to have its effects, and as certain romantic notions persisted, the position of women was somewhat improved.

Changes in familial patterns came slowly. Besides her major role of bearing and training children, the woman was obedient to her husband and a heavy contributor to the economic activities of the household, at least in all but the highest social class. She had no property rights of her own, and in law she was treated as a minor. She could not enter into a contract to do work or perform other services, and wages paid her went to her husband. She had no political rights or duties, such as voting or jury service. (Myrdal, 1944)

With the Industrial Revolution came the gradual emancipation of women from complete dominance by father or husband; the attainment, finally, of political rights such as the vote; the gradual relaxation of the more severe Christian taboos on sex for both men and women; and the urbanization of population, with its effects on the economics of the household and on the decline of the importance of the home in education, religious training, and recreation.

In short, then, role expectations and familial functions have changed in relative importance. Sexual relations, childbearing, and child rearing have proportionately a much larger place in total family life than they once had. In contrast, the economic function of the family and the home has become steadily less important. Comparable changes have occurred in other familial functions: religion and occupational training, for example.

Mate Selection

Research indicates a strong tendency for people to select as spouses persons similar to themselves. That is, like marries like. (This is technically known as *homogamy.*) "Like" refers to such sociological variables as age, education, social class, race, religion, previous marital status, and area of residence. (Burma, 1952; Hollingshead, 1950; Kennedy, 1952; Landis and Day, 1945; Park and Glick, 1967; Udry, 1971)

How mate selection is affected by residential propinquity, for example, is shown by a number of studies. When J. H. S. Bossard examined 5,000 consecutive marriage licenses issued in Philadelphia, he found that more than 17 per cent of the couples gave residential addresses within one block of each other, 23 per cent within two blocks, and over one-third within five blocks. More than half (52 per cent) lived within 20 blocks of each other. Only 17 per cent resided in different cities. (Bossard, 1932) Moreover, there is some evidence that the tendency of people to marry those in the same vicinity has actually increased, at least in certain cities. Ray H. Abrams found this to be true for Philadelphia, as did Ruby Jo Reeves Kennedy for New Haven. (Abrams, 1943; Kennedy, 1943)

Apparently not only distance but also density of population influences the relative rates of selection of those nearby. On the basis of his studies in New England, John S. Ellsworth concludes tentatively, "Other things being equal, the possibility of marriage between persons living in different population groupings decreases as the distance between them increases but tends to increase with the number of persons available at given distances." (Ellsworth, 1948; Stouffer, 1940)

It is not mere propinquity or density, however, which determines the selection of a mate. Rather, it is that people of similar race, nationality, occupation, religion, and social class tend to live in the same neighborhoods. In short, the ecological factors of segregation have a place in this process.

While homogamy prevails in mate selection so far as social characteristics are concerned, it does not necessarily follow that like marries like in so far as psychological variables are concerned. For example, while a young person is likely to marry another young person of the same social class, same religion, and comparable education, he or she may marry a person whose personality tends to be opposite to rather than similar in make-up. If a submissive man marries a dominant woman or a deferent woman marries a hostile man, we may say that their motivations or needs are complementary. (Winch, 1971)

Marital Adjustment

Various attempts have been made to determine the specific elements which make marriage a success or failure in U.S. society. These studies deal chiefly with middle-class urban families. (Kirkpatrick, 1963; Burgess and Wallin, 1953) They throw light on the possibility of predicting marital satisfaction on the basis of premarital experiences and situations, since they indicate some of the factors making for success or failure in wedded life.

The researchers report that a high degree of marital happiness between one's parents, absence of conflict with parents, adequate sex information in childhood, approval of the marriage by parents and other significant persons, personal happiness in childhood, and strong attachments to mother or father are predictive of success in one's own marriage. They find that having had firm but not violent discipline and parental instruction in sexual matters is important. It must be stressed that no one of these factors is crucially important in itself, but that combinations of them may be highly significant. Of all the factors, probably happy home life and similarity in socialization are the most important.

Marriage and Family in the United States

In spite of some popular notions about the ill effects of divorce and the emancipation of women on the American family generally, more than 90 per cent

17-4 CHECKING IT OUT: Median Age at First Marriage by Sex for the United States: 1890 to 1970

Year	*Males*	*Females*	*Difference*
1890	26.1	22.0	4.1
1900	25.9	21.9	4.0
1910	25.1	21.6	3.5
1920	24.6	21.2	3.4
1930	24.3	21.3	3.0
1940	24.3	21.5	2.8
1950	22.8	20.3	2.5
1960	22.8	20.3	2.5
1970	23.2	20.8	2.4

SOURCE: U.S. Bureau of the Census, *Current Population Reports*, Population Characteristics, Series P-20, No. 72 (Washington, D.C.: U.S. Government Printing Office, December 21, 1956), p. 3; "U.S.A. Population Changes: 1950–1960," *Population Bulletin*, XIX (1963), 32; and U.S. Bureau of the Census, *Statistical Abstract of the United States, 1971* (Washington, D.C.: U.S. Government Printing Office, 1971), p. 60.

of the population will marry at some time during their lives. The median age at marriage, which had dropped slowly but steadily at least since 1890, has gone up slightly in the past decade. The median age at first marriage for men declined from 26.1 years in 1890 to 22.8 in 1950 and after a decade of stability, increased slightly to 23.2 in 1970. The corresponding figures for women reveal the same trend: a change from 22.0 years in 1890 to 20.3 years in 1950, and then after a decade of stability a slight increase to 20.8 years in 1970. One trend that has remained unchanged in the past 80 years is that the age difference at marriage between men and women has been decreasing. In 1890 the male was typically 4.1 years older than the female at the time of marriage, but in 1970 the difference was only 2.4 years.

The relatively early marriage age in the United States results in a high proportion of married persons in the total population. The situation is quite different in most other industrialized countries where an aging population, less national wealth, and lower standards of living probably play a part in delaying entrance into matrimony. To cite a few comparative figures from the late 1940s: For males aged 20–24 and 25–29 who had ever married, the United States percentages were 28 and 64 respectively. In England and Wales the percentages for these two age groups were 53 per cent; in France, 21 and 64 per cent—much nearer our own. For females aged 15–19 years and 20–24 years, the United States percentages were 12 and 55 respectively; for England and Wales, 2 and 26; for France, 6 and 49. (*Stat. Bulletin*, 1947)

Although the marriage rate has been high, the average size of the American family has been shrinking. At the time of the first census in 1790, the average number of persons per family was 5.7. A hundred years later it was 4.9. By 1940 it had fallen to 3.8, and by 1969 to 3.2.

The changes in family size are correlated, of course, with (1) childless marriages—the extent of which is indicated by the fact that 15 per cent of American women who marry bear no children; (2) an aging population, which means that more families with no minor children survive than formerly; (3) an increase in the average span of time between marriage and birth of the first child; (4) the general decline in the rate of population growth; and (5) "a growing tendency for old people to live in independent households instead of as dependents with their married children." (Goldthorpe, 1968, p. 84)

FAMILIAL INSTITUTIONS

Sexual relations and marriage must not be confused. Traditionally, marriage has been a group-sanctioned bond establishing the family relations, especially with reference to offspring. Sexual relations have not necessarily led to marriage. Indeed, marriage in most societies is not generally encouraged for sexual or romantic reasons. It is not sexual gratification that has been the primary purpose of marriage but rather the legitimacy of the offspring and their care and training through the early years. In the words of Malinowski, "Marriage on the whole is rather a contract for the production and maintenance of children than an authorization of sexual intercourse." (Malinowski, 1929) In our own culture, however, the sexual and affectional phases of marriage may become more important with the decline of parenting and related functions of the family. Scanzoni and Scanzoni (1976) have chosen to view marriage as a social exchange situation. Where persons maintain ongoing expressive (sexual and emotional) and instrumental (economic and task-oriented) exchanges, a marriage exists.

In many societies, marriage is a secular, not a religious, contract. Religious sanctions, true enough, are often added, but marriage is not universally supported by religion. When religion has a part, as in Judeo-Christian religions, it may serve to increase the emotional bonds and to put more weight behind the community controls over the family.

Marriage implies a welding of two lives together in reference to certain obligations and duties. Since people think concretely, this union is usually expressed by a symbol. In various parts of the world one finds such rites as the bride and groom eating out of a common bowl, drinking from the same vessel, mixing clay or earth together from two separate lots, performed as symbolic of the union. Marriage symbolism is illustrated in our own society by, among other things, the use of engagement and wedding rings.

Marriage Sanctions

No society permits absolutely free selection of mates. As we have seen, close degrees of blood relationship, age differences, class differences, and wider kinship relations limit this choice. The *incest taboo* is without doubt the most nearly universal restriction on mating. It prohibits marriage chiefly between parent and child and between brother and sister. Yet it often reaches out to more remote blood relatives. The few historical instances of sanctioned incest, as among the ruling families of ancient Egypt, Peru, and Ireland, were not the result of primitive conditions but of a belief in divine powers that would be dissipated by marriage outside the royal line. And in the case of ancient Egypt, brother-sister marriages had the consequence of preserving the economic advantage of the family. (Middleton, 1962) Daughters usually inherited a substantial part of the family estate and marriage to their brothers prevented splintering the estate into small and economically unproductive units. The very intensity of the incest taboo is some indication that the rules are sometimes broken. Social workers, psychiatrists, lawyers, clergymen, and others dealing with more intimate family problems report that incest is not unknown in present-day society; nor is it confined to any one social class.

Exogamy is the type of union in which a person marries someone outside his or her own group, whether the group be family, clan, village, or other social unit. The opposite type of union, in which a person mates within his or her own group, is called **endogamy.**

Tribal endogamy is almost universal. In the more rudimentary societies it is a natural outcome of isolation and strong in-group solidarity. Within the tribe or larger society, where a clan system develops or where professional or aristocratic ranking or economic status or a caste system arises, endogamy is generally required or at least strongly encouraged.

Exogamy arises wherever groups of persons are believed sufficiently related to be forbidden to marry, with a consequent insistence on their mating in other groups within the wider community. It is usually found in association with wider kinship and clan relations. In the American bilateral system, formal exogamy is in little evidence, marriages between distant relations usually not being considered incestuous.

Two factors that govern the selection of a spouse are (1) the degree to which the normative structure of the society allows one a free choice, on the one hand, or, on the other, allows one's parents, priest, employer, or someone else to decide whom one should marry; and (2) the degree to which the norms rule ineligible some persons whom one might marry. Linton Freeman has cited four extreme situations which can arise from variations of these two factors. (1958)

When a man from the Yaruro Indian tribe of Venezuela is of marriageable age, his mother's brother picks one of his daughters for the young man, and the bridegroom moves into his uncle's household. The only females who are eligible brides are his mother's brother's daughters, and he does not even select the one he will marry. The Hottentots also marry within a small field of eligibles determined by kinship, but within the field one is allowed free choice of mates. In feudal Japan the field of eligibles was wide, but the participant had his spouse selected by his family. In the United States a situation opposite to that of the Yaruro prevails: an open field of eligible mates and the individual free to select his or her own spouse. Aside from the incest taboos concerning sexual relationships within the immediate family or between close cousins, which are enforced by custom and by law, people in the United States are not required to select their mates within determined limits.

When a Marriage Ends

Marital Dissolution

There are several ways in which marriages end. Among these are death of one partner, desertion, and divorce. Desertion occurs when one partner leaves the home and does not return. Traditionally, husbands have been the ones who deserted. But today the runaway wife is a growing problem. Because the law gives the husband the right to establish domicile, if a husband finds work in another city and his wife does not accompany him, she can be charged with desertion. The ending of marriage through death affects American women more than American men—roughly 80 per cent of those losing spouses through death are women. There are two reasons for this. First of all, females outlive males of the same age. Also it is clear that in the United States, women tend to marry men who are older than they are, thus increasing the possibility that they will be widows.

Divorce

The view of marriage as a sacrament or holy ceremony is commonly held by religious traditionalists in many Western societies. However, this is in fact a relatively modern view, which dates from the middle of the sixteenth century. Before that time, marriage and divorce involved secular, not religious, contracts. For example, in ancient Greece and ancient Rome, divorces and marriages were arranged privately between families. However, at the Council of Trent in the sixteenth century, the canon law of the Catholic Church established that marriage was sacred and could only be ended by death. When adultery, heresy, or cruelty were discovered, legal separation was possible but marital partners were unable to remarry. The Protestant churches of Europe have traditionally considered adultery, desertion, and cruelty as grounds for divorce. However, until recent times, an ecclesiastical or church court controlled the dissolution of marriage. In America, from the colonial period divorce procedure has been determined by the individual states. Marriage has not been viewed as a private family matter as in ancient Rome. Rather the state has functioned as an interested third party with a stake in preserving marital ties. The state grants marriage licenses and decrees of divorce and assumes some responsibility in the case of abandoned families, widows, and orphans.

The divorce rate has been rising steadily in this country, and in 1976, for the first time, the number of divorces exceeded one million—almost three times the number in 1950. Approximately 40 per cent of marriages now end in divorce and 3 out of 10 women separate from their husbands before the age of 30. Though the rate of remarriage has also been rising, it does not approach the divorce rate. An astonishing new phenomenon increasingly accompanies divorce proceedings—"the unwillingness of either parent to take custody of the children." (Bronfenbrenner, 1976)

No-Fault Divorce Until no-fault divorce came into existence in the United States, divorces were obtained in an adversary situation in which husband and wife faced each other as plaintiff and defendant. The hostility that was apt to result from such contests served to widen the gulf between couples, even forcing children to choose between parents and take sides in the dispute. In recent years, a number of states have enacted reforms in their divorce laws. In California, the Governor's Commission on the Family (1966) recommended that as a major reform no-fault divorce be instituted. In 1969, California passed a law that incorporated this suggestion. The idea of plaintiff and defendant was abandoned and the need to establish the guilt of one of the parties was removed. When it can be shown that a marriage has "irreparably failed," it may be dissolved. Other no-fault grounds are incompatibility and separation (which is not viewed as desertion).

THE FUTURE OF THE FAMILY

Is the Family Dying?

In the midst of the many and varied changes the family has undergone during the past century, much has been written and spoken about its future. Exactly what the future of the family is and how it will be organized is a matter of considerable speculation and there are those who write of "The Death of the Family." (Cooper, 1970) The marriage rate, however, tells us something about the changes in the modern family. The marriage rate rose at the beginning of the 1960s and leveled off by the end of the decade; but by the early 1970s it began to decline, especially among 20-year-olds. Fewer and fewer young people appear to see a need to get married. If, in an earlier day, marriage and child rearing were unquestioned experiences that the young female prepared for, today's career possibilities give women additional choices in the kinds of lifestyles they will adopt. Mobile and career-minded females may choose to remain single; they may marry but elect not to have children; or they may become single parents; or they may combine marriage, a family, and a career. However, the desire of many to avoid the legal tie of marriage has led to an increase in the numbers of couples living together without marrying. At the same time that legal marriage is being questioned, the traditional expectation of parenthood has also changed. Population considerations make unplanned and prolific childbearing disadvantageous for the society. The desire for a comfortable standard of living make this behavior disadvantageous for the couple involved. While a sentimental appreciation for the family as an institution probably still is widespread in our culture, and mediates against its abolition, the family does appear to be changing and many alternatives to the traditional nuclear family may now be found in the United States. Some of these will be discussed below.

Alternatives to the Traditional Marriage

Remaining Single In 1971, 5 per cent of the population of 30 or older were unmarried. The very high marriage rate of the 1960s has not been equalled in the 1970s; in fact, the marriage rate has been falling. Between 1960 and 1970, the number of single men under 35 increased by 5 per cent. The number of single women of the same age increased by 7 per cent. (*Current Population Reports,* 1972) Certain patterns are becoming clear for this social category. The traditional definition of marriage as the only acceptable state is changing. Remaining single has become a desirable alternative for many. Of those preferring singlehood, many have chosen to live alone. Others choose to live with a mate; still others have begun communal arrangements. The Women's Movement has been influential in suggesting options other than traditional marriage; in the case of females, living alone has lost the "Old Maid" connotation of earlier times. The "swinging single" or "bachelorette" has emerged. Though this group has been little studied by social researchers, it is apparent that many women live alone as a matter of preference. Social Exchange Theory offers the concept of "profit" to describe the ratio of rewards to costs in exchange situations. (Homans, 1961) Because some single females may perceive marriage as a "low profit" situation (more punishments then reward), the desire for marriage is lessened. A study by Elizabeth Havens (1973) relates the economic independence of women to their desire to remain single. It appears that "the higher the economic achievement of females, the less their desires to accept the confining traditional familial sex-role of wife-mother-homemaker or to be evaluated solely in terms of that sex role."

Homosexual Marriage The new militancy of homosexuals has made them anxious to challenge norms and laws that they feel are discriminatory. They reject cultural mores that limit emotional attachments and sexual relationships to those of the opposite sex. Because they are asserting themselves regarding rights they feel have been denied, it is not surprising that homosexuals are now demanding the right of legal marriage. The inability to marry appears to have specific consequences for gays. Simon and Gagnon report the results of a study of white males "with extensive histories of homosexuality." Just about half of these men acknowledged that 60 per cent of their sexual partners were individuals with whom they had only one sexual experience. (1972, p. 562)

Such promiscuous behavior is common in the homosexual community and may be related to the lack of public recognition for stable and deep emotional commitments on the part of homosexuals. Dennis Altman, in *Homosexual Oppression and Liberation* (1971), comments that while it is not possible to know how much relationships may be strengthened simply because they are publicly acceptable, nevertheless he suspected "that after a time lovers have a real psychological need for the support that comes from being recognized as such."

Because the possibilities of legal marriage do not exist, other strategies have evolved. One homosexual individual may legally adopt another, thereby insuring the inheritance of common property and allowing one of the partners a lawful change of name. Other homosexuals participate in formal marriage ceremonies. Because the need for a community-wide recognition of their relationship does exist, male homosexuals and lesbians may be married in churches that serve the homosexual community.

Swinging One of the most titillating events of the 1950s was the media coverage of a new recreational pattern in the affluent suburbs of the United States—wife-swapping. While this behavior was not really new, the increasing numbers of middle-class couples who appeared to be participating suggested that wife-swapping or "swinging" might be a further proof of the death of the American family. Swinging involves the willing relinquishment of sexual rights to one's marriage mate, and the understanding that others will share these rights temporarily. (Palson and Palson, 1975) Swinging takes many forms. Couples may separate and engage in intercourse in separate bedrooms or they may have group sex. Females are more likely to exhibit homosexual behavior in swinging situations than are men. One of the most interesting questions to researchers has been to discover how swingers avoid jealousy. Palson and Palson determined that with those couples who had developed such satisfying emotional relationships that each felt irreplaceable, jealousy ceased to be a problem. They called this a tendency to *individuation.* Carol Symonds (1968) has distinguished between recreational swingers and utopian swingers. Recreational swingers have stable relationships but find marriage sexually restrictive; swinging allows them variety without endangering their marriage. Utopian swingers attempt to establish meaningful relationships with other marital pairs. One of the results of swinging may be that couples radically change the form of their marriage. Swinging could conceivably give way to a group marriage in the case of utopian swingers, thus challenging the monogamous marriage even more.

Open Marriage The best-selling book *Open Marriage*, written by the O'Neills, shows an open rejection of the traditionally monogamous marriage on several levels (1972). The monogamous marriage has demanded an exclusive relationship between partners. The open marriage encourages friendships outside the marriage for both partners, with sex a possibility though not a necessity. Open marriage encourages the growth of the individual through an avoidance of sex-role stereotyping. Masculine roles, such as washing the car, and feminine roles, such as taking care of the children, are discarded. The O'Neills believe that both sexes would "benefit enormously if they shared and openly displayed the admirable qualities that each sex is supposed to have separately." (p. 146) Open marriage discourages the "togetherness" of the 1950s by suggesting that marital partners should free themselves from restrictive sex-roles and actively seek independent lives. By doing some things together and other things apart, the O'Neills suggest that marriage will be a less restrictive and more enriching experience.

Whither the Nuclear Family? Jessie Bernard (1973) voices the view of most sociologists when she states that the future in marriage is in no way threatened by the proliferating alternative family styles. An intimacy is developed in marriage that seems permanently attractive for many. Indeed the traditional conception of marriage with its expectation of sexual fidelity is still viewed as the most desirable arrangement by most Americans. (The Roper Organization, 1974)

INTERPRETIVE SUMMARY

The familial structure normally consists of a mother, a father, their children, and, in some societies, certain members of one parent's extended kinship group. Where the system is patrilineal, control is likely to be patriarchal, and the wife may live with her husband's extended kinship group. In matrilineal societies, the reverse tends to be the norm. Bilateral structures have historically been patriarchal, though the household itself has tended to exclude all but the two parents and their children. Monogamy is the most common type of marriage. Polygyny and polyandry exist in some societies, an individual taking multiple spouses for purposes of prestige and/or economic aid. All societies have some prohibitions involving mate selection. One almost universal prohibition is that against incest, within or without marriage; however, the definition of incest varies. Many societies further restrict eligibility along class or other in-group lines. Finally, a society may require that an individual's parents or some extended kinship group select his mate. Most societies have some provision for dissolution of marriage, though what constitutes justification for dissolution varies.

Reproduction is the one social function unique to the family in all societies. In some societies, there are more or less severe sanctions to ensure that reproduction does not occur outside marriage. In other societies premarital relations are encouraged with pregnancy seen as preparatory to marriage. Probably the next most important function is socialization of offspring. From early social experiences within the family, the child learns what his or her statuses and probable life chances are, and develops a self-image. Historically, the family has been the basic economic unit, though this function has diminished in urban societies. As this and other functions have been removed from the family, its function of satisfying the basic human need for affection has become especially important.

The family in the United States is conjugal in nature. Descent is traced patrilineally, though the husband's and wife's kinship groups are both important, and the control of the father over the family is partial and by no means absolute.

Most of the characteristics of the contemporary American family can be traced to economic upheavals such as the Industrial Revolution and to related ideational forces, particularly romanticism, the Renaissance, and the Protestant Reformation. For example, the emphasis on individualism has increased individual choice in mate selection, except for certain incest taboos. The belief in individual value has also led gradually, and so far incompletely, to increased freedom and privileges for women. High standards of living, medical advances, and other factors have caused the marriage age to drop and the size of the family to decline.

Researchers have found that the factors most responsible for happy marriages in our country are similarity of social background, previous happy family life, and healthy attitudes toward sex. Though individuals in the United States tend to marry people with socially similar backgrounds, the divorce rate in this country is relatively high. Although the rate of remarriage has also been rising, it does not approach the divorce rate. The dissolution of marriage through divorce has been controlled, in America, by the individual states since colonial times. Traditionally, divorce proceedings have been adversary situations with the state functioning as an interested third party with a stake in perserving the marriage. Recently, however, the no-fault divorce has been instituted by some states and the adversary form of divorce abandoned.

Where the death of the modern family is discussed, a concern for the family as a basic societal institution is being expressed. Rather than marriage and child-rearing as unquestioned experiences for the young, the traditional nuclear and monogamous family style is changing and alternative styles are proliferating. Among these are remaining single, homosexual marriage, swinging, one-parent families, and open marriage.

QUESTIONS

1. Is marriage necessary? What are the advantages of marriage today for American males and females?
2. What cultural events have changed our views about child rearing?
3. What are some of the varieties of family forms to be found in human societies? How can we explain the differences that we find?

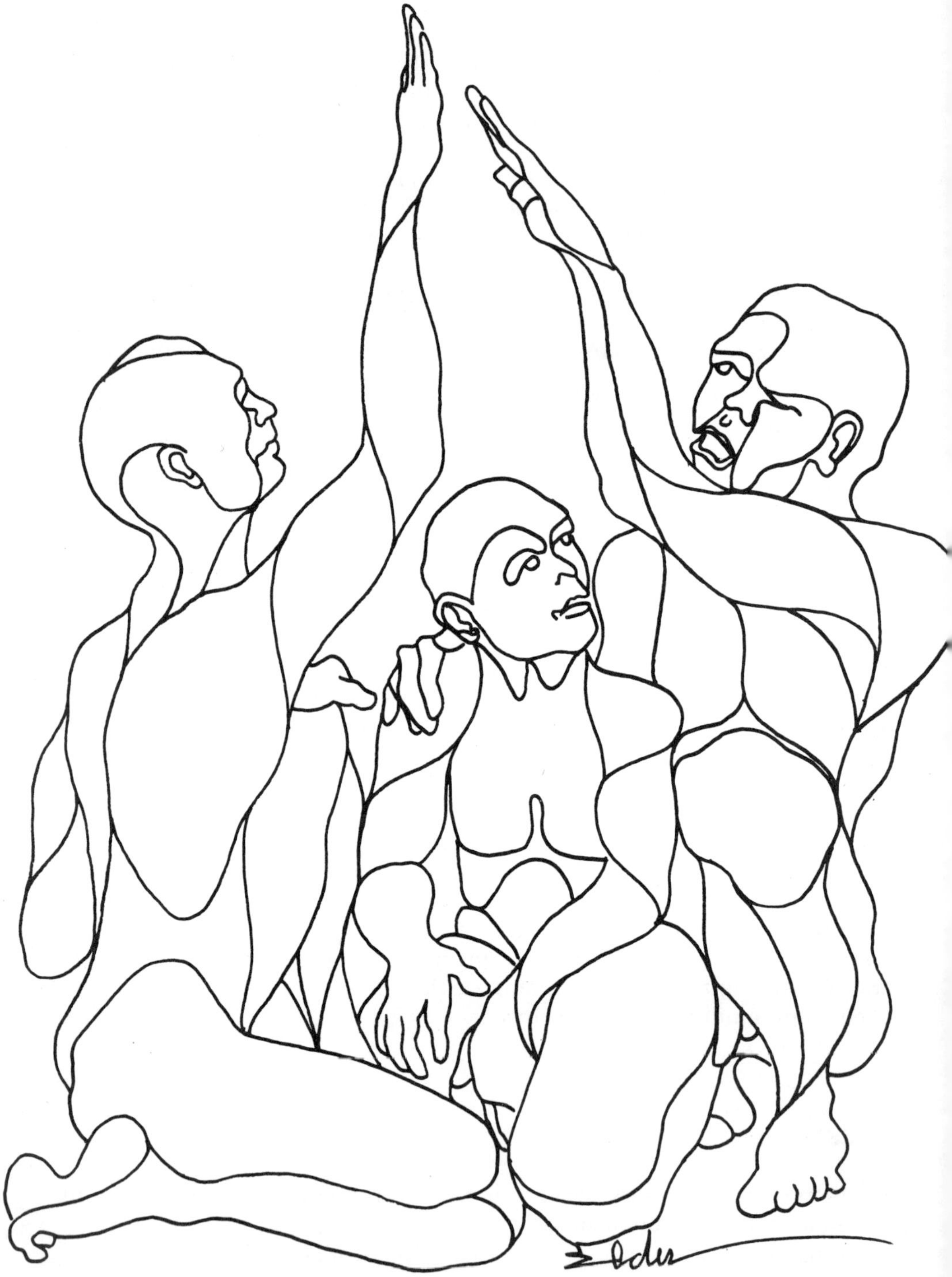

18

Education and Society

There is considerable variation in the social structure of societies. Some are small in numbers, some relatively large; some permit polygyny, some are strictly monogamous; some have a rigid stratification system, in others the class system is relatively loose and flexible; and so on. But regardless of size and the combination of choices from the cultural spectrum that prevails in any society, some structures to provide the function of socialization will be present. Each individual must learn the lore accumulated by his ancestors, must practice certain skills, must be indoctrinated with the values of his group, and must learn the expectations associated with the roles he will play.

EDUCATIONAL STRUCTURES

The transmission of culture can be only partially delegated to formal organizations, such as school systems or religious organizations. Much education always takes place in informal structures, such as play groups, in which the person learns by imitating his older playmates. Even in structures specifically set up to perform the function of socialization, there is, in addition to conscious and formal transmission of culture, a great deal of nondeliberate and informal passing-on of knowledge, skills, and values. In U. S. schools, for instance, both competition and cooperation are stressed. The first is found in strong rivalry for rewards, such as grades for academic work or success in athletics. Cooperation is taught through stress on group spirit and teamwork.

Informal Groups

Nonliterate Societies All nonliterate peoples have some form of transmission of culture, but the functions we think of as "educational" fall to the family, clan, or vocational or religious guild. While there are many variations, the fundamental content of folk education is not unlike that of urban societies: folklore, mythology, history, manual skills, appropriate manners, and instruction and practice in the folkways and mores.

The differences in education among nonliterate people rest, as they do with other peoples, on their views of the child. Some, like the Plains Indians, regard the child as a miniature adult, with much the same motives as an adult. Such tribes give much time to deliberate instruction in legends, moral tales, and religion. The Bantus of South Africa view the child as an irritating creature who is unaccountable in his conduct and subject, as are adults, to deception, threats, and intimidation. The Arapesh of New Guinea, in contrast, look on the child as one to be carefully guarded and gently instructed, since his function will be to take over the care and protection of his elders.

Sometimes the work of teaching is done by the parents, with one or the other taking the main responsibility; sometimes it is in the hands of uncles or aunts or grandparents. Though formal schools as we know them are entirely lacking, some differentiation of specialists is present. Such are the craftsmen of certain guilds who teach the crafts, shamans or priests who instruct in magical or religious rituals, and war leaders who train youth in skills of warfare.

Formal Organizations

Formal Education in the Ancient World Education as a special function of a particular group or agency did not arise until the invention of writing and arithmetic and advances in agriculture, metallurgy, and commerce. All the ancient civilizations—Egypt, Babylonia, Assyria, Persia, India, China, Greece, and Rome—had systems of formal education. In all these, however, it was confined to the privileged and leisure classes; and much of what has now become a part of formal schooling, such as vocational and civic training, was left to other groups: familial, religious, political, and economic. The upper classes tended to stress philosophy and ethics, art and music, rhetoric, mathematics, and gymnastics and military arts—studies considered proper interests of the ruling classes.

Formal Education in Western Europe In Europe, education in the Middle Ages was in the hands of the Roman Catholic Church. At first it was rather meager, consisting of simple instruction of the illiterate masses in church regulations and intellectual and moral initiation of individuals into the priesthood and orders of the church.

The serious beginnings of modern education, both elementary and higher, had to await the Renaissance, the Reformation, and important economic changes. Protestantism, with its emphasis on individualism in religion, the rise of trade and city life, and the Industrial Revolution, which freed the individual from serfdom and feudalism, began to break the upper-class and the theological holds on education. It became increasingly apparent that neither a sound representative government nor an efficient business or industry could be managed without literate and technically trained individuals.

Today all urban societies have extensive educational facilities: the school plant, a wide variety of curricula and methods of teaching, a specially trained personnel for management and instruction, and a rationale or philosophy of the aims, methods, and values of education.

Supplements to Formal Structures

The existence of schools, formal organizations that have as their principal function the education of the population, does not mean that all or even most socialization is provided by them. Both in folk and urban societies, most individuals receive their essential early training from their families and others. From parents and brothers and sisters people learn to walk and talk, and to distinguish the basic concepts of right and wrong which prevail in their societies. Even those who live in societies having elaborate formal educational systems get a large proportion of their knowledge and ideas of good and evil outside the school—from friends, elders, and from observing people in everyday situations.

In addition to learning in primary groups and in school, the individual in a literate society is exposed to an enormous amount of facts and opinions through the mass media. It makes good sense to consider newspapers, television and radio corporations, book publishers, and similar organizations as supplementary educational structures.

The Press

Books are pouring from American presses at the rate of about 15,000 titles a year. Nearly one-third of them are of a more or less technical character. These books furnish material for formal education, and the reading habits set up in school carry over to provide a means of further acquisition of skills, knowledge, and entertainment. Perhaps even more important than books are magazines and newspapers, which have been increasing in circulation in recent decades.

Books, magazines, and newspapers flood us with a stream of words that cannot fail to leave their impression. This material is constantly providing not only facts but myths, legends, and stereotypes that are reflected sooner or later in political, economic, religious, and moral attitudes and behavior. Reverence for the printed word is one of the reasons propaganda and advertising are very effective.

Movies, Radio, and Television

The Influence of the Media In addition, the motion picture, radio, and television have become powerful media of mass communication. During the week-long presentation which began on January 23, 1977, 130 million Americans saw some segment of the celebrated "Roots." Never before in history had a drama been seen and heard by so many people at the same time. But it is not in entertainment alone that such a gigantic visual impact has influence on people. The death of President Kennedy brought an estimated 90 per cent of the nation together in a common beholding of the funeral and a common mourning of the late President by way of television. The close-ups of police in Selma, Alabama, chasing black people with gas, clubs, pistols, and riot guns made that city an instantaneous symbol of moral indignation for many Americans. Within a week thousands of people poured into that small city from all over the country to demonstrate their sense of outrage. Clearly, the mass media has a substantial impact on the beliefs and behavior of people. In addition to their functions of newscasting and entertainment, both radio and television have been increasingly used in schools and universities to supplement formal instruction.

Never before has the world had such an array of agencies for mass impression. Oratory, formal teaching, religious exhortation, and all other methods of arousing groups of people with the same stimuli at the same time pale into insignificance beside these mighty forces. Whoever controls these media determines in large measure the mentality of people. In the United States, while formal education is predominantly state-controlled, these other means of stimulation are, with few exceptions, in the hands of private enterprise. But to an increasing extent, other nation-states are taking over control of the newer devices, combining them with the traditional educational system, sometimes in order to bend them to the ends of their particular political and economic systems.

The Control of Education

It would be a mistake to assume that there are no class and other group controls determining the character of education in a representative democracy. There are. In some European countries the class structure is more rigid than it is in the United States. In Britain, for example, both the Anglican Church and the upper class have, in the past, largely determined policy and practice in education. While the Industrial Revolution brought an increasing extension of school opportunities for the middle and lower classes, the system itself changed slowly toward a pattern more democratic in aim, content, and procedure.

In the United States, education was at first largely in the hands of the church and the local community; and it tended to be restricted to the rich and affluent. Free public education was not considered essential until it became clear to leaders and masses alike that universal literacy goes hand in hand with universal suffrage, participation in civil life, and complex technology. In most democratic countries the abolition of property qualifications for voting and office-holding is correlated with the demand for compulsory publicly financed elementary education.

While the classroom subject matter has changed through the decades, American education has revolved around the concepts of sound knowledge, public welfare, training in basic skills, and indoctrination in the fundamental values of democracy. An educated citizenry in a democracy means persons with not only sound knowledge and skill but also the ability to combine individual choice and freedom with a sense of personal and public responsibility for their judgments and actions. This does not imply that everyone will finish the same grade with the same education. Rather, it indicates that every means possible should be used to provide equality of opportunity in education for all the children of all the people, with due regard for individual differences. It is presumed that out of such a system will come intelligent citizens who will be capable of managing their own affairs and who at the same time will be voluntary participants in the larger concerns of the community and the nation.

Despite the many sharp and striking contrasts between education under representative democracy and under dictatorial systems, the aim of mass education is always to prepare the young for later participation in adult society. Hence the school will carry society's values to its charges. The aims and values may seem bizarre or dangerous to outsiders. For example, some nations that stress cooperation might be aghast at the degree to which Americans emphasize rivalry and competition in schools; while most Americans would certainly oppose the even greater degree to which competition is stressed in Japan, for example, where suicides because of college failure are common. But as long as a cultural system persists, the school will be its servant. Moreover, the moral principles of loyalty, obedience, patriotism, and a whole host of codes of good manners and mutual participation in group life have much in common in both systems. For example, many of the "Rules for School Children" adopted in 1943 by the Soviet leaders could fit, with slight modification, the democratic schools. The stress on diligence, obedience, personal cleanliness, good posture, use of proper language, and like matters is pretty much the same general tradition as our own. (Yesipov and Goncharov, 1947)

Illiteracy

The availability of education, especially basic education, in various countries is very much related to the economy of the society. Literacy and industrialization, for instance, go hand in hand. In 1969, one per cent (1,433,000 persons) of all U.S. citizens 14 years of age and older were illiterate. (The figure for the United States given in 18-1 is for the year 1969 to make it comparable to the other data in the

18-1 CHECKING IT OUT: Illiteracy in Selected Countries

Country	*Per Cent Illiterate**	*Year*
Argentina[1]	8.4	1971
Brazil	33.8	1970
Bulgaria	9.4	1965
Chile	11.9	1970
Dominican Republic	32.8	1970
Ecuador	32.5	1972
France	3.6	1946
Greece	15.6	1971
Hungary	2.0	1970
India	66.6	1971
Indonesia	43.4	1971
Iran	63.1	1971
Iraq	75.8	1965
Israel[2]	15.8	1961
Italy	6.1	1971
Japan	2.2	1960
Liberia	91.1	1962
Mexico	25.8	1970
Morocco	78.6	1971
Nicaragua	42.5	1971
Niger	98.6	1962
Pakistan	81.2	1961
Panama	21.7	1970
Paraguay	19.9	1972
Peru	27.6	1972
Philippines	17.4	1970
Poland	2.2	1970
Portugal	29.0	1970
Romania	11.4	1956
Senegal	94.4	1961
South Africa	43.0	1960
South West Africa	61.6	1960
Spain	9.8	1970
Sudan	85.3	1966
Syria	60.0	1970
Taiwan	46.1	1956
Thailand	21.4	1970
Turkey	48.7	1970
U.S.S.R.[3]	0.3	1970
United Arab Republic	80.5	1960
United States[1]	1.0	1969

Country	Per Cent Illiterate*	Year
Uruguay	9.7	1963
Venezuela	23.5	1971
Yugoslavia	16.5	1971

* Per cent illiterate refers to the per cent of the total population 15 years of age and older (except as noted) unable to read and write.
[1] Population aged 18 and older.
[2] Population aged 14 and older.
[3] Population aged 9–49.
SOURCE: Statistical Office of the United Nations, New York, N.Y., *Statistical Yearbook*; United Nations Educational, Scientific, and Cultural Organization, Paris, France, *UNESCO YEARBOOK*.

table.) Cultural and structural variations are seldom completely distinctive and unique. So it is with matters of education.

Like social institutions, the educational institution performs functions other than those for which it was manifestly created and intended. Formal school systems ordinarily have several latent functions. For one thing, beyond the elementary grades, schools serve as a marriage market. People tend to select spouses of a class and educational status approximately equal to their own, and there is no more likely place to find them than at school. Both high schools and colleges afford opportunities to meet and get to know persons of the opposite sex in one's age category and educational status.

A related latent function of educational structures is to provide an opportunity to widen the student's circle of acquaintances. One usually leaves college, for example, with a set of friends different from and broader than the set with which one left high school. Related to this consequence is, for many, the function of forming relationships with people who will become business or professional contacts in the future.

One latent function of the educational system of the United States is that schools keep a sizable and fairly predictable proportion of young people out of the labor force. Imagine the unemployment problem if more than 14 million young people 14 to 18 years of age who are now attending school were part of the labor force.

Education and Status

Other than socialization, probably the most important function of educational structures is conferring status. The amount of formal education one has is highly correlated with his class position. Research indicates that this is true not only in the United States but in Japan, Germany, the Soviet Union, and other industrial societies. Actually, education is related to one's position in the stratification structure in two ways: (1) a portion of people's evaluation of one's status derives directly from how much and what kind of education he or she has received, and (2) many of the other important criteria of class position, such as occupation, income, and style of life, are partially consequences of the type and amount of education one has had.

A majority of male college graduates, for example, have professional jobs while less than one-tenth of those with a high-school education attain such prestigious occupations. Similarly, men who finish college earn substantially more than men who have only a grammar-school education. The cash value of education, however, is not the same for everyone. At every educational level, the

18-2 CHECKING IT OUT: Median Income of Year-Round Full-Time Workers by Educational Attainment, 1976

Item	*Women*	*Men*
Elementary		
Less than 8 years	5,644	8,991
8 years	6,433	11,312
High School		
1–3 years	6,800	12,301
4 years	8,377	14,295
College		
1–3 years	9,475	15,514
4 years or more	12,109	19,338

SOURCE: U.S. Bureau of the Census, *Current Population Reports*, Series P-60, Nos. 80, 114, (Washington, D.C.: U.S. Government Printing Office, 1977).

annual income for women is less than what it is for men. Moreover, this income difference is not solely due to the lack of full-time employment opportunities for women. As the table indicates, the annual income for year-round, full-time women workers is lower than the annual income for men (including those who do not have year-round, full-time employment) at every educational level. Women with a high-school education earn less than men who have only a grade-school education and female college graduates with full-time employment have lower incomes than men with only a high-school education.

Perhaps the surest indicator of the importance of education in the stratification system is the eagerness with which newly wealthy but relatively uneducated people surround themselves with the trappings of learning: a library, paintings, a symphony subscription, and so on. Nor is this deference to education confined to the wealthy. Parents of moderate means who never graduated from high school see to it that their children attend college.

Education, then, not only helps one acquire income and occupational prestige; the education itself confers status, as illustrated in the concept "educated person."

EDUCATION IN THE UNITED STATES

Formal education in the United States has developed through three major phases. During colonial times and even during the first 50 years of our history as a nation, the support and control of education was almost entirely local. Between 1830 and 1880 the foundations of the modern school system were laid down, paralleling in development the nation's expanding industrial life. During this period the states more and more assumed control over their educational systems.

After about 1880 there was growing recognition of the central importance of schooling. Child labor was gradually abolished, girls and women were afforded more—but not equal—educational opportunities, and the curriculum was broadened to include health and vocational education. There was a great increase in the total amount of time spent in school. There was even greater attention to high-school training; and there has come, since World War II, a great increase in enrollments in colleges and universities. Recently the belief has spread that education should be a continuous process from infancy throughout life, and there has been a tremendous growth in programs of formal adult education.

18-3 CHECKING IT OUT: Per Cent of All 17 Year Olds Completing High School, 1870–1975

Year	*Per Cent*
1870	2.0
1880	2.5
1890	3.5
1900	6.4
1910	8.8
1920	16.8
1930	29.0
1940	50.8
1950	59.0
1960	65.1
1970	75.6
1975	74.4

SOURCE: U.S. Bureau of the Census, *Statistical Abstract of the United States, 1971* (Washington, D.C.: U.S. Government Printing Office, 1977), p. 153; and U.S. Bureau of the Census, *Historical Statistics of the United States* (Washington, D.C.: U.S. Government Printing Office, 1960), p. 207.

The Increase of Formal Education

One indication of the emphasis that people in the United States put on education is the fact that in 1970 more than 58 million persons were enrolled in schools and colleges. Nearly three-fifths (58.9 per cent) of all Americans between the ages of 5 and 34 were enrolled in some program of formal education. College enrollment in the U.S. more than doubled between 1960 and 1970 and the enrollment of women during this time increased one and one-half times while the college

18-4 CHECKING IT OUT: Educational Attainment of U.S. Adult Population, 1970*

	Per Cent Completing Each Educational Level				
Year of School Completed	*All Persons*	*White Males*	*White Females*	*Black Males*	*Black Females*
Elementary					
Less than 5 years	100.0	100.0	100.0	100.0	100.0
5–7 years	94.8	94.0	96.2	81.5	87.9
8 years	85.7	85.2	88.4	65.5	70.6
High School					
1–3 years	72.3	71.3	75.0	54.4	59.3
4 years	55.2	57.2	57.7	32.5	34.8
College					
1–3 years	21.2	26.3	18.7	10.0	10.4
4 or more years	11.0	15.0	8.6	4.6	4.4
Median School Years Completed	12.2	12.2	12.2	9.6	10.2

* Persons 25 years of age and older.
SOURCE: U.S. Bureau of the Census, *Statistical Abstract of the United States, 1971* (Washington, D.C.: U.S. Government Printing Office, 1971), p. 108.

enrollment of black Americans nearly tripled. Of all children in the U.S. between the ages of 7 and 14 more than 99 per cent are enrolled in school. In 1920, 18 per cent of all 18- and 19-year-olds were enrolled in school and 50 years later nearly one-half (48 per cent) were enrolled. In no other country in the world and at no other time in history has such a large proportion of a population been in school. This reflects an amazing faith in the value of formal education.

School opportunities have been expanding for the past hundred years. In 1870, 57 per cent of all persons in the United States between the ages of 5 and 17 were enrolled in school; by the end of World War I two-thirds of these young people were in school. By the end of World War II the number had risen to 80 per cent; in 1970 more than 95 per cent were enrolled in school. In 1870, 2 per cent of all 17-year-olds were high-school graduates and 100 years later 77 per cent of all 17-year-olds had completed high school.

Elementary education had become firmly established in the United States by the turn of the nineteenth century and secondary enrollments had been going up slowly since 1880. In 1890 there were about 400,000 high-school students; in 1910 about 900,000. In 1940 there were 6.6 million; by 1970 there were more than 14 million. The growth of college and university enrollments has also been impressive. In 1900 there were only about 200,000 students in this category. The next 40 years saw a million added to this number. In 1950 there were more than 2.2 million students in American colleges and universities; and in 1970 college and university enrollments reached a record high of over 7 million.

Changes in Curriculum

A Child-Centered Curriculum Since what is taught in school is largely a reflection of the norms of the larger society, changes in the curriculum are indicators of the total institutional structure of our society. In the recent past the main shifts in elementary-secondary education have been from curricula oriented around subject matter to those focused on the child as a growing personality. The former stressed content and capacity to reproduce what had been read or heard. Today the school is more child-centered, with stress on the self and on social development. In methods, the shift has been from a rather severe authoritarianism to a more permissive practice, in which the child has a larger degree of participation. "Progressive education," though now largely discarded as a formal technique, has influenced even the more conservative public and parochial schools. Motivation, cooperative learning, and mental hygiene are given much attention.

Changing Course Content The rapid rise in high-school population, especially after 1910, led to a proliferation of separate courses and various groupings of courses of study, such as liberal or college-preparatory, commercial, vocational, and fine arts. In the first half of the century, there had been a drift away from courses designed to prepare the pupil for higher education to those having a more practical usefulness in jobs or in the home and giving the future citizen some preparation for his public and political rights and duties. The ancient languages, algebra, geometry, trigonometry, and formal political history have tended to give way to modern languages, "modern" mathematics (with emphasis on understanding rather than mere mastery of operations), and social studies with emphasis on current problems. Intense competition with the Soviet Union, in the 1950s, led to reexamination of the desirability of a stronger curriculum in science and mathematics. After Sputnik, it was contended in many high quarters of government and education that the Soviet "superiority" or "success" was due to the fact that students in the USSR were far more thoroughly trained in the natural sciences, mathematics, and technology than those in the United States.

Junior High Schools and Junior Colleges Along with these trends has gone considerable reorganization of the institutional framework. The secondary school is being extended downward to include the last two years of the traditional elementary program, and upward to cover the first two years of college. The former we know as the junior high school; the latter, the junior or community college. In the U.S., junior colleges have grown rapidly. In 1928 they had an enrollment of about 50,000; four decades later their enrollment was 1,300,000. Under the growing pressure for college education, many communities have established a two-year college course, sometimes in connection with their high schools. It may well be that these "community colleges" will come to be the typical terminus of formal education for many in the population.

While development of high schools has been, to some extent, a hit-or-miss affair, and while there has been some confusion of purpose, the leaders of American education have come more and more to take the position that virtually every person should have at least a high-school education, and an ever-growing portion of our young people at least two years of college. Indeed, a college education is being thought of increasingly as a "right" rather than a "privilege." (Clark, 1960) The trends in secondary education look largely to occupational preparation, but it is assumed that citizens must have some general education as well. Programs to meet this need include literature, history, and science and also try to stress social values that lead to a "well-rounded" personality.

Colleges and Occupational Preparation Like the secondary schools, colleges have witnessed considerable changes in the course of study, though these have been less drastic than in high schools. There has been a shift from classical courses to those of a more applied or "practical" sort. There has been a considerable increase in preprofessional and professional courses in medicine, engineering, journalism, art, agriculture, social work, and teaching. As new specialized vocations arise—for example, in personnel and other administrative work, in computer sciences, marketing and accounting, in public relations for business and government, and in radio and television—the colleges and universities provide training for these new occupations.

The Decline of Reading and Writing In 1957, the average verbal score on the national Scholastic Aptitude Tests was 473. In 1973, the average had dropped 33 points to 440. In 1976, the results of a four-year study conducted by the U.S. Office of Education showed that 23 million persons in America are functionally illiterate. Such statistics demonstrate a decline in academic achievement which is apparent across the nation. They may, in fact, be the result of curriculum changes reflecting quite different attitudes about the role of teachers and the functions of schooling. A critic of the contemporary educational system recently identified the factors most responsible for the decline in student performance. They were the lack of emphasis on the traditional disciplines and the concentration rather on educational innovations. (Armbruster, 1977) For example, instruction in traditional courses of grammar has diminished greatly. Some teachers of English reject the notion of one correct grammar and one standard of word usage. Such teachers give the speech patterns of all individuals equal respect and stress that students should not be made to feel inferior because of the way they speak or write. The controversy surrounding Black English is related to the awareness that in learning standard English, minority children must quickly infer that the English that they speak is incorrect. Critics of this view stress the lessened occupational mobility for those who cannot use the standard English demanded by employers.

The lower level of academic achievement is not a problem specific to minority students. The reluctance of educators to stress grammar or to assign homework has contributed to poor reading and writing skills in middle- and upper-class schools as well as in ghetto schools.

Adult Education

In 1957, a public opinion poll reported that "more than two out of every five adults in the voting population expressed the desire to engage in some kind of study." The survey also showed that more women than men wanted adult education; that the 21-29 age group expressed the greatest demand; and that the more schooling a person had, the more additional education he or she wanted. In subject matter, social science stood first, with professional fields second. (Kurtz, 1957)

There are various reasons for this interest in adult education. Desire to improve one's knowledge and skill with respect to job or profession is one. Wide public interest in domestic and foreign affairs, coupled with the growing belief that only through an informed citizenry can the country solve its problems, is another. Then too, people have much more leisure than formerly. Forced retirements, technological unemployment, as well as a growing population of senior citizens have created a new group of educational consumers who want to prepare for new careers, want exposure to the experiences of college, or who want to take up reading, crafts, arts, or other activities to enrich their lives. The press, radio, television, and the motion picture provide some of the needed information, but not enough. More formal school facilities are also required.

In the early days there were lecture series and chautauqua, educational-recreational assemblies of several days' duration. Then came public forums and more formal adult education under both private and public sponsorship. Various universities set up extension and correspondence courses. Every state now has some facilities for extension work. While many students work for credit in these courses, many others enroll for the satisfaction of getting additional knowledge.

Another adult education effort has been the Americanization program, especially during the decades when this country was receiving thousands of European immigrants each year. More recently, various plans to combat discrimination against minority groups and to foster good will have been attempted under such titles as "Intercultural Education" or "Equal Opportunity Programs."

There is a wide variety of technical institutes, both public and private, which as yet have not been integrated into the formal educational system. In addition, many industrial and business firms have programs of apprentice and in-service training for specialized vocations.

EDUCATION AND STRATIFICATION

One of the consequences of formal education has been the conferral of status. An examination of the system of formal education in U.S. society reveals that the amount and quality of education one receives varies with income, occupation, sex, race, and region. Each of these variables has consequences for the stratification system, not only in its own right but to the degree that it influences educational opportunity and hence life chances.

Income

It can generally be said that the lower the income the higher the fertility rate. This creates a relative concentration of school-age children in low-income families. Thus the families which can least afford to send even one child through school are those most likely to have a number of children. Not only is the family hard put to finance a college education for any of its members, but their children have higher probabilities of terminating their educations prior to college.

The family income is related not only to the amount but to the kind of education one is likely to receive. Students from higher-income families can afford more education and are hence more likely to aspire to the professions, which require more years of preparation and more expensive schooling. Students from families with lower incomes usually have little choice but to enroll in commercial and industrial courses. (Warner, Havighurst, and Loeb, 1944)

Occupation

Income and occupational prestige are positively correlated and there is a direct relationship between the occupational status of the parents and the amount of

18-5 CHECKING IT OUT: Father's Education and Son's Education

Son's Educational Attainment	Educational Status of Father: Not High-school Graduate	High-school Graduate But No College	Some College	College Graduate
No high-school diploma	42.6	10.3	6.5	4.0
High-school diploma but no college	34.1	36.1	23.8	8.2
At least some college attendance	23.3	43.7	69.7	87.9

SOURCE: Murray Gendell and Hans L. Zetterberg, eds., *A Sociological Almanac for the United States*, 2nd ed. (New York: Charles Scribner's Sons, 1964), p. 80; based upon men twenty to twenty-four years of age, October 1960.

education children receive. The lower the occupational level of the parents, the less the educational attainment of their children. Research at Indiana University shortly after World War II revealed that 14 per cent of the student body was composed of sons of professional men, although professionals constituted only 4 per cent of the state's population. On the other hand, only 13 per cent of the students were sons of semiskilled and unskilled laborers, although such workers constituted 44 per cent of the population. This situation existed despite the fact that government aid had greatly increased the number of students from lower-class homes attending college: the G.I. Bill of Rights had nearly doubled the proportion of students from the lower occupational strata attending the university. (Mulligan, 1951)

These occupational and income data indicate, of course, that the class structure has functions for the educational institutions themselves. Studies have shown that most public-school teachers in the United States come from middle-class families. It is not surprising, then, that the schools are oriented to middle-class norms. (Hollingshead, 1949; 1975)

Region

Even desegregation will not alone wipe out inequalities in opportunity according to race. Nearly one-half of all black Americans still live in the Southern region, and in terms of the ranking of the regions according to the quality of formal education, the South stands at the bottom. The Southern states, for the most part spend less for schools and invest less per pupil than most states in other sections.

This situation exists in the South partly as a reflection of rural-urban differences. The South is heavily rural and, throughout the United States, the proportion of individuals enrolled in school for each age category is highest in urban and lowest in rural-farm areas.

Clearly, a sizable proportion of the population is capable of acquiring more formal education than it is now given opportunity to secure. The stratification system operates to remove some of these people from school before they have an opportunity to realize their educational potential.

Race

The Roots of the Problem Black Americans have long been discriminated against in education as well as in most other areas of American life. Although the situation has changed in recent years, discrimination persists. Evidences of this oppression, as it relates to education, may be found in Perkinson's book, *The Imperfect Panacea: American Faith in Education, 1865–1965.* (1968) Looking at Perkinson's material, we may relate the racial problems of the nation's schools to the Southern strategy following the Civil War. At a time when most of America's blacks lived in the rural South (90 per cent in 1900), Perkinson comments that "it became necessary to ensure the perpetuation of the ignorance of one race and the enlightenment of the other. Education would ensure that each race remained 'in its place.' " (p. 21) Perkinson says that all the education bills passed at this time revealed the white strategy of "constraining the Negro by curtailing his educational opportunities while at the same time providing liberal educational opportunities for whites." Texas set up a public school fund for the education of "white scholastics," and Georgia planned for the schooling of all those from the ages of 6 through 21 as long as they were "free white inhabitants." But just as the Southern whites saw the reestablishment of white supremacy in the inferior education of blacks, the black Reconstructionists saw their only hope in education. In two states, South Carolina and Louisiana, blacks were able to secure state constitutions insuring integrated schools. They sought to avoid segregated schools that would stigmatize blacks as "second-class citizens." In Florida and Mississippi state constitutions were interpreted to allow mixed schools. However, without compulsory education laws, whites kept their children home. The laws were openly flouted by the creation of all-white schools.

Passage of the Civil Rights Act of 1875 included a plank prohibiting segregated schools; this was removed before passage. When President Hayes removed Northern troops from the South in 1877, Reconstruction ended, and with Reconstruction ended any hopes that Southern blacks might have had for educational power. They were systematically disenfranchised (poll tax, grandfather clause). In 1896 in Louisiana there were 130,334 black voters. In 1904 there were 1,342. In 1896 black registrants were a majority in 26 parishes; by 1900 in none. As blacks lost political power, school funds allocated to black schools were diverted and spent in white schools.

From 1877 to 1885 the average monthly salaries of black and white teachers were identical. In 1886, Mississippi adopted a law permitting separate salary scales. By 1895 white teachers were earning $33.04 monthly, black teachers $21.46. Without political power, terrorized and discriminated against, blacks steadily lost ground. In some counties of Mississippi in 1907 from $30 to $38 was spent on the education of each white child. Expenditures for black children ranged from 27¢ to one dollar. This should to some degree explain the educational deprivation of blacks as they began migrating to the urban centers of the North.

And yet in this situation, the *North* also has much to be ashamed of. Over the past 70 years as blacks have escaped North in the hope of educational and vocational opportunities, they have been effectively kept powerless by their relegation to urban ghettos and de facto segregation in the schools. Dr. Kenneth Clark has pointed out that a systematic study of the consequences of schools segregated in fact, compared with the consequences of schools segregated by law, finds that the psychological consequences are the same. De facto segregated schools generally create as high a percentage of woefully retarded children as did de jure segregation. "The basic story of academic achievement in Harlem is one of inefficiency, inferiority, and massive deterioration" (Clark, 1965, p. 119).

The Coleman Report

A Historic Survey The Coleman Report (1966) has been a significant educational document for the country in its examination of quality education and integration. It has had an important effect on the integration of schools, particularly where busing has occurred. The Coleman Report was the result of a massive study of 4,000 American schools all across the country. The study surveyed over a half million students and 71,000 teachers and principals. For the first time in American history, a systematic effort was made to find out what effect different school characteristics had on what black and white students learned. There was also an attempt to diagnose those factors that make students learn.

School Facilities Schools attended by blacks across the nation have fewer of the facilities that seem related to achievement (i.e., fewer books per pupil in libraries, less access to chemistry and language laboratories) but the differences are not very large. In some cases, blacks are better off than whites. In the South the average school plant of blacks is apt to be newer. In the North, the black elementary school is apt to be older. Nationwide, the average black school is more likely than the average white to have a library and a full-time librarian (pp. 10–11).

Staff Teachers of blacks are on the whole inferior to teachers of whites, but the differences are small and far from uniform. Teachers of blacks score lower on tests of verbal ability, think worse of the colleges they attended, have lower morale, and are more eager to transfer to another school. In the urban North, black students have one chance in three of getting a black teacher. White students have one chance in 50. Black teachers are drawn from the middle of the black ability distribution. White teachers are also drawn from the middle of the white ability distribution. It seems that the best black college students are not becoming teachers any more than the best white students are.

In the South There were a lot of surprises. In the rural South, black males were more apt to be in school at 16 and 17 than were whites. Perhaps because of the desire to move to the North, a diploma is felt to be more important to blacks. In the urban South black females were more apt to stay in school longer than white females (possibly with the realization that they would work after marriage). Furthermore, while blacks were more apt (nationwide) to drop out of school, and less likely to go to college, they were no less eager than whites to stay in school and expressed more of a *desire* to enter college.

Tests As part of their study the researchers included a battery of tests (verbal and nonverbal ability, reading comprehension, math, natural sciences, social studies, humanities). While the researchers found small external differences between schools, blacks according to these tests were learning substantially less than whites. The average scores of blacks were one standard deviation below those of whites, meaning that 85 per cent of black scores were below the white average. Only one-sixth of black first graders scored above the national average on tests of verbal ability. The same was true for black high-school seniors. Of all the tests that they administered the researchers found that *verbal ability* was the best measure of a school's effectiveness. They could correlate verbal ability of students to quality of school. If we accept the premise that schools are the means to upward mobility in the society, verbal ability is then crucial to success in school, to intellectual attainment, and to college entrance and job success. It was found that the state of the physical educational plant had little to do with the attainment of verbal skills. The student culture was a key factor. And the difference was greater for blacks than for whites. Blacks did better if they had middle-class schoolmates.

This was the major finding of the report: Black students did better in predominantly middle-class schools and worse in predominantly lower-class schools, but that racial integration had little or no independent effect. Integrating poor blacks with poor whites, in other words, probably does no good.

Integrating poor blacks with middle-class blacks might do as much good as integrating them with middle-class whites, but as a practical matter there aren't enough blacks to go around. (One reason for this is that 40% of all white collar blacks send their children to private schools.) For the forseeable future, social class integration will be impossible without racial integration as well.

Other Important Revelations:

1. Self-concept—black students did not show as much confidence as whites that their personal behavior would affect what happened to them. They were more likely to feel that "people like me don't have a chance to be successful in life." They were more likely to feel that success is more dependent on luck than hard work and they were more likely to feel that "every time I try to get ahead something or somebody stops me." (p. 289)

2. A black child's achievement was closely correlated to his feeling that he could control his own destiny. The report suggests that blacks are somewhat more likely to feel they can control their fate if they attend racially integrated schools.

3. Pouring money into black schools will probably accomplish little or nothing. The report provides much indirect evidence that such innovations have made little difference in the past.

4. Middle-class children do as well in heavily integrated schools as elsewhere.

18-6 CHECKING IT OUT: Denver School Busing Succeeds; Social Mixture Called a Factor

While Bostonians resisted, Denverites desegregated their schools this fall under a busing program that has caused some complaints and tension but no violence or overt displays of racial hatred.

Many pupils and parents here say they do not like busing and many have moved to the suburbs to avoid it, but there is pride here that when legal avenues of opposition were exhausted, residents obeyed court edicts and are thus far giving desegregation a chance.

Why? The answers most Denverites give are tied to the city's racial and social mixture. The city lacks a key ingredient found in Boston's troubles: a substantial number of lower-class whites. Most either moved to the suburbs years ago or are too old to have children in school. If Denver's almost totally white suburbs were forced to accept minority students from inner city schools, there would almost certainly be trouble, observers believe.

Another factor is that the population of the city of Denver is more than 80 per cent white. It is relatively affluent and has one of the highest education levels of any city in the nation. Most of those who stay or who move in decide consciously that they want to live in an intergrated inner city.

In any case, whites in Denver generally do not feel threatened by minority group members.

The 1970 census showed a minority population of 16.8 per cent, of which Mexican-Americans accounted for 11.3 per cent and blacks wer 4.1 per cent. The blacks are relatively affluent and upwardly mobile, compared with the Mexican-American community, which has voted for antibusing school board candidates and tends to favor bilingual, bicultural compensatory education programs in schools where their children form a majority.

Denver resisted desegregation for more than six years. The change was first proposed by Rachel Noel, the school board's first black member, on April 25, 1968, and approved in a 5-to-2 vote of the school board a month later.

This fall, after a long series of legal battles that went all the way to the United States Supreme Court, a desegregation program involving busing went into effect under close supervision by Federal District Judge William E. Doyle.

A boycott, led by an antibusing group, called the Citizens Association for Neighborhood Schools, came apart under a series of restraining orders issued by Judge Doyle against organizing of boycotts.

SOURCE: James P. Sterba, *The New York Times,* October 26, 1974, p. 34.

The Effects of the Coleman Report The Coleman Report proved to be a major influence on the educational development of the nation's schools in the decade following its publication. It stimulated the use of **busing** as a means of achieving more racially integrated schools. It has contributed to the dramatic change in the racial composition of Southern schools. It is a curious fact that while 38 per cent of Southern white parents and 24 per cent of Northern white parents say they would not object to sending their children to a school where as many as half the students are black, only 4 per cent of Americans favor busing as a means of integrating schools (Gallup Opinion Index, 1976). The majority of busing programs have been accomplished in the nation's schools without incident. However, the violent resistence of Northern "white ethnic" communities, as in Boston in 1976, have clearly indicated the racism in segments of the country's population, and also the depth of white fears about the impact of lower-class children on the educational quality of middle-class schools. This latter consideration has had an unforeseen result. Court-ordered integration of urban schools has resulted in the more rapid movement of middle-class whites out of the cities. Finally, empirical studies on the effects of integration and desegregation on black students have been controversial and uneven in their conclusions. Some studies find that blacks have benefited; other studies reveal negative results academically and psychological stress. (St. John, 1975)

Race and Intelligence—Scientific Racism?

Just as physical anthropologists have carefully described physical differences among human groups in an attempt to develop or dispute racial categories, so too have other social scientists devoted attention to the differing achievements of racial minorities, attempting to relate cultural abilities, athletic prowess, and intellectual accomplishments to inborn characteristics. Certainly the Social Darwinist ideologies of the nineteenth century caused many English-speaking whites to accept the view that they were intellectually superior to nonwhites that they were colonizing. The acceptance of the belief that there are inherited differences among the races has most often related to intelligence. In the United States the differences in intelligence between blacks and whites has been a continuing source of controversy. Some people have chosen to take the fact that whites are more often found in high economic or educational statuses than are blacks as evidence of racial superiority. Social scientists, however, accept the economic differences between the races as the consequences of social stratification, not biology.

One situation, in which differences in intelligence between blacks and whites were empirically examined, occurred when an enormous number of American draftees were given tests measuring intelligence after World War I.

18-7 CHECKING IT OUT: Average Scores on Two Army Intelligence Tests of 1,750,000 Men During World War I

Category	*Alpha Test (for literates)*	*Beta Test (for illiterates)*
White	59	43
Northern Negro	39	32
Southern Negro	12	20

SOURCE: Robert D. North, "The Intelligence of American Negroes," *Research Reports*, 1955, 3:2–8. Tables from p. 4. By permission.

18-8 CHECKING IT OUT: Contrasts of Whites from Three Lowest Scoring States with Negroes from Three Highest Scoring States on Army Alpha Test of Intelligence During World War I

	Whites			*Negroes*	
State	*Number of Cases*	*Median Score*	*State*	*Number of Cases*	*Median Score*
Arkansas	618	41.0	New York	850	44.5
Kentucky	832	41.0	Ohio	152	48.8
Mississippi	665	40.8	Illinois	578	46.9

SOURCE: North, "The Intelligence of American Negroes," p. 4.

The table seems to indicate that whites are more intelligent than blacks. But the fact that the differences between Northern and Southern blacks are even greater than those between Northern blacks and whites raises a question: how much of the differences in intelligence test scores is attributable to differences in cultural experience? There is no evidence to support the theory that the more intelligent blacks move North. How much of the Southern black's poorer test performance, then, is traceable to inferior schools, less well-educated teachers and parents, fewer years of formal education, and so on? The answer is apparent from the table, which contrasts blacks from the three highest-scoring states with whites from the lowest-scoring states. Several other studies made at different times in various parts of the country indicate that differences in performance on intelligence tests by race, as well as differences by region, are attributable to environmental factors. It should be stressed that differences in cultural experience make it just as difficult to prove that there are not inherited differences between races as to prove that there are. But there has been no scientific evidence to support the belief that such inherited differences exist. The controversy surrounding race and intelligence was revived recently when Arthur Jensen (1969), an educational psychologist at the University of California at Berkeley published a lengthy research paper in the *Harvard Educational Review*. After noting that the average score for whites on intelligence tests (I.Q.) was ten to fifteen points higher than the average score for blacks, Jensen suggested that the differences in scores was the result of genetic or inherited differences, with blacks being genetically the intellectual inferiors of whites.

Intelligence—The Result of Nature or Nurture?

This extraordinary conclusion must be related to the concept of intelligence as it is generally understood. First of all, social scientists continue to disagree about the definition of intelligence. Although some recognize intelligence as "that which intelligence tests measure," this is not considered helpful for purposes of analysis. Intelligence has many dimensions and can variously be defined as the capacity to think in abstract terms, the capacity to learn, to solve problems, to adapt to the environment. Just as there is disagreement about the properties of this element of personality, there is also disagreement about the degree to which it is an inherited or a learned ability. Jensen believes the contribution of genetic factors to intelligence as it is measured by I.Q. tests is .81; Christopher Jencks (1972) thinks .45 is a more reasonable figure. Jensen is then suggesting that "nature," or what is inherited from parents, most crucially determines intelligence, with the effects of learning and environment, or "nurture" to be much less important. He then theorizes that "genetic factors are strongly implicated in the average Negro-white intelligence difference" (p. 82). Scholars like Jencks do not discount the influence of genetic inheritance on test performance but rather they disagree about the extent to which environment affects the way blacks and whites test. This is because intelligence tests are in fact aptitude tests tapping specific areas of achievement (i.e., language, reasoning abilities, spatial relationships, symbolic, and mathematical knowledge). We might remember that such tests do not tap intellectual abilities like creativity and social interaction skills. Because I.Q. tests depend on language abilities and assume a basic fund of information in a particular age group, they are *culture bound.* They tap the abilities and cultural learning of the American middle class. Because blacks and others are less often to be found in the middle class and because the language, vocabulary, and information contained in the test are more accessible to middle-class individuals, the I.Q. test is not tapping intelligence at all but the cultural learnings of the middle class.

Jerome Kagan (1973) demonstrates the degree to which I.Q. tests tap middle-class skills in the pre-test activities of Ernest Haggard. Haggard spent con-

18-9 CHECKING IT OUT: Subcultural Learnings Reflected in Adrian Dove's "Chitling Test"

1. Who did "Stagger Lee" kill?
(A) His mother (B) Frankie (C) Johnny (D) His girlfriend (E) Billy
2. A"gas head" is a person who has a
(A) Fast-moving car (B) Stable of "lace" (C) "Process" (D) Habit of stealing cars (E) Long jail record for arson
3. If a man is called a "blood," then he is a
(A) Fighter (B) Mexican-American (C) Negro (D) Hungry hemophile (E) Redman or Indian
4. If you throw the dice and 7 is showing on the top, what is facing down?
(A) Seven (B) Snake Eyes (C) Boxcars (D) Little Joes (E) 11
5. Cheap chitlings (not the kind you purchase at a frozen-food counter) will taste rubbery unless they are cooked long enough. How soon can you quit cooking them to eat and enjoy them?
(A) 45 minutes (B) 2 hours (C) 24 hours (D) 1 week (on a low flame) (E) 1 hour
6. "Down home" (the South) today, for the average "soul brother" who is picking cotton (in season) from sunup until sundown, what is the average earning (take home) for one full day?
(A) $.75 (B) $1.65 (C) $3.50 (D) $5 (E) $12
7. A "handkerchief head" is
(A) A cool cat (B) A Porter (C) An Uncle Tom (D) A hoddi (E) A preacher
8. "Jet" is
(A) An East Oakland motorcycle club (B) One of the gangs in "West Side Story" (C) A news and gossip magazine (D) A way of life for the very rich
9. "And Jesus said, 'Walk together children . . .' "
(A) "Don't get weary. There's a great camp meeting" (B) "For we shall overcome" (C) "For the family that walks together talks together" (D) By your patience you will win your souls" (Luke 21:19) (E) "Mind the things that are above, not the things that are on earth" (Col. 3:3)

10 If a pimp is up tight with a woman who gets state aid, what does he mean when he talks about "Mother's Day"?
(A) Second Sunday in May (B) Third Sunday in June (C) First of every month (D) None of these (E) First and fifteenth of every month

11. Jazz pianist Ahmad Jamal took an Arabic name after becoming really famous. Previously he had some fame with what he called his "slave name." What was his previous name?
(A) Willie Lee Jackson (B) LeRoi Jones (C) Wilbur McDougal (D) Fitz Jones (E) Andy Johnson

12. What is Willie Mae's last name?
(A) Schwartz (B) Matsuda (C) Gomez (D) Turner (E) O'Flaherty

13. What are the "Dixie Hummingbirds"?
(A) A part of the KKK (B) A swamp disease (C) A modern gospel group (D) A Mississippi paramilitary group (E) Deacons

14. "Bo Diddley" is a
(A) Game for children (B) Down home cheap wine (C) Down home singer (D) New dance (E) Mojo call

15. "Hully gully" came from
(A) East Oakland (B) Fillmore (C) Watts (D) Harlem (E) Motor City

16. Which word is most out of place here?
(A) Splib (B) Blood (C) Gray (D) Spook (E) Black

The answers

1. (E)	**3.** (C)	**5.** (C)	**7.** (C)	**9.** (A)	**11.** (D)	**13.** (C)	**15.** (C)
2. (C)	**4.** (A)	**6.** (D)	**8.** (C)	**10.** (E)	**12.** (D)	**14.** (C)	**16.** (C)

SOURCE: *New York Times,* July 2, 1968.

siderable time explaining test procedures to lower-class children, attempting to allay the fears associated with intelligence tests and motivating better performance through promise of rewards. This preparatory activity resulted in an average improvement from 15 to 20 points. Adrian Dove also focused on cultural learnings when he developed his "Chitling Test." This measure, which is standardized on the cultural information of ghetto inhabitants, would frustrate most white and many black middle-class pupils. This kind of cultural bias indicates that intelligence tests do not, in themselves, allow us to differentiate between what is "caught" through inheritance and what is "taught" through training and education.

CURRENT ISSUES IN EDUCATION

There are numerous issues in educational ideology that continue to be topics of public discussion.

Social Action vs. Conformity

In examining the place of the school in the community, there is the perennial question of the treatment of public issues in the classroom. The problem of academic freedom usually arises whenever special-interest groups in the community object to teachers' discussing topics which such groups consider either "dangerous" or none of the school's business.

In the matter of social action the taboo is even more severe. Direct participation in reform on the part of teachers usually meets with strong opposition from those who control the schools at every level. High-school or college students have only recently begun to take part in conflicts between labor unions and employers or become active in political campaigns. This is not true, of course, in some countries, where the institutions of higher learning especially are often the seedbeds of progressive and even radical movements.

Federal Aid and Local Control

Another problem has to do with the nature and kind of federal aid that public education may or should receive. In the past, the major support of education has come largely from local and state sources. While most states have tried to equalize educational opportunities within their own boundaries, marked differences among states and regions continue, as we have seen. Out of an awareness of this differential and out of general concern about further extension of schooling has come a growing pressure for more federal funds for the schools.

There has been much opposition to such proposals from business interests that object to further federal taxation and from many educators who believe that, if such aid were given, the federal government would play an even larger part in the direct control of the schools. There is, in other words, some anxiety that further governmental control of the school might be a threat to traditional freedom of education. Nonetheless, academic deficiencies in large numbers of public school students stimulate pressure for federal aid.

Public vs. Private Schools

What is the relation of private to public education in a democracy? The courts have more or less consistently contended that education is a function of the nonpolitical groups of our national society, as well as of the government. (Young, 1956) There can be no doubt that privately endowed institutions of higher learning have played an important part in our national life. Yet mounting costs of schooling have led some to argue in favor of government aid to such institutions. Again, the fear of direct control makes many people connected with privately supported schools hesitate to press for government help. Since a good deal of the private schooling in this country is in the hands of religious denominations, there is the further complication of government support for church activities.

Indeed, there has been a good deal of sharp public debate, as well as a number of court cases, dealing with tax aid to private schools. Such matters as teachers' salaries, provision of school buses, free textbooks, and free lunches are controversial. Many parents believe that since they pay taxes to support the public schools even though they send their children to private schools for which they must pay fees, it is only just and proper that aid be given to the private schools.

Deschooling Society

While it is true that colleges and universities participate in the training of many specialists who function in technological society, it has also been true that a liberal arts degree is a passport to a better job and higher socioeconomic status. There has been growing criticism of U.S. schools as discriminatory structures that block advancement and deny access. Ivan Illich has repeatedly asserted that "almost the entire American structure of schooling is irrelevant for gaining competence in the vast majority of American jobs (Illich, 1970, p. 37) Both Illich and Paul Goodman (1968) advocate less schooling. Both use the example of the law as a profession that can be adequately learned without benefit of law school. Illich notes that the legal schooling of some of our great jurists has been "negligible." If students can learn through apprenticeships (i.e., as a clerk to a lawyer), the educational experience can be more meaningful and less discriminatory.

Open Admissions

Because Americans have always used the educational system to resolve pressing social problems, the lack of mobility of minorities, particularly blacks, has become a concern of educators. It is clear that socioeconomic status is closely related to the level of education attained. In order to enjoy the financial and social rewards of the society to a greater degree, it was necessary for minorities to have access to higher education. A solution to this problem has been attempted through open admissions programs. In New York, where open admissions was instituted in 1970, all graduates of the city's high schools were guaranteed a seat in one of the local colleges. The underlying reason for this innovation has been that all may have access to higher education, and where educational deficiencies occur, remedial help and support services will be made available; then demands for competency and ability will come at the end of the educational experience in college rather than at the beginning. Thus a true chance at educational opportunity will be given to those put at a disadvantage by inferior schools and teachers. By instituting open admissions, both New York and California gave unique opportunities to black students and to disadvantaged white students, too. The Fleischmann report revealed that whereas only

10 per cent of seniors at East Harlem's Benjamin Franklin High School applied to colleges before open admissions and only 1 per cent were accepted, the new system caused 76 per cent to apply. (1973)

Affirmative Action—The Bakke Case

Affirmative action programs constitute another response in this society to the question of how best to provide significant opportunities for the advancement of minorities. Both in the case of admissions to colleges and professional schools and in the case of occupational hiring practices, the use of race as a factor in admissions and hiring has been another contemporary attempt to offer access to those who have been traditionally excluded. And yet there has been little consensus on the best way to employ "race consciousness" in providing opportunities for mobility. Professor Ralph R. Smith of the University of Pennsylvania Law School and the National Conference of Black Lawyers suggests three current points of view in his article "Bakke's Case vs. the Case for Affirmative Action" (1978). Some academics and educators take the view that equality of opportunity is possible only if "race were used to make compensatory adjustments in test scores and admission standards . . ." This is akin to the traditional policy of adding a fixed number of points to the scores of Armed Forces veterans on Civil Service tests. A second approach to race consciousness in admissions and hiring is to be aware of race and to consider it as one factor among many to take into account. A third view recognizes the effects of discrimination on minorities historically and accepts "more stringent measures up to and including the designation of a given number of places for minorities" (p. 3).

In the case of Allan Bakke, the Supreme Court was being asked to affirm or deny the constitutionality of college admissions programs that used policies of "race consciousness" in an attempt to remedy past discriminations against blacks. In 1972, Bakke, a white man, first applied to eleven medical schools, among them the University of California at Davis. After two rejections by Davis, Bakke retained a lawyer to file suit against the university. He charged that the allocation of 16 positions in the freshman class of the medical school to minorities was unconstitutional. Bakke charged that all applicants to the program had not been judged by equal standards and indeed the affirmative action program of the university violated the Constitution's Fourteenth Amendment, which guarantees equal protection.

On June 28, 1978, the Supreme Court in a 5–4 vote affirmed the constitutionality of affirmative action programs. Justice Powell's opinion, which became the official statement of the Court, accepted the principle that universities could consider race as a factor in making decisions about applicants for admission. Justice Powell cited Harvard University's admissions policy, where an applicant's race was considered along with other nonacademic factors, as "an illuminating example" of "diversity without fixed quotas" (Knight, 1978). Of 1,628 admissions to Harvard and Radcliffe for September 1978, only the first 150 would be entering solely on the basis of "academic merit." For the rest, other factors, in addition to academic merit, would be used ". . . Geographic origin, class, and professional and extracurricular interests have long been used," the brief said, "with race added only in recent years" (*New York Times,* June 29, 1978, p. A23). This policy is analogous to the second view outlined by Professor Smith above.

In the second part of the Court's decision, the majority held that Bakke should be admitted to the medical school at Davis. Davis' policy, similar to Professor Smith's third view, set aside 16 of 100 places within the freshman class for minorities. Bakke was unable to compete for these places though minority individuals could have access to them or also could compete for the 84 regular admissions slots. Because five of the Justices found that the allocation of places based on race (a quota situation) was a violation for the Civil Rights Act of 1964, they judged that Bakke's rights had been violated and ordered him admitted to Davis. This historic decision, which will be the source of continuing debate, was meant to further ecourage equality of opportunity. "Affirmative action can proceed, with due regard for the fine line the Court has drawn: minorities may be helped through the doors of opportunity but not through a separate door that is racially reserved for them alone" (*New York Times,* June 29, 1978, p. A24).

Community Control of Schools and Decentralization in Urban Schools

As hopes of integrating inner-city schools began to evaporate in the 1960s, minority leaders began to demand community control of schools. The notion here was that minority children had much to gain from programs that were controlled by minority members. Such adults would be ego-models to the young and encourage them to learn the skills that the schools provided, realizing that there were status and economic rewards possible. With control of schools assured, parents could expect accountability from school personnel when students were not learning. More importantly, parents could be a part of the educational process and exercise more control over the education of their children. Decentralization of schools is a response to the rigid bureaucratic organization of Boards of Education. Central boards are often asked to make decisions about supplies, curriculum, and staffing of schools even though their members are often far removed from local problems. Trivial decisions such as provisions for light bulbs, erasers, or transportation facilities for students may have to be made by Boards of Education; and these decisions might be months in coming. (Rogers, 1968) With decentralization and community control, community school boards have the right to determine policy, budgets, personnel appointments, and educational innovations. These boards are made up of local teachers and parents who are elected within their communities. It is perhaps too early to assess the effectiveness of these programs. They have only been in existence since 1965. Many mistakes appear to have been made and some successes recorded. However, the pressure for decentralization of the nation's school systems has increased as the awareness of the inefficiency and rigidity of centralized educational systems becomes apparent.

INTERPRETIVE SUMMARY

All societies have some provisions, formal or informal or both, for socialization of individuals. In dictatorial societies, a central purpose of education is to develop loyalty and subservience to the state. In democracies, the purpose of education is to develop individuals who are both self-sufficient and capable of making the democratic system work.

The emphasis in the United States upon individual worth has led to increased education for all classes. However, the situation even today, with a larger proportion of the population in school or part-time school than at any other place at any time, is still not ideal. Accessibility of education is still limited by one's race, sex, region, and the occupation and income of one's family. The fact is particularly sobering when the latent functions of education are considered.

Increased school enrollment is only one of the changes that have occurred in the U.S. educational system. Many of these changes were related to the belief in universal education. For example, the recognition that many people ended their formal education at the high-school level, led to emphasis on useful subjects, particularly vocational subjects, and on new methods that were expected to help the average child understand his schoolwork more easily. The teaching of traditional subjects, such as grammar and spelling, diminished as controversy about the appropriateness of one standard and correct grammar developed among educators. Traditional liberal arts subjects have been revamped, and sometimes combined, with the average student in mind. The number of junior colleges and relatively inexpensive two-year community colleges is increasing. Still other changes, such as increased specialization in curricula and emphasis on mathematics and science, may be traced to specialization in all areas of U.S. culture and to competition with the Soviet Union. An important recent trend has been the widespread growth of adult education programs in community and four-year colleges.

In addition to changes in the duration and the context of education, the 1960s brought demands for increased educational opportunities from blacks and other minorities. The Coleman Report, a significant educational survey, attempted to assess the effects of various characteristics on student achievement. A major conclusion was that racial integration of schools was a way of accomplishing social integration. The social class of pupils was found to be related to academic achievement. Blacks did better with middle-class schoolmates.

One aspect of U.S. education that has not changed substantially is its source of control, which has always been local and state. In fact, both teacher behavior and curriculum have historically been controlled by the more conservative elements in the community, and often federal aid has been resisted on the grounds that it would lead to federal control. Certain subgroups have set up private schools in order to increase control over their children; for them the dilemma posed by federal aid has been an especially difficult one.

In the past decade the education system has been an arena wracked with continuing controversies, as interest groups have sought to resolve social problems through educational means. A rejection of the schools as credential-granting institutions has led some critics to recommend "deschooling" society. Open admissions, busing, community control and decentralization of schools have been advanced as solutions giving U.S. minorities more educational opportunity, and more control over the quality of education received.

QUESTIONS

1. How does ascription influence educational opportunities? What is the relationship between socioeconomic status and education?
2. What are some of the manifest functions of education in U.S. society? What are some latent functions?
3. What were some of the surprising findings of the Coleman Report? What effects has Coleman's educational survey had on U.S. educational systems?

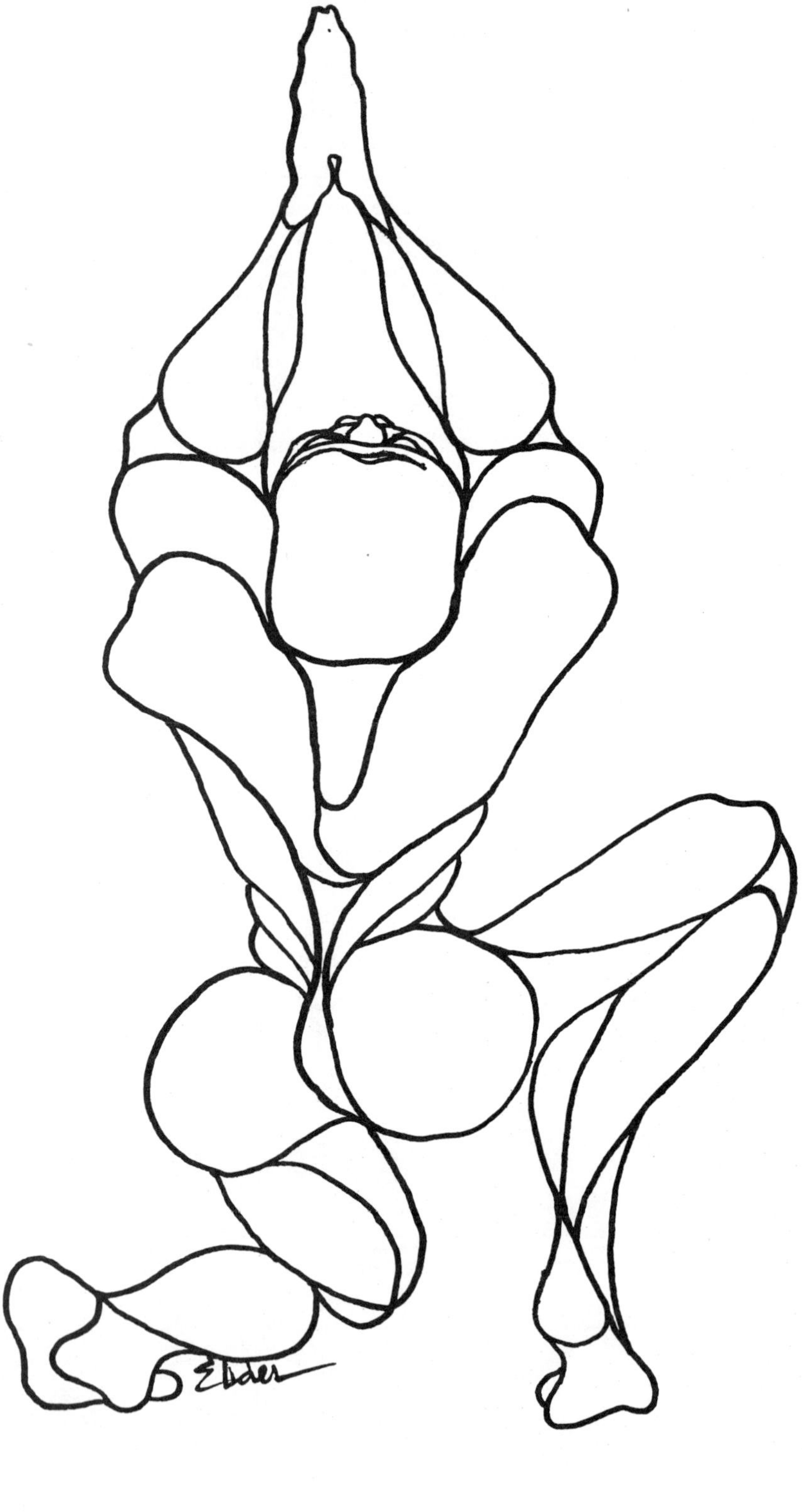
Elder

19

Religion and Society

In the course of trying to satisfy the more immediate needs of sustenance, shelter, reproduction, and group and personal safety, prehistoric people found themselves confronted with many forces in nature that they did not understand. They speculated, and that was the beginning of philosophy. They put forth a finger to investigate, and that was the beginning of science. They experienced awe and fear, and these were the beginnings of religion.

In his classic study of religious behavior first published in 1912, Durkheim defined religion as "... a unified system of beliefs and practices relative to sacred things, uniting into a single moral community all those who adhere to those beliefs and practices." (Durkheim, 1947) Religion concerns belief in supernatural forces that influence human events. Many societies have a wide range of organizations associated with religion, including special officials, forms of worship, ceremonies, sacred objects, tithes, pilgrimages, and the like. In literate societies, religious leaders have developed elaborate theories or theologies to explain humankind's place in the universe. Furthermore, the great world religions—Hinduism, Buddhism, Confucianism, Judaism, Christianity, and Islam—are cores of elaborate cultural systems that have dominated whole societies for centuries.

RELIGIOUS STRUCTURES

Religion in nonliterate societies rests on belief in personal and impersonal powers which play a part in human life. Belief in personal powers is called animism and it is illustrated by belief in spirits, ghosts, and demons which bring

19-1 CHECKING IT OUT: Religious Population of the World

Religion	*N. America*	*S. America*	*Europe*	*Asia*	*Africa*	*Oceania*	*Total*
Total Christian	231,099,700	158,980,000	348,059,300	89,909,000	137,460,300	18,112,600	983,620,900
Roman Catholic	131,631,500	147,280,000	182,514,300	47,046,000	53,740,000	4,475,000	566,686,800
Eastern Orthodox	4,189,000	552,000	50,545,000	1,894,000	15,255,000	380,000	72,815,000
Protestant	95,279,200	11,148,000	115,000,000	40,969,000	68,465,300	13,257,600	344,119,100
Jewish	6,641,118	727,000	4,082,400	3,203,460	294,400	84,000	15,032,378
Muslim	249,200	238,300	8,283,500	433,001,000	134,285,200	103,000	576,160,200
Zoroastrian	250	2,000	6,000	224,700	600	—	233,550
Shinto	60,000	92,000	—	55,004,000	—	—	55,156,000
Taoist	16,000	12,000	—	31,088,100	—	—	31,116,100
Confucian	96,100	85,150	25,000	173,940,250	500	42,200	174,189,200
Buddhist	155,250	195,300	200,000	260,117,000	2,000	16,000	260,685,550
Hindu	81,000	782,300	260,000	515,449,500	483,650	841,000	517,897,450
Totals	238,398,618	161,114,050	360,916,200	1,561,937,010	272,526,650	19,198,800	2,614,091,328

SOURCE: *Encyclopaedia Britannica Book of the Year*, 1978, p. 616.

good or bad luck. Impersonal power, called *mana* (Melanesian), *orenda* (Iroquois), *manitou* (Algonquian), and other names, manifests itself in natural objects, and not necessarily through people, spirits, or ghosts. In Polynesia and Melanesia, for example, mana refers to an extraordinary force yielding extraordinary results and may be located in any object—person, plant, rock, music, or animal.

> If a man's pigs multiply and his gardens are productive, it is not because he is industrious and looks after his property, but because of the stones full of mana for pigs and yams that he possesses. Of course a yam naturally grows when planted, that is well known, but it will not be very large unless mana comes into play: a canoe will not be swift unless mana be brought to bear upon it, a net will not catch many fish, nor an arrow inflict a mortal wound. (Codrington, 1965)

Among nonliterate peoples, the various phases of life are not sharply divided, as they typically are in industrial societies. Work and art, play and religion, magic and toolmaking are all closely interwoven. Economic activities are often surrounded by noneconomic rituals. Recurrent events in the life of the group, such as birth, death, illness, marriage, and seasonal changes, have special emotional significance. Ceremonies connected with these events become part of the folkways.

Magic

Surrounded as they were by forces of nature and of other people, forces which they did not fully understand, early people probably did not distinguish in any logical way between natural and supernatural elements. In fact, it is difficult to sort out the religion of nonliterate people from the other phases of their rudimentary culture. In particular, what we call magic permeates both religion on the one hand and practical behavior on the other.

Magic is invented or discovered in the same way other techniques are invented or discovered. An act is performed, either accidentally or because imagination suggests that it might be successful. If it seems to work, it is adopted as a rule of action. If, for example, it is discovered that friction produces heat, this may suggest fire. The imagination furnishes a clue that proves valid in overt action. But imagination suggests also that if one were to burn a wax effigy of an enemy, one would be doing that enemy harm and that if a barren woman has a wooden image of a child placed in her lap, she will bear a child (as the Batak of Sumatra believe). If the intended victim actually does fall ill or if the woman does conceive, the practice is regarded as successful. We call fire-making naturalistic or realistic because its action is fully explained by present-day physical science. We call effigy-making magic because any success it may seem to have is outside the cause-and-effect relations known to science.

Because members of nonliterate societies do not ordinarily organize secondary groups as a setting for religious interaction, there is seldom any sense of the separation of religious norms from other norms, of religious groups from other groups, or of religious activities from other activities. One would never hear in such a society the sentiment, often voiced in ours, that "we should bring business and religion closer together." In folk society they have never been separated.

Religious Organization

From Sect to Church In the United States, religious belief and expression have become institutionalized into secondary organizations called churches. The term **church** has different meanings for different people. Some consider a church to be (1) a body of devotees (2) organized for a religious purpose and developing as an agency for this with (3) a hierarchy of officials and leaders and (4) a body of doctrine and philosophy that ties the whole together into a systematic unit. In popular speech, too, the term *church* is sometimes used to mean a unit of common religious beliefs and practices, as when we speak of the Christian Church. At other times, *church* refers to a more limited body of believers within this larger grouping, such as the Presbyterian or the Methodist Church. (These, properly speaking, are denominations.) In a fourth sense, *church* refers to a congregation or locally organized body of worshipers—and, of course, to the building where these people gather for religious services.

The most basic distinction in the forms of religious organization is that of church and sect, which comes from the work of the German scholar Ernst Troeltsch. (Troeltsch, 1931) Many scholars also subclassify churches into two main types, the **ecclesia** and the **denomination**. The ecclesia, in principle, is universal, has complete unity with the rest of society (including the state), and possesses universal membership. The Roman Catholic Church of the Middle Ages is the closest actual approximation of an ecclesia. The denomination is positioned between the ecclesia and the sect. It seeks neither to control the world nor to withdraw from it. Instead, it attempts to co-exist with other churches and openly approves of the separation of church and state. The major religious bodies of the United States are examples of denominations.

19-2 CHECKING IT OUT: From Sect to Church

	Sect		Church
From:	Membership composed chiefly of the propertyless	To:	Membership composed of property owners
From:	Economic poverty	To:	Economic wealth, as disclosed especially in the value of church property and the salary paid to ministers

19-2 CHECKING IT OUT: From Sect to Church (continued)

	Sect		*Church*
From:	The cultural periphery	To:	The cultural center of the community
From:	Renunciation of prevailing culture and social organization, or indifference to it	To:	Affirmation of prevailing culture and social organization
From:	Self-centered (or personal) religion	To:	Culture-centered religion
From:	"Experience"	To:	A social institution
From:	Noncoöperation, or positive ridicule, toward established religious institutions	To:	Coöperation with the established churches of the community
From:	Suspicion of rival sects	To:	Disdain or pity for all sects
From:	A moral community excluding unworthy members	To:	A social institution embracing all who are socially compatible within it
From:	An unspecialized, unprofessionalized, part-time ministry	To:	A specialized, professional, full-time ministry
From:	A psychology of persecution	To:	A psychology of success and dominance
From:	Voluntary, confessional bases of membership	To:	Ritual or social prerequisites only (such as a certificate of previous membership in another respected denomination, or training in an educational process established by the denomination itself)
From:	Principal concern with adult membership	To:	Equal concern for children of members
From:	Emphasis on evangelism and conversion	To:	Emphasis on religious education
From:	Stress on a future in the next world	To:	Primary interest in a future in this world—a future for the institution, for its members, and for their children
From:	Emphasis on death	To:	Emphasis on successful earthly life
From:	Adherence to strict Biblical standards, such as tithing or nonresistance	To:	Acceptance of general cultural standards as a practical definition of religious obligation

19-2 CHECKING IT OUT: From Sect to Church (continued)

	Sect		*Church*
From:	A high degree of congregational participation in the services and administration of the religious group	To:	Delegation of responsibility to a comparatively small percentage of the membership
From:	Fervor in worship services	To:	Restraint
From:	Positive action—a comparatively large number of special religious services	To:	Passive listening—a program of regular services at stated intervals
From:	Reliance on spontaneous "leadings of the spirit" in religious services and administration	To:	A fixed order of worship and of administrative procedure
From:	The use of hymns resembling contemporary folk music	To:	The use of slower, more stately hymns coming out of more remote liturgical tradition
From:	Emphasis on religion in the home	To:	Delegation of responsibility for religion to church officials and organizations

SOURCE: Liston Pope, *Millhands and Preachers. Copyright* © 1942 by Yale University Press. Reprinted by permission.

The **sect** is at odds with the institutionalized church on almost every count: it is a primary group whose institutions refuse integration with the institutionalized church's social order and reject cultural values which are at variance with its religious ideology. Today's sect is likely to be tomorrow's church. The whole history of the development of the Protestant denominations, as indicated by their name, is a story of groups objecting to certain ways of a church and breaking away to start sects. In time, a sect makes its peace with the wider society and becomes a church itself; later, a new generation of people may break away from it and form another sect. Indeed, Christianity itself was first a sect that emerged in a time of social discontent as the religion of the poor, the dispossessed, and the outcast.

A *sect* is a body of believers that grows up within the larger church. (Wilson, 1959) Certain persons, often few in number at first, begin to disagree about points in the main ceremonials and doctrine of the parent organization. At the outset they do not think of themselves as outside their denomination: only as they come into conflict with the ecclesiastical officials of the principal body does the idea of separation arise. Often it is only after they have been expelled from the organized church that they formulate their own creed, their own official hierarchy, and take on a distinctive name and become a new "denomination."

Religious Roles

Religious norms and practices give rise to distinctive social roles. As an elderly Maori once remarked to a white man, "Gods die if there are no priests to keep them alive." (Thomas, 1937) Social roles in religion fall into two general categories: the religious thinkers and mystics, found in both formal and informal religious structures, and executives or operators, who are by definition more prevalent in formal structures. The former category includes the mystics proper, the prophets, and the messiahs. The later category includes the priests, pastors, formal teachers, missionaries, and various administrators. Mystics are likely to be innovators and disturbers of the established order. Religious executives are generally conservative, preferring the old and tried to the new. There is, in fact, something of a continuing struggle in religious organizations between these two kinds of social roles. Some would confine religious expression within rather definite limits set by symbols, rites, traditions, and established theology. Others would not unduly hamper religious experience by such established patterns of thought and action but would leave much room for the individual's unique experience.

The **priest, rabbi**, or **pastor** fills the role expectations of carrying on the religious rituals and expounding theology. He or she is the special person who officiates at the church ceremonies and cares for both spiritual and temporal affairs.

Religious teachers or **philosophers** have played a central part in the rise of the great world religions. Jesus, St. Paul, Mohammed, and Buddha are all familiar instances. The *missionary* is a special teacher whose business it is to carry the message, rituals, and symbolism of an established religion to nonbelievers.

The **religious executive** may be, like St. Paul, both missionary and organizer. In many Protestant churches in which a priestly hierarchy is not developed or is practically nonexistent, the affairs of the church organization are carried on by executives whose work combines that of priest or pastor with social-service activities and management.

The **mystics** play a special part in the growth of religion. They identify themselves or come into union with the god, or with the world-spirit, or with the Absolute—however the culture phrases the idea of supernatural forces. The mystic illustrates the place in a society of the divergent person who may initiate changes in culture. Mystics believe that, through their dreams, visions, and other unique mental experiences, they come into direct personal communication with divine powers.

The **prophet** is an important religious leader. While prophets may be priests, often they are mystics. They serve as intermediary for some divine power, issuing warnings, giving commands, and revealing the course of future events. Obviously, the prophet's role is set by the culture. When there is a strong priestly hierarchy, as among the Ekoi of West Africa or in the Roman Catholic Church, there is little opportunity for such persons to appear.

The **messiah** is the divine leader or prophet who is recognized as having supernatural attributes, who foretells some catastrophic end of the world and often assumes the role of final judge. The messiah ordinarily comes from among the people themselves, who in a time of crisis look to him to save the society from disaster. Mohammed, for example, was the messiah of the people who came to call themselves, after him, Mohammedans. Christ, of course, is the messiah of Christians.

Basic Religious Patterns

The institutional practices and formal theories that have grown up about religion are many. The most important are ceremonials, symbolism, sacred objects and buildings, and creed and theology.

Ceremony or **ritual** is a standardized and accepted action directed toward some specific end. (Rituals and ceremonies are not confined, of course, to religion). In religion, ritual is a settled manner of entreating or controlling the supernatural powers in regard to some particular situation. Ordination, the sacraments, various forms of sacrifice, and penance call for special rituals. In some churches, such as the Greek Orthodox or Roman Catholic, the ceremonials are elaborate. In other churches, like those of the Quakers or Calvinists, the forms play only a slight part in religious life.

Throughout religion, **symbolism** is important. Symbols are substitutes for or representations of objects or situations. They may be verbal or tangible. A commonly recognized religious symbol helps worshipers identify themselves with their fellows and so promotes a sense of solidarity. Often it comes to stand not alone for the particular object or situation to which it was originally attached but for the whole group and its culture: the cross stands for Christianity, the crescent for Islam. The symbol in the mind of the user may serve either an intellectual or an emotional purpose. For the religious worshiper, the object and its symbols are combined into an indivisible emotional experience, which asserts itself whenever the symbol is brought forth. The Eucharist, for example, symbolizes for the Christian the supreme sacrifice of Jesus, and in this ritual the worshipers identify themselves intellectually and emotionally with one of the main tenets of their theology.

19-3 CHECKING IT OUT: Religious Beliefs in America

1. I know God really exists and I have no doubts about it
2. Jesus is the Divine Son of God and I have no doubts about it
3. Jesus was born of a virgin*
4. Jesus walked on water*
5. I believe that Jesus will actually return to the earth some day*
6. There is a life beyond death*
7. The Devil actually exists*
8. A child is born into the world already guilty of sin*
9. Belief in Jesus Christ as saviour is absolutely necessary for salvation
10. Being of the Jewish religion definitely prevents salvation
11. Being anti-Semitic definitely prevents salvation
12. Practicing artificial birth control definitely prevents salvation
13. Discriminating against other races definitely prevents salvation

Religious Organization	Per Cent Holding Religious Belief												
	1	2	3	4	5	6	7	8	9	10	11	12	13
Congregationalists	41	40	21	19	13	36	6	2	38	1	23	0	27
Methodists	60	54	34	26	21	49	13	7	45	3	23	0	25
Episcopalians	63	59	39	30	24	53	17	18	47	3	26	2	27
Presbyterians	75	72	57	51	43	69	31	21	66	7	20	1	22
American Baptists	78	76	69	62	57	72	49	23	78	7	13	1	17
Southern Baptists	99	99	99	99	94	97	92	43	97	25	10	5	16
Sects**	96	97	96	94	89	94	90	47	96	23	26	4	29
Catholics	81	86	81	71	47	75	66	68	51	1	20	23	24

* Per cent who said "completely true."

** Sects include The Assemblies of Gods, The Church of God, The Church of Christ, The Church of the Nazarene, The Foursquare Gospel Church, and one independent Tabernacle.

SOURCE: Charles Y. Glock and Rodney Stark, *Religion and Society in Tension* (Chicago: Rand McNally, 1965).

Sacred objects associated with the various religions have symbolic power insofar as they evoke memories of a religion's history and traditions. The Hebrew ark of the covenant and the phylactery, the Christian candles, altar, and especially the cross play important parts in many religious ceremonials. For their religious exercises people often repair to special sacred localities: mountaintops, mineral springs, groves of trees, river banks, seashores. Special buildings are erected, such as the tabernacle of the ancient Hebrews; the temples of ancient Babylonia, Egypt, Greece, and Rome; the synagogues of the Jews; and the cathedrals and churches of Christians.

Theology is the systemic explanation that religious leaders work out to show the human relation to god and to the universe. Often this includes some account of the origin of the world and of humanity, such as the stories of creation in the Bible. It represents the *creed*, or body of beliefs and doctrines of the church. The written words become the sacred scriptures.

RELIGIOUS FUNCTIONS

Religious structures exist in every society, and they function for the continuity of the society. The supernatural laws and beings around which such structures are oriented supply an ultimate idea of reality to which the cultural values and social norms can be related. Religion provides a higher court of appeal when one feels one's fellows have treated one unjustly and promises better things in the future. It provides the individual with an institutionalized crystallization of hopes and an outlet for fears in ways that almost predetermine the choice of immediate goals.

> Throughout most of the world religious education, broadly conceived, helps the individual make sense of much instruction which might otherwise appear to him as a meaningless and arbitrary assortment of directions and prohibitions. If, for instance, a child learns (as in some Christian denominations) that the attainment of salvation is the main goal of life and that to that end he is to attend church regularly, read the Bible and pray daily, honor and love his parents, work hard, live frugally, refrain from dishonest conduct, unchastity and riotous behavior, avoid dancing, drinking and card-playing, his social development is not only given a very definite direction but a certain internal consistency. (Nottingham, 1954)

Sanctions for the Mores

Religion and Morality Religion has frequently been a powerful factor in lending emotional support to the moral code. In all the great religions there is an intermingling of religion and morals. There is little doubt that the belief in a god influences moral conduct. Among the Ekoi of West Africa, where magic is considered very powerful and where spirits are used for malevolent ends, people believe in benign spirits who counteract the evil ones and aid humankind in more humane ways. So too, some nonliterates of relatively simple culture, such as the Australian Bushmen and the Andaman Islanders, believe in spirits that are considered guardians of morality.

As the concept of an ethical god develops, the relation of religion to morality becomes more important. By identifying oneself with such a god, one may modify one's conduct. Among the Hebrews, Jehovah, at first a tribal god of vengeance, gradually emerged as a universalistic god of high moral qualities.

In Christian theology the struggle between the forces of God and the forces of Satan symbolizes the conflict within the individual between the moral and the immoral, between the spirit and the flesh, between good and evil. Throughout Christian history the role of God and the saints as standards of virtue has been highly important. A personal deity becomes an ideal with which one may compare one's own conduct.

Any scheme of otherworldly reward or punishment for conduct becomes a powerful aid to morality. But although the idea of continuity of life after death is rather widespread, not all groups have the notion of retribution or divine judgment. Indeed, this idea came rather late in cultural development.

In many religions the belief in a final judgment, with its terrible punishments for the evil and glorious rewards for the virtuous, is pictured in bold and striking manners. Without doubt, the fear of hell fire and damnation has been a powerful factor in the control of conduct. Associated with fear, systems of penance and absolution have been developed to remove or at least lighten the burden of future punishment.

The virtues of honesty, fair-dealing, conformity to sexual codes—in short, all the accepted details of moral conduct of the community or society—may become integrated with religious beliefs and practices. Today there is a tendency to integrate principles of social welfare, the morality of fairer distribution of wealth, of sound and honest politics, of high community standards of health and conduct into the religious ideals of the church.

Religion and Economy— Weber's Sociological Analysis

Protestantism and Capitalism In nonliterate societies nearly every feature of life is intermixed with religion. This is clearly evident in the economy: food-gathering, hunting, fishing, herding, agriculture, trade, and barter—each is directly related to the gods. It is not always so apparent that religion also plays a part in our more complex captialistic economy, but Max Weber, a German sociologist, R. H. Tawney, a British economist, and others have argued that there is a parallel between the development of Protestant ideas and practices and the rise of modern capitalism in Western Europe and America. (Weber, 1930; Tawney, 1926) The individualism of Protestantism goes hand in hand with the rise of nationalism and the change from the relatively rigid class structure of the Middle Ages to the open-class system of the Industrial Revolution. The otherworldly asceticism of Catholicism, in which emphasis was put on confession of sins and absolution as preparation for the hereafter, gave way to what Max Weber aptly calls "worldly asceticism," in which, while the moral virtues of hard work, honestly, truthfulness, and steadfastness of purpose are retained, activity is directed toward the affairs of this world instead of the hereafter.

Weber, a seminal theorist in sociology, whose work in other areas we have already studied, wrote a very important work called *The Protestant Ethic and the Spirit of Capitalism* (1930). In this essay, he examined the degree to which elements of Protestantism (specifically the religious values of Calvinism) affected the rise of capitalism.

The central doctrine of Calvinism is that of *predestination.* According to this belief, the "elect"—or those selected for salvation in the life to come—are chosen with no regard for earthly behavior. We, then, cannot effect our own salvation; it is predetermined by the Creator. And yet the inability to affect one's fate must have created feelings of anxiety and powerlessness in early Calvinists. Such a constant state of uncertainty about the future must have been unbearable, so that certain beliefs were developed to cushion the religious believer and give direction to behavior. Calvinism is an ascetic belief system, which rejects luxury, amusements, wealth, and pleasure. Acquisition of worldly goods as an end in itself is considered sinful. Calvinists are taught to think of themselves as custodians of the goods and wealth that come through God's grace. One is expected to acquire but to limit consumption and live simply. The concept of the "calling" further enhances this ascetic life style. Because the all-important concern of the Calvinists and other Puritan sects is salvation, all activity centers around this preoccupation. The notion grew that labor and salvation are connected. The treatment of labor as a "calling" identified it as the best means of attaining grace. This means that the lowliest occupation must be pursued with intensity and seriousness and that the accumulation of wealth might be a sign of God's blessing. Being rich might be a sign that one is among the elect. Weber quotes John Wesley, the father of Methodism, to show the paradoxical nature of this ascetic ideal:

> We ought not prevent people from being diligent and frugal; we must exhort all Christians to gain all they can, and to save all they can; that is, in effect, to grow rich.

Weber is clear in his belief that the unique doctrines accepted by ascetic Protestants, such as the Calvinists, caused social behavior that has contributed to the development of modern Western capitalism. Hard work, sacrifice of present pleasure for future profits in a business, honesty in business dealings, and other homely virtues became the daily morality of the pious Protestants, especially the Calvinists, the Quakers, and the Separatists.

The Significance of Weber's Theory Frequently Weber in his theoretical formulations seems to be responding to Karl Marx. He questions Marx's assertion that the economic institutions of society influence all other institutions. In the case of ascetic Protestantism it appears *that the religious institution* *had a pivotal influence on the economic institution.* The hard work, delay of gratifications, honesty in business, and frugality caused Protestants (the Calvinists in particular) to accumulate the economic surpluses that have aided in the growth of Western capitalism. Thus economic behavior has been strongly influenced by values located within the religious structure. This insightful discussion further illustrates the power of cultural values within societies.

The Protestant Ethic in America Capitalism, Protestantism, and political democracy, bound together by certain accidents of history and certain similar ideologies, came to full bloom in America. The emphasis on religious piety, individualism, liberty and activity, and the worship of material success, coupled with almost unlimited natural resources, made early America a living example of this combination of the repression of pleasure-seeking and the direction of energy into hard work, success, and religious satisfaction. Nowadays, however, one cannot assume the existence of any direct cause-and-effect relationship between the Protestant and Catholic faiths and role behavior in contemporary American society. Research indicates that whatever influence these two religious subcultures have on their adherents in our society is overriden by the general ethos. (Mack, et al., 1956) There is no evidence that the so-called Protestant ethic is participated in any less by Catholics than by Protestants or Jews in the contemporary United States.

Yet institutions are interrelated, and there remains in our normative structure not only some connection between economic and religious institutions, but a belief on the part of many that such a relationship ought to exist. Yet there are many who believe that capitalism has been injurious to the true aim of religion. The inequalities of wealth and the exploitation of people, both as workers and as consumers, by business interests have led some church leaders and others to give thought to reforms in the economic order. In the early twentieth century there arose among certain American Protestant groups what was known as the "social gospel" movement, which contended that human rights should come before those of property; that mutual service, not profit, should be the chief economic motive; and that cooperation, not competition, should be the mode of economic production and distribution.

Yet as long as the church gets its chief support from the dominant capitalist class, it is not easy for it to go far in economic views from those who pay its bills. If the church, like the traditional school, continues to reflect the dominant economic and political views of those in power, it will consume much of its time and energy defending the prevailing economic and political order.

Religion and Education

Socialization Functions Formal teaching has long been a prerogative of organized religion. In Christian history, the church has played a decisive part in education. The cathedral schools of the Middle Ages were used for religious and moral training, and early Protestantism fostered elementary learning so that members might read the Bible. The Sunday School was established in 1780 by an Englishman, Robert Raikes, with a view to more formal religious and moral education. The movement soon spread to America and in a past religious census in the United States (1936), about four-fifths of the congregations had Sunday Schools. (U.S. Government Printing Office, 1941)

Even more influential than the Sunday School has been the parochial school, organized to fulfill the legal demands for formal schooling but offering children of various churches religious and moral instruction not available in public schools. The philosophy underlying this form of education was set forth in the "Encyclical on Education" (1930) by Pope Pius XI:

> It is necessary that all the teaching and whole organization of the school, and its teachers, syllabus and textbooks in every branch, be regulated by the Christian spirit, under the direction and maternal supervision of the Church; so that Religion may be in very truth the foundation and the crown of youth's entire training; and this in every grade of school, not only in the elementary but in the intermediate and the higher institutions of learning as well. (*Current History*, 1930, p. 1101)

Closely related to more formal religious education has been the development of such organizations as the Young Men's Christian Association, the Catholic Youth Organization, and the Young Men's Hebrew Association. There are, in addition, vacation schools, clubs, and forums, and the churches sponsor other activities in which more formal education is supplemented with opportunities for discussion of current moral, religious, and economic problems.

The Boy Scouts, Girl Scouts, and Camp Fire Girls, though not strictly religious organizations, have much in common with these other agencies. These groups carry on chiefly leisure-time activities but relate these activities rather explicitly to the ethical and religious principles taught in the church. The Boy Scouts, for instance, are taught to respect their parents, to have reverence for God, and to play fairly.

It is significant that religious organizations are taking over some of the functions formerly located in the home, in the neighborhood, and even in the school. For many Americans, religious activity serves as a focus for the integration of a host of other activities.

RELIGIOUS PATTERNS IN THE UNITED STATES

Community and Church

In the primary community of medieval Europe the Church was the focus of much of the people's lives. In Protestant countries it continued to serve important functions, although where rival denominations and sects arose, the integrating benefits of religion and church organization were often lost in theological conflicts. In spite of the continuation of these divisive tendencies, churches in the United States have served the community as the center not only of religious thought and action but also of moral standards. Today the primary-community church reflects the changes that have gone on in the wider world outside. Open-country churches, for example, are declining, while village and town churches are becoming the center of both farm and village religious activity. The rural and village church has added educational, recreational, and social-service activities to its functions.

Formerly the church was the focus of much of the neighborhood life. The Catholic churches have continued to be particularly effective as neighborhood centers, since the membership is divided geographically into parishes, in the same manner as voting precincts or school districts are laid out. This gives the pastor an opportunity to serve the people who are themselves neighbors and who already have attitudes of solidarity growing out of common life. The urban Protestant parishes, for the most part, are not divided on geographic lines, with the result that members are often drawn from widespread areas. As long as the population remained fairly stationary, this handicap was overcome by the fact that the church buildings were located in the residential sections in which most of the members lived. In rapidly growing U.S. cities the situation is quite different. Many church edifices are left stranded in the midst of retail or wholesale districts or in cheap rooming-house or emerging slum areas just beyond the retail business section. The members often live so far from the home church that they drift away to other parishes nearer by or give up their church affiliation entirely.

In many other ways the city church is also affected by changes in the society, especially in the growing emphasis on secondary-group organization. Many sophisticated urban people are skeptical of what organized religion has to offer. There is frequently a conflict within the church body itself as to whether it should liberalize its dogma, taking up social-service and educational and recreational programs, or stick by the old and tried at the cost of younger membership and at the risk of slow decay and perhaps final disappearance.

Religious Participation

Difficulties in Opinion Polling For several reasons, statistics on church membership are not a very dependable measure of the extent of participation in organized religious groups. First, there is no adequate census of church members throughout the world—nor, for that matter, in the United States. There has been strong opposition in the United States to a scientifically conducted census of religious membership. Religion is regarded as a form of individual and group activity which has no relationship to the government, except insofar as the state protects churches, like any other accepted institution, from interference in their activities. As a result, members of many denominations, as well as a number of citizens concerned with civil liberties, view an objective census of church membership as none of the state's affair.

Second, there is little agreement among denominations as to what constitutes membership. Some groups count anyone born or baptized into their fold as a member, even if that person denies membership and/or has not participated in church activities for years.

Also, there is the question of a satisfactory measure of participation. Is the indifferent member to be equated with the ardent one? In the Gallup survey taken in 1968, 43 percent of Americans attended church weekly. (Sigelman, 1977) However, church attendance reveals little about intensity of belief or of commitment.

Religion and Stratification

A considerable body of research offers evidence that religious beliefs, as well as religious participation, vary from stratum to stratum in the class structure. (Herberg, 1956) Research has shown, for example, that acceptance of the sect type of organization is associated with low socioeconomic status, while acceptance of the church type of structure is more frequently found among those with more formal education who fill occupational statuses of higher prestige. (Dynes, 1955) Research also indicates a direct relationship between incidence of church membership and economic status or prestige (Cantril, 1943) Church attendance is highest in the middle class. One careful and detailed research project found that religious interest was related to social mobility. Indeed social class mobility, not religious ideas, significantly influenced members to switch denominations within Protestantism (i.e., As lower-class members of fundamentalist groups prosper they shift their affiliation to middle-class denominations; middle-class members shift to prestigious affiliations like Episcopalianism). Certainly the denomination to which one belongs is a salient factor of social status. (Glock and Stark, 1970)

RELIGIOUS CONFLICT

Like all social institutions, religion is both a source of social integration and a source of social division within society. Indeed, James S. Coleman has argued that cleavage and conflict are inherent in the existence of religious groups, and there is much evidence to support his thesis. (Coleman, 1956) Religious bodies are usually no different from others in their jealous regard for power and control. Frequently, when a church group is threatened, it responds, as do other groups, by avoidance, escape, or some kind of aggressive counteraction. How violent religious conflict may become is witnessed in Western history by the Crusades of the Middle Ages against the infidel and by the bloody and violent Thirty Years'

War between Catholic and Protestant monarchs following the publication of Martin Luther's famous *Theses* in 1517. More recently the bitter conflicts between Moslems and Hindus in India, between Arabs and Jews in the Near East, and between Catholics and Protestants in Northern Ireland show that religion, when linked with economic and political aims and institutions, may be a powerful element in open conflict.

Given the numerous religious subcultures in the United States, the norms governing behavior in the religious realm are anything but universal. Sets of values have clashed in several areas, including the role of religion in socialization, the denominational differences in dogma, and the competition of religion and science as structures meeting the necessary function of providing a sense of purpose.

Separation of Church and State

Historically, Christianity has frequently been involved in a conflict between church and state. The controversy over the claims of the Roman Catholic Church to temporal power—that is, political control—went on all through the Middle Ages. Protestantism arose, in part, out of this struggle. Today the separation of church and state is a basic tenet of all democratic countries. Yet difficulties arise from time to time regarding the place of the church in education. Many believe that all basic education in a democratic country should take the form of public schooling. But various churches have long contended that the home and the church are the essential and proper agencies of education. Efforts to close parochial schools by legislation have met with failure. For example, an Oregon law of 1922 provided that after 1926 all parents must send their children to public schools. Yet the Supreme Court held as follows:

> As often heretofore pointed out, rights guaranteed by the Constitution may not be abridged by legislation which has no reasonable relation to some purpose within the competency of the state. The fundamental theory of liberty upon which all governments in this Union repose excludes any general power of the state to standardize its children by forcing them to accept instruction from public teachers only. The child is not the mere creature of the state; those who nurture him and direct his destiny have the right, coupled with the high duty, to recognize and prepare him for additional obligations. (268 *U.S. Reporter* No. 510)

It is clear that education continues to be regarded in this country as a family and religious prerogative, in spite of the theory of public schooling for all. But the matter has not rested there. Since the Oregon case was settled, many problems regarding religion and education have arisen.

One of these has to do with provision for religious instruction. The system of "released time," as it is called, is an arrangement under which time is allowed from the regular school hours for children to attend classes in religion taught by people from their respective denominations. In most states such instruction is not permitted in public-school buildings but must be elsewhere, in places determined by the churches concerned. Children are required either to attend or do their regular schoolwork in this period. In Illinois such instruction was permitted, for a time, in the school building. But in a test case, the Illinois enabling law was declared unconstitutional by an 8 to 1 decision of the United States Supreme Court. (333 *U.S. Official Reporter* No. 2) The decision held that the Illinois law contravened the First Amendment to the Constitution, which had "erected a wall between church and state," as Justice Hugo Black put it in the majority opinion.

Aside from the legal aspects, there has been considerable controversy over the value of the released time plan of religious instruction. While there is much support for it from some leaders of all three major faiths, there is growing criticism from many educators who believe that such a program actually stimulates a sense of religious difference among children and thereby fosters prejudice.

In 1964, a case protesting the saying of prayers in public school was brought before the Supreme Court and won. The decision is significant not only in that it upholds the fundamental separation of church and state, but in that it recognizes the rights of nonbelievers in the society: most prayers in the public schools had been short and nonsectarian, and only nonbelievers and those opposed on philosophical grounds had objected in the first place.

Yet the courts have approved legislation that provides for free textbooks and free bus transportation for children who attend parochial schools. Moreover, there is a growing pressure from some Catholic leaders for federal and other tax aid for parochial schools, on the grounds that such schools deserve public aid, since they provide education for a large number of young people. To counteract this trend, many Protestant groups take a firm stand against any plan to permit the use of public funds for parochial schools.

The whole conflict reveals many of the basic difficulties in a highly diverse culture. The plea for cultural diversity must always face the counterargument that, to survive, a culture system must also have a large degree of uniformity and agreement within its institutional systems.

Denominations and Dogma

While conflict has marked the relations between many religious bodies, cooperation is by no means lacking. In U.S. Protestantism there has been a trend toward consolidation and cooperation. Indeed, there has been considerable support for consolidation for some time. For instance, more than 40 per cent of those asked in a 1948 poll of Protestant churchgoers favored a combination of all Protestants in the United States into one church. Denominations have frequently federated for various purposes and for longer and shorter periods of time. For example, the National Council of Churches of Christ, established in 1950, consists of 29 Protestant and certain Eastern Orthodox denominations. This organization represents about three-fifths of all Protestant church members. It has four divisions: Christian Education, Christian Life and Works, Home Missions, and Foreign Missions. (*The World Almanac,* 1961)

Another instance of cooperation is the "community church" that emerges with the union of separate Protestant groups. Such action sometimes takes place, of course, when the separate denominations become too weak to keep going by themselves. But sometimes the union is born of a strong public view that a community-wide church will serve the religious needs of people more effectively than separate denominations. The community church often stimulates public forums, offers recreational facilities to the young people of the entire city, and undertakes preventive programs in health and delinquency. This is a far cry from the church which functioned only as the dispenser of dogma, moral advice, and unregulated charity.

Cooperation across the traditional barriers between Catholic and Protestant or between Christian and Jew has been much less frequent. Recent decades have seen a tendency toward certain joint action among these churches. The organization of local ministerial associations is a step in this direction. The National Conference of Christians and Jews, founded in 1928, has tried to develop tolerence and cooperation. In the late 1930s the Methodist Episcopal Church, the Methodist Episcopal Church South, and the Methodist Protestant Church merged after a long split over slavery. One of the largest mergers of the 1940s occurred between the Evangelical Church and United Brethren, resulting in the Evangelical United Brethren. During the 1950s another religious merger resulted in the United Presbyterian Church of North America. In the 1950s and the early 1960s there were a number of mergers within various Lutheran bodies culminating in 1962 with the formation of the Lutheran Church of America. During the papacy of John XXIII there was also a significant diminution of Catholic-Protestant church conflicts, and delegate-observers from numerous Protestant organizations attended the first Ecumenical Council in 100 years in Vatican City. Nonetheless, most such efforts have been limited by strong interfaith rivalry.

The distinctive features of the major religions reflect the larger cultures of which they are a part. Yet, as some of the barriers of prejudice and isolation have disappeared, certain tendencies toward worldwide cooperation have arisen. Such gatherings as world religious conferences, in which representatives of all the major religions have participated, are evidence of a growing awareness of common problems in religion in spite of differences of creed. But such efforts must of necessity remain largely verbal so long as political conflict continues on the international scene.

Religion and Science

Galileo and the Inquisition There is still a widespread belief that religion and science are in fundamental conflict. Many feel that, as science is more and more applied to solving modern problems—both technological and social—there is less need for religion. When people talk about religion and science as being in conflict, they usually refer to the fact that church officials have at various times opposed certain scientific findings that the church officials regard as contravening the long-established creed or dogma of their organizations. In this sense history is indeed full of conflicts between theology and scientific findings. For example, when Galileo was taken before the Court of Inquisition for his scientific work, he was indicted

> . . . for holding as true the false doctrine taught by many—namely, that the sun is immovable in the center of the world and that the earth moves and also with a diurnal motion; . . . following the hypothesis of Copernicus, you include several propositions contrary to the true sense and authority of the Holy Scripture. . . . The proposition that the sun is the center of the world and immovable from its place is absurd philosophically, false and formally heretical because it is expressly contrary to the Holy Scriptures. . . .

Galileo recanted and renounced his heresy. But Bruno, who refused to renounce Copernican cosmology, was burned at the stake in Rome, and as late as 1819 the books of Galileo, Copernicus, and Kepler were on the Catholic *Index* of forbidden books. However, neither Martin Luther, whose break with Catholicism started the Protestant Reformation, nor the Orthodox Jews of the time were any more sympathetic toward the discoveries of science.

Science and Church Dogma Because science depends on maximum freedom of thought and because its findings run counter to many church dogmas, perhaps it was inevitable that conflict should arise. **The Copernican system**, which replaced the older view of the cosmos, reduced the earth to a mere speck in the total universe and robbed humanity of much of its former importance. Later, in the nineteenth century, **the Darwinian theory of evolution** placed human beings in the animal kingdom. And during the past seventy-five years, psychology and the social sciences have shown that the mental life and behavior of humans can be studied and understood in large part through the method of science.

Religion and science do not always conflict, however. For instance, Merton has argued that the Puritan religion of seventeenth-century England was one important element in the rise and spread of modern science. According to Merton, "the deep-rooted religious *interests* of the day demanded in their forceful implications the systematic, rational, and empirical study of Nature for the glorification of God in His works and for the control of the corrupt world." (Merton, 1957) On a more personal level, consider the following observation of Albert Einstein.

> Whoever has undergone the intense experience of successful advances in this domain of scientific thought is moved by profound reverence for the rationality made manifest in existence. By way of the understanding, he achieves a far-reaching emancipation from the shackles of personal hope and desires, and thereby attains that humble attitude of mind toward the grandeur of reason incarnate in existence, which, in its profoundest depths is inaccessible to man. This attitude, however, appears to me to be religion in the highest sense of the word. (Einstein, 1940)

Belief as a Universal Function

The mystic identification with power outside may offset or balance the disappointments, heartaches, and pain of daily living, in which half-measures, compromises, and self-denials are common. It is easy for the critic of religion to point out that this sort of thing is "an escape from reality," a mass neurosis, or, as Freud argued, a mere "illusion." (Freud, 1930) But cultural reality is not something material or made up of biological reactions to food, drink, and sexual objects. It is a matter of socially learned beliefs, attitudes, ideas, meanings. It exists in the minds of men. One cannot, therefore, blandly dismiss religious experience as an unfortunate illusion without at the same time raising the question whether art, philosophy, and most of the other fundamentals of social organization and family life are not illusions also. Faithfulness to a mate, loyalty to a country, or belief in a bank note can be shown by this logic to be illusions too.

One need not affiliate with a religious organization in order to survive. But everywhere people believe in something that imbues them with a sense of purpose, be it science, religion, or philosophy. An explanation of reality is a part of every culture, and the student of society must take that explanation into account if he or she is to understand social structure.

Religious explanations of reality have greatly interested sociologists as they have examined the cultures of groups and societies. J. Milton Yinger (1977) hypothesized that though the differences between the religions of the world were vast, they were alike in their attempts to deal with the facts of human suffering, meaninglessness, and injustice in the world. Indeed where no religious belief was professed, concern with meaninglessness, suffering, and injustice persisted. In his cross-national survey of students, questionnaires were submitted to Buddhists, Hindus, Jews, Muslims, Protestants, Roman Catholics, and agnostics and atheists. Only 8 percent of those sampled failed to refer to these themes when asked to indicate the "basic and permanent question for mankind" (p. 72). Because these themes are basic to the different forms in which religious activity is expressed, Yinger sees them as "the roots of religion." Nearly three-fourths of the responses were in the "religious direction" as students determined that "behind the difficulties and the disorder there is another kind of reality that supersedes or redefines experience" (p. 77).

Secularization

Like all social institutions, religion has undergone important changes in the great transition from communal to associational forms of social organization. Increasingly, people question the relevance of religion in the modern world and conclude that religion is no longer a central institution in the secular societies of the twentieth century. Religion has become highly secularized in the United States; the heavy church participation in such secular matters as civil rights, education, welfare, recreation, drug rehabilitation, and other social issues of the day and the de-emphasis of purely sectarian matters underscore this fact. For many Americans religion has become separated from a large area of their life. But reported church membership in the United States has been increasing for a century and it is now higher than it has been at any time since at least 1850. (Salisbury, 1964) It is difficult to know how to evaluate these statistics because, as Herberg pointed out, "church membership does not mean the same today as it meant in the eighteenth or early nineteenth century, when something of the older sense of personal conversion and commitment still remained." Nevertheless, Herberg goes on to report that 95 per cent of all Americans identify themselves as a member of some religious group. (Herberg, 1956) The contrast between the legal separation of church and state in American society and the continuous use of religious symbols in government and political life to glorify the American experience to some suggest a lack of commitment to religious doctrine and possibly the acceptance of a "civil religion."

19-4 CHECKING IT OUT: Civil Religion in America

While some have argued that Christianity is the national faith, and others that church and synagogue celebrate only the generalized religion of "the American Way of Life," few have realized that there actually exists alongside of and rather clearly differentiated from the churches an elaborate and well-institutionalized civil religion in America. This article argues not only that there is such a thing, but also that this religion—or perhaps better, this religious dimension—has its own seriousness and integrity and requires the same care in understanding that any other religion does . . .

As S. M. Lipset has recently shown, American religion at least since the early nineteenth century has been predominantly activist, moralistic, and social rather than contemplative, theological, or innerly spiritual.[1] De Tocqueville spoke of American church religion as "a political institution which powerfully contributes to the maintenance of a democratic republic among the Americans"[2] by supplying a strong moral consensus amidst continuous political change. Henry Bargy in 1902 spoke of American church religion as *"la poésie du civisme"* [the poetry of nationalism—Editor's note.][3]

It is certainly true that the relation between religion and politics in America has been singularly smooth. This is in large part due to the dominant tradition. As de Tocqueville wrote:

The greatest part of British America was peopled by men who, after having shaken off the authority of the Pope, acknowledged no other religious supremacy: they brought with them into the New World a form of Christianity which I cannot better describe than by styling it a democratic and republican religion.

The churches opposed neither the Revolution nor the establishment of democratic institutions. Even when some of them opposed the full institutionalization of religious liberty, they accepted the final outcome with good grace and without nostaligia for an *ancien regime.* The American civil religion was never anticlerical or militantly secular. On the contrary, it borrowed selectively from the religious tradition in such a way that the average American saw no conflict between the two. In this way, the civil religion was able to build up without any bitter struggle with the church powerful symbols of national solidarity and to mobilize deep levels of personal motivation for the attainment of national goals.

1. Seymour Martin Lipset, "Religion and American Values," Chapter 4, *The First New Nation* (New York, 1964).
2. Alexis de Tocqueville, *Democracy in America,* Vol. 1 (New York, 1954), p. 310.
3. Henry Bargy, *La Religion dans la Sociète aux États-Unis* (Paris, 1902), p. 31.

SOURCE: Robert N. Bellah, "Civil Religion in America,"*Daedalus: Journal of the American Academy of Arts and Sciences,* Boston, Mass. (Winter, 1967), p. 1

Robin Williams is probably correct in his estimation that "neither mass religiosity nor complete secularism appear to be permanent historical possibilities." (Williams, 1960) Religion in the secular societies of the mid-twentieth century is no longer a faith that permeates every aspect of life. But people who expect the secularization of religious life to continue unabated might well consider Kingsley Davis's answer to the question of how far this secularization can go.

> The answer, I think, is that it can go a long way but that there is ultimately a limit. If the population becomes too matter-of-fact in its attitudes, too calculating in its behavior, too sophisticated in its values, it is likely not to stick together sufficiently to maintain order and protection. The resulting social disorder may give rise to new religious sects that preach a return to the pristine values and promise salvation if the people will listen to the message of the supernatural. The rise of Christianity in Rome was at the start just such an emergence of an obscure sect preaching its doctrine to a sophisticated civilization. Within a remarkably short time it was the state religion of the Empire. (Davis, 1949)

After Secularism . . . What?

Political assassinations, wars that seem meaningless, corruption of public officials, escalating crime rates, unsatisfying drug experiences, world-wide poverty, all have contributed to a revived interest in religion in America. The need to probe life's meaning and seek explanations for widespread immorality and suffering is contributing to a major revival of religious interest.

Andrew Greeley (1972) is one of the sociologists who questions the degree to which secularization continues to influence the institutionalized forms of religion in this society. Because secularized religion rejects sacred experience and the awe-inspiring "intrusion of the transcendental" into everyday life (p. 153), those with this perspective approach life and its experiences from a rationalistic and scientific base. Greeley maintains that there are other people who have retained the capacity to "be surprised by the strange and unexpected, to be frightened by the destructive, to be awed by the beautiful and to be puzzled by the ultimate, [thereby experiencing] a strong urge to establish and maintain contact with the 'really real' " (p. 159). Edward Shils (1968) calls this capacity for religious experience "the need to reaffirm contact with the stratum of the

19-5 CHECKING IT OUT: Responses to Religious Orthodoxy Items by Sex, 1970–1973: Percent Agreeing or Strongly Agreeing

Statement of the Item	*Boys*		*Girls*	
	1970 (N = 989)	*1973 (N = 941)*	*1970 (N = 927)*	*1973 (N = 1,035)*
With the second coming of Christ, the dead will live again.	41	48**	40	49***
To me, the most important work of the church is saving sinners.	41	46*	45	45
I believe there is a devil who tries to lead men into sin.	45	53***	48	54**
I believe there is a hell where men are punished for their sins.	51	59***	58	65**
I believe there is a life after death.	55	60*	59	63
The Bible is God's word and what it says is true.	63	65	72	70
I believe there is a Divine plan and purpose for every living person and thing.	59	63	70	71
God is a heavenly Father who watches over and protects us.	75	66***	82	78*

* = $p < .05$: a statistically significant level of differences (z scores) between percentages, 1970–1973.
** = $p < .01$
*** = $p < .001$

SOURCE: Mary M. Zaengler, Arthur M. Vener, Cyrus S. Stewart, "The Adolescent and his Religion: Beliefs in Transition," *Review of Religious Research,* 1975, 17:56–57.

'serious' in human existence." Greeley emphasizes that in addition to a renewed interest in the sacred and the supernatural, contemporary Americans are once again reaffirming the most basic aspects of religious dogma. Table 19-5 illustrates the significantly greater number of positive responses to fundamental questions of dogma in a sample of adolescents over a three-year period (Zaengler, Vener, and Stewart, 1975) as religious beliefs have intensified.

The need to experience the sacred and the supernatural seems apparent in the growing multitude of bizarre or fundamentalistic or cultist movements as well as the movements concerned with experiencing new levels of consciousness. Because a tolerance for religious diversity is typical of modern society, cults and sects like Hare Krishna and the Unification Church of Rev. Moon, The Divine Light Mission of Maharaj Ji, but also covens of witches, and consciousness movements like Transcendental Meditation, est, Yoga, abound, and draw followers. Let us examine a few of these:

Witchcraft The practice of witchcraft has been revived in the United States and Great Britain and appears to have the status of a religion for its practitioners. This formerly forbidden worship is apparently a survival of the Celtic pre-Christian nature religions that were widely practiced in ancient Britain and appear to have continued as an unofficial religion as Christianity became the established religion. In earliest times no distinction was made between benevolent witchcraft (the use of magical arts to cause love, to prophesy) and malevolent witchcraft (to seek revenge, to cause harm). By the fourteenth century the Christian Church was powerful enough to try, convict, and execute alleged witches. Seventeenth-century Massachusetts was infamous for its hanging of witches. Contemporary covens of witches have tended to emphasize benevolent witchcraft.

The Moonies "Moonies" are members of the Unification Church of Rev. Sun Myung Moon, a Korean religious leader with a large American following. This cult is composed largely of adolescents who leave home to join an ascetic organization within which they must practice self-denial and commit themselves totally to a life style in which their actions are rigidly controlled (i.e., they must be members for seven years before receiving permission to marry). Moonies are subjected to an intense socialization experience as they convert to the beliefs of this group. They are expected to accept Rev. Moon as a messiah who has come to save the world. Parents of Moonies have accused the Unification Church of "brainwashing" their children and have in some cases resorted to kidnapping and "deprogramming" their children, that is, reversing the effects of the experience with Moon (Rice, 1975). And yet Moonies express contentment as they engage in fund-raising activities, secure in a drug-free, sex-free environment where they have found purpose and a sense of community.

est (Erhard Seminars Training) Est is one of several quasi-religious movements that are committed to changing the individual consciousness. Est training was created by Werner Erhard in 1971 and offers trainees the chance to transform the quality of their lives. Training sessions involve a 60-hour group experience which is spaced over two consecutive weekends. Est training is not like an encounter group, which encourages confrontations between people, or an effort at group therapy. Yet like Transcendental Meditation, Yoga, and Zen, est training blends the discipline of mind and body garnered from Eastern religions with psychological insights.

INTERPRETIVE SUMMARY

Throughout history, religions have served the functions of explaining the unknown and making it less terrifying, of defining our place in the universe and giving us a sense of purpose. Religions have provided people with standards of morality and, conversely, have frequently lent sanctions for already existing political, economic, and other mores of a society. Finally, in order to preserve their more general functions, religious organizations have increasingly entered the areas of recreation and social work.

Religions differ in theology. Many religions have tried to answer such questions as: Is there one god, or more than one? If so, is God good or bad, carnate or incarnate, etc? Is there an afterlife? What is it like? Upon what is admission based? To what extent should I work now to gain entrance?

In folk societies, worship of intangible divinities tends to go along with belief in animism and magic. As might be expected, formal religious structures often do not exist, although religion itself may pervade all areas of life. Religious leaders may be mystics or priests; in more complex societies, the former are generally outside the pale of the established churches, which tend to be conservative. All religions, folk and urban, rely on ceremonies, with their attendant symbols, sacred objects, special locales or buildings, for perpetuation.

Historically, religious conflict is more common than cooperation; in fact, the history of religion involves a series of bitter conflicts within established organizations, gradual splits, and emergence of sects into new denominations. More recently there has been a trend toward consolidation of similar groups and there has even been limited cooperation among dissimilar national and international organizations for specific purposes.

In the United States, the influence of religion on human behavior is especially difficult to assess, since the Protestant Ethic is by now firmly a part of the American ethos. Figures concerning the number of individuals participating in each church are also inexact, since individuals are reluctant to give "private" information about their religious habits, and since churches differ on the question of what constitutes membership. However, available statistics indicate that the United States has hundreds of denominations, that Christianity is the largest single category, and that middle-class individuals and upwardly mobile individuals tend to be the most avid participants. As for the social location of churches, Protestants have largely discarded the "community church" of earlier times in favor of denominational churches, although recently there has been a slight reversal. Catholics have retained the community church, as well as church-run community schools. The Supreme Court has banned prayer in public schools and the use of public-school facilities for sectarian religious training, but the right of private groups to build private schools which include religious training has been considered basic, and heated and sometimes bitter arguments have arisen concerning financial responsibility of the federal and state governments for these parochial schools.

Recent trends in America show much diversity in the range of choices of religions available. Fundamentalist groups continue to grow. Also cults and sects are proliferating. Among these are the Moonies, Hare Krishna, est, and even witchcraft.

QUESTIONS

1. In what way does Weber disagree with Marx's analysis of the factors that contributed to the rise of capitalism?
2. What is the interest of the sociologist in religion?
3. In which ways is religion different from science? From magic?
4. Are Americans losing interest in religion? Is secularization growing? Give examples to justify your answer.

Part IV

Social Change and Social Problems

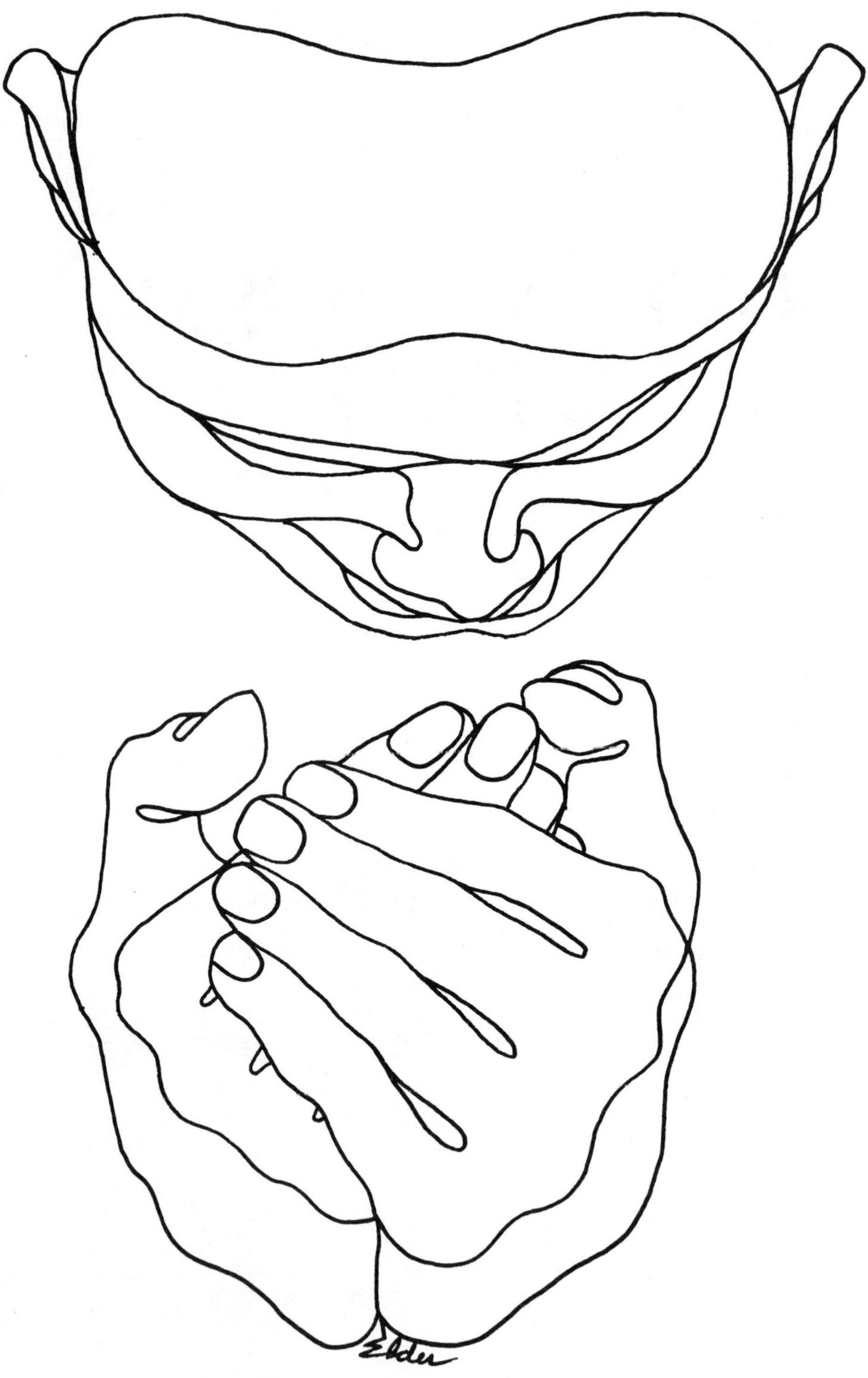
Elder

20

Social and Technological Change

While social life contains many elements of permanency and stability, it is also characterized by aspects of social change. Every society is characterized by an interplay of those forces that create cultural stability and those that create change. Culture is never wholly static. Yet, for purposes of indicating broad differences, we say a culture is *stable* when a condition of equilibrium of patterns and processes is its basic feature. In contrast, a culture marked by rather extensive alteration of its patterns and resulting disequilibrium is said to be *dynamic*. Many nonliterate peoples, especially those living under conditions of isolation, have remained relatively unchanged for long periods of time. Such were the Australian aborigines before the arrival of the white people. Certain relatively complex cultures continued a long time without any striking changes. This was the situation in Egypt during long periods of its ancient history. Yet it would be a mistake to assume that the culture of any society, large or small, is ever completely stable and static. Therefore, it will be our task in this chapter to examine the ways in which societies change and the causes of such change. We will be interested in theories of social change and factors within societies that contribute to change.

Two major factors of interest will be diffusion—that is, borrowing traits or patterns from other cultures—and the invention or discovery of new cultural elements within the society. In either case, social change will be the result: the addition of traits or patterns to the culture will produce modifications in the social structure.

THEORIES OF SOCIAL CHANGE

From the coming of the Industrial Revolution to the present day, the societies of the Western world have had to adjust to rapid social change resulting from an expanding technology. Everything has changed: from farmhouse to factory, from horse-drawn wagons to supersonic transports, from country fiddles to stereos, from homespun clothes to synthetics. There has been a continuing attempt on the part of social scientists to analyze and understand the patterns of change. Of the various theories that attempt to discover the regularities in social change, the following four will be discussed: evolutionary, equilibrium, conflict, and cyclic (rise-and-fall) theories. In general, these theories are closely related to the social conditions that existed at the time that their originators were writing and thinking about society.

Evolutionary Theories

Many of the theoretical explanations of social change that were developed in the nineteenth century were closely related to the discoveries and technological advances of the day. For example, Darwin's *Origin of Species* did not begin the discussion of evolution. At the time that Darwin published his masterwork, a number of influential anthropologists and sociologists had already begun grappling with the principles of sociocultural evolution. The writings of nineteenth-century travelers, explorers, and missionaries and their descriptions of exotic preindustrial societies had caused theorists to attempt to explain the startling differences among societies and the manner in which changes occurred in them. An often repeated notion was that social change was cumulative so that societies developed into higher and higher forms.

In the early part of the nineteenth century Auguste Comte had described three stages of development through which societies passed. These were a theological stage, when the supernatural was used to explain phenomena; a metaphysical stage, where abstract concepts were used to explain the operation of the universe; and, finally, a positive stage, where scientific explanations were most acceptable. We have already encountered Herbert Spencer's doctrine of evolution (Chapter 1) and are aware that it stresses the *direction* of social change—from the simple to the complex, from the uniform to the multiform, from the unstable and homogeneous to the complex and heterogeneous. Both Comte and Spencer typify the strongly held belief of early social scientists that social change was tied to progress and was a positive force in human social life. Anthropologist Lewis H. Morgan (1877) described the increasing complexity of societies through the evolutionary stages of *savagery, barbarism,* and *civilization* as, with progress and change, they move toward greater perfection.

It was clear to many of the social thinkers of the nineteenth century who accepted the notion of evolutionary development, from Comte to Durkheim, that the Industrial Revolution had pushed Western Europe closer to that perfection. By the end of the century the belief in ever-continuous progress had fostered an ethnocentrism, which emphasized the differences between the West and less developed societies and chose to believe that the industrial societies were more advanced, therefore superior. The imperialistic subjugation of other societies by the Western nations is closely tied to such ethnocentric beliefs. Spencer's evolutionary assumption of "the survival of the fittest" was used to justify territorial aggression. Those who felt themselves to be the "fittest" verbalized the responsibility of "the white man's burden" to bring civilization to the barbarians and the savages. If, as Spencer's principle of Social Darwinism suggested, there is a natural selection operating to produce some that are more "fit" than others, this view also gave justification to wealthy industrialists who disregarded the safety, health, and basic needs of their industrial laborers.

Equilibrium Theories

Equilibrium theory in sociology grows out of an understanding of biological structure. In the analogy that can be drawn between biological organisms and entities like families or societies, the emphasis is on the social system, that whole which is made up of parts that are interrelated. And where change takes place in one part of a biological organism or a society, it leads to change in other parts. In general, in these situations of change, there is continual adjustment ocurring so that an integration of parts will be accomplished and the system can continue to function in a harmonious way. Talcott Parsons (1902–), who was Sorokin's colleague at Harvard, differs markedly from Sorokin in his fundamental concern with the equilibrium of social systems rather than social change. As the leading functionalist theorist in American sociology during the middle portion of the twentieth century, Parsons devoted much attention to the needs and functions of social systems. His functional imperatives outline those problems of function that must be solved if the system is to continue in equilibrium. Alvin Boskoff (1969) has used the example of the American university to illustrate Parson's "functional imperatives" and their contribution to social stability:

> ... The adaptive function (emphasis on means with respect to outside conditions) would be illustrated by the provision of heating or air-conditioning for classrooms and offices; the goal-attainment function (emphasis on achieving group ends with respect to external reality) might be pursued through research and services that enhance the prestige of the university; the pattern-maintenance and tension-management functions (which focus on developing proper motivation and acceptance of the normative structure of the system) would be performed by orientation sessions, allocation of rank and salary increases to the staff, and by machinery for handling grievances; and finally, the integrative function (stressing the emotionally satisfying nature of coordinated activities of all the members) would be served by the honorific use of the university name, by symbolic reference to "school colors," by rallies, convocations, and commencement exercises (p. 188).

During the decade of the 1960s, the work of Parsons was subjected to considerable criticism. Parsons' theoretical analyses seemed primarily to be concerned with social stability and social order. He theorized that where conflict threatened to destroy social equilibrium, adjustments would be made so that social stability was restored. During the political and social disorder of the 1960s, American sociologists began to raise many questions about the processes of change. Parsons' theory did not appear to account for the violent upheavals and societal dislocations of the time. In fact Parsons had stated earlier that both the concepts of sociology and the data that existed were inadequate for use in a carefully developed theory of social change.

20-1 CHECKING IT OUT: Two Views of Human Society and Social Change

The Consensus View of Society	*The Conflict View of Society*
1. Every society is a relatively persistent, stable structure of elements.	1. Every society is subject at every moment to processes of social change: social change is ubiquitous.
2. Every society is a well-integrated structure of elements.	2. Every society experiences at every moment social conflict: social conflict is ubiquitous.
3. Every element in a society has a function, i.e., contributes to the maintenance of the society.	3. Every element in a society contributes to its disintegration and change.
4. Every society is based on the consensus of values among its members.	4. Every society rests on the coercion of some of its members by others.

SOURCE: Adapted from Ralf Dahrendorf, "Towards a Theory of Social Conflict," *Social Change*, edited by A. Etzioni and Eva Etzioni (New York: Basic Books, Inc., 1964), p. 103.

Conflict Theories

If equilibrium theory has tended to stress the orderliness and stability of social systems, conflict theories have stressed a perspective that is diametrically opposed to notions of social equilibrium. As it has been observed in Chapter 1, conflict theory focuses, not on cooperation and the interdependence of parts of systems, but rather on the competition and conflict that occurs as group interactions develop. However, this perspective highlights the value of conflict and struggle. Conflict is recognized as a basic mechanism of society and an effective means by which social change can be introduced.

Conflict theorists acknowledge a theoretical debt to Karl Marx. Marx's dialectical process offers an explanation of the manner in which conflict is generated, and the way in which social change occurs. As opposing elements within society become increasingly polarized within society, they ultimately clash. Marx's most dramatic confrontation was to be between the bourgeoisie, the owners of the means of production (factories, technology), and the proletariat (industrial workers without power). By controlling the economic resources of societies, the bourgeoisie had been able to control all other societal institutions, so that religious systems, political systems, and even the intellectual products of a society served the interests of the bourgeoisie. The exploitive relationship of the dominant class and the continual impoverishment of the working class would eventually lead to revolution, but not before the workers had developed a sense of "class consciousness" and a strong political awareness of themselves as a group. Marx believed that beneficial social change would come about as a result of revolution. Capitalism would be replaced by socialism and in time a communist society would be established where the resources of society would be shared in a more humane way.

Cyclic Theories

Spengler During the first half of the twentieth century, many theories were proposed to explain the ways in which cultures, societies, and civilizations changed. Oswald Spengler (1880–1936) was among those theorists who developed an explanation based upon the cyclic rise and fall of societies as their cultures changed. Spengler compared cultures to human organisms; each had its own childhood, youth, maturity, and old age. Spengler believed that each culture had a life span of possibly 1,000 years. In its final stage of old age, a society possessed a dying culture. This view of European culture is captured in the title of his influential book, *The Decline of the West.* (1926) We should remember that Spengler, a German scholar, had lived through the widespread destruction and social upheavals caused by World War I. His view of change, as principally determined by destiny, is unacceptable to modern social scientists.

Toynbee Arnold Toynbee, a British historian (1889–1975), developed a more optimistic view of social change in his massive work, *A Study of History.* (1946) Toynbee's unit of analysis is the civilization and he examines twenty-one civilizations (e.g., Western, Mayan, Hellenic, Hindu, Egyptian, Eskimo, Polynesian). Toynbee agrees with Spengler that civilizations pass through stages of development and ultimately decline, but he places no predetermined time limit on these stages. Rather the growth of a civilization is related to the kind of challenge that it must meet. A challenge may be found in the climate or in the presence of hostile and aggressive neighbors. Two things contribute to the growth of the civilization. One is that the challenge must not be too demanding. For example, the severity of the arctic weather and the constant fight for survival have limited the development of the Eskimo people. The other element in the development of civilization is a creative minority, able to lead and inspire the majority. When this minority loses creativity in its responses to environmental challenges the decline of the civilization begins. The minority might retain power by force but lack of vitality in the minority eventually causes the death of the civilization. Toynbee reasoned that the dying phase might last hundreds of years, as in the case of the Greek civilization.

Toynbee has been criticized for substantiating his theory with examples drawn mainly from Western and Hellenic cultures. He selectively fitted examples to theory and ignored realities that lay outside his theory. And yet his ambitious attempt to unearth causal factors to explain the development of complex and productive societies must be applauded for its breadth of vision and the magnitude of the attempt.

Sorokin Pitirim Sorokin (1889–1968), a Russian-born sociologist transplanted to Harvard, developed an explanation for social change in which the unit of analysis is, as it was for Spengler, the culture. Sorokin (1937) describes the pattern of change as a fluctuation between ideational culture and sensate culture. *Sensate cultures* value the results of sensory experiences so that such cultures might be characterized by scientific development, materialism, hedonism, and skepticism. *Ideational cultures* emphasize spiritual and metaphysical values. Therefore religion flourishes within such cultures. Mysticism, supernaturalism, and idealism are valued, and the truths of faith are more important than the truths of science. Sorokin saw cultures as fluctuating between these two extremes in a pendulum-like way, but he also described periods in which a culture might be poised between these two extremes. This was an *idealistic culture*, with a mixture of sensate and ideational values. Sorokin's discussion of social change is less than satisfying because he does not really explain the process of social change. The moving force of social change is not clear. Sorokin insists that cultures change because it is within their nature to do so. Also he is very dogmatic. Everything that he admires is ideational; everything that he does not like is sensate. And yet regardless of his conclusions, Sorokin makes an impressive contribution to sociology by asking the right questions.

CAUSES OF CHANGE—DISCOVERY AND INVENTION

It is not always easy to draw a distinction between discovery and invention. The former represents perception of relationships between elements not previously recognized or understood. The relationship may have been deliberately sought or it may have been found accidentally. On the other hand, invention is a combination of known elements or devices into some new form. In a sense, discovery is fundamental to invention, since people must have certain knowledge and skill regarding things, people, and situations before they can put that knowledge and skill to work to produce something novel. Yet the discovery of new facts or relations may depend on the invention of new methods of thinking or acting. For our purpose, the term *invention* will serve both for the discovery of some fact or principle and for the creation of a new device or pattern.

Since technology has made a striking impression on daily life in our time, people sometimes get the notion that invention involves only mechanical devices. But inventions occur in both material and nonmaterial phases of culture. The automobile and the telephone seem—and are—highly significant inventions. But so, too, are the Australian ballot, intelligence testing, and chainstore merchandising.

Basic Features of Invention

Inventions may be classified into two sorts: empirical and planned. Until the rise of modern science, most inventions were of the former type. Empirical invention generally grows out of trial-and-error attempts to improve some device or institution already at hand, or out of accidental discovery of a technique. Science has now provided us with the means of planning or directing and even predicting many of our inventions.

We may well ask what stimulates inventiveness. The old saying that "necessity is the mother of invention" requires qualification. Recurrent need may or may not induce inventiveness. The long-continued use of old and ineffective ways of doing things is ample evidence that sheer necessity does not always give birth to efficient invention. The truth is that very often, in the words of Thorstein Veblen, "Invention is the mother of necessity." That is to say, once an invention has become accepted as a new element in a culture, it may set up wants and motives not previously present in the society. The whole expansion of human needs under conditions of modern industry and merchandising is evidence enough of this fact.

It is the cultural and social situation that makes invention possible. The existence of sufficient leisure for calm and deliberate examination of various possibilities is important. An element of curiosity must be present. Without doubt, "just monkeying around" with mechanical devices or ideas has brought about valuable new combinations. In trial-and-error invention, as in all hit-or-miss learning, accidental combinations are often significant. False combinations may even suggest correct solutions later. Musing or daydreaming is also important. Getting "hunches" or making guesses is as necessary, especially in the early phases, as actual manipulation of physical objects or of social situations.

Yet neither pressing necessity nor mental reverie alone, nor the two together, fully account for invention. Such advances depend on two major factors: culture and the individual. These are closely interrelated, but for purposes of discussion we shall deal with (1) the general cultural base; (2) the culture's values and attitudes toward invention—that is, the interest or run of attention; and (3) the place of special and high intellectual abilities.

The Cultural Base

With reference to the effect on culture and society, inventions may be classed as primary or basic, and as secondary—that is, derived, or "improving," as Ralph Linton calls them. (1936) **Primary inventions** are illustrated by such things as the discovery of the use of fire, the discovery of ultraviolet rays, and the invention of the phonetic alphabet; the wheel; the means of smelting iron ore; and the zero, negative numbers, and calculus. **Secondary inventions** are those which have to do with improving or modifying other inventions, such as air conditioning or the introduction of the automatic transmission in the automobile.

An invention, if it is to survive, must have relevance to the existing culture. There is, in fact, a selective process going on at all times with reference to inventions in any society. If there is strong intellectual or emotional resistance to change, an invention may be dropped before being tried out. If, on the other hand, a society is receptive, the invention may effect profound changes. So too, the use of an invention in the total culture is important. The Greeks, for example, invented a steam engine but limited its use to religious rituals. Their culture was not ready for its application to modes of transportation or machine production.

Both basic and improving inventions depend on the state of knowledge and skill in a given society. The effect of the lack of scientific knowledge and techniques is illustrated in the work of Leonardo da Vinci. Certainly he was intellectually capable of inventing a successful flying machine—in fact, he did construct some interesting models of airplanes. But they were not workable, because he lacked the necessary tools of modern mathematics and mechanics. As a painter, however, Da Vinci was one of the greatest masters of all time, and his contributions to the study of human anatomy and to military techniques were outstanding. For these attainments there was an adequate cultural foundation.

Not only do potential inventors sometimes lack the mechanical principles or methods, but the essential materials may not be at hand. The lack of essential materials usually reflects cultural retardation in some related skill or knowledge. Thus hard steel could not be produced until certain alloys were developed.

In our society, extensions of inventions depend on the ever-larger cultural base from which they emerge, on cultural acceptance of inventions in general, and on the stimulation of capitalistic enterprise which seeks to apply inventions in order to make greater profits. Capitalism has been a stimulant to both science and technology. In all societies inventions have resulted from efforts to improve public welfare. The Soviet successes in rocketry and space technology are dramatic examples of great strides in science and engineering under a non-capitalistic system.

Planned Invention and Science

Until the rise of modern science, most inventions were empirical. Science now provides us with a means of directing and even predicting many inventions. Of course, one discovery or invention often has to wait for another. The photoelectric cell, for example, long known to physics, was not perfected for practical use until the invention of a vacuum-tube amplifier.

The planning of inventions for the larger needs of society has only begun. An early example was the designing and testing of the Liberty motor during World War I. Under a governmental directive, a number of engineers and other experts cooperated to develop a more satisfactory airplane engine. The development of the submarine detector during the same war was another case of necessity followed by planned and cooperative research. During World War II there was much more of this sort of thing. The outstanding example was the Manhattan Project, out of which came the atomic bomb.

Such planned invention is not the product of wartime needs only. In agriculture, too, there are a considerable number of planned inventions. One of the most striking is the development of hybrid corn, which has made possible an increase in yield of nearly 30 per cent. This new corn was developed by controlling the process of pollination so as to secure vigor, uniformity, and other desired characteristics. So far, most of our planned inventions have had to do with mechanical and biological problems.

Values and Run of Attention

Along with the necessary culture base in knowledge and skill, the social values regarding invention are important. From our standpoint, nonliterate people had a real need for public health measures to prevent disease, reduce the death rate, and improve their physical well-being. That they did not obtain these measures was partly because they lacked information and techniques but partly also because their ideas and values regarding birth, death, and disease were vastly different from our own. What a culture demands and what it values will help direct its inventors. Among the Crow Indians, for example, there was considerable stress on individual visionary experience, which encouraged the introduction of a new religious cult. In Samoa there is some allowance for innovation in ritual and decorative arts, yet "in the decorative arts, the freedom given to the individuals is rendered nugatory by the absence of cultural recognition to the innovator and by the strong prejudice against active imitation so the gifted individual receives but passing praise for his work." (Mead, 1928)

The Samoan attitude grows out of the general cultural patterning that stresses individual conformity to tradition and cooperative relations. Americans, in contrast, put much emphasis on interpersonal competition for attainment, especially in mechanical invention and business enterprise. However, there is no reward of either money or honor for those who suggest sharply different institutional norms.

It is evident, then, that what W. I. Thomas calls "the run of attention" in a society has much to do with the particular direction that inventions will take.

The entire matrix of technology and money-making sets the framework within which potential innovators growing up in American society will operate. Were we to fix our present material culture at about its present level and turn our inventive attention elsewhere, we might experience greater and more numerous changes in patterns of political, religious, artistic, or recreational activities.

20-2 CHECKING IT OUT: Mechanical Invention as a Combination of Known Elements

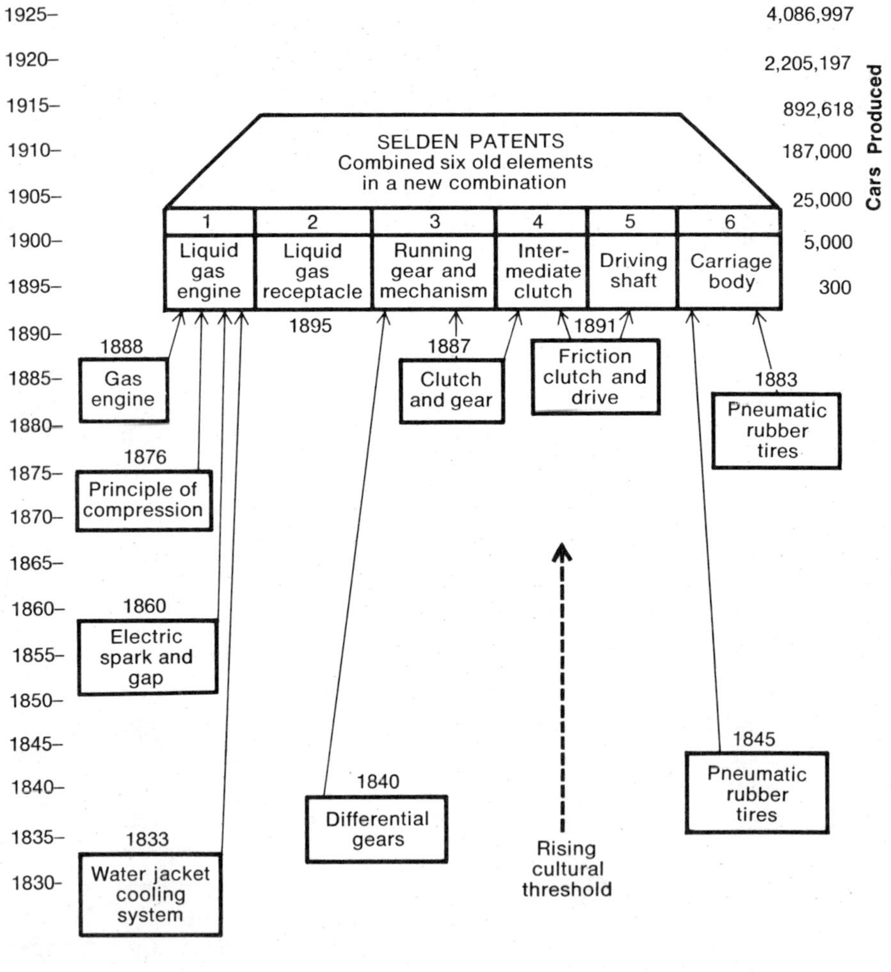

SOURCE: F. Stuart Chapin, *Cultural Change* (New York: The Century Company 1928).

Intellectual Ability and Inventiveness

To recognize that the particular run of attention will be determined by culture does not deny the importance of persons of superior mental endowment in producing new inventions. One may well ask what place special ability or so-called inventive genius has in invention. It is very easy to assume that inventions are the result of the innate ability of a few chosen persons. There is no doubt that, given the proper cultural encouragement, intellectually gifted persons become inventors. Yet who these people are and what they do with their capacity depends on the society. It is hardly conceivable that the genius of the jungle would become a great physician, though he might well become a military leader or the inventor of a new religious ritual. Due to the lack of social opportunities, it is no surprise that there are proportionately fewer women inventors in twentieth-century United States than there are male inventors. Men, of course, are not proportionately more intelligent than women.

The relation of culture to individual ability raises the question of the "great-man theory" of history—that is, does history make great men or do great men make history? Confining ourselves only to the matter of invention, the particular direction of inventions and their nature are determined by culture. Often we forget the slow accumulation of basic knowledge by less well-known men who made possible the more spectacular work we hear about. The inventions of Thomas A. Edison in electricity, for instance, would have been impossible without hundreds of researches in the century before him.

Clearly, inventions and discoveries do not depend on one particular exceptional person but on the nature of the culture out of which the new elements in the invention arise. Advances in invention depend so much on minor accretions to the total body of knowledge that it is indeed doubtful that any one particular inventor is essential at a given time. "Great men" alone do not make inventions. As Ralph Linton once wrote:

> Unpleasant as the realization may be to egotists, very few individuals can be considered as more than incidents in the life histories of the societies to which they belong. Our species long ago reached the point where organized groups rather than their individual members became the functional units in its struggle for survival. (Linton, 1945, p. 12)

DIFFUSION

Social and cultural change occurs not only by invention or discovery but also by diffusion. *Diffusion* is the borrowing and adopting of cultural traits or patterns from other social units. Ordinarily, diffusion is thought of as a movement of traits through *space*. In this sense it is not to be confused with *transmission* of culture, which has to do with passing traits and patterns through *time*—that is, from generation to generation. Thus, formal education is not diffusion but transmission.

The Spread of Culture

The elements of culture may diffuse among nations and regions, from class to class, from community to community, and among any other associations of people. For example, Christianity and, later, industrialism spread from Europe and the United States to Japan and China. Much of the system of education in the United States was borrowed from nineteenth-century Germany. As a rule, social fashions spread from the upper to the working classes. Urban ways are diffused to rural localities.

Diffusion can be either direct or indirect. Direct diffusion occurs when groups have physical contact. Indirect diffusion is the spread of traits without group contact. The first is illustrated by migration and colonization, by contact through war and trade, and by the work of religious missionaries. The second is witnessed in the spread of printed materials, by radio and television, and by the infiltration of ideas and goods in commerce carried on without direct personal contact. Indirect diffusion accompanies the development of secondary-group organization.

The spread of culture is not always just from Western societies to nonliterate societies. It is often reciprocal. While Western people have diffused their culture, especially the material phases, over most of the earth, nonliterate peoples have contributed heavily to literate societies. The contribution of this kind most obvious to us is, of course, the large number of cultural items received from Native Americans. These include, among many other things, maize or Indian corn and many methods of its cultivation, potatoes, beans, tomatoes, and tobacco. These people also gave us the game of lacrosse, and taught colonists new methods of stalking game and enemies in dense woods.

In turn, the white man brought the Native American the horse and saddle and firearms. These items produced great changes in the culture of the tribes on the Great Plains, giving them mobility, adding to their efficiency in game hunting, and stimulating their interest in warfare. On the other hand, these very alterations probably retarded any incipient tendencies toward more settled community life and agriculture. The whites also brought Christianity; but, as elsewhere, it tended in many instances to be fused with the native religion, an indication that the items which are diffused sooner or later merge with the indigenous culture patterns if they do not replace them.

War and conquest have been important factors in diffusion. The Roman legions spread Latin culture around the Mediterranean and beyond. Not only new political systems but also new economic organization and religion have followed in the wake of war.

Diffusion is generally more important than invention in the total building of any culture: of all the items in any given culture, more are borrowed from other peoples than are invented. Very often culture traits that are thought to have arisen from geographical conditions or from crises actually have come from other culture groups. Some anthropologists go so far as to lay down a kind of rule that, other things being equal, it is easier to borrow than to invent. Perhaps because of the inertia of habit and man's lack of originality, it seems more common to look around and find some method already in use than to think up an entirely new device to meet the situation.

Rates of Diffusion

Culture traits and patterns diffuse at different rates. As a rule, material traits spread much more quickly than those which have to do with forms of the family, political organization, art, religion, or recreation. Native peoples, for example, often readily accept firearms, utensils, tools, and cloth, but at the same time retain their own language, kinship organization, religion, and art. The diffusion nearly always involves some modification. Rarely is any trait, unless it is of a material nature, borrowed by people without some modification at their hands.

Diffusion may go on in an informal and almost unconscious way, or it may be the result of a conscious attempt to foist an alien culture on another society. Spreading by trade and migration is often of the first sort; that fostered by organized religion or by a conquering state usually is more deliberate.

There are also certain hindrances to diffusion, such as inadequate transportation and communication, complete isolation, taboos on change, and resistance to foreign ideas and techniques. So too, displacement of one pattern by another prevents the further spread of the pattern displaced. The practice of drinking coffee is not likely to spread rapidly in a country such as China, long addicted to tea.

The factors affecting rate of diffusion may be summarized as follows: (1) availability of transportation and communication, including distance and barriers to travel such as mountains or sea; (2) resistance to culture changes, such as taboo, sense of superiority, and general cultural inertia; (3) prestige of the lending culture and its people; (4) conquest of one people by another; (5) migration, especially when *en masse*, as in the Teutonic invasions of the Roman Empire, in modern immigration, or in enforced moving of large populations from one region to another; (6) the need for some new element to meet a critical situation; and (7) adaptability of the recipients of the new culture, as in the ready adoption of Western industrialism by Japan.

As a matter of fact, the cultural elements operating in diffusion are not unlike those which more or less determine invention. That is, the broad cultural base of prior skill and knowledge must be taken into account. So too, the basic values of potential recipients are important. Persons of high status, scholars, political and industrial leaders, war chiefs, and religious functionaries will usually be in the vanguard of reception. Finally, since nearly all borrowed traits are subject to some modification in their new setting, special ability will play a part in adapting the item to the new situation.

FACTORS INFLUENCING INNOVATIONS

The acceptance of innovations is qualified by the nature and extent of the changes, by the rate at which they are introduced, and by the degree of readiness of groups. We have already indicated that societies differ in their receptiveness to change. In a society oriented to modern technology, new cultural elements that contribute to further technology are more acceptable, on the whole, than radical innovations in institutions that support the moral system of the society. So too, changes of wide scope will tend to induce more reaction than will minor changes. One factor contributing to present-day anxieties is the fact that people cannot readjust themselves fast enough to the large number of innovations to which they are exposed. In personal terms this means that individuals cannot do the "unlearning" necessary for the acquisition of the many new thoughts and patterns of social interaction without becoming confused and distressed in the process.

Cultural Lag

Whether induced by political revolution or by slower methods, changes in one field often induce dislocations in another area of behavior. For example, the last 150 years have seen a tremendous burst of material inventions in western Europe and America which have altered the nature of technological culture the world over. In sharp contrast, corresponding modifications in the nonmaterial culture have been slow, halting, and ineffective. Often new needs arising from rather sudden material changes have not been adequately satisfied. In other words, the previous integration of the major parts of a total culture has been disturbed by these changes.

This differential in the rate of change W. F. Ogburn termed *cultural lag*, which he defined in these words:

> The thesis is that the various parts of modern culture are not changing at the same rate, some parts are changing much more rapidly than others; and that since there is a correlation and interdependence of parts, a rapid change in one part of our culture requires adjustments through other changes in the various correlated parts. ... Where one part of culture changes first, through some discovery or invention, and occasions changes in some part of culture dependent upon it, there frequently is a delay in the changes occasioned in the dependent part of the culture. (*Social Change*, pp. 200–201)

Many of the contemporary problems of society can be viewed in terms of "cultural lag." There is today a wide range of new patterns of social interaction and new ideas fostered by material alterations which were not anticipated and for which there has been no preparation. This dislocation is largely a result of differentials in rates of change. In fact, *social disorganization* is often characterized as the breakdown of societal order to such an extent that the former social controls are dissipated and social disorder arises.

Few people would deny that advantages have accrued from technological innovations: lessening of the severity of work and hours of labor, increase in leisure, widespread education, mobility and travel, increased "animation" of life, extension of contacts, and a higher standard of living for millions. But it is also true that many dislocations have arisen from the failure of the nonmaterial culture—especially that connected with societal organization—to keep pace with these new material culture patterns. Social mobility has decreased the significance of the neighborhood and community for many people, weakened social controls, and fostered certain types of crime. Changes in industrial production have caused technological unemployment, pollution, and alienation.

The political order, too, is marked by many dislocations: the continuance of outworn political units of voting, the restriction of residence for office-holders, and the persistence of many governmental forms that belonged to the horse-and-buggy era. The lag in laws and administration of justice and in the correction and care of dependents, delinquents, and criminals is compounded by the lack of personnel adequately trained for work in a complex society.

When new patterns are believed to threaten old values and long-accepted ways of doing things, resistance is bound to arise. The receptivity to social change is a function of the existing social situation. In U.S. society change has at times been resisted by business, labor, class and community interests, as well as by government bodies and by scientific experts.

Changes in Technology

There are hundreds of instances of opposition to technological change in the history of modern industry. The major aim of profits often blinds entrepreneurs to new opportunities to make money and to serve the public more efficiently at the same time. The major consideration is often not "Will it work?" but "Will it pay?" Various factors enter into this inertia. Among them are: the large capital investments in going concerns already providing goods and services; the cost of putting new plants into operation and of selling the product or service; the desire to maintain a dominant position over existing or potential competitors; the somewhat unwieldy ways and means; and the trouble smaller businesses have securing capital to start new enterprises. There are almost endless illustrations of such resistance; we shall select but a few from the history of transportation.

The introduction of the railroad into the United States met with great opposition. In 1812 John Stevens' proposal to introduce railway lines into New York State was flatly turned down by such leaders as DeWitt Clinton, Gouverneur Morris, and Robert R. Livingston. When later—1815 in New Jersey and 1823 in Pennsylvania—Stevens obtained charters, he had difficulty persuading capitalists to invest in his enterprises. The owners of canal barges and of stagecoach lines were particularly bitter about the railroads. The rationalizations of potential investors who objected to the railway were many and ingenious: fear of speed, of setting fire to towns, of disrupting the local life, and so on.

Once the railroads had become fairly well established, moreover, a process of crystallization set in. Owners and investors opposed further advances. Commodore Cornelius Vanderbilt, one of the early railroad magnates, dismissed George Westinghouse and his air-brake invention with the remark that he had no time to waste on fools. Eli J. Janney, the inventor of the car-coupler, had to wait ten years before he could get a foundry to manufacture it for him. Until very recently, the design of the Pullman sleeper was pretty much the same as it was in 1859. Electric locomotives, streamlined trains, and other improvements were adopted very slowly. When the autobus came into use, railway executives and employee unions alike opposed the extension of bus lines because it was felt that their competition would ruin the railroads.

The automobile presents another story of long, slow development. As early as 1769, Nicholas Joseph Cugnot invented a three-wheeled vehicle powered by two steam cylinders. But he got no popular support for his device. Other steam-propelled carriages were tried out with only limited acceptance. When the internal-combustion engine, in combination with other inventions, made the automobile practicable, years went by before the new vehicle was accepted. The automobile was "a rich man's toy" which would never have any practical use. The first U.S. automobile manufacturers got a cool reception from the Wall Street bankers. In 1908, John Pierpont Morgan and his partners refused to buy a block of securities priced at $5,000,000 in a concern that was later consolidated into General Motors.

As with the railroads, improvements in the automobile were opposed by corporate owners, although the lag in accepting what people called "refinements" was less than with many other mechanical devices. Yet the self-starter, six- and eight-cylinder engines, four-wheel brakes, balloon tires, and automatic transmission were slow to be adopted.

The story of the airplane parallels these others. This radical departure in the means of transportation and communication seemed fantastic even to a generation already attuned to rapid technological changes, and all the early airplane manufacturers had difficulty financing their inventions.

Laborers, like investors, have often been slow to accept new technologies. The factory system in England and elsewhere met with much opposition from the workers. The most recurrent opposition to modifications in industrial processes has come from labor unions. In the 1870s, the introduction of labor-saving devices in the boot-and-shoe industry was bitterly opposed by the workers' unions. Silk workers went on strike against the three- or four-loom system. Building and construction workers have fought a steady battle against the introduction of machine processing into their work. Agreements with union painters have dictated the width of brushes so that workers would not be able to cover more surface than the unions considered fair. Union painters have long opposed the introduction of spray guns. The history of trade unionism is filled with such cases.

The introduction of the diesel engine was opposed by the railroad unions because it threatened the fireman's job. Indeed, it was only after the railroads agreed to keep firemen on the engine crews that diesels were put into wide use.

Political Resistance

Political factors have also played a part in retarding industrial advancement. Public officials have felt pressures of two sorts: from the people in general, and from such vested interests as those of business or labor. Public opposition to the railroad as dangerous and disruptive of custom and tradition delayed legislation that would have facilitated the railroad's development. Some states even passed laws against this new form of transportation. For example, since the state of New York had gone into heavy public debt to subsidize the Erie Canal, it wrote into early railroad charters and franchises restrictions that made it practically impossible for the railroads to compete with the canal barges. A tonnage tax so high it was impossible for railroads to carry freight was one of these restrictions. When the railroad unions became strong, they agitated in Congress to limit the length of trains and to determine the size of train crews—at the very time when improved roadbeds, more powerful locomotives, and safety devices made possible longer trains and smaller crews. This is a kind of socially induced cultural lag.

Inertia Among the Experts

A most interesting aspect of this entire subject is the frequent resistance of experts themselves. Scientific training is highly specialized; and people who for years have done work in one particular line, especially if they have obtained high prestige, often oppose changes if these run counter to their professional or other beliefs.

In 1826 an engineer said of the railroad that "a rate of speed of more than six miles an hour would exceed the bounds of providence," and the suggestion of John Stevens that trains might travel 20 miles an hour was met with derision. A notable instance of scientific authority invoked against an invention was the astronomer Simon Newcomb's criticism of the airplane. In 1906 Newcomb publicly declared that neither the laws of physics nor the state of the industrial arts made it practicable for man to "fly long distances through the air."

The history of modern medicine is replete with illustrations of hostility to innovations. Opposition greeted the pioneer work of Louis Pasteur in the field of bacteriology and immunology. In the study of mental diseases an interesting instance is the ridicule which greeted Dr. Sigmund Freud when, before a distinguished group of neurologists in Vienna, he reported a case of male hysteria. He was informed in no uncertain terms by the most eminent neurologists of the day that this was impossible, since hysteria was associated only with female physical functions. Freud lived long enough to see complete verification of his contention and recognition of his competence in the field of mental disease.

Class and Community Resistance

Not only do vested economic interests, political organizations, and experts often resist cultural change, but the general population also frequently does so, often taking its justification for opposition from these other groups.

Class factors enter very thoroughly into resistance. An amusing and revealing class attitude was expressed in the English Parliament by Craven Fitzhardinge Berkeley in these words: "Nothing is more distasteful to me than to hear the echo of our hills reverberating with the hissing of railroad engines running through the heart of our hunting country, and destroying that noble sport, fox hunting, to which I have been accustomed from my childhood." (Stern, 1937, p. 40) The royalty of Europe long opposed the substitution of automobiles for horse-drawn carriages on state occasions.

Class resistance to institutional modifications is well-known. Attempts to modify the system of private enterprise have met with recurrent criticism from the propertied classes, and agitation to abolish the capitalistic system has led to legal and violent extralegal means to silence such ideas.

The opposition of the general public at times is no less vigorous than that of the privileged classes. When the railroads first came into rather general use, preachers, merchants, and the man in the street often denounced them as instruments likely to destroy their way of life. There are numerous examples in the history of education of negative reactions to new pedagogical practices. In one community the system of staggering the time for recess so as to allow more play space for the children had to be abandoned because some parents who saw children on the playground all though the day spread the word that this "new-fangled" plan meant all play and no work. The introduction of a course of study which would lessen the emphasis on such subjects as Latin and incorporate vocational subjects, art, music, and the like had to overcome opposition in community after community before being accepted.

Not every innovation is met by strong resistance, however. Many changes are facilitated by the pressure of grave economic-political crises. The establishment of the Securities and Exchange Commission, following the stock market crash of 1929, is a case in point. But on the whole, the more drastic the change, the more intense the emotional opposition is likely to be. In spite of the American belief in progress and the stress progress gets in both formal and informal education, alterations which touch our more basic values arouse anxiety, hostility, and negative feelings. The most acceptable changes are those which are in line with principles already taken for granted. The knowledge of science remains far in advance of application.

TECHNOLOGY AND INSTITUTIONS

New technological or other devices, whether originating within a society or borrowed from outside, obviously set up a network of effects. Innovations influence one another and constantly alter the culture and social structure.

Culture and Technology

The influences of innovations are both direct (primary) and indirect (secondary). Direct or primary influences are evident in such an invention as the cotton gin, which almost completely replaced former production techniques. So too, if a state changes from a representative democracy to a dictatorship, many former institutions will be liquidated and others replaced, although some old ways of doing things will continue alongside the new.

The secondary or derivative influences are even more striking. These have to do with extension of effects to other technologies and institutions or associations. For example, the cotton gin stimulated cotton raising and the large plantation system; it influenced slavery and so had a great effect on political and everyday life, not only in the South but in the North as well.

In recent decades we have witnessed profound modifications in life as a result of the introduction of motor vehicles. The automobile, at first considered a luxury, soon became a routine necessity. To mention only a few of its more obvious effects: It led to the building of hard-surfaced, all-weather roads, which permitted higher speeds. This in turn led to further improvement of highways: the elimination of sharp turns, the construction of super-highways, the production of more automobiles, and, of course, increased air pollution. New elements in a culture often have far-reaching effects. The automobile may reduce the revenue of the railroads and hence influence the consumption of coal. On the other hand, the automobile "causes" an extension of pipelines for oil, increases the consumption of gasoline, and creates a need for experts to control pollution. The introduction of two items serving the same end, such as gas and electricity for household use, sets up a struggle for dominance. Such competition serves a selective function.

The motor vehicle also influenced the displacement of draft animals on the farm and in our cities altered the importance of forage crops and pasturage in the rural economy. The automobile has increased the mobility of people—daily, seasonally, yearly. Because it increased congestion in urban centers, it aided the decentralization of population and so affected the growth of suburbs. It has influenced home life, made union school districts possible, and so on and on. It

20-3 CHECKING IT OUT: How the Automobile Affected American Culture

. . . But all the new products, services, and entertainments paled when placed beside the automobile—the economic and social wonder of the age. Invented in Europe, the gas-powered horseless carriage was a curiosity on American streets through the early 1900s. Then, in 1908 Henry Ford introduced the Model T, an inexpensive, durable motor car, built by an assembly line of machines and workers. This manufacturing process, according to Ford, applied "the principles of power, accuracy, economy, system, continuity, speed, and repetition." By atomizing production into a smoothly flowing stream of simple, repetitive tasks, Ford was able to fashion more cars for cheaper costs, while raising the wages of his workers. He had democratized the automobile.

Between 1920 and 1930 automobile registrations in this country nearly tripled, from eight to twenty-three million. The effects on the economy were extraordinary. By the mid-twenties the automobile industry used 20 percent of the nation's steel output, 80 percent of the rubber, and 75 percent of the plate glass. It revamped the petroleum industry from one of illumination and lubrication to one of propulsion. It created a vast new service network of filling stations, repair shops, and parts and accessories dealers. Unlike their European counterparts who viewed the automobile as an item of luxury, American manufacturers, such as Ransom E. Olds and Henry Ford, intended their product for a mass market . . .

. . . The automobile also influenced social attitudes. Contemporaries believed the '20s to be an age of revolt, when youths snubbed traditional manners and morals. Moral critics believed motor cars were contributing to this revolt, especially in the cities. In 1919 one in ten cars had closed tops; by 1927 five of every six were covered, giving the inside of autos new secrecy. Although alarmists probably exaggerated the extent of misdeed by youths who parked in darkened lanes away from adult eyes, the car provided a new source for parental anxiety. More importantly, for many families the automobile symbolized social freedom and self-respect. Historian John B. Rae has noted that in 1906 Woodrow Wilson expressed fear that possession of a motor car would bring on socialism because it would provoke envy of the rich. Instead, says Rae, it incited the common man to "desire to own an automobile, not to change the social system." In urban-industrial America the car, inexpensive and available, became a badge of equality, the ultimate expression of mobility. As one writer suggested in 1924, "It is hard to convince Steve Popovich, or Antonio Branca, or plain John Smith that he is being ground into the dust by Capital when at will be may drive the same highways, view the same scenery and get as much enjoyment from his trip as the modern Midas."

SOURCE: Howard Chudacoff, *The Evolution of American Urban Society* (Englewood Cliffs, N.J.: Prentice-Hall, 1975), pp. 190-192.

is clear that the effects of this invention on life styles and social attitudes has been as profound as its effect on the economy.

Or take the changes brought about by the radio. Radio waves are used in guiding ships to port, in flying airplanes, as danger signals when navigators are in distress, and in exterminating parasites. Radio and television have also brought in new words: *broadcast, newscaster, shortwave, frequency modulation, televise, stereophonics, communications satellite.*

With regard to advances in communication and transportation, modern man has not yet fully understood what increased speed through space may mean for future economic and political organization or for human personality itself. Certainly the contraction of space as measured by time may bring about great changes in many of our institutions. One can only imagine the political and social changes that simultaneous worldwide telecasting may bring.

Advances in the biological sciences have also been striking. Medical research, coupled with public health programs, has eliminated contagious and infectious diseases to a degree literally undreamed of a century ago. The changes influence the age distribution of the population and hence affect the entire social structure.

20-4 CHECKING IT OUT: How the New Microtechnology Will Transform Society

. . . The miracle chip [or microcomputer] represents a quantum leap in the technology of mankind, a development that over the past few years has acquired the force and significance associated with the development of hand tools or the discovery of the steam engine. Just as the Industrial Revolution took over an immense range of tasks from men's muscles and enormously expanded productivity, so the microcomputer is rapidly assuming huge burdens of drudgery from the human brain and thereby expanding the mind's capacities in ways that man has only begun to grasp. With the chip, amazing feats of memory and execution become possible in everything from automobile engines to universities and hospitals, from farms to banks and corporate offices, from outer space to a baby's nursery.

Those outside the electronic priesthood often have trouble grasping the principles of the new microtechnology or comprehending the accomplishments of the minuscule computers. The usual human sense of scale, the proportion between size and capability, the time ratio assumed between thought and action, are swept into a new and surreal terrain. Consequently, people tend to anthropomorphize the computer; they are superstitious about it. In *2001: A Space Odyssey,* the companionable computer Hal turns rogue in outer space and methodically begins assassinating its masters. In a B-movie called *Demon Seed,* the world's most advanced computer actually impregnates a scientist's wife, played by Julie Christie; it is so smart that it yearns to be alive—and scarily succeeds. . .

. . . All of the prodigies of technology leave many people not only nostalgic for simpler times but alarmed by the unknown dangers that "progress" may bring with it. Those who first used fire must have terrified their generation. Practically any breakthrough in knowledge carries with it the possibility that it will be used for evil. But with microcomputers, the optimists can argue an extemely persuasive case. The Industrial Revolution had the effect of standardizing and routinizing life. Microtechnology, with its nearly infinite capacities and adaptability, tends on the contrary toward individualization; with computers, people can design their lives far more in line with their own wishes. They can work at terminals at home instead of in offices, educate themselves in a variety of subjects at precisely the speed they wish, shop electronically with the widest possible discretion. Among other things, microtechnology will make the mechanism of supply and demand operate more responsively; customers' wishes will be registered at the speed of light.

Some, like Sociologist Seymour Martin Lipset, envision a "more egalitarian society" because of the computer. Transferring so much work to the machines, thinks Lipset, may produce something like Athenian democracy; Athenians could be equal because they had slaves to do their work for them.

Says Isaac Asimov, the prolific author and futuristic polymath: "We are reaching the stage where the problems that we must solve are going to become insoluble without computers. I do not fear computers. I fear the lack of them." Many people have great expectations and doubts about the new technology, especially in a century when they have felt themselves enslaved and terrorized by the works of science. Stewart Brand, creater of the Whole Earth Catalog, argues for a longer perspective: "This is a story that goes back to the beginning of tool-using animals, back to the rocks the earliest man picked up in Africa. As soon as he started picking up rocks, his hands started changing, his brain started changing. Computers are simply a quantum jump in the same co-evolutionary process."

There seems little doubt that life in the U.S., then in the rest of the industrial world and eventually all over the planet, will be incalculably changed by the new microtechnology. . . .

SOURCE: *Time,* February 20, 1978, pp. 44-5. Reprinted by permission from TIME, The Weekly Newsmagazine; Copyright Time Inc. 1978.

Daniel Bell (1973) has recently characterized our nation as a "post-industrial society" dependent on a complex technology controlled by an elite of scientists and technocrats. In the world of the future, sociologists like Bell envision a freer, leisure-oriented society where automation will enable citizens to develop and enrich themselves. The new microtechnology will allow people to design their own lives in positive and productive ways.

Material and nonmaterial changes influence one another. The nonmaterial effects of mechanical inventions are of varying degrees and kinds. The introduction of the typewriter first changed the habits of clerks, who had formerly used pen and ink. Later, it gave rise to a class of special workers, mostly women.

Lag in Application

These examples are striking but one must not assume that invention necessarily means use. New devices often fail to become part of the technology or institu-

20-5 CHECKING IT OUT: Innovation Incubation Intervals (approximate)

Innovation	*Conception*	*Realization*	*Incubation Interval (years)*
Antibiotics	1910	1940	30
Automatic transmission	1930	1946	16
Ball-point pen	1938	1945	7
Cellophane	1900	1912	12
Cotton picker	1924	1941	17
Crease-resistent fabrics	1918	1932	14
Dry soup mixes	1943	1962	19
Filter cigarettes	1953	1955	2
Fluorescent lighting	1901	1934	33
Frozen foods	1908	1923	15
Gyrocompass	1852	1908	56
Heart pacemaker	1928	1960	32
Helicopter	1904	1941	37
Hybrid corn	1908	1933	25
Instant camera	1945	1947	2
Instant coffee	1934	1956	22
Liquid shampoo	1950	1958	8
Long-playing records	1945	1948	3
Magnetic recordings	1900	1937	37
Minute rice	1931	1949	18
Nuclear energy	1919	1965	46
Nylon	1927	1939	12
Penicillin	1928	1943	15
Photography	1782	1838	56
Radar	1904	1939	35
Radio	1890	1914	24
Roll-on deodorant	1948	1955	7
Safety razor	1895	1906	11
Self-winding watch	1923	1939	16
Silicone	1904	1942	38
Stainless Steel	1904	1920	16
Telegraph	1820	1837	17
Television	1884	1947	63
Transistor	1940	1956	16
Video tape-recorder	1950	1956	6
Xerox copying	1935	1950	15
Zipper	1883	1913	30

SOURCE: Stephen Rosen, *New York Times*, June 18, 1976, p. 38.

tions. For example, the recall of judges, which once attracted great public interest, did not persist. So too, as noted above, resistance may long delay otherwise useful changes. With regard to technology, there are other factors to be taken into account. A new instrument or machine must be durable, simple, safe, and economical to install, operate, and repair. Then also, there must be the materials needed for its manufacture, and it generally must be capable of mass production.

The application of knowledge of nuclear physics is an interesting case in point. Its first use in war was not followed by any rapid application to peacetime industry, partly because of its possible use in future wars and partly because of the high cost of building plants and of switching over to this form of power.

INTERPRETIVE SUMMARY

No society is completely static. Social and technological change is evident in all societies; however, the rate of change and the direction of change vary in different societies. There is a continuous interplay between forces that contribute to cultural stability and forces that lead to social change.

Theories of change may be grouped into four categories: evolutionary, equilibrium, conflict, and cyclic. *Evolutionary* theories flourished in the nineteenth century and related social change to progress and the increasing perfectability of social structures. Spencer's doctrine of evolution identifies the direction of social change to be unilinear, from simple to complex forms. The rapid development of the West, due to the Industrial Revolution, caused Social Darwinists, Spencer among them, to conclude that Western societies, because of their social differentiation and complexity, were the most advanced. This ethnocentric view was accepted as a justification for imperialistic aggression against nonwhite and weaker nations. *Equilibrium* theories stressed that social change is essentially a harmonious process. Talcott Parsons, a contemporary theorist, concerned himself with the equilibrium of social systems rather than with social change. Parsons observed that if conflicts occur in one part of the social structure changes may also occur in other parts; however, changes are structured to restore social stability and harmony. *Conflict* theories stress the fact that social conflict is a natural process and ubiquitous. This view is based on Marx's conclusion that social changes emerge from conflict situations. According to Marx's dialectical process, opposing elements (e.g., the bourgeoisie and the proletariat) will clash. The revolution resulting from the clash leads to beneficial social changes. *Cyclic* theorists, such as Spengler and Toynbee, viewed social change as part of an inevitable process whereby civilizations develop, flourish, and then decay. Sorokin's cyclic explanation of change described the dramatic fluctuations that occur as cultures alternate between polar opposites. Sorokin stressed a movement away from ideational cultures emphasizing spiritual values toward sensate cultures which value sensory experiences, materialism, and science.

Because no society is completely static, a culture never accepts all potential innovations, and those that are used enter at varying rates. Social need is not the only factor affecting acceptance. Material innovations are accepted more readily than concomitant changes in basic values and beliefs, regardless of need. Both material and ideological innovations may be resisted because the "run of attention" of the society lies elsewhere. Vested interests, such as business, labor, scientific groups, social classes, or communities, may resist change because of the fear of losing an investment, prestige, or other security, or inability to see that a "far-fetched" idea might work. A society's political structures, also having investments to protect or not wishing to alienate the public for other reasons, may resist change. Of course, an innovation may also be rejected because it really is not practical or relevant to a culture.

Cultures are modified in two general ways: by invention and by diffusion, wholesale or modified adoption of elements from outside cultures and from subcultures within the society. Invention is stimulated or discouraged by the factors above, as well as by the "cultural" base, which includes the cumulative knowledge, skills; and materials present in a culture at a given time. The scientific method is now an invaluable part of the cultural base of many societies. Diffusion, which is responsible for most cultural changes, is affected by the basic factors influencing all innovation and by certain other factors, notably prestige of the lending culture and immigration.

Innovations are likely to have more widespread effects than those that were specifically intended. For example, one material change may cause far-reaching changes in a culture's basic institutions and structures. Conversely, when a material innovation is accepted but necessary changes in institutions are resisted or people are unable to carry out institutional changes quickly enough, a society may undergo a long period of deleterious cultural lag or even become disorganized.

QUESTIONS

1. What social factors cause the phenomenon of cultural lag? In what ways is cultural lag dysfunctional?
2. In examining the four theories of social change, which best describes the United States since the Revolutionary War? Russia in the twentieth century? Contemporary Egypt?
3. What can you predict about the rate at which inventions will occur in U.S. society? Why?

21

Collective Behavior and Social Movements

People live most of their lives within the confines of normative social structure and within the routines that yield form and stability to social life. Social behavior is usually, but not always, institutionalized. Smelser reports that "in all civilizations men have thrown themselves into episodes of dramatic behavior, such as the craze, the riot, and the revolution." (Smelser, 1963, p. 1) The clash of striking workers and police that results in shouting, the destruction of property, the use of tear gas and night sticks, and personal injury is an example of behavior which is violent and not routinized by the social norms that govern more institutionalized behavior. Other less dramatic examples of collective behavior include the movie audience, the crowd leaving a football game, the skillful manipulation of public opinion by the propagandist, the movements of minorities for equal rights and social status. The major areas of collective behavior include crowds, publics and public opinion, and social movements.

CROWD BEHAVIOR

Relatively impermanent and unstructured forms of human association are usually classified according to the intensity, frequency, duration, and focus of the interaction occurring among the people involved.

Audience

An audience is a number of persons in physical contiguity (that is in the same place at the same time) all of whom are subject to the same stimulus. It is therefore proper to speak of a theater audience, a football audience, or, during a sermon, a minister's audience. It is not correct, in sociological language, to refer to everyone in the United States who is watching a play on Saturday night as a television audience, because the viewers are not in physical contiguity. And even though one member of the group attending a football game is gazing into his girl friend's eyes instead of focusing on the stimulus being shared by the others, this group is still a football audience.

The intensity of interaction among the members of an audience is, in general, fairly low. On occasion, the wild screaming of others in a stadium may stimulate someone to a like response. But most of the time the members of an audience interact only at the level of being aware that others are there, and hence modifying their behavior to the extent, say, of not removing their shoes at a concert as they might if they were not in interaction with the rest of the audience.

The focus of an audience is the common stimulus of the play, concert, baseball game, or whatever its members came to see. Because of this focus, the duration is usually relatively brief. Ordinarily, the members of an audience interact as such on only one occasion, an obvious exception being the audience with concert series tickets or season passes to sports events.

Crowds

A crowd is a number of persons interacting on only one occasion, and at a very low level of intensity. A crowd is of brief duration. The members of the group are in physical contiguity, but they seldom have a shared and definite focus; hence they are characterized by relatively random activity, or milling. After the common stimulus has been withdrawn, a group which has been an audience becomes a crowd. The people leaving a football stadium or a theater are a crowd. People standing on a street corner waiting for a bus are a crowd. A number of persons pushing past one another in a department store constitutes a crowd. They are aware of one another's presence, but their level of interaction is not at all intense. They certainly are not organized with relation to one another in a manner comparable to a club. They do not have a focus, as an audience does. Each member of the crowd may have a purpose, as in the case of a shopping crowd, but the members are not subject to a common stimulus in the same sense as are people attending a concert.

Mobs

Like crowds, mobs usually interact on only one occasion, and ordinarily for a brief time. Unlike crowds, however, mobs pitch their interaction at a high level of intensity; they are characterized by a display of emotion, usually accompanied by violent behavior. Mobs usually have a leader or leaders who help them focus their emotions and violence on a goal or target.

On a typical night in a college town, you can find an audience at the movie theater. Here is a group of persons in physical contiguity, together temporarily to focus on a common stimulus, the movie. Their interaction is not very intense; each person there is scarcely aware of the others. Yet this awareness will inhibit each person in some of his behavior: if the music on the sound track were on the radio at home, a couple might get up and dance to it; they will not do so here. On the other hand, being a group member encourages some behavior: one is more likely to laugh if the rest of the audience laughs than if he were alone.

Suppose the film breaks. Some members of the audience will whistle; others will shout. A few will throw their empty popcorn boxes at others' heads. Most people will turn to chat with their companions. Some will leave to get a drink of water or buy more popcorn. The common focus for the group is gone; people mill around. The audience has been transformed into a chattering and very loosely structured crowd.

Suppose at this point the lights go on, and the theater manager appears and says, "We can't repair the film, so there will be no movie tonight. We're sorry, but we can't give you your money back." Someone jumps up on his seat and shouts, "Let's fix him!" and with a roar the movie-goers surge toward the stage to revenge themselves on the theater manager. The crowd has become a mob.

Any relatively impermanent group, such as an audience, crowd, or mob, is composed of individuals who are also members of more permanent social structures, such as families, friendship groups, and organizations. This seems obvious enough, but we sometimes forget it when emotion dims rationality. It is easy to hate a lynch mob by thinking of it as composed of bestial persons who are full-time lynch mob members. It is more difficult to understand such a mob, since its participants spend the greatest portion of their social lives as members of families and other primary groups.

The interaction which converts a crowd into a mob often seems trivial: an argument over who will dance with whom, rough treatment of a traffic violator by a policeman, the shutting off of fire hydrants around which slum children are frolicking on a hot day, an exchange of verbal insults between adolescent gang members. In recent years interracial mob behavior erupted in Rochester, Jersey City, Elizabeth, Paterson, the Dixmoor suburb of Chicago, North Philadelphia, the Bedford-Stuyvesant section of Brooklyn, and Harlem. Violence ranged from Danbury, Connecticut, to the Watts area of Los Angeles; again in east Brooklyn, Chicago, and in Cleveland; Des Moines, Omaha; and Troy, Newark, and Detroit.

A good deal is known about the social structure of slum tenements, economic discrimination, and educational deprivation that provide a basis and context for such consequences. What patterns can we identify as associated with the process of mob formation, rioting, and its aftermath?

A look at the **race riots** widespread in the United States in 1919 is instructive. The number of violent racial confrontations one counts in the United States that year depends on one's definition of a riot. The author of *From*

Race Riot to Sit-in, 1919 and the 1960's: A Study in the Connections between Conflict and Violence (Waskow, 1966) presents brief descriptions of sixteen others in an appendix of his book, but focuses on the seven cases where blacks and whites actively fought one another in groups: Charleston, Knoxville, Omaha, Chicago, Washington, D.C., Longview, Texas, and Elaine, Arkansas. A number of patterns emerge.

1. Violence usually erupted during a period of stiflingly hot weather.

2. Gangs of black and white adolescents were involved.

3. Communists were frequently blamed for inciting the violence.

4. Local police were rarely neutral, were vigorous in enforcing the law, and were often replaced by troops.

5. The standard post-riot public response was a demand for more repressive police action.

21-1 CHECKING IT OUT: KKK: Nightgown Crusaders

From 1955 through 1958 the Klu Klux Klan was revived in the South. In the wake of the revival came an outbreak of bombings, cross burnings, torchlight rallies, whippings, and beatings. For example, Judge Aaron, a mentally retarded Negro handyman, was abducted and castrated on Labor Day, 1957. Testimony at a subsequent trial revealed that the klansmen had been out to find just any Negro as their victim. Ten men, members of the Ku Klux Klan of the Confederacy, had held a special Labor Day meeting where, agitated by "integration talk" about Birmingham, they designated six of their number to find "some damn Negro to scare the hell out of." Stopping at a drugstore, the six secured razor blades and turpentine and then drove about in search of a Negro. When Aaron was sighted walking with a girl companion, the klansmen forced him into the car and drove to a Klan-built concrete-block shelter. Here one of the klansmen, Bart A. Floyd, performed the castration as part of a test to prove himself "worthy of becoming assistant exalted cyclops." The klansmen were subsequently convicted of mayhem and given the maximum sentence of twenty years imprisonment.

In another case in 1958, in Charlotte, North Carolina, klansmen, under cover of darkness, undertook to plant a two-stick dynamite bomb at a Negro elementary school. Authorities, tipped off by an undercover agent, laid in wait at the school and apprehended the conspirators. The klansmen had planned the retaliatory venture after Lumbee Indians subjected the Klan to national ridicule—the nation's press depicted klansmen as scampering in disarray before Lumbee war whoops and gun shots. The embarrassed Klan was out to make headlines because, according to one of the conspirators, "the Klan was dying on the vine." Authorities also implicated klansmen in church bombings in Montgomery and Atlanta, although acquittals were returned in these cases. Similarly, at least three floggings were linked with the Klan.

SOURCE: James W. Vander Zanden, *Race Relations in Transition* (New York: Random House, 1965), pp. 37–38. Reprinted by permission of Random House, Inc.

21-2 CHECKING IT OUT: Lynching in the United States, 1882–1951

	Total Number Lynched	*Average Annual Number Lynched*	*Number Negroes Lynched*	*Negroes as a Percentage of those Lynched %*	*Number Whites Lynched*	*Whites as a Percentage of those Lynched %*
1882–1890	1299	144.3	619	47.7	680	52.3
1891–1900	1599	155.9	1132	72.6	427	27.4
1901–1910	846	84.6	752	88.9	94	11.1
1911–1920	606	60.6	554	91.4	52	8.6
1921–1930	275	27.5	248	90.2	27	9.8
1931–1940	114	11.4	103	90.4	11	9.6
1941–1951	31	2.8	29	93.5	2	6.5
TOTAL	4730		3437	72.7	1293	27.3

SOURCE: Tuskegee Institute, *1952 Negro Year Book* (Tuskegee, Alabama: The Negro Year Book Publishing Company, 1952), p. 278.

One of the major manifestations of mob behavior has been the **lynch mob**. Although many people associate lynching only with hanging, lynching includes a broader range of violent behavior. The Tuskegee Institute, which probably has the most complete data on the subject, classifies as lynching all those events in which (1) there is legal evidence that a person was killed; (2) the victim met his death through illegal means; (3) a group participated in the killing; and (4) the group acted under the pretext of service to justice, race, or tradition. (*Negro Year Book*, 1952) The social character of lynching in the United States from 1882 (the first year for which reliable statistics are available) to 1951 are shown in Table 21-2.

Crowd Behavior Control

The maintenance of social control in crowd situations is usually the responsibility of law enforcement agencies, The actions of police have sometimes contributed to crowd action, as they did with striking crowds during the period from 1890 to 1940. The police have spurred crowd behavior by demonstrating hostility to the crowd, thus making themselves a target of hostility and focus of action, by not being present in time to provide protection, or by doing little when they were on hand. The sentiment of the authorities has much to do with the action of a crowd. Many a lynching occurred because the sheriff arrived too late to protect the victims from attack.

One set of procedures for controlling and/or terminating mobs was developed by Joseph Lohman for use by police departments:

1. Removal or isolation of the individuals involved in the precipitating incident before the crowd has begun to achieve substantial unity.

2. Interruption of communication during the milling process by dividing the crowd into small units.

3. Removal of the crowd leaders, if it can be done without the use of force.

4. Distracting the attention of the crowd from its focal point by creating diversions at other points.

5. Preventing the spread and reinforcement of the crowd by isolating it. (Turner and Killian, 1957, p. 144)

PUBLICS AND PUBLIC OPINION

Socialists use the concept of **public** in two essential ways; first, to refer to a physically dispersed number of people who share an interest in a given topic. In this sense a public is composed of a number of persons who are subject to a common stimulus but are not in physical contiguity. A public, then, is an aggregate rather than a group, because its members do not interact with one another. A speaker in an auditorium addresses an audience; a speaker on a radio broadcast addresses a public. Not all the readers of a newspaper interact with one another; a newspaper public is therefore not a group. Accordingly, one speaks of a concert *audience,* a lecture *audience,* a movie *audience,* but of a newspaper *public,* a radio *public,* and a television *public.*

Secondly, the term public is used to refer to a collection of people who are concerned about, divided upon, and engaged in direct and indirect communication and discussion about an issue. Publics arise through spontaneous reaction to debatable issues. There is no "public" in the sense of one all-encompassing public—there are publics. Each issue has a public and there are as many publics as there are issues. Typically, different (public) issues are of concern to different segments of the society; gun control, personal property, taxes, foreign trade regulations, and equal rights for women are all issues which do not concern the same people.

As the members of a public consider, discuss, and form opinions about the issue, a public opinion is developed. Although the objective of a public is to arrive at a prevailing collective opinion concerning an issue, decisions are not unanimous. When such a composite point of view is reached as the result of discussion, it is called a public opinion.

Propaganda

The formation of public opinion is never a spontaneous process left only to chance. Instead, it is shaped and influenced by propoganda. Propaganda is the deliberate use of communciation to persuade people to favor one predetermined line of thought or action over another. The essence of propaganda is intent. Propagandists use an extensive repertoire of techniques to influence and control public opinion, all of which "involve either the control of fact or the control of interpretation" (Davis, 1949, p. 160).

SOCIAL MOVEMENTS

Crowds, audiences, and publics do not exhaust the major forms of collective behavior. Another major form is the social movement. Social movements refer to "a collectivity acting with some continuity to promote or resist a change in the society or group of which it is a part." (Turner and Killian, p. 308) Social movements "have their inception in a condition of unrest and derive their motive power on one hand from dissatisfaction with the current form of life and on the other hand, from wishes and hopes for a new scheme or system of living." (Blumer, 1951, p. 199) Social movements include the civil rights movement, the peace movement, the ecology movement, and the feminist movement.

Like the mob, the social movement begins as a response to a collectively

21-3 CHECKING IT OUT: Propaganda: The Tricks of the Trade

Name-calling—giving an idea a bad label—is used to make us reject and condemn the idea without examining the evidence. Symbolized by the ancient sign of condemnation used by the Vestal Virgins in the Roman Coliseum, a thumb turned down.

Glittering generality—associating an idea with a "virtue" word—is used to make us accept and approve the idea without examining the evidence. Symbolized by a glittering gem that may or may not have much intrinsic value.

Transfer—associating an idea with a person, image, or symbol which is respected and revered making us accept or reject the idea not on its own merit, but on the basis of the authority and prestige that has been transferred to it. Symbolized by the theatrical mask.

Testimonial—having some loved or hated person approve or condemn a given idea. Symbolized by a seal and ribbons, the "stamp of authority."

Plain folks—attempting to convince one's public that one's ideas are good because they are those "of the people." Symbolized by the traditional analogue for an old friend, an old shoe.

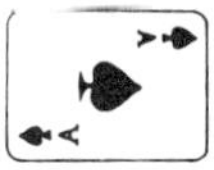

Card-stacking—the use of only such highly selected material, whether true or false, as supports one's case. Symbolized by the ace of spades, the card traditionally used to signify treachery.

Band wagon—"Everybody's doing it," with the implication that we must therefore "jump on the band wagon." Symbolized by a bandmaster's hat and baton, used on old-fashioned band wagons.

SOURCE Reprinted by permission from *The Fine Art of Propaganda* by Alfred McClung Lee and Elizabeth Briant Lee. Copyright by the authors 1939, 1967. (New York: Octagon Books, 1972.) The propaganda symbols were designed by Lee and Lee.

perceived problem, something in the prevailing social order which appears unjust. But the aims and the method of the mob are more short-lived, more specific, and more intense than those of the social movement. The mob lacks the sustaining ideology, official rationale, and long-term objectives of the social movement as well as its structure and social organization.

A social movement tends to arise in response to some sort of perceived oppressive or threatening condition that members of the movement wish to overthrow or ameliorate. Social movements are unified and relatively long-lasting manifestations of collective behavior which have (1) a distinctive perspective and ideology, (2) a strong sense of solidarity and idealism, and (3) an orientation toward action. The ideology of a movement gives it direction, cohesion, and self-justification, and it offers hope and inspiration. Members of a social movement are typically persons who have a strong sense of commitment to the "cause." Social movements are a "group venture extending beyond a local community or a single event and involving a systematic effort to inaugurate changes in thought, behavior, and social relationships." (King, 1956, p. 27)

TYPES OF SOCIAL MOVEMENTS

The Women's Movement

Lucy Komisar predicted the influence of the women's movement on the consciousness of the United States with her assertion, "If the 1960's belonged to the blacks, the next ten years are ours" (1970). While Komisar has perhaps underestimated the intensity and continuing drama of the black struggle, she has perceptively gauged the explosive impact of the women's movement on this society. As a contemporary social movement, reawakened after decades of quiescence following the successful achievement of women's suffrage, this struggle for liberation has emphasized two goals. One is defined by the doctrine of *feminism* or the equality of the sexes. Here women demand economic and political equality stressing equal employment opportunities, equal access to colleges and professional schools, and equality before the law. The second goal is the end of sexism, the domination and exploitation of women by men because they are perceived as inferior. Members of the women's movement are vigorously emphasizing the need to achieve social equality. An important step in this direction is thought to be the elimination of the sex-role stereotyping built into the socialization of American children. (Freeman, 1970) The social demand that females be feminine and males masculine has led to role behavior patterns that have severely limited women as the social and economic equals of men. (See Chapter 6.)

The women's movement identifies closely with the ideology found in Simone de Beauvoir's *The Second Sex* (1953), Betty Friedan's *The Feminine Mystique* (1963), and Kate Millet's *Sexual Politics* (1970). And yet it is a whole made up of diverse subgroups, with differing priorities and action programs. Among these are the National Organization of Women (NOW), often likened to the NAACP as a moderate and mainly political structure, numerous consciousness-raising groups, *Ms. Magazine,* and a variety of study groups. These smaller units may choose to describe themselves as Marxist or non-Marxist, lesbian or straight, radical or reformist.

The Marcus Garvey Movement

An authentic social movement, which was extremely influential among American blacks in the 1920s was founded by Marcus Garvey (1887–1940), a black man born in Jamaica, British West Indies. A printer by trade, Garvey had studied at the University of London, and had maintained a correspondence with Booker T. Washington, the influential black educator. In 1917, Garvey organized The Universal Negro Improvement Association in New York's Harlem. In response to the precarious existence of American blacks, during a period when lynching, floggings, and murder went unpunished, Garvey envisioned a return by American blacks to Africa. He was committed to the development of a powerful black civilization there, which would also provide aid and assistance to black populations around the world. Garvey's "Back-to-Africa" movement was strongly nationalistic and stressed a self-help orientation among blacks. Garvey rejected white philanthropy, would permit no white members in his Improvement Association, and in fact was contemptuous of interracial organizations like the NAACP. Garvey's appeal was directed to the ordinary black citizen and his ambition and daring plans created a sense of pride and hope in the black masses. When the second Universal Negro Improvement Association convention was held in New York in 1921, 25,000 blacks from North and South America, the West Indies, and Africa attended. Garvey's grass-roots appeal was so great that on this occasion when the Garveyites paraded to Madison Square Garden for a rally, Harlemites joined them and together a throng of 50,000 marched through the streets of New York. Although Garvey was attacked as a "charlatan," a "thief," and a "madman" by black leaders, he was hailed as a "Black Moses" by the masses. Gilbert Osofsky (1967) notes that no black leader in American history has been able to develop a mass movement as large as Garvey's. Indeed, "at a time when the NAACP annual budget was $50,000 to $60,000, Garvey was able to raise more than $1,000,000 *within* the Negro community itself" (p. 262). Garvey's great appeal for blacks lay in his stress on racial pride and his glorification of blackness. As racial confrontation escalated after World War I, when blacks attempted to maintain the economic and social gains that they had made during the war years, Garvey offered important psychological support to an oppressed people.

The Garvey movement was hailed by such white reactionaries as the Ku Klux Klan as a way of solving the race problem. Ultimately Garvey was convicted in federal court of using the mails to defraud in connection with the Black Star Steamship Line, a business venture developed to provide transportation back to Africa. He was deported to Jamaica in 1927.

Nazism

Before Hitler and his National Socialist Party came to power in 1933 and completely dominated the political institution of Germany until 1945, they were part of a charismatic social movement. In his discussion of "The Nazi Party: Its Leadership and Composition" (1969), Hans Gerth described the Hitler movement as "a fusion of two types of domination, namely, the charismatic and the bureaucratic types" (p. 258). Hitler was regarded by his followers as an extraordinary leader able to break through existing structures and create new ones. Gerth notes that Hitler, like other charismatic leaders, refused to be identified with contemporary offices or positions, so that as Reich-Chancellor he did not become President or Kaiser. He chose to be called Der Führer. With the assumption of power, the Nationalist Socialist Party moved into the bureaucratic structure of government that existed and merged with it. The party became the bureaucracy, and the members of Hitler's inner circle strengthened their positions by immediately beginning to enlarge and solidify the bureaucratic units of which they were given control.

As a social movement, however, the National Socialist Party had been committed to an action-oriented program for change. Gerth notes that many of the leading positions went to individuals who had been failures in occupational and other pursuits. Such people had less commitment to the moral and social conventions of the time and were expected to carry out party orders with less inhibitions. Also, these followers who saw themselves as disadvantaged would be willing to gamble on a charismatic leader. The Nazi party was very much a middle-class political movement, with elementary-school teachers "the best represented of all professional groups composing the Nazi Party. . ." (p. 263). As career bureaucrats who had to compete within the educational structure, this group could be expected to be frustrated and angry about the lack of movement upwards within the bureaucracy. In its early stages this was primarily a young group. Before the party assumed power, 42 per cent of the membership was between 18 and 30 years of age (p. 266). After 1935, older and more experienced men began to join in large numbers. The Nazi party was seen as a "salvationary" movement which promised social and economic security and high social status to those elements long denied these advantages. Such "unsuccessful" persons were to be found in every stream of German society. Princes without thrones, indebted and subsidized landlords, indebted farmers, virtually bankrupt industrialists, impoverished shopkeepers and artisians, doctors without patients, lawyers without clients, writers without readers, unemployed teachers, and unemployed manual and white-collar workers: all joined the movement (p. 264).

Gerth notes that this extremely dissatisfied group, unable to successfully compete for the financial and social rewards that were available, would not resist Hitler's totalitarian regime, realizing that, as a unified party, they could take what they felt had been denied them. Such acceptance of totalitarian methods made possible the unrestrained butchery of the succeeding years, with the destruction of national states, the incarceration and murder of millions, and the involvement of most of the civilized world in a bloody and tragic war.

LEADERSHIP AND COLLECTIVE BEHAVIOR

All in all, leadership is a combination of ability and opportunity. When class structure is rigid, dominance tends to be associated with a particular class or caste, and followership and submissiveness with membership in the lower ranks. In a democratic system, where class lines are somewhat vague and loose, leaders may and do arise from any class provided they follow the accepted patterns of the culture. Leaders in American society, however, are much more likey to be recruited from the upper and middle classes than from the lower classes. (Warner and Abegglen, 1955)

Types of Leaders

There have been many attempts to classify leaders. An early effort using social role categories was E. B. Gowin's distinction between the "intellectual" and the "executive." In the former he included scientists, authors, philosophers, and artists; in the latter corporation presidents, governors of state, high religious officials, and top trade-union officials. (Gowin, 1915) O.L. Schwartz distinguished between "men of thought" and "men of action;" (Schwartz, 1916) and Sir Martin M. Conway, an English popularizer of social psychology, in discussing crowd behavior used as a three-fold classification: "crowd representative," or group organizer; "crowd compeller," one who persuades or forces a group to follow him; and "crowd exponent," one who, perceiving the motives and frustrations of the masses, becomes their leader because he verbalizes and crystallizes their desires and shows them how to act. (Conway, 1915)

A contemporary writer has come up with a three-way typology of "Princes," "Heroes," and "Supermen." The first are men motivated to dominate others; the second are dedicated to great and noble causes; and the third are iconoclasts who break down old norms and values. (Jennings, 1960)

Still another typology has been proposed by Charles M. Bonjean on the basis of an empirical study of community leaders in a medium-sized city. The data consisted of ratings by known leaders and nonleaders of a specified number of local "leaders." The author found that leaders fall into three categories: (1) *visible leaders,* who are playing widely perceived and accepted roles in the community; (2) *concealed leaders,* who have more power or leadership function "within the leadership circle or power elite" than is commonly realized; and (3) *symbolic leaders,* who do not wield "as much influence in the community as the community at large thinks they do." (Bonjean, 1963, p. 678)

From studies of small groups, ranging in size from three-man to six-man groups, Robert F. Bales and his co-workers found that participants differentiate between "idea specialists" and "best-liked men." While the former are highly regarded for their aid in solving problems presented to the group, they are not, on the whole, the best-liked. (Bales and Slater, 1955)

In his discussion of political leadership, H. D. Lasswell developed a five-fold typology: (1) The *bureaucrat,* or *administrator,* operates an institution or agency along precise, orderly, and fixed lines. (2) The *boss* is a hard-headed opportunist concerned with the manipulation of political power by direct or indirect means. (3) The *diplomat* is concerned with the manipulatin of political power through suave manner, calmness, patience, and clever and sometimes insincere use of conversation and social graces. (4) The *agitator* strives for reform or revolution, is adept in the use of programs, catchwords, and suggestive slogans. The agitator paints the *status quo* as completely evil and decadent, the future as a new heaven on earth. And (5) *the theorist* who makes a systemic analysis of the environment from which he or she formulates a logical and consistent picture of the world of people and events. (Lasswell, 1930)

None of these classifications of leadership is completely satisfactory. Far too little is known about the causal sequences in the life course of leaders, the criteria for determining types, and the divergent historical situations in which leaders operate. Moreover, it is evident that the various classificatory schemes reflect both the culture and the personal experience of those who construct them.

Thus, whether there are general traits of leadership remains a moot question. There is one generalization we *can* make. Followers may *ascribe* to those in positions of dominance over them personality traits and powers that the latter may not possess. This is a familiar phenomenon: a distinguished natural scientist or engineer is expected by the masses to be expert also in international relations, labor-management problems, or the effect of comic books on children's conduct.

Once traits and powers are attributed to leaders, they may capitalize on these projections from their followers and assume knowledge, skill, and leadership in fields where they have no actual competence. Sometimes, too, individuals who are the beneficiaries of such projection of potency attain at least a modicum of capability in the areas in which wisdom has been attributed to them. (Merton, 1968)

Leadership in Mass Society

While Lasswell's classification of leaders is by no means to be regarded as final, a modification of it seems applicable to modern mass societies, both democratic and authoritarian. The three most significant types of leaders today seem to be the administrator, the expert, and the agitator. The unprecedented expansion of large-scale industry and business has placed managerial personnel in a highly strategic position in the power structure of economic enterprise. So too, the extension of political controls over new areas of social life has resulted in an increase in administrative functionaries, with all this implies as to further power of the govenmental bureaucracy.

Complicated industrial, political, and military systems cannot operate without the expert. (Janowitz, 1960) One's role as a specialist requires that one be completely objective, dispassionate, and unconcerned, in that role, with the moral implications of one's function. While one occupies a position of control absolutely vital to the operation of a complex culture, as an expert one is set apart from the moral order. Such a person symbolizes the highest degree of impersonality and segmentalization in a mass society.

On occasion the agitator will assume an important role in mass society, particularly in time of grave economic and political insecurity. In such situations the agitator easily changes into a would-be dictator and, with appealing slogans and fine promises, may capture the support of the masses in a personal drive for power. If the agitator combines talents with those of an organized revolutionary minority, he or she may become the agent for producing great changes, both political and economic. Often the mass of followers do not understand the changes that are brought about once the demagogue gets in power.

Relationship Between Leaders and Followers

The distribution of power among leaders and heads of organizations in a mass society suggests the whole problem of the relationship of those in positions of power to their followers. In societies where there is wide participation of the masses in politics, economic life, and religion, the role of the persuasive and responsible leader is especially vital. Such a leader crystallizes the vague feelings and attitudes of the masses when they are confronted with situations they cannot handle.

The followers find in the leader and program an image that they can follow. So too, in setting the role and giving prestige, they project upon the leader many qualities they believe a leader should have. Then, by identification, the followers seem to themselves to share these qualities. Their projection affects the leader, of course, who to be successful must assume these roles and accept the attendant status. As George C. Homans puts it, "The leader is the [person] who, on the whole, best lives up to the standard of behavior that the group values." (Homans, 1950, p. 169) Such leaders as *symbols* provide a focus for feeling and acting conjointly. Around them followers build up patterns of response which yield results and give much satisfaction as well.

Of course, in every society leaders are separated from their followers only in degree. They share with them a participation in society and culture. Nevertheless, they embody distinctiveness and variability in thought and action which the followers like and admire. A leader's behavior becomes a focus for the identification of the followers and hence encourages effective group activity and solidarity.

INTERPRETIVE SUMMARY

The character of collective behavior is suggested by consideration of such topics as crowds, audiences, mobs, publics, and social movements. Collective behavior refers to the relatively impermanent and unstructured activities wherein the norms and expectations that ordinarily define and limit human conduct are not operative.

An audience is a collectivity of persons in physical continuity with a common focus of attention, such as spectators at a baseball game who are in the stadium. A crowd refers to a number of persons, also in physical contiguity, without a specific and shared focus of attention—such as a crowd leaving the baseball stadium. Mobs are collectivities where there is a high level of intense interaction and are typically characterized by violent behavior. The term "public" refers to a collection of people with the same interest who are not in physical contiguity, such as a radio public. A social movement is defined as a "collectivity acting with some continuity to promote or resist a change in the society or group of which it is a part." Social movements are the most structured and permanent forms of collective behavior. Social movements of the early twentieth century include the Garvey Movement and Nazism. Among current social movements are the women's movement and the determined efforts of the handicapped.

Leadership everywhere is a combination of opportunity and ability. Followers tend to care less how their leaders were chosen than how they treat them. They want above all to feel secure, which means that they want their leader to be fair, supportive, understanding, and interested in them. They will be more effective as a group if they have such a leader. This is particularly true in a highly specialized society where work is noncreative and relations impersonal; in fact, in such task-oriented groups workers will frequently band together defensively, informally choosing a leader who can fulfill needs their formal leader does not recognize. Followers feel secure with a leader who is like themselves, yet more knowledgeable and bolder.

QUESTIONS

1. Why has the Communist Party failed to develop as a significant social movement in the United States?
2. Compare these social movements: the women's movement, the Black Muslims, and the Jesus movement. In what ways has each changed over time? Why is each an authentic social movement? From which segment of the population does each draw its members?
3. How would a sociologist describe 100,000 fans at a stadium football game? Do these people comprise a group?

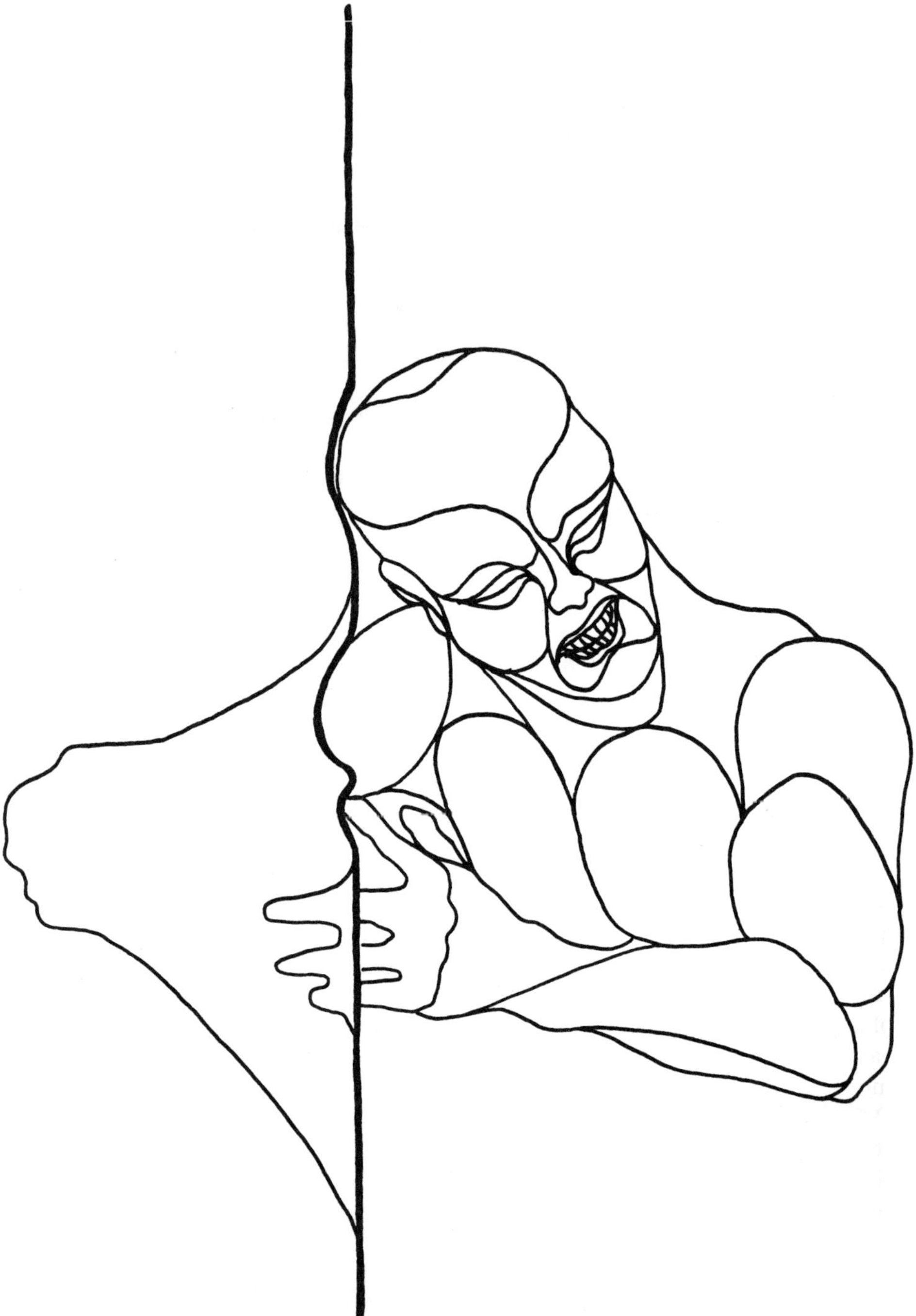
Elder

22

Social Deviance and Contemporary Social Issues

Most of us live in a world of order most of the time. We live in a normative world of group-shared expectations. Yet the fact that a social group expects certain behaviors from an individual or from another group does not always mean that its expectations are met. No norm is *always* obeyed; individuals do not *always* conform to every set of expectations.

There are several reasons why the behavior of some people never conforms perfectly to the norms of the society in which they live. For one thing, norms are general, while an individual's behavior in any situation is specific. An expectation, if it is to apply to different people in varying situations over a period of time, must be conceived in quite general dimensions. Each of us learns the rules of his society as a set of broad (and usually "flat") generalizations: "You should eat meat with a fork, not with your fingers," or "Honor thy father and thy mother." But there are situations in which deviation from the norms is tolerated. One can eat meat with one's fingers at a picnic, and no one would expect a starving man to eschew food because he did not have a fork. Indeed, there are situations where violation of the norm becomes itself an expectation: in many societies, the son whose father commits treason is expected to reject, not honor, his father.

THE DEFINITION OF DEVIANCE

The generalized nature of norms is only one factor which can help us explain deviation. Another is variation among individuals and groups in their perception

22-1 CHECKING IT OUT: Nakedness—Norm Violation in New York

A 37-year-old man stripped off all his clothes outside the New York Hilton Hotel on the Avenue of Americas at 53d Street yesterday afternoon and staged a nude, one-man Thanksgiving Day parade through midtown Manhattan.

Bathed in bright autumn sunlight and nuzzled by temperatures in the low 50's, the man—short and stocky with dark hair and a stubble of beard—dumped his clothes in a trash basket outside the hotel and set off at a smart pace.

He walked south on the avenue, east on West 52d Street past the fashionable "21" Club and other restaurants, then north on Fifth Avenue.

Passers-by gaped, gawked, smiled and shook their heads in bewilderment. Several people with cameras followed him, taking pictures, but many in the sparse holiday sidewalk crowds just ignored—or pretended to ignore him.

One observer noted that the stroller heeded each "WALK" and "DON'T WALK" street-crossing sign he encountered and generally was a model pedestrian.

But the 10-minute outing in the buff ended abruptly about 2:45 P.M. when a couple of police officers and two ambulance attendants caught up with the stroller outside a Fifth Avenue jewelry store near 54th Street.

The ambulance men took him by the arm and led him away. He struggled only slightly and was taken to St. Clare's Hospital. No charges were filed by the police, who retrieved the man's clothes from the trash basket.

A spokesman for the hospital later said the man had been "treated and released." Asked what treatment had been administered, the spokesman said: "A doctor talked to him, got him dressed and sent him home."

SOURCE: *The New York Times,* November 25, 1977, p. B19.

of what the norms are and their interpretation of what they mean. It is possible, for reasons ranging from mental incompetence to geographic (and hence social) isolation, for a person to be unaware of some of the societal norms. In U.S. society, for example, an illiterate is cut off from an important source of information about what is expected of a citizen. Many Americans are aware of the norm "Keep the sabbath day to sanctify it, as the Lord thy God hath commanded thee," but there is widespread variation in the interpretation of this rule.

Then too, norms differ in the degree to which they are considered obligatory. Considerably weaker sanctions are imposed on a person who deviates from a folkway, such as a clothing fashion, than on one who violates one of the mores. As one moves down a scale of tolerance toward the point where a custom passes from a folkway to a cultural alternative, deviance becomes more and more likely.

Cheating on examinations or term papers is not an unusual phenomenon on college campuses. One 1966 nationwide study concluded that nearly half of all college students cheat. (Harp and Taietz, 1966) Research reports show the following incidence of cheating by seniors: Columbia—26 per cent, Cornell—30 per cent, Fordham—52 per cent, Notre Dame—54 per cent.

When a norm is this widely violated, does it mean that it is not really a norm at all? No, because there is agreement, even among the cheaters, that cheating is wrong. Research covering a number of universities concludes that the majority of students believe that students are normally obligated not to cheat. What, then, is the difference between those who cheat and those who do not? One difference is a clearly sociological one; i.e., rates of cheating vary according to the different groups with which a student is affiliated. Recent research at three colleges in an Ivy League university reveals marked differences in rates of cheating on term papers by the students' major. Following the freshman year, 42 per cent of the students in Agriculture reported cheating; 50 per cent of those in Engineering did so; but only 26 per cent of those in Arts and Sciences did. Other studies have also shown that students in vocational or career-oriented fields are more likely to cheat than students majoring in the humanities and that fraternity members report a higher incidence of cheating than nonfraternity members. This is true in all three colleges, but the fraternity members with the highest incidence of cheating are in Agriculture and Engineering.

One cannot understand the amount of deviance in a mass society without noting the extent to which it is the product of differing subcultures. Normative standards vary by social class, by ethnic group, by degree of urbanization, by region, by age group, by sex, and by occupation. A group-shared expectation in a company store patronized by sharecroppers in rural Arkansas may be a violation of the norms in a Park Avenue gift shop catering to wealthy New Yorkers. Taking a hubcap from an automobile in a lower-class area is stealing; taking a piece of the goal posts (much more expensive than hubcaps) after a football victory at a college stadium is only a high-spirited prank. In this case, what is or is not criminal is influenced by class position. In a multi-group society such as that of contemporary United States, with racial, ethnic, class, occupational, and regional subcultures, deviance is more than a little in the eye of the beholder.

Albert Cohen insists that "much—probably most—deviant behavior is produced by clinically normal people." (Cohen, 1959, p. 463) According to Cohen:

> . . . we must always keep as our point of reference deviant behavior, not kinds of people. A major task before us is to get rid of the notion . . . that the deviant, the abnormal, the pathological, and, in general, the deplorable always come wrapped in a single package. (p. 463)

THEORIES OF DEVIANCE

Anomie Theory

Anomie was a concept first used by Emile Durkheim. (1893) Durkheim defined anomie as *normlessness.* There were times when the cultural norms of a society were in disarray. Sometimes the norms were no longer operating; sometimes they were in conflict as rapid social changes occurred. At such times social order was threatened, as the ordinary constraints on behavior no longer applied. Durkheim's concept of anomie has been revived in contemporary sociology by Robert K. Merton. (1968) Merton, a functionalist theorist, has used the concept of anomie to explain deviance within society. According to Merton, society presents culturally defined goals to its members. These goals reflect the values and beliefs that are current. People in the United States are generally encouraged to strive for the goals of wealth, prestige, education, fame, a position high on the socioeconomic ladder. Our culture also indicates the acceptable means by which these goals are to be attained. The norms or rules by which these goals can be attained have been institutionalized in clear and patterned behavioral expectations. For example, in progressing through the educational structure of a college, the use of force or fraud in advancing is normatively unacceptable behavior. We are expected to conform to institutionalized means for achieving cultural goals (by studying, performing well on tests). Merton has formulated a typology of conformity and deviation. He contends that anomie is likely to be most severe when the culture, while prescribing certain ends or goals, does not provide certain individuals access to legitimate means for achieving these ends. For instance, a poor youth may turn to illegitimate means to obtain a part of the American dream when legitimate means are not available to him. Or a society may dictate that members must be literate while denying the schools, books, and teachers to large numbers of people. The consequence is severe stress for impoverished persons trying to reach the goal of literacy while having to spend most of their waking hours working to stay alive.

Merton mentions that while the society of the United States encourages everyone to aspire to wealth and social position, the culturally legitimate means are so restricted that many people—the poor, women, minorities—are denied opportunities for achieving them. In this sense, the problem is not that people are unwilling to accept the values of the society but that social inequality prevents certain people from following the norms they willingly accept. According to Merton,

> It is only when a system of cultural values extols, virtually above all else, certain common success-goals for the population at large while the social structure rigorously restricts or completely closes access to approved modes of reaching these goals for a considerable part of the same population, that deviant behavior ensues on a large scale. . . .
>
> The moral mandate to achieve success thus exerts pressure to succeed, by fair means if possible and by foul means if necessary. (Merton, 1968)

Merton suggests five ways in which an individual can deal with the cultural goals and the institutionalized ways of reaching them. A person can accept both the ends and the means for reaching them, **conformity**; one can accept the goals but reject the accepted ways of achieving them and invent methods of one's own,

22-2 CHECKING IT OUT: A Typology of Modes of Individual Adaptation

Modes of Adaptation	*Culture Goals*	*Institutionalized Means*
I. Conformity	+	+
II. Innovation	+	—
III. Ritualism	—	+
IV. Retreatism	—	—
V. Rebellion	±	±

SOURCE: Robert K. Merton, *Social Theory and Social Structure*, rev. ed. (Glencoe, Ill.: The Free Press, 1957), p. 40.

22-3 CHECKING IT OUT: Innovation, Retreatism and Rebellion in Japan

Japan's youth, once obedient and disciplined, have become increasingly alienated, aimless, and dissatisfied, according to a government study.

Disillusionment of the young, the report warns, is being expressed by the rising crime rate, terrorism by extremist groups, and mounting emphasis on money and pleasure.

The warning is underlined in the official report prepared by the prime minister's office. The report recommends fundamental changes in attitudes by older Japanese towards youth and their problems.

Serious concern is being expressed by police about the increase in crime among teen-agers between 14 and 15 years old.

In 1971, a total of 107,107 young people were charged with crimes and delinquency—a slight decrease on the overall figures for the previous year.

But, crimes committed by youngsters of 14 and 15 represented 36.4 per cent of the total.

Two-thirds of the crimes were classified as theft; most of the remainder were connected with acts of violence.

The report said many young people today lack social solidarity, their sense of dissatisfaction is mounting, and they have a growing feeling of emptiness in their lives.

These trends were a reflection of the confusion of values brought about after World War II and drastic social changes, it said.

There is a decline of power and capability of parents in postwar education and leadership at home that is promoting an unhealthy mental growth among young people, the report said.

It led to bizarre acts of terrorism, such as last May's massacre at Tel Aviv Airport, when three Japanese youths killed 26 people, and the series of incidents involving the extremist "Red Army" clique last February, in which at least 17 people were killed.

Other manifestations were an upsurge in reckless road racing by teen-age drivers that has spread like wildfire across the country in the past few months, as well as frequent suicides by high school students and a tendency among young workers to change jobs frequently.

The prime minister's office called for measures to channel youthful energy into more creative and positive activities.

This included facilities for self-training, sports and recreations, creation of youth organizations, more international youth organizations, and greater youth participation in the shaping of administrative policies and regional social life.

Japanese newspapers, however, were disappointed that the report failed to make proposals for reforming the education system, which retains much of its prewar character.

They particularly wanted an end to the so-called "examination hell," which demands arduous preparation by young people to insure progression through the right schools to the right job.

An increasing number of young Japanese simply drop out of the system. Some commit suicide. An average of 3,000 run away from home every year.

Escapism through sniffing paint thinner or similar chemicals has been attracting police attention for some years. However, Japan's drug problem is not yet considered serious.

Commenting on the education system, an Ashai Shimbun editorial said: "Millions of junior high and high school students are spending for meaningless tests the hours which are most important for formation of personality."

The Yomiuri Shimbun said: "Parents are concerned that schools have become merely the means for climbing the social ladder and do not provide the education to build character.

"They have no confidence in schools which have been transformed into diploma mills producing students only good at passing tests for advancement into higher schools," the paper said.

Japan's population under 25 at present is 45,030,000—42.9 per cent of the total—but this will decrease because of a declining birth rate. The number of college and university students last year was 1,700,000, about one-fourth of the high school graduates.

SOURCE: *Chicago Tribune,* February 14, 1973, p. 2.

innovation; one can cling to the institutionalized means as ends in themselves while forgetting the goals for which they were originally intended, **ritualism**; a person can reject both cultural goals and the forms appropriate to them, **retreatism**; or one can abandon both the cultural goals and means but take the position of a revolutionary and try to introduce new ones, **rebellion**.

While the first type is the true conformist, the third usually passes for one. Many people looked on in their society as deviants—the drug pusher, the racketeer seeking upward mobility, for instance—constitute the second type. Retreatists include tramps, hermits, "drop-outs," and drug addicts, and the fifth type is characterized by the rebel with a cause. Political radicals such as the Weather Underground exemplify the deviance of the rebel.

Critique of Anomie Theory Merton's approach to deviance is that it is a response on the part of individuals when the routes to legitimate aspirations are blocked. His view of deviance is consistent with his view of society as a generally stable system in which societal goals are accomplished because of a high degree of consensus about goals, and also about means to these goals. Merton's functionalist view assumes that the conduct of people in society is guided by norms and that there is consensus about these norms. There is also much social pressure causing people to conform to the norms. Therefore, deviants are those people who violate social norms. But there are other sociologists who do not accept the functionalist assumption that the deviant is the one who violates social norms. These sociologists are aware that many people break the rules but are never categorized as deviants. An individual engaged in adultery may violate the social norm of marital fidelity and no one may ever know, so the person never gets branded as a deviant. Some people break the rules and are only midly sanctioned for their behavior (as in the case of Spiro Agnew).

Labeling Theory

One of the most important studies in the area of deviant behavior in recent years is a provocative work by Howard Becker entitled *Outsiders: Studies in the Sociology of Deviance.* (1963) Becker does not accept society's definition that people are deviant, but he recognizes the fact that society does label people as deviants and that this labeling is consequential for the people who are so labeled. Becker uses a fascinating example drawn from Malinowski's anthropological study of the Trobriand Islanders (1926): Kima'i, a young man of that group, had a sexual relationship with his cousin (the daughter of his mother's sister). This occurred in a society where such a relationship with a clan-member was considered incest. The relationship was no secret to other tribe members but nothing had been done about it until a jealous ex-lover of the girl confronted Kima'i publicly and accused him of incest and then hurled at him "certain expressions intolerable to a native." (p. 10) The insults and the social ostracism caused Kima'i to take his own life. Here Becker points out that breaking the rules is not enough to make a person a deviant. Members of his group knew that Kima'i was having a relationship with his cousin and the relationship was disapproved of. But it was only when the young man was publicly accused that the social group turned against the couple. Deviants are then those who have been so labeled. Goffman (1963) has observed that possession of unacceptable characteristics (i.e., scars, blackness) causes some persons to be "stigmatized" and labeled as deviants. Much, therefore, depends on the rules of labeling and who applies the rules. As Becker wrote:

> . . . social groups create deviance by making the rules whose infraction constitutes deviance, and by applying those rules to particular people and labeling them as outsiders. From this point of view, deviance is not a quality of the act the person

commits, but rather the consequence of the application by others of rules and sanctions to an "offender." (Becker, 1963, p. 9)

Consequences of Labeling The sociologist who accepts the labeling perspective is less interested in the causes of deviance and more interested in what happens when a person is labeled deviant and in the consequences of being so labeled. Edwin Lemert, an important labeling theorist (1951), makes a distinction between *primary* and *secondary* deviance to emphasize the consequences of labeling. Primary deviance is situational. It is often temporary behavior and easily concealed from others. Homosexual practices while the person is confined in prison is an example of primary deviance because it may or may not make the individual who participated feel like a deviant. Smoking pot at a party probably would not make the smoker feel like a deviant, or be considered a deviant by society. Secondary deviance is really the consequence of reactions to primary deviance. If the person is publicly labeled, if a new status must be added to the status set ("hooker," drug addict, thief, "homo") because the individual has been arrested, or has "been caught in the act," or is identified by significant others, two things may happen. The individual may be treated differently by those who are important to him or her. There may be a "degradation ceremony" (Garfinkel, 1956) in which the person is publicly accused, possibly punished, but certainly forced to recognize that the accusers consider themselves superior to the accused. A second result of labeling is that the self-concept of the individual may change. The individual may accept the label ("If I have the name, I may as well have the game"). There is a "self-fulfilling prophecy" operating here: a deviant label has been applied, then accepted so that behavior is altered or expanded to fit the label. As secondary deviance, deviant behavior becomes habitual; the drug user who has been publicly labeled may enter the subculture of drug takers and begin a career of deviance with new habits and a new life style. Here the labeling process has caused the deviant to be rejected by "straight" society and then to assume a deviant identity.

A Critique of Labeling Theory While labeling theory is useful in making clear the capacity of society to manufacture deviance and while this perspective offers insight into the development of secondary deviance, it reveals certain limitations under scrutiny. One of these relates to the assumption that the process of labeling leads to secondary deviance. Milton Mankoff, among others, has suggested that rather than accepting the label and taking on a deviant life style, the process of labeling may in fact end the devaint behavior. (1971) Edward Sagarin offers several criticisms of labeling theory which are worthy of interest. He finds that labeling theory generates an "underdog ideology." (1975) Sociologists with this perspective appear to see deviants as victimized by labeling. They take the side of the deviant. Sagarin believes that in attempting to remove the onus from the deviant to a hostile society, a distortion may be introduced into the research. Even though the sociologist accepting the labeling perspective states his bias and puts everyone on notice, "truth cannot be attained by taking the perspective of either a victim or a victimizer... but rather requires a synthesis of the perspectives of all those involved in an activity." (p. 133) Sagarin further comments that it may be difficult to understand property crimes and violent crimes using the labeling perspective. While this perspective is valuable in understanding homosexuality, it may not be helpful in explaining rape.

Theories of Deviant Subcultures

Edwin H. Sutherland, a major American criminologist, proposed a theory of *differential association* to explain criminal and delinquent behavior. This theory was developed in his famous *Principles of Criminology* (1947), a pioneering work which sought to refute the common acceptance of criminal behavior as the result of inherited traits, personal pathology, or psychological maladjustment. Essentially, he proposed that criminality was the result of social learning. It was through association with others in intimate group settings that attitudes, values, and motives were shaped. A consistent enough and intimate enough environment could be thought of as a learning laboratory where socially acceptable and law-abiding behavior might be internalized, or where deviant norms might be absorbed. Differential association was, then, stressing the fact that differences, in those with whom we associate, influence our own conduct. Sutherland's emphasis on the group-relatedness of crime and delinquency has provided a fruitful direction for other social scientists. And the whole notion of deviant subcultures such as gangs, cliques, and peer groups grows out of his work.

The Subculture of Juvenile Delinquency Albert K. Cohen and James F. Short, Jr., (1958) have used the concept of the deviant subculture to describe a variety of delinquent subcultures. These include the *parent male subculture*, so called because it is the most common form in the United States—the hedonistic, often destructive, small gang. The *conflict-oriented subculture* was another form and described the large gang structure that has a hierarchal structure and differentiation of roles (e.g., President, War Counselor). Such subcultures were highly organized, had territorial limits, and distinctive names.

22-4 CHECKING IT OUT: Police Link South Bronx Youth Gangs to Soaring Crime

A 37-year-old drug pusher is fatally struck by six bullets that shape a cross on his body. A bus is invaded and its driver held at gunpoint while passengers are relieved of wallets, watches and other valuables, Wild West style. A runaway girl is crippled after being beaten with belts and chains.

These acts of violence, all committed last month, were among more than 800 reported examples of violent crimes last year that have been linked by the police to the youth gangs that have been proliferating in the South Bronx.

Police Inspector Robert H. Johnson, who is in charge of the 90-man youth gang task force in the Bronx, says the 130 gangs in the South Bronx last year accounted for more than 30 murders, 22 attempted homicides, 300 assaults, 10 rapes, and 124 armed robberies. In all, some 1,500 gang arrests were made.

The police believe that the largest number of youth-gang homicides in any one previous year was 12 for the entire city in 1962.

The resurgence of street-gang warfare became a national problem last year. But many police observers believe that the growth began in the rubble-strewn, graffiti-splattered, disease-ridden streets of the South Bronx. Many South Bronx gangs now have "divisions" in other parts of the city.

Street gangs have terrorized slum areas, including the South Bronx, during the nineteen-fifties and early sixties. Many experts say these gangs broke up after their members became addicted to heroin and in their drug-induced torpor dropped out. But now, specialists at Lincoln Hospital and other health and community officials in the South Bronx say they have observed a marked increase in youth violence that has accompanied a marked decrease in overdose cases and other indicators of narcotics use.

There are those in the South Bronx who credit the gangs with routing drug pushers and restoring a feeling of pride. But others contend that few gangs are drug-free and that some of them are used by drug dealers as armies to consolidate their power.

Many residents also complain that the gangs have unleashed a reign of terror on their neighbors, menacing merchants, assaulting students in virtually all of the borough's schools and, in some cases, wounding women and children caught in the gunplay.

All residents, however, feel that the reappearance of the gangs represents an important symptom of the sickness of the South Bronx. To many residents, too many youngsters in their community are faced with only two choices—the walking death of narcotics or the violent world of the street gangs.

The police say that the gangs, which call themselves "cliques," have 9,500 members, ranging in age from 13 to 30. Most of them are Puerto Ricans, many are homeless and almost all are estranged from their families. Most gangs are headquartered in abandoned buildings, some of which were vacated after the gangs moved in.

To gang members, headquarters is home, a haven against the biting winds, an emotional sustenance against the isolation from society that they feel. Most headquarters are heated by gas ovens, with mattresses tossed in disarray on the floor. The black walls are covered with day-glo paintings, with violent and obscene themes illuminated by fluorescent lighting.

Each gang has its own "colors," or insignia, which appear on walls in the gang's turf and on the backs of the dungaree jackets they favor—a sartorial cue from the Hell's Angels. With their colors massed on their own turf, the gangs walk down desolate Fox Street in Hunts Point and into stores on Southern Boulevard, terrorizing residents and intimidating shopkeepers.

The gang names themselves are chosen to inspire fear and respect: Savage Skulls, Black Assassins, Savage Nomads, Majestic Warlocks, Brothers of Satan, Reapers, Henchmen, Black Spades, Dirty Dozen.

SOURCE: *The New York Times,* January 16, 1973, p. 1.

Cohen and Short also identified *drug-addict subcultures* and *semiprofessional theft subcultures* that provided training in illegal activities leading to adult careers in crime. There was the *middle-class delinquent subculture,* a rapidly growing phenomenon though not clearly developed at that time and *female delinquent subcultures,* also underresearched empirically. Female subcultures might be organized along the lines of males and closely identified with male groups (as in The Noble Lord Debs) or they might be organized for sexual, drug, or other activities.

Delinquents as "Gentlemen of Leisure" Sociologists David Matza and Gresham M. Sykes (1961) questioned the standard view of the delinquent as one in opposition to the norms and values of society and committed to violating the laws. They suggested rather that many delinquents are essentially in agreement with social norms. This is to say that they accept prevailing norms and the belief systems of which they are a part. However, such delinquents "neutralize" the norms that exist and the emotional responses that they might have to their own deviance by rationalizing their actions. The delinquent uses these techniques of neutralization: (1) denial of responsibility—the old "I'm depraved, 'cause I'm deprived" response of *West Side Story* fame; (2) denial of injury—i.e., homeowners are not really injured by a burglary because they are insured; (3) denial of the victim—here the perception of the situation is altered so that the victim deserved injury (was being punished for prior transgressions); (4) condemnation of the condemners—if the police are "pigs" and immoral and corrupt, their right to judge the delinquent is denied; (5) the appeal to higher loyalties—while social norms are accepted in principle, subcultural norms take precedence. Thus, while injuring another person is wrong, revenge has to be exacted or self-defense is the main consideration. Matza and Sykes also believed that the values of delinquents were less deviant than had been supposed. Rather they resembled the code of "the gentleman of leisure" described by Thorstein Veblen by emphasizing adventure, daring, rejection of disciplined work, enjoyment of luxury, and gaining prestige through a show of masculinity. These were not necessarily deviant values, though the forms of expressing them might be deviant.

Critique of Theories of Deviant Subcultures Sutherland's theory of differential association is different from the contributions of Matza and Sykes or Cohen and Short in that it is primarily a theory describing social processes. Here delinquency grows out of social interaction within the group. Delinquency is learned behavior, acquired in intimate association. However, Sutherland does not explain how some youths can associate with, even live with others who are delinquent and not become delinquent. In addition, Sutherland's intimate association involves a face-to-face situation in which delinquent behavior is learned. This view does not account for the strong influence of a medium such as television through which antisocial behavior can be learned in isolation.

CRIMINAL BEHAVIOR

If sociologists are to explain the consequences of social structure, they must understand patterns of deviation from society's norms as well as patterns of adherence. A theory which accounts for conformity to the folkways and mores as a function of the way society is put together ought also to treat violation of norms as a consequence of the social structure.

To maintain internal social order, modern societies have developed written codes specifying what must or must not be done by an individual to another individual or to the state. Rules regarding wrongs committed against another individual are called torts. Taken together, they are known as civil law. Legal rules dealing with wrongs committed against the society as a whole are called criminal law; violation of one of these is a crime. Obviously, there is considerable overlap here. Some crimes are acts committed against an individual—for example, rape—but, because such crimes are considered threats to the social order, they are treated in criminal law. In the United States, crimes are divided into relatively serious violations, called felonies, and less grave offenses, known as misdemeanors.

Violation of a criminal law does not in itself constitute a crime. With few exceptions, the perpetrator of an act in violation of the criminal code must have *intended* to violate the law for his act to be considered a crime. It is this provision concerning criminal intent that is important in the definition of juvenile delinquency. In many states it is assumed that a person under a certain age (usually sixteen) is incapable of having criminal intent, and hence cannot commit a crime.

PATTERNS OF CRIMINAL BEHAVIOR

The Uniform Crime Report

Statistics on crimes are not complete indicators of criminal activity. A number of crimes never come to the attention of law enforcement authorities. Con-

22-5 CHECKING IT OUT: National Crime, Rate, and Percent Change

	Estimated Crime 1976		*Percent Change Over 1975*	
Crime Index Offenses	*Number*	*Rate Per 100,000 Inhabitants*	*Number*	*Rate*
Total	11,304,800	5,266.4	+ .4	− .3
Violent	986,580	459.6	− 3.9	− 4.5
Property	10,318,200	4,806.8	+ .9	+ .1
Murder	18,780	8.8	− 8.4	− 8.3
Forcible rape	56,730	26.4	+ 1.1	+ .4
Robbery	420,210	195.8	− 9.6	− 10.3
Aggravated assault	490,850	228.7	+ 1.3	+ .6
Burglary	3,089,800	1,439.4	− 5.0	− 5.7
Larceny-theft	6,270,800	2,921.3	+ 4.9	+ 4.2
Motor vehicle theft	957,600	446.1	− 4.3	− 5.0

SOURCE: *Crime in the United States: Uniform Crime Reports* (Washington, D.C.: U.S. Government Printing Office, 1976), p. 35.

siderably fewer than half the crimes reported to the police result in arrests. Many persons who are arrested are dismissed without ever being prosecuted in court. Of those prosecuted, many are acquitted. Yet even with these limitations, crime statistics do have some value. The agency that has been authorized by Congress to develop official statistics on national crime is the Federal Bureau of Investigation (FBI). Acting as a national clearing house, the FBI compiles and publishes reports submitted from over 13,000 enforcement agencies each year. This report, which is called *Crime in the United States: Uniform Crime Reports,* does provide the most comprehensive overview of crime across the nation available. Of particular value are the reported Crime Index Offenses. The Crime Index reports on seven crimes judged as most serious by the FBI. These are murder, forcible rape, robbery, aggravated assault, burglary, larceny-theft, and motor vehicle theft. Crime Index offenses, then, provide information that indicates the *rate* at which crimes occur per 100,000 of population. Crime rates are helpful in describing the changing patterns in crime; they offer comparisons between geographic regions, states, and cities. In examining crimes occurring in 1976, for example, we find that there were 18,780 murders. This becomes 8 murders for every 100,000 people in the population. Notice that there was an 8 per cent decrease in the numbers of murders compared with 1975.

Limitations of the Uniform Crime Report While the Uniform Crime Report does offer information about the character of crime in the United States, there are serious limitations connected with these statistics. Probably the most serious is the fact that the FBI statistics are the result of self-report. Law enforcement agencies compile and submit their own reports of known criminal activity, although the FBI examines each report "not only for arithmetical accuracy but also, as a possible indication of error, for deviations from the experiences of similar agencies." (p. 3) However, the validity of self-reported statistics is questionable wherever police administrators may benefit from underreporting crime (e.g., where the crime rates of middle- and upper-class suburbs are escalating).

A study completed for the President's Crime Commission attempted to determine the accuracy of official crime statistics by conducting a house-to-house survey and asking people if they had been victims of certain major crimes. This "victimization rate" was then compared with the official "crime rate." The comparison showed that the official rates for murder and auto theft appeared to be quite accurate, but about half again as many robberies, twice as many serious thefts and serious assaults, three times as many burglaries, and four times as many rapes occur as FBI reports indicate. The study also found that in some central cities, the reported victimization rate was as much as ten times greater than the reported crime rate. (Wilson, 1967)

Although the existing records are clearly inadequate, they are the only systematic data available. The disposition of the nearly 1,855,890 Crime Index offenses reported to police officials in 1976 is as follows:

365,321	arrests made (remainder unapprehended)
166,450	arrests of persons under 18
331,638	cases formally presented to juvenile and adult courts
109,606	persons guilty as charged
11,692	persons guilty of lesser offenses
43,834	persons acquitted or case dismissed
110,052	juveniles referred to juvenile court

Types of Crime

Crimes Against Persons Crimes involving physical violence, while the backbone of the mystery novel trade, are relatively rare. In the United States, assault is the most common of these crimes. Rape is second (counting both forcible and statutory), and the least common is felonious homicide.

Murder In 1976 there were 18,780 murders committed in the United States. The number of murders decreased 8 per cent from 1975 to 1976. Males were the victims of murder in three out of four cases. Study of the murder situation shows that of 4,997 white victims, 4,454 were murdered by white offenders and of 5,628 black victims, 5,412 were murdered by blacks. In 49 per cent of cases, the murder was accomplished with a handgun.

Rape The number of forcible rapes (56,730) showed a 1 per cent increase over

1975, but a 21 per cent increase over 1972. As a violent crime against the person, rape is one of the most underreported crimes. This is probably the result of fear on the part of victims, embarrassment, and also because of the way victims have been handled by law enforcement officials in the past. Some attempts to change procedures related to the handling of rape victims have been made by some departments (e.g., female officers to interview victims). Of the total rapes reported in 1976, in 51 per cent of cases an arrest was made. Fifty-one per cent of those arrested for forcible rape were white and 47 per cent were black. Though the vast majority of these cases were prosecuted, acquittals and/or dismissals resulted in 49 per cent of cases.

Crimes Against Property Far more numerous than assaults, rapes, or murders are crimes against property, of which the most frequent are auto theft, burglary, and larceny. Note that these crimes, unlike offenses against the person, do not necessitate face-to-face interaction between the criminal and the victim. One strong pressure to confrom, internalized through the process of socialization, is the guilt an individual may feel at violating a norm in the presence of another. Thus it is not only safer but probably easier psychologically for most people to violate a social expectation when the victim is absent and anonymous.

Organized Crime A type of crime somewhat different from crimes against the person or against property is the crime against public safety and morals. It is in this realm that we find organized crime. At the core of what is usually called organized crime in America, is an organization, sometimes called "Cosa Nostra," sometimes called "The Mafia," or "The Syndicate." Donald Cressey (1972) insists that this organization is only part of a larger whole but it may still be described as one of America's largest business enterprises. The Cosa Nostra controls almost all of the illegal gambling in the United States. This shadow organization also controls usury or loansharking, is the major importer and wholesaler of narcotics, and controls selling and dispersal of stolen goods. The Cosa Nostra or the Mafia, in addition to illegal businesses, has develped a monopoly of some legitimate businesses in this country (e.g. vending machines, juke-boxes) and they have a wide range of legitimate businesses such as "restaurants and bars, banks, hotels, apartment houses, trucking companies, financial corporations, food corporations, linen supply houses, office buildings, factories, and even garbage collection routes." (p. 22)

It is by using profits as a measure that the Mafia can be considered one of the nation's largest businesses. The Task Force on Organized Crime of the 1967 President's Commission noted that organized crime cost U.S. taxpayers an estimated 9 billion dollars annually. This amount is double the amount spent for police, court, and correctional services for this country in that year. The success of criminal organizations like the Mafia results from their ability to provide services that the public demands. And the customers of organized crime (those citizens that gamble, those that buy drugs) often cooperate with the Mafia against the police and the courts. For organized crime to exist, large numbers of people must patronize the criminals; and the people charged with finding, arresting, prosecuting, and convicting them must be failing to carry out their responsibilities.

Not all the crimes against public safety and morals occur as organized criminal activity, but probably most such offenses are in this pattern. It is easy to see a similarity between criminal activity and other economic activity: organized crime imitates in its organization the legitimate means of producing and distributing goods and services. The top executives in an illegal gambling operation engage in occupational role behavior not unlike that of the managers of a legitimate corporation. Indeed many of the characteristics of bureaucratic organization may be found within the structures of organized crime (See Chapter 9.) One of these is that, like other large-scale organizations, the Mafia hierarchy is composed of positions or offices that exist independently of their incumbents. Cressey notes that this bureaucratic feature enables the criminal organization to function that much more effectively. "For example, the arrest, conviction, incarceration and deportation to Italy of New York's Charles Luciano only resulted in passing of Cosa Nostra leadership to Frank Costello. And neither the imprisonment of Cosa Nostra boss Vito Genovese in 1959, nor his death a few years later, had any discernible effect on the amount of crime committed by his 'family' " (p. 100).

The essential difference between organized crime and other groups of criminals (such as bank robbers, embezzlers, burglars, counterfeiters) is that organized crime operates as a monopoly. It allows no competition. Thomas Schelling applies to it adjectives that define any business monopoly—"ruthless, unscrupulous, greedy, exploitative, unprincipled." (1974, p. 421)

One important reason for the continued existence of organized crime in this society is the systematic corruption of public officials. The Task Force reports state this loudly and clearly. Commissions like the Knapp Commission have made the public more aware of the extent of this corruption, but if a serious effort is ever to be made to eliminate organized crime, the analyses of sociological researchers may provide crucial answers. One such is offered by Cressey. He is convinced that the pursuit of individual criminals within organized crime will be fruitless. Cressey stresses that criminal organizations must be dealt with as organizational structures. He notes that "social problems disappear only when their place in a social system disappears." (p. 105) Cressey supplies an example of this in the case of the robbery of bus drivers. By changing the interaction system, so that exact fares were required and bus drivers were no longer handling money, the incidence of robberies was dramatically decreased. Similarly, the activities of hijackers would be greatly affected if one structural position in the criminal hierarchy could be eliminated, that of the *fence*. Any attack on organized crime must consider structural arrangements and the systematic, rational, and sophisticated organization that has developed.

White Collar Crime In the last quarter of the nineteenth century, a number of home-grown millionaires flourished in the United States. These wealthy industrialists dominated such fields as banking, railroads, steel, petroleum. They have become known to succeeding generations as the "robber barons." Shady and illegal business practices were well known to these men and they could be called the most spectacular of the white collar criminals produced in this country. A. B. Stickney, a railroad president, is reputed to have said at a meeting of sixteen other railroad presidents, gathered in the home of J. P. Morgan, "I have the utmost respect for you gentlemen individually, but as railroad presidents, I wouldn't trust you with my watch out of my sight." (Sutherland, 1949, p. 42) The Sherman Antitrust Law of 1890 was enacted to curtail the most blatant of the robber barons' activities; and yet the criminal actions of industrialists, corporations, and others in the business world have continued to the present. Edwin Sutherland, a leading American criminologist who defined *white collar crime*, insisted that conventional explanations of criminal behavior were inadequate in this case. Social scientists had persisted in associating crime with poverty and personal pathology when, in fact, individuals on all social levels could be found to have committed criminal acts. However, the type of criminal offenses committed by the middle and upper classes were apt to be different. Upper status people were less apt to be connected with crimes of violence (e.g., aggravated assault). Upper status people were more often engaged in white collar crime, or violations of the law while pursuing legitimate occupational activities. Such crimes included embezzlement, tax evasion, price-fixing, misrepresentation in advertising. In addition to the crimes related to the Watergate episode, former President Nixon was guilty of tax evasion when he backdated material and then donated it to the National Archives. In this

22-6 CHECKING IT OUT: A Violation of Law: Misrepresentation in Advertising

. . . [S]ome advertisements exaggerate the values of the products, and this is equivalent to giving short weights. An extreme case of advertisements of this nature was a case decided against two hoodlums in Chicago about 1930. They sold a bottle of medicine at a price of $10 to a blind man with the claim that this would cure his blindness. When analyzed, the medicine was found to consist of two aspirins dissolved in Lake Michigan water. The hoodlums were convicted and sentenced to six months' imprisonment. The advertisements by large corporations are frequently of this class, except that they are not so extreme and are not followed by convictions in criminal courts and imprisonment. Garments advertised and sold as silk or wool are almost entirely cotton. Alligator shoes not made from alligator hides, walnut furniture not made from walnut lumber, turtle-oil facial cream not made from turtle-oil, Oriental rugs not made in the Orient, Hudson seal furs not made from the skins of seals are further instances of such misrepresentation.

Caskets advertised as rustproof are not rustproof, garments as mothproof when they are not mothproof, garden hose as three-ply when it is only two-ply and radios as "all-wave reception" that do not receive all waves. Electric pads are advertised with switches for high, medium, and low heat, when in fact they have only two degrees of heat. Storage eggs are sold as fresh eggs, old and reconditioned stoves as new stoves, and worn and reconditioned hats as new hats. Facial creams sold as skin foods, corrective of wrinkles, do not feed the skin or correct wrinkles. Some coporations advertise that their tea is made from tender leaves, especially picked for these corporations, when in fact their tea is purchased from lots brought in by importers who sell the same tea to other firms.

SOURCE: Edwin H. Sutherland. "The Crime of Corporations," *Problems in Political Economy: An Urban Perspective,* ed. David M. Gordon (Lexington, Mass.: D. C. Heath & Co., 1971), p. 304.

instance, the government encourages the socially desirable objective of having the personal records of prominent people available to the public by allowing notables to donate material to the national repositories, then to deduct the loss of the commercial value of these materials on income taxes.

Sutherland (1956) found that since 1932 the 70 largest corporations had received adverse court decisions 980 times. This means that they had been found guilty of violations of law in 980 cases. If the courts defined a habitual criminal as someone convicted four times of felonies then 90 per cent of the 70 corporations were habitual criminals. The kinds of crimes involved included unfair labor practices, misrepresentation in advertising, restraint of trade, infringements (e.g., in the case of patents), and fraud.

Sutherland felt that there were two important reasons why corporate and white collar crime continued unabated. Unlike professional thieves, businessmen consider themselves honest men. They may acknowledge themselves to be lawbreakers. However, they feel the laws are wrong or that while the laws might restrict others, the laws should not restrict them. The business man "does not think of himself as a criminal, because he does not conform to the popular stereotype of the criminal. This popular stereotype is always taken from the lower socioeconomic class." (p. 310) In addition, there is little stigma attached to white collar crime. Such crimes are tried in civil, not criminal courts. Sutherland illustrates this with a statement from an official of the Department of Justice who advocated abandonment of criminal prosecutions for antitrust violations. "While civil penalties may be as severe in their financial effects as criminal penalties, yet they do not involve the stigma that attends indictment and conviction. Most of the defendants in antitrust cases are not criminals in the usual sense. There is no inherent reason why antitrust enforcement requires branding them as such." (Sutherland, 1949, p. 43)

22-7 CHECKING IT OUT: Two Views of Prostitution

The functional analysis of prostitution. The functional analysis of prostitution views prostitution as a social institution serving certain needs of the society. Kingsley Davis (1937), who has provided us with a classic functional analysis in *The Sociology of Prostitution,* wonders why a practice that causes such social disapproval, that is so frequently "outlawed," continues to exist. Davis argues that institutions are not maintained only if they are socially acceptable, but often persist because they satisfy needs not met by legitimate institutions, needs which legitimate institutions, in a sense, create. Prostitution must be analyzed in relation to other institutions involving sexual relations. However, it differs from the legitimate sexual institutions of courtship and marriage in that intercourse is engaged in for nonsocial purposes (personal pleasure or money). These very "gesellschaft" qualities of prostitution (i.e., segmented relations, emotional indifference) contribute to its vitality. Where sexual experiences are unavailable "due to defects of person or circumstance," prostitution serves a precise function. Circumventing the rituals of courtship and the emotional involvement of sexual attraction, prostitution guarantees physical release and demands only the "cash." For those desiring sexual variety, satisfactions considered perverse, as well as intercourse free from pretense or entanglements, prostitution satisfies the desire for sexuality in unsanctioned ways.

The functional analysis of prostitution must also look at the "demand" side of the equation. Prostitution can be eliminated only when the needs for it have disappeared. Eliminating the "supply" by encouraging women into more legitimate occupations will cause little change. Davis believes that prostitution will persist as long as (1) there is institutional control over sexual expression and (2) some people are more sexually attractive than others. As a functional institution prostitution would be greatly affected by increased sexual freedom in society. The greater the possibilities for free, mutually satisfying sex, the lesser is the demand for prostitutes. In status societies where the institution of the family is strong, prostitution and the family frequently function side by side. In such societies women have either a place within the family system or they function outside it as prostitutes, as members of a separate caste. In such societies there are few intermediate statuses and the two institutions are staffed by different personnel so that they function side by side, without confusion. Where familial controls are weak, the system of prostitution tends to be poorly defined and it is easier to satisfy one's desire outside the family with a respectable member of society. Davis does not expect sex freedom to displace prostitution because there will always be reproductive institutions controlling sexual liberty and a system of dominance which creates motives for selling sexual favors. But finally prostitution is economical. It enables a small number of women to service many men and provides a sexual outlet for strangers, perverts, and the physically repulsive, a function no other institution performs.

The interactionist approach to prostitution. Whereas the functional approach to prostitution (as stated by Davis) focuses on the *demand* side of prostitution, the interactionist approach centers on the *supply* aspect. Why do some women become prostitutes? What is the social-psychological process by which some women become prostitutes? The interactionist approach is best seen in the work of Edwin Lemert (1972) and Karen Rosenblum (1975). Utilizing the distinction between "primary" and "secondary" deviance (introduced by Lemert), Rosenblum argues that "all women, to the degree to which they reflect the contemporary female sex role, are primary deviants." That is, prostitution must be analyzed as a form of female deviance, which in turn must be seen as an aspect of the female sexual role. Rosenblum analyzes female sex-role behavior using Lemert's definition of "primary" and "secondary" deviance. The individual who experiences role or value conflict may seek a resolution of the conflict in a situation involving some risk. **Primary deviations** relate to those situations where risk-taking, if discovered, might be thought undesirable but would be socially excusable. **Secondary deviance** involves an organization of life around the deviance. Deviant behavior has become a central fact of existence, and social control in the form of stigmatization, punishment, or social segregation has contributed to some alteration in the psychic structure of the deviant (the self-concept). Primary deviance does not result in such a change in status and self-regard. Also primary deviance need not lead to secondary deviance. Rosenblum then applies this theoretical distinction to the domain of prostitution. She begins with an identification of the characteristics of secondary deviance within prostitution, examines the transition from primary to secondary deviance, then working backward attempts to grapple with the concept of primary deviance.

The following manifestations of "secondary deviance" can be delineated: (1) the sex act comes to be defined in highly impersonal and structured terms; (2) the routine and scheduling of everyday life becomes restructured so as to maximize "business" opportunities; (3) a subculture develops whose solidarity is both emotional and economic in nature; and (4) an ambivalence, about one's own self-worth and the merits of the occupation, develops.

Two major precipitating factors leading to the adoption of this occupation are the desire for independence (the desire to avoid a permanent relation) and the potentially lucrative nature of prostitution (money could be earned far in excess of what could be earned in nondeviant occupations). The nature and quality of contacts with women already in the business are also relevant.

Rosenblum's analysis of the female sex role focuses on the fact that women are not socialized to expect sexual gratification routinely but are nevertheless expected to give much attention to the cultivation of sexual desirability. While men are also concerned with their sexual desirability, their self-conceptions are not anchored to that desirability but rather to occupational achievements. Because the latter alternative has been less available to women, unusually high value has been placed on sexual desirability. In the case of one type of deviant, the call girl, as well as in the case of the nondeviant woman, this desirability is measured by physical appearance and the ability to make a man feel "masculine." Although neither the call girl nor the nondeviant woman have "high expectations" about receiving sexual gratification, both expect some "pay off" if they are preceived as desirable (the call girl's payment is monetary). Rosenblum finds that in these two cases the difference between the way sexuality is utilized and expectation regarding sexuality is only one of degree. Therefore the decision to become a call girl involved only an exaggeration of behavior and attitudes also to be found in nondeviant women. Rosenblum concludes by pointing out that primary deviance in the case of prostitution occurs when a woman who, while exchanging sexual favors for pay, does not see herself as a prostitute or structure her life around prostitution. However, it is difficult to determine what is precisely meant by "sexual favors" or "pay." In summing up, Rosenblum finds prostitution a uniquely female form of deviance because of the relationship between the attributes built into the female role and the requirements of the occupation of prostitution. Where secondary deviance develops out of primary deviance, precipitating factors such as previous contacts with prostitutes may be found. However, the sociologist must not ignore those aspects of the female sex role that allow such factors to have the influence that they do.

Crimes Without Victims Edwin M. Schur (1965) has developed a category of deviance called "crimes without victims." He discusses abortion, homosexuality, and drug addiction as victimless crimes, or interactions "in which one person obtains from another, in a fairly direct exchange, a commodity or personal service which is socially disapproved and legally proscribed." (p. 170) Because there is no victim in these situations, Schur comments that they might readily be identified as "exchange crimes" or "business crimes." It is clear that criminal laws reveal both a societal judgment about behavior deemed unacceptable and those considered to be victimized by such behavior. Indeed, the official designation of a victim is one indication that the stability of society has been challenged by such behavior. (Quinney, 1972) In the case of robbery, the victim and the victimizer are recognized with little difficulty. Schur notes that in the case of statutory rape—intercourse with a minor, or underage, female—the factor of her consent blurs her role as a victim. In the case of abortion, homosexuality, or drug addiction, the idea of victimization is blurred even more. First of all, there is a continuing debate about the degree of harm to the self in each of these activities. Secondly, a particularly disturbing feature of victimless crimes is the difficulty in enforcing the criminal laws connected with them. Because the exchange that takes place occurs in privacy and involves consent on the part of those involved, the laws defining the deviance are unenforceable. In the case of an illegal abortion, the chance of the formerly pregnant female becoming a complainant against the abortionist is slim. The lack of a complainant in the case of consenting homosexuals is obvious. For these reasons, Schur suggests that legal reforms are needed so that homosexuals may conduct relationships without interference and so that medical practitioners can replace those who illegally supply goods and/or services to addicts and women seeking abortions.

Differential Rates of Crime

Regional Differences in Crime Rates Sanctions, or rewards and punishments, exist to inhibit the commission of crimes. When such social controls

22-8 CHECKING IT OUT: Crime Rate by Region, 1976 (Rate per 100,000 inhabitants)

Crime Index Offenses	*North-eastern States*	*North Central States*	*Southern States*	*Western States*
Total	5,157.7	4,922.9	4,783.4	6,782.8
Violent	523.6	381.7	429.3	548.3
Property	4,634.1	4,541.2	4,354.1	6,234.5
Murder	7.0	7.4	11.3	8.5
Forcible rape	20.4	23.4	26.3	38.9
Robbery	288.1	175.8	139.9	206.8
Aggravated assault	208.1	175.1	251.7	294.1
Burglary	1,446.7	1,195.2	1,346.2	1,962.1
Larceny-theft	2,541.9	2,944.0	2,716.6	3,740.0
Motor vehicle theft	645.5	402.1	291.3	532.4

SOURCE: *Crime in the United States: Uniform Crime Reports* (Washington, D.C.: U.S. Government Printing Office, 1976), p. 34.

are relatively weak, we can expect more violations of the law. As we have noted, differences among subcultures may account for variations in how seriously people view the norms. There is some evidence that crimes of violence, for example, differ by social class: middle-class people may abuse one another verbally in situations where lower-class people might use blows. There are also regional variations in the United States in crimes against the person: the West has significantly higher rates of rape, robbery, and aggravated assault than the rest of the country. The South has been traditionally more tolerant than the rest of the society of the expression of physical violence.

The Influence of Age It is widely believed that young people are more likely to be criminals than old people, but this is another generalization that requires cautious evaluation. In the first place, amateur or inexperienced criminals are more likely to be arrested, and hence influence crime statistics, than are older, professional criminals. Second, it is true that most persons arrested in the United States are under 35 years of age, but then, most people in the United States are under 35 years of age.

Sex and Crime Nearly 90 per cent of the persons arrested in the United States are men. This sex difference in criminality has generally been accepted as a social and cultural phenomenom. Because cultural practices have forced women into passive, dependent, and less aggressive roles, crime statistics have traditionally reflected these traits in the low level of violent crimes committed by women. Women have been prone to commit so-called "typical female" crimes

22-9 CHECKING IT OUT: Females and Murder

"The change here has been very obvious for anyone who has been in the system for a few years," explained Mrs. Claudia McCormick, director of the women's facility. "Now while most of our women are in here for murder, it is not stranger-to-stranger murder. In a large number of cases, it was the husband, boyfriend, or child whom they killed. I've heard it said, 'Well, that's how it always has been.' That really isn't so. Not many years ago, we'd get an awful lot of women who had *hurt* their child or husband and only a very few who had actually killed them. There was something that stopped the women short of actually murdering. Whatever that 'something' was is gone. They murdered pretty easy now. Then in the other twenty per cent of our population you'll find an unusually high number of women in for armed robbery. Now you never saw that before at all.

"At the same time, it's hard to really put your finger on, but there is a new attitude among these women. Like, you'll hear them talking of their first murder, saying, 'Well, you know, the first one gets to you but afterward, it just don't touch you.' It's become a status symbol in their peer group to murder. Now, no matter how you cut it, that is a drastic change from the way things used to be with females here."

SOURCE: Freda Adler, *Sisters in Crime* (New York: McGraw-Hill, 1975) p. 183.

such as shoplifting, forgery, embezzlement, and small thefts. Male juvenile delinquents have been typically arrested for offenses involving stealing and mischievous acts. Female delinquents have been typically involved in sex offenses, hidden under the labels "incorrigibility" or "running away." Throughout the criminal justice system women have not been processed and handled in the same ways that men have been. This differential treatment may reflect behavior that is truly different or may continue because social control agents have a sexual double standard. It has been frequently noted that elements of chivalry and paternalism work to give women a somewhat favored status within the system. (Chesney-Lind, 1973; Nagel and Weitzman, 1972; Reckless and Kay, 1967) Freda Adler in *Sisters in Crime* (1975) proposes that the sharp rise in female crime must be related to the fact that "the social revolution of the sixties has virilized its previously or presumably docile female segment." (p. 87) At the same time the "baby boom" increased the juvenile population, and unemployment has reduced job opportunities. Adler gives much weight to the influence of the women's movement on female criminality and delinquency. She parallels the new feminism and the changes that it has brought to the status of women within families and on the job with the changed behavior of female criminals (i.e., those who now reject prostitution and shoplifting in favor of assault and robbery). Adler has identified a "sharply rising crime rate" for women that is growing "at an alarming rate."

The idea of the "new female criminal" have been rejected by Joseph Weis (1967), who finds the relationship between the women's movement and the changing female criminal to be "tenuous." He notes that official statistics still show women to be typically nonviolent criminals. Where they have shown increases in criminal activity, these have been in the areas of larceny (thefts), fraud, and forgery. "National arrest data and self-reports of delinquent behavior show that the 'new female criminal' is an invention and that the women's movement cannot be held responsible for changes in female criminal behavior which data indicate simply have not happened." (p. 17)

The Influence of Social Class

Probably the best predictor of criminal behavior is position in the stratification system. Occupation, race, education, income, and other indicators of one's position in the stratification structure are closely correlated with life chances. Among the consequences of low status is, for example, more frequent and direct contact with criminality. (Sutherland and Cressy, 1960) It is perhaps not the years of schooling, the amount of money, or the standing of the job itself that are so important here as the intervening variables: the social factors that are themselves a consequence of low socioeconomic status, such as overcrowded housing in blighted neighborhoods; loss of self-respect; the squelching of ambition in a bright child attending a badly equipped and poorly staffed school; or the differential and unequal treatment that the poor and minorities receive from law enforcement officers. Police typically overestimate the arrest rates of minority groups.

Social Control

The Public Regulation of Deviance Deviant behavior has impact on the social structure far beyond the deviant act itself. The process of dealing with deviants has its own consequences. Because the power of the state supports their actions, agencies of social control have been developed to take action against deviants; these agencies must catch deviants, process them, and then control or contain them. Deviance thus becomes bureaucratized. And deviants are handled by bureaucratic structures characterized by hierarchy, impersonality, specialization, and systematic rules. In addition to the fact that the regulation of deviance is a gigantic industry, commanding a sizable amount of the citizen's tax dollar, social control creates jobs for police personnel, correction and probation officers, judges, lawyers, and court personnel. It is important to note that social structures created for the control of deviance evolve their own norms and ultimately leave their mark upon the culture in which they originate.

Prisons

The penal system in America is the largest in the world. With 400 major penal institutions, 800 juvenile detention and correctional structures, and 3,900 local jails, on any specified day there are about 400,000 Americans incarcerated in correctional facilities across the country. Twice as many are on probation and are being supervised on parole. (Carney, 1977)

The dimensions of the criminal justice problem can be gauged by the fact that 1,855,890 Crime Index offenses were recorded by the police in 1976. Of the 1,203,880 individuals who were formally charged by the police only 17 per cent were acquitted or dismissed. Where convicted offenders must be incarcerated, the cost is high. Carney notes that in 1973 it cost taxpayers $10,000 annually to care for a child detained in a correctional facility and approximtely the same for an adult.

The Functions of Imprisonment A chief structure within the penal system is the *penitentiary,* a massive state or government facility erected to contain long-term prisoners. The term "penitentiary" reflects the intentions of

22-10 CHECKING IT OUT: A Prisoner Looks at Prisons

A. Living in prison is like living on another planet.
   a. Life in prison is totally isolated from "outside."
   b. Community standards and life styles are not recognized here.
   c. A prisoner must conform to the life style created for them while living here.
   d. That the rules and regulations, style of living, etc., are totally alien is of no consequence to the system; the sooner a prisoner learns to live within the prison, the sooner he can get out because, without exception, rehabilitation is measured by the administration in terms of a prisoner's adjustment to this alien world which they have created.

B. Requirements for survival in this alien world amount to little more than brainwashing.
   a. Responsibility is not allowed (personal responsibility). Every move, every decision, every aspect of life in prison is controlled and decided by the administration.
   b. The only decision a prisoner has to make is whether or not he can live without personal responsibility.
      i. First alternative: Become totally irresponsible and defer all decisions to the administration. (Become totally dependent upon others to "decide.")
      ii. Resist irresponsibility and insist upon making some decisions for oneself (second alternative)
   c. Choice of the wrong alternative earns an administratively manufactured label and insures a longer stay.

SOURCE: This analysis was made by a prisoner currently serving a sentence in Rahway State Prison, New Jersey.

nineteenth-century correctional authorities. The prison experience was supposed to produce penitence and remorse in the prisoner and lead to a reformation of character. Therefore, through disciplined work, religious instruction, medical assistance, and exposure to conditions of cleanliness, the prison experience was expected to be meaningful. In earlier times in the U.S., jails and workhouses were foul places where prisoners were idle with no work, where debtors and hardened criminals were jailed together, and where the sexes were not separated. Liquor was readily available and incarceration provided the opportunity for "promiscuous and unrestricted intercourse, and universal riot and debauchery." (Sutherland, 1947) Contemporary attitudes about prisons still reflect the expectation that the prison experience will change the convicted person. Americans, in general, see imprisonment as serving these functions:

1. Providing punishment for committing a crime.
2. Deterring others by providing an example of what can happen if the law is violated.
3. Removing criminals from society, thereby safeguarding the majority.
4. Rehabilitating prisoners so that they will be law-abiding upon release.

Punishment—Yes! Rehabilitation—No! And yet while providing punishment and removing criminals from society, the penal system has failed dramatically in its attempts to rehabilitate or to deter those who might commit crimes. Carney comments that the prisons in the U.S. are becoming "centers of violence." For example, between December, 1972, and July, 1973, there were 118 stabbings in the California prison system. Of this number, 17 were fatal. A "Mexican Mafia" has been identified within this same prison system which consists of 200 members and which has a "death code for betrayal."(p. 11) This in the penal system which is credited with being perhaps the best in the country. In New York, the bloody events at Attica Correctional Facility, in which 43 people were killed, seem an "outer limit" demonstrating the possibilities for violent encounters in the nation's prisons. If the purpose of incarceration is to

22-11 CHECKING IT OUT: Behind the Explosion at Attica—The New Breed of Inmate Versus Conventional Correction Officers

There were many men in Attica in 1971 who held the view that they were victims of society. They must be distinguished, however, from the small group who, like Samuel Melville, were totally committed to a firm political ideology of revolution. Melville had been convicted of bombing public buildings for political purposes. The bond between these two brands of self-proclaimed political prisoners was their common rejection of established authority and their denunciation as barbaric of the wages, programs, hygiene, medical care, censorship, and other conditions at Attica.

In contrast to this new breed of inmate were the older inmates—black, white, and Spanish-speaking—who had come to accept prison conditions: they made few demands upon officials, proclaimed at most their innocence, but not society's guilt, kept their frustration and anger to themselves, and accepted the word of the guards as law. Many who were interviewed by the Commission expressed deep antagonism toward younger inmates who were not prepared to "do their own time," and insisted on defying authority.

The older inmate may have remembered when prison conditions were worse, but the improvements made no impression on the younger one. It did not matter to the younger inmate that he was not required to move in a lockstep shuffle; that he was not required to work 12 to 14 hours a day; that he had a makeshift handball court and a basketball hoop and television in his exercise yard; that there was a prison library and commissary for his use. To the young inmate, it was enough that he was still a faceless number in a silent formation of marching men; that he was assigned to meaningless, unpleasant work details for reasons of administrative efficiency having nothing to do with rehabilitation; that for many months of the year his exercise yard was buried in four feet of snow; that he was entitled to only one shower a week in all seasons of the year; that he was paid, on the average, 25¢ a day for his labor, half of which officials saved for his release, and was expected to buy his own cigarettes and toiletries from his wages; and that he saw a correction staff that did not include one black or Puerto Rican officer and that exhibited the same "remember your place and do as you're told" attitude that his people had been rebelling against for the last decade. The new inmate was not about to submit to these conditions simply because he had been convicted of a crime. . . .

The Commission discussed the problem of the new inmate and the "political prisoner" with more than 200 of Attica's correction officers. Their responses varied from understanding to racist interpretations of inmates' complaints. But one theme stood out above all others and made any meaningful meeting of minds between inmates and correction officers almost impossible: "These men are not in here for missing Sunday School," said one officer. Another exclaimed, "No one comes here for just playing jacks on the sidewalk." An inmate's very presence at Attica was regarded as sufficient evidence that he had voluntarily forfeited, by his own actions, many of the rights the new inmate insists upon retaining. In speaking of the rights of prisoners, correction officers often turn the question to the rights of their victims. "They cry about their rights," correction officers say, "but what about the rights of their victims? Did they worry about the rights of the man they killed or the woman they raped?" The inmate who refused to regard himself only as a criminal simply cound not relate in any meaningful, constructive manner with a prison staff that could not regard him as anything else.

Thus, correction officers frequently found themselves demanding adherence to rules which inmates would not accept. As the number of confrontations increased during this period, so did the intensity. An officer's orders to stop talking, for example, were first questioned, later ignored, and finally ridiculed.

SOURCE: *Attica,* The Official Report of the New York State Special Commission on Attica (New York: Bantam Books, 1972), pp. 118–120.

rehabilitate so that offenders will go on to productive and crime-free careers, then the system seems totally ineffectual. The Uniform Crime Reports for 1974 documents this failure in its report of recidivism, the relapse into criminal activity after release from prison. Of 207,748 offenders who had been arrested between 1970 and 1974, 65 per cent had been arrested two or more times. Indeed the average number of arrests was four times each.

It is perhaps to be expected that within the present system, rehabilitation is impossible for most prisoners. Today's prisons are abnormal environments in which prisoners of one sex are confined; the majority are economically deprived, young, and from minority groups treated differentially by the larger society. Erving Goffman (1961) calls prisons one of the forms of *total institutions*. They are in part residential communities and in part formal organizations or bureaucracies where all activities are conducted within the same facility and under the same authority. Conformity of behavior is demanded and inmates move through a tight schedule of activities in the company of others like themselves. All total institutions (such as the military, religious orders, mental institutions, prisons) subject newcomers to a system of "mortifications" intended to turn the person into a tractable and conformng individual. Goffman says that the bathing, disinfecting, haircutting, issuing of institutional clothing, substitution of a number for a name, are part of "an obedience test and even a will-breaking contest: an inmate who shows defiance receives immediate visible punishment which increases until he 'cries uncle' and humbles himself." (p. 17)

However, in prison the ritual mortification rarely has the desired effect. Too frequently the horrors of the prison experience destroy the possibilities of rehabilitation. We have recently witnessed the unmasking of guards in a northern prison as members of the Klu Klux Klan. In 1976, U.S. District Judge Frank Johnson called Alabama's prisons "unfit for human habitation." It is well known that the young and defenseless new inmate is faced with the possibility of rape. Indeed, it has been estimated that between 30 and 45 per cent of the inmate population participate in homosexual interactions. (1972) An unanticipated consequence of such brutalizing experiences is a mounting bitterness and anger in the prisoner. Goffman quotes Richard McCleery on the effects of this anger " '[The prisoner] decides to "get even" for his unjust treatment in prison and takes reprisals through further crime at the first opportunity. *With that decision he becomes a criminal.*' " (p. 57)

Future Developments in Criminal Justice As John Conrad has observed in his article "Corrections and Simple Justice," while rehabilitation continues to be a worthwhile objective, it appears unlikely that this is possible within existing correctional facilities. (1974) This view has led to the development of community-based rehabilitation programs. The notion here is that particularly nondangerous prisoners (e.g., those convicted of embezzlement, forgery, gambling) might be better off working in the community and making restitution to their victims than becoming hardened criminals in prison. A strong

22-12 CHECKING IT OUT: A Warden's View of Reform

[Warden] Brierton's whole management technique contributes to the demystification of the prison. He has deemphasized the need to punish prisoners for violation of rules, while focusing on the need to restrain those who can be shown to be a threat to institutional security. He is not committed to a particular standard of living that prisoners "deserve." That is a matter for the courts and the legislature.

To be sure, the bureaucratization and professionalization of the prison has not reached its limits. While a few college graduates are present among the guard force, the great majority of employees are poorly educated and weakly integrated into the bureaucratic structure. The greatest obstacle to the emergence of a period of restoration under Brierton is the traditional task orientation and lack of specialized expertise of the staff. There has in the past been a strong tendency toward cooptation of the new professionals on the staff by the old Ragenites. Some new staff members, anxious to earn acceptance, have been led to accept the long-term employees' definition of the situation. There is sharp collegial pressure to be seen as realistic, tough, and pragmatic.

The professional administrators identify with the inmates far less than do the counselors and teachers, whose roles are constructed around providing services to their inmate-clients. The professionalization of the administration has *not* resulted in a monolithic group of "reformers" committed to "treatment" on the one hand, and a monolithic group committed to "punishment" on the other.

Brierton has brought a new definition of administration to the prison. He stresses efficient and emotionally detached management. He has attempted to remove the affect attached to handling inmates. Whether this type of detached bureaucratic administration will ultimately be successful in a people-processing institution may be the crucial question facing corrections in the years ahead.

SOURCE: James B. Jacobs, *Statesville: The Penitentiary in Mass Society* (Chicago: University of Chicago Press, 1977), p. 104.

22-13 CHECKING IT OUT: A Prisoner Outlines Prison Reforms

March 8, 1977

John Horn, Commissioner
Dept. of Labor and Industry
State House
Trenton, N. J. 08625

Dear Commissioner Horn:

There are about 6,000 able-bodies men in our State Prisons today who are, for. all intents and purposes, unemployed. Meaningful, productive, competitive wage-producing work has been traditionally withheld from prisoners. This economic deprivation has always been considered to be a part of the punishment of imprisonment. However, I believe the endorsement of this ancient policy has reached the point, in today's economy, where the taxpayer is being more severely economically punished than the prisoners.

The corrections budget for the coming fiscal year to maintain these men is reported to be in excess of 67 million dollars. That figure does not include the unknown welfare cost of maintaining prisoners' families. As a prisoner at the Rahway State Prison, many men have expressed to me their willingness and desire to support themselves and their families through honest, productive work. As it stands, we earn about 12¢ an hour on the average in return for performing often meaningless tasks. The present wage in this prison amounts to little more than a handout with which to buy razor blades and soap.

At a recent Penal Reform meeting held in this institution, I had the opportunity to suggest a possible alternative to Senator Herb Buehler. The alternative, in capsule, is this:

Bring private industry into State institutions and allow prisoners to work in a productive, competitive wage-producing capacity. Preliminary figures show that: if 5,000 men are allowed to earn only $100 per week, a weekly taxable payroll of half a million dollars would be generated or, 26 million dollars a year. Of that figure, it is estimated that about 90 per cent would be returned to the State in the form of taxes, reduction of welfare costs, restitution to crime victims and in direct payment to the state in self-support in a manner similar to the one used in the work release program.

The positive prospects for both the community and prisoners abound. Not only would the taxpayer costs for prisons be reduced, but a system of restitution to crime victims could be worked out; any business willing to participate in such a trial program would be assured of a steady work force, low absenteeism, a low labor force turnover, and maximum return on training programs. The prisoners would be permitted to learn good work habits, regain a measure of self-esteem, retain their family position as "bread winner" and, perhaps most importantly of all, be able to identify with working society as a member who is "pulling his own weight."

Senator Buehler was quite enthusiastic toward the idea. Since organized Industry and Labor would, of necessity, have a voice in any practical application of such a program, the Senator has suggested that I write to you for your observations and comments.

I would appreciate it, therefore, if you will be kind enough to give me an idea of the position of the Department of Labor and Industry toward the implementation of such a program.

SOURCE: This letter was sent by a prisoner at Rahway State Prison, New Jersey

argument is being made that carefully supervised probation and parole programs offer ex-offenders the best chance of rehabilitation. Whereas prison locks criminals together in "intimate association," prisons also separate prisoners from law-abiding folk. Because the ex-offender must develop a noncriminal career, this must be undertaken, with guidance and supportive services, right in the community.

It seems clear that agencies of social control have little chance of changing criminal behavior as long as so little is known about the process of rehabilitation. Therefore a pressing need for research and experiment by social scientists continues, so that changes in criminal careers may become a reality.

The Functions of Deviance

The dysfunctions of deviance for the society are perhaps obvious. Owners of stores account for shoplifting and hijacking by raising prices. Homicide disrupts family life. Juvenile gangs terrorize neighborhoods and destroy the stability of communities. In general, the stable functioning of any society is bound up in the conformity of its members to societal standards. And most people conform to most of the norms most of the time. And yet deviance is also functional for societies. Durkheim presented this argument in 1893 in *The Division of Labor in Society.* He stressed that as the community mobilized in reaction to a crime that had been committed, important and useful things were happening. The outrage and anger expressed by community members made clear the unacceptability of the criminal behavior and served to reaffirm the norms and standards. The criminal law had two functions. It established the punishment to be accorded the criminal and it also aided the community that had been distressed by the crime. The limits beyond which behavior was unacceptable were again made clear. Thus crime and its punishment contributed to the integration of society.

INTERPRETIVE SUMMARY

No society expects all members to conform to all of its norms all of the time. Norms do not apply to all situations; they vary in importance and often conflict with subcultural norms. Deviance, then, is behavior that violates the norms of a given group or society in a given situation. The types of behavior labeled deviant depend upon the definition and interpretation of norms by various groups in various situations.

In developing *anomie theory,* Merton constructed a typology of deviant behavior which seems applicable to those situations in which an individual is mentally and intellectually capable of recognizing society's goals. While conformists work for accepted goals in accepted ways, deviants either use unacceptable tactics or actively attempt to change the goals.

Labeling theory questions the assumption that deviants are those who violate social norms. Rather the labeling perspective views deviance as a consequence of the way society treats the offender.

Sutherland's theory of differential association focuses on deviant subcultures (e.g., delinquent gangs) and relates deviant behavior to social learning in intimate group settings. In such groups, norms, contrary to those of the larger society, might be internalized. Cohen and Short have described a variety of delinquent subcultures. Matza and Sykes suggest that deviants may not be rejecting social norms, but "neutralizing" existing norms and rationalizing their actions.

Crimes considered serious in the United States are those involving violence against individuals, crimes against property, and crimes threatening the public safety and morals. In the last category are such offenses as organized crime, white-collar crime, and those crimes (abortion, homosexuality, drug addiction) characterized as "victimless crimes." In the United States, there are class and regional differences in the rates and kinds of crimes. Statistics concerning age differentials are necessarily inaccurate, but men seem to engage in this type of behavior more frequently than women do. A rise in female crime has been identified, but within the criminal justice system women are processed and handled differently from men.

In regulating deviant behavior, agencies of social control have been devised which catch, process, control, and contain deviants. These bureaucratic structures form a huge industry. Prisons and penitentiaries have been constructed to contain prisoners. Though punishment and containment have been recognized as important functions of prisons, rehabilitation of deviants is expected by the populace, but thwarted in the abnormal, violent environments that prisons have become.

Community-based rehabilitation programs are now being discussed as one possible way to remove some prisoners from the "intimate association" of hardened and violent criminals. The need for further research and experiments in order to learn more about the process of rehabilitation is needed.

QUESTIONS

1. Is it possible to create a society in which deviant acts seldom occur? What are the functions of deviance?
2. An individual has been mugged and beaten on a street corner. What insights could (a) an anomie theorist, (b) a labeling theorist, (c) a differential association theorist offer about the person or persons who committed this deviant act?
3. What are some possible results should the "victimless crime" be decriminalized?
4. Give a theoretical explanation that clarifies the difference between committing a deviant act and beginning a deviant career.

Glossary

Accommodation Used in two senses: (1) As a condition, a state of equilibrium between individuals or groups in which certain working arrangements have been agreed upon or accepted. (2) As a process, the social adjustment between individuals or groups aimed at the temporary suspension of conflict. Also called "antagonistic cooperation." Some common forms of accommodation are tolerant participation, compromise, arbitration, and conciliation.

Acculturation The process in which those of one culture absorb the traits of another.

Achieved statuses Statuses and roles that are open to achievement.

Amalgamation A biological fusing or merging of groups.

Anomie A condition of society marked by normlessness or lack of values and goals; characteristic of some members of mass society.

Anomie theory Robert Merton's view of deviance as a normal or expected reaction when societal goals such as wealth and prestige cannot be attained by legitimate institutionalized means.

Ascribed statuses Those positions that are assigned to an individual regardless of his or her own abilities or performance.

Assimilation The process by which a group, voluntarily or involuntarily, assumes the behavior, attitudes, and cultural styles of a more dominant group so that both groups are merged into one group with a common identity.

Audience A number of persons in physical contiguity all of whom are subject to the same stimulus.

Authoritarian personality A personality type characterized by intense hatred of outgroups and by opinions, attitudes, and values that show a consistent pattern tied to deep-seated psychological needs.

Authority Power that is seen as legitimate.

Bilateral descent Descent determined equally by the mother's and the father's line.

Bureaucracy A formal, rationally organized social structure involving clearly defined patterns of activity, characterized by rules, a hierarchy of offices, and centralized authority.

Caste A closed, endogamous category resulting from stratification in which status in a hierarchy of power relations is defined and permanently fixed by ancestry.

Charismatic authority Authority seen as legitimate because of the special qualities possessed by an individual. Charismatic leaders have been thought to possess qualities that go beyond the normal, even to the supernatural.

Class A category resulting from stratification in which the status, while often determined at birth or during early life, is not so completely or irrevocably fixed as in caste.

Class consciousness The perception and awareness individuals have of their position in the social class system, together with a sense of solidarity and shared interests with those of the same class.

Competition The act of striving for some object that is sought for by others at the same time; a contention of two or more persons or groups for the same object or goal.

Conflict Direct and open antagonistic struggle of persons or groups for the same object or end. The aim of the conflict is the annihilation, defeat, or subjection of the other person or group as a way of obtaining the goal.

Consanguine family A form of family organization in which several generations make up a single household.

Consciousness of kind A concept used by Franklin H. Giddings to designate a strong sense of unity felt by group members because of a feeling of identification with others who are similar.

Control effect A problem encountered in

participant observation. The researcher runs the risk of changing group interaction by his or her presence. Control effect is lessened when the researcher "takes a role."

Control group In an experiment, a group of subjects used for purposes of comparison. The control group, which is identical to the experimental group, is not subjected to the experimental treatment (independent variable).

Corporation A type of formal organization that functions as a recognized legal entity, empowered to transact business and engage in trade.

Counterculture A subculture whose beliefs and behavior patterns are in conflict with the dominant culture.

Crowd A number of persons whose interaction is of brief duration and low intensity. The members are in physical contiguity but seldom share the specific focus typical of an audience.

Crude birth rate The number of births per thousand members of the population at a given period.

Crude death rate The number of deaths per thousand members of the population at a given period.

Cultural alternatives Various possibilities of action with reference to the same object, situation, or problem, all of which are approved by the society in question. In other words, the group or the individual has a choice among a number of permitted courses of action.

Cultural complexes The combining of cultural traits to form a larger unit. The phenomenon of football forms a cultural complex in the United States.

Cultural integration That situation in which the parts or components of culture (i.e., norms, values, beliefs) function in harmony. If new cultural elements produce conflict and tension, the resolution of these conflicts contributes to cultural integration.

Cultural lag A condition of disequilibrium arising out of an unequal or uneven rate of change in two or more cultural elements that are functionally interrelated.

Cultural relativism A principle which affirms that elements of culture are best described when related to the larger social and cultural system. A particular custom of a society cannot be validly judged without reference to the values, needs, and morality of that culture.

Culture trait The simplest unit or element of culture used in an analysis.

Culture The social heritage of a people. Culture encompasses the beliefs, values, knowledge, norms, symbols, and artifacts that are shared within a particular group or society.

Demographic transition A process describing population change. Populations go through three stages: (1) a preindustrial stage when both mortality and birth rates are high; (2) an early industrialization stage when mortality declines but birth rates remain high; and (3) a mature industrialization stage when low mortality is balanced by a low birth rate.

Dependent variable In cause-and-effect terms, the dependent variable is the "effect" variable. Changes in the dependent variable result from changes or variations in the independent variable.

Deviant behavior Behavior defined as departing from or running counter to the norm and the accepted and expected ways of a group or society.

Differential association Edwin H. Sutherland's theory that deviance is the result of social learning in primary group situations rather than the result of biological inheritance or personality traits.

Differentiation The process of developing different sets of rights and duties associated with various statuses.

Diffusion The spread in space of culture patterns from one society to another.

Discrimination Behavior towards a minority based on a prejudiced attitude; or the differential treatment of minorities.

Discovery The perception of relations among elements not previously recognized or understood.

Division of labor A concept used in the discussion of social organization to refer to the differentiation of roles.

Dyad The smallest group possible and the simplest sociological unit. A dyad consists of two persons who are interacting.

Dysfunction Any activity or consequence associated with a structure or system that is judged to hinder its integration and stability.

Endogamy Marriage within the tribe, class, or group.

Estates A kind of stratified society that is less rigid than a caste system but more rigid than a class system. Medieval feudal society is the classic model of the estate system. Social position is based on relationship to land.

Esteem The evaluation of an individual's role behavior in a given status; the community judgment of how well one fulfills the expectations of his or her role.

Ethnocentrism Belief that one's race, society, culture, etc. is superior to all others; the tendency to judge other cultures by the standards prevalent in one's own.

Ethnic group Ethnic group status results from cultural characteristics such as national origin, language, or religion. Members of ethnic groups recognize a common cultural past.

Ethos Those predominant characteristics of a whole culture system that distinguish it from other culture systems.

Exogamy Marriage outside the tribe, class, or group.

Experimental group In an experiment, a group of subjects is exposed to a treatment (the independent variable) that is withheld from a *control* group. The control group, which is similar in all other respects to the experimental group, is then compared with the experimental group to determine the effect of the treatment.

Fecundity The potential capacity for reproduction.

Feminism An ideology that stresses equality of the sexes.

Feral children Children who have reputedly been reared by animals and not socialized within human society; refers also to neglected children who have been reared with minimal human contact.

Fertility Indication of the actual use of powers of fecundity; measured by the rate of reproduction.

Field experiment An experiment that is conducted outside of the laboratory in a situation not created by the researcher.

Folkways Norms that can be violated without stringent punishment; minor rules of behavior.

Function The consequences of the operation or existence of a component in a social system for the whole or for other components. The functioning of the component parts determines the stability and equilibrium of the whole.

Functionalism A macro-theory in sociology that views society as composed of interrelated elements, each of which functions to maintain itself and to satisfy basic needs that are vital to the stability of the overall system.

Gemeinschaft A kind of social group described by Ferdinand Toennies. Gemeinschaft societies are folk or primary societies where social relationships are long-lasting, personal, and face-to-face and social controls are mainly informal (gossip, ridicule) but with a strong degree of consensus. The Gemeinschaft is most often approximated in rural-agricultural societies.

Gender identity Taking on the nonbiological characteristics associated with sexual differentiation—masculinity or femininity.

Genocide The extermination of a minority group by a majority group.

Gesellschaft This ideal type of urban society is characterized by a large population; thus, face-to-face interactions by all members are impossible. Secondary relationships predominate and social interactions are formal, contractual, expedient, and segmented. The population of the Gesellschaft is heterogeneous and a complex division of labor predominates.

Group Two or more individuals who share a common feeling of unity and identity and who interact in patterned ways based on shared expectations about each other's behavior.

Homogamy The selection of a mate from among those sharing factors such as race, ethnicity, religion, education, age, and class.

Hypothesis An unproven statement or proposition that predicts a relationship between certain variables. A hypothesis frequently takes the form of an "if–then" statement.

Ideal-type An analytical construct of a "pure" form of some social phenomenon. The essential features of the construct are then compared with observed reality.

Ideational cultures Cultures, as described by P. Sorokin, where spiritual and metaphysical values predominate. In such cultures, interest in the supernatural, mysticism, and religion take precedence over interest in science.

Ideology A system of ideas (i.e., beliefs, principles) that is reflected in, and justifies, the activity of a social group or category in society.

Independent variable In cause-and-effect terms, the independent variable is the "cause" variable. Manipulation of this variable in experimental designs results in changes in the dependent variable, the "effect" variable.

In-group Any group toward which a person has a strong sense of belonging and of common ends; developed by identification. The opposite of out-group.

Institutional racism Racial discrimination that results from the day-to-day operations of institutions rather than from specifically prejudiced attitudes. Institutional racism results from indirect processes rather than institutional policy.

Instrumental relationships Relationships typical of the Gesellschaft that are goal or task-oriented. Interactions are begun for specific and limited purposes. Therefore emotional involvements with others are less likely to occur than in the Gemeinschaft.

Intergenerational mobility The movement up or down a system of stratification from one generation to the next. Traditionally the son's occupational mobility has been compared with his father's.

Invention A combination of known elements or devices into some new form.

Labeling theory A theoretical view of deviance that stresses the effects of being labeled a deviant. Imposition of social labels by others may have greater consequences for the deviant than the violation of the norm itself.

Laboratory experiment A controlled experiment that features the construction of an environment by the researcher and deliberate manipulation of that environment for the purpose of testing or establishing a hypothesis.

Labor force That fraction of a society's population engaged in producing and distributing goods and services for remuneration.

Latent function The unintended or unanticipated consequence or end of particular social arrangements.

Laws Prescribed rules of conduct or norms that are established by the State to protect the rights, duties, and liberties of societal members. Violation of these norms is punishable.

Legal-rational authority Authority that is derived from a system of rules and procedures from laws or norms. Legal-rational authority relates to the status or position held by the leader rather than personal qualities.

Life chances The possibilities that exist throughout the life cycle based on social class position—i.e., the chance to stay alive during the first year of life.

Life style Max Weber's concept that describes the goods and services consumed by individuals, the manner in which this occurs, and the values underlying such consumption patterns.

The looking-glass self The self-concept that emerges from social interaction. The fully developed self results from the ability to see one's self reflected in the eyes of important "others."

Magic A practice believed to produce effects by the assistance of supernatural beings or by a mastery of secret forces in nature.

Matriarchal family A form where the mother has primary authority and power within the family.

Matrilineal The family form in which descent is traced through the mother's lineage.

Matrilocal residence A custom which directs the husband and wife to reside with the wife's family.

Mechanical solidarity Durkheim's term for the social cohesion found in traditional or preindustrial societies where pressures for sameness or homogeneity in behavior and attitudes prevail.

Megalopolis The ecological unit which results from the linking of metropolitan areas.

Migration The movement of individuals or groups in space.

Minority Those members of society who are prevented from participating fully and equally in all phases of social life due to prejudice and discrimination.

Mob An emotionally aroused crowd with some purpose such as attack on a person or group, or property; or such as escape from danger—for example, a panic crowd.

Monogamy The marriage form in which the norms require the union of one man and one woman.

Mores Norms which have strong moral meaning and whose violation results in severe sanctions.

Mortality The death rate; usually computed as the number of persons per thousand who die in a given year.

Norms Group-shared expectations or rules about conduct. Folkways, mores, and laws are examples of norms.

Nuclear family A family form comprised of a married couple and their children.

Organic solidarity Durkheim's term for the social cohesion of modern industrial societies where there is a complex division of labor and a large number of specialized roles so the cooperation and interdependence is emphasized.

Out-group Any group toward which a person feels a strong sense of avoidance or opposition. Opposite of in-group.

Participant observation An empirical method in which the researcher becomes a member of the group under study in order to participate in and observe the group's activities. Group members may or may not know that they are being observed.

Patriarchal family Where the father has primary authority and power within the family.

Patrilineal The family form in which descent is traced through the father's lineage.

Patrilocal residence A costom which directs the husband and wife to reside with the husband's family.

Personality Totality of habits, attitudes, ideas, and characteristics of an individual which grow out of the interplay between one's constitutional make-up and one's role and status in the various groups of which one is a member and which determine one's sense of self.

Pluralism A social situation where ethnic and racial groups are accorded equal rights and priveleges and no minorities exist.

Polyandry The marriage form in which the norms permit the union of one woman with two or more men.

Polygyny The marriage form in which the norms permit the union of one man with two or more women. Popularly known as "polygamy."

Population In demography, all the members residing in a geographical area, for example, a nation, a city, a community. In survey research, the total number of those possessing the characteristic(s) under study. It is from the population (sometimes referred to as the universe) that a sample is drawn.

Positivism A philosophical position developed by Auguste Comte that required the use of the methods of the physical sciences in sociological inquiry. Knowledge was to be gained from observation and analysis of social behavior in order to discover the fundamental laws of historical development.

Power The ability to control and dominate others, even if they resist.

Prejudice An emotional, rigid attitude toward a group of people; a misjudgment that one defends.

Prestige The evaluation of a status; the judgment within a society's norms of the desirability of a given status.

Primary deviance Situational deviance that is often temporary and easily concealed. Homosexuality while in prison may or may not make the participant feel like a deviant.

Primary group Basic social group operating through intimate, face-to-face contacts. The source of the early personal-social and cultural training which the individual receives from others; for example, the family, neighborhood, and play group.

Proletariat Marx's term for society's working class that is propertyless and exploited by the bourgeoisie.

Propaganda Open or veiled suggestions and other means of inducing modification or acceptance of certain beliefs, attitudes, and practices.

Public An aggregation of individuals, not necessarily contiguous in space or time, held together through some more or less common interest or common stimulus.

Race A race is a number of people who share a set of innate physical characteristics (i.e., skin color) which are not exclusive to any racial group but overlap among the major groups; there is, however, a higher percentage of certain characteristics in each major group.

Racism An ideology which justifies domination of one race by another on the grounds that the more powerful race is superior.

Random sample A part of a population selected by a technique that gives each member of the population an equal chance to be chosen for the sample.

Recidivism The return to crime which occurs after a prisoner has been released from prison.

Reference group A social group or social category to which the individual refers in regard to attitudes, beliefs, values, and behavior. It is not necessary to be a member of one's reference group.

Representative sample A part of a population whose characteristics accurately correspond to the characteristics of the whole population of interest.

Role The behavior attached to a status; the expectations which are a consequence of occupying a given position in a social structure.

Sample A portion of a population that is studied to gain information about the whole.

Sanctions The rewards or punishments used to enforce the norms in a society.

Scientific theory A logically related set of established or verified statements based on empirical data and offered to explain phenomena or that which has been perceived by the senses.

Secondary deviance When deviant behavior has resulted in labeling of the individual by others, the deviance has become habitual and the life style of the person has been altered to include the deviant behavior.

Secondary group Group founded on conscious common interest, not necessarily dependent on face-to-face relations. Many secondary groups are related to institutions—for example, state, church, and education.

Sect A religious organization with primary group characteristics that is at odds with the institutionalized church. Though a sect may finally break away and establish itself separately, today's sect could be tomorrow's new church.

Segregation In urban ecology, the process in which areas of a city become specialized in relation to population so that residents share common social, ethnic, or racial characteristics, or specialized in relation to services offered.

Sensate cultures Cultures, described by P. Sorokin, in which interest in the results of sensory experience and empirical investigation predominate. In such cultures scientific investigation, skepticism, atheism, and hedonism are valued.

Sexism An ideology or set of beliefs that accepts the domination of males in the social world as the result of a "natural" superiority over females.

Situs A set of related occupational specialities arranged hierarchically.

Social category A plurality of persons, sharing a common characteristic but who do not interact socially, who share no common sense of membership and who have no consciousness of kind.

Social control Formal (police department) or informal (ridicule) social arrangements utilized by society to get individuals and groups to conform to societal norms.

Social dynamics Analysis of social processes producing social change.

Social group A plurality of persons involved in a pattern of social interaction (and shared understandings), conscious of sharing common membership and accepting the rights and obligations that accrue only to members.

Socialization The interactional process by which the individual learns the social–cultural qualities (habits, ideas, attitudes, and so on) that make him or her a member of society and hence a human being.

Social mobility Movement from status to status within the social structure.

Social movement A form of collective behavior where masses of people join to resist or bring about social change.

Social process Modes of action, operation, or interaction among individuals or groups.

Social statics The analysis of social structure revealing elements that produce order and social stability.

Social status (1) A position in a social structure; (2) social honor, prestige, or esteem. Here status connotes evaluations received by individuals.

Social stratification The unequal distribution, persisting over time, of the valued things in society. Social stratification is a form of structured social inequality.

Social system A view of society, as a whole comprised of interrelated parts, much discussed by Talcott Parsons. However, systems theory may also be applied to structures such as the family, the classroom, the bureaucracy.

Society The general term for people living in social interaction. More specifically, the largest social group or aggregate in which more or less common culture patterns are found covering the fundamental institutions.

Sociology The scientific study of the social aspects of human life. The analysis of the structure of social life—the way in which groups are put together—and the way in which they function.

Status conflict Strain resulting from attempts to reconcile the demands and expectations of different statuses.

Status-set The complex of statuses or positions occupied by an individual.

Structure The way the parts of a whole are put together; the relationship of the parts to one another.

Subculture Shared, learned patterns of behavior common to a specific group or category within the larger culture.

Survey research A research method in which the attitudes and behavior of respondents are probed through use of questionnaires. These are either self-administered or administered by trained interviewers.

Symbol Any object, picture, gesture, sign, mark, printed or written matter, or sound which stands for another or serves to recall another, and which directs mental and actional associations.

Symbolic interactionism A theoretical perspective that focuses on the interaction between individuals through symbols, mainly language. Symbolic interactionism stresses the shared significance of day-to-day communications among people interacting in face-to-face situations.

Theology The study of the relationship between human beings and the supernatural forces and beings of the sacred world.

Toleration A form of accommodation in which opposing groups agree to avoid further conflict and "live and let live."

Total institutions Erving Goffman's term for such residential communities as prisons and mental hospitals where all of an individual's activities take place.

Traditional authority Authority that is bestowed through ancient custom. Traditional authority is accepted as legitimate in societies where the norms are believed to be sacred.

Trend data Information gathered in survey research where a time variable has been introduced in the study design. By this method, changes in the attitudes, behaviors, and opinions of respondents may be analyzed.

Triad A group of three persons interacting.

Unidimensional Refers to a test or scale in which a series of items "hang together" to reveal one dimension. Authoritarianism is a single dimension comprised of several distinctive traits.

Urbanization The process of becoming urban.

Validity The correspondence between what a test is supposed to measure (i.e., intelligence) and what it really measures.

Values The quality of desirability (or undesirability) believed to inhere in an idea, object, or action. Values are accepted, in time, by the group in certain orders of priority.

Bibliography

ABRAMS, R. H. Residential propinquity as a factor in marriage selection: Fifty-year trends in Philadelphia. *American Sociological Review*, 1943, *8*, 288–294.

ADLER, F. *Sisters in crime: The rise of the new female criminal.* New York: McGraw-Hill, 1975.

ADORNO, T. W. et al. *The authoritarian personality.* New York: W. W. Norton, 1950.

ALLIHAN, M. A. *Social ecology: A critical analysis.* New York: Columbia University Press, 1938.

ALTMAN, D. *Homosexual oppression and liberation.* New York: Avon, 1971.

Americans marry young, *Statistical Bulletin*, 1947, *28*, No. 2, p. 9.

ANDERSON, C. A. A skeptical note on the relation of vertical mobility. *American Journal of Sociology*, 1961, *66*, 560–570.

ANDERSON, E. L. *We Americans: A study of cleavage in an American city.* Cambridge: Harvard University Press, 1937.

ANDERSON, N. *Desert saints.* Chicago: University of Chicago Press, 1942.

ARMBRUSTER, F. E. The more we spend, the less children learn. *New York Times Magazine*, August 28, 1977, pp. 9–11; 53–60.

ARRINGTON, L. J. *Great basin kingdom: An economic history of Latter-Day Saints, 1830–1900.* Cambridge: Harvard University Press, 1958.

BALES, R. F. & SLATER, P. E. Role differentiation in small decision-making groups. In T. Parsons & R. F. Bales (Eds.), *Family, socialization, and interaction process.* New York: Free Press of Glencoe, 1955.

BALTES, P. B. & SCHAIE, K. W. Aging and IQ: The myth of the twilight years. *Psychology Today*, 1974, 7, 35–40.

BANDURA, A. *Aggression: a social learning analysis.* Englewood Cliffs, N.J.: Prentice-Hall, 1973.

BARNES, H. E. *An introduction to the history of sociology* (Abridged Ed.). Chicago: University of Chicago Press, 1967.

BARRY, H., III, BACON, M. K. & CHILD, I. L. A cross-cultural survey of some sex differences in socialization. *Journal of Abnormal and Social Psychology*, November 1957, *55*, 327–332.

BARUCH, G. *Correlates of girls' evaluation of their competence.* Unpublished manuscript, Radcliffe Institute, 1974.

BASS, B. M. *Leadership, psychology, and organizational behavior.* New York: Harper, 1960.

DE BEAUVOIR, S. *The second sex.* New York: Knopf, 1953.

BECK, B. Welfare as a moral category. *Social Problems*, 1967, *14*, 258–277.

BECKER, H. S. *Outsiders: Studies in the sociology of deviance.* New York: Free Press, 1963.

BELL, W. Familism and suburbanization: One test of the social choice hypothesis. *Rural Sociology*, 1956, *21*, 276–283.

BELL, N. W. & VOGEL, E. F. *The family.* New York: Free Press, 1968.

BENEDICT, R. *Race: Science and politics.* New York: Viking, 1940.

BENEDICT, R. *Patterns of culture.* Baltimore: Penguin Books, 1946.

BENET, S. Why they live to be 100, or even older, in Abkhasia. *New York Times Magazine*, December 26, 1971.

BERGER, B. ET AL. Child-rearing practices of the communal family. In I. L. Reiss (Ed.), *Readings on the family system.* New York: Holt, 1972.

BERGER, P. L. *Invitation to sociology: A humanistic perspective.* Garden City, N.Y.: Doubleday, 1963.

BERLE, A. A. JR. *Power without property.* New York: Harcourt, 1959.

BERNARD, J. *The future of marriage.* New York: Bantam, 1973.

BERREMAN, G. D. Caste in India and the United States. *American Journal of Sociology,* 1960, *66,* 120–127.

BERRY, B. *Race and ethnic relations.* (2nd ed.). Boston: Houghton Mifflin, 1958.

BESLE, A. A. & MEANS, C. C. *The modern corporation and private property.* New York: Macmillan, 1933.

BESTOR, A. E. *Backwoods utopias: The sectarian and Owenite phases of communitarian socialism in America, 1663–1829.* Philadelphia: University of Pennsylvania Press, 1950

BETTLEHEIM, B. Feral children and autistic children. *The American Journal of Sociology,* 1959, *64,* 467.

BIERSTEDT, R. *Emile Durkheim.* New York: Dell, 1966.

BIRNBAUM, J. Life patterns, personality style and self-esteem in gifted family-oriented and career-committed women (Doctoral dissertation, University of Michigan, 1971).

BLAU, P. M. *The dynamics of bureaucracy.* Chicago: University of Chicago Press, 1955.

BLAU, P. M. *Bureaucracy in modern society.* New York: Random House, 1956.

BLAU, P. M. *Exchange and power in social life.* New York: Wiley, 1964.

BLAU, P. M. The flow of occupational supply and recruitment. *American Sociological Review,* 1965, *30,* 475–490.

BLAU, P. M. & SCOTT, W. R. *Formal organizations: A comparative approach.* San Francisco: Chandler, 1962.

BLAUNER, R. *Racial oppression in America.* New York: Harper, 1972.

BLOOM, L. & RIEMER, R. *Removal and return: The socio-economic effects of the war on Japanese Americans.* Berkeley: University of California Press, 1949.

BLUMER, H. Collective behavior. In A. M. Lee (Ed.), *Principles of sociology* (Rev. ed.). New York: Barnes and Noble, 1951.

BOAS, F. *Race, language and culture.* New York: Mecmillan, 1948.

BOGUE, D. J. *The population of the United States.* Glencoe: The Free Press, 1959.

BONJEAN, C. M. Community leadership: A case study and conceptual refinement. *American Journal of Sociology,* 1963, *68,* 672–681.

BOSSARD, J. H. S. Residential propinquity as a factor in marriage selection. *American Journal of Sociology,* 1932, *38,* 219–224.

BREDEMEIER, H. C. & STEPHENSON, R. M. *The analysis of social systems.* New York: Holt, 1964.

BRONFENBRENNER, U. The changing American family. *AFL-CIO American Federationist,* February, 1977, 7–11.

BROWN, J. K. Iroquois women: An ethno historic note. In R. Reiter (Ed.), *Toward an anthropology of women.* New York: Monthly Review Press, 1975.

BURGESS, E. W. & WALLIN, P. *Engagement and marriage.* Philadelphia: Lippincott, 1953.

BURKEY, R. *Ethnic and racial groups: The dynamics of dominance.* Menlo Park, California: Cummings, 1978.

BURMA, J. H. Research note on the measurement of interracial marriage. *American Journal of Sociology,* 1952, *57,* 587–589.

BURNETTE, R. *The tortured Americans.* Englewood Cliffs, N.J.: Prentice-Hall, 1971.

BUTTERFIELD, F. Newark's new minority, the Italians, demands equity. *The New York Times,* August 28, 1971, p. B27.

CANTRIL, H. Education and economic composition of religious groups: An analysis of poll data. *American Journal of Sociology,* 1943, *48,* 574–579.

CARMICHAEL, S. & HAMILTON, C. *Black power: The politics of liberation in America.* New York: Random House, 1967.

CARNEY, L. P. *Corrections in the community.* Englewood Cliffs, N.J.: Prentice-Hall, 1977.

CENTERS, R. Occupational mobility or urban occupational strata. *American Sociological Review,* 1948, *13,* 197–203.

CENTERS, R. *The psychology of social classes.* Princeton: Princeton University Press, 1949.

CHESNEY-LIND, M. Judicial enforcement of the female sex role: The family court and the female delinquent. *Issues in Criminology,* 1973, *8,* 51–69.

CHINOY, E. The tradition of opportunity and the aspirations of automobile workers. *American Journal of Sociology,* 1952, *57,* 453–459.

CHINOY, E. *Society: An introduction to sociology.* New York: Random House, 1963.

CHRISTENSEN, H. T. Mormon fertility: A survey of student opinion. *American Journal of Sociology,* 1948, *53,* 270–275.

CLARK, B. R. The "cooling-out" function in higher education. *American Journal of Sociology, 65,* May, 1960, 569–576.

CLARK, K. B. *Dark ghetto: Dilemmas of social power.* New York: Harper, 1965.

CLARK, M. & ANDERSON, B. *Culture and aging.* Springfield, Ill.: C. C. Thomas, 1967.

CLAY, HENRY. *Economics for the general reader.* New York: Macmillan, 1918.

Closeups of corporate bias. *Business Week*, November 24, 1975, p. 63.

COATES, C. H. & PELLEGRIN, R. J. Executives and supervisors: A situational theory of differential occupational mobility. *Social Forces*, 1956, *35*, 121-126.

CODRINGTON, R. H. Man. In W. A. Lessa & E. Z. Voqt (Eds.), *Reader in comparative religion* (2nd ed.). New York: Harper, 1965.

COHEN, A. K. The study of social disorganization and deviant behavior. In R. K. Merton, L. Broom, & L. S. Cottrell, Jr. (Eds.), *Sociology Today*. New York: Basic Books, 1959.

COHEN, A. K. & SHORT, J. F. JR. Research in delinquent subcultures. *Journal of Social Issues*, 1958, *14*, 20-37.

COLEMAN, J. *U.S. National Center for Educational Statistics: Equality of educational opportunity*. Washington, D.C.: U.S. Government Printing Office, 1966.

COLEMAN, J. S. Social cleavage and religious conflict. *Journal of Social Issues*, 1956, *12*, 44-56.

COMFORT, A. *A good age*. New York: Crown, 1976.

CONRAD, J. P. Corrections and simple justice. *Aldine Crime and Justice Annual 1973*, 1974, p. 516.

CONWAY, M. M. *The crowd in peace and war*. New York: Longmans, Green, 1915.

COOLEY, C. H. *Human nature and the social order*. New York: Charles Scribner's Sons, 1902.

COOLEY, C. H. *Social organization*. New York: Charles Scribner's Sons, 1909.

COOLEY, C. H. *Sociological theory and social research*. New York: Henry Holt, 1930.

COOLEY, C. H. *Human nature and the social order*. New York: Schocken, 1964.

COON, C. S. & PUTNAM, P. The pygmies of the Ituri forest. In C. S. Coon (Ed.), *A reader in general anthropology*. New York: Henry Holt, 1948.

COOPER, D. *The death of the family*. New York: Random House, 1970.

COSER, L. A. Social conflict and the theory of social change. *The British Journal of Sociology*, 1957, *8*, 197-198.

CRESSEY, D. R. *Criminal organization: Its elementary forms*. New York: Harper, 1972.

Crime in the United States: Uniform Crime Reports. Washington, D.C.: U.S. Government Printing Office, 1976.

DAHRENDORF, R. Toward a theory of social conflict. *Journal of Conflict Resolution*, 1958, *2*, p. 218.

DALLIN, D. *The real Soviet Russia*. New Haven: Yale University Press, 1944.

DARWIN, C. *The origin of species* and *The descent of man*. New York: Modern Library, 1948 (*Origin* originally published 1859; *Descent* originally published 1871).

DAVIDSON, P. E. & ANDERSON, H. D. *Occupational mobility in an American community*. Stanford, Calif.: Stanford University Press, 1937.

DAVIE, M. R. The pattern of urban growth. In G. P. Murdock (Ed.), *Studies in the science of society*. New Haven: Yale University Press, 1937.

DAVIS, A., GARDNER, B. B. & GARDNER, M. R. *Deep south*. Chicago: University of Chicago Press, 1941.

DAVIS, K. The sociology of prostitution. *American Sociological Review*, *2*, 1937, 744-755.

DAVIS, K. Extreme social isolation of a child. *American Journal of Sociology*, 1940, *45*, 554-565.

DAVIS, K. Final note on a case of extreme isolation. *The American Journal of Sociology*, 1947, *52*, 432-437.

DAVIS, K. *Human society*. New York: Macmillan, 1949.

DAVIS, K. The origin and growth of urbanization in the world. *American Journal of Sociology*, 1955, *60*, 429-437.

DAVIS, K. The unpredicted pattern of population change. *Annals of the American Academy of Political and Social Science*, 1956, *305*, 53-59.

DAVIS, K. The theory of change and response in modern demographic history. *Population Index*, 1963, *29*, 345-366.

DAVIS, K. & MOORE, W. E. Some principles of stratification. *American Sociological Review*, 1945, *10*, 242-249.

Department of Mass Communication, UNESCO. *What is race? Evidence from scientists*. Paris: United Nations Educational Scientific and Cultural Organization, 1952.

DEWEY, R. Peripheral expansion in Milwaukee county. *American Journal of Sociology*, 1948, *54*, 118-125.

DEWHURST, J. F. *America's needs and resources: A new survey*. New York: The Twentieth Century Fund, 1955.

Do Americans go to church? *Catholic Digest*, 1952, *7*, 1-7.

DOBZHANSKY, T. *Genetics of the evolutionary process*. New York: Columbia University Press, 1970.

DRUCKER, P. *Concept of the corporation*. New York: John Day, 1946.

DUBOIS, W. E. B. *The suppression of the African slave trade 1638-1870*. New York: Schocken, 1969 (originally published 1896).

DUNCAN, O. D. The trend of occupational mobility in the United States. *American Sociological Review*, 1965, *30*, 498.

DUNNELL, K. & CARTWRIGHT, A. *Medicine takers, prescribers, and hoarders*. London: Routledge and Kegan Paul, 1972.

DURKHEIM, E. *The elementary forms of religious life*. New York: The Free Press, 1947.

DURKHEIM, E. *The division of labor in society*. Glencoe Ill.: Free Press, 1949 (originally published 1893).

DURKHEIM, E. *Suicide: A study in sociology* (trans. John A. Spaulding and George Simpson). New York: Free Press, 1951 (originally published, 1897).

DYNES, R. R. Church-sect typology and socioeconomic status. *American Sociological Review*, 1955, *20*, 555–560.

EDWARDS, A. D. Ecological patterns of American rural communities. *Rural Sociology*, 1947, *12*, 150–161.

EDWARDS, D. A. Early androgen stimulation and aggressive behavior in male and female mice. *Physiology and Behavior*, 1969, *4*, 333–338.

EINSTEIN, A. Science and religion. *Science Newsletter*, September 21, 1940, p. 182.

ELIOT, G. *Felix Holt, the radical* (3 vols.). Edinburgh: William Blackwell, 1866.

ELKINS, S. *Slavery: A problem in American institutional and intellectual life*. Chicago: University of Chicago Press, 1969.

ELLSWORTH, J. S. The relationship of population density to residential propinquity as a factor in marriage selection. *American Sociological review*, 1948, *13*, 444–448.

ERIKSON, E. *Childhood and society*. New York: Norton, 1950.

EVANS, B. *The natural history of nonsense*. New York: Vintage Books, 1946.

EVANS-PRITCHARD, E. E. *The Nuer: A description of the modes of livelihood and political institutions of a Nilotic people*. Oxford: Clarendon Press, 1968.

FARLEY, R. & HERMALIN, A. The 1960s: A decade of progress for Blacks? *Demography*, 1972, *9*, 353.

FAVA, S. F. Suburbanism as a way of life. *American Sociological Review*, 1956, *21*, 34–37.

296 Federal Reporter 929. *Society of the sisters of the Holy Names of Jesus and Mary V. Pierce, Governor of Oregon*. Case affirmed in 268 U.S. Reporter 510.

FIREY, W. *Land use in central Boston*. Cambridge: Harvard University Press, 1947.

FLEISCHMANN, M. ET AL. *The Fleischmann report on the quality, cost and financing of elementary and secondary education in New York State*, Vol. 1. New York: Viking, 1973.

FOGEL, R. W. & ENGERMAN, S. L. *Time on the cross: The economics of American Negro slavery*. Boston: Little, Brown, 1974.

FREEMAN, J. Growing up girlish. *Transaction*, 1970, *8* (1+2), 36–43.

FREEMAN, L. C. Marriage without love: Mate selection in non-western societies. In R. F. Winch, *Mate selection: A study of complementary needs*. New York: Harper, 1958.

FREUD, S. *The future of an illusion* (W. D. Robson-Scott, trans.). New York: Liveright, 1928.

FREYRE, G. *The mansions and the shanties*. New York: Knopf, 1963.

FRIEDAN, B. *The feminine mystique*. New York: Dell, 1963.

FRIEDL, E. *Women and men: An anthropologist's view*. New York: Holt, 1975.

GALBRAITH, J. K. *The new industrial state*. Boston: Houghton Mifflin, 1967.

GANS, H. J. *The Levittowners: Way of life and politics in a New York suburban community*. New York: Pantheon, 1967.

GARDNER, R. A. & GARDNER, B. Teaching sign language to a chimpanzee. *Science 165*, 664–672.

GARFINKEL, H. Conditions of successful degradation ceremonies. *American Journal of Sociology*, 1956, *61*, 420–424.

GERTH, H. H. & MILLS, C. W. (eds. & trans.). *From Max Weber: Essays in sociology*. New York: Oxford University Press, 1946.

GERTH, H. H. & MILLS, C. W. *Character and social structure*. New York: Harcourt, 1954.

GIBBS, J. P. & DAVIS, K. Conventional versus metropolitan data in the international study of urbanization. *American Sociological Review*, 1958, *23*, 504–514.

GIDDINGS, F. H. *Principles of sociology*. New York: Macmillan, 1896.

GILLIAM, D. B. *Paul Robeson: All-American*. Washington, D.C.: New Republic, 1976.

GIST, N. Ecological decentralization and rural-urban relationships. *Rural Sociology*, 1952, *17*, 328–335.

GLENN, N. D. Aging, disengagement, and opinionation. *Public Opinion Quarterly*, 1969, *33*, 17–33.

GLENN, N. D. & GRIMES, M. Aging, voting, and political interest. *American Sociological Review*, 1968, *33*, 563–575.

GLICK, P. C. & LANDAU, E. Age as a factor in marriage. *American Sociological Review*, 1950, *15*, 517–529.

GOFFMAN, E. *Asylums: Essays on the social*

situation of mental patients and other inmates. Chicago: Aldine, 1961.

GOFFMAN, E. *Stigma: Notes on the management of spoiled identity.* Englewood Cliffs, N.J.: Prentice-Hall, 1963.

GOLDMAN, I. The Zuñi Indians of New Mexico. In M. Mead (Ed.), *Cooperation and competition among primitive peoples.* New York: McGraw-Hill, 1937.

GOLDTHORPE, J. E. *An introduction to sociology.* Cambridge, England: 1968.

GOODMAN, M. E. *Race awareness in young people.* Reading, Mass.: Addison-Wesley, 1952.

GOODMAN, P. *People and personnel* and *Like a conquered province.* New York: Vintage Books, 1968.

GORDON, M. J. *Assimilation in American life.* New York: Oxford University Press, 1964.

GOWIN, E. B. *The executive and his control of men.* New York: Macmillan, 1915.

GREELEY, A. M. *Unsecular man: The persistence of religion.* New York: Schocken, 1972.

GREELEY, A. M. *Ethnicity in the United States: A preliminary reconnaissance.* New York: Wiley Interscience, 1974.

GREENBLATT, M. & GLAZIER, E. The phasing out of mental hospitals in the United States. *American Journal of Psychiatry,* 1975, *132,* 1135–1140.

GREENE, F. *The Far East.* New York: Rinehart, 1957.

GRODZINS, M. *Americans betrayed.* Chicago: University of Chicago Press, 1949.

HAMMOND, D. & JABLOW, A. *Women in cultures of the world.* Menlo Park, Calif.: Cummings, 1976.

HAMMOND, P. Aging and the ministry. In M. W. Riley et al. (Eds.), *Aging and society II: Aging and the professions.* Russell Sage Foundation, 1969.

HARE, A. P. *Handbook of small group research.* Glencoe, Ill.: Free Press, 1962.

HARLOW, H. F. & HARLOW, M. K. Social deprivation in monkeys. *Scientific American,* 1962, *207,* November, 137–147.

HARLOW, H. F. & ZIMMERMAN, R. Z. Affectional responses in the infant monkey. *Science,* 1959, *130,* 421–432.

HARP, J. & TAIETZ, P. Academic integrity and social structure: A study of cheating among college students. *Social Problems,* 1966, *13,* 365–373.

HARRIS, M. *Patterns of race in the Americas.* New York: Walker, 1964.

HATT, P. K. Spatial patterns in a polytechnic area. *American Sociological Review,* 1945, *10,* 352–356.

HATT, P. K. The concept of natural area. *American Sociology Review,* 1946, *2,* 423–427.

HAVENS, E. Women, work and wedlock: A note on female marital patterns in the United States. *American Journal of Sociology,* 1973, *78,* 975–981.

HAWLEY, A. H. *Human ecology: A theory of community structure.* New York: Ronald Press, 1950.

HEILBRONER, R. L. *The making of economic society.* Englewood Cliffs, N.J.: Prentice-Hall, 1962.

HELLE, H. J. *Die unstetig beschäftigten Hafenarbeiter in den nordwest-europäischen Häfen: eine industrie-soziologische Untersuchung in Antwerpen, Bremen, Bremerhaven, Hamburg und Rotterdam* (The unsteadily employed longshoremen in the ports of northwestern Europe: An industrial sociological investigation in Antwerp, Bremen, Bremerhaven, Hamburg and Rotterdam). Stuttgart: G. Fischer, 1960.

HENNESSY, B. *Public opinion* (2nd ed.). Belmont, California: Wadsworth, 1970.

HERBERG, W. *Protestant, Catholic, Jew.* Garden City, N.Y.: Doubleday, 1956.

HERBERG, W. *Protestant–Catholic–Jew: An essay in American religious sociology.* Garden City, N.Y.: Doubleday, 1957.

HERTZLER, J. O. *Social progress.* New York: Appleton-Century-Crofts, 1928.

HERTZLER, J. O. Some tendencies toward a closed class system in the United States. *Social Forces,* 1952, *30,* 313–323.

HINTZE, H. *Regionalism.* Vol. 13. *Encyclopedia of the social sciences.* New York: Macmillan, 1934.

HOLLINGSHEAD, A. B. *Elmstown's youth.* New York: Wiley & Sons, 1949.

HOLLINGSHEAD, A. B. Cultural factors in the selection of marriage mates. *American Sociological Review,* 1950, *15,* 517–529.

HOLLINGSHEAD, A. B. Age relationship and marriage. *American Sociological Review,* 1951, *16,* 492–499.

HOLLINGSHEAD, A. B. *Elmtown's youth* and *Elmtown revisited.* New York: Wiley, 1975.

HOMANS, G. C. *The human group.* New York: Harcourt, 1950.

HOMANS, G. C. *Social behavior: Its elementary forms.* New York: Harcourt, 1961.

Homosexuality in prisons. U. S. Department of Justice, National Institute of Law Enforcement and Criminal Justice. Washington, D.C.: U.S. Government Printing Office (February, 1972), 12–13.

HORNER, M. *Sex differences in achievement motivation and performance in competitive and non-competitive situations.* Unpublished doctoral dissertation, University of Michigan, 1968.

HORNER, M. Fail: Bright women. *Psychology Today,* 1969, *3(6),* 36–38; 62.

HORNER, M. Toward an understanding of achievement-related conflicts in women. *Journal of Social Issues,* 1972, *29,* 157–175.

HOROWITZ, I. L. The life and death of Project Camelot. *Transaction,* 1965, *3,* 3–7.

HOROWITZ, I. L. & RAINWATER, L. Journalistic moralizers. In I. L. Horowitz & C. Nanry (Eds.), *Sociological realities II: A guide to the study of society.* New York: Harper & Row, 1975.

HOYT, H. *The structure and growth of residential neighborhoods in American cities.* Washington, D.C.: Federal Housing Administration, 1939.

HUMPHREYS, L. *Tearoom trade: Impersonal sex in public places.* Chicago: Aldine, 1970.

HUNTER, F. *Community power structure: A study of decision makers.* Chapel Hill: University of North Carolina Press, 1953.

HURD, R. M. *Principles of city land values* (4th ed.). New York: Real Estate Record and Guide, 1924.

HYMAN, H. The value systems of different classes. In R. Bendix & S. M. Lipset (Eds.), *Class, status and power.* Glencoe, Ill.: The Free Press, 1953.

ILLICH, IVAN. *Deschooling society.* New York: Harper & Row, 1970.

Illinois ex rel. McCollum V. Board of Education, school District No. 71, Champaign County, Illinois, et al. *333 U.S. Official Reporter,* No. 2, 203–256.

INGRAHAM, J. C. Autos in urban regions rule and frustrate living. *New York Times,* January 28, 1957, p. 1.

INKELES, A. Social stratification and mobility in the Soviet Union: 1940–1950. *American Sociological Review,* 1950, *15,* 465–470.

INKELES, A. & ROSSI, P. H. National comparison of occupational prestige. *American Journal of Sociology,* 1956, *61,* 329–339.

JACKSON, E. F. & CROCKETT, H. J., JR. Occupational mobility in the United States: A point estimate and trend comparison. *American Sociological Review,* 1964, *24,* 25.

JAMES, J. A critique of Firey's land use in central Boston. *American Journal of Sociology,* 1948, *54,* 228-234.

JANOWITZ, M. *The professional soldier: A social and political portrait.* New York: Free Press of Glencoe, 1960.

JENCKS, C. ET AL. *Inequality: A reassessment of the effect of family and schooling in America.* New York: Harper & Row, 1972.

JENNINGS, E. E. *An anatomy of leadership.* New York: Harper & Row, 1960.

JENSEN, A. R. How much can we boost I.Q. and scholastic achievement? *Harvard Educational Review,* Winter, 1969, *39,* 1–123.

KAGAN, J. & LEMKIN, J. The child's differential perception of parental attributes. *Journal of Abnormal and Social Psychology,* 1960, *61,* 440–447.

KANTER, R. M. Commitment and social organization: A study of commitment mechanisms in utopian communities. *American Sociological Review,* 1968, *33,* 499–517.

KANTER, R. M. Communes for all reason. *Ms,* 1974, *3,* 62–67.

KARDINER, ABRAM. *The individual and his society.* New York: Columbia University Press, 1939.

KATZ, M. L. *Female motive to avoid success: A psychological barrier or a response to deviance.*

KELLOGG, W. N. & KELLOGG, L. A. *The ape and the child.* New York: McGraw-Hill, 1933.

KENNEDY, R. J. R. Premarital residential propinquity and ethnic endogamy. *American Journal of Sociology,* 1943, *48,* 580–584.

KENNEDY, R. J. R. Single or triple melting pot? Intermarriage in New Haven, 1870–1950. *American Journal of Sociology,* 1952, *58,* 56–59.

KERCKHOFF, A. C. Nuclear and extended family relationships: A normative and behavioral analysis. In E. Shanas & G. Streib (Eds.), *Social structure and the family: Generational relations.* Englewood Cliffs, N.J.: Prentice-Hall, 1965.

KING, C. W. *Social movements in the United States.* New York: Random House, 1956.

KINSEY, A. C., POMEROY, W. B. & MARTIN, C. E. *Sexual behavior in the human male.* Philadelphia: W. B. Saunders, 1948.

KINSEY, A. C. *Sexual behavior in the human female.* Philadelphia: W. B. Saunders, 1953.

KIRKPATRICK, C. *The family as process and institution.* New York: Ronald Press, 1963.

KISER, C. V. & WHELPTON, P. K. Social and psychological factors affecting fertility, II: Variations in the size of completed families of 6,551 native white couples in Indianapolis. *Milbank Memorial Fund Quarterly,* 1944, *22,* 72–105.

KNIGHT, M. Harvard admissions plan held a model of flexibility. *New York Times,* June 29, 1978, A23.

KOHLBERG, L. & GILLIGAN, C. The adolescent as a philosopher. The discovery of the self in a post conventional world. *Daedalus* (Fall, 1971), 1051–1086.

KOMISAR, L. The new feminism. *Saturday Review*, 1970, *53*, 27–30, 55.

KOVEL, J. *White racism*. New York: Pantheon, 1970.

LABOVITZ, S. & HAGEDORN, R. *Introduction to social research*. New York: McGraw-Hill, 1971.

LAMPARD, E. E. *Industrial revolution: Interpretations and perspectives*. Washington, D.C.: American Historical Association, 1957.

LAMPMAN, R. Changes in the share of wealth by top wealth-holders 1922–1956. *Review of Economics and Statistics*, 1959, *41*, 379–392.

LAMPMAN, R. J. Income distribution and poverty. In M. S. Gordon (Ed.), *Poverty in America*. San Francisco.: Chandler, 1965.

LANDECKER, W. S. Class boundaries. *American Sociological Review*, 1960, *25*, 868–877.

LANDIS, P. H. & DAY, K. H. Education as a factor in mate selection. *American Sociological Review*, 1945, *10*, 558–560.

LASSWELL, H. O. *Psychopathology and politics*. Chicago: University of Chicago Press, 1930.

LASSWELL, T. E. A study of social stratification using an area sample of raters. *American Sociological Review*, 1954, *19*, 310–313.

LEAF, A. Getting old. *Scientific American*, 1973, *229* (No. 3), 44-52.

LEHRMAN, R. L. *The long road to man*. New York: Basic Books, 1961.

LEMERT, E. *Human deviance, social problems and social control*, Englewood Cliffs, N.J.: Prentice-Hall, 1972.

LEMERT, E. M. *Social pathology*. New York: McGraw-Hill, 1951.

LENSKI, G. E. American social classes: Statistical strata or social groups? *American Journal of Sociology*, 1952, *58*, 139–144.

LENSKI, G. E. Social correlates of religious interest. *American Sociological Review*, 1953, *18*, 533–544.

LENSKI, G. E. *Power and privilege*. New York: McGraw-Hill, 1966.

LEVITAN, S. A. & HETRICK, B. *Big brother's Indian programs—with reservations*. New York: McGraw-Hill, 1971.

LICHTHEIM, G. *Marxism: A historical and critical study*. New York: Praeger, 1969.

LICHTHEIM, G. *A short history of socialism*. New York: Praeger, 1970.

LIEBOW, E. *Tally's corner*. Boston: Little, Brown, 1967.

LINTON, R. *The study of man*. New York: Appleton-Century-Crofts, 1936.

LINTON, R. *The cultural background of personality*. New York: Appleton, 1945.

LIPSET, S. M. & BENDIX, R. Social mobility and occupational career patterns. *American Journal of Sociology*, 1952, *57*, 366–374, 494–504.

LITWAK, E. Three ways in which law acts as a means of social control: Punishment, therapy, and education. *Social Forces*, 1956, *34*, 217–223.

LORENZ, K. *On aggression*. New York: Bantam, 1966.

MACCRONE, I. D. *Race attitudes in South Africa*. Oxford, 1937.

MACIVER, R. M. & PAGE, C. H. *Society*. New York: Holt, Rinehart and Winston, 1949.

MACK, R. W. Housing as an index of social class. *Social Forces*, 1951, *29*, 391–400.

MACK, R. W., FREEMAN, L. & YELLIN, S. *Social mobility: Thirty years of research and theory*. Syracuse: Syracuse University Press, 1957.

MACK, R. W., MURPHY, R. J. & YELLIN, S. The Protestant ethic, level of aspiration, and social mobility: An empirical test. *American Sociological Review*, 1956, *21*, 295–300.

MACK, R. W. & SNYDER, R. C. The analysis of social conflict—Toward an overview and synthesis. *Journal of Conflict Resolution*, 1957, *I*, 212–248.

MACLEISH, K. & YOUNG, K. *Culture of a contemporary rural community*. No. 3 Rural life studies. Washington, D.C.: Dept. of Agriculture, 1942.

MALINOWSKI, B. Marriage. *Encyclopaedia Britannica*, 14th ed., 1929, *14*, 940–950.

MALINOWSKI, B. Culture. *Encyclopedia of the Social Sciences*. New York: Macmillan, 1931.

MANARD, B. B. & KART, C. S. Social factors and institutionalization of the elderly. In C. S. Kart & B. B. Manard (Eds.), *Aging in America*. New York: Alfred, 1976.

MANKOFF, M. Societal reaction and career deviance: A critical analysis. *Sociological Quarterly*, 1971, *12*, 204–218.

MANNEY, J. D., JR. *Aging in American society*. Ann Arbor, Mich.: The Institute of Gerontology, The University of Michigan–Wayne State University, 1975.

MARDEN, C. F. & MEYER, G. *Minorities in American society*, fifth edition. New York: D. Van Nostrand, 1978.

MARSHALL, G. Racial classifications, popular and scientific. In M. Mead, et al. (Eds.) *Science and the concept of race*. New York: Columbia University Press, 1968.

MARSHALL, J. B. America's best managed companies. *Duns Review and Modern Industry*, 1960, *75*, 38–40.

MARSHALL, S. L. A. *Crimsoned prairie: The Indian wars on the great plains*. New York: Scribner's 1972.

MARTIN, K. & VOORHIES, B. *Female of the*

species. New York: Columbia University Press, 1975.
MARTINDALE, DON. *The nature and types of sociological theory.* Boston: Houghton Mifflin, 1960.
MARX, K. *Capital, the Communist manifesto and other writings* (M. Eastman, Ed). New York: Modern Library, 1959.
MASON, M. K. Learning to speak after six and one-half years of silence. *Journal of Speech Disorders,* 1942, *1,* 295–304.
MATZA, D. & SYKES, G. M. Juvenile delinquency and subterranean values. *American Sociological Review,* 1961, *26,* 712–719.
MAXFIELD, F. N. *What happens when the social environment of a child approaches zero.* Unpublished manuscript. Cited by K. Davis, *Human Society.* New York: Macmillan, 1948, p. 206.
MAY, M. A. & DOOB, L. W. *Competition and co-operation* (Bulletin No. 25). New York: Social Science Research Council, 1937.
MAYER, A. J. & HAUSER, P. Class differentials in expectation of life at birth. In R. Bendix & S. M. Lipset (Eds.), *Class, status and power.* Glencoe, Ill.: The Free Press, 1953.
MAYER, K. B. *Class and society.* New York: Random House, 1955.
MAZUR, A. & ROBERTSON, L. S. *Biology and social behavior.* New York: Free Press, 1972.
McCLUSKY, H. Y. Adult education. In R. H. Kurtz (Ed.), *Social Work Year Book, 1957.* New York: National Association of Social Workers, 1957.
McKEE, J. B. *Introduction to sociology.* New York: Holt, Rinehart and Winston, 1969.
MEAD, G. H. Mind, self, and society. In C. W. Morris (Ed.), *From the standpoint of a social behaviorist.* Chicago: University of Chicago Press, 1934.
MEAD, M. The role of the individual in Samoan culture. *Journal of the Royal Anthropological Institute of Great Britain and Ireland,* 1928, *58,* 481–495.
MEAD, M. *Sex and temperament in three primitive societies.* New York: Morrow, 1935.
MEAD, M. (Ed.) *Co-operation and competition among primitive peoples.* New York: McGraw-Hill, 1937.
MECHANIC, D. *Medical sociology.* New York: The Free Press, 1968.
MERTON, R. K. *Social theory and social structure* (Rev. ed.). New York: Free Press, 1957, 1967.
MIDDLETON, R. A deviant case: Brother-sister and father-daughter marriage in ancient Egypt. *American Sociological Review,* October, 1962, *27,* 603–611.
MILLER, D. *Handbook of research design and social measurement.* New York: David McKay, 1964.
MILLER, S. J. The social dilemma of the aging leisure participant. In A. M. Rose & W. Peterson (Eds.), *Older people and their social worlds.* Philadelphia: Saunders, 1965.
MILLET, K. *Sexual politics.* Garden City, N.Y.: Doubleday, 1970.
MILLS, C. W. *The power elite.* New York: Oxford University Press, 1956.
MILLS, C. W. *The sociological imagination.* New York: Oxford University Press, 1959.
MOBERG, D. O. Religiosity in old age. *The Gerontologist,* 1965, *5,* 78-187.
MONEY, J. Sexual dimorphism and homosexual gender identity. *Psychological Bulletin,* 1970, *74,* 425–440.
MONEY, J. & EHRHARDT, A. A. *Man and woman, boy and girl.* Baltimore: Johns Hopkins, 1972.
MOSCA, G. *The ruling class.* New York: McGraw-Hill, 1939.
Moving the masses in modern cities. New York: American Transit Association, n.d., pp. 24, 25 (pamphlet).
MUKERJEE, M. Population theory and politics. *American Sociological Review,* 1941, *6,* 784–793.
MULLIGAN, R. A. Socio-economic background and college enrollment. *American Sociological Review,* 1951, *16,* 188–196.
MURDOCK, G. P. *Social structure.* New York: The Free Press, 1965.
MYRDAL, G. *An American dilemma.* New York: Harper & Brothers, 1944.
NAGEL, S. S. & WEITZMAN, L. T. Double standard of American justice. *Society 19,* 1972, *5,* 18–25.
NANCE, J. *The gentle Tasaday: A stone age people in the Phillippine Rain Forest.* New York: Harcourt, 1975.
NATIONAL RESOURCES COMMITTEE. *Regional factors in national planning and development.* Washington, D.C.: U.S. Government Printing Office, 1935.
NATIONAL RESOURCES COMMITTEE. *Urban government.* Washington, D.C.: U.S. Government Printing Office, 1939.
NEWMAN, O. *Defensible space.* New York: Macmillan, 1972.
A new twist to the double helix. *Matrix: A report on research at Rutgers.* New Brunswick, N. J.: Department of Public Information, 1977.
NISHIMOTO, R. S. & THOMAS, D. S. *The salvage.* University of California Press, 1946.
NORTH, C. G. & KATT, P. K. Jobs and occupations: A popular evaluation. *Opinion News,* 1947, *9,* 3–13.
NOTESTEIN, F. W. Problems of policy in relation to areas of heavy population pressure. In

Demographic studies of selected areas of rapid growth. New York: Milbank Memorial Fund, 1944.

NOTTINGHAM, E. K. *Religion and society.* New York: Random House, 1954.

NOVAK, M. *The rise of the unmeltable ethnics.* New York: Macmillan, 1974.

O'DEA, T. F. *The Mormons.* Chicago: University of Chicago press, 1957.

OGBURN, W. F. *The social characteristics of cities.* Chicago: International City Manager's Association, 1937.

OGBURN, W. F. *Social change.* New York: Viking Press, 1950.

OGBURN, W. F. The wolf boy of Agra. *The American Journal of Sociology,* 1959, *64,* 449–454.

O'MALLEY, L. S. S. *Indian caste customs.* London: Cambridge University Press, 1932.

O'NEILL, N. & O'NEILL, G. *Open marriage.* New York: Avon Books, 1972.

ORTNER, S. B. Is female to male as nature is to culture? In M. Z. Rosaldo and L. Lamphere (Eds.), *Woman, culture and society.* Stanford: Stanford University Press, 1974.

OSOFSKY, G. *The burden of race: A documentary history of Negro-white relations in America.* New York: Harper & Row, 1967.

PAGE, C. H. Bureaucracy's other face. *Social Forces,* 1946, *25,* 88–94.

PALSON, C. & PALSON, R. Swinging in wedlock. In I. L. Horowitz and C. Nanry (Eds.), *Sociological realities II: A guide to the study of society.* New York: Harper & Row, 1975.

PARKE, R., JR. & GLICK, P. C. Prospective changes in marriage and family. *Journal of Marriage and the Family,* 1967, *29,* 249–256.

PARSONS, T. *The social system.* New York: The Free Press, 1951.

PARSONS, T. & BALES, R. F. *Family, socialization, and interaction process.* Glencoe, Ill.: Free Press, 1953.

PATTERSON, G. R. ET AL. Assertive behavior in children: A step toward a theory of aggression. *Monographs of the Society for Research in Child Development,* 1967, *32,* serial no. 113.

PECHMAN, J. The rich, the poor, and the taxes they pay. *The Public Interest,* 1968, *17,* 21–43.

PERKINSON, H. J. *The imperfect panacea: American faith in education, 1865–1965.* New York: Random House, 1968.

PETER, L. J. & HULL, R. *The Peter principle.* New York: William Morrow, 1969.

PIAGET, J. & INHELDER, B. *The psychology of the child.* New York: Basic Books, 1969.

POPE, L. Religion and the class structure. *Annals of the American Academy of Political and Social Science,* 1948, *256,* 84–91.

The Pope's encyclical on education. *Current History,* 1930, *31,* 1101.

Population still moving westward. *Statistical Bulletin,* 1955, *36,* p. 8.

PORTEUS, S. D. *The psychology of a primitive people.* London: Longmans, Green & Co., 1931.

PRESTHUS, R. *The organizational society.* New York: Knopf, 1965.

QUINN, J. A. *Human ecology.* Englewood Cliffs, N.J: Prentice-Hall, 1950.

QUINNEY, R. Who is the victim? *Criminology,* 1972, 314–323.

RECKLESS, W. C. & KAY, B. A. *The female offender.* President's Commission on Law Enforcement and Administration of Justice. Washington, D.C.: U.S. Government Printing Office, 1967.

RESKIN, B. F. Scientific productivity, sex and location in the institution of science. *American Journal of Sociology,* 1978, *83(5),* 1235–1243.

RICE, B. Messiah from Korea: Honor thy father Moon. *Psychology Today,* January, 1976, *9,* 36–47.

ROETHLISBERGER, F. J. & DICKSON, W. J. *Management and the worker.* Cambridge: Harvard University Press, 1939.

ROETHLISBERGER, F. J. & DICKSON, W. J. *Management and morale.* Cambridge: Harvard University Press, 1943.

ROGERS, D. *110 Livingston Street.* New York: Random House, 1968.

ROGOFF, N. *Recent trends in occupational mobility.* Glencoe, Ill.: Free Press, 1953.

THE ROPER ORGANIZATION, *The Virginia Slims American women's opinion poll.* New York: The Roper Organization, 1974.

ROSALDO, M. Z. & LAMPHERE, L. *Woman, culture and society.* Stanford: Stanford University Press, 1974.

ROSE, A. M. *Sociology: The study of human relations.* New York: Knopf, 1956.

ROSE, P. I. *They and we: Racial and ethnic relations in the United States.* New York: Random House, 1974.

ROSEN, G. The evolution of social medicine. In H. E. Freeman, S. Levine & L. G. Reeder (Eds.), *Handbook of medical sociology* (second edition). Englewood Cliffs, N. J.: Prentice-Hall.

ROSENBLUM, K. E. Female deviance and the female sex role: A preliminary investigation. *British Journal of Sociology,* 1975, 169–185.

ROSS, E. A. *Tests, and challenges in sociology.* New York: Appleton-Century-Crofts, 1931.

ROSZAK, T. *The making of a counter culture: Reflections on the technocratic society and its youthful opposition.* New York: Doubleday, 1969.

SAGARIN, E. *Deviants and deviance: An introduction to the study of disvalued people and behavior.* New York: Praeger, 1975.

SALISBURY, S. *Religion in American culture.* Homewood, Ill.: The Dorsey Press, 1964.

SARGENT, S. S. Class and class-consciousness in a California town. *Social Problems,* 1953, *1,* 22–27.

SCANZONI, J. &. SCANZONI, L. *Men, women and change.* New York: McGraw-Hill, 1976.

SCHEFF, T. *Being mentally ill.* Chicago: Aldine, 1966.

SCHELLING, T. C. What is the business of organized crime? In J. B. Williamson et al. (Eds.), *Social problems: The contemporary debates.* Boston: Little, Brown, 1977.

SCHERMERHORN, R. A. *These are our people.* Boston: D. C. Heath, 1949.

SCHNEIDER, L. Institution. In J. G. Gould & W. L. Kolb (Eds.), *A dictionary of the social sciences.* New York: The Free Press, 1964.

SCHNORE, L. F. The functions of metropolitan suburbs. *American Journal of Sociology,* 1956, *61,* 453–458.

SCHNORE, L. F. The growth of metropolitan suburbs. *American Sociological Review,* 1957, *22,* 165–173.

SCHUR, E. M. *Crimes without victims: Deviant behavior and public policy.* Englewood Cliffs, N. J.: Prentice-Hall, 1965.

SCHWARZ, O. L. *General types of superior men.* Boston: Richard G. Badger, 1916.

SCHWENN, M. *Arousal of the motive to avoid success.* Unpublished junior honors thesis, Harvard University, 1970.

SCUDDER, R. & ANDERSON, C. A. Migration and vertical occupational mobility. *American Sociological Review,* 1954, *19,* 329–334. (a)

SCUDDER, R. & ANDERSON, C. A. The relation of being known to status rating. *Sociology and Social Research,* 1954, *38,* 239–241. (b)

SCUDDER, R. & ANDERSON, C. A. Range of acquaintance and of repute as factors in prestige rating methods of studying social status. *Social Forces,* 1954, *32,* 248–253. (c)

SELLTIZ, C., JAHODA, M., DEUTSCH, M. & COOK, S. W. *Research methods in social relations.* New York: Holt, 1959.

SHEVKY, E. & WILLIAMS, M. *The social areas of Los Angeles: analysis and typology.* Berkeley: University of California Press, 1949.

SHEVKY, E. & BELL, W. *Social area analysis: Theory, illustrative application and computational procedures.* Stanford: Stanford University Press, 1955.

SHILS, E. *The present state of American sociology.* Glencoe, Ill.: Free Press, 1948.

SHILS, E. Ritual and crisis. In D. R. Cutler (Ed.), *The religious situation: 1968.* Boston: Beacon Press, 1968.

SHOCK, N. W. The psychology of aging. *Scientific American,* 1962, *206* (No. 1), 110.

SIGELMAN, L. Multi-nation surveys of religious beliefs. *Journal for the Scientific Study of Religion,* 1977, *16* (3), 289–294.

SIMMEL, G. *Conflict* (K. H. Wolff, trans.). Glencoe, Ill.: Free Press, 1955.

SIMMEL, G. *The sociology of Georg Simmel* (K. H. Wolff, trans.) New York: Free Press, 1950.

SIMON, W. & GAGNON, J. H. Homosexuality: The formulation of a sociological perspective. In I. L. Reiss (Ed.), *Readings on the Family System.* New York: Holt, 1972.

SIMPSON, G. E. & YINGER, M. J. *Racial and cultural minorities: An analysis of prejudice and discrimination.* New York: Harper & Row, 1972.

SINGH, J. A. L. & ZINGG, R. M. *Wolf children and feral man.* New York: Harper and Brothers, 1942.

SMALL, A. W. *General sociology.* Chicago: University of Chicago Press, 1905.

SMELSER, N. J. *Theory of collective behavior.* New York: Free Press, 1963.

SMITH, R. R. Bakke's case vs. the case for affirmative action. *New York University Education Quarterly,* 1978, *9* (2), 2–8.

SOROKIN, P. A. *Social and cultural dynamics.* New York: American Books, 1937.

SOROKIN, P. A. *Society, culture, and personality.* New York: Harper & Brothers, 1947.

SPENGLER, J. J. Sociological presuppositions in economic theory. *Southern Economic Journal,* 1940, *7,* 131–157.

SPENGLER, J. J. Malthus's total population theory: A restatement and reappraisal. *Canadian Journal of Economics and Political Science,* 1945, *11,* 245.

SPENGLER, J. J. Aspects of the economics of population growth, part 1. *Southern Economic Journal,* 1947, *14,* 123–147.

SPENGLER, J. J. Aspects of the economics of population growth, part 2. *Southern Economic Journal,* 1948, *14,* 233–265.

SPENGLER, O. *The decline of the West.* New York: Knopf, 1926.

SPITZ, R. A. *Hospitalism* (Vol. 1): *The psychoanalytic study of the child.* New York: International Universities Press, 1945.

SPITZ, R. A. *Hospitalism: A followup report* (Vol. II): *The psychoanalytic study of the child.* New York: International universities Press, 1946.

STAMPP, K. M. *The peculiar institution: Slavery*

in the antebellum South. New York: Random House, 1956.

Statistical Abstract of the United States, 1971. Washington, D.C.: U.S. Government Printing Office, 1971.

Statistical Abstract of the United States, 1977. Washington, D.C.: U.S. Government Printing Office, 1977.

Statistical Bulletin. New York: Metropolitan Life Insurance Company, Vol. 58, pages 10-11, 1977.

STEINFELS, P. Introduction. In P. Steinfels (Ed.), *The concept of health.* Hastings Center Studies, Vol. 1, No. 3, pp. 3-6, 1973.

STERN, B. J. Resistances to the adoption of technological innovations. *Technological Trends and National Policy.* Washington, D.C.: U.S. Government Printing Office, 1937.

STEVENSON, G. H. *The imperial administration. The Cambridge ancient history,* Vol. 10. Cambridge, England: Cambridge University Press, 1934.

STEWART, G. R. *Man: An autobiography.* New York: Random House: 1946.

STOGDILL, R. M. Leadership, membership and organization. *Psychological Bulletin,* 1950, *47,* 1–14.

STOUFFER, S. A. Intervening opportunities: A theory relating mobility and distance. *American Sociological Review,* 1940, *5,* 845–867.

STOUFFER, S. A. *Studies in social psychology in World War II* (4 Vols.). Vols. 1 & 2. *The American Soldier.* Princeton, N.J.: Princeton University Press, 1949.

STOUFFER, S. A. Some observations on study and design. *The American Journal of Sociology,* 1955, *55,* 355–361.

Summary and detailed tables, religious bodies, 1936. Vol. 1. Washington, D. C.: U.S. Government Printing Office, 1941.

SUTHERLAND, E. H. The crime of corporations. In A. K. Cohen, et al (Eds.), *The Sutherland papers.* Indiana University Press, 1956.

SUTHERLAND, E. H. *Principles of criminology.* Philadelphia: Lippincott, 1947.

SUTHERLAND, E. H. *White collar crime.* New York: Holt, Rinehart, 1949.

SUTHERLAND, E. H. & CRESSEY, D. R. *Principles of criminology* (6th ed.). Philadelphia: Lippincott, 1960.

SYMONDS, C. *Pilot study of the peripheral behavior of sexual mate swappers.* Unpublished M. A. Thesis, University of California, Riverside, 1968.

TANNENBAUM, F. *Slave and citizen: The Negro in the Americas.* New York: Knopf, 1947.

TANNER, N. Matrifocality in Indonesia and Africa and among Black Americans. In M. Z. Rosaldo and L. Lamphere (Eds.), *Woman, culture and society.* Stanford: Stanford University Press, 1974.

TAUSSING, F. W. & JOSLYN, C. S. *American business leaders.* New York: Macmillan, 1932.

THOMAS, W. I. *Primitive behavior.* New York: McGraw-Hill, 1937.

THOMPSON, W. S. *Population problems* (4th ed.). New York: McGraw-Hill, 1953.

TIGER, L. & FOX, R. *The imperial animal.* New York: Holt, 1971.

TINBERGEN, N. *The study of instinct.* Oxford: Clarendon, 1951.

Toward a code of ethics for sociologists. *The American Sociologist,* 1968, 316–318.

TOYNBEE, A. *A study of history.* New York: Oxford University Press, 1946.

TOZZER, A. M. *Social origins and social continuities.* New York: Macmillan, 1925.

TROELTSCH, E. *The social teaching of the Christian churches* (O. Wyon, trans.). New York: The Macmillan Company, 1931.

TUMIN, M. M. Some principles of stratification: A critical analysis. *American Sociological Review,* 1953, *18,* 378–394.

TURNER, R. H. & KILLIAM, L. M. *Collective behavior.* Englewood Cliffs, N.J.: Prentice-Hall, 1957.

Tuskegee Institute. *1952 Negro year book.* Tuskegee, Ala.: The Negro Year Book Publishing Co., 1952.

TYLOR, E. B. *Primitive culture.* New York: Brentano's, 1924.

UDRY, J. R. *The social context of marriage.* Philadelphia: Lippincott, 1971.

UDY, S. H. JR. *Organization of work.* New Haven, Conn.: HRAF Press, 1959.

U.S. Bureau of the Census, *General population characteristics,* United States summary, 1970 U. W. Census, Table 53, 1970.

U.S. Bureau of the Census, *Projections of the population of the U.S. by age and sex, 1972–2020.* Table 53, Series P-25, 493, 1973.

U.S. Department of Labor, Bureau of Labor Statistics. *Economic forces in the U.S.A. in facts and figures.* Washington, D.C.: U.S. Government Printing Office, June, 1955, 62–63.

VAN ARSDOL, M. D., JR., CAMILLERI, S. F. & SCHMID, C. F. The generality of urban social area indexes. *American Sociological Review,* 1958, *23,* 277–284.

VANDER ŽANDEN, J. W. *American minority relations: The sociology of racial and ethnic groups.* New York: Ronald Press, 1972.

Vital Statistics—Special Reports, 1956, *42* (no. 15), 327.

VITELES, M. S. *Motivation and morale in industry.* New York: W. W. Norton, 1953.

VON HOFFMAN, N., HOROWITZ, I. L. & RAINWATER, L. *Sociological snoopers and journalistic moralizers.* In I. L. Horowitz and C. Nanry (Eds.), *Sociological realities II: A guide to the study of society.* New York: Harper, 1975.

WALLAS, G. *Our social heritage.* New Haven, Conn.: Yale University Press, 1921.

WARNER, W. L. *Democracy in Jonesville.* New York: Harper & Brothers, 1949.

WARNER, W. L. & ABEGGLEN, J. C. *Big business leaders in America.* New York: Harper & Brothers, 1955. (a)

WARNER, W. L. & ABEGGLEN, J. C. *Occupational mobility in American business and industry 1928–1952.* Minneapolis: University of Minnesota Press, 1955. (b)

WARNER, W. L., HAVIGHURST, R. J. & LOEB, M. B. *Who shall be educated?* New York: Harper & Brothers, 1944.

WARNER, W. L. & LOW, J. O. *The social system of the modern factory.* New Haven: Yale University Press, 1947.

WARNER, W. L. & LUNT, P. S. *The social life of a modern community.* New Haven: Yale University Press, 1941.

WARNER, W. L. & LUNT, P. S. *The status system of a modern community.* New Haven: Yale University Press, 1942.

WARNER, W. L., MEEKER, M. & EELLS, K. *Social class in America: A manual of procedure for the measurement of social status.* Chicago: Science Research Associates, 1949.

WARNER, W. L. & SROLE, L. *The social systems of American ethnic groups.* New Haven: Yale University Press, 1945.

WASKOW, A. I. *From race riot to sit-in, 1919 and the 1960's: A study in the connections between conflict and violence.* Garden City, N. Y.: Doubleday, 1966.

WEBER, M. *The Protestant ethic and the spirit of capitalism* (T. Parsons, trans.). New York: Scribner's, 1930.

WEBER, M. In H. H. Gerth & C. W. Mills (eds. and trans.), *From Max Weber: Essays in sociology.* New York: Oxford University Press, 1958 (originally published 1946).

WEBER, M. *Bureaucracy* (Vol. III). In G. Roth & C. Wittich (Eds.), *Economy and society: An outline of interpretive sociology* (3 vols.) New York: Bedminister Press, 1968.

WEIS, J. G. Liberation and crime: The invention of the new female criminal. *Crime and Social Justice: Issues in Criminology.* Fall-Winter 1976, No. 6, 17–27.

WEST, J. *Plainville, U.S.A.* New York: Columbia University Press, 1945.

WHITE, L., with DILLINGHAM, B. *The concept of culture.* Minneapolis: Burgess, 1973.

Why do you do what you do. Sociology: A new theory of behavior. Time, August 1, 1977, pp. 54–63.

WILENSKY, H. C. Work as a social problem. In H. S. Becker (Ed.), *Social Problems.* New York: Wiley, 1966.

WILLIAMS, R. M. JR. *American society: A sociological interpretation.* New York: Knopf, 1970.

WILSON, B. R. An analysis of sect development. *American Sociological Review,* 1959, *24,* 3–15.

WILSON, E. O. *Sociobiology.* Cambridge, Massachusetts: Belknap Press of Harvard University Press, 1975.

WILSON, J. Q. A readers guide to the Crime Commission reports. *The Public Interest,* 1967, *Fall,* 67.

WINCH, R. F. *The modern family.* New York: Holt, 1971.

WIRTH, L. Urbanism as a way of life. *American Journal of Sociology,* 1938, *44,* 17.

WIRTH, L. The urban society and civilization. In *Eleven twenty-six: A decade of social science research.* Chicago: University of Chicago Press, 1940.

WOOFTER, T. J. *Landlord and tenant on the cotton plantation* (Vol. 5., Research monograph, 1936). Washington, D.C.: Works Progress Administration, Division of Social Research, 1936.

The world almanac, 1961. New York: New York Telegram and Sun, 1961.

WRONG, D. H. The functional theory of stratification: Some neglected considerations. *American Sociological Review,* 1959, *24,* 772–782.

YANKELOVICH, D. *The new morality: A profile of American youth in the 70's.* New York: McGraw-Hill, 1974.

YESIPOV, B. P. & GONCHAROV, N. K. *I want to be like Stalin.* New York: John Day, 1947.

YINGER, M. J. Comparative study of the substructures of religion. *Journal for the Scientific Study of Religion,* 1977, *16* (1), 67–86.

YOUNG, K. Society and the state: Some neglected areas of research and theory. *American Sociological Review,* 1946, *2,* 137–146.

YOUNG, K. *Isn't one wife enough?* New York: Henry Holt, 1954.

YOUNG, K. *Social psychology* (3rd ed.). New York: Appleton-Century-Crofts, 1956.

YUAN, D. Y. Voluntary segregation: A study of New York Chinatown. In M. Kurokawa (Ed.), *Minority Responses.* New York: Random House, 1970.

ZAENGLER, M. M., VENER, A. M. & STEWART, C. S. The adolescent and his religion: Beliefs in transition. *Review of Religious Research,* 1975, *17,* 56–57.

Index